DANTE
The Poet, the Political Thinker, the Man

Dante from a sketch by Seymour Kirkup of a portrait by Giotto

DANTE

The Poet, the Political Thinker, the Man

Barbara Reynolds

I.B. TAURIS
LONDON · NEW YORK

Published in 2006 by I.B.Tauris & Co. Ltd
6 Salem Road, London W2 4BU
175 Fifth Avenue, New York, NY 10010
www.ibtauris.com

ISBN 10: 1 84511 161 3
ISBN 13: 978 1 84511 161 8

A full CIP record for this book is available from the British Library

Typeset in Adobe Caslon Pro by A. & D. Worthington, Newmarket, Suffolk
Printed and bound in Great Britain by TJ International Ltd, Padstow

Contents

Illustrations

To the memory of my many students
for whom I wish I had been more courageous

Acknowledgements

I acknowledge with thanks the kind permission of David Higham Associates to reproduce translations by Dorothy L. Sayers and myself from the three volumes, *Hell*, *Purgatory* and *Paradise*, published by Penguin Classics. I am indebted also to the same publisher for permission to publish a development of part of the Introduction to the new edition of my translation of *La Vita Nuova*.

The illustration on the cover of Dante studying is reproduced from the fresco by Luca Signorelli on the wall of Orvieto Cathedral. The Frontispiece is reproduced from a sketch by Seymour Kirkup of Dante as a young man, after Giotto. The photographs of the Baptistery of Florence and of the decorations on the cupola are reproduced from Piero Bargellini's *Questa è Firenze*, published by G.C. Sansoni, 1968. The photograph of the statue of Pope Boniface VIII by Arnolfo di Cambio is reproduced from T.S.R. Boase's book, published by Constable and Co. in 1933. The drawing of the Emperor Henry VII is reproduced from Kurt-Ulrich Jäshke's *Europa und das römisch-deutsche Reich um 1300*, published by W. Kohlhammer, 1999, supplied by courtesy of Professor Janos Bak. The illustrations of the Journey of St Paul are reproduced from the article 'La Descente de Saint Paul en Enfer' by P. Meyer, *Celtica*, s.d. The photographs of the mosaics relating to the former tomb of Matilda are independently produced. The mosaic of Justinian and his retinue is a reproduction from the panel in San Vitale, Ravenna. The masque of Dante is reproduced from the Palazzo Vecchio in Florence. The diagrams of Wilfrid Scott-Giles from the three Penguin volumes are reproduced by kind permission of his son, Giles Scott-Giles.

The text of the *Commedia* is taken from the edition by John D. Sinclair, London, John Lane, The Bodley Head, 3 volumes, revised edition, 1948. Lyrics by Dante, if not otherwise acknowledged, are to be found in *Dante's Lyric Poetry*, edited by Kenelm Foster and Patrick Boyde, Volume I, Oxford, Clarendon Press, 1967.

What is important is not proof (for who can be said to have *proved* anything?) but what is most probable to the rational, informed mind.

Louise Baron

Entia non sunt multiplicanda praeter necessitatem.

William of Ockham

Introduction

This book offers a new look at Dante. After a professional life spent lecturing and teaching on Dante, dutifully passing on what was then received opinion, I decided to read all his works again, this time with an independent mind. This is difficult to achieve. We carry a lot of excess baggage when we set out on such a journey and I still cling to some of it. Nevertheless, I believe that what I here present is a portrait of Dante, the poet, the political thinker and the man, which has not been seen before. Almost every chapter contains new ideas and fresh insights, some of them radical, many controversial.

Among the discoveries which I have made are two which offer a fundamental challenge. They concern the famous enigmas: the *veltro* and the DVX, the first a prophecy by Virgil, the second by Beatrice, of a leader who was to bring peace and order to the world. Many learned and ingenious attempts have been made to identify him, but no definitive conclusion has been reached. By keeping an open mind, I have, almost by accident, hit upon what I consider are the solutions to both conundrums. Their very simplicity has caused them to be overlooked for nearly seven centuries. They are bound to meet with disagreement, perhaps with instant dismissal. I hope that they will at least arouse discussion and so lead on to further perceptions.

Almost every factual statement concerning Dante has been disputed and many continue to be controversial. The accepted opinion regarding Beatrice, the Florentine girl with whom he fell in love and who was the main inspiration of his poetry, is that she was the daughter of Folco Portinari, that she married Simone Bardi and died in 1290 at the age of 24. But it has also been maintained that she did not exist at all, being merely an allegorical figure signifying Theology. In this book I suggest that Beatrice plays not one but many roles in the *Commedia*, some of them not defined before.

It is said that Dante's early poems were set to music and sung by his friend Casella, the composer: there is no proof that this is so. Dante had five, six, seven children: according to recent opinion, he had only two sons and one daughter. Dante studied for a time in Paris (Gladstone even believed that he studied at Oxford): according to other opinion, he never left Italy. Several works and letters attributed to him have been judged to be forgeries and some are still the subject of controversy. Dante and his friend Forese Donati exchanged a series of obscene sonnets. When discovered they were rejected as spurious, then accepted as genuine; they are once again the subject of discussion. All such disputes, and there are many, give the biographer a free hand, but it requires courage to use it, rather than simply weigh one view against another and reach no decision.

Taking a new look at one of Dante's minor works, his treatise on the art of writing in the vernacular, *De Vulgari Eloquentia*, I realized for the first time that it was written originally as a lecture. Read in this light, it reveals him vividly as a public speaker. We become suddenly aware of his ability to entertain an audience, his talent as a mimic, his acute sensitivity to accents as he walks about Bologna, noting the differences in pronunciation from district to district. It also reveals him as an irate personality, downright in his opinions and impatient of disagreement.

Another minor work, long considered spurious but now accepted as authentic by most Dante scholars, is his address to Can Grande della Scala, the ruler of Verona and Dante's patron. I offer here a totally new view of it. I consider that it has been wrongly defined as an 'epistle': it is, on the contrary, an oration, delivered in Verona by Dante himself in an attempt to gain promotion and financial aid for the third part of his poem, *Paradiso*.

There has long been a mystery concerning Dante's philosophical work, *Il Convivio*, intended, when he began it, to be his *magnum opus*. Why did he leave it unfinished and turn to writing the *Commedia*? I offer a solution which has not been suggested before. Again, it is a simple one. Dante, the exile, cut off by then from the funds of fellow exiles, with whom he had quarrelled, was hard pressed for money. He hoped to generate income by giving a course of lectures on subjects arising from his *canzoni*, philosophy, allegory, astronomy and ethics, and by selling copies of his text as he progressed. Unfortunately he misjudged his market. Audiences dwindled, sales fell off and he was obliged to turn to a more successful kind of entertainment: the story of a journey into the world of the dead. Investing what was a primitive form of pop art with the dignity of Virgil's story of the journey of Aeneas into Hades and making it a vehicle for his own profound ideas, he created a new form of literary art which this time held his audience and has continued to do so ever since.

I use the word 'audience' advisedly. In Dante's time, owing to the expense of manuscripts, works were read aloud in public more often than perused in solitude. This accounts for the many varied sound effects perceptible in Dante's style. It is also possible to see how he adjusted the work to the responses it received as it progressed. Modern readers, limited to the page-to-eye-to-mind experience, tend to overlook the importance of the relation-ship between an author and a *listening* public. To hold their attention, Dante had need of variety. This he achieved by changing his style from canto to canto. Most effective of all was the fact that he told the main story in the first person: 'I was there … I saw … I heard'. Read aloud by Dante himself, the *Inferno* especially must have been compelling. Stories are inserted within stories, startling encounters are contrived between himself and personages not long dead. He reduced the traditional figures of personification allegory ('perambulating labels') and replaced them by real characters, who, while being themselves, at the same time represented abstract concepts. Though remote from us now, they still hold our fascinated attention, owing to skilful character drawing and to dialogue that brings personalities to life by differ-ent styles and tones of voice. An element of drama is perceptible throughout. There is also the fact that Dante had quite a few personal scores to settle.

It was not his intention simply to preach a parable about punishments for sin and rewards for virtue. He was deeply concerned about the state of the world and believed that he had found a solution: the acceptance throughout Europe of the supreme secular authority of an Emperor. His chief aim in writing the *Commedia* (as it was to have been in *Il Convivio*) was to promote this belief among as wide an audience and readership as possible. He held that mankind was created for happiness and that the highest joy was to be found in the use of reason and the pursuit of truth. His reading of the mystics and his own gift for contemplation enabled him to conclude the work with a vision of the Trinity, a vision which he may actually have expe-rienced.

Views differ as to whether he did or not. There is no conclusive proof and I leave the question open. I suggest, however, a possibility which does not appear to have been presented before. From his earliest writings, in particu-lar in his visionary imaginings of Beatrice conveyed in *La Vita Nuova*, there are indications that Dante, perhaps in company with his fellow poets, may have indulged in herbal stimulants which induced a heightened state of consciousness. There is an intriguing clue, hitherto unnoticed, in the first canto of *Paradiso*, which points in that direction.

In my descriptions of the *Commedia* and of Dante's minor poetry I have aimed at presenting the traits of his personality as well as the qualities of his narrative and literary skills. In several chapters I offer new insights, of which one of the most important is my discovery of the source of his story of the last journey of Ulysses. The translations, unless otherwise indicated, are my own, some of which are published here for the first time.

Since this book is the result of independent observation, I give no bibli-ography. The sources of quotations and, where appropriate, of information and occasionally of opinion, are provided in the notes. In order not to hold up the narrative, I have relegated to an appendix basic information about Guelfs and Ghibellines, Popes contemporary with Dante, Emperors mentioned by him, together with a chronology, so far as it is known, of his works and of the chief events of his life.

Several professional friends have read the work in full or in part and have made valuable suggestions, in particular Jill Paton Walsh and A.N. Wilson. I wish especially to thank Professor Andrew Lewis for his guidance on matters relating to mediaeval law. I have also benefited from an exchange of views with colleagues and am grateful to them for their help and encouragement, as well as for their warnings and misgivings. They are (or were): Catherine Aird, Professor Janos Bak, the Rev. Robert S. Beresford, Professor Patrick Boyde, George Bull, Christopher Dean, Dr John Keast-Butler, Professor E.M. Peters, Dr Roger Poole, Professor Jonathan Saylor, Professor John Scott, Dr Prue Shaw, Professor Ruggero Stefanini, Canon John A. Thurmer and Dr Richard Webster. I also thank Dr Louise Baron for allowing me to quote her wise saying as an epigraph. I also thank my literary executors, Kerstin Lewis and Adrian Thorpe, for following my undertaking with a watchful eye.

My thanks are also due to I.B.Tauris for their enterprise in publishing this book, expecially to Alex Wright and his colleagues, and also to Alison and David Worthington for their careful typesetting of the text.

Barbara Reynolds
Cambridge 2006

CHAPTER I

The Early Years

Dante Alighieri believed that he was a direct descendant of the ancient Romans. According to family tradition, a great-great-grandfather on his father's side could trace his origins to the Elisei, one of the Roman families reputed to have founded Florence. This illustrious ancestor, Cacciaguida, was born towards the end of the eleventh century. A Florentine, he served, as other Tuscans did, in the Second Crusade, was knighted and killed in battle. His wife, Alighiera Alighieri, came from the region of the Po Valley, possibly Ferrara, and some of her descendants adopted her family name. Derived from the Latin word *aliger*, it means 'winged'. Dante owed his Christian name to his mother's side. A shortened form of Durante, it means 'enduring'. The notion of ancient lineage, whether Roman or not, and names charged with such significance must have inspired in him a strong sense of destiny.

He was born in the year 1265. The precise day is not known but since he claimed the constellation of Gemini as his natal stars[1] it must have been between May and June. He was christened the following year in the Baptistery of San Giovanni, one of the earliest buildings in Florence, where he believed that his ancestor Cacciaguida too had been baptized.[2] The Cathedral, as we know it today, had not then been built and the Baptistery was more prominent than it is now.[3] Dante called it his 'beautiful San Giovanni' and looked back to it from exile with longing, hoping one day to receive the poet's crown of laurel there.[4]

The original baptismal font is no longer in place, though broken segments of it are said to be in the Museum of the Works of the Cathedral. It was a low octagonal structure, like the font in the Baptistery at Pisa,[5] and inside it, as at Pisa, were stone cylinders. Multiple baptisms were held twice a year, on Easter Eve and on the Eve of Whit Sunday, when the Baptistery was crowded with families and godparents. It has been said that the baptizing priests stood in the cylinders and leant forward to the water in the font. It is more likely that the priests stood in the dry font, facing the congregation and baptizing with water contained in the cylinders. One day someone (it

Fig 1. The Baptistery in Florence

has been said a child) fell into a cylinder and was unable to extricate himself. Dante smashed it with an axe to release him, an action that was considered sacrilegious. He makes a point of justifying himself in *Inferno*, where holes in the rock containing Popes guilty of simony remind him of these cylinders, one of which he broke, he says, to save someone who was drowning:

... e questo sia suggel ch'ogn' uomo sganni.

... and by this seal let all be undeceived.[6]

His father, Alighiero Alighieri, was about 45 years old when Dante was born. A man of property, both inside Florence and in the countryside beyond, he added to his income by lending money, an activity which Dante later condemned as usury. By means of it, however, the father maintained his family in comfort and left them modestly provided for. Dante's mother, named Bella, was the daughter of Durante Scolaro, said to be related to a distinguished family, the Abati. She died when Dante was a child, some time between 1270 and 1275, and his father married again. His second wife was Lapa, the daughter of Chiarissimo Cialuffi. She bore him two children: a son, Francesco, and a daughter, Gaetana. Another daughter (possibly of his first wife), whose name is unknown, married Leone Poggi. Their son, Andrea, was said by Giovanni Boccaccio, Dante's first biographer, to look marvellously like the poet.

Boccaccio was eight years old when Dante died in 1321 and had never set eyes on him. Nevertheless, in preparation for his biography, he questioned many people who had known him, including his nephew Andrea. He describes Dante's appearance as follows:

This our poet, then, was of middle height; and when he had reached maturity he went somewhat bowed, his gait grave and gentle, and ever clad in most seemly apparel, in such garb as befitted his mature years. His face was long, his nose aquiline, and his eyes large rather than small; his jaws big, and the under lip protruding beyond the upper. His complexion was dark, his hair and beard thick, black and curling, and his expression was always melancholy and thoughtful.[7]

From measurements taken of Dante's skeleton in 1921,[8] his height was between 1.644 and 1.654 metres, roughly the equivalent of five feet five inches. Measurements of the upper part of the skull confirm that his face was long. The nasal cavity suggests that the nose slanted slightly to the right and that it was large and aquiline. The orbits of the eyes show that they were large; also that the right eye was larger and slightly lower than the left. The cheek bones were prominent. The lower jaw is missing so its size cannot be verified. Calculations of the skull indicate that his cranial capacity was 1,700 cubic centimetres. The weight of his brain has been estimated as a possible

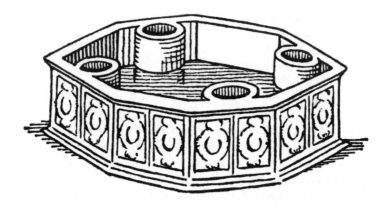

Fig 2. Baptismal Font in Pisa

1,470 grams. These measurements suggest that his brain was above average in size and weight.[9]

In his youth he was not bearded, as can be seen from the portrait of him, said to have been painted by his friend Giotto, on the wall of the Bargello in Florence. This was damaged and badly restored in 1841 but some idea of what it was like originally can be seen from a sketch which the artist Seymour Kirkup was able to make of it before the damage had gone too far.[10] This shows a sensitive, oval face, beardless, with a straight nose and firm chin. The prominence of the under lip, to which Boccaccio refers, can be seen in potential and this perhaps developed as he grew older.

There is no evidence that Dante felt himself an outsider among his father's second family. An allusion in one of his poems to a sister standing at his bedside while he lay ill indicates, on the contrary, an affectionate relationship:

Donna pietosa e di novella etate,
adorna assai di gentilezze umane,
ch'era là 'v'io chiamava spesso Morte,
veggendo li occhi miei pien di pietate,
e ascoltando le parole vane,
si mosse con paura a pianger forte.

A lady, youthful and compassionate,
much graced with qualities of gentleness,
who where I called on Death was standing near,
beholding in my eyes my grievous state,

hearing babbled words of emptiness,
began to weep aloud in sudden fear.

These lines are the beginning of a *canzone* which Dante included in a selection of his early poems, entitled *La Vita Nuova*.[11] In a prose commentary he explains that this 'kind and gracious young woman' was closely related to him. The traditional interpretation is that she was his half-sister, Gaetana, who in the year of Dante's illness, 1290, would have been about 15. Apart from this brief and tender reference, Dante does not mention his siblings, though it is said that his half-brother Francesco visited him in his exile and negotiated a loan for him. He refers to his parents once only, in *Il Convivio*, a work he wrote in the early years of his exile. Explaining why he is writing in the vernacular instead of in Latin, he gives as one reason his intimate love of his native speech, which he feels is part of his very being. This is literally true, he says, because his parents spoke it and this brought them together and so was responsible for his existence:

> Questo mio volgare fu congiugnitore de li miei generanti, che con esso parlavano … per che manifesto è lui essere concorso a la mia generazione, e così essere alcuna cagione del mio essere.

> *This vernacular of mine brought my parents together, for they spoke in it … so it is obvious that it had a share in begetting me and thus is a cause of my existence.*[12]

In these words we can sense Dante's longing to hear the Florentine speech again. It may even be that he is here recalling an echo of his mother's voice: *con esso parlavano*: he seems to be remembering his parents talking *together*. If so, this must be one of his earliest childhood memories.[13]

His father died some time between 1281 and 1283, leaving Dante, then in his late teens, under the authority of a guardian, as the law required, until he was 25 years of age.[14] From the many images of parenthood that occur in the *Commedia* it would seem that the early loss of his mother and later of his father left Dante with an emotional need. Several times he writes of himself as a child: held in the protective arms of Virgil, carried sleeping up part of Mount Purgatory by St Lucy, turning to Beatrice like a little boy to its mother for reassurance in a moment of panic; once he even compares himself to an infant hungrily mouthing for the breast.

After the death of his mother, his most important childhood experience was his meeting with a little girl of eight when he himself was nearly nine. Describing this event later in *La Vita Nuova*, when the child, grown to womanhood, had married and had died, Dante, by then an established poet, idealized the feelings she aroused in him at this first meeting as the beginning of a life-long submission to the power of love. In a realistic sense, it may have been his first awareness of the stirrings of puberty. Later in life, in a sonnet addressed to a poet friend, Cino da Pistoia, he admits that the origins of his feelings for her were sexual.[15] In another poem he even traced her influence upon him to the day of her birth, when, he says, his little childish body felt a strange tremor and he fell to the ground.[16] Since he was then only about nine months old, he could not have remembered this. If there is any truth in it, he may have suffered an infantile convulsion about which his nurse or his mother told him later. He describes himself as having a tendency to faint when overcome by strong emotions, as when in *La Vita Nuova* he sees Beatrice unexpectedly at a wedding, or within the fiction of *Inferno*, when Francesca da Rimini comes to the end of her piteous story and Dante says of himself: 'I fell as a dead body falls':

e caddi come corpo morto cade.[17]

He says in *La Vita Nuova* that when he first saw Beatrice she 'was dressed in a very noble colour, a decorous and delicate crimson, tied with a girdle and trimmed in a manner suited to her tender age'. She has been identified as the daughter of Folco Portinari, a banker and a prominent citizen of Florence. Boccaccio relates that the meeting took place at a May Day party held in the Portinari home. She was one of 11 children: five sons and six daughters.[18] One of the sons, either Manetto or Ricovero, who were both of an appropriate age, was a close friend of Dante's.[19] Folco Portinari held government office and was elected Prior in August 1282. In 1288 he founded the hospital of Santa Maria Nuova.[20] There is a tradition that he was persuaded to do so by Beatrice's nurse, Mona Tessa, who, aided by the Sisters of the Order of Oblates, looked after the first patients. To this day, every year the Sisters celebrate Mona Tessa's birthday (3 July) in the little church of Santa Margherita, situated between the Portinari and the Alighieri houses,[21] where Dante and Beatrice both worshipped. There is a memorial tablet and an effigy of Mona Tessa on the original building of the hospital. Folco died on 31 December 1289. In his will, which is dated 15 January 1288, it is shown that Beatrice, to whom he bequeathed 50 Florentine pounds, was by then married to Simone Bardi, a member of a prominent family of bankers. Dante does not mention her marriage.

He does mention her father's death, in *La Vita Nuova*, where he describes a group of women mourners returning from a visit of condolence to Beatrice, with whom he deeply sympathized. Several years had passed since the death of his own father but it seems that he felt regret for what might have been, for he says: 'No friendship is as intimate as that between a good father and a good child.' It was a few days after Folco's death that Dante fell ill and lay babbling in the delirium that frightened his sister. He had perhaps caught a cold in the winter weather, as he stood watching the mourners, and may have succumbed to pleurisy or pneumonia. The piercing winds that whistle down the narrow streets of Florence in winter are dangerous still today.

The image of the 'angelic child', as he called her, stayed with him throughout his childhood, eclipsing another important event, which he never mentions: his betrothal at the age of 12 to Gemma, a daughter of the Donati family, arranged by his father and hers. In due course, Boccaccio says after the death of Beatrice in 1290, but probably earlier, he and Gemma married. She brought him a substantial dowry and they had several children, the exact number of whom has not been verified. There were certainly two sons: Iacopo, who became a priest and had only illegitimate issue, and Pietro, who prospered as a judge and built a villa at Gargagnago, near Verona, where his descendants, the Serego-Alighieri, still live. There has been mention of two other sons, Giovanni and Gabriello, but it is thought that they may have been the offspring of someone of the same name as Dante. If this is the case, they may have been cousins. It has been said that there were two daughters, Antonia, and Beatrice who became a nun in Ravenna. The more recent opinion is that there was only one daughter and that it was Antonia who took the veil under the name of her father's celebrated love. Boccaccio, on little evidence, as he admits, says that the marriage was unhappy and that for this reason Gemma did not join her husband in exile, though her sons and one daughter did.[22] Whatever the truth, marriages were arranged for financial or political reasons and were not an occasion for romantic expectations.

As the son of parents who prided themselves on distinguished lineage, Dante was instructed in the Trivium and the Quadrivium, a course of study consisting first of grammar (that is, Latin), logic and rhetoric, followed by arithmetic, geometry, astronomy and music. His earliest Latin grammar book is likely to have been the *Ars Grammatica* by Donatus, the fourth-century grammarian, for long in use. Dante places the soul of Donatus among the learned in *Paradiso*, an unusual tribute to the author of a Latin primer.[23] He was less kind to Priscian, to whose more advanced work he probably progressed, for he places him in *Inferno* on the burning sand among the sodomites.[24] The texts he read could have included a Latin translation of Aesop's fables, a collection of moral precepts by Dionysius Cato,[25] a book of eclogues which drew parallels between classical mythology and Scripture, and a work entitled *Facetus*, which taught good manners.

He seems not to have made much progress in Latin as a boy, for he said that when as an adult he tried to read Cicero and Boethius he found them difficult. With later study he became a proficient reader of the classics, particularly of Virgil, Ovid, Lucan, Cicero and of the later poet Statius; he also learnt to write Latin prose and verse with competence. He knew no Greek, apart from a few words, but that was usual in his period. There was no university in Florence, but he was able to continue his education by attending lectures at the schools of the Franciscans in Santa Croce and the Dominicans in Santa Maria Novella. One of the canons of Santa Maria was the preacher Remigio de' Girolami, who had studied in Paris and may have heard St Thomas Aquinas lecture on Aristotle there. On his return to Florence he took up a post as lecturer in theology at the Dominican school. If Dante heard him, there is the intriguing possibility of a close link between St Thomas and Dante the student of theology and philosophy. He admired Brunetto Latini, an eminent scholar, notary, magistrate and man of letters. When Dante knew him he was in his 60s, about the age his father would have been. He encouraged the boy in his studies and saw a great future for him in his horoscope. Dante draws an affectionate though painful portrait of him among the sodomites in *Inferno*,[26] where he expresses sorrow and, it seems, surprise at his plight, as well as profound respect and indebtedness, as though to a surrogate father, whose 'dear, benign, paternal image' he still keeps in his heart, recalling how he hourly taught him the art 'by which men become immortal'.[27]

Dante was deeply moved by music, especially by singing, which seems to have induced in him a trance-like state of bliss. He is not known to have played any instrument, though he may have done, for one of his friends was a maker of lutes.[28] Many of his poems were set to music, one at least by his friend Casella, who was a singer as well as a composer.[29] The musical setting of a *ballata* included in *La Vita Nuova*[30] is mentioned both in the poem and in the prose commentary. A *ballata*, as the word implies, was not only sung but was accompanied also by a performance of dancers.[31]

Leonardo Bruni, his fifteenth-century biographer, says that Dante drew excellently and there is an allusion to this skill in *La Vita Nuova*, in which he speaks of himself drawing figures of angels on wooden boards.[32] He calls it *la mia opera* ('my work'), which sounds like something more than doodling. It may have been work commissioned by a church. He was later to depict angels in words, notably two in *Purgatorio*, arrayed in garments 'green as fresh leaves new-budded on a wand', which trailed behind them, fluttered by green wings, their hair golden, their faces so dazzling that the eye of the beholder was confounded.[33] If this was how he also painted angels his 'work' must have been colourful. He was knowledgeable about contemporary artists and the materials used for paints. In *Purgatorio* he gives a list of colours which the flowers in the Valley of the Rulers surpassed: 'gold and fine silver, cochineal and white lead, indigo, bright and clear emerald when it is newly split'.[34] Two of his friends were artists: the miniaturist, Oderisi of Gubbio, and Giotto, whom he is said to have watched at work on the frescoes in the Scrovegni Chapel in Padua. Nothing remains that is known to be in his handwriting but Leonardo Bruni, who had seen 'certain epistles', says that he wrote 'a finished hand, with thin, long letters, perfectly formed'.

Though not tall, Dante must have been robust for he was trained in horsemanship for battle and in the use of the lance, the sword and the mace. Such skills required strength, dexterity and years of practice. In 1289, when he was 24, he fought in the first rank of the Florentine cavalry against the Ghibellines of Arezzo at the Battle of Campaldino. In a letter which Bruni saw, he described the battle and drew a plan of it, saying that though he was then no novice in arms he at first felt great fear, which changed to exultation when the cavalry, routed in the beginning, regrouped and charged, defeating the enemy. Dante had thus done his share of hacking and slicing. It has been suggested that it may even have been Dante himself who slew the Ghibelline warrior, Buonconte da Montefeltro, whose moment of death he describes so poignantly in *Purgatorio*.[35] In *Inferno* he mentions being present at the siege of the fortress of Caprona, when, later in the same year, the Tuscan Guelfs, led by Lucca and Florence, invaded Pisan territory and captured several strongholds.[36] Leonardi Bruni regrets that Boccaccio did not say more in his biography about Dante's military valour.

A vigorous and active man, Dante also took part in sports, such as hunting, both with hounds and hawks. In one of his sonnets he reproaches himself for spending too much time in such masculine pursuits, to the neglect of the company of women:

Sonar bracchetti, e cacciatori aizzare,
lepri levare, ed isgridar le genti,
di guinzagli uscir veltri correnti,
per belle piagge volgere e imboccare,
assai credo che deggia dilettare
libero core e van d'intendimenti!
Ed io, fra gli amorosi pensamenti,
d'uno sono schernito in tal affare,
e dicemi esto motto per usanza:
'Or ecco leggiadria di gentil core,
per una sì selvaggia dilettanza
lasciar le donne e lor gaia sembianza!'
Allor, temendo non che senta Amore,
prendo vergogna, onde mi ven pesanza.

Huntsmen hallooing, hounds that bark and bay,
hares from their cover leaping, shouts of glee,
swift, eager greyhounds from the leash set free,
coursing the sunlit slopes to snatch their prey,
such things give ample pleasure, I dare say,

to hearts untouched as yet by gallantry.
But I, whose thoughts of love encumber me,
by one of them am mocked on such a day.
It says, in teasing words which well I know:
'Oh, what a faithful lover we have here,
who for rough country sport prefers to go,
forsaking the fair sex who pleased him so!'
And then, afraid that Love will overhear,
I feel ashamed and heavy-hearted grow.

He enjoyed coarse company, as well as manly sport. With one his friends, Forese Donati, a cousin of his wife, he exchanged a series of vulgar and sexually insulting sonnets. This was a literary game known as a *tenzone*, a contest between poets who vied with each other, not always in abuse, sometimes in courteous argument. When first identified in the nineteenth century these sonnets caused so much outrage to Dante scholars that they refused to believe they were genuine. Later accepted for many years, they are once again the subject of controversy.[37]

A significant event in Dante's years as a young adult was his admittance into the society of poets who were experimenting with new concepts. The literary fashion of courtly love, as cultivated by troubadours in aristocratic centres in Provence, had spread to Northern Italy and Sicily. The stereotyped homage paid to an unnamed married woman was developed and refined by Italian poets in the thirteenth century, particularly by Guido Guinizelli of Bologna,[38] whose verses expressed a new reverence for female beauty and virtue. Love came to be seen as an ennobling experience of which only a *cor gentile* (gentle, or noble heart) was capable. Such rarefied emotion, distinguished from lust, gave rise to intense visionary and dream-like imaginings, sometimes mystical and verging on the religious. Poets who cultivated such experience, possibly with the stimulus of love potions,[39] were known as the *Fedeli d'Amore* (the Faithful Followers of Love), who acknowledged obedience to Love, personified as a feudal lord or some other figure of authority. In Florence the poets exploring such concepts formed a self-consciously élite group and were sometimes mocked by other, more earthy versifiers, as was Dante.

Hoping to become one of the elevated circle, Dante, at the age of about 17, began circulating some of his sonnets, at first anonymously. On receiving replies, he grew bolder and sent other poems to a wider group. One is a sonnet relating a dream which he asks the recipients to interpret. He later introduced it as the first poem in *La Vita Nuova*, saying there that it relates to Beatrice, though originally it may have been just an exercise in the conventional narration of a vision:

A ciascun'alma presa e gentil core
nel cui cospetto ven lo dir presente,
in ciò che mi rescrivan suo parvente,
salute in lor segnor, cioè Amore.
Già eran quasi che atterzate l'ore
del tempo che onne stella n' è lucente,
quando m'apparve Amor subitamente,
cui essenza membrar mi dà orrore.
Allegro mi sembrava Amor tenendo
meo core in mano, e ne le braccia avea
madonna involta in un drappo dormendo.
Poi la svegliava, e d'esto core ardendo
lei paventosa umilmente pascea:
appresso gir lo ne vedea piangendo.

To every captive soul and gentle lover
within whose sight this present rhyme may chance,
that, writing back, each may expound its sense,
greetings in Love, who is their Lord, I offer.
Already of those hours a third was over
wherein all stars display their radiance,
when lo! Love stood before me in my trance:
recalling what he was fills me with horror.
Joyful at first he seemed and in his keeping
he held my heart, while in his arms there lay
my lady in a mantle wrapped, and sleeping.
Then he awoke her and, her fear not heeding,
my burning heart fed to her reverently.
Then he departed from my vision weeping.

Among the poets who replied was Dante of Maiano, who took a coarse, jocose tone and, in a parody of medical advice, told his young namesake to give his testicles a good wash to see if that would clear his head; if not, he suggested he should see a doctor and present a specimen of his urine,[40] thus mockingly diagnosing a pathological sexual condition.

A serious reply came from Guido Cavalcanti,[41] which began:

Vedeste, al mio parere, onne valore
e tutto gioco e quanto bene om sente,
se foste in prova del segnor valente
che segnoreggia il mondo de l'onore …

You saw, in my view, all the good there is,
all joy and virtue that a man can know,
since that great Lord had taken you for his,
to whom in honour all obedience owe …[42]

This response was welcome to Dante for two reasons: the meaning of his dream had been taken seriously by the most eminent among the poetic group he wished to join; it also marked the beginning of a friendship.

Guido Cavalcanti, a member of an aristocratic and prosperous Guelf family, was Dante's senior by about ten years. Male comradeship was important to Dante and this early friendship was one of the most influential. 'My first friend', Dante called him, meaning not so much the first in time as the first in order of affection. They talked about poetry, love and religion. Cavalcanti's father, an Epicurean, believed that the soul died with the body and Guido was also suspected of being an unbeliever.[43] His love poetry expressed conflict between idealism and desire, which resulted in more torment than joy. Dante became his protégé and responded to his guidance as a poet. Something of their relationship is perhaps reflected in the pupil–teacher relationship between Dante and Virgil in the *Commedia*.[44]

From Cavalcanti he could have heard family reminiscences of the Ghibelline warrior Farinata degli Uberti, the imposing personage who in *Inferno* rises from the burning tomb of heretics, 'seeming to hold all Hell in scorn'.[45] Guido had been espoused in childhood to his daughter in the hope of creating amicable relations between two families of opposing political allegiance. Guido could also have told Dante tales of the troubadour Sordello, whose mistress, Cunizza da Romano, passed her old age in the Cavalcanti household. Sordello, though a Mantuan, wrote poems in Provençal, a language that Dante also mastered. So greatly did he admire him that he chose him as a figure worthy to embrace Virgil, a fellow Mantuan, on Mount Purgatory, making the meeting an occasion for an impassioned outburst of patriotic wrath. The celebrated lines describing the dignified disdain of Sordello as they approach him could have been derived from Cunizza's own words about him, as remembered by Cavalcanti:

> ... o anima lombarda,
> come ti stavi altera e disdegnosa
> e nel mover degli occhi onesta e tarda!
> Ella non ci dicea alcuna cosa,
> ma lasciavane gir, solo sguardando
> a guisa di leon quando si posa.

> *... o soul of Lombardy,*
> *what pride and scorn thy attitude avouched,*
> *and in thy slow regard what dignity!*
> *He said no word to us as we approached,*
> *but merely fixed his gaze upon us both,*
> *after the manner of a lion couched.*[46]

Cunizza herself had led a colourful life, having had four husbands and two lovers, one of whom was Sordello, for whom she left her first husband. Dante derived a sympathetic account of her, perhaps from Cavalcanti's memories, for he places her in the Heaven of Venus in *Paradiso*, an example of human love set in perfect relation to the divine. Something of Cunizza's authentic personality may be reflected in the joyous utterance in which she forgives herself, since the love by which she sinned is now her beatitude.[47]

The love life of the group of poets extended beyond the vision of one idealized woman. In a charming and subtly erotic sonnet Dante expresses a wish that he, Guido and Lapo Gianni, another poet friend, might sail away together in a boat, accompanied by three women whom they loved: Giovanna (for Guido), Lagia (for Lapo) and, for himself, 'she who is number thirty on the list'. We do not know her name. We know only that it was not Beatrice.

Guido, i' vorrei che tu e Lapo ed io
fossimo presi per incantimento
messi in un vasel, ch'ad ogni vento
per mare andasse al voler vostro e mio,
sì che fortuna od altro tempo rio
non ci potesse dare impedimento,
anzi, vivendo sempre in un talento,
di stare insieme crescesse 'l disio.
E monna Vanna e monna Lagia poi
con quella ch'è sul numer de le trenta
con noi ponesse il buono incantatore:
e quivi ragionar sempre d'amore,
e ciascuna di lor fosse contenta,
sì come i' credo che saremmo noi.

Guido, I wish you, I and Lapo could,
by virtue of enchantment, taken be
and placed upon a boat, to sail the sea,
no matter what the wind, where'er we would.
And that no tempest or ill-omened flood
might put our voyaging in jeopardy,
but, living ever in such harmony,
we'd find our pleasure day by day renewed.
And that the kind magician might convey
Giovanna, Lagia in the boat with us,
and her who's number thirty in my rhyme.
Then in Love's converse we would spend our time,
making all three content and bounteous,
while we, I vow, would joyful be as they.

The 'number thirty' refers to a poem, mentioned in *La Vita Nuova* but no longer extant, in which he had listed the names of the 60 most beautiful women of Florence. Who they were (apart from Beatrice) we do not know, nor what the number 60 signified. The idea may have arisen from a pageant or a dramatic representation of some kind. The name of Beatrice coincided with the number nine, which as the square of the Trinity signified a mystical quality attaching to her, not her position in a beauty competition; indeed he says elsewhere in the same work that her loveliness was like a miracle beyond compare. However, it is plain that his interest in women was not confined to her alone.

Florence in Dante's youth was a prosperous and powerful city state, both beautiful and terrible. The chronicler Giovanni Villani[48] records that the population in his day was about 900,000, not counting the religious orders of monks and nuns in monasteries and convents. In addition he estimated that there were some 1,500 foreigners, travellers and soldiers staying or passing through Florence. Boys and girls of reading age numbered between 8,000 and 10,000. Those learning arithmetic are said to have been between 1,000 and 2,000; those learning Latin and rhetoric in four large schools between 550 and 600. There were 110 churches in the city and its environs, including abbeys. Some 200 or more workshops for woollen manufactures employed more than 30,000 people. Dino Compagni, another chronicler, describes the city as follows:

> a city of invigorating air, well-mannered people, beautiful, well-dressed women, magnificent houses decorated by skilled craftsmen, a city different from others in Italy. From far and wide people come to visit it, not from necessity but for the sake of its many arts and crafts and the ornamental beauty of its buildings.[49]

This is an idealized picture, rather like an extract from a travel leaflet. Nevertheless it is not surprising that Florence had even then become something of a tourist attraction. Florentine buildings, with their geometrical patterns of dark green or rose marble on white, the painted interiors of churches, glittering with frescoes and mosaics, were and are still a brilliant sight. There were festivals, such as the processions of the *Fedeli d'Amore*, with Love garlanded and garbed in white, accompanied by his followers; the celebration of the Resurrection on Easter Sunday with a pageant of eminent citizens and members of guilds, accompanied by dancing and singing. On 24 June, the Feast of St John the Baptist, the patron saint, a horse race, like the one in the Campo of Siena, was run along the Corso, finishing in the centre of the city. There were also spectacular pageants on the river Arno. Men and women, robed and masked, represented qualities of valour, loyalty, virtue and perfection, inspired by the chivalric tradition. Life was lived in public; funerals, weddings, festivals, processions engaged and heightened the emotions; joy, triumph, grief, anger were all expressed with theatrical display.

There was also a dangerous and sinister aspect to Florence: a forest of stone, it has been called. The noble and powerful families built houses with immensely tall towers, examples of which may be seen to this day in San Gimignano. Erected as a defence against rival families, they served as ambush points from which bolts from crossbows or flaming arrows were shot across the narrow streets, darkened by overhanging balconies. Shouting, rioting and the clatter of horses was continuous. The arrogant Filippo Argenti of the wealthy Adimari family is said to have shod his horse with silver and was famed for riding dangerously through the crowded alleys, making those on foot flatten themselves in terror against the walls.[50]

Public executions of a horrific nature were usual, as in other cities. Dante says that he saw people burned alive. He had also witnessed the fearful death of assassins, who were killed by being planted head down, with only their legs protruding. An example of this ghastly fate is depicted in one of the bronze panels on the doors of the church of San Zeno in Verona. In *Inferno* Dante says that the legs of sinners, which he sees sticking out of holes in a rock, remind him of this punishment. As he bends to talk to one of them, he compares himself to a priest leaning down to catch the last words of a condemned man, who prolongs his confession in order to defer the terrible moment when the earth is shovelled in and smothers him.[51] Dante was familiar with instances of torture, death by starvation, murder, treachery, adultery, sodomy and bestiality.[52] Images of evil were depicted everywhere. In particular, the cupola of the Baptistery was decorated with mosaics arranged in rectangles, placed symmetrically, representing Hell, Purgatory and Paradise, the Last Judgement and, of special importance for the *Commedia*, a grotesque figure of Satan, with three mouths, two protruding snake-like from the sides of his head, each devouring a sinner, an image with which Dante was familiar from earliest childhood.[53] His representation of Lucifer in *Inferno* resembles it closely, even to the sinners being crunched in his three mouths.[54]

The devils and torments in *Inferno* are not Dante's own inventions. Such terrifying warnings were not only displayed in frescoes and mosaics: they were recited in rhyme by street entertainers, they were the subject of sermons and they were enacted.[55] The chronicler Giovanni Villani describes a festival held in 1304 in which were represented

> scenes and figures of Inferno, with fires and other punishments and tortures, with men disguised as devils horrible to look at and others representing figures of naked souls, enduring various torments with great shrieking and screaming and commotion, hateful and terrifying to hear and see.[56]

But Florence was also a joyful and brilliant city, full of prosperous, sophisticated and talented people, accustomed to luxuries, such as gold, silver and pearls; fine wool imported from England and Spain; silk, perfumes and spices imported from the Far East. Its wealth was created by craftsmen, organized into guilds, of which one of the most powerful was the guild of wool merchants. There were also cloth-makers, silk merchants, furriers, leather-makers and the guild of physicians, surgeons and apothecaries. Only members of the major guilds could take part in government, and Dante became a nominal member of the last mentioned when he decided to enter public life. Banking, scarcely organized elsewhere, was well advanced in Florence, with connections all over Europe. Women wore costly embroidered gowns, cut low to reveal the breasts; they wore jewels, they used makeup, they dyed their hair blond or auburn. The young men wore fitted hose and jerkins so short, Boccaccio says disapprovingly, that no woman could be in doubt as to their gender, even though their hair was long.[57] Significantly, in his biography he says that Dante's dress was always seemly. He may be speaking of Dante's middle and later years, when he wore the long dignified robe called a *lucco*, associated with the office of magistrate. In the portrait attributed to Giotto, Dante is shown wearing what appears to be a formal gown and his hair is concealed beneath the characteristic Florentine hood. It would be surprising, however, if as a young man he did not dress like his contemporaries on informal occasions. From his conversation with Forese Donati on the Mountain of Purgatory,[58] it is clear that in later years Dante also took a censorious view of ostentation and immodesty; and in *Paradiso*, through the words he gives to his ancestor Cacciaguida,[59] he nostalgically refers to the days when men wore plain buff coats, girt with leather belts, bone-buckled, and their wives wore clothes of home-spun thread and put no makeup on their faces. We do not know how he felt about such matters when he was young. We know only that he sought and enjoyed the company of beautiful women.

The poet Folgore da San Gimignano[60] has provided in a series of sonnets a radiant picture of social life in Tuscany. Known as 'The Garland of the Months',[61] they are addressed to a group of nobles in Siena but the details which emerge would apply equally well to Florence. We see the interior of houses, warmed by fires in January and lit by torches, beds laid with silk sheets and coverings of fur. In February there is hunting of the hare, deer and boar, the riders, clad in sturdy buskins and short jerkins buttoned close, coming home, their servants laden with the prey, to feast and drink wine and carouse. In March there is fish to be had from teeming rivers: lampreys, salmon, eel, trout and sturgeon. April is a month for sporting on the grass beside a fountain in the company of women; there are Spanish palfreys, the latest fashions from France, singing and dancing in the style of Provence, accompanied by music played on the newest instruments from Germany. May is the month of tournaments, with women looking on and joyfully embracing the victors. In June the fruit is ripe: lemons, oranges and dates; and in the shade of trees men and women sprawl at leisure. In July white Tuscan wine is brought up from cellars, cooled with ice; pheasant, partridge and capons in aspic, and veal flavoured with garlic are on the menu. In August, to escape the heat, people go into the mountains and take pleasure in riding from morning to eve. September is the time for hunting with falcons, astors, merlins, sparrowhawks or with hounds. October, November and December are the months for keeping warm indoors with wine, log fires and whole pigs roasting on the spit.

Dante as a young man took part in such pleasures, as far as his means permitted. His life is unlikely to have been limited to the rarefied occupation of writing idealistic love poems. In fact we have a suggestion that it was not, for once Guido Cavalcanti rebuked him in a sonnet for wasting his talents:

> I' vegno il giorno a te infinite volte
> e trovote pensar troppo vilmente;
> allor mi dol de la gentil tua mente
> e d'assai tue vertù che ti son tolte.
> Solevanti spiacer persone molte,
> tuttor fuggivi la noiosa gente ...

> *I come to thee by daytime constantly,*
> *but in thy thoughts too much of baseness find:*
> *greatly it grieves me for thy gentle mind,*
> *and for thy many virtues gone from thee.*
> *It was thy wont to shun such company,*
> *and all such sorry concourse ill inclined ...* [62]

Such was the environment in which Dante was born and grew to maturity. The contrasts between joy and horror are reflected in the conflicting aspects of his personality: on the one hand, realistic, earthy and sensual, and on the other, righteous, idealistic and visionary. His background accounts for him to some extent, but it cannot explain how, sharing these influences with his contemporaries, he yet so outstripped them as to become one of the greatest poets of the Western world. There is no explanation for genius but some clues as to why Dante developed as he did can be traced in the political events of his life and in his writings. The earliest of these were his love poems, particularly his selection and interpretation of them known as *La Vita Nuova*. This is the subject of the next chapter.

CHAPTER 2

Dante and Guido Cavalcanti

ante's first book, *La Vita Nuova*, written between 1292 and 1294, was the direct outcome of his friendship with Guido Cavalcanti. A treatise by a poet, written for poets, on the art of poetry, it is composed of a selection of Dante's early poems, accompanied by a commentary in prose. This is of two kinds. First, he narrates the events and feelings that led him to compose each poem; next, he analyses each poem from the point of view of structure and content.

The title, translated literally, means 'The New Life', but it is not even certain that Dante intended it to be the title of the whole work. It arises from the Latin words *Incipit vita nova*, which he says stand as a heading near the beginning of his book of memory. It may therefore be only an introduction to the first few chapters, which cover his childhood. There are at least two other indications later in the work that other headings were intended. The Latin word *novus* means not only 'new' but also 'first', 'inexperienced', 'untried'; it can also mean 'wonderful', 'marvellous', 'unheard of'. The Italian phrase *vita nuova* does not, in fact, occur anywhere in the text itself, but Dante refers to it with that title in *Il Convivio* ('The Banquet'), a philosophical work he wrote in the early years of his exile.[1] The phrase is used again, though ambiguously, in *Purgatorio*, where Beatrice, speaking of Dante to the angels, says:

> 'Questi fu tal nella sua vita nova
> virtualmente, ch'ogni abito destro
> fatto avrebbe in lui mirabil prova.'

> *'This man in his new life potentially,*
> *was such that every worthy gift from grace*
> *a wondrous bounty should have proved to be.'*[2]

In this context it seems to mean youth, or perhaps it is an allusion to the work itself. Whatever the explanation, an element of novelty, of things discovered and untried, is certainly a feature of *La Vita Nuova*.

The Italian vernacular was only about half a century old as a literary language when Dante and his contemporaries began writing verse. Compared with Old French and Provençal, it was limited in range and quality. Brunetto Latini, for instance, may have taught Dante many things but how to write verse was not one of them. His poem in Italian, *Il Tesoretto*, consists of a primitive jog-trot of seven-syllable couplets which give no inkling of how poets would transform the language within a generation.

When Dante first began circulating his poems, he entered into an exchange of sonnets, a *tenzone*, on the subject of love, with the same Dante of Maiano who returned such a coarse comment on Dante's account of his dream.[3] These early attempts show no great talent or originality on either side, but as soon as Dante came under the influence of Cavalcanti his knowledge widened and his verse improved. The Florentine circle and their contacts beyond Florence were professional men of distinction: Dino Frescobaldi was a member of a banking family, Lapo Gianni was a notary, Cino da Pistoia was an eminent scholar in jurisprudence. They were influenced by poets of an earlier generation, Guittone of Arezzo and especially Guido Guinizelli of Bologna, another lawyer. Cavalcanti himself was witty and profound, a student of philosophy, a reader of Albertus Magnus and Averroës. In his own poems he showed how terms from physiology and psychology could provide a new vocabulary in which to analyse the effects of love, terms which Dante borrowed.

Under the influence of Cavalcanti he tried his hand at the *canzone*. This was derived from the Provençal *canso*, a poem intended to be sung, as the word indicates. The structure was elaborate and in strict accordance with musical form. In common with all his educated contemporaries, Dante had been instructed in music. Like the other three components of the Quadrivium (arithmetic, geometry and astronomy) it was a study based on proportion and relationship. Number, conceived as the essence of all things, provided the key to an understanding of the universe. It also unlocked beauty. St Thomas Aquinas had said, 'The senses delight in things duly proportioned.' The creative challenge to link the potential of the new, untried language with concepts that embraced infinity and the cosmos must have been exhilarating indeed.

Conversation between Cavalcanti and Dante, as they stood on the brink of these uncharted waters, was destined to lead, in the case of Dante, to unprecedented exploration. In *La Vita Nuova*, if we listen carefully, we can hear snatches of their talk. Discussing the question of personification, Dante says that since the ancient Latin poets used it (and he gives examples), there is no reason why it should not also be used in vernacular rhyme, though never as a mere ornament: it must always be possible to reveal the true meaning that lies beneath.

I will add that the Latin poets did not write in this manner without good reason, nor should those who compose in rhyme,[4] if they cannot justify what they say; for it would be a disgrace if someone composing in rhyme introduced a figure of speech or rhetorical ornament, and then on being asked could not divest his words of such covering so as to reveal the true meaning. And this friend of mine and I know quite a number who compose rhymes in this stupid manner.[5]

In its colloquial tone, the last sentence (*E questo mio amico e io ne sapemo bene di quelli che così rimano stultamente*) is like an extract from a tape recorder, or even a video, for we not only hear them talking, we see them and sense Dante's gratification at being in agreement with his distinguished friend.

Not only is *La Vita Nuova* the outcome of such conversations. There is more than one hint that the work is written in accordance with Cavalcanti's advice. Dante says, for instance, that when Beatrice died he wrote a letter of lament in Latin, but he does not include it because it was his intention from the beginning to write this work only in Italian:

I am well aware, too, that my first friend, for whom I write this work (*a cui io ciò scrivo*), also desired that I should write it entirely in the vernacular.[6]

The words *a cui io ciò scrivo* have been understood to mean that Dante 'dedicated' the book to Cavalcanti. They may not bear such a formal significance but it is clear that the figure of his 'first friend' was at his elbow as he wrote. Even so, Dante does not entirely do without the authoritative *imprimatur* of the senior language. The book begins and ends with a Latin phrase and there are quotations from the Vulgate and classical authors in the course of the work; his faculties, personified as 'spirits' (a conceit he borrowed from Cavalcanti), and the figure of Love address him in Latin, as though the vernacular were too familiar for such high and significant converse.

By the time Beatrice died in 1290, aged 24, Dante had become recognized in Florence as a leading poet. His verses were sung, recited and memorized not only by men but also by women, some of whom commissioned him to write for them. That is to say, he now had a public. He and they realized that he was venturing into new territory.

In the beginning, like his Florentine friends, he had written within the conventions inherited from the troubadours and their Sicilian and Italian imitators. The stock situations were: the torment of unrequited love, the obligation to keep secret the name of the beloved, the device of a 'screen-love' to deceive the inquisitive, the personification of Death as a pitiless destroyer of youth, misunderstandings with the beloved, intolerable ecstasy in her presence and anguished mortification at her mockery. But a new ingredient had been added by Guido Guinizelli, who created the concept of the *cor gentile* ('gentle' or 'noble heart'), a quality of mind and soul that alone made it possible to experience the elevating effect of love.

The avant-garde poets who gathered round Cavalcanti saw themselves as an in-group who had special understanding of this concept. They perhaps met in Cavalcanti's house, bringing their latest compositions to be read aloud or more probably sung, for example by Casella, whose soul, 'met in the milder shores of Purgatory', Dante woos to sing again as he used to do in Florence, soothing Dante's longings with his songs of love.[7] Women were welcomed as members of the audience, and some of Dante's poems were addressed exclusively to them. They were not only sung but, in the case of *ballate*, accompanied by dancing. Possibly they were also expounded and discussed. If this is so, the prose sections of *La Vita Nuova* may be a development of such gatherings, which must have been rather in the nature of concerts or recitals. When a poet sent a composition directly to his lady the occasion was similar to an *aubade* or a serenade. Minstrels were employed on regular wages in a sizable household and accounts often furnish names and sometimes specify the instruments played. Whether such minstrels were employed by Cavalcanti is not known.

It is easy to forget that these poets led everyday lives, pursued their professions, took part in politics, attended social functions, met and courted attractive women, married and had love affairs. Guido Cavalcanti and Lapo Gianni, for instance, who were both married, are said to have shared the same mistress. Like the others, they separated their real from their imaginative lives, in which the experience of love, analysed in terms of new concepts, underwent a process of spiritualization.

The society in which Dante moved was small and closely knit. People took a keen interest in one another's affairs, especially love affairs, and there was much gossip. When at the age of 18 Dante realized that he was in love with the adult Beatrice, he tried to conceal his feelings from all except his poet friends. He only once disclosed her name in writing (and that in the abbreviated form of Bice[8]) while she was still alive. This was in accordance with the rules of the literary game, but may also reflect what he actually did. What distinguishes *La Vita Nuova* is the amount of vivid social detail it provides.

He describes being in church one day, sitting where he could gaze at Beatrice, who was also present. Another woman, who sat in his line of vision, thought he was gazing at her and this gave him the idea of making her his 'screen-love', to deceive those who were taking too much interest in him. The scene is not difficult to imagine: the other woman who in her vanity thought Dante was attracted to her, the friends who thought so too, the nudges and raised eyebrows, the chatter and laughter as they came out of church. Not much attention can have been paid to the sermon that day.

The 'screen-love's' delusion must have been confirmed by the poems that Dante wrote for her. Possibly it was not a delusion and he did make his feelings known to her. Why not? He says that her appearance was very pleasing; he was a young man, much given to philandering, according to Boccaccio. The pretence, if it was pretence, was maintained, he says, for 'several years and months'. When she left Florence he admits he was more dismayed than he would have believed possible and, to keep up appearances, he wrote a lament.

Eventually he replaced her by another 'screen-love'. His way of narrating this is figurative. He says that he was riding on a journey with a company of people, feeling despondent because he was leaving the city where his true love lived. Along the way, he met Love dressed in humble, travelling clothes, who advised him to take a new 'screen-love'. He named her; it was someone Dante knew well. On his return to Florence he played the part of her admirer so ardently that malicious gossip reached the ears of Beatrice, who cut him in the street.

Her refusal to greet him upset him deeply. He fled to the privacy of his room where he lay on his bed and wept, falling asleep 'like a little child that has been beaten'. In his sleep, he dreamt that Love stood beside him in the figure of a young man dressed in white. He gazed pensively at Dante, then, sighing, spoke to him in Latin, saying: 'My son, it is time for our false images to be set aside.' He then wept and when Dante asked him why, he said, again in Latin: 'I am like the centre of a circle, to which the parts of the circumference are related in similar manner; you, however, are not.' When Dante asked what these words meant, Love replied, in the vernacular: 'Do not ask more than is useful for you'. He then explained why Beatrice had withdrawn her greeting: his attentions to the 'screen-love' had given rise to scandal and she feared her own name might suffer likewise.

Since Dante's long-kept secret was already partly known to Beatrice, Love advised him to write a poem addressed indirectly to her, saying that he had loved her ever since his boyhood and that when his gaze rested on another woman Love made him see in her face the face of Beatrice: 'In this way she will come to know your true desire and will see how mistaken are those who speak ill of you.' He is to take special care that the poem is set to harmonious music. Since it is a *ballata*, it will be accompanied by dancing, as well as sung.

This imaginary dialogue between himself and the figure of Love represents Dante's guilt and embarrassment. He has been indiscreet in his affair with the new 'screen-love'; he knows that he has been deceiving himself in pretending that his love is always pure and ennobling, though he believes that there is a perfect state of mind and soul in which all love is good.

He personifies the *ballata*, requesting it to seek the company of Love. Together they are to visit Beatrice and ask her forgiveness. When Beatrice has heard the song performed, Love is to explain the reasons for Dante's apparent love of other women. Beneath the complex poetic figure may be glimpsed the picture of Beatrice receiving the dancers and singers into her home or perhaps her garden, watching and listening to them. From an event which followed soon afterwards it does not seem that she was much affected.

A friend invited Dante to accompany him to a wedding reception. Among the guests was Beatrice. He sensed her presence even before he saw her and became so faint that he had to lean 'for support against a fresco painted in a frieze round the walls of the house'. This was observed by other women who laughed at him, and Beatrice too, alas, joined in their mockery. He was so overcome that he thought he was dying. His friend had to take him by the hand and lead him away. He returned to his room, where again he wept, in an agony of shame. It occurred to him that if he explained to Beatrice why the sight of her had so overwhelmed him she might have compassion on him. Although Love had told him it would not be fitting to address her directly (that is, it was contrary to convention to do so), he did now address three sonnets to her. The first of these, reproaching her for her mockery, begins:

> Con l'altre donne mia vista gabbate,
> e non pensate, donna, onde si mova
> ch'io vi rassembri sì figura nova
> quando riguardo la vostra beltate.
> Se lo saveste, non poria Pietate
> tener più contra me l'usata prova,
> chè Amor, quando sì presso a voi mi trova,
> prende baldanza e tanta securitate. ...

> *With your companions you make fun of me,*
> *not thinking, Lady, what the reason is*
> *I cut so strange a figure in your eyes*
> *when, raising mine, your loveliness I see.*
> *If you but knew, Pity no more could be*
> *severe towards me in her usual guise.*
> *Finding me near you, Love his weapons tries,*
> *gaining in boldness and temerity. ...*[9]

Bewildered by the effect which the sight of Beatrice has upon him, Dante converses with himself, asking, 'Since I take on such an absurd appearance whenever I am near her, why do I still try to see her? If she asked you this, what would you say to her?' He expresses this bewilderment in the other two sonnets addressed to her.

Later a group of women, perhaps those who were present at the wedding, asked him what the point of his love was, since he was overcome by faintness in his lady's presence. He replied that his joy originally lay in her greeting but now that this was denied him he found all his beatitude in writing words in praise of her. One of the women retorted: 'If that were true, your verses would be very different.' With feminine directness, she had put her finger on the nub: his poems up to then had been self-pitying laments. The dialogue suggests that Dante may have met with a similar challenge at one of the poetry recitals.

Thinking the matter over, Dante realized that the women were right: the time had come for him to concentrate in his poems on the beauty and virtue of Beatrice and forget his sufferings. But the more he thought about it, the more afraid he was to begin, as though he were verging on an enterprise that might prove beyond his powers. Then one day, as he walked by a stream of very clear water, his tongue, as though moved of its own accord, uttered the words:

Donne ch'avete intelletto d'amore.

Ladies who understanding have of love.

This seemed to him to be an excellent beginning for a poem, as well as for the new direction he wished to take. He stored the line away in his mind for several days until he found the resolve to continue. The completed poem is the first canzone in *La Vita Nuova* and ushers in what have been called the poems of praise.

There was nothing new in poems of praise. This was a very usual theme in the poetry of the time. What is different is that the imaginative transforma-tion of Dante's experience of love had entered a new stage. Beatrice was now more than the focus of a conventional, poeticized love. In thinking of writ-ing poems in praise of her he came to realize that she represented something beyond herself: ideal virtue, incomparable beauty, a paradisiacal being for whose presence in Heaven the angels and the saints were clamouring. This is Dante's first step towards a new form of allegory: it is not personification or symbolism, but the perception that actual persons can be images of qualities beyond themselves, not only in masques and pageants but in real life. This would immensely enlarge his range, leading eventually to the creation of the convincing, unforgettable characters who people the *Commedia*, and at the same time represent sins or virtues.

Years later, when he was two-thirds of the way through his major work, Dante looked back to this *canzone* and recognized it as a turning point. In *Purgatorio*, on the Cornice of the Gluttons, he introduces the soul of the poet Bonagiunta of Lucca, to whom he gives the following words:

> 'Ma dì s' i' veggio qui colui che fore
>   trasse le nove rime, cominciando
>   *"Donne ch'avete intelletto d'amore."'*

> *'But say, do I see here the man who wove*
> *the strands of those new verses which begin,*
>   *"Ladies who understanding have of love?"'*

Dante answers:

>   ... 'I' mi son un che, quando
> Amor mi spira, noto, e a quel modo
> ch'e' ditta dentro vo significando.'

>   ... *'I am one who when*
> *Love breathes in me, take note, and in the way*
> *that he dictates I say what his words mean.'*[10]

Bonagiunta answers: 'Oh, now I see what is meant by what they call the *dolce stil nuovo.*'

The Italian phrase, *dolce stil nuovo*, is usually translated into English as 'sweet new style', but that is not what it means. In Italian, as in French, when there are two or more adjectives it is the final one that carries the emphasis. In English, this is the function of the first adjective. The point is that there was already a *dolce stile* ('a sweet style'), as there was an *aspro stile* ('a harsh style'). What Dante had initiated was a *new* sweet style.

Dante da Maiano was not the only one who made fun of him. Cecco Angiolieri, who wrote comic verse, teased him about an apparent contradiction in one of his sonnets and quoted some of his words in gentle mockery. Dante did not expect (or even want) many of his readers to understand him and he said so more than once. Sometimes he said that a poem was written only for a specially chosen group of readers, such as women who understood the meaning of love. At the same time, Dante did not always take himself as solemnly as some of his commentators do. He wrote some teasing lines to a certain Brunetto Brunelleschi, accompanying a poem he knew would be beyond his wits. In another sonnet he made fun of himself for absent mindedly gazing up at the leaning Carisenda tower in Bologna, oblivious to what was going on around him. Perhaps he was absorbed in watching the effect of a cloud passing over in a direction contrary to the tower's slant, which makes it seem as if the tower is falling. He was to remember this effect in describing the stooping of a giant in *Inferno*.[11] A delightful tease, unnoticed by Dante scholars, occurred in the eighteenth century, when Lorenzo da Ponte (who was well read in Italian literature) wrote his charming parody of '*Donne ch'avete intelletto d'amore*' in the words he gives the love-sick Cherubino to sing to 'his' ladies in *Le Nozze di Figaro*:

Voi che sapete che cosa è amor ...

When the *canzone* had been heard by several people, a friend asked Dante to write a poem defining love. To do so he had recourse to a definition already provided by the predecessor from whom he and his friends acknowledged derivation: Guido Guinizelli. He does not give his name but refers to him as *il saggio* ('the wise man') and quotes his concept of the 'noble heart':

Amor e 'l cor gentil sono una cosa,
sì come il saggio in suo dittare pone,
e così esser l'un sanza l'altro osa
com'alma razional sanza ragione.
Falli natura quand' è amorosa,
Amor per sire e 'l cor per sua magione,
dentro la qual dormendo si riposa
tal volta poca e tal lunga stagione.
Bieltate appare in saggia donna pui,
che piace a li occhi sì, che entro al core
nasce un disio de la cosa piacente;
e tanto dura talora in costui,
che fa svegliar lo spirito d'Amore.
E simil face in donna omo valente.

Love and the noble heart are but one thing,
even as the wise man tells us in his rhyme,
the one without the other venturing
no more than reason from a reasoning mind.
Nature, disposed to love, creates Love king,
making the heart a dwelling-place for him
wherein he lies quiescent, slumbering
sometimes a little, now a longer time.
Then beauty in a virtuous woman's face
pleases the eyes, striking the heart so deep
a yearning for the pleasing thing may rise.
Sometimes so long it lingers in that place
Love's spirit is awakened from his sleep.
By a worthy man a woman's moved likewise.[12]

The last line seems an off-hand, last-moment attempt to imagine a reciprocal response on the part of a woman. This is unusual and the idea is not developed. Dante and his fellow poets wrote of love from the man's point of view. The women they praised were beautiful, virtuous, gracious and modest;

the love they inspired was elevating and transforming. What they themselves experienced does not seem to have been a subject for poetry. In the previous generation there had been a woman poet, known as *la compiuta donzella* ('the accomplished damsel'), but only three sonnets by her remain and they were not influenced by Guinizelli.

What Beatrice felt about Dante and about his idealization of her we can only guess. Perhaps it was a matter of pride, both to her and to her husband, that she should be the object of the outstanding devotion of so admired a poet. We see her first as an adult walking down a street in Florence, dressed in white, decorously accompanied by two older women; she turns on noticing Dante and greets him graciously. Next she is offended by the excessive attention he pays to a 'screen-lady' and we see the scornful toss of her head as she cuts him in the street. Then we find her laughing, unkindly, with other women at his trembling embarrassment in her presence. In a sonnet, not included in *La Vita Nuova*, we see her among a group of beautiful women, she the most beautiful of them all, at a celebration of All Saints' Day, when Dante dares to look her directly in the face and sees an image of an angel. Wherever she goes she inspires virtue. Her greeting, when she is disposed to grant it, bestows salvation and fills him with love of the whole world. In one sonnet he describes his happiness on seeing her walking behind Giovanna, whom Cavalcanti once loved, and in the commentary he interprets the occasion as a revelation of Christ preceded by St John the Baptist. By the time he wrote the commentary, his perception of the natural as an image of the supernatural had reached an advanced stage. To understand how Beatrice is related to this image and to other visions of her, he resolved to devote himself to a period of study and reflection, in order, as he says at the end of the work, to prepare himself to write of Beatrice what had never before been written in verse of any woman.[13]

As to Beatrice's appearance, Dante says that her complexion was pearllike, but not pale to excess. In *Purgatorio* he refers to her eyes as *smeraldi* ('emeralds'). If this means that her eyes were green (though, like so many things concerning Beatrice, this has been disputed), then it may be that her hair was auburn. This would account for the pale skin, which is a feature of people with reddish hair. She was devout and had a profound veneration for the Virgin Mary. We do not know where she was educated: most probably by nuns at a convent school. When her father died she was deeply grieved, although she was by then married and had left her family home.[14] She herself died the following year. We do not know whether she had children; it may be that she died in childbirth. Dante says, in the third *canzone*, that she had suffered no chill or fever; she simply died suddenly.

In the prose which follows the third *canzone* he says that he does not intend to discuss 'her departure from us', *la sua partita da noi*, a phrase interpreted as referring to her death. It is more likely, however, that it refers to her funeral. He gives three reasons for not discussing it: first, it is outside the subject of his book; secondly he does not possess adequate words to treat of it; and thirdly, to do so would involve him in self-praise. This has been unconvincingly interpreted as meaning that for him she had become such that to speak of her death would reflect glory upon him as well as upon her. He limits himself to showing that the date of her death, at the ninth hour on 9 June 1290, calculated by the Arabian, Syrian and Roman calendars, corresponds in hour, day, month and year with the number nine, 'with which number she was always associated'.

Funerals were very public affairs in Florence and the mourning for a beautiful young woman, whose father had been renowned, whose husband also was an eminent citizen, must have been widespread. Dante, the distinguished poet, whose poems to her were so much admired, and who was also a close friend of one of her brothers, is likely to have been an honoured guest, perhaps even one of the chief mourners. How could it have been otherwise? It is possible even that one of his poems to her was recited or sung, or, more probably, the lament in Latin which he says he wrote after her death was read out at her funeral.[15] To have spoken of this would indeed have been to speak in praise of himself and this may well be what he means when he speaks so mysteriously of his third reason for not discussing what he calls 'her departure from us'. This cannot simply mean her death, about which, in fact, he goes on to speak at some length.

In writing previously of the death of the father of Beatrice, he does discuss public aspects of that event, explaining that it was the custom in Florence for women and men to mourn the dead separately.[16] Thus it is that he sees a group of women returning from mourning with Beatrice and hears them exclaiming about her grief, saying 'How bitterly she weeps!' It makes Dante himself weep to hear them and they are amazed, on passing him, to observe his grief and say to each other, 'Look at this man. He is so distressed that you would think he had seen her weeping as we have.' Dante would have liked to speak with them but that would not have been fitting, for at such moments men and women did not mingle.

Nevertheless, grief was as freely manifested in public as in private and it was the pious duty of relatives and friends to wail and lament out loud, or, to use the Irish word, to 'keen'. After this ritual, came the funeral, the coffin being carried through the streets, followed by a long procession in which members of the public joined, as may still be seen in Italy to this day. The funeral of Beatrice would have been an event of great social importance in Florence. Dante in fact speaks of the city as being widowed by her loss.

In the second *canzone*, which occupies a central position in the book, he describes the nightmare he suffered during his illness, in which he saw Beatrice lying dead. His commentary contains details which suggest that he may actually have gone to her house and witnessed the ritual of her laying-out:

> I seemed to go to see the body in which that most noble and blessed soul had been; and the illusion was so powerful that I saw my lady lying dead, and women seemed to be covering her, that is, her head, with a white veil. ... When I had seen all the sorrowful necessities completed which it is necessary to perform for the bodies of the dead, I thought I returned to my room.[17]

He insists that all this was the vain imagining of a nightmare, but some commentators believe that this poem was written after her death and inserted into *La Vita Nuova* as a pseudo-prophetic vision. If this is the case, he may have converted what actually happened to the status of a dream. From an episode related earlier in the work, it appears that he had paid at least one such visit of respect, on the occasion of the death of a young woman 'who had graced the city with her loveliness':

> I saw her lifeless body lying where many women were mourning piteously over it. When I remembered that I had seen her formerly in the company of my most gracious one I could not help shedding a few tears.[18]

And as he wept he decided to compose something about her death.

His grief on the death of Beatrice is overpowering. He makes no attempt to conceal it; on the contrary he deliberately makes it public and seems to take comfort in the fact that people are concerned at his forlorn aspect. He has reached the stage where the merest glance of sympathy sets him weeping again, when he catches sight of a beautiful woman looking at him from a window with every appearance of compassion.

He never names this woman, probably because she was still alive; she is referred to simply as *la donna gentile* ('the gracious lady'). He finds himself drawn more and more to her; he writes sonnets to her; he debates with himself as to the nature of this new attachment. It must, he thinks, be a very noble love, but he then declares that his heart is the enemy of his reason[19] and he reproaches himself with infidelity to the memory of Beatrice. Finally he has a vision of her as a child, as he first saw her, and this makes him resolve to put an end to the affair.

In *Il Convivio* Dante interprets the *donna gentile* as Philosophy. He does not deny, however, that she was a real woman. This is another example of perceiving an actual person as an image of something beyond herself. He says that she replaced Beatrice and that this can be confirmed by reference to the end of *La Vita Nuova*. This is one of the most disputed passages in

Dante's writings. At the end of the earlier work Dante says that his love for Beatrice ended by being victorious over his feelings for the *donna gentile*, not the other way round. Attempts have been made to reconcile the two texts. It has even been suggested that there was an earlier version of *La Vita Nuova*, which Dante then altered. The apparent contradiction can be solved, however, if we understand that in *Il Convivio* he is referring to his resolve to put off writing poems about Beatrice until he had completed a period of study. In other words, it is a question, not of one woman replacing another, but of one activity (the writing of love poems to Beatrice) being superseded by another (the study of philosophy).[20]

Why did Dante introduce the *donna gentile* into *La Vita Nuova* at all? Probably because the poems he wrote to her had been heard by many people, who were also aware of his new attachment. The poems needed to be explained, as did the affair. For a real affair it probably was and, as affairs do, it came to an end. Nevertheless the consolation he derived from it was later perceived by him to be an image of the consolation he derived at the same period from his study of philosophy, and this is a concept he pursues, not without further obfuscation, in *Il Convivio*.

His affair with the *donna gentile* had brought his grieving to an end. If, as seems likely, he was by then married to Gemma Donati, it must have tried her patience to have a husband continually in tears. Perhaps Guido Cavalcanti suggested writing *La Vita Nuova* as a remedy. Many poets, Ted Hughes, to take a modern example, have tried a similar therapy. In Dante's case, there seems to have been a need to reveal as well as a desire to conceal and mislead. Both poems and explanations are equivocal.

Up to this point, Dante's poems had been known more by ear than by eye. Parchment was expensive and even paper was scarce, so few written copies can have been in circulation. *La Vita Nuova*, on the other hand, was intended as a permanent document, to be referred to by those who wished to know how the poems came to be written and how they should be understood. At the same time, it is also possible that the work was read aloud, possibly by Dante himself. The analytical sections represent what was known as a *divisio textus*, a division of the text into parts according to content. Contemporary readers, accustomed to this method of clarification, no doubt found it enlightening. Modern readers find it tedious. It is said that when Dante Gabriel Rossetti was at work on his translation, he found these passages so uninspiring that he asked his brother William to translate them for him.

What is intriguing is that the divisions do not correspond to the formal structure of the poems. The emphasis is on the argument and its development. Dante evidently thought it necessary to make clear where these articulations occur, as though the metrical form of the poem or its musical setting would obscure the meaning. It may also be that the analyses were intended as a guide to those who wished to read the poems aloud, or to composers invited to set them to music. Whatever their function, they play an important part in the structure and design of the work.

The arrangement of *La Vita Nuova* is based on an elaborate pattern, of which the number nine (the square of three, the symbol of the Trinity) is the key. The 31 poems are placed in the following sequence: ten short poems, one *canzone*, four short poems, one *canzone*, four short poems, one *canzone*, ten short poems. The mid-point of this series is the second *canzone*. With its supporting eight short poems, four preceding and four following, it is the centre of a central group of nine. This central group is flanked by two ones, which are in turn flanked by two tens, thus:

$$10 + 1 + 9 + 1 + 10$$

which can also be arranged as:

$$1 + 9 + 1 + 9 + 1 + 9 + 1$$

in which the number nine occurs three times.

The second *canzone* is the central panel of a triptych, of which the first and third *canzoni* are the supporting panels to the left and right. This can be taken to signify the division of Dante's life into two parts, the period before Beatrice's death and the period after it. The pattern is further emphasized by a bilateral symmetry in which the earthly life of Beatrice at the beginning is mirrored by her celestial nature at the end. The mirror-imaging is further managed by the position of the analyses of the poems, which before Beatrice's death follow them and after her death precede them, in order, Dante says, that the later poems may seem more 'widowed'.

This fascination with numerical pattern is characteristic not only of Dante but of his contemporaries. By understanding the virtue of numbers, the relationship between them, their squares and their cubes and what was known as mystic addition,[21] it was possible to see that the same mathematical laws governed all life. In making a work of art it was necessary to employ a numerological symbolism in order to control the relationship of its parts to the whole. Such patterns of thought had been inherited from Pythagoras and preserved for the Middle Ages by St Augustine and Martianus Capella, among others. The doctrine of the Trinity led Christian writers to perceive patterns of three throughout creation and to construct their works according to a triple pattern. What is unique in Dante is the extraordinary skill he would eventually show in applying such control to the construction of the *Commedia*.[22]

We do not know how Guido Cavalcanti received *La Vita Nuova*. He must have been gratified that it was written in accordance with his advice. He was not to know, however, that it was the first step on an unprecedented journey, for he died in 1300. The circumstances of his death, in which Dante was tragically involved, are part of Florentine politics, the subject of the next chapter.

CHAPTER 3

Disaster

I t was 1295. Dante was now 30. In 12 years, from being a young unknown versifier, he had become an admired member of a distinguished group of poets. His poems were sung, recited and memorized; copies were made of them, even beyond Florence. He had given permanent form to a selection of them in an elegantly constructed memorial to his lady. He was married and had a young family. He had moved on from writing poetry to Beatrice and was devoting himself to the study of philosophy and to the writing of odes with a philosophic and social content. Now of mature age, he had attained full citizenship of the Republic of Florence and was eligible to take part in public duties. Perhaps it was now that he began to wear the long dignified robe called the *lucco*.

Something very splendid had happened in the spring of 1294. Charles Martel, great-grandson of King Louis VIII of France, who had been crowned King of Hungary at the age of 19 and was also heir to the Kingdom of Naples and to the County of Provence, visited Florence, where he remained for three weeks, awaiting the arrival from France of his father, Charles II of Anjou. The Florentines were overjoyed to welcome the young royal. He arrived accompanied by 200 French and Neapolitan knights arrayed in scarlet and dark green, their horses' saddle cloths embroidered with gold lilies bordered with gold and silver.[1] Magnificent entertainments were organized. Dante, the distinguished poet, was invited to take a prominent part and one of his *canzoni* was performed.[2] A friendship developed and Dante perhaps hoped that Charles would offer him patronage in some sphere of public life. Any hopes he may have had were blighted the following year when Charles died of plague in Naples. Regret for what might have been is poignantly conveyed in *Paradiso*, where the soul of Charles Martel, in the Heaven of Venus, greets Dante by quoting the first line of the *canzone*,[3] recalling their affection and lamenting his early death, but for which Dante's life might have been very different.

This heady moment of finding himself close to power and in the midst of splendour may have led to Dante's decision to enter public life. To do so it was necessary to join one of the guilds. He chose that of the Physicians and Apothecaries. It has been said that the reason for his choice was that manuscripts were sold at apothecaries' shops; another may have been that painters were also members of this guild. It is more likely that his new studies in philosophy rendered him eligible to the fellowship of men of science, or 'natural philosophy' as it was called. To his distinction as a poet he was adding the *gravitas* of the status of a student of philosophy. This enlarged his professional as well as his intellectual range.

Dante's family and that of his wife were Guelfs. The Guelf party had held power in Florence for a quarter of a century, but the threat of reprisal by Ghibelline exiles was always present. There had been an attempt in 1289, repulsed at the Battle of Campaldino, in which Dante had fought in the cavalry. There was also the delicate problem of defending the independence of Florence against the ambitions of the Pope while at the same time relying on Papal influence to discourage plans of the Emperor's supporters to encroach upon Tuscany.

Power within Florence itself swayed between magnates and commoners. The oppression of the people by the nobles had recently provoked a rebellion, led by Giano della Bella, himself a member of a noble family, who brought about a reform of the government, enacted in a series of new laws known as the *Ordinamenti della Giustizia* (Ordinances of Justice). These provisions had come into effect in 1293, only two years before Dante became involved in political matters. All members of noble families were now excluded from office, and harsh penalties were imposed on any manifestation of resistance. On the other hand, participation in government was opened to wider sections of the community than ever before. One result of these changes was to set Guido Cavalcanti and Dante Alighieri on different sides. Guido, a member of a noble family, was barred from office; Dante, of distinguished but lesser lineage, was eligible for membership of a guild and so for participation in government.

The structure of the new Florentine government consisted of a *Gonfaloniere di Giustizia* (Standard-bearer of Justice), who was an elected official with an army of 1,000 to enforce the Ordinances, supported by six Priors, elected by the major guilds, who held office for two months. There were three councils: one of 100 members which was responsible for finance; one of 300 members which advised the official known as the *podestà* (elected as an independent arbiter from outside Florence); and one of 150 members which advised an official known as the *Capitano del Popolo* (Captain of the People). Each council was re-elected every six months and no councillor could be re-elected to the body on which he had just served. Power was thus effectively distributed, balanced and curtailed, and members of the government were vigilant in defence of their new constitution.

Official documents record that Dante spoke in a number of debates. A supporter of the White Guelfs, he was elected a member of the executive body known as the Council of the Hundred and became recognized as an eloquent and persuasive speaker. In May 1300 he was sent as a delegate to San Gimignano where he addressed the commune on a matter relating to the Tuscan Guelf League. After five years of active participation he was elected one of six Priors, to hold office from 15 June to 15 August 1300.

By then the situation in Florence had become difficult and dangerous. The Guelf party had split into two factions, known as the Whites and the Blacks.[4] The Blacks were reputed to be more militant and aggressive than the Whites but in that respect there was little to choose between them. The leader of the Blacks in Florence was Corso Donati, handsome, popular, aggressive and ambitious, the brother of Dante's friend Forese and a cousin of Dante's wife. Like Dante, he had fought with valour at the Battle of Campaldino.[5] The leader of the Whites was Vieri de' Cerchi, a member of a family that had recently come into wealth and prominence and whose ostentatious lives aroused resentment and envy. Guido Cavalcanti, though disbarred from government, was an active supporter of the Whites. Corso Donati was a bitter enemy of Cavalcanti, whom he dubbed insultingly *'Cavicchia'* (a word meaning peg, an equivalent presumably of 'prick') and it is said that he attempted to have him murdered. Cavalcanti, in retaliation, aimed a spear at Corso, but missed. The magnates, or grandees, resented being excluded from government and there were continual riots and protestations.

The office of Prior, representing the highest status in the Florentine Republic, carried great prestige, but since it was tenable only for two months it was held in turn by a fair number of persons. Election signified, therefore, little more than good standing and the trust of one's fellow participants in public life. While it lasted the position was princely. Throughout their two months in office Priors were obliged to live in seclusion, in the Torre della Castagna, forbidden to accept private invitations or to have contact with outsiders, rather like a jury under English law, protected from intimidation, bribery or any other form of corrupt influence. When they walked abroad they were distinguished by their coats of crimson cloth, adorned with ermine linings, collars and cuffs. The Palazzo della Signoria, on which construction began in the 1290s, was intended as an improved official residence for the Priors. What is now called the Piazza della Signoria was known in Dante's time as the Piazza dei Priori.

Even after his term of office, Dante was called upon to serve the Republic in various ways. In April 1301 he was appointed to superintend the widening and straightening of a road in Florence, undertaken so that reinforcements could be brought in easily to protect the city against attacks by the magnates or against the return of exiled Ghibellines. On 19 June of that year he spoke in two debates. On both occasions he opposed the application of Pope Boniface VIII for support from Florence for a campaign he was waging against personal enemies. A motion to send money and troops was carried but Dante's vote was recorded as a decided negative. This may be an example of the kind of imprudence of which he later accused himself, in a letter seen by Leonardo Bruni, in which he traced all his misfortunes to his election as Prior.

His most painful duty befell him while he still held office. On May Day 1300, six weeks before his election, violent rioting broke out in the city. The hostility between the Black and White Guelfs came to a head and the Pope sent Cardinal Matteo of Acquasparta to make peace; he did not succeed. On 23 June, the Eve of the Feast of St John the Baptist, the processing heads of the guilds were set upon by some of the nobles, who shouted: 'We won Campaldino and now you keep us out of office!' The Priors, in an attempt to restore calm, decided to banish the leaders of both sides. The most prominent of the Blacks were confined to Castel della Pieve in Umbria; the leaders of the Whites, including Guido Cavalcanti, were sent to Sarzana in the Lunigiana.[6] This was a malarial district and Guido fell ill. In consequence, he was allowed to return to Florence, where he died at the end of August 1300.

This was a tragic ending to a friendship that had been so important to Dante in his early years. He refers to it obliquely, with moving subtlety, in *Inferno*. The fictional date of the journey through Hell, Purgatory and Paradise is Easter Week of the year 1300. When he began writing the *Commedia* Dante had been in exile for several years. This gap between fictional and real time enabled him to contrive pseudo-prophecies, making his created *persona*, the character Dante, unaware of what was to happen. One of the most memorable of these occurs in the Circle of the Heretics, whose souls are entombed in burning sepulchres. The scene is dominated by the towering figure of Farinata degli Uberti, the Ghibelline warrior who led a crushing defeat of the Guelfs at the Battle of Montaperti in 1260.[7]

The proud heretic, who seems to hold all Hell in scorn, challenges the traveller, whose voice he has recognized as Tuscan. 'Who were your ancestors?' he asks. Dante informs him. Farinata slightly raises his eyebrows and says scornfully: 'They were fierce enemies of mine, but twice I scattered them.' Dante, the Guelf, collects his self-command and replies, no less challengingly: 'They twice returned, but your party has not learned that skill.' This is a painful thrust: Farinata's party had been in exile for 40 years. Ghibelline and Guelf are now locked eyeball to eyeball and there is silence.

The scene must have been full of drama for contemporary listeners, especially Florentines. The Battle of Montaperti and the intention of the victorious side to raze Florence to the ground had not been forgotten. Members of the Uberti family were permanently exiled and their property destroyed. Farinata himself had been posthumously declared a heretic and his bones disinterred from hallowed ground and scattered.

Before Farinata can retort, another soul rises from the same tomb, a less impressive figure, reaching about up to Farinata's chin. 'I think,' says Dante, 'that he was kneeling.' Looking bewilderedly round, as though searching for someone, this second soul asks, in quavering tones, 'If loftiness of intellect gives thee the right to walk through this dark prison ...

'mio figlio ov'è? Perchè non è ei teco?'

Where is my son? Why is he not here with thee?[8]

The thin, whining tones of the repeated vowel *e* in the original Italian are skilfully suggestive of a querulous old man.

Dante realizes that this is the father of Guido Cavalcanti, reputed to have been a heretic, and he answers, somewhat enigmatically: 'I am not here by my own virtue. He who waits there is leading me to her for whom perhaps your Guido felt disdain.' His use of the past tense (*forse cui Guido vostro ebbe a disdegno*[9]) plunges the father into confusion and despair. Is his son then dead? Dante hesitates in his reply and the soul falls back into the tomb in grief.

Farinata, who has stood motionless, unmoved by this interruption, resumes his confrontation of Dante, saying: 'The continued exile of my party torments me more than this tomb which is my bed; but within fifty months you will know how difficult an art it is to return from banishment.'

This is a forecast of Dante's own exile. Before he can reply, Farinata asks him why the Florentines are so hostile to his descendants. Dante answers, 'They have not forgotten the great slaughter that stained the river Arbia red with blood.' Farinata sighs and shakes his head: 'I was not alone in that,' he says, 'but when it was decided to destroy Florence, then I stood alone against the council and faced them openly.'

Dante then conveys a perplexity, the reply to which contains what is in fact a moving farewell to Guido, but so veiled that it has gone unnoticed: 'You souls in Hell, it seems, can see the future, but are confused as to the present.' Farinata confirms that they are like people who have long sight: they can see events far off but as things draw near their vision of them grows dim. Dante now understands the other soul's bewilderment and requests Farinata to tell him that his son is still among the living.

That was true in the timeframe of the story, but what Dante the character does not know is that Guido's exile too is approaching, a sentence that would be signed by Dante himself as Prior, and which would result in his death. This is a hidden prophecy, impossible for the father to foresee because it will happen so soon, of no concern to the haughty Ghibelline, though he was Guido's father-in-law, too painful for the writer Dante to convey more plainly.

It is interesting to notice that when addressing both Farinata and Cavalcanti senior, Dante uses the respectful *voi*, whereas they both address him as *tu*. The same occurs in his conversation with Brunetto Latini,[10] with Guido Guinizelli,[11] with Dante's crusader ancestor Cacciaguida,[12] and with Beatrice (except in his farewell prayer to her). Here is an echo of the social etiquette of Dante's time. His form of address to Virgil, however, for all his reverence of him, is the intimate *tu*, expressive of the close bond between them.

The year 1300 was of unique significance for the Christian world. Pope Boniface had declared a Jubilee, offering plenary absolution to all repentant pilgrims who visited the shrines of St Peter and St Paul and made a full confession of their sins. There had been no such event on such a scale before. The response was immediate and immense. Rome was crowded throughout the year with pilgrims from all over Europe. Florentines too set out in great numbers, on horseback, in carriages, on foot, staying at hostelries along the way or camping out. Among them was Giovanni Villani. He was so affected by the sight of Rome that he decided to write a chronicle, just as Edward Gibbon, 500 years later, sitting among the ancient ruins, resolved to write his history of the Empire's decline and fall. Recalling his impressions, Villani wrote:

> Finding myself on that blessed pilgrimage in the holy city of Rome, beholding the great and ancient things therein, and reading the stories and the great doings of the Romans, written by Virgil and Sallust and Lucan and Titus Livius and Valerius and Paulus Orosius, and other masters of history ... I resolved myself to preserve memorials ... for those who should come after.[13]

Villani estimated that on every day of the Jubilee no fewer than 200,000 pilgrims thronged the streets. He himself had been in danger of being trampled underfoot. Another chronicler, Guglielmo Ventura of Asti, estimated that the total number for the whole year amounted to about 2 million.

Among the pilgrims from Florence was Dante. The first sight of Rome to a traveller from the north was from Montemario. He would later make his ancestor Cacciaguida allude to it in *Paradiso*.[14] Crossing the bridge of Castel St Angelo, Dante was impressed by the method of crowd control, whereby the traffic was regulated into two columns, facing opposite directions. He was to make satirical use of this in the arrangement he provides for the panders and seducers in *Inferno*.[15] But his attitude to Rome was not scornful; quite the contrary. In *Il Convivio* he refers with awe to the 'noble city ... the holy city, of which the very stones of the encircling walls are worthy of reverence and the soil on which she stands more hallowed than has ever been acknowledged'.[16]

The vast crowds of pilgrims from near and far, mainly burghers and simple peasants, with their clamour of foreign tongues, their alien dress and aspect, provided Dante with his first physical awareness of the variety and dimensions of the European world. Of this world Rome was the spiritual and historical centre, an inspiring vision that transcended local politics and ambitions. By the time he returned to Florence his world view had been enlarged and altered in ways that would ultimately provide him with powerful themes for the *Commedia*. The spectacle of thousands of penitent pilgrims, himself among them, arriving to make full confession of their sins and to receive absolution, made an imaginative and spiritual impact upon him. It is not surprising that when he came to write the allegory of his own life-pilgrimage and of world disorder he should choose for its chronological setting Easter Week of the year 1300.

In the meantime, there were the dangers of Florentine politics. In the disaster that was about to take place, three figures played prominent roles. They were Pope Boniface VIII, Charles of Valois (the brother of the King of France), and Corso Donati. Dante, esteemed and respected as a poet, but otherwise at that time a minor figure, was about to be caught up in intrigues of international politics over which he had no control but which were to change his life for ever.

Benedict Caetani was elected Pope with the name of Boniface VIII in 1294. The nephew of a bishop, he had a successful career in the secretarial and diplomatic service of the Church, for which his study of canon law had prepared him. He advanced from modest incumbencies to responsibilities involving a range of diplomatic skills. In 1265 he was sent to England with Cardinal Ottobono Fieschi (later Pope Clement IV) who was charged to pledge Papal support to Henry III in his conflict with Simon de Montfort. There they remained for three years, during which time the Cardinal and Caetani were imprisoned in the Tower of London. They were rescued by Prince Edward (later King Edward I). In 1276 Ottobono became Pope and entrusted Caetani with the responsibility of collecting Papal tithes from France. His experience was thus early involved with the role of the Papacy in Europe. In 1281 Simon de Brie, a French friend of his early years, became Pope Martin IV. His election was disputed and Caetani supported him. In return the Pope created him Cardinal Deacon, and Charles II of Anjou (the

Fig 3. Pope Boniface VIII

grandson of the King of France) entrusted him with confidential business. He became involved as curial agent in conflicts between France, Sicily and Aragon and observed with interest the prominent part played by Charles of Valois, to whom at one point the Kingdom of Aragon was assigned. He increased his personal fortune, holding a plurality of benefices, in France, Italy and even one in Towcester, in the diocese of Lincoln, England.

His enemies accused him of simony (the trafficking of ecclesiastical preferment in return for money or power) and of the aggrandizement of members of his family. His election to the Papacy was beset with controversy. After the death of Pope Nicholas IV in 1292, the cardinals, in conclave for two years, failed to agree on a successor. Finally an eccentric choice was made. Pietro Morrone, a saintly hermit aged 80, who lived in a cell in the mountains of the Abruzzi, was elected as Pope Celestine V. The office was beyond his powers and after five months he abdicated. It was said that Caetani put pressure on him to do so and that he intrigued to secure his own election, which took place a few days later. Dante certainly believed this to be the case and never forgave him for the part he was to play in the fate of Florence. Of all the evil-doers in the *Commedia* he is the most repeatedly reviled and execrated.

The turmoil in Florence was of grave concern to Boniface. He suspected the White Guelfs of anti-Papal ambitions and determined to support their opponents, the Blacks. Their leader, Corso Donati, who had been banished from Florence in 1299, broke bounds and went to Rome to conspire with the Pope. Boniface decided to empower Charles of Valois as an intermediary and peacemaker. The Whites grew anxious about the independence of Florence and their newly established constitution, for which they suspected the Pope held no respect. They did not trust Charles of Valois either, and they were right.

Heavy-featured, tall and thick-set, Charles shared the handsome looks of his brother the king (known as Philip the Fair) but in a coarser mould. A courageous soldier, ambitious and already powerful, he had been in the sights of Boniface for some time as a useful tool. In October 1301 Corso Donati, having negotiated with the Pope, visited Charles in Siena, bringing promises of Papal favour and offering 70,000 florins from the Blacks for his support in Florence.

In the same month the Whites, anxious and in a weak position, sent an embassy of three to Pope Boniface, requesting his assurance that Charles, if he came as peacemaker, would be charged by His Holiness to uphold the Florentine constitution. It is said that Dante was a member of the trio. If so, it must have been a striking face-to-face encounter: the Pope, majestic, five feet ten inches tall, florid-faced,[17] Dante, five inches shorter, dark in complexion, bearded by then, lean-faced and lantern-jawed, contemplating him with his dark, deep-set eyes. According to tradition, the Pope received the emissaries coldly. His plans had been made and he had no intention of changing them. It is said that he dismissed two of the group but detained Dante, possibly judging that he might prove hostile and uncompromising if allowed to return to Florence, possibly also intending to involve him in some compact or concession, or misleading him by flattery and diplomatic skill into believing that this was so.

Meanwhile in Florence on 1 November, All Saints' Day, Charles of Valois arrived at the gates, ostensibly as a peacemaker. He gave a pledge of fair conduct and the Whites had no option but to admit him. In addition to his own troops, he was accompanied by 200 knights from Perugia and others from Lucca and Siena, who had come, it was said, to do honour to the brother of the King of France. He was lodged at the house of the Frescobaldi family, across the river Arno. The Priors, one of whom was the chronicler Dino Compagni, were alarmed by his military entourage. Charles invited them to dine but they were prevented by their oath of office from accepting. They agreed to meet him at Santa Maria Novella, and there in public assembly they handed control of the city over to him. He swore to preserve the peace but immediately gave orders for his followers to stand ready for action. Three days later, Corso Donati arrived, illegally, accompanied by other exiled Blacks, who were armed. It was a *coup d'état*. They flung open the prisons, releasing more supporters, and set about pillaging the city, murdering the Whites, and plundering and burning their houses. Charles did nothing to restrain them. By 8 November new Priors had been elected (all of the Black party) and plans were at once set in hand to pass sentences of banishment upon the Whites.

Among them was Dante Alighieri.

CHAPTER 4

The First Years of Exile

Pope Boniface may have received the embassy not in Rome but in Anagni,[1] where it was his habit to withdraw to his family palace. Anagni is some 30 miles south-east of Rome, on a hill in the province of Frosinone, commanding a superb panorama of the valley of the river Sacco and of Mounts Laziali and Lepino. There in his moments of leisure Dante may have walked along the narrow streets of the walled city and prayed in the Cathedral, noting its aisled nave, its alternating square and column-shaped piers, its three eastern apses, its spectacular crypt with a multicoloured mosaic pavement, its walls decorated with frescoes of Biblical scenes and allegories of the sciences and figures of the evangelists and saints. The Caetani palace no longer exists,[2] but at the time when Dante and his two fellow delegates may have been received there it glittered with Papal splendour. The city was soon afterwards to be the scene of a sensational outrage.

Released at last, Dante rode northwards along the wintry roads, accompanied by an armed escort[3] and carrying in his saddle-bags the few garments and belongings he had brought for what he had assumed would be a brief stay. On reaching Siena he received news of the disaster that had befallen the White Guelfs in Florence. The murderous violence, the plunder and destruction of houses, including his own, made it impossible for him to return there. He had no way of making contact with his wife. Since Gemma was a Donati and a cousin of Corso, he could hope that she and the children had been granted shelter and protection. This seems in fact to have been the case. For himself, his only immediate option was to join his fellow exiles who were gathering in Gargonza, near Siena. As he rode on, shocked and anguished, he reviewed in his mind what had occurred. He knew that Charles of Valois had been charged to respect the constitution of Florence and to function justly as peacemaker. It was now obvious that he had had no intention of doing so. This was deliberate treachery and Dante would later refer to him contemptuously as being 'armed with the lance of Judas'.[4] But he saw clearly now that the real villain was Pope Boniface, who had all along schemed and intrigued to gain control of Florence, even to the point of preventing Dante, the most able of the deputies, from putting his fellow Whites on their guard. A fierce hatred, never to be extinguished, flared up in Dante's heart and would ultimately fuel the great work he was to write.

His arrival at Gargonza must have caused a stir of interest and excitement. Here was Dante Alighieri, the distinguished and eloquent man of letters, invested with the dignity of a former Prior, who had recently parleyed with the Pope. Exile was a common weapon in those days. The community that received him was only one of many such groups of political refugees, experienced in the routine of supplying shelter, food and clothing and of sharing funds. They at once involved him in their plans for a return to Florence, whether by negotiation or by force. They were too few to take action on their own. The only thing to do, however distasteful it might be, was to make common cause with previously exiled Ghibellines, some of whom were now of the second or third generation, their banishment having lasted since their defeat by the Guelfs at the Battle of Benevento in 1266.[5] Their first joint meeting probably took place in February 1302. There was no doubt a difference between those newly exiled, with the shock and pain fresh upon them, and those who had come to terms with their predicament and made lives and careers for themselves, though nurturing still a desire for vengeance and hopes of an eventual triumphant return.

A second joint meeting took place in June 1302 at San Godenzo, 20 miles to the north-east of Florence. Plans were made for military action. Thus Dante, the former cavalryman, found himself at the age of 37 caught up once more in a world of combat and military strategy. By then two sentences of banishment had been passed on him. On 27 January 1302 he and four others were accused *in absentia* of corruption, prohibited from ever again holding public office in Florence, fined 5,000 florins and banished from Florentine territory for two years. They were required to appear before the new Priors within three days to pay the fines. If they failed to do so their property would be confiscated. On 10 March the banishment against him and 14 others was extended to perpetuity, with the further decree that if they returned to Florence they would be burned alive.

Dante could only co-operate with his fellow exiles. More and more kept arriving, bringing continued reports of rioting, murder and the burning of property. They began to organize their campaign. There were several minor skirmishes but for the most part the Blacks maintained the advantage. In the summer of 1302 there was further inconclusive fighting in the Mugello area,[6] which continued until September. It has been said that Dante took part in these early combats, though he seems somewhat over-age to have done so. He was probably more usefully employed as a delegate and spokesman. In the autumn of 1302 he went to Forlì, in Romagna, 20 miles north-east of San Godenzo. His mission there was to enlist the help of Scarpetta Ordelaffi, head of a Ghibelline family, whom the White Guelfs were willing to accept as their commander-in-chief. Plans were made for an attack against Florence in March 1303. Known as the Second War of Mugello, it was a humiliating failure for the exiles.

By May or June 1303 Dante was in Verona, at the Ghibelline court of Bartolommeo della Scala. He was to speak of Verona as his first refuge and it seems that Bartolommeo extended a generous welcome to the celebrated poet from Florence.[7] His original purpose may have been to enlist Bartolommeo's help against the Blacks. He found other Florentines in Verona,[8] including members of the Alighieri family, cousins on his father's side. Also in Verona was Lapo degli Uberti, the son (or nephew) of the famous warrior Farinata, the victor of the Battle of Montaperti against the Guelfs of Florence in 1260, whom Dante was to evoke so powerfully in *Inferno*.[9] Conversation with Lapo and other members of the Uberti family no doubt provided him with a vivid impression of the personality of the Ghibelline who by force of character had reversed the decision of the victorious side to raze Florence to the ground. Why, his descendants asked, did the Florentines persist in so ferocious a vendetta against them? In Canto X of *Inferno*, as has been shown, Dante gave this question to the soul of Farinata and contrived for him to make what is in effect a plea for forbearance.[10]

As the renowned author of love poems, he would have been a figure of interest, especially to women, some of whom may have aspired to console him for the loss of Beatrice. There is a tradition in the family of the painter Altichiero[11] that they are descended from an illegitimate offspring born of Dante from this period of his life. Some sexual release he must have sought and love affairs are reflected in several of his poems written during his exile.[12]

While he was still a guest at the court of Bartolommeo, an event occurred that shocked the Christian world. Known as the Scandal of Anagni, it was a sacrilegious attack upon the person of Pope Boniface which led to his death. Among the enemies of Boniface was Philip IV of France who persisted in the taxation of clergy without Papal consent. Boniface issued a Bull forbidding such procedure under penalty of excommunication. In reply Philip forbade the export of currency and valuables, thereby reducing the Papal revenue. Boniface made certain concessions, being obliged to do so by his war against the Colonna family, bitter enemies of the Caetani. Boniface led a successful campaign against them and in 1298 they surrendered. They were absolved but not reinstated in their possessions. Some fled to France and conspired with Philip against Boniface.

To further his own interests, Philip called a general council to investigate charges of heresy and profligacy against Boniface, who promptly announced his excommunication. On the eve of the publication of the Bull, Boniface was attacked in his residence in Anagni. The date was 6 September 1303. The coup was led by Sciarra di Colonna and the French emissary Guillaume de Nogaret. They were supported by a number of Italians who had grievances against Boniface. They also had allies inside Anagni itself.

At 6 o'clock in the morning, 300 armed men on horseback and 1,000 men on foot entered the town of Anagni by a gate left open by treachery and thronged the narrow streets. An Englishman, William Hundleby, proctor of the Bishop of Lincoln, sent back an agitated account:

> Men and women were leaping from their beds and opening the doors, asking the cause of such hubbub, and it was discovered that Sciarra Colonna … had entered the town with a great force acquired through the King of France, to seize the Pope and bring about his death.[13]

Bells rang and people rushed out into the market place. Some of the inhabitants, including members of the Papal guard, welcomed the intruders. The houses of cardinals were plundered and three of them were obliged to make their escape. The attackers arrived at the Caetani palace, where they found Boniface, with only two cardinals in attendance.

Boniface was then in his 80s,[14] suffering severe pain from a stone in the bladder. He faced his enemies with dignity and courage and asked what they wanted. Their demands were that he should reinstate the Colonna family in their possessions, surrender Church treasure, renounce the Papacy and give himself up as a prisoner. The Pope refused all their demands and the attack was renewed. Only a few faithful retainers remained to defend him.

By 6 o'clock in the evening, Sciarra Colonna and Guillaume de Nogaret, with their followers, forced their way into the Pope's own chamber. He had put on his Papal robes and confronted them seated on a throne, the crown of Constantine on his head and the Keys and the Cross in his hands. He said: 'Since, like Jesus Christ, I am to be taken by treachery and put to death, I will at least die as Pope.'[15] It is not known whether he was physically assaulted but he was put under guard as a prisoner and his treasures were plundered. By now the people of Anagni had begun to rally to his defence and decided to rescue him. Nogaret was wounded but both he and Sciarra made their escape. The Pope was escorted to the market place, where he absolved the people, the French banner was trailed in the mud and women brought gifts of food and wine. Boniface asked the people to restore any treasure they had stolen and many did so. On 16 September Boniface left Anagni under the protection of a guard sent from Rome. On the 18th he reached his palace in the Lateran and on the 21st he moved into the Vatican. He did not long survive the effects of the attack and on 12 October he died.

News of the scandal aroused general consternation. Resentment against Boniface was forgotten. There was criticism of the outrage even in France. Christ had been assailed in the person of His vicar. The new Pope, Benedict XI, who as Cardinal Nicholas Boccasini had been an eyewitness, preached this view of the event in his sermons. Strange to say, Dante took his line from him.

In *Purgatorio*, on the Cornice of the Covetous, Dante encounters the soul of Hugh Capet, ancestor of the Capetian kings of France, who prophesies and laments the sins committed by his descendants. Among them, he foresees the outrage committed by Philip IV, 'the new Pilate':

> 'e nel vicario suo Cristo esser catto;
> veggiolo un'altra volta esser deriso;
>   veggio rinovellar l'aceto e 'l fele,
>   e tra vivi ladroni esser anciso ...'
>
> *'and in Christ's Vicar, Christ a captive made;*
> *I see once more the mockery and the railing,*
>   *I see renewed the vinegar and the gall,*
>   *'twixt two live thieves I see his deadly nailing ...'*[16]

In these words Dante is echoing a hymn written by Boniface himself, in which he describes a vision of the Virgin Mary standing at the foot of the Cross beholding 'once more' the sufferings of her Son: *vede l'aceto ch'era di fiel misto* ('she sees the vinegar mingled with gall'). The thrust of Hugh Capet's reproach is directed at Philip IV and his agents, the 'two live thieves', Sciarra Colonna and Guillaume de Nogaret. Talk about the outrage must have been lively at Verona. Dante could scarcely help having mixed feelings about it. However greatly he despised and hated Boniface, he deeply revered the sacred office he held. When he came to write the passage in *Purgatorio* he expressed horror at the sacrilege but he also mocked the man himself by making his own words echo back at him. He had already bitterly reviled him in *Inferno*; nor had he finished with him yet.

On 31 January 1304 the new Pope appointed Cardinal Niccolò da Prato as peacemaker in Tuscany, specially charged with reconciling the opposing factions in Florence; for there was now much quarrelling among the Blacks themselves, owing to the increasing ambitions of Corso Donati. The Cardinal arrived in Florence on 10 March. This raised the hopes of the Whites who looked to him not only to pacify the Blacks but to bring about reconciliation with all the Tuscan Guelfs, thereby facilitating their return to Florence.

Bartolommeo della Scala died on 7 March that same year and Dante soon afterwards left Verona. He went almost certainly to Arezzo, which was now the headquarters of the Whites. He had become one of their 12 councillors and it was on their behalf that he wrote a letter to the Cardinal[17] expressing readiness to abide by his arbitration and promising a truce from warfare on their part. From the text of the letter it is apparent that a communication from the Cardinal had been conveyed to the exiled Whites by an unnamed envoy (who has not been identified), referred to as 'Brother L'. The letter is a reply to an admonishment urging desistance from further military action and is headed:

> To the most reverend Father in Christ, their most blessed Lord, the Lord Nicholas, by divine grace Bishop of Ostia and Velletri, Legate of the Apostolic See, and by Holy Church ordained Pacificator in Tuscany, Romagna, the March of Treviso, and the regions circumadjacent, his most devoted sons, Alexander the Captain,[18] the Council and the whole body of the White Party of Florence, commend themselves in all devotion and zeal.

The text begins:

> In submission to salutary admonishment[19] and in response to the Apostolic Holiness, after consultation which we held to be of value, we reply ... to the sacred communication you have addressed to us.

Lest the reply has seemed slow in coming, the writer of the letter (Dante) begs indulgence, given

> ... the number and nature of the consultations and communications necessary for the proper conduct of the affairs of our brotherhood and for the observance of good faith with the league.

These words convey the tension and complexity of the discussions, with messengers scurrying from post to post. Nevertheless the exiles reached a consensus and commissioned Dante to say that the Cardinal's letter had filled their minds with joy:

> ... for the healing of our country, for which we have yearned, longing for it as it were even in our dreams, in the course of your letter ... is more than once promised us.

They undertook to cease from all assault and acts of war and, as lovers of peace and justice, to submit themselves to the Cardinal's judgement and commands:

> With filial voice ... we most affectionately implore that your most merciful Highness may bedew with the calm of tranquillity and peace this Florence so long tempest-tossed; and that as a loving father you may keep under your protection ourselves, who have ever been defenders of her people, and all who are under our authority.

The appeal is earnest, heartfelt and moving. Hopes have been raised. But the Cardinal was unsuccessful in his mission: the Blacks would not agree to the return of the Whites. Some had gone to Florence in advance as delegates and on 8 June the Cardinal advised them to leave. Two days later the Blacks renewed their burning of houses and the Cardinal departed, placing the city under an interdict.

Soon afterwards Alessandro da Romena died and Dante wrote a letter of condolence to his nephews, Guido and Uberto.[20] Praising his virtues and professing lasting remembrance, Dante laments the passing of so great a Tuscan, in whom he, an undeserving exile (*exul immeritus*),[21] had placed his hopes of a return. He also excuses himself for not having attended Alessandro's funeral. It was not lack of respect or ingratitude that kept him away but the poverty of exile, depriving him of horses and arms,[22] a poverty from which he struggles with all his strength to free himself, without success.

On 7 July Pope Benedict died. His peacemaking attempts had failed and the exiles did not know what to expect from Benedict's successor, whoever he was to be.[23] On 20 July they made one last determined effort to re-enter Florence, Dante having advised delay. White Guelfs and exiled Ghibellines from Florence, reinforced by troops from Bologna, Arezzo, Pisa, Pistoia and elsewhere, gathered at Lastra, near Fiesole, a few miles to the north of Florence. Though planned carefully, the attack failed and some 400 Ghibellines and White Guelfs were slain.

It was about this time that Dante quarrelled irrevocably with his fellow exiles and broke away from them, forming, as he said, 'a party of himself alone'.[24] The disappointment of so many defeats, the compromises between exiled Guelfs and Ghibellines, the failure of the peace mission of Cardinal Niccolò da Prato, which had raised their hopes, and Dante's advice to defer action, which they considered responsible for their most recent failure, led inevitably to recriminations, suspicion and calumny. Dante would speak later of his former companions with extreme contempt and bitterness, calling them vicious, violent fools and rejoicing in their ultimate failure.[25] The quarrel must have been violent. Possibly they had accused him of trying to negotiate a return to Florence for himself in return for betraying their military plans. To have been accused, unjustly, of corruption by the Blacks, and now, possibly, to be made a scapegoat by his companions in misfortune would have been hard to bear. One result of this rupture was that he was no longer eligible for a share of the funds that the exiles made available to those who co-operated in their cause. It is significant that shortly before the break Dante's half-brother, Francesco, was in Arezzo in May negotiating a loan on his behalf.

Dante was now on his own. There was no future for him in politics or military combat. He must rely on his own abilities. He had been able to add to his income now and then, as the opportunity arose, by undertaking secretarial and diplomatic (possibly even secret) commissions. In Forlì he served Scarpetta Ordelaffi in some such capacity. It is possible that in Verona Bartolommeo also employed him in a similar manner. The relatively tranquil period of his first sojourn there, the respect accorded to him as a poet and philosopher, had led him to reconsider his future. It may have been then, or soon afterwards, that manuscripts which he had left behind in Florence came once more into his hands.

According to tradition, Dante's nephew Andrea was asked by Gemma Donati to look for certain documents she had hurriedly stored away in a chest. Among various materials he came on papers in Dante's writing. Boccaccio at first identified them wrongly as the first seven cantos of *Inferno*. They were probably sonnets and *canzoni* that he had written after the death of Beatrice. Perhaps they were brought to him by Francesco when he visited him in Arezzo in May 1304. It is unlikely that he came empty handed. Indeed, the meeting between the brothers must have been charged with emotion. Francesco was able to give him up-to-date news of his wife and children and Dante could ask what chances he had of being recalled to Florence. These were remote: even his two sons, Pietro and Jacopo, had been included in a recent sentence of banishment when they should reach the age of 14.

Turning over his manuscripts again and re-reading his poems, in particular his philosophic odes, he experienced a resurgence of his literary powers. They were further stimulated by a renewal of his friendship with Cino da Pistoia.

Cino da Pistoia[26] was a member of a wealthy Guelf family, of the Black faction, who took an active part in politics and was exiled from Pistoia for three years, from 1303 to 1306. He was a distinguished jurist, whose *Lectura in codicem*[27] is a commentary, still of fundamental importance to legal historians, on the first nine books of the *Codex* of Justinian. He was also a lyric poet, admired by both Dante and later by Petrarch. He and Dante had been friends for many years and had exchanged poems, continuing to do so even during Dante's exile. It was once thought that Cino was among those who replied to Dante's earliest sonnet.[28] When Beatrice died he sent Dante a *canzone* in condolence, from which Dante quotes a line in *De Vulgari Eloquentia*.[29]

They met again in Bologna, during Cino's exile there, between 1304 and 1306. The change of environment offered refreshment to Dante's mind and senses. The city, with its Roman street plan, its 170 towers, its buildings and arcades of russet and pink-toned local sandstone, was dignified and prosperous. It was also a city with a university, one of the oldest in Europe,[30] famous as a centre of jurisprudence, where Cino was teaching Roman law. Dante could mingle with other intellectuals, lawyers, physicians and men of letters. He had access to manuscripts. He could attend lectures, including those delivered by Cino. University and legal texts were reproduced quickly and efficiently, being distributed in parts, to allow several scribes to work from a single copy. Bibles, choir books, guild statutes and registers were produced more slowly, many of them beautifully illuminated, by Oderisi of Gubbio, whom Dante met, and later by Franco Bolognese.[31] Here he was a witness to the handing down of the principles of Roman civilization to the contemporary world torn by tumult and disorder. Conversations with Cino, it may reasonably be assumed, enriched and enlarged his hopes for the future.

The fact that Cino was a member of the Black Guelfs of Pistoia made no difference to their friendship. Their mutual concerns transcended party politics. They shared an interest in the traditions linking the ancient Roman Empire with the authority vested in the Emperor of contemporary Europe. Cino as a poet was closely associated with Dante's literary past. In a sense he was a replacement for Guido Cavalcanti but destined to be even more influential. Two works which Dante began in Bologna were the outcome of this renewed relationship. One of these, *De Vulgari Eloquentia*, is the subject of the next chapter.

CHAPTER 5

Language and Poetry

In the university city of Bologna, surrounded by scholars, Dante felt drawn to resume intellectual activity. His renewed contact with his friend and fellow poet, Cino da Pistoia, revived his memory of the style that they and other members of the *Fedeli d'Amore* had developed for their poems. It occurred to him that no one had written on their literary use of the vernacular, nor had even defined what that literary vernacular was. He now undertook to do so. The result of his resolve was a work in Latin prose, *De Vulgari Eloquentia* ('On the Art of Writing in the Vernacular').

It shows many signs of having been delivered orally, as a course of lectures, and later published in a reader's edition.[1] This is not the usual view but once it is accepted as a possibility many unnoticed features of the work, as well as aspects of Dante's personality, leap from the page. Dante's position in relation to the University was equivalent to the modern situation of a poet in residence. Here was a poet-scholar, recently arrived in Bologna. His friend Cino, who as well as being a poet was also a learned professor of jurisprudence, was in a position to recommend and sponsor him.[2] Having quarrelled with his fellow exiles, he was no longer eligible for a share in their funds and needed to earn what money he could.

The work begins with an announcement of novelty:

> Since I do not find that anyone before me has dealt with the doctrine of the vernacular language ... and since it is my wish to enlighten to some little extent the discernment of those who walk through the streets like blind men, generally fancying that things which are in front of them are behind them,[3] I will endeavour, the Word aiding me from Heaven, to be of service to the vernacular speech.[4]

Vernacular speech he identifies as 'that which we acquire without any rule, by imitating our nurses'. From this is derived a 'secondary speech', which the Romans called 'grammar'. This, he states, is artificial and it is the natural speech he first undertakes to define and describe.

To explain the variety of languages throughout the world, he has recourse to the story of the Tower of Babel in Genesis, a story he takes literally. This is not surprising, any more than his literal belief in Adam, 'the man who had no mother, was never suckled, who never saw either childhood or youth', and who received the gift of speech direct from God. The language he spoke, Dante says, was Hebrew. He was to change this belief when he wrote in *Paradiso* of his encounter with the soul of Adam, who reads in his mind the desire to know, among other things, what language he spoke in the Garden of Eden. From Adam's words it is apparent that Dante later thought that language was a product of human reason and, as such, susceptible of change and decay.[5]

What is surprising, and delightfully so, is to find him, in *De Vulgari Eloquentia*, vividly imagining the workmen building the Tower of Babel:

> Some were giving orders, some were acting as architects, some were building the walls, some were adjusting the masonry with rules, some were laying on the mortar with trowels, some were quarrying stone, some were engaged in bringing it by sea, some by land ...[6]

Having surveyed the main linguistic groups of Europe, he discusses change and development. Just as manners and dress alter, as he has noticed, travelling from one part of Italy to another, so do languages, with time and place. Of this he gives an eerie example, which must have stirred the imagination of his listeners:

> I boldly affirm that if the ancient inhabitants of Pavia were to rise from the dead they would speak another, different language if they talked to Pavians of the present day.[7]

Because of gradual, imperceptible change it became necessary to devise rules ('grammar') to secure a fixed identity of language. As in the case of Latin, literary forms were developed also for French, Provençal and Italian. French, identified by its affirmative *oïl*,[8] is pleasant and easy, a fit vehicle for the translation of the deeds of the Trojans and Romans, of works of history and learning and of 'the most beautiful adventures of King Arthur' (*Arturi regis ambages pulcerrimae*), a hint of the pleasure Dante took in Arthurian romances. Provençal, identified by its affirmative *oc*,[9] a sweet, polished language, has served the art of the troubadours. Italian, identified by its affirmative *sì*,[10] the sweetest of all three, has been the medium of the subtlest poets, 'like Cino da Pistoia and his friend (*amicus ejus*)', namely Dante himself. This graceful compliment to Cino, accompanied by the reference to their friendship, occurs several times in the work. If Cino was in the audience, as he may have been, this would have made the allusion all the more meaningful. There is an echo here of the references in *La Vita Nuova* to Guido Cavalcanti as his 'first friend'.

He next moves to a consideration of the many forms of Italian vernacular speech, in order to discover which one, if any, is fit to be the basis of a literary language for writers all over Italy. He compares the search for an ideal vernacular to a hunt (he later compares it to hunting a panther), saying:

> [I]n order that we may be able to have a practicable path for our hunt, let us first clear the bushes and brambles out of the wood.[11]

The 'bushes and brambles' (*frutices atque sentes*) are the dialects he dislikes most and he gives examples: the speech of Rome, Spoleto, Ancona, Milan, Bergamo, Aquileia, Istria, the Casentino and Prato. He is particularly contemptuous of the vernacular of Rome:

> [T]he vulgar tongue of Rome, or rather their hideous jargon, is the ugliest of all the Italian dialects.[12]

He also feels great scorn for the Sardinians ('who are not Italians'), though he is not known ever to have been to the island. He has heard that their original language has died out and says disdainfully that they now attempt to speak Latin, 'as apes imitate men'.[13]

Wandering from place to place, he has become aware of many different accents and idioms. Why does speech differ so greatly in Italy, he asks, as for instance between Pisa, Padua, Milan, Verona, Rome and Florence? And, what is even stranger, why does it differ between parts of the same city, as for instance in Bologna, where speech alters between one district and another, such as Borgo San Felice and Strada Maggiore? Here is a local example, chosen specially for a Bolognese audience, conjuring up the figure of Dante walking about the city, listening, like a mediaeval Professor Higgins, to the passers-by and noting with surprise the variations in their talk. The tone of this section of the work is so informal and intimate that it brings us alongside Dante, listening with him. It is likely that in quoting examples of local barbarisms, as he calls them, he imitated the various accents.

He knows too how to amuse an audience. Concerning the speech of Genoa he says:

> [I]f the Genoese were so careless as to lose the letter z, they would have either to be dumb altogether, or to invent some new kind of speech, for z forms the greatest part of their dialect and this letter is uttered with great harshness.[14]

The towns at the extremities of Italy, such as Trent, Turin and Alessandria, are situated so near the frontiers that they cannot possess pure languages:

> Even if their vernaculars were as lovely as they are hideous, I would still say that they were not truly Italian because of the foreign elements they contain.[15]

And he adds, with arrogant finality:

If anyone has any doubt about this, I do not consider him worthy of any reply from me.

As for the Venetians, there are not many who would put in a claim for their language, but

> if any of them, trusting in error, should cherish any delusion on this point, let him ask himself if he has ever said
> *Per le plaghe de Dio tu non veràs.*
> By God's wounds thou shalt not come.[16]

It is difficult to see what he found so offensive about this example, at least in its written form, which is quite similar to Tuscan, which he himself spoke and wrote: *Per le piaghe di Dio tu non verrai.* It must have been the Venetian accent which he found objectionable and which he mimicked.

Love of one's mother tongue, that is to say the vernacular one learns in childhood, should not lead one to rate it above all others. In speaking of his own he gives moving expression to his love of Florence, which nevertheless he does not allow to prejudice him:

> [T]hough I drank of the river Arno before I cut my teeth, and though I love Florence so dearly that for the love I bore her I am wrongfully suffering exile, I rely on reason rather than sentiment. And although as regards my own pleasure and physical comfort there is no more agreeable place in the world than Florence, yet when I unroll the volumes[17] of poets and other writers who describe other places in the world it is my considered and firm opinion that there are many countries and cities both nobler and more delightful than Tuscany and Florence, and also that a great many nations and races use a speech more agreeable and serviceable than Italians do.[18]

Dante here thinks back, imagining himself as an infant hearing the Florentine voices of his nurse, his mother, his father and other members of the household long before he could understand them. As he says also in *Il Convivio*, a work he was writing concurrently with this, the vernacular his parents spoke brought them together and thus resulted in his own existence. He retained his Florentine way of speaking and it is intriguing to realize that in lecturing in Latin to a Bolognese audience he would have pronounced it with a Florentine accent.

Although he dearly loves Florence, and would later recall with regret the pleasure and comfort of living where bread did not taste of salt and where the stairs of his house were familiar beneath his feet, he is bitterly scathing about the claims of Tuscans that their vernacular is superior to all others:

> [I]nfatuated in their frenzy they arrogate to themselves the title of the illustrious vernacular; and in this matter not only the minds of the common people are crazed, but many distinguished men have also embraced this delusion.[19]

He cites as examples Guittone of Arezzo,[20] Bonagiunta of Lucca,[21] Gallo of Pisa,[22] Mino Mocato of Siena[23] and even his revered Brunetto of Florence,[24] all of whose style he terms merely municipal. With scorn he cites in rapid succession discordant examples of the speech of Florence, Pisa, Lucca, Siena and Arezzo. It is as though he is reading from an actor's script, cued for the imitation of five different accents. He acknowledges, however, that though 'almost all the Tuscans are obtuse as regards their degraded dialect', several writers have selected its better qualities and made good use of them; in this connection he names Guido Cavalcanti, Lapo Gianni and 'another' (himself), who are all Florentines, and Cino who is a native of Pistoia.

Leaving Tuscany, he moves next to the eastern territories of the Italian peninsula:

> Crossing now the leaf-clad shoulders[25] of the Apennines, let us continue our hunt on the left side of Italy, beginning from the east.

In Romagna he finds two types of dialect with opposite characteristics. One, because of the softness of its words and pronunciation, seems so feminine that it makes a man sound like a woman. He has noticed this especially in Forlì. (This is perhaps a jibe at Scarpetta Ordelaffi who failed in the attack he led against the Florentines in March 1303.) He greatly dislikes the speech of Brescia, Verona, Vicenza and Padua. With their ugly contractions of endings in *-to* and *-tà*, their dialects are bristling and shaggy and with their rough harshness distort a woman's speech, making her sound like a man. He also condemns the Trevisans, who like the Brescians and their neighbours, pronounce *v* as *f*, as in *nof* for *nove* and *vif* for *vivo*, which he regards as a gross barbarism. He singles out for special praise one writer of the Veneto who has striven to depart from his mother tongue and to use a justly balanced (his word is 'curial') vernacular, namely Aldobrandino of Padua.

This is an intriguing allusion. His name is unlikely to have been familiar to his Bolognese audience but it had a special significance for Dante. Aldobrandino dei Mezzabati of Padua held the office of Captain of the People in Florence from May 1291 to May 1292. Dante met him then and may have renewed acquaintance with him during his first visit to Verona. A sonnet of Dante's, written possibly during this period (or in Florence in the 1290s), was known to Aldobrandino, who replied to it. It concerns the attempt of a woman named Lisetta to gain Dante's affections but, finding him attached to someone else, 'she turns away, her face suffused with shame'.[26] Aldobrandino, in his reply, encourages Lisetta to try again. This was perhaps a private jest. However it may have been, whether a real or an imagined episode, here is the name of an obscure versifier, caught and held for ever in the amber of Dante's Latin prose.

Next comes a handsome compliment to the people of Bologna which must have gratified his listeners. Their speech, he says, is more beautiful than the others, containing elements borrowed from Imola, Ferrara and Modena and resulting in a dialect tempered to a praiseworthy sweetness: 'and this without hesitation I judge to be the case'. In this Dante may have been sincere as well as politic. The speech of the people of Bologna to this day is particularly pleasing, being low and rich in tone, in comparison with which the speech of Florence tends to be harsh and strident.

But, Dante continues, Bolognese speech is superior only when compared with the other dialects. This does not mean that it is in itself the ideal literary language of Italy. If this had been so, Bolognese poets would not have departed from it, as did Guido Guinizelli and his cousin Guido Ghisilieri,[27] Fabruzzo[28] and Onesto. The last mentioned, a Doctor of Laws, is known to have been living in Bologna in 1301. If he was still there in 1304 Dante may have met him. He is the only one of the last three mentioned whose poems are known to have survived. Both Cino and Petrarch praised them.[29]

Resuming his metaphor of the chase of the panther, 'who is fragrant everywhere but nowhere apparent',[30] Dante recommends that we should take up our hunting spears and encircle our prey in a systematic manner. Like Italian characteristics in general, which are not peculiar to any one town but are common to all, so the ideal vernacular of which he is in search is not particular to any one region but is discernible in all. For this language he invents four adjectives: illustrious, cardinal, courtly and curial.

These are not rhetorical categories or definitions. They are descriptions, verging on metaphors. An 'illustrious' vernacular is that which is illuminated by power, illuminates others and sheds lustre on the user. Examples of writers who have made excellent selective use of it are, once again, Cino da Pistoia and his friend (himself), as may be seen in their *canzoni*. A 'cardinal' vernacular is one upon which all the others hang and turn, as a door turns on its hinge.[31] 'Courtly' is that which is appropriate to a court: 'hence it is that all who frequent royal palaces always speak the illustrious vernacular'. 'Curial' is that which is well balanced, as are scales that are found in the most excellent courts of justice.

In the following section,[32] Dante proposes to say who is worthy to use the ideal vernacular, for what subjects, as well as how, where, when, and to whom it should be addressed. He considers first the use of it in verse, which he regards as a model for prose. Those to whom Dante himself has addressed his poems are fellow poets, a woman, or a particular group of men and women, personifications and supernatural beings. Not all who write verse are at liberty to use the ideal vernacular, nor is it appropriate for all subjects, as for instance dwellers in mountains who would write of rustic matters:

> [L]anguage is as necessary an instrument of our thought as a horse is of a knight, and since the best horses are suited to the best knights ... the best language will be suited to the best thoughts.[33]

Dante had served in the first rank of the Florentine cavalry and ridden the finest horses available. In his present poverty he can no longer afford a horse of any kind, but his thoughts are elevated above those of many who can, for the best are to be found only in a writer in whom knowledge and genius are combined (a clear reference to himself). The illustrious language confers the highest adornment but should not be used for inferior subjects. For instance:

> [W]e would not describe an ox with trappings or a hog with a belt as adorned, rather we laugh at them as disfigured; for adornment is the addition of something appropriate.[34]

His next example of unsuitable adornment gives us a disconcerting glimpse of what Dante's attitude was to women when he was not writing poems about them:

> As to the statement that superior things mixed with inferior ones bring about an improvement in the latter, that is true if the mingling is well judged, as when for instance we mix gold and silver together; but if it is not, the inferior things appear worse, as when for instance beautiful women are seen in the company of ugly ones ... or when an ugly woman is decked out in gold or silk.[35]

He then moves to consider which subjects are appropriate for the illustrious vernacular. He identifies three groups, under the headings Arms, Love and Virtue (prowess in war, amorous passion and rectitude). As an instance of the first category, he quotes the name of the Provençal poet Bertran de Born. No Italian poet, he says, has written on the subject. He also cites two other Provençal poets: Arnaut Daniel, who has written on love, and Giraut de Borneil, who has written on rectitude. Of Italian poets he cites only Cino da Pistoia, who writes on love, and himself ('his friend'), who writes on rectitude. He is alluding here to his philosophic *canzoni*, composed after the death of Beatrice, presenting himself in a new role: no longer primarily a love poet but a poet of righteousness.

Of the various forms in which poets have written, the *canzone*, the *ballata* and the sonnet, Dante considers the *canzone* the most excellent. One reason he gives for this is particularly interesting because of the light it sheds on poetry as a performing art. If we take a right view of poetry, Dante says, it is nothing more than a rhetorical composition set to music. Only the *canzone*, however, has its individual melody (often surviving in manuscript).

The *ballata* is performed by dancers, who also sing the words, but the melody is either well known and used for many different *ballate*, or improvised.[36] Modern readers, for whom Dante's poems are reduced to a page-to-eye-to-mind experience, are deprived of a great deal of their original effect, which must have been most beautiful, being not only sung but sometimes danced, and accompanied on a musical instrument. It is possible that Dante, while composing a *canzone*, had a melody in his head, or that indeed he sang as he worked. When he comes to describe its structure, it is clear that the musical setting is the first consideration.

Introducing this subject, he has recourse to a picturesque image: 'We will now,' he says, 'unlock the workshop of this craft (*illius artis ergasterium reseremus*).' Like promising apprentices we enter his workshop and are first of all solemnly admonished. Writing poetry, in particular a *canzone*, is a discipline and must not be undertaken casually (*casualiter*). To attain perfection we must copy the great poets of the past. As teachers of rhetoric we must also follow their teaching. A poet must be careful to choose a subject suited to his strength (as Horace advised in his *Ars poetica*), 'lest he fall into the mud'.

Having thus induced in his audience a respectful attitude to the craft of poetry, he defines three styles or levels of diction. The usual translation for the Latin terms he uses is tragic, comic and elegiacal. This is misleading. Even in classical Latin the adjective *tragicus* meant 'grand, lofty, sublime', as well as 'tragic'. The adjective *comicus* not only meant 'comic' but was used of the subject of comedy, that is to say, ordinary or everyday. The word *elegia*, in mediaeval Latin usage, could mean not only an elegy but also a composition that was merry or lascivious, that is to say, lowly or vulgar. For subjects of the first category only the illustrious vernacular will do. For those of the second category, an everyday vernacular may be combined with the lowly. For subjects of the third category, only a lowly vernacular may be used.

It was Dante's intention to give examples of all three levels, but unfortunately the work does not proceed beyond Chapter 14 of the second book, in which only the *canzone* and the illustrious vernacular are discussed. This is a sad loss because Dante was to make use of all three categories of the vernacular when he came to write the *Commedia* and it would have been interesting to have his further comments in advance. He had already begun to adopt a violent and lowly style in some of his *canzoni*, as for instance in the one beginning *Doglia mi reca nel core ardire* ('Grief brings boldness to my heart'), which he quotes in this work as an example of a poem on righteousness.[37]

He continues his consecrated approach to the composition of poetry. Talent by itself is not sufficient. The writer must exercise caution and discretion. He must make strenuous efforts to develop his inborn genius; he must practise his craft with diligence; he must acquire the mental training of a man of learning: *hoc opus, hic labor est* ('this is a task, here is toil').[38] Dante is here quoting from Virgil's *Aeneid*, where the Sibyl addressing Aeneas speaks of the few whom kindly Jupiter or their own shining worth lifts up into the heavens as sons of the gods. Dante interprets these fortunate few as poets who are fit to sing of the highest subjects in the highest style. It is evident that among them he includes himself. The Sibyl's words are immediately preceded by a prophecy of the task that awaits Aeneas:

> ... facilis descensus Averno;
> noctes atque dies patet atri janua Ditis;
> sed revocare gradum, superasque evadere ad auras,
> hoc opus, hic labor est ...

> *... easy is the descent to Avernus;*
> *night and day the doors of gloomy Dis stand open;*
> *but to retrace thy steps and pass out into the upper air,*
> *this is the task, here is the toil ...*[39]

The importance of this passage in relation to the *Commedia* can hardly be overstated and it is fascinating to catch a glimpse of Dante's mind already engaged with it. For the present, however, he is concerned merely to express scorn for those who being nothing more than geese aspire to soar like an eagle to the stars.

Only the *canzone* is appropriate for the loftiest subjects, which must be sung in the illustrious language, and only the best poets are fit to undertake the task. Illiterate writers who burst forth into ill-constructed *canzoni* are to be laughed at, 'as we laugh at a blind man making distinctions between colours'.[40] Here is another instance of a disconcerting insensitivity on the part of Dante, all the stranger when we recall the delicacy of his approach to the blind on the Cornice of the Envious in *Purgatorio*:

> A me pareva andando fare oltraggio,
> veggendo altrui, non essendo veduto.

> *To me to pass on seemed discourteous,*
> *since I saw them but they could not see me.*[41]

He moves on to instruct his listeners on the tools of the craft. First, the length of the lines: those of 11 syllables are the stateliest, though those of five, seven or three syllables are also admissible. Next, the arrangement of words in sentences: this varies from flat, moderately ornate, pedantic to elegant. The first examples he gives are in Latin prose, one concerning his exile, one concerning the negotiation of Charles of Valois with the Marquis of Este, who lent him 10,000 gold florins, and the last concerning the treacherous overthrow of Florence by Charles and the subsequent failure of his campaign in Sicily. The use of such events as examples of the technique of Latin style show how bitterly the recent disasters were rankling in Dante's soul.

He also quotes examples of excellence in sentence structure from six Provençal poets and from four Italians: Guido Guinizelli, Guido Cavalcanti, Cino of Pistoia and lastly, once again, himself. He recommends aspiring writers to read Latin poets, such as Virgil, Ovid, Statius and Lucan, as well as writers of lofty prose, such as Livy, Pliny, Frontinus,[42] Orosius, 'and many others whom friendly solitude leads me to seek out'. The words 'friendly solitude' (*amica solitudo*) evoke a touching picture of a lonely Dante finding consolation in seeking out manuscripts in the University or in the shops of apothecaries where manuscripts were sold. The chapter ends with a scornful reference to those who in their ignorance praise Guittone of Arezzo and others like him, who never managed to avoid plebeian words and constructions.

We learn next about the classifications of words and how to discern which are worthy to be used in a *canzone*. He identifies three main groups: childish, feminine and manly. Examples of childish words are *mamma* and *babbo*, which are to be excluded altogether. Feminine words, such as *dolciada* and *placevole*, are too soft. Sylvan words, such as *greggia* and *cetra*, are too rough. Urban words, which alone are admissible, he divides into groups for which he uses terms associated with the cloth trade, with which, as a Florentine, he was familiar: they can be combed-out and glossy, or shaggy and rumpled, descriptions which indicate on Dante's part a sensuous, tactile response to words. It is as if, when he writes, he fingers the nap of what he weaves. The combed-out and the shaggy words are the noblest and they alone belong to the illustrious vernacular. By 'combed-out' he means words that have, preferably, three syllables, which are without an aspirate,[43] which do not contain the letters *z* or *x*, double liquids, or a liquid immediately after a mute letter. Such words produce a sweetness, as in the case of *amore*, *donna*, *disio*, *vertute*, *letitia*, *salute*, *securitate*, *defesa*. Shaggy words are either necessary monosyllables, or words that may have a certain roughness, yet, when mixed with combed-out words, produce a pleasing harmony. Examples are: *terra*, *honore*, *speranza*, *gravitate*, *alleviato*, *impossibilità*, and even words of many syllables, such as *sovramagnificentissimamente*, which has 11.

In quoting the last example, Dante resembles a collector who proudly takes from his cabinet one of his most unusual specimens and holds it up for admiration. There is even, he adds, a word of 12 syllables in Italian and 13 in Latin, but this falls outside the present discussion, as it would not fit into a line of 11 syllables. The word in question is *honorificabilitudinitate*. This is a joke word and one can imagine a smile on Dante's lips as he uttered it. It is a word that also amused Shakespeare, who used it in its 13-syllable Latin form in the ablative plural: *honorificabilitudinitatibus*.[44]

We next learn how closely the construction of a *canzone* is related to musical form. The music by itself does not constitute the *canzone*: no trumpeter, organist or lute player would claim as much (and here we have a fleeting glimpse of the musicians who accompanied the singers of poems). Nevertheless, the whole art of the *canzone* depends on three things: first, the division of the melody; second, the relation of the parts; third, the number of lines and syllables.[45] And since a *canzone* is a joining together of stanzas, it is necessary to say what a stanza is.

The Italian noun *stanza*, from the verb *stare*, 'to stand', is primarily a standing, or pausing. By development it came to mean a place where a pause is made, or where one stands. By further development it came to mean a room or a division of a house. That is the meaning that Dante attaches to the stanza of a poem. It is interesting that he envisages it in this concrete sense, for it indicates the architectural nature of his art, a feature particularly evident in the *Commedia*. A *canzone* is thus a structure like a house in which one moves from room to room, all designed in a unifying style.

The kinds of stanza used depend on the musical setting for which they are designed. The musical form may consist of one continuous melody without repetitions or it may be divided into two different melodic sections, which Dante calls *odi*, a word that normally means 'odes' but here means 'musical phrases'. According to where the repetition occurs, the stanzas are divided into sections for which he uses the terms *pes, volta, frons, sirma, coda*.[46] These variations in structure are so intricate that an audience could not have understood them without the help of musical accompaniment. Dante has already mentioned three instruments, any one of which could have been have been used for the purpose: a trumpet, a lute or an organ, that is, an *orgue portatif*, a small portable keyboard instrument.

Concerning rhymes, Dante says that the poet relies on them for the sweetness of the whole harmony of his composition. The pleasure Dante takes in them and in their unifying effect, the beautiful linkage (*concatenatio pulcra*) of one stanza with another, the final couplet of each stanza which 'with rhyme falls into silence' makes this section of the work one of the most intimate and revealing. It also anticipates the importance that rhyme will have in unifying the cantos of the *Commedia* in the interweaving pattern of *terza rima*, which Dante has yet to invent.

Just as he is about to discuss the number of lines and syllables a stanza should contain the work comes to an end. We have only time to learn that this depends on the subject. If it is a sinister theme calling for rebuke, irony and invective, it should be brief. If it is a pleasing theme, calling for the expression of joy and praise, the stanza should flow gradually with a fitting richness to its conclusion.

It is not known why the work is unfinished. Certainly his plan for its completion was clear in his mind. Of the manuscript only three examples are extant, but they are not in Dante's handwriting, of which, surprisingly, no example is known to have been preserved. It is not impossible that a complete version did once exist.

Enough remains to provide a portrait of the man he was in 1304: harsh and embittered by his misfortunes, arrogant and dismissive, keenly aware of his talent, determined to gain recognition, but at the same time intellectually enamoured of the high calling of poetry which he felt himself endowed to serve.

CHAPTER 6

Invitation to a Banquet

D ante's first book, *La Vita Nuova*, was written for fellow poets. His second, *De Vulgari Eloquentia*, was written in Latin for a learned audience and learned readers. Before he began it he wrote the first section of another book and continued writing the two works together. The title was *Il Convivio* ('The Banquet') and he wrote it in Italian. It was intended for readers who had no opportunity or time to learn Latin, for 'princes, barons, knights, and many other noble folk, not only men but also women, who use the vulgar tongue and are not scholars'.[1] He had taken on the role of moralist and educator and was addressing the widest public he had ever attempted to reach.

His plan was to write 15 sections in all, beginning with an introduction and proceeding with an interpretation of 14 of his *canzoni*. The interpretation is in two parts, literal and allegorical, and offers both scientific information and moral instruction. The educative purpose was noble and generous-minded: his mind is radiant with the joy of communicating what he believes to be true and of using his genius to persuade us how the world may be put right. The volume would have been immense if he had finished it. In fact, only three *canzoni* are interpreted, making a work of four sections in all. Completed, it would have totalled at least 300,000 words. It was to have been his *magnum opus*.

A question arises: how did he propose to reach so wide an audience? Did he at first offer the work as extra-mural lectures? There are several signs in the text that this may have been the case. At one point he uses the word *voluptade* ('pleasure') and adds: 'I don't mean *voluntade* ['will'], I spell it with a p.'[2] At another point, using the word *adorna* ('adorns') he says: 'This word is a verb, not a noun, a verb, I mean, in the present tense of the indicative, third person.'[3] Both these interpolations suggest someone delivering a lecture and might have been copied unnecessarily into a reading text. In addition, in the first section, as will be shown below, he expresses embarrassment about his impoverished appearance.

An oral delivery would not alone have been sufficient for his purpose, however. To have a lasting effect, the work would have to be circulated, read and discussed. There were plenty of scribes in Bologna, but how did he manage to pay them? Perhaps money he received from the University for his work on the Italian vernacular was put to this use. If so, that would explain why he began writing both works in tandem. As soon as parts of both texts were copied, they could have been offered for sale and a source of income thereby created. Demand may have dried up and that was perhaps why neither work was completed. No other convincing explanation has been suggested.

He had a personal as well as a public agenda in writing *Il Convivio*. The poems inspired by the *donna gentile*, written after the death of Beatrice, had been read aloud and circulated in manuscript. Rumours had reached him that he was being criticized for being unfaithful to his first great love. He undertook to show that this was a misunderstanding. He also wished to set his *canzoni* in a context of high cultural importance.

He was sensitive not only to public opinion of his writings but also to the impression he made on those who saw him. He plays for sympathy near the beginning in words that are so direct and intimate that it is as though we hear and see him being interviewed:

> If the Disposer of the Universe had willed otherwise, men would not have acted wickedly towards me and I should not have unjustly suffered punishment, the punishment, I mean, of exile and poverty. Ever since the citizens of the fairest and most renowned daughter of Rome, namely Florence, chose to cast me out of her sweet bosom, wherein I was born and nurtured to manhood and where, if she is willing, I long with all my heart to rest my weary soul and end my allotted days, through nearly all the regions to which this language extends I have been wandering, a pilgrim, almost a beggar, displaying against my will the blows of fortune, which are often judged to be the fault of the injured person himself. In truth I have been a ship without a sail, without a rudder, blown to different ports and inlets and shores by the parching wind of grievous poverty. And many people who have set eyes on me, imagining from my reputation that my appearance would be different, have thought poorly of me and my works, both those I had already written and any I might write in the future.[4]

This, then, is how he thinks people think of him as he begins the work by which he hopes to establish his reputation and even, perhaps, to earn an honourable recall to Florence. He exaggerates a little about his wanderings as an exile, since by 1304 he had sought refuge only in Tuscany, Venetia and Romagna; but he had been dependent, first on his fellow exiles and next on the hospitality of Bartolommeo della Scala, and on whatever he could borrow or earn. Once he went attired in the scarlet, ermine-trimmed mantle of a Prior of Florence and lived in privilege in the Torre della Castagna. Now his clothes are shabby and he has no home.

But he could give a banquet, a feast of the mind, the food of angels, for which all humans hunger, namely knowledge. He does not consider himself a philosopher, except in the sense that he is a lover of wisdom, but he has sat at the feet of those who feed on the bread of angels and has eaten the scraps that fall from their table.

His *canzoni* will be the main courses of the feast and his interpretation and commentary the bread. At actual banquets which he had attended, as for instance the one given in honour of Charles Martel in Florence or at others in the Scala court in Verona, bread, baked in the form of trenchers, was brought to the table unclean, bearing the marks of ashes from the oven, and those serving had to cut away the dirt before the main course could be placed on it, rather like scraping a piece of toast that has got burned. This he must now do with his commentary before the feast can begin.

The first objection, or 'stain' (*macula*), as he calls it figuratively, is that he will be obliged to speak of himself. This is contrary to the rules of rhetoric, and to justify himself he refers to two illustrious predecessors: St Augustine and Boethius. Although he had spoken of himself continually throughout *La Vita Nuova* he had then felt no need to apologize, but this is to be a more serious and adult work. The second 'stain' is that the commentary is in a lofty, grave and difficult style. He justifies this by saying that it is necessary for him to clear himself of imputations of insincerity by expounding his *canzoni* in terms that will lend him authority. He fears also that his air of poverty will disappoint those who have heard of his fame and may cause them to take a disparaging view of his work. All the more need, therefore, that his style should be dignified.

The flour from which the bread is made also requires to be justified, for it is produced from barley, not wheat; that is to say, the commentary is written in the vernacular, not in Latin, which was the usual language for commentaries. He had already departed from this tradition in *La Vita Nuova*, relying then on the authority and advice of his friend Guido Cavalcanti. He now proposes to go further and make the vernacular a medium for philosophy, science and ethics, an extension for which he had few predecessors.[5] It was a bold step, but his love for the vernacular and his confidence that he had mastered it in its highest form gave him the necessary resolve.

He finds it necessary to defend the vernacular against widespread disparagement, inspired mainly by ignorance and incompetence. Those who cannot write it well blame their failure upon the language itself, 'as the bad smith blames the iron which he has to use, and the bad lute-player blames his lute'. Others, to show off their knowledge, praise foreign languages (such as Provençal or French) as superior to Italian. Still others are motivated by envy or meanness of spirit. All such detractors of the vulgar tongue he condemns as 'execrable wretches ... adulterers ... by whose wicked guidance' the blind are led astray.[6]

Latin, he maintains, would not have been a suitable medium for a commentary on his *canzoni* because they are written in the vernacular, a language which is subject to change, whereas Latin is stable and in a superior category, unsuited to perform a subsidiary service to an inferior medium:

> [I]f we look back attentively over some fifty years, we see that many words have become extinct and have come into existence and been altered. ... Thus I say that if those who departed this life a thousand years ago were to return to their cities, they would believe that they had been occupied by some foreign people, because the language there would be so different from their own. This will be much more fully discussed elsewhere in a book which I intend to compose, God permitting, about the Vulgar Tongue.[7]

This is the first reference to *De Vulgari Eloquentia*, from which it is evident that it was in his mind when he began *Il Convivio*. He uses the same striking instance of the dead rising and finding the language of their cities greatly changed, though in the Latin work he transfers the shock to the living and gives as a specific example the city of Pavia.[8]

A commentary in Latin would have been intelligible only to learned readers and there are many others who wish to understand his *canzoni*. It is true that Latin can be read by speakers of other languages, such as German and English, but the *canzoni* would have to be translated for their benefit.[9] And here Dante utters a condemnation in words that strike submission into the heart of all translators, yet fail to deter them:

> Let it be known that nothing that has been harmoniously composed in poetic form can be translated from its own language to another without destroying its sweetness and harmony. And this is the reason why Homer has not been translated from Greek into Latin like the other writings which the Greeks have bequeathed to us; and this is the reason why the verses of the Psalter have none of the sweetness and music of harmony, for they were translated from Hebrew into Greek and from Greek into Latin, and in the first translation all that sweetness disappeared.[10]

He could, of course, have written the commentary in Latin, leaving it to others to translate it for unlearned readers, but

> I took the precaution of composing it [in the vernacular], trusting to myself more than to anyone else.

He is convinced that in his mastery of the vernacular, both in prose and in his *canzoni*, he has brought the language to a new level of eloquence and beauty. It is his intention now to gain renown for it.

His main purpose, however, is to 'lead men to knowledge and virtue', and only those who are noble in character can benefit from such guidance. What he means by 'noble' he will explain, he says (and he does so), in the fourth section, one of several indications that the plan of the book was complete in his head. The knowledge of Latin is not in itself a guarantee of superiority. Indeed, there are many who learn Latin purely for motives of gain or prestige. Such people should not be called men of letters,

> just as no-one should be called a lute-player who keeps a lute at home in order to lend it out on hire.[11]

To ask him if he loves his native tongue is as foolish as to ask, on seeing flames coming out of the windows and doors of a house, whether it is on fire. He loves it for its intimate relationship to himself and to the persons who are nearest to him, that is, his parents, his fellow citizens and his own people. He loves it also for its intrinsic qualities,

> and here we must understand that every good quality that is peculiar to anything is part of its beauty, as in the male sex having a handsome beard, and in the female sex being quite free of facial hair, or as in a hound having a keen scent, and in a wolf-hound the ability to run fast.[12]

He feels not only love for his own language, but *lealtà* ('loyalty' or 'obligation'), a virtue which he says he will discuss in the 14th section.

At last, having cleansed the bread of stains and justified the ingredient of which it is made, he is ready to serve the banquet, by which thousands of guests will be fed, leaving baskets full of fragments over for himself. And from this miracle a new sun will rise, giving light to those who sit in darkness. The Biblical echoes with which Dante ends the first section show the solemnity and joy with which he sets out on his task and his confidence that it will bring him recognition and acclaim.

The *canzoni* that provide the first three courses of the banquet (as far as it goes) were all written in Florence after the death of Beatrice. The first of these, beginning *Voi che 'ntendendo il terzo ciel movete* ('O you who by understanding the third heaven move'), is the one which may have been sung in honour of Charles Martel on the occasion of his visit to Florence in 1294.[13] When he came to write *Paradiso*, Dante would use this first line in the greeting by which the soul of Charles welcomes him in the Heaven of Venus.[14]

All three *canzoni* had been performed and discussed at gatherings of his fellow poets and friends in Florence. Thus they had given rise to gossip about Dante's fidelity as a lover and were continuing to do so. More than ten years had passed since he wrote them, and recent tragic events had cut him off from his life as a renowned poet and prominent citizen of Florence. As he re-read them in his present circumstances, they took on a different aspect and he saw that they could serve a new purpose. Since the subject was the relationship between love and righteousness, he saw that he could make of them, and others (for he continued to write *canzoni*), material from which to construct an ambitious moral and educational programme.

When Beatrice died in June 1290, Dante found consolation in love for her successor, a woman who is never named[15] but is called *la donna gentile* ('the kind', or 'gracious lady'). He suffered agonizing feelings of disloyalty to the memory of Beatrice and wrote several poems to express this conflict. Some of these are included and explained in *La Vita Nuova*.[16] The *canzone* beginning *Voi che 'ntendendo*, though not included there, belongs to the same period and continues the theme of emotional conflict. It is, however, less personal, since his love for the *donna gentile* had become associated with a dedication of another kind.

At the end of *La Vita Nuova* Dante relates that his infatuation with the *donna gentile* was vanquished when a vision of Beatrice as a child appeared to him. A further vision of her in Heaven made him resolve to write no more of her in verse until he could do so worthily:

> And to this end I apply myself as much as I can, as she indeed knows. Thus, if it shall please Him by whom all things live that my life continue for a few years, I hope to compose concerning her what has never been written in rhyme of any woman.[17]

When he wrote these words he had already entered upon a course of study in philosophy. His mind became so enamoured that it seemed to him as though he had fallen in love again. He identified the experience with his love for the *donna gentile*, with which it appears to have been contemporary. This 'double vision', so to call it, he now undertakes to interpret in *Il Convivio*, a work which will be written in a more mature style than *La Vita Nuova*. He does not mean by this to disparage the earlier work but to illuminate its meaning by means of the new. The conflict that took place between his love for Beatrice and his love for the *donna gentile* is said in *Il Convivio* to have ended in the victory of the latter. This has been held to contradict what he says at the end of *La Vita Nuova*. The problem is resolved, however, if we understand him to mean that when he began to study philosophy his poems were inspired by a new kind of love.[18]

He first explains that writings can be understood and ought to be expounded in four senses, which he calls literal, allegorical, moral and anagogical.[19] The literal sense is 'a beautiful fiction'; beneath that, disguised as by a cloak, is the allegorical meaning. He cites as an example Ovid's tale of Orpheus who with his lyre made wild beasts tame and caused trees and stones to move towards him; of this the true meaning is that a wise man by his voice makes cruel hearts mild and humble and moves at his will those who have no knowledge or art. Why poets chose to conceal their true meaning in this way he intended to discuss in the 14th section.

To illustrate the moral and the spiritual interpretations, he uses two texts from Scripture. Teachers, he advises, should look carefully for the moral sense for their own as well as their hearers' benefit. As an example he cites the Gospel story of Christ's ascent of the mountain where the transfiguration occurred, on which occasion he took with him only three of his apostles; of this the moral meaning is that for our most secret affairs we should have only few companions.

The anagogical or spiritual sense can be perceived in writings that already in their literal meaning relate to higher matters. As an example he cites Psalm 104: 'When Israel went out of Egypt, the house of Jacob from a people of strange language; Judah was his sanctuary, and Israel his dominion.' Though it is plain that the literal sense of this is true, the spiritual sense is no less true,

> namely, that when the soul issues forth from sin she is made holy and free as mistress of herself.

From these examples it appears that at the time of writing *Il Convivio* Dante did not consider that one and the same text would yield all four interpretations. When he came to explain the meaning of the *Commedia* in his so-called epistle to Can Grande della Scala he showed that the same text could in fact be understood in four senses.[20]

He proceeds next to expound the literal meaning of the first *canzone*. He begins by reminding readers of the closing chapters of *La Vita Nuova*, in which he writes of the *donna gentile* and of her compassion for him after the death of Beatrice. In the conflict between his memory and his new love he addressed the angelic beings who move the sphere of the planet Venus, from which the force of love derives. This leads him to his first passage of scientific information. The subject is astronomy.

Like all his educated contemporaries, Dante had been taught that the earth was a globe, motionless in the centre of the universe. Encircling it were eight concentric spheres carrying seven planets, the Moon, Mercury, Venus, the Sun, Mars, Jupiter, Saturn, and in the eighth sphere the constellations. Beyond that was believed to be a ninth sphere, the Crystalline Heaven or Primum Mobile, which imparted movement to the others. The spheres circled the earth all together once every 24 hours, from east to west. As well as this diurnal motion, the planets and the stars moved back along their spheres from west to east, at different speeds. The planet Venus performed a still more complicated movement, whirling also in its epicycle, a smaller sphere which was thought of as attached to the main one. This was the basic explanation, inherited from the generations of astronomers who preceded

Copernicus, of the movements of the heavenly bodies as perceived by the naked eye. Dante would have been instructed in such matters in his youth when he studied astronomy as one of the four subjects of the Quadrivium. By the time he came to write *Il Convivio* he had learnt a great deal more about the subject, both from reading and from his own observations.

Poring over manuscripts late into the night by candlelight, as well as naked-eye gazing at the stars, fatigued his eyes, as he says:

> A star sometimes appears blurred on account of the eye which from weakness or weariness undergoes a change and exhibits some colour and some lack of power. For example it sometimes happens that when the sheath of the pupil becomes much bloodshot through infirmity caused by weakness almost all things appear ruddy, and so the star appears tinged with colour. And because the sight is weakened, some dispersion of the visual spirit takes place in it, so that an object is no longer seen as concentrated, but appears diffused, almost in the same way as our writing on damp paper. And this is the reason why many persons when they wish to read remove the writing to a distance from the eye in order that the image may enter the eye more smoothly, and in a finer shape. … Of this I myself had experience … for, through greatly overtaxing my sight by studious reading, I so weakened the visual spirits that the stars all appeared to be discoloured by a kind of white haze. And by giving my eyes a long rest in dark and cool rooms, and by cooling the ball of the eye with pure water, I regained the former healthy condition of my sight.[21]

Astronomy had a powerful influence upon his creative imagination. Intertwined with it were profound concepts of philosophy and theology. The mediaeval notion of the universe seems limited to us with our present-day instruments and exploration of outer space, but for Dante and his contemporaries the cosmos reached beyond the physical into the infinite and the eternal. His authority on the subject was Alfraganus,[22] an Arab author whose work on the elements of astronomy consists of 30 chapters. Based on the principles of Ptolemy, it was translated from Arabic into Latin about the year 1142 by, it is supposed, Johannes Hispalensis, under the title *Alfragani Elementa Astronomica*. This version was in common use during the Middle Ages and is the one that Dante studied.[23] He refers to it several times in *Il Convivio* and some of the information he provides about the heavens in this work and in *La Vita Nuova* is translated almost word for word from the Latin text. It is as though we see him in his study looking from one book to another, as Luca Signorelli portrays him in the fresco in the Cathedral of Orvieto.[24]

Alfraganus quotes from Aristotle, from whom the concept of a tenth heaven was derived. This was known as the Empyrean, a word meaning a sphere of fire. It was thought of as the abode of God, which existed neither in time nor space. When God, who is Himself timeless, changeless and infinite, created the universe, time and change began. Simultaneously with primal matter and the material heavens, God created angels, who function as His agents operating through nature. Among their activities is to diffuse their influence upon the heavenly bodies which in their turn influence life on earth. Thus astronomy is identified with astrology, in which Dante believed, though not to the exclusion of free will.

He considered it appropriate to address his *canzone* to the angelic beings, also called Intelligences, who move the sphere of Venus, since this was the planet, named after the goddess of love, which had infused in him his love for both Beatrice and for the *donna gentile*. Such concepts would be familiar to his contemporaries. Though the names of the planets are derived from Roman deities, or, as Virgil was to call them in *Inferno*, 'false and lying gods',[25] the angels were as real to Dante the Christian believer as the heavenly bodies themselves. They can be apprehended by human senses, for

> there shines in on our intellect light which emanates from their living essence … just as a man who has his eyes shut is aware that the air is luminous because a gleam from its brightness reaches him … just as a ray of light passes through the pupil of a bat.

He explains the transference of his love for Beatrice to the *donna gentile* by saying that whereas the latter still lived on earth and was subject to the influence of the movers of Venus, Beatrice was now in Heaven, beyond their power. This leads him to a digression about the immortality of the soul, in which he has absolute belief. He berates as 'most brutish, vile, foolish and pestilent' all those who think otherwise. He quotes as sources for his conviction Aristotle's *De Anima* ('On the Soul'), the beliefs of the Stoics, Cicero's *De Senectute* ('On Old Age'), as well as the beliefs of Jews, Saracens, Tartars,

> or of any others who live according to law of any kind. If all of these were deceived, an impossibility would follow which would be horrible even to mention.

Nature has implanted hope of immortal life in the human mind, a hope that sets man apart from the animals. This hope is further confirmed by dreams,

> which we could not have if there were in us no immortal part, inasmuch as, if we think about the matter exactly, the medium of revelation whether corporeal or incorporeal must needs be immortal.

Above all, assurance is given us by 'the most veracious doctrine of Christ',

> a doctrine which we cannot perfectly behold while our immortal is mingled with our mortal part; but we behold the immortal perfectly by faith, and by

reason we behold it touched with the shadow of darkness which falls upon it owing to the mixture of mortal and immortal: and this ought to be our strongest argument that both one and the other exist in us. Thus I believe, thus I affirm, thus I am assured, that I shall pass to another better life after this where that glorified lady survives, of whom my soul was enamoured.[26]

Not only were the writings of poets to be interpreted allegorically. Reality itself, history, present events and persons all had multiple significance. This is different from the traditional personification allegory, that is, the representation of an abstract concept in the figure of a person, as when Boethius represents Philosophy in the figure of a woman. The form which Dante here adopts might be called revelation-allegory, that is, the recognition of meanings beyond the literal and actual. He makes systematic use of this type of allegory in his commentary in *Il Convivio*. The nine heavens, which he believes actually exist, are identified with abstract concepts, namely the sciences which compose the totality of knowledge which is accessible to reason. The seven planets are said to correspond to the seven branches of learning known as the Quadrivium and the Trivium: the Moon to grammar, Mercury to logic, Venus to rhetoric, the Sun to arithmetic, Mars to music, Jupiter to geometry, and Saturn to astronomy; the constellations correspond to physics and metaphysics, the Primum Mobile to ethics; ultimately, beyond space, is the Empyrean, which corresponds to theology. The movers of the sphere of Venus, whom Dante addresses in his *canzone*, are in this allegorical sense understood to be masters of the art of rhetoric, in particular Cicero and Boethius, by whose writings he was first drawn to the study of philosophy. The *donna gentile*, of whom he was in actual life enamoured after the death of Beatrice, is identified with Philosophy itself.

This form of allegory was first consciously explored by Dante as a poet in the composition of the *canzoni* he wrote after the death of Beatrice. His most striking and creative use of it would be made later in the *Commedia*. What he discovered in his allegorical interpretation of the *donna gentile* led him to the revelation of the meaning of Beatrice.

Why, then, did Dante omit all reference to the *donna gentile* in the *Commedia*? The answer is that he did not.

Two of his *canzoni*, which were inspired by his love for her, in fact the very first two which he interprets in *Il Convivio*, are quoted in the *Commedia*. '*L'amor che nella mente mi ragiona*' is sung by Casella on the shore of Mount Purgatory; the first line of '*Voi che 'ntendendo il terzo ciel movete*' is quoted by Charles Martel in the Heaven of Venus. Dante could not have forgotten, nor could he assume that his readers had forgotten, that in *Il Convivio* he had equated the *donna gentile* with Philosophy, 'the fairest and most honourable Daughter of the Emperor of the Universe'. It was impossible that such a sublime figure should not appear in his poem as having played a major role in his salvation, but since she was still alive in the fictitious year of the story she could not (in the poetic convention of the time) be introduced as her actual self.

At the beginning of the *Commedia* Virgil tells Dante that the Virgin Mary has commanded Lucia, the enemy of all who are cruel and whose *fedele* ('devotee') Dante is, to urge Beatrice to go to the rescue of one who for love of her *uscì della volgare schiera* ('departed from the common herd').[27] Lucia has been traditionally identified as St Lucy of Syracuse, a third-century martyr, the patron of persons with weak sight. As such, she has been interpreted as signifying illuminating grace. Such a meaning can also be attached to philosophy, which illumines the mind, as Dante makes clear in his *canzone 'Amor che nella mente ...'*, using several dazzling images of light to do so. It was his study of philosophy that enabled him to write 'more worthily' of Beatrice, as he said he hoped to do at the end of *La Vita Nuova*. He could now perceive her as a figure of revealed theology, as the *donna gentile* was a figure of philosophy.

Lucia's role in the *Commedia* is not limited to sending Beatrice to Dante's aid. It is she who carries the sleeping Dante up the lower slopes of Mount Purgatory, leaving him to awaken at the gate which leads to the seven cornices. It is through philosophy, 'the blessedness of the intellect', she 'who gently turns round all those that have been deflected from the right way' (as he says in *Il Convivio*), that Dante represents himself as progressing towards an understanding of sin and righteousness, reaching at last a readiness for confession, contrition and absolution. In the story of the *Commedia* a stage in this spiritual journey is achieved while he is sleeping, just as in an actual *metanoia* the soul moves through several stages without being consciously aware of it.

Lucia may also be *la donna santa e presta* ('the lady holy and alert') who appears to Dante in a dream on the Mountain of Purgatory.[28] She is the last of the souls pointed out to Dante by St Bernard as seated in the Celestial Rose in *Paradiso*.[29] On her right is St John the Baptist, the Forerunner, and on his right is St Anne, the mother of the Virgin, another forerunner. It is significant too that Lucia 'faces Adam', since philosophy, as Dante says in *Il Convivio*, 'was in God's thought when He created'.

We do not know the name of the *donna gentile*. It is not impossible that it was Lucia.

CHAPTER 7

Main Dishes and Trenchers

The metaphor of a banquet hangs like a tapestry as a visual background to the intellectual feast that Dante prepared. In his day such an occasion was an art form, stately and elaborate. The main dishes were carried into the hall in splendour, sometimes on the back of a horse. They made, in the traditional phrase, an 'entrée', accompanied by servitors, musicians, even by acrobats. At the most festive banquets entertainments were provided between the courses, such as dances accompanied by singing, or miniature pageants.

At Dante's banquet 14 main dishes have been prepared, that is, his 14 *canzoni*, to be eaten on trenchers of bread, namely, his commentary. As befits such an occasion, every *canzone* is a thing of beauty, perfectly concocted, a worthy offering to his guests. It is to be imagined, it may even have happened, that each *canzone* was sung to an accompaniment before the reader (Dante himself) passed to the prose, a possibility that would heighten the pleasure of the repast. The recipe is provided in *De Vulgari Eloquentia* but it required a master chef to create so exalted and varied a selection of courses. It seems, sadly, that the guests had appetite for no more than three.

The first dish, '*Voi che 'ntendendo il terzo ciel movete*' ('You who by understanding the third heaven move'), is an early example of his new form of allegory.[1] He was writing consciously in a double sense: the conflict between his old love and the new, in which the occasional lack of response from the *donna gentile* is an image of his difficulties with the study of philosophy. His second main dish is the *canzone* beginning *Amor che nella mente mi ragiona* ('Love which discourses to me in my mind'). Like the first, it draws the listeners' thoughts up into the heavens, raising their imagination to the sun circling the earth. This is the song which the soul of Casella sings on the shore of the Mountain of Purgatory.[2] It is appropriate that it should be sung on Dante's arrival in the southern hemisphere, for the astronomy of that region is brilliantly visualized both in the *canzone* and in the commentary that follows it. In fact, the description of the yearly spiralling of the sun has been called the most remarkable passage of scientific prose before the time of Galileo. To make clear the changing distribution of light between the northern and southern hemispheres, Dante asks his listeners to imagine two cities, one at the north pole and one at the south, divided by the equator. Mysteriously, instead of designating these two positions on the globe 'A' and 'B' or 'X' and 'Y', he personifies them with the names 'Maria' and 'Lucia'. His intention may have been to indicate that the passage is more than an astronomical explanation. The light of the sun, shed equally and alternately upon Maria and Lucia, may signify the power of God diffused now upon divine grace, the Virgin Mary, now upon illuminating grace, Lucia. If this is so, it is all the more appropriate that in the *Commedia* Lucia should come to Dante's aid on Mount Purgatory in the southern hemisphere.[3] The clarity of his explanation of the sun's positions through the year as it spirals north and south of the equator is again demonstrated there in Virgil's exposition and in Dante's ready grasp of it, a conversation overheard and amiably mocked by his indolent friend Belacqua.[4]

Expounding his *canzoni* in his present circumstances was a nostalgic task for Dante, but the opportunity to display their beauty was some consolation to his pride. So musical is the sequence of words, so exquisite the linking of the lines that from the page alone they rise like songs, though voice and accompanying instrument have long been silent. The second *canzone* is a hymn to Philosophy:

> Suo esser tanto a Quei che lel dà piace,
> che 'nfonde sempre in lei la sua vertute
> oltre 'l dimando di nostra natura ...
> Cose appariscon ne lo suo aspetto
> che mostran de' piacer di paradiso ...
> Elle soverchian lo nostro intelletto,
> come raggio di sole un frale viso:
> e perch'io non le posso mirar fiso,
> mi conven contentar di dirne poco.

> *Her being so pleases Him who gave it her,*
> *in her unceasingly He infuses power*
> *beyond our nature's measure to conceive ...*
> *Such things within her aspect are perceived*
> *as demonstrate the joys of Paradise ...*
> *These overpower our human intellect,*
> *as sunlight with its beam confounds weak sight:*
> *and since I cannot fix them with my gaze,*
> *I must contented be with but few words.*[5]

This allusion to his weak sight offers yet another interesting link between the *donna gentile* and St Lucy, the patron of those with failing vision. It is on interpreting these lines that Dante speaks of the condition of his own eyes, weakened by constant reading and star-gazing.[6]

The lady who is Philosophy is she who humbles all who are wicked; she was in the mind of Him who set the universe in motion:

Questa è colei ch'umilia ogni perverso:
costei pensò chi mosse l'universo.[7]

In *Inferno*[8] Lucia, whose *fedele* ('devotee') Dante is said to be, is designated *nimica di ciascun crudele* ('the enemy of all who are cruel'), a phrase that closely resembles *colei ch'umilia ogni perverso* ('she who humbles all who are wicked'), applied here in the *canzone* to Philosophy.

Having placed before his guests these two celestial dishes, Dante next offers more terrestrial fare: a *canzone* on the subject of nobility. The opening lines, *Le dolci rime d'amor ch'i' solia/cercare ne' miei pensieri,/convien ch'io lasci* ... ('The sweet love-poems for which I used to search my thoughts I must now forsake'), introduce a change of style as well as of theme: he will now speak in harsh and subtle verse concerning the quality that makes a man truly noble. This poem is allegorical only in the sense that by the word *donna* the meaning 'Philosophy' is intended, 'that most powerful light, Philosophy, whose rays cause the flowers to bloom again and to bear fruit in the true nobility of men' (*quella luce virtuosissima, Filosofia, i cui raggi fanno ne li fiori rifronzire e fruttificare la verace de li uomini nobilitade*). Having made this clear, Dante proceeds to expound and enlarge on the literal sense, which is didactic and polemical.

The concept of *gentilezza* (of which 'nobility' is one meaning) had been raised by Guido Guinizelli in the poem which the *Fedeli d'Amore* took as their inspiration, *'Al cor gentil ripara sempre Amore'* ('Love in the gentle heart his refuge always seeks').[9] He denied there decisively that *gentilezza* was derived from lineage. It is to be expected that Dante would follow him in this, but there was another reason why the concept of nobility exercised his mind. He wrote this *canzone* soon after 1295, when those of noble birth had just been excluded from the government of Florence as a result of the Ordinances of Justice introduced by Giano della Bella in 1293.[10]

The third *canzone*, when he wrote it, was thus of immediate and topical interest. He had already entered public service and was concerned with questions of social justice and political life. A great deal of Provençal poetry had been of a moral or political nature and the tradition had already been developed in Italy by Guittone of Arezzo and his imitators. What made this *canzone* an innovation on Dante's part was his decision not to limit himself from now on to the one subject favoured by the *Fedeli d'Amore*, namely love, and to extend the range of his diction accordingly.

When he came to comment on it in *Il Convivio*, about ten years had passed and his life had undergone a drastic change. The political and ethical concerns of the poem had acquired tragic overtones, not only for him personally but for the social and political state of Italy. It was more than ever necessary to give the lie to false assumptions and establish the true principles by which men should govern themselves and one another. He speaks of his *canzone* as medicine which he wishes now to provide speedily in order to restore good health. In the metaphor of the banquet, it is a plain dish, intended to provide substantial nourishment after the rich fare of the two preceding courses.

The commentary is carefully constructed, with many sub-divisions and digressions, rising frequently to the eloquence of an oration. Speaking of himself as he was when he wrote the *canzone*, he says that in his devotion to Philosophy, in whom all reason dwells and rectitude has its source, he came to love the followers of truth and to hate the followers of error, though reminding himself that hatred should be directed not at those who commit errors but rather at error itself. (It must be acknowledged that when he came to write the *Commedia* he failed on several occasions to follow this precept.)

One error he condemned above all: a mistaken belief concerning the origin of nobility, as a result of which the good were held in contempt and the evil were honoured and exalted. This was the worst confusion in the world, as anyone could see who considered the consequences.

The erroneous opinion had been attributed to the Emperor Frederick II,[11] who on being asked what nobility was is said to have replied: 'Ancestral wealth and fine manners'. This had been widely accepted, though the second part of the definition was usually disregarded. Dante set out to refute the Emperor's opinion, but in order to clear himself of a charge of disrespect he now, in his commentary, first analyses the basis of imperial authority and secondly shows that it does not extend to the matter in hand. In the first part of his argument he sets forth important new beliefs which he has formed during his exile.

In his 'friendly solitude' (*amica solitudo*), as he calls it in *De Vulgari Eloquentia*,[12] he had spent much time pondering moral obligations, the problems of civil unrest, the principles of government and the purposeful design of history. Before his exile, on entering on his study of philosophy, he had found enlightenment in the writings of Cicero and Boethius. He had also begun a close study of Virgil's *Aeneid* and the Roman historians, especially Livy. In philosophy his supreme authority was Aristotle, whom he quotes 40 times in *Il Convivio*, referring to him as 'the chief Philosopher', 'the leader of all philosophers', 'he who brought moral philosophy to perfection', 'the guide and conductor of the world', 'the most worthy of trust and obedience, whose words are the supreme and highest authority', 'the master and leader of human reason'. His opinion is to be preferred above all others:

> [I]n any matter on which the divine judgement of Aristotle opens its mouth it seems best to me to set aside that of everyone else.[13]

This is he whom he will call *il maestro di color che sanno* ('the master of those who know') when he sees his soul in Limbo in *Inferno*.[14]

It is to Aristotle that he looks for guidance as to the first principles of government. Quoting his definition of man as 'a social animal' (Dante's word is *compagnevole*), he lists the needs of the individual for the domestic companionship of a family (of which Dante was now deprived), of the household for a neighbourhood, of the neighbourhood for a city, of the city to further its crafts and strengthen its self-defence, for interchange and brotherly relations with neighbouring cities. Such connections lead to the formation of kingdoms, which by desire for increased territory are led to make war upon one another. Thus the happiness of individuals, for which they were created, is impeded. The only remedy is that a single monarch should govern the whole world:

> a single prince, who having nothing further to desire would keep kings confined within their borders and hence at peace with one another, and such peace would lead to mutual love and to happiness.[15]

Such universal and incontestable office of command is known as Empire, the command of all other offices of command, held by an Emperor who declares and enforces law for all.

Dante is next obliged to prove that such authority was rightfully lodged in the hands of the Emperors of ancient Rome and subsequently rightfully inherited by the elected rulers of the Empire of the Christian world. He had formerly believed that the power of Rome had been established by force, but his reading of Virgil and Livy caused him to alter his view. The supremacy of the Romans, descendants of the lofty lineage of Troy, he now believed, was ordained by God for the perfecting of human life on earth. As the mind of a smith is the efficient and moving cause in hammering out a knife, while the blows of the hammer are but the instrumental cause, so not force but reason and, moreover, divine reason, was the efficient and moving cause in the creation of the Roman Empire.

The subject calls for a digression which he says will provide 'both profit and enjoyment'. This quotation of the words of Horace[16] introduces one of the most important chapters in the work. It begins with a discourse on Divine Providence, whose works are often incomprehensible to us. How indeed could human reason discern eternal counsels? Quoting from

Proverbs, 'Hearken because I have to speak of great things',[17] he links the wisdom of the ancient pagan world with that of the Old Testament and the foundations of the Christian faith.

His vision of continuity leads him to identify the time chosen by God for His Incarnation with the period when the authority of Rome was established under an Emperor. Earth was then in its best conjunction of elements; universal peace reigned as it had never done before nor ever would again, 'for the ship of human society was speeding over a smooth track to its destined port'. He further identifies the birth of Rome, that is, the coming of Aeneas to Italy, as contemporary with the birth of David, the ancestor of the Virgin Mary. He greatly marvels at the wisdom of God in bringing these two events together and calls down curses upon those who have the presumption to disbelieve:

> Oh, ineffable and incomprehensible wisdom of God who didst so long ago prepare for Thy coming a single moment yonder in Syria and here in Italy! Oh, most foolish and degraded beasts who pasturing under the guise of men, presume to speak against our faith and, spinning and delving, claim to know what God with so much foresight has ordained! Accursed be you, your presumption and those who put their trust in you![18]

There follows a long, eloquent passage in glorification of Roman history, from the time of Romulus to that of the first Emperor. It is evident, he says, that Rome was blessed not with human but with godlike citizens, who in their devotion to her were inspired not with human love but with divine. In an accumulation of powerful statements he lists the heroes and their deeds,

> which were not done without some light from the divine goodness over and above their own natural goodness. And it ought to be manifest that these most eminent men were the instruments by which Divine Providence worked in the Roman Empire, where often the arm of God appeared to be present.[19]

Rhetorical questions follow one upon another in a mounting crescendo of oratorical effect:

> Who will say that Fabricius was under no divine inspiration? ... Or Mucius when he set fire to his own hand? ... Who will say that Torquatus, when he sentenced his own son to death, could have endured to do so without divine assistance? ... Did not God put His own hand to the task when the Franks, after taking the whole of Rome, endeavoured to enter the Capitol by stealth, and only the cry of a goose made it known? And did not God put His own hand to the task in the war of Hannibal with the Romans? ... And did not God put His own hand to the task when a new citizen of small standing, namely Cicero, defended the liberty of Rome against so great a citizen as Catiline? Yes, without doubt. And I indeed believe that the stones of her walls

are worthy of reverence, and that the soil on which she stands is worthy beyond all else that has been proclaimed and praised.[20]

Legends drawn from Livy's history of Rome and accepted by Dante on the same footing as facts are here set out in an exalted example of the new vernacular prose he is creating. The effect strongly suggests a passage written to be read aloud. The same events would be cited again in his Latin treatise on world government, *Monarchia*.[21] They would also appear in epic style in *Paradiso*,[22] where he gives to the soul of Justinian, Emperor and lawgiver, the task of unrolling the scroll of Rome's history from its earliest beginnings, linking it with the age of Charlemagne and with Dante's own, thereby proclaiming Roman justice the earthly symbol of the divine.

Dante was not only expounding a political theory. By the time he wrote *Il Convivio* he had come to believe that he understood God's plan for the world and that he, a descendant of the 'godlike citizens' of Rome, was destined to reveal it. This vision was a sacred truth which the banquet was designed to celebrate.

Having established the lawful grounds of imperial authority, Dante next undertakes to consider the status of philosophy. Reviewing the development of the ancient schools, he shows that the highest and most trustworthy master is Aristotle. Philosophical authority is not opposed to imperial; on the contrary, the two reinforce each other and when conjoined reach their fullest strength. Thus it is that in the Book of Wisdom Solomon says, 'Love righteousness, ye that judge of the earth.'[23]

This statement of the basis of justice will be given spectacular presentation in *Paradiso*, where the souls in the Heaven of Jupiter spell out in a pattern of lights the words *Diligite iustitiam qui iudicatis terram*, in which wisdom and kingship combined are shown to constitute perfect justice.[24] This image is forcibly contrasted by the execration of unworthy rulers on earth, just as in *Il Convivio* Dante follows the quotation of the words attributed to Solomon by the condemnation of two contemporary rulers, Charles II of Anjou and Frederick of Aragon and other unnamed tyrants, who lack all philosophical authority in their exercise of power.

Reverting to his *canzone*, Dante points out how it refutes the opinion of what he calls 'the common people' (*il vulgo*) concerning the origin of nobility. There is danger, he says, in allowing false opinions to take hold, for they spread like weeds in a field, suffocating the crop, that is, truth. It is a mighty task to weed an overgrown field of popular opinion, so long left destitute of tillage. He does not intend to clear the whole field but to free only those blades of the plant of reason which have not been completely smothered. The rest deserve no more care than beasts, for it is impossible to communicate with anyone in whom reason is extinct. It would be like calling back to life someone who has lain four days in the tomb.

To be devoid of reason or to refuse to apply it is to renounce life as a human being, for it is reason that distinguishes man from the beasts. In fact, to reject reason, as to commit evil, is to be dead, even though the body walks the earth. This terrifying image is used to great effect in *Inferno*, where the soul of Branca d'Oria, who invited his father-in-law to a banquet and murdered him, is pointed out to Dante among the traitors.[25]

After describing the fruits of reason, among which are discernment and reverence of the lesser for the higher, Dante is ready to refute the false opinion that nobility is conferred by wealth. Before doing so, as though to gather together all his strength, he uses a striking military metaphor, drawn from his own experience in battle:

> We will now charge full front at depraved opinions and throw them to the ground, in order that by means of this victory the true opinion may hold the field in the minds of those in whose interest it is right that the truth should prevail.[26]

The manoeuvres of the combat, which is prolonged, are mapped in the next chapter.

CHAPTER 8

The True Definition of Nobility

Dante next sets himself to refute the opinion that nobility is derived from wealth and possessions. Riches, being base, are the very opposite of what is noble. To begin with, there is no justice in the distribution of wealth. It can be acquired by chance, by inheritance or by unlawful means. Lawful gains, it is true, do arise from skill, commerce and service but the greatest riches are obtained without equity. He himself has seen the place in Falterona[1] where a lowly peasant digging in the soil found a bushel of silver coins. There is no justice in such chance events. Bequests and succession, too, devolve more often on the wicked than on the good. Would that the words of a certain Provençal troubadour were heeded: 'He who does not inherit goodness should forfeit inheritance of wealth.' Unlawful gains never come to those who are virtuous, for they would reject them, while lawful gains seldom come to the virtuous either, who are concerned with more important matters.

By the time Dante wrote his commentary he had spent nearly two years in Bologna, where he had opportunity to study the matter profoundly. He himself was impoverished by then and though this caused him pain and embarrassment he still denounced greed for money and possessions. This is the sin of avarice, which endangers and destroys cities, regions and individuals, continually inspiring desires for greater and greater wealth, which cannot be satisfied, and this is the important point, *without injury to others*. Discussing the matter, as he probably did with his friend Cino and other scholars in jurisprudence, he had come upon the safeguard against this most dangerous of evils. It stood plainly stated in the texts of canon and civil law:

> [F]or what else were they designed to remedy so much as that cupidity which grows by the amassing of riches? Certainly both branches of the law make this sufficiently plain when we read their origins (*cominciamenti*), that is, the origins of their written record.[2]

Texts of canon and civil law were readily available in Bologna. Copies were being made continually by students for their own use and were also on sale. Perusing them, Dante found a structure for the well being of society. Avarice could be checked by civil law if a righteous Emperor, who alone could declare and enforce it, came to power. By partnership between canon and civil law and given an ideal relationship between Church and State, evil could be eliminated from the world. In words which have puzzled readers for centuries, Dante would express this hope in the form of an enigmatic prophecy uttered by Virgil in the first canto of *Inferno*.[3]

In spite of his personal misfortunes, brought about by the ill doing of his enemies, Dante asserts his unshaken belief in ultimate good. The highest desire of every soul is to return to God who created it, yet it is liable in its journey to take the wrong path. In a pleasing simile, Dante compares the soul to a traveller

> who takes a road along which he has never gone before and thinks that every house he sees in the distance is an inn and, finding he is mistaken, fixes his eyes trustfully on another and so on from house to house until he arrives at the inn he is seeking.

The same errors can be observed in children who first desire an apple, then a bird, then, as they grow older, a horse, then a mistress, then wealth and still more wealth. Our desires are as though heaped in the form of a pyramid, the object of least value being at the apex, leading towards God who is the base of all. As we proceed through life we desire greater and greater things but in this progress we may be led by the wrong desire because 'the path is lost in error like the roads on earth' (*questo cammino si perde per errore come le strade della terra*):

> [I]n human life there are diverse paths, one of which above all is the right road, and another the wrong, and certain other paths which are more or less wrong or right.[4]

The image of the right path that has been lost, an image of Biblical origin which is repeated several times by Boethius, would be used by Dante in the opening metaphor of the first canto of *Inferno*, in three lines which must be among the best known in Western literature:

> Nel mezzo del cammin di nostra vita
> mi ritrovai in una selva scura
> chè la diritta via era smarrita.

> *In the middle of our path in life*
> *I woke to find myself in a dark wood*
> *for the way which leads us straight was lost to sight.*[5]

The metaphor is anticipated in *Il Convivio* again in a phrase describing the soul entering upon a new and hitherto untrodden path of life (*nel nuovo e mai non fatto cammino di questa vita*), and so also is the image of the dark wood, when he speaks of the young man 'who enters into the wrong forest of this life (*l'adolescente che entra ne la selva erronea di questa vita*) and cannot keep to the right path unless it is pointed out to him by his elders'.[6]

From Boethius, Dante had learnt that there were above all three wrong paths: the desire for pleasure, the desire for fame and the desire for material possessions. In the first canto of *Inferno* he would represent them as three wild animals which impede his progress up a mountain: a leopard, a lion and a she-wolf. The last of these terrifies him more than the others, driving him step by step back down into the valley.[7] Boethius too, comparing vices to animals, had said that a man burning with greed for other men's possessions was like a wolf.[8] (The coming event of the *Commedia* casts many of its shadows before.)

The evils of wealth are well known. Those who possess it are hated and live in fear of losing it. Merchants who carry their money with them about the world are afraid of every rustle of leaves, but if they travel without it they enliven their journey with song and converse. The man who possesses nobility of soul is not discomposed if he loses his wealth, for such a loss cannot rob him of his nobility, a thought from which Dante himself could now draw moral courage.

The belief that nobility is derived from ancestral wealth is easily shown to be false, since a logical consequence would be that no humbly born man could ever become noble, which is to say that nobility can never have a beginning. To anyone holding such a foolish opinion,

> one would wish to reply not with words but by taking a dagger to such brutish ignorance.[9]

It is difficult at this distance in time to know whether this is an example of Dante's sardonic humour or yet another expression of the contempt he felt towards those who lacked the ability to reason and towards those who disagreed with him.

Let us consider, he says, the case of Gherardo da Camino. Nobody could deny that he was a noble man, and even if his origin had been humble nobody would have dared to say otherwise. Gherardo, cited here as a model of excellence, and referred to in the past tense, had died in March 1306. Thus it is possible to determine that this passage and the remaining chapters of *Il Convivio* were written after, probably quite soon after,[10] that date. This tribute to him is in the nature of an obituary, of immediate significance to Dante's contemporary readers, but requiring for us the resource of archives to bring him back to life. Born about the year 1240, Gherardo was Captain-General of Treviso from 1283 until his death. He was respected and well known, in Tuscany as well as in his own region, as a champion of the

White Guelfs. He was also celebrated as a patron of poets and other writers; in this capacity Dante may have known him and perhaps had reason to feel indebted to him. He thought so highly of him that he would refer to him again in *Purgatorio*, where Marco Lombardo speaks of him as *il buon Gherardo*.[11] In 1300, the fictional time of the *Commedia*, he was still alive but Dante represents himself as not then having met him or even heard of him. This may be an example of the many oblique allusions to his exile and to those who will befriend him in his misfortune.

In the *canzone*, having demonstrated the falsity of the opinions he contests, Dante says 'it is clear to all sound minds (*intelletti sani*) that such statements are vain':

> ... per che a 'ntelletti sani
> è manifesto i loro diri esser vani.[12]

In his commentary he explains what he means by minds that are sound and by minds that are not. The phrase is of special interest because he uses it again in *Inferno*, where he draws the attention of those who have 'sound minds' to the teaching that is hidden beneath the veil of certain mysterious lines:

> O voi ch'avete li 'ntelletti sani,
>   mirate la dottrina che s'asconde
>   sotto 'l velame de li versi strani.[13]

By *intelletto*, he explains in *Il Convivio*, he means

> the noble part of our soul which may be designated by the common term 'mind'. The intellect may be termed 'sound' when no evil disposition of mind or body impedes it in its operation, which is to discover what things are, as Aristotle says in the third book of his *De Anima* ['On the Soul'].[14]

He has observed an evil disposition of the soul attended by three terrible kinds of sickness of the mind. The first of these is a boastfulness that leads people to believe that they know everything and to affirm as certain things that are not. Cicero condemns such people in the first book of his *De Officiis* ('On Duties'), as does St Thomas Aquinas in *Contra Gentiles* ('Against the Gentiles'):

> [T]here are many who by their natural dispositions are so presumptuous as to believe that they can gauge everything by their intellect, believing everything true that seems to them true, and false everything that does not.[15]

Such people never attain to learning, believing they are already sufficiently instructed; they never ask questions, they never listen, they never desire to be questioned, and if they are, they reply before the question is concluded and their answer is wrong.

The second sickness he has observed is caused by a natural dejection of the mind, which leads people to deny the possibility that anything can be known, by themselves or by others. They never enquire or reason or heed what others say. Such people, Aristotle said, were not qualified to be students of moral philosophy, for they live in ignorance like beasts and despair of all learning.

The third sickness is a kind of levity or superficiality of mind which leads people to pass all bounds in their reasoning, leaping to a conclusion before they have framed a syllogism, flying off to another conclusion, believing they are arguing most subtly when they do not start from any principle. With those who deny first principles, as Aristotle said, it is useless to argue. Among them are many uneducated people who do not know their A B C and yet would dispute about geometry, astrology and physics.[16]

In addition, there are infirmities of the body, such as congenital defects, as in the case of half-wits, and the derangement of the brain, as in the case of madmen. For such cases the law provides in the *Infortiatum*,[17] from which he quotes: 'In one who makes a will, at the time when the will is made soundness of mind, not of body, is required.'[18] With this specific reference to a text in the second section of the *Digest* we have evidence that while in Bologna Dante read and noted legal texts.

Moving to the positive definition of nobility, Dante states that 'wherever virtue is, there is nobility'. It is a grace received by the individual soul direct from God. Virtue is derived from nobility, but the reverse is not true. He illustrates this in the *canzone* by an image of the sky in which many stars are shining. When he comments on it in *Il Convivio* his imagination takes wing, his style soars and his very voice can be heard:

> How fine and appropriate an illustration! For truly nobility is a heaven in which many and divers stars are shining. There shine in her the intellectual and moral virtues; there shine in her good dispositions bestowed by nature, namely, piety and religion, and praiseworthy feelings, shame and pity, and many more; there shine in her bodily excellences, namely beauty, strength, and almost perpetual health. And so many are the stars which spread themselves over her sky, that surely we cannot wonder if they make many and divers fruits grow on human nobility, so many are their natures and potencies, concentrated and united in one simple substance; and on them as on divers branches she bears fruit in divers ways. In very truth I dare affirm that human nobility, when its importance is measured by the number of the fruits which it bears, surpasses that of angels, although the nobility of an angel is more divine in its unity. And this the Psalmist recognized when he began 'O Lord our God, how admirable is Thy name in all the earth. ... Thou hast made man a little lower than the angels and hast crowned him with glory and honour and hast set him over the works of Thy hands.'[19] Indeed, therefore, the comparison of human nobility to

the heavens was most beautiful and appropriate![20]

This is the exultant Dante admiring his own poetic simile, the Dante who will go on to create sublime passages of contemplation in *Paradiso*. His prose too at this point has reached a level hitherto unknown in the vernacular.

Nobility, then, is bestowed by God upon the individual soul and is the source of virtue. Those who possess it are almost like gods. In contemplating this wonder, Dante again rises to new levels of joyful eloquence. The creation of the soul stirs in him a sense of marvel that defies his powers of expression:

> Let no one marvel if I speak of things that are hard to understand. To me it seems wondrous that such matters [as the creation of the soul] can be inferred and perceived by the intellect. This is not a thing for language to make plain, I mean the language of the people. Therefore I say with the Apostle, 'Oh, the heights of the riches of the wisdom of God, how incomprehensible are Thy judgements, and Thy ways past finding out!'[21]

The thought of the soul receiving the gift of nobility direct from God leads Dante to marvel at the wonders of human procreation, a subject he will expound also in *Purgatorio*.[22] That his knowledge of biology was at fault and that his ideas of the relationship between corporeal and spiritual forms were derived from ancient philosophers, especially Aristotle, is relatively unimportant. What matters to readers separated from him by seven centuries is to see his mind radiant with the joy of perceiving and communicating what he believes is true. This is 'the mind in love' (*la mente innamorata*)[23] which will create the great hymn in praise of intellectual and spiritual understanding which is *Paradiso*.

> When God sees His creature made ready to receive His gift, He bestows it with a bounty proportionate to the soul's readiness to receive it. [Such bounty], called the Gifts of the Holy Spirit, were identified by Isaiah as Wisdom, Understanding, Counsel, Strength, Knowledge, Piety, Fear of God.[24] Oh excellent harvest! Oh excellent and wonderful seed! Oh admirable and gracious Sower, who waitest only for human nature to prepare the ground to be sown! How blest are they who duly cultivate such seed![25]

The noblest offshoot of such seed is an appetite of mind, which in Greek is called *hormen*.[26] If this is not properly tended the seed is of little worth, but strengthened by good habit it will bear fruit and from the fruit will come the enjoyment of happiness.

Like a host who eagerly provides for the enjoyment of his guests, Dante says:

> It is a precept of the moral philosophers who have spoken about giving, that a man should bestow care and trouble on rendering the gifts he confers as useful

as he can possibly make them to the receiver. Thus I, desiring to obey such a command, strive to make this banquet of mine in each of its parts as useful as I can. And since in this portion of my subject it chances that I am able to offer some remarks on the sweetness of human happiness, I think that no discourse I could utter would be more useful to those who are not acquainted with it.

The 'sweetness of happiness' is to be found in the use of the mind. Such activity can be either practical or contemplative. Both give delight, though in contemplation the delight is greater, for it is more charged with spiritual light that anything else on earth. The practical use consists of acting virtuously by our own will, with prudence, temperance, courage and justice; the contemplative use consists in reflecting on the works of God and Nature.

Such contemplation cannot be fully realized in this life for it consists in beholding God, Who is beyond our power to know. All our mind can do is to meditate on Him and behold Him through His effects. This we long for as our highest beatitude.[27]

In the last complete stanza of the *canzone* Dante describes the ways in which nobility is displayed in the soul at succeeding stages of life. These lines, written by a poet in his early 30s, still confident in his career and esteemed by his fellow poets, in full command of his style, possess a particular clarity and beauty. Read in the light of his commentary, written ten years later and after such a reversal of fortune, they become an even more moving statement of his still unshaken belief in potential human goodness.

L'anima cui adorna esta bontate
non la si tien ascosa,
chè dal principio ch'al corpo si sposa
la mostra infin la morte.
Ubidiente, soave e vergognosa
è ne la prima etate,
e sua persona adorna di bieltate
con le sue parti accorte;
in giovinezza, temperata e forte,
piena d'amore e di cortese lode,
e solo in lealtà far si diletta;
è ne la sua senetta
prudente e giusta, e larghezza se n' ode,
e 'n se medesma gode
d'udire e ragionar de l'altrui prode;
poi ne la quarta parte de la vita
a Dio si rimarita,
contemplando la fine chè l'aspetta,
e benedice li tempi passati.

The soul whom this nobility adorns
does not conceal it in herself,
for from the moment when she joins the body
she displays it till she dies.
Obedient, gentle and restrained
she is in her first age,
and her person she adorns
with every seemly loveliness.
Next in her youth, strong, temperate,
replete with love and praised for courtesy,
in lawful living only she finds joy.
And at the start of her old age,
prudent and just, known for her generous gifts,
joy she feels within herself
when hearing and speaking of another's good.
Arrived then at the fourth part of her life
God's bride she is anew,
and meditates on her awaited end,
blessing the years which she has passed.

In his commentary Dante defines precisely four stages of life, which he calls adolescence, youth, old age and decline, comparing each period to the span of an arch, rising to an apex and descending. Adolescence, or the period of growth, lasts from infancy until the age of 25. During this time the rational part of the soul cannot perfectly exercise discrimination. It is for this reason that the law ordains that in the performance of certain duties a man must defer to a father or a guardian until he has passed into the period called youth.[28] Setting aside what philosophers and physicians have said and relying on his own reason, Dante states that this second span of life lasts from 25 to 45 years. Of this, and of the whole of life, the mid-point is 35. The third stage, that of old age, lasts from 45 to 70. Finally comes decline, from the age of 70 until death.

Listing the attributes desirable in each of the four ages, Dante builds up an ideal world of virtuous behaviour, sadly remote from the reality he sees around him. Now and then he bursts into lamentations, bitterly contrasting the real state of affairs with the ideal. His evocation of a world that could yet come to be reveals his most deeply felt concerns and the matters on which he set the highest value. It also reveals his courageous resolve to show how things can be put right. Most remarkable is his faith in the power of reason.

Among the qualities bestowed by nobility upon the soul of an *adolescente*, good manners (*soavi reggimenti*), modesty, courteous speech, respect for elders, control of the passions and penitence for faults, the most striking is what he terms *stupore*, that is to say,

> an amazement (*stordimento*) of the mind on seeing or hearing great and wonderful things, or feeling them in some way ... which leads to reverence and a desire to know and learn.[29]

In mapping the ideal foundation for life during the period he called *adolescenza* Dante had the living examples of his own two sons. It is not known when Pietro and Jacopo were born but they must by now have passed the age of 14 and so become subject to the decree of exile from Florence. They may have joined their father in Bologna, or possibly in Verona, where they may have been left under the protection of Alighieri cousins who were living there. Dante does not mention them in any of his works; nor does he ever refer to his wife.

When he wrote *Il Convivio* Dante himself was in his early 40s, an age, he says, when reason, like a good horseman, should direct desire with bridle and spur. The bridle is called Temperance, the spur is Courage, the virtue which shows us where we should make our stand and fight. As an example he quotes the tale of Aeneas as related by Virgil:

> What a bridling that was when Aeneas, after he had received such pleasure from Dido, as will be told later in the seventh section, and was experiencing such enjoyment with her, tore himself from her in order to follow an honourable, laudable and profitable course, as is related in the fourth book of the *Aeneid!* And what a spurring that was when the same Aeneas had the courage to enter alone with the Sibyl into Hell in quest of the soul of his father Anchises, encountering such dangers as are described in the sixth book!

This is an age too when love should govern us: a 'young' man should love his elders,

> from whom he has received his being, nurture and teaching, lest he should appear ungrateful. He should also love his juniors, in order that through loving them he may impart kindness to them and on this account be supported and honoured when his prosperity wanes.[30]

Of this, as for the qualities of courtesy and *lealtà* (obedience to the law), Dante again takes as examples episodes from Virgil's story of Aeneas.

His comments on the period of old age are largely inspired by Cicero's *De Senectute*. This is a time when a man should seek to be useful not only to himself but also to others, his country and the entire world, modelling himself on the example of Cato of Utica, about whom Dante read in Lucan's *Pharsalia*.[31] In this connection Dante twice uses a very pleasing simile. A man in old age who offers counsel to others

> opens out like a rose which can no longer stay closed and diffuses its perfume

which is generated within ... as a rose which renders up her fragrance not only to him who goes to her for it but also to anyone who passes her way.[32]

Prudence is the source of right counsel which guides an old man himself and others to a prosperous end in human affairs and actions:

It is right at this age that a man's judgments and authority should be a light and a law to others. And because this unique virtue was perceived by philosophers in antiquity to show itself in perfection at this age, they committed the government of the state to those who were of this age, and therefore the assemblage of rulers was called a 'Senate'.

At this point Dante breaks forth into one of his bitter lamentations:

(Oh wretched, wretched country of mine! What pity for thee wrings my heart whenever I read, whenever I write anything that bears on civil government!)

But, he continues, since he intends to treat of justice in the last section but one he will say no more about it for the present.[33]

On the age of decline, Dante again draws on Cicero who said that natural death is our haven after a long voyage and our repose:[34]

And just as a good mariner when he draws near to harbour lets down his sails[35] and enters it gently with slight headway on, so also ought we to let down the sails of our worldly pursuits and turn to God with all our understanding and heart, so that we may come to that haven with all composure and with all peace.[36]

Death in this age, without pain or bitterness, is like a ripe apple detaching itself lightly, without force, from its bough. It is also like the return of a man from a long journey who is met at the gate of his own city by her citizens, or like one who seems to be departing from an inn and returning to his own mansion:

Oh vile wretches who run into port with sails full set, and in the harbour where you ought to repose, wreck and destroy yourselves with the force of the wind at the spot to which you have been so long journeying!

As two examples of those who behaved with wisdom in this respect he cites Lancelot, who became a hermit in old age, and Guido da Montefeltro, 'our noblest of Latins':

Both these noble men indeed shortened the sail of their worldly occupations for in their extreme age they surrendered themselves to religion, laying aside all worldly delights and pursuits.[37]

Guido da Montefeltro, a renowned leader of the Ghibellines, entered the Franciscan Order in 1298, the year he died. Dante presents him in *Inferno* as a victim of the deceit of Pope Boniface VIII, who prevailed on him to instruct him in tricking his enemies. In the tale which the soul of Guido himself relates to Dante, he uses the same metaphor of lowering sail as one approaches death:

> 'Quando mi vidi giunto in quella parte
>   di mia etade ove ciascun dovrebbe
>   calar le vele e raccoglier le sarte ...'
>
> *'When I reached the age when it is meet*
>   *for every mariner, with his port in sight,*
>   *to lower sail and gather in the sheet ...'*[38]

Dante's reference to him in *Il Convivio* as 'our noblest of Latins' may show that he regarded him as an example of a virtuous man who was still capable of being led astray by someone as evil and astute as Pope Boniface. It is more probable that Dante heard only later of the trickery of the Pope, by which Guido was led to break his vows.

There comes next a beguiling allusion to marriage, mentioned nowhere else in *Il Convivio*. The bonds of matrimony may still constrict a man in old age but this does not excuse him from entering a religious life, for even those who are married can do so, 'since God requires only the profession of the heart'. It has been said that in his youth Dante became a novice of the Franciscan Order and then withdrew. This reminder that the religious life may be entered into even by those who are married is perhaps an indication that Dante was himself considering doing so in the last stages of his life.[39]

Interpreting the line in the *canzone* which refers to the remarriage of the soul to God in the age of decline (*a Dio si rimarita*), Dante takes as an example the desire of Marcia, the divorced wife of Cato of Utica, to return to him at the end of her life. He had read the story in Lucan's *Pharsalia*[40] and relates it here in detail, explaining it allegorically as signifying the desire of the noble soul to return to God:

> And what earthly man is so worthy to signify God as Cato? Certainly none.[41]

The fourth section of *Il Convivio* ends with a brief interpretation of the *congedo* of the *canzone*, which he calls an ornament,

> for every good workman tries to ennoble and embellish his task at the end as far as he can, in order that it may be the more valued when it leaves his hands.

Dante follows this example, sending his *canzone* forth to where his Lady (Philosophy) dwells. It is useless, he says in the commentary, to go elsewhere, for as Christ has said, we should not cast pearls before swine, and as Aesop has said, 'To a cock a kernel of corn is worth more than a pearl.' Philosophy is found only among the wise and among those who feel love for her. He bids the *canzone* tell his Lady that he now discourses on her friend,

> for truly Nobility is her friend, since the one is so deeply enamoured of the
> other that Nobility is ever calling for her and Philosophy turns her fondest
> gaze to no other quarter. Oh, how great and how beautiful an ornament is
> this which is bestowed upon her at the end of this *canzone*, where she is called
> the friend of her whose own mansion is in the most secret place of the divine
> Mind!

With this impressive flourish, calling for applause for the conclusion of his
canzone, Dante reaches the end of what remains of *Il Convivio*. He had so
much more to say, stored in his mind and prepared in his notes. He had
given several indications of how he intended to proceed. The sense of loss is
very great, until we realize that nothing at all has been lost. Everything that
he wrote in *Il Convivio*, everything that he intended to write in continuation, with much else, will be found, in another form: the *Commedia*.

CHAPTER 9

Injustice and Avarice

The subject of the 14th section of *Il Convivio* was to have been justice, and Dante had a *canzone* prepared. Beginning *Tre donne al cor mi son venute* ('Three women have gathered round my heart'), it was written during his exile, probably while he was in Bologna. He is concerned about the wrongs of society, his resentment at the injustice he himself has suffered and his growing conviction that God's plan for the world is the establishment of peace under a single, righteous ruler.

His *canzone* on the subject is like a *tableau vivant*, beautiful and at the same time mysterious. Written in the form of personification allegory, it introduces three statue-like female figures. One, the mother and grandmother of the others, speaks weeping, leaning upon her hand like a lopped rose, her bare arm a column of grief, drenched with the storm of tears that falls from her face, her hair dishevelled and her feet unshod. She is *Drittura* (Justice). Her daughter is *Larghezza* (Generosity) and her grandchild is *Temperanza* (Temperance), both born beside the river Nile, whose source is in the Garden of Eden. All three figures are so beautiful and of such noble bearing that Love, who rules in the poet's heart, is overcome and cannot speak. Once they were welcome in the world, but now they are hated and reviled. They have come as to the house of a friend to speak of their sorrowful state. Hearing the words of Justice and gazing at the beauty of the three figures, one of whom dries her eyes on her blond hair, the poet feels it an honour to share with them the condition of exile:

L'essilio che m'è dato onor mi tegno.

Exile on me imposed I hold an honour.

To share misfortune with those who are virtuous is also a matter of pride:

Cader co'buoni è pur di lode degno.

To fall with the good is worthy too of praise.

The figure who speaks tells Love she is the sister of his mother Venus, namely Astraea, the last of the immortals to leave the earth. She represents divine and natural law, her daughter the law of nations and her granddaughter human law. Love tries to hearten them, saying that though Generosity and Temperance and others born of their blood, which he too shares, must now go begging, it is mankind that should weep, not they, who are of the eternal citadel. Though they and he are wounded, a race will return that will keep bright his arrows which are tarnished now.

If this were all, the poem would be simply a blend of personification and myth, the meaning plain enough, but Dante adds an image which is unlike anything in his other lyrics. The garment of Justice, coarse and with a plain girdle, hangs in such tatters that the part of her body *che il tacere è bello* ('which it is decent not to name') is uncovered. This physical humiliation may be intended to signify that Justice has been prostituted. He refers to it a second time, in overtly sexual terms. In the first of the two *congedi* he commands the poem to permit no man to pull aside its garment to reveal what a fair woman conceals; those parts which are uncovered must suffice; the sweet fruit to which all hands reach out must be denied. But if the poem meets with someone who is a friend of virtue, it may put on fresh colours and, thus arrayed, allow the flower, so beautiful to behold, to be desired by hearts which love. This erotic image may signify that Justice is in danger of being corrupted and is secure only if administered by the righteous.

A second mystery concerns an admission by Dante that he has erred, several months previously, but has repented:

> ... s'io ebbi colpa,
> più lune ha volto il sol poi che fu spenta
> se colpa muore perchè l'uom si penta.

> ... *if guilt was mine,*
> *through several moons the sun has turned since when*
> *it cancelled was, if blame dies with remorse.*

It is not known to what guilt Dante here refers. Since the words come soon after a mention of his exile, his fault would seem to have been political rather than moral or religious. In the second *congedo* Dante asks forgiveness of the Black Guelfs. For what? Not, surely, for the crimes of which he was falsely accused and on the pretext of which he was banished – misappropriation of funds, extortion and bribery – but perhaps for having joined with exiled Ghibellines and White Guelfs in an attempt to force an entry back into Florence:

> Camera di perdon savio uom non serra,
> chè 'l perdonare è bel vincer di guerra.

> *A wise man does not bar the room of pardon,*
> *for pardon is fair victory in war.*

In the last section of *Il Convivio* Dante intended to deal with the virtue of liberality.[1] For this, too, he had a *canzone* ready. Beginning *Doglia mi reca ne lo core ardire* ('Grief brings boldness to my heart'), it is quoted in *De Vulgari Eloquentia*.[2] This shows that it was written by 1304. Reference to the humiliation of having to ask for favours and being granted them grudgingly suggests that it was written after he had quarrelled with his fellow exiles and was now dependent upon charity.

It is a very angry and bitter poem. The style is abrupt, in places violent. He warns readers that he intends to speak out against almost everyone. Like many of his earlier lyrics it is addressed to women, but with a startling difference. Despairing of the moral degeneration of men, he commands women to withdraw from them, hiding their beauty and even going so far as to deface it. He reproaches them for desiring men who are unworthy. Beauty was given to them, as moral strength had been given to men, in order that these two constituents of perfection might blend under the power of love. Now that there is no honesty in men, there can be no love between the sexes, unless one gives the name of 'love' to bestial appetite.

Men who depart from goodness are like evil beasts. From being masters they have chosen to become slaves; to life they have preferred death. Goodness, created by divine Love, is both his servant and high minister. With joy she steps forth from the fair portals of Love's domain and visits the human soul; with joy she travels and returns; with joy she carries out her service, preserving, adorning and enriching what she finds. She is the reverse of Death and never heeds him:

O cara ancella pura.
colt'hai nel ciel misura;
tu sola fai segnore, e quest è prova
che tu se' possession che sempre giova.

O precious and pure handmaid,
who from heaven hast thy rule;
thou only dost nobility confer,
thus thou a gift art, which can never fail.

Whoever departs from such a handmaid is the slave not of a lord but of another slave. Consider what he who strays from her must lose: his eyes which should illumine his mind remain closed and he walks at the whim of one whose eyes are fixed only on folly.

Recalling that he is addressing women, Dante moves from the abstract to the particular, for it is rarely, he says, that obscure words penetrate the minds of those who wear the wimple:

Ma perchè lo meo dire util vi sia,
discenderò del tutto
in parte, ed in costrutto
più lieve, sì che men grave s'intenda:
chè rado sotto benda
parola oscura giugne ad intelletto;
per che parlar con voi si vole aperto.

But that my words may be of use to you,
I will descend from general terms
to details and to simpler form,
that less remote my meaning may appear:
for rarely does an obscure word
achieve an entry to a wimpled brow;
and so with you plain speaking is required.

It had long been a commonplace that women are by nature less capable than men of abstract thought. St Thomas Aquinas had said that women were influenced more by their feelings than by their reason. From this *canzone* it appears that Dante followed his view and yet, when he began to write *Il Convivio*, he explicitly included women among those whom he wished to address, though even here he refers slightingly to their capacity when he speaks of the vernacular as being a language which 'even women speak'. Women who inspire the highest love are beautiful and virtuous, even saintly, as Beatrice is shown to be in *La Vita Nuova*. They know by insight what love is, and Dante addressed several of his poems to them as well as to Beatrice. It is noticeable, however, that such poems require no powers of abstract reasoning for their comprehension. How this view of women is to be reconciled with the role which Beatrice will play as theological guide, informant and counsellor in *Purgatorio* and *Paradiso* will be considered later in the present work.[3]

In the present *canzone*, Dante asks his women readers, for their own good, not certainly for his, to despise and scorn all men. So enslaved have men become that they resemble a miser running blindly after money. This leads Dante to deplore the vice he has come to regard as the most destructive of all, namely avarice. His poem from here on grows increasingly harsh, even ferocious in expression. His language seems scarcely suitable for the *canzone* or characteristic of the *volgare illustre*:

Corre l'avaro, ma più fugge pace;
oh mente cieca, che non pò vedere
lo suo folle volere
ch 'l numero, ch' ognora a passar bada,
che 'nfinito vaneggia!

The miser runs, but peace runs faster still.
Oh! blinded mind, that cannot see
in its mad longing
that the sum it strives to pass
vanishes to infinity!

He personifies Death, who makes equals of us all, and challenges the miser:

Dimmi, che hai tu fatto,
cieco avaro disfatto?
Rispondimi, se puoi, altro che 'Nulla'.
Maladetta tua culla
che lusingò cotanti sonni invano!
Maladetto lo tuo perduto pane,
che non si perde al cane!
Chè da sera e da mane
hai raunato e stretto ad ambo mano
ciò che sì tosto si rifà lontano.

Tell me, what hast thou done,
thou miser, blind, undone?
Answer me, if thou canst, apart from 'Nil'.
Cursed be thy cradle which
beguiled so many dreams in vain!
Cursed be the bread that on thee wasted was,
Though not upon a dog!
For thou, from morn to eve,
hast gathered in and clutched with both thy hands
what slips away so fast, beyond thy grasp.

Misers not only accumulate their wealth beyond measure; they also hoard it, thus causing servitude to others, from which escape can be made only with difficulty. He addresses Death and Fortune, rebuking both:

Morte, che fai? Che fai, fera Fortuna,
che non solvete quel che non si spende?
Se 'l fate, a cui si rende?
Non so, poscia che tal cerchio ne cinge
che di la sù ne riga.

Death and savage Fortune, what are you about,
that you do not disperse what is not spent?
Or if you do, to whom?
I do not know, for we are locked within
a circle by the powers above.

Reason should intervene to remedy the unjust distribution and inheritance of wealth. But Reason says, 'I am powerless':

Ah, come poca difesa
mostra segnore a cui servo sormonta!

Ah, what trivial defence
a master makes surmounted by a slave!

And now in words of exceeding bitterness he rebukes the wealthy who watch the blameless poor run naked over hill and marsh, while they themselves wrap garments round the worthless clay that is their flesh. In a miniature allegory, Dante describes the efforts of Virtue to lure the miser to liberality. She walks round, calling persistently. She throws a morsel of bait towards him, but the miser makes no move towards it. If, after she departs, he does approach, he is so pained by the thought of making a gift to anyone that no praise results when he does. This is Dante's picture of Scrooge. He knows him well. 'I want you all to hear me', he cries:

I' vo' che ciascun m' oda:
chi con tardare, e chi con vana vista,
che con sembianza trista,
volge il donare in vender tanto caro
quanto sa sol chi tal compera paga.
Volete udir se piaga?
Tanto chi prende smaga,
che 'l negar poscia non li pare amaro.
Così altrui e sè concia l'avaro.

Heed all of you what I now say:
Some misers with delay, some with disdain,
some with a sullen brow,
convert their gift into a costly sale,
so high the price he only knows who pays.
And would you learn the pain?
So much it injures him who takes
that afterwards refusal has no bitterness.
To this a miser comes and others brings.

Dante's humiliation at the hands of those on whom he depends for charity runs deep. The result is that the unjust distribution of wealth becomes one of his greatest concerns. The gap between rich and poor, the selfishness of the rich, the inescapable poverty of the helpless and deserving were problems to which, at the time of writing this *canzone*, he could see no remedy. By the time he began *Il Convivio* he had come to see and hope for a solution. The two final sections were to have been a triumphant proclamation of this vision and this hope, a vision and a hope he then transferred to the *Commedia*.

In the meantime, his poetry remains swathed in allegory and his style has become awkward and obscure. In contrast, clarity and directness are about to take command of his imagination as he embarks on his new work.

CHAPTER 10

Dante the Showman

D ante's disappointment at the lack of response to *Il Convivio* must have been deeply demoralizing. It was his most ambitious enterprise to date and he had invested in it his highest hopes, his profoundest learning and his finest talent. Some inkling he must have had that his audience was dwindling and sales of manuscript were falling off: the reference towards the end of the last chapter to casting pearls before swine is significant.

The blow was further exacerbated in October 1306 when the Florentine government brought pressure to bear on the Bolognese to expel all White Guelfs who had taken refuge there. This added to the difficulty of continuing *Il Convivio*, not to mention his lectures on the Italian vernacular. Possibly forewarned, Dante had already kicked the dust of Bologna from his heels and had accepted the hospitality of Franceschino Malaspina in his castle at Sarzana in the Lunigiana.[1] Looking back over his shoulder, he retained a memory of several unworthy Bolognese whom he would later locate in *Inferno*: Francesco d'Accorso, the sodomite,[2] Venedico di Caccianemico, who sold his sister to the Marquis Obizzo d'Este and boasts in Hell of the great number of pimps from Bologna who share his punishment,[3] and two Bolognese friars among the hypocrites.[4]

Sarzana was a place of sad association for Dante, for it was here that his friend Guido Cavalcanti was exiled and had caught malaria, returning to Florence only to die.[5] While there, Dante was employed as an intermediary in a dispute between the Malaspina family and the Bishop of Luni.[6] Documents dated 6 October 1306 attest that the negotiation was successful. Here is further indication that Dante eked out his income when he could by such commissions.

It is not known how long he remained at Sarzana, probably not beyond the summer of 1307. During his stay he had become acquainted with Franceschino's cousin, Moroello. A Guelf, he had captained the Florentines in their campaign against the Ghibellines of Arezzo; in 1297 the Guelfs of Bologna had elected him Captain-General in the war against the Marquis

Azzo of Este; the following year he was appointed *podestà* of Bologna; in 1299 he was captain of the Milanese forces in a conflict with the Marquis of Montferrat; from 1301 onwards he was frequently in arms on behalf of the Blacks of Tuscany and by 1307 he was made captain of the Guelf League. All such exploits gained for him a reputation for military valour and political skill. Dante, once a combatant in arms himself, was an admiring observer of his career. He introduces the soul of his cousin Currado among the Late Repentant in *Purgatorio* and takes the opportunity to pay honour to the family for their courage and generosity.[7] There is also a reference in *Inferno* to Moroello's military prowess.[8]

This valiant man of arms must also have been a man of letters, for Dante sent him an epistle accompanying a *canzone* on the subject of his feelings for a young woman he had met in the Casentino region after his departure from Sarzana. Beginning *Amor, dacchè convien pur ch'io mi doglia* ('Love, since grief is once again to be my fate'), it is thought to be his last *canzone*. Boccaccio said that it was Moroello who encouraged him to resume work on the *Commedia* when the first seven cantos were sent on to him from Florence. This is a misunderstanding on Boccaccio's part, for there is no sign that Dante began the work before his exile. He may have done so soon after leaving Bologna and perhaps it was this commencement that Moroello saw and encouraged him to continue. Boccaccio also said that he had been told that Dante dedicated *Purgatorio* to him but there is no confirmation of this. That the tradition exists is an indication that relations between them were those of a literary companionship. Cino da Pistoia also knew him and addressed a sonnet to him, to which Dante, at Moroello's request, wrote a reply. There are signs here of a poetic liaison between the three men, of which we have only the residue of two sonnets and one *canzone*.

In his letter, written in Latin, to Moroello, whom he addresses ceremoniously as 'Your Magnificence', Dante apologizes for his silence after leaving the court at Sarzana, to which he has since looked back with nostalgic regret, and where, as Moroello remarked, he was both dependent and yet free. His silence is not due to neglect but to the fact that he has fallen violently in love and is still a victim of this new passion. His first sight of the young woman was like a flash of lightning, followed by a thunder clap. All his resolve to remain aloof from women and to cease from writing poems about them has been shattered; gone too are his continuous meditations on the things of heaven and earth. He is now once again and more than ever the helpless prisoner of love, with no will of his own. The reference to his meditations (*meditationes assiduas quibus tam coelestia quam terrestria*) suggests that Moroello had read part at least of *Il Convivio* or was aware of its existence, he being, though Dante addresses him, out of protocol, in Latin, an example of the 'princes, barons, knights and many other noble folk' whom he had hoped to reach.

On leaving Sarzana Dante became the guest of the Guidi family in their castle at Poppi, in the Casentino region in the north-east of Tuscany, not far from the battlefield of Campaldino, where Dante as a young man had fought against the Ghibellines of Arezzo.[9] The Guidi were a powerful family, of Lombard origin, who in the course of centuries had gained possession of castle after castle. Their strongholds were solid and impressive; they grew more and more wealthy and members of their widespread family occupied important positions in a number of cities in Romagna and Tuscany. It is not known what commissions Dante undertook for his host on this occasion but when he returned a second time to benefit again from his protection he acted as secretary to Count Guidi's wife, the Countess Battifolle.

On his first visit to Poppi, released from his intellectual concerns at Bologna and from his duties at Sarzana, Dante, now aged 42, found himself in the upper valley of the Arno, among the slopes of the Etruscan Apennines, a beautiful region, tantalizingly near Florence, where he longed to return. And there, he says in the poem, walking along the bank of the river, he met a young woman who affected him like a *coup de foudre*. We do not know her name. The region is one in which Dante had always felt vulnerable to the power of Love but now there are no friends, as once there were, neither women nor men, no fellow poets, to whom he can unburden himself or to whom he can look for sympathy and understanding. In the *congedo* he bids his *montanina canzon* ('mountain song') go forth. Perhaps it will see Florence, *la mia terra* ('my city'), which, lacking all love and pity, locks its gates against him. If it should enter there he bids it say: 'No longer can my lord wage war on you. Where I come from, a chain so binds him that even if you relent in your cruelty he no longer has the freedom to return.'

This is not an allegorical poem. The subject is not ethics, nor moral obligations, nor justice, nor God's plan for the world; nor does the lady symbolize Philosophy. This is a poem about carnal love, disguised in conventional phraseology, sent, man to man, to Moroello who will understand its hidden meaning. The code words are 'death', 'dying', 'failing strength', 'revival', long used in love poetry as euphemisms for sexual orgasm. The poem expresses a sense of shock and bewilderment. After a long period of abstinence, love has caught him off guard. While still in Bologna he had not entirely given up writing poems on the subject of love, such as a group of sonnets he had exchanged with Cino, but compared with this *canzone* those are mere poetic exercises in which he is seen to be emotionally detached.

After the failure of *Il Convivio* and the spiritual crisis it probably occasioned, Dante gave thought to his next undertaking. He knew that he had misjudged his public. The 'princes, barons, knights and many other noble folk, not only men but women' whom he had hoped to reach had not responded. Long discussions on astronomy, morals, law and Roman history, even though varied by beautiful poems and personal revelations, had failed to hold attention. Too popular to attract the learned and too learned for popular taste, *Il Convivio* had missed its market. But the vast material he had prepared for it need not be wasted.

There had long been a popular demand for tales of marvels. The street entertainers developed their skills to meet it. Their repertoire was extensive: they could sing, play musical instruments, perform acrobatics; they had a supply of stories by heart, in which the magical and the fabulous predominated. A favourite was a horror story of a journey into the world of the dead, with gruesome descriptions of the punishment of unrepentant sinners. Such tales were recited with realistic gusto, accompanied by tears and groans, the rudimentary dialogue enlivened with gestures; even masks were worn. Sometimes the story was fully acted with theatrical props and effects. Giovanni Villani describes such a performance in Florence in his *Chronicle*.[10] Damned souls tormented by demons and virtuous souls welcomed by joyful angels into Heaven were everywhere a familiar sight in mosaics and frescoes, not only in Italy but elsewhere in Europe. In England they were known as Doom paintings.

One of the most successful was the tale of St Paul's visit to Hell in the company of an angel. Already known in the fourth century in two Greek versions, it was mentioned, with scorn, by St Augustine of Hippo. Another early version existed in Syriac. Latin versions abounded in the early Middle Ages, as well as translations in Old French, Early English, Provençal and Italian, both in prose and verse.[11]

One version in Old French, in rhyme, accompanied by a translation and commentary in Latin prose, evidently intended as material for a sermon, dates from the early fourteenth century. The manuscript is illustrated with miniatures which could easily serve for Dante's *Inferno*. It is God's will that St Paul shall see the punishments of Hell. His guide, in this version the Archangel Michael, leads him by the hand and shows him first the open gates. He sees a tree on fire, festooned with crucified bodies hanging from the branches, some by their feet, others by their hands, their arms, their tongues, their ears, their hair. In a furnace burning with flames of seven different colours St Paul sees rows of heads of damned souls. He gesticulates in horror and asks who they are. The Archangel replies that they are the souls of sinners who died before they could repent. They long for death but the dead cannot die a second time. They weep, they moan, they groan. St Paul tries to cover his eyes with his mantle, but the Archangel pulls him firmly along.

Next he sees a horrible river in which diabolical monsters swim like fish and gobble up the damned souls without mercy. It is spanned by a bridge, along which naked souls crawl. The virtuous ones make it to a door which leads to Paradise. The others fall into the river and stand immersed at different levels, some to their knees, some to their bellies and navels, some to their eyebrows. St Paul weeps piteously and asks the meaning of the different levels. The Archangel explains that they represent different sins: envy, deceit, fornication. (The Latin commentary adds: neglect of church attendance and confession, inattention to sermons.) St Paul weeps and says: 'Alas for the souls for whom such torments are prepared!'

In a fiery furnace stand more souls of the damned, visible from their navels up, biting their tongues and grimacing in torment. In a miniature a demon is shown beating them from above while below two other demons keep the fire hot with poker and bellows. Further on is a dark place where women, dressed in black, are covered with pitch and sulphur, with snakes and vipers curled about their necks. The Archangel explains that these are the souls of women who lost their virginity before marriage and who gave the bodies of their children to pigs and dogs or threw them in a river. A miniature shows a wheel with damned souls clinging to it while three demons make it whirl without pause. Next, in a place of ice, one part of which is on fire, are the souls of those who injured widows and orphans. Men and women, gathered on the banks of a river, reach out to a fruit tree but cannot grasp the fruit.[12] They are souls who did not keep their fasts. One old man tormented by four demons was a bishop who did not obey the law of God, who was unchaste in body, words and thoughts, who was avaricious, proud and criminal: hence the severity of his punishment. St Paul weeps. The Archangel asks: 'Why do you weep? You have not yet seen the worst sins of Hell.'

They come to a deep pit from which flames are leaping. The Archangel says: 'Stand back a while so that you can endure the stench.' A miniature shows St Paul blocking his nose with his mantle. In another place St Paul sees men and women being devoured by worms and serpents. Other souls are packed together, heaped high, groaning and sighing with a sound like thunder. One soul is being pulled along by seven demons. A list of his sins is presented to him, which he reads and makes his own judgement as to his place of punishment. The devils seize him and rush him along to where there is wailing and gnashing of teeth. Still other souls, all tonsured, are tormented by two demons while another is roasted on a spit, turned by two small demons. St Paul asks, 'Tell me, who are these men I see?' The Archangel replies: 'They were ordained ministers of the church who neglected their priestly duties, loved folly and excess and spent their time in wanton ways.'

Fig 4. St Paul and the Archangel Michael

In a continuation, souls dressed in white robes are seen in Heaven, kneeling before Christ. The damned souls cry out for mercy: 'Jesus, Son of God, who didst descend into Hell, with a diadem on Thy head, have mercy on us!' A reprieve is granted for relief from suffering from the ninth hour of Saturday to the first hour of Monday. The manuscript, which is incomplete, breaks off near this point.

The verse is crude and the narrative lacks organization. Many such texts were similar in these respects. But this is material that Dante used for his *Inferno* when he came to write it. Like a masterly showman, he takes the primitive scenario and develops it into a well-organized production. And with it he combines something else.

Other stories of journeys into the world of the dead had been inherited from antiquity. Among the best known were Homer's account of the descent of Odysseus, the myth of Orpheus who went to recover his wife Eurydice and, above all, Virgil's description of the journey of Aeneas into Hades in search of his father Anchises.[13] This last for Dante had supreme significance.

In the second canto of *Inferno* Dante draws back in fear from the enterprise to which Virgil has committed him: 'You say that Aeneas went to the world of the dead, and did so in the body. But it is clear to anyone why God allowed this for he was chosen as the father of Rome and of her Empire, whence came the Papal See. The Chosen Vessel[14] went there too, that he might bring back confirmation of the faith that leads to salvation. But why should I go? Who allows it? I am not Aeneas, I am not Paul': *Io non Enea, io non Paolo sono*.[15]

Modern commentators are united in relating the reference to St Paul to 2 Corinthians XII, verses 2–4, in which speaking of himself the Apostle says:

> I knew a man in Christ above fourteen years ago (whether in the body I cannot tell; or whether out of the body, I cannot tell: God knoweth); such a one caught up to the third heaven. ... How that he was caught up into paradise, and heard unspeakable words, which it is not lawful for a man to utter.

Dante's first listeners, however, would undoubtedly have taken his reference to St Paul to be an allusion to the familiar tale of his journey into Hell, of which they would recognize many details in the story they were about to hear. By placing Aeneas and St Paul together in this one line, Dante, in a stroke of genius, combines the classical and the mediaeval, the august and the lowly, in what was to prove a new form of literary art.

The shadowy figure of Virgil who stands in the wooded valley in the first canto of *Inferno*, silent, as is the way of ghosts,[16] until Dante speaks to him, is not the Virgil we know from our classical sources. For Dante and his contemporaries he was something different. More than any other ancient writer, he was a link between the pagan past and the present, between the *dei falsi e bugiardi* ('lying and false gods') and the true God of the Christians. He, it was believed, had prophesied the birth of Christ, in his fourth eclogue, in which, in mysterious words which have never been convincingly explained, he foretells the birth of a child who will bring to pass a new age of gold. The belief that this was a prophecy, unwitting on the part of Virgil, of the birth of Christ was current already in the fourth century. The Emperor Constantine accepted it. Because of it, Virgil came to be known as the Prophet of the Gentiles. In Rheims Cathedral his name was included in prayers for the prophets. In Liège, in the eleventh century, he appeared as a character in a Nativity play. In Spain, in the fourteenth century, he was classed among the Old Testament prophets.

Gradually throughout the Middle Ages, Virgil acquired the reputation of a fabulous figure. Already in classical times he had been regarded as an oracle. He became famed in legends, accepted by the learned as well as by the illiterate, as a sage, an astrologer, a protector, a magician, a prophet. All this mediaeval attire he wore in the eyes of Dante's earliest audience when he revealed himself in the opening canto of the *Commedia*:

'Poeta fui, e cantai di quel giusto
   figliuol d'Anchise che venne da Troia,
   poi ch 'l superbo Ilion fu combusto.'

'I was a poet and I sang in praise
   of Anchises' just son, who came from Troy,
   when Ilium the proud was set ablaze.'[17]

To Dante he is the great poet whom he greets with bowed head and reverent words:

'Or se' tu quel Virgilio e quella fonte
   che spandi di parlar sì largo fiume?'

'Art thou indeed that Virgil and that fount
   who pourest forth so broad a stream of speech?'[18]

He is also the glory and the light of other poets, whom Dante has long studied and loved, on whom alone he has based his own style which has earned
him honour. But he is also the figure invested with an aura of power who can
now help Dante in his peril. Driven back down the mountain by three wild
animals, terrified above all by the she-wolf, he implores:

'Aiutami da lei, famoso saggio!'

'Rescue me from her, o thou famous sage!'[19]

Thus he appeals to Virgil as a wise man, a magician. This would not surprise
his listeners. They would expect it. Nor would they be surprised by Virgil's
mysterious prophecy of the hound that will one day drive the she-wolf from
the world. Virgil was known to utter mysterious prophecies. Nor would it
puzzle them that Virgil, empowered by authority from Heaven, would be
Dante's guide and guardian and, having led him to the gates of Hell, would
take him by the hand and lead him *dentro alle segrete cose* ('in among the
secret things').[20] That was how the Archangel led St Paul. This was going to
be a good story, of the kind they were used to.

   This time Dante the showman had captured his audience and he would
hold it for seven centuries.

CHAPTER 11

The Return of Beatrice

One thing is certain, and few things are, concerning Beatrice: she plays no part in *Il Convivio*. At the end of *La Vita Nuova*, as we have seen, Dante said he would write no more poetry concerning her until he had studied enough to write what had never been written in verse of any woman, *sì com' ella sae veracemente* ('as she truly knows'). By the time he began *Il Convivio*, his studies had been extensive, but he was ready then only to draw a distinction between his love for Beatrice and his love for the *donna gentile*. About Beatrice, the glorified soul in Heaven, he would say no more at present.

When he began his new work his plan changed. The design was vast in structure and elaborated in minute detail. His story of a journey to the world of the dead was to have perfectly organized apparatus and scenic effects, of sufficient grandeur to carry his vision for the salvation of the world and of his own soul. He would tell it in the first person, obtaining thereby the utmost verisimilitude. Unlike the story of St Paul's journey, it would encompass Purgatory and Paradise, as well as Inferno. In Inferno and Purgatory the pagan and partly Christianized Virgil could be his guide. For Paradise another figure would be required. The question was: who? There were many possibilities: St Thomas Aquinas? St Bernard? Angelic beings? Indeed, they and quite a few other figures do play minor roles as mentors and intermediaries. He needed many voices among which to allocate what he had learnt from his studies and the beliefs he had formed; for this purpose he assembled an immense cast. But for his own role in the drama he needed someone of personal significance: the time had come to bring forward Beatrice as his leading lady.

A compelling feature of the *Commedia* is the force of the narrative. But it is not one single narrative: it is studded with minor stories, even stories within stories, in dialogue or told in the first person, some by mythological figures but the majority by the souls of people recently dead and well known. One linking theme, drawn from folklore and also found in Arthurian and other tales of chivalric adventure which Dante knew well, was the quest of the knight for his lady, who sends a messenger to bring him to her and from afar guides him through the realm of the dead or of faerie. At their meeting, the lady rebukes her lover for his infidelity, he confesses his fault and they are reconciled. This is the basic story of the journey of Dante, led by a messenger (Virgil) to Beatrice.[1] Structurally it serves to draw the main story onward, as hints and allusions placed at critical points keep the audience in anticipation of what is to come. One instance, in *Inferno*, shows that despite his meticulous planning Dante occasionally changed his mind as the poem progressed. When Farinata degli Uberti hints at Dante's exile, Virgil tells him he will learn more about the course of his life from Beatrice:

'La mente tua conservi quel ch'udito
    hai contra te', mi comandò quel saggio.
    'E ora attendi qui', e drizzò il dito:
'quando sarai dinanzi al dolce raggio
    di quella il cui bell' occhio tutto vede,
    da lei saprai di tua vita il viaggio.'

'Keep in thy mind what thou against thee now
    hast heard', that man of wisdom counselled me,
    'and mark', he said, his finger raised, 'when thou
in her sweet radiance shalt come to be,
    whose lovely eyes behold all things that are,
    from her thou'lt learn the path ahead of thee.'[2]

But in *Paradiso* it is Dante's ancestor Cacciaguida who unfolds his future to him, not Beatrice.[3]

We first see Beatrice in the *Commedia* through the words of Virgil. To reassure Dante that his journey has the highest authority in Heaven, he describes the visit of a blessed soul who sought him in Limbo. For the first time we hear words spoken by her, reported by Virgil, who describes her voice as sweet, low and angelic, her eyes as brighter than the stars. Her speech is elaborately courteous. She is aware of his fame as a poet. She expresses loving concern for Dante's danger and is anxious lest she may have come too late. And she tells him who she is:

'I' son Beatrice che ti faccio andare.'

'I Beatrice am who send thee on this quest.'[4]

Virgil continues to relate that in reply to his enquiry as to why she was unafraid to descend into Hell she described a heavenly scene which led her to do so. The Virgin Mary in her compassion called to St Lucy who in her turn urged Beatrice to go to the rescue of one who so loved her that for her sake he rose to distinction, or as Dante makes St Lucy say, *uscì per te della volgare schiera* ('for thee departed from the vulgar herd').[5] Alerted by St Lucy to Dante's extreme peril, Beatrice instantly left her throne in Heaven in search of Virgil, trusting to his power as a poet which honours him and all those who have heard him. Ending her appeal, she turned her countenance away, her eyes brimming with tears.

This is not the scornful young woman of *La Vita Nuova*, the Beatrice who cut Dante in the street, who mocked and laughed at him when he trembled in her presence. Almost 20 years have passed. Dante's thoughts concerning her have led him to create a new Beatrice, beatified and invested with the divine qualities he had already associated with her but which formerly he had not understood. As *Il Convivio* developed, the exalted meaning of the *donna gentile* was his foremost consideration, but his mind, radiant with the contemplation of philosophic truth, was at the same time alert to the truths of theology. We do not know whether he intended to introduce theological doctrine into *Il Convivio*. If so, he would not then have drawn an allegorical connection with Beatrice, for he said that he intended not to mention her further in that work. When and why did he decide to give Beatrice the role of expounding theological doctrine in *Paradiso*?

Before his exile, while he was still in turmoil with the conflict between his love for Beatrice and his love for the *donna gentile*, he had a vision of Beatrice in Heaven,

> clothed in the crimson garments in which she first appeared before my eyes; and she seemed as young as when I first saw her.[6]

This was followed by a 'marvellous vision' in which he saw things that made him decide to write no more poetry concerning Beatrice until he could do so worthily.[7] He does not describe this vision, but it follows a sonnet in which he tells how a thought, which he calls a sigh, ascended into Heaven like a pilgrim spirit, and there beheld a lady in glory, so beautiful and possessed of such attributes that his intellect was dumbfounded,

> for our intellect in the presence of those blessed souls is as weak as our eyes before the sun. ... I say [in my sonnet] that although I cannot comprehend the place to which my thought takes me, that is into the presence of her miraculous nature, I understand this at least, that this thought of mine is entirely concerned with my lady, for frequently I hear her name.[8]

These visions of Beatrice remained latent in his mind as he studied philosophy and wrote *Il Convivio*. By the time he began to plan his new work he had realized their significance: she had become both an instance and an image of creation glorified by love.

Beatrice, the Florentine child, girl and woman, with whom Dante fell in love, was educated, as has been presumed, at a convent school, where she would have learnt her catechism and as much Latin as was needed for her prayers and the litany. There is an enormous gap between her and the Beatrice of the *Commedia*, who on one occasion speaks in Latin,[9] prophesies the coming of a Benefactor, instructs Dante on the metaphysics of the moon and the chain of cause and effect between the angelic beings and life on earth; on the eternal existence of the souls in the Empyrean and their temporary presence in the spheres for Dante's benefit; on the doctrine of unfulfilled vows; on the Atonement, the Just Vengeance, the Resurrection of the body; on the Angelic Hierarchy; on the Creation; who, with startling inappropriateness, launches into a sarcastic diatribe against unworthy preachers who in their sermons rely more on their own jokes than on the Gospel; whose last words are a bitter gibe at Pope Boniface VIII.[10] This, again, is not the Beatrice of *La Vita Nuova*. Who then is she?

In one of her roles she is the voice of Dante's intellect. In *Il Convivio* his knowledge, acquired by study after the death of Beatrice, undertaken for her sake and continued during his early years of exile, is expounded directly, in the first person. In the *Commedia* he apportions it among a series of personages, of whom the most continuous are Virgil and Beatrice. The doctrinal and instructive parts of his work thus take on the form of dialogues, thereby introducing an element of drama, which heightens the power of the narrative.

The light of theological truth that now radiates his mind, his understanding of the universe, his gradual approach to a vision of God, all this he owes to the memory of Beatrice, for it was in order to understand her significance that he persisted in his studies. As the character Dante rises through the spheres of Heaven, shedding error after error, growing continually in understanding, so the beauty of Beatrice, of her smile and of her eyes, grows ever more dazzling. By means of this image Dante the poet reflects his intellectual exultation and spiritual joy at the increasing clarification of his mind.[11]

But in the *Commedia* Beatrice, as Dante creates her, plays many roles. The simplest and for some readers the most appealing is the Beatrice whom Dante continues to love, remembering the beautiful Florentine girl, now a soul in Heaven who, he believes, watches over him and tries to guide him, but from whose memory he has often strayed. This basic theme, linking the work together, runs from Virgil's description of her at the beginning of *Inferno* to our last glimpse of her in *Paradiso*, where, returned to her throne, she folds her hands in prayer, with all the heavenly host, that the Virgin Mary may intercede for Dante that he may behold God. This is the Beatrice of Dante's early love poetry, in whom he perceived the immanence of divine glory and who continues to inspire some of his most exalted lines in the

Commedia. At a supreme moment he links the two together. In *Paradiso*, when he enters the Empyrean, he turns to look at Beatrice and finds her beauty so transfigured that it defeats all his power to describe it. Not all that he has ever written of her would suffice:

Se quanto infino a qui di lei si dice
  fosse conchiuso tutto in una loda,
  poco sarebbe a fornir questa vice.
La bellezza ch'io vidi si trasmoda
  non pur di là da noi, ma certo io credo
  che solo il suo fattor tutta la goda.
Da questo passo vinto mi concedo
  più che già mai da punto di suo tema
  soprato fosse comico o trageda;
chè, come sole in viso che più trema,
  così lo rimembrar del dolce riso
  la mente mia di sè medesmo scema.
Dal primo giorno ch'i' vidi il suo viso
  in questa vita, infino a questa vista,
  non m'è il seguire al mio cantar preciso;
ma or convien che mio seguir desista
  più dietro a sua bellezza, poetando,
  come all'ultimo suo ciascuno artista.

Were everything I've ever said of her
  rolled up into a single jubilee,
  too slight a hymn for this new task were there.
Beauty past knowledge was displayed to me –
  not only ours; the joy of it complete
  her Maker knows, I think, and only He.
From this point on I must admit defeat
  sounder than poet wrestling with his theme,
  comic or tragic, e'er was doomed to meet;
for her sweet smile remembered, as the beam
  of sunlight blinds the weakest eyes that gaze,
  bewilders all my wits and scatters them.
From the first hour I looked upon her face
  in this life, till that vision, I could trust
  the poet in me to pursue her praise;
now in her beauty's wake my song can thrust
  its following flight no farther; I give o'er
  as, at his art's end, every artist must.[12]

Soon afterwards, realizing that Beatrice has left him to return to her throne in Heaven, Dante looks up at her and offers the following prayer, in which the whole of this theme is gathered up in a farewell:

'O donna in cui la mia speranza vige
  e che soffristi per la mia salute
  in inferno lasciar le tue vestige,
di tante cose quant'i' ho vedute,
  dal tuo podere e dalla tua bontate
  riconosco la grazia e la virtute.
Tu m'hai di servo tratto a libertate
  per tutte quelle vie, per tutt'i modi
  che di ciò fare avei la potestate.
La tua magnificenza in me custodi,
  sì che l'anima mia che fatt' hai sana,
  piacente a te dal corpo si disnodi.'

'O thou in whom my hopes securely dwell,
  and who, to bring my soul to Paradise,
  didst leave the imprint of thy steps in Hell,
of all that I have looked on with these eyes
  thy goodness and thy power have fitted me
  the holiness and grace to recognize.
Thou hast led me, a slave, to liberty,
  by every path, and using every means
  which to fulfil this task were granted thee.
Keep turned towards me thy munificence
  so that my soul which thou hast remedied
  may please thee when it quits the bonds of sense.'[13]

Beatrice, it seemed to him, although so distant, smiled, 'then to the eternal fountain turned her head'. It is significant that in these last words of loving gratitude, the honorific pronoun *voi* by which he has addressed Beatrice throughout the poem is here replaced by the intimate pronoun *tu*. She is here once again the Florentine girl and woman whom he loved.

The meeting between Dante and Beatrice in the *Commedia* occurs in the Garden of Eden at the summit of the Mountain of Purgatory. Occupying a central position in the work, it brings together the unexpected departure of Virgil, Dante's shock and grief, the entry on the stage of Beatrice in disguise, her reproaches, his humiliation, confession of infidelity and reconciliation. For this crucial and complex *scène à faire* and for the allegorical spectacles which follow, Dante uses many different forms of creative art: narrative, drama, pageant, masque and dumb-show. In each of them Beatrice plays a different role, though Dante's personal vision of her, as he had come to think of her, remains unchanged.

The implications of these paradoxes will be considered in a subsequent chapter.[14]

CHAPTER 12

The Story Begins

The most carefully planned feature of the *Commedia* is its structure. The number of cantos, the regions of the dead, the form of the verse, are based on the figure three and its multiples: 33 cantos to each of the three main sections (*cantiche*), plus one introductory canto, bringing the total to 100, the perfect number. Most striking of all is the verse. Known as *terza rima* (triple rhyme), it was Dante's invention. In a long verse narrative there is always danger of monotony. Couplets are a particular peril. Blank verse was not used in vernacular writing. Dante loved rhyme, *concatenatio pulcra* ('beautiful linkage'), as he called it.[1] It is also an aid to memory and a safeguard against omissions and alterations by copyists. The separation of each couplet by a new rhyme which hooks over on to the next, pulling the narrative forward, was a brilliant solution. It gives individual unity to every canto, while linking them all in an identical pattern. The effect is that of woven fabric.

He chose the 11-syllable line (*endecasillabo*) for the entire work. This had long been part of his repertoire. He had used it in sonnets, *canzoni*, *ballate* and *sestine* and valued it for its stateliness. He would now test its versatility to the full. Narrative, dialogue, epigrams, enigmas, outbursts of wrath, satire, humour, farce, caricature, scenes of horror and of beauty, exultation, flights of poetic imagination and lyrical rapture all had to be accommodated, usually in end-stopped lines, sometimes flowing over into paragraphs of three lines or more. His range of diction too would be far more extensive and varied than he had previously allowed himself. No longer limited to the *volgare illustre*, it would include the speech of every day, some of it lowly, some of it even coarse, as well as diction that is delicate, noble and exalted. The form of the work was to be part narrative, part descriptive, part dramatic, part epic, part exhortatory, part satiric and part lyric. The language that would be adequate for such variety was that of comedy, as he had defined it in *De Vulgari Eloqentia*.[2] That is why he called the work a *commedia*. It was Boccaccio who first added the word *divina*.

How did Dante become such a superb master of the art of storytelling, of dialogue, of characterization, of cliff-hanging moments of suspense? Nothing in his earlier poetry, not even the narrative of *La Vita Nuova*, gives any inkling that he had this ability. One can only cast about for models. There were the stories of the Old Testament, many of them told in dialogue, almost like mini-dramas. There were the vivid descriptions of transformation related by Ovid in his *Metamorphoses*, a work which Dante knew well. There was the epic account of Roman history by Lucan in his *Pharsalia*. Above all, there was Virgil's *Aeneid*. The mediaeval *chansons de geste*, the Arthurian and other stories of chivalrous romance, the accounts of distant journeys, were a treasure-house of narrative. There were also traditions of popular storytelling, such as the *Legenda Aurea* ('Golden Legends'), containing lives of the saints and ecclesiastical lore, the *Gesta Romanorum* ('Deeds of the Romans'), compiled in Latin by monks as recreational reading and as material for sermons. There were mediaeval morality and miracle plays, with farcical interludes of devil-play. Whatever his models, Dante added material of his own, some of it invented, some of it sensational and immediate, creating thereby a mixed composition that is totally unprecedented in literature.

The story opens with the character Dante lost in a dark wood, wild, rough and dense. He had wandered in while in a state of sleep and came to himself on reaching the foot of a hill, of which the upper slopes were lit by the morning sun. He takes courage and begins to climb but is chased back by three wild animals: a leopard, a lion and a she-wolf. This last of the three is the most frightening, the more so as it is a female wolf, an image revered in ancient Rome for nurturing Romulus and Remus but here deformed into a ravening beast. He stumbles back down the valley and sees a figure in the shadows. It does not speak and whether it is a spirit or a living man Dante does not know. He calls out to it for help.

Thus begins one of the most famous double acts in all literature. This is the poet Virgil, who will accompany Dante through Hell and Purgatory, instructing, explaining, protecting, exhorting, sometimes scolding, but becoming, as the story progresses, a loving and beloved companion. On learning who he is, Dante is overcome with awe. He greets him as the poet whose work he has read from end to end, from whom he has learnt the *bello stile* ('beautiful style') which has brought him honour. This cannot mean the style of the *Commedia*, for that is not yet written; it can only refer to Dante's earlier poems, especially his *canzoni* on moral subjects, written with a loftiness and gravity that he has learnt from Virgil.

It is to Virgil the wise man, the *saggio*, however, that he appeals for help from the wolf. And it is Virgil the prophet who replies. The animal kills all those who cross its path,

'e ha natura sì malvagia e ria,
   che mai non empie la bramosa voglia,
   e dopo 'l pasto ha più fame che pria.'

'and has so vile a nature, framed for ill,
   she never satisfies her ravening greed,
   and after eating is more hungry still.'[3]

As befits his oracular role, Virgil foretells in mysterious words that a *veltro* ('hound') will come to destroy the wolf:

'Molti son li animali a cui s'ammoglia,
   e più saranno ancora, infin che 'l veltro
   verrà, che la farà morir con doglia.
Questi non ciberà terra nè peltro,
   ma sapienza, amore e virtute,
   e sua nazion sarà tra feltro e feltro.'

'With many creatures she is known to breed
   and will with others yet, until the hound
   shall come to ravage her and leave her dead.
He will not feed on wealth, nor yet on ground,
   but wisdom, charity and righteousness;
   'twixt felt and felt his naissance will be found.'[4]

The phrase *tra feltro e feltro*, a conundrum unsolved for nearly seven centuries, has given rise to many fanciful and ingenious speculations. It has long been assumed that the hound is the figure of some political or spiritual leader who will rid the world of avarice, the usual interpretation of the she-wolf. The leopard and the lion probably represent the other two false desires which Dante found identified by Boethius: the desire for pleasure and the desire for fame, said to pose less danger than the desire for wealth.[5] The two nouns *feltro* and *feltro* are sometimes printed with a capital F because they have been identified with the place-names Feltre in Venetia and Montefeltro in Romagna, an area within which it has been conjectured that the Benefactor would be born. Other commentators interpret the word *feltro* as indicating coarse felt clothing worn by those who renounce wealth. Another interpretation is that the Benefactor will be born under the constellation of the Twins, called *fratres pilleati*, the brothers Castor and Pollux, who wear felt skull caps. According to yet another view the phrase refers to felt-lined urns in which votes for magistrates were collected.

Identifications of the Benefactor have included Can Grande della Scala, that is, the Ghibelline ruler of Verona whom Dante greatly admired (the coincidence of his name 'Great Dog' seeming to many to be convincing), the Emperor Henry VII, Christ in His Second Coming, and even Dante himself. None of these identifications sheds any light on the meaning of the phrase *tra feltro e feltro*, except possibly that of Dante, who was born under the constellation of the Twins. It is far from certain, however, that when he wrote these words Dante had any specific Benefactor in mind. The assumption that he had has led to much erroneous speculation and confusion.

In the fourth section of *Il Convivio*, which he had recently written, probably in 1306,[6] Dante had stated that the only remedy for the problems of wars and their causes was imperial authority, invested in a single monarch who,

> possessing everything, and having nothing left to desire, would keep kings confined within the borders of their kingdoms, so that peace would reign between them, and cities would rest in peace, and while they so rest neighbourhoods would love each other, and in this mutual love families would satisfy all their wants; and when these are satisfied, a man would live happily, which is the end for which he is born.[7]

The remedy for avarice, which more than anything else 'endangers and kills cities, countrysides and individuals', is found to lie in the texts of canon and civil law:

> [F]or what else were the two branches of Law, I mean Canon and Civil Law, designed to remedy so much as that cupidity which grows by the amassing of riches? Certainly both branches of the law make this sufficiently plain where we read their origins (*cominciamenti*), that is, the origins of their written record.[8]

The explanation of the words *tra feltro e feltro*, understood in this context, is very simple, so simple that it has been overlooked. It is to be found in the technique of papermaking.[9] A mould was dipped into a vat of pulp and to absorb the moisture the paper was couched on a sheet of felt. Another felt sheet was placed on top and another piece of paper on top of that. When a pile of alternating pieces of felt and paper had been thus constructed, it was placed in a press by which most of the remaining moisture was removed. The sheets of paper were then hung to dry. If the paper was not perfectly dry, the ink blurred on it, as Dante says in *Il Convivio*, in connection with his eyesight:

> [B]ecause the sight is weakened, some dispersion of the visual spirit takes place in it, so that an object is no longer seen as concentrated, but appears diffused, *almost in the same way as our writing on damp paper*.[10]

The process of making paper was widely known in Italy by the early fourteenth century. There were paper mills in operation in Fabriano in 1276 and in Bologna in 1298. Dante's contemporaries would have known that between felt and felt one found paper, that is to say, texts. Later commentators, losing sight of this simple explanation, and assuming that Dante was referring to a particular person, had recourse to sophisticated interpretations in which numberless commentators have confounded their readers ever since.

In other words, the remedy for avarice is to be found precisely where, in *Il Convivio*, Dante said it was: in the texts of canon and civil law. The hound prophesied by Virgil is a figure of a righteous emperor, described in *Il Convivio* as desiring neither riches nor land, a Benefactor for whom Dante hopes but who has not yet come. He will declare and enforce the law as laid down in the Codex of Justinian, maintaining a balance with canon law as set out in the *Decretum* of Gratian, that is to say, *tra feltro e feltro*, between layers of felt which dry the paper on which writing will then be legible.

Virgil tells the frightened Dante that there is no way past the she-wolf except through the world of the damned and the repentant. That is to say, he must be brought face to face with the results of avarice and other sins. Through these two regions, Inferno and Purgatory, Virgil will lead him. From there on a worthier spirit will take over, for into Heaven Virgil may not go. He dwells, we are soon to learn, in Limbo, with others like himself who lived outside God's law. Dante in his desperation consents to go with him and the first canto ends:

> allor si mosse, e io li tenni retro.

> *then he moved on and I behind him went.*[11]

But then, as has been said, Dante has misgivings. Who is he to undertake such a journey? He is neither Aeneas nor St Paul.

When Virgil reassures him that his journey is authorized by powers on high, the hidden implication is that he *does* in fact combine the functions of Aeneas and St Paul. Dante the writer has had a vision of God's purpose in linking the birth of the Roman Empire with the foundation of the Christian faith, a vision he began to impart in *Il Convivio* and which he will now make the main theme of the *Commedia*.

Virgil reproaches Dante for his cowardice in terms so direct and colloquial that we catch the rhythm of everyday speech and even the gestures of exasperation:

> 'Dunque che è? Perchè, perchè ristai?
>   Perchè tanta viltà nel cuore allette?
>   Perchè ardire e franchezza non hai,
> poscia che tai tre donne benedette
>   curan di te ne la corte del cielo,
>   e 'l mio parlar tanto ben t'impromette?'

'What ails thee then? Why, why, dost thou hold back?
 Why does such fear take hold within thy heart?
 Why courage and decision dost thou lack,
since three such blessèd women take thy part
 in Heaven's court, concerned for thy sad plight,
 and promise of such good my words impart?'[12]

The effect on Dante is delicately conveyed by a simile that lifts the reader out of the dark valley into a meadow lit by the morning sun:

Quali i fioretti, dal notturno gelo
  chinati e chiusi, poi che 'l sol li 'mbianca
  si drizzan tutti aperti in loro stelo,
tal mi fec'io di mia virtute stanca ...

As little flowers, in the frost of night
  drooping and closed, stand open and erect
  when the sun touches them with morning light,
so did my failing courage resurrect ...[13]

Dante is reassured. His will and Virgil's are now one:

'Tu duca, tu segnore, e tu maestro.'

'Leader and lord and master be thou then.'[14]

And they set off along the densely wooded path.

CHAPTER 13

Limbo

The two poets arrive before the gateway to Hell. The words inscribed above it fill Dante with dread. The gate, as though speaking, conveys its grim warning:

Per me si va nella città dolente.
  Per me si va nell'eterno dolore.
  Per me si va tra la perduta gente.
Giustizia mosse il mio alto fattore.
  Fecemi la divina potestate,
  la somma sapienza e 'l primo amore.
Dinanzi a me non fuor cose create
  se non etterne, e io etterno duro.
  Lasciate ogni speranza voi ch'entrate.

Through me the way to the abode of pain.
  Through me to where all woes eternal prove.
  Through me the way to where the lost remain.
Justice inspired my maker high above.
  By divine power I was created there,
  by highest wisdom and by primal love.
Made before me was nothing whatsoe'er
  but things eternal and I eternal bide.
  All hope abandon ye who enter here.[1]

Prominent in this daunting message is the word 'justice'. The damned are those who died unrepentant. God's forgiveness cannot reach them for they have rejected it. That is why they have no hope. Virgil defines the damned as those who *hanno perduto il ben dell'intelletto* ('have lost the good of the intellect'), namely truth.[2]

Dante's first impression on entering Hell is of sighs and lamentations echoing through the starless air, strange voices, terrifying tongues, words of grief and rage. This is what St Paul experiences on his journey with his angelic guide and, also like St Paul, Dante asks who these souls are and what it is that makes them lament so loudly. He is told that they are those who lived without praise or blame. Mingled with them are the angels who when Lucifer rebelled were neither for him nor for God, but merely for themselves.

This reference to what were known as 'neutral angels' is of special interest. Belief in them was widespread and occurred in a number of mediaeval works such as the *Voyage of St Brendan* and *Parzifal* by Gottfried von Eschenbach. They symbolized the concept of an area between good and evil. Belief in them came to be considered heretical and it is interesting that Dante silently drops all mention of them in *Paradiso*. As late as the fifteenth century they were portrayed by the Florentine painter Francesco Botticini in human form among the heavenly host,[3] the belief then being that though granted a second chance by God they were unworthy to return to their original angelic nature.

Dante sees a whirling banner, after which comes a train of souls, so long he could scarcely believe death had undone so many.[4] Dante recognizes (*vidi e conobbi*, 'I saw and knew') one

che fece per viltà il gran rifiuto.

who out of fear the great refusal made.

He has been identified as Pope Celestine V, who abdicated in 1294, thus making way for the election of Boniface VIII.[5] Other identifications include Esau and Pontius Pilate, but the immediacy of the words *vidi e conobbi* suggests someone of recent significance to Dante. If the soul is that of Celestine V, this is an early and oblique introduction of the theme of Boniface, which will gain in momentum as the work progresses.

No other soul among this group is named. Virgil scorns them:

'Non ragioniam di lor, ma guarda e passa.'

'Let us not talk of them; look and pass on.'[6]

Peering ahead, Dante sees people crowding at the bank of a great river as though eager to cross. He asks again who they are but is told to wait until they reach the sad shore of the Acheron. Feeling rebuffed, Dante remains silent. Suddenly a boat is seen, oared by a ferryman, who chants:

... 'Guai a voi anime prave!
Non isperate mai veder lo cielo.
I' vegno per menarvi all'altra riva
nelle tenebre etterne, in caldo e 'n gelo.'

... *'Woe to you, base souls!*
Hope not the heavens ever to behold.
I come to take you to the other shore,
into eternal darkness, heat and cold.'[7]

Startled by the sight of Dante, a living man, the oarsman breaks his rocking rhythm and shouts:

'E tu che se' costì, anima viva,
    pàrtiti da cotesti che son morti.'

'And thou who standest there, a living soul,
    be gone from all these others who are dead.'[8]

When Dante does not move he tells him he is destined for another voyage, from another port, and by a lighter craft. And now Virgil, the magician, utters a formula of power, naming the ferryman:

… 'Charon, non ti crucciare:
vuolsi così colà dove si puote
ciò che si vuole, e più non dimandare.'

    … *'Charon, thyself do not torment:*
thus it is willed where power and will are one,
so ask no more and with this be content.'[9]

Charon, of the shaggy jaws and eyes ringed with flame, is at once subdued, but the damned souls burst forth blaspheming God, cursing their parents, humankind, the place, the time, the seed of their begetting and their birth. In crowds they clamber on to the boat, Charon beating lingerers with his oar. This rough description is followed by a simile, not lowly-mediaeval but Virgilian:

Come d'autunno si levan le foglie
    l'una appresso dell'altra, fin che 'l ramo
    vede alla terra tutte le sue spoglie,
similmente il mal seme d'Adamo
    gittansi di quel lito ad una ad una,
    per cenni come augel per suo richiamo.

Just as in autumn, leaves lift, one by one,
    until the branch sees on the ground below
    where all its former vesture now is gone,
so do the wicked progeny of Adam throw
    themselves in turn from off that shore, just as
    a bird, at signals, to its lure will go.'[10]

The boat-load moves off over the dark water and Virgil tells Dante to take courage, for Charon's words to him promise well for the future destiny of his soul.

At this the earth shakes, there is a gust of wind, and a crimson flash deprives Dante of his senses. He falls like someone overcome by sleep. He is awakened by a clap of thunder and finds himself on the other side of the river Acheron. How he was transported there we are not told. He peers down into a deep dark abyss resounding with innumerable cries of woe. Virgil, leading the way, turns pale. Dante, thinking he is afraid, feels fear himself, but Virgil says, 'What you mistake in my face for fear is pity for the souls below', adding impatiently:

'Andiam, chè la via lunga ne sospigne.'

'Let us move on, for we have far to go.'[11]

And they enter Hell's First Circle, which is Limbo.

The continuity between the ancient and the Christian world was part of Dante's vision in *Il Convivio*. It is carried over into the *Commedia* where it takes on a personalized, dramatic form. God's plan for the world existed before time and is eternal. In the experience of humanity, however, there is before and after: the Incarnation happened in time and place. Those who lived and died before Christ had not known Him. Those who lived after Him had access to the Truth. This was an inexorable division, inescapable in fact and logic.

'Limbo' is a theological term denoting the abode and condition of souls who though choosing virtue are yet excluded from the bliss of the presence of God. The word is derived from the Latin *limbus*, meaning border or edge, and such souls were visualized as dwelling in an upper fringe of Hell, experiencing no torment other than a perpetual longing. Dante accepted this belief but it pained and puzzled him. In the *Commedia* he displays it in individual terms, relating particularly to the fate of Virgil. This introduces a tension of anxiety lasting throughout *Inferno* and *Purgatorio* which is eventually resolved in *Paradiso*.[12]

Dante describes Limbo as a place of darkness, filled with the sighing of vast crowds of men, women and children. They are the virtuous unbaptized and those who, living before Christianity, did not worship God aright, and of these, Virgil says, 'I myself am one.' Dante the character is seized at the heart with grief when he hears this, for he knows that people of great worth are here. Seeking to overcome his doubt, he asks Virgil for reassurance:

'Dimmi, maestro mio, dimmi signor',
   comincia' io per volere esser certo
   di quella fede che vince ogni error:
'uscìcci mai alcuno, o per suo merto
   o per altrui, che poi fosse beato?'

'Tell me, lord, master,' thus did I begin,
   that I might certain be and reassured
   about that faith that conquers every sin,
'did any go forth hence, as a reward
   for his or other's merit, to be blessed?'[13]

Virgil understands his covert meaning.

The belief that between Christ's death and Resurrection He visited Limbo to release the souls of those who had believed in His coming became orthodox in about the fourth century and found its way into the Apostles' Creed, in the words 'He descended into Hell'. Dante would many times have seen this scene represented in painting and sculpture. It was a favourite subject of mediaeval legend and drama and is known in English by the agricultural metaphor, 'The Harrowing of Hell'. In a brilliant stroke of verisimilitude, Dante imagines that Virgil, who had died 19 years before the birth of Christ, was a witness of this spectacular event:

> Rispuose, 'Io era nuovo in questo stato,
>   quando ci vidi venire un possente,
>   con segno di vittoria coronato.'

> *'I was but new to this estate', said he,*
>   *'when one of power I saw descending here,*
>   *with round his head a sign of victory.'*[14]

He saw this 'one of power' draw forth Adam, Abel, Noah, Moses, Abraham, David, Jacob with his father and his sons, Rachel and many others who were all made blessed. 'And I would have thee know,' Virgil adds, 'that before then no human souls were saved.' He does not know who the mysterious figure was and Dante does not say, but his audience would understand that Virgil at that supreme moment had, without knowing it, looked on the face of Christ, just as, in his fourth eclogue, he had unknowingly foretold His birth.

Making their way through the crowd of souls, dense as a forest, they come to a blaze of light where others are set apart. These are souls who are specially honoured in consequence of their fame on earth. Dante hears a voice call out:

> 'Onorate l'altissimo poeta:
> l'ombra sua torna, ch'era dipartita.'

> *'Pay honour to the loftiest of poets:*
> *his spirit now returns that had departed.'*[15]

Four souls draw near, their demeanour neither sad nor joyful. Virgil names them: they are Homer, Horace, Ovid and Lucan, an august reception committee advancing to welcome Virgil back, paying him honour in the name of poet which they all share, and in this, says Virgil, 'they do well'.

These shadowy figures form a *tableau*, like a faded mural painting. They speak with Virgil for a while, then turn to greet Dante, at which Virgil smiles.

E più d'onore ancora assai mi fenno,
   ch' e' sì mi fecer della loro schiera,
   sì ch'io fui sesto tra cotanto senno.

And still more honour yet to me they paid,
   for to their group they then admitted me
   and sixth among such wisdom I was made.[16]

There was a time, many years before, when Dante, young, unknown and at the beginning of his career, was admitted to a distinguished group of *rimatori* (rhymesters) in Florence. Now he imagines himself admitted to the company of five of the greatest poets of the ancient world, and *made one of them.*

The choice of poets is significant. Homer, the narrator of the defeat of the Trojans by the Greeks; Virgil, who related the journey of Trojan Aeneas to the West and his descent into the world of the dead, where he was told of his mission to found the Roman race; Lucan, who narrated the history of the Roman civil war which led ultimately to the establishment of the Empire; Ovid, who narrated ancient tales of myth and legend; Horace, the moralist and author of the *Ars Poetica* ('The Art of Poetry'). Of this sublime group Dante is now a member. Dante the character is modestly overcome with awe. Dante the writer will draw on them for much of his material and will even at times set himself to surpass them. He is also making a decisive statement about his own standing and mission. The meaning of the link between the ancient and the Christian world is to be mediated through him. His position amongst them is thus a just acknowledgement. He is no longer a mere rhymester, but a poet in the classical sense, an important distinction.

The company of six move on together, talking of things which were fitting for that place but on which it is now well to be silent. This is a tantalizing exclusion of the reader from the author's confidence. *What* did they talk about? And in what language? Latin, we may suppose, with translation into Greek for the benefit of Homer. These are professional secrets which it is not suitable for us to know.

They come to the foot of a noble castle, encircled seven times by high walls, defended by a beautiful stream, which they cross as though on firm ground. Dante, with the five poets, enters seven gateways. Within is a meadow of bright green grass where souls are gathered, their eyes grave and contemplative, and in their aspect great authority; they speak rarely and in gentle voices. This is Dante's version of the ancient concept of the Elysian Fields. A paradise inhabited by the elect and virtuous after death, it is described by Virgil in the *Aeneid* as a land of joy, of green meadows and happy dwellings of the Blessed.[17] Here were the souls of the Trojan ancestors, of heroes who had fought for the fatherland, of priests and poets and philosophers. In Virgil's vision these ancient souls are joyful and fulfilled. In Dante's, they are serene but grave, longing for unattainable fulfilment. Between the two visions stands the Christian faith.

The group of six draw to one side and ascend a mount from which the *spiriti magni* ('great spirits'), assembled on the enamelled green, are visible and can be pointed out to Dante, one by one. The memory of having seen them fills him now with exultation. The list of names that follows seldom has this effect on a modern reader, but if we bear in mind that these are the souls selected by Dante as those he would above all rejoice to see, we can enter into the reverent wonder in which he holds the ancient world.

He mentions first Electra, the mother by Zeus of Dardanus, the ancestor of the Trojan race. She is in the company of her descendants, including Hector and Aeneas, the latter Dante's predecessor, seen here among his august lineage. It has been shown elsewhere that Dante accepted mythological and historical personages on the same level. That is why he moves on straightaway to mention Julius Caesar, whom he regarded as the first Roman Emperor, 'armed and with hawk-like eyes', for he, as God designed, was a result of the founding of the Trojan race. Next are two women warriors: Camilla, who fought against Aeneas and was killed, and, opposite her (*dall'altra parte*), Penthesilea, Queen of the Amazons, who assisted the Trojans after Hector's death and was killed by Achilles. Next he names Latinus, the King of Latium, who welcomed Aeneas on his arrival and offered him the hand of his daughter Lavinia, who sits near him. In the union between Aeneas and Lavinia, the Trojan and Latian lines were united and the way was opened for the foundation of the city and empire of Rome. But many heroic deeds were needed before that could be accomplished. Brutus, who roused the Roman people against Tarquinius Superbus, whose son had raped Lucrece, is named. Other heroic Roman women listed are: Julia, the daughter of Caesar and wife of Pompey, who laments that she did not live to reconcile her father and her husband; Marcia, whose return in old age to her husband Cato Dante had interpreted allegorically in *Il Convivio* as the return of the soul to God; and Cornelia, the daughter of Scipio Africanus and mother of two renowned Tribunes, Tiberius and Caius Gracchus, celebrated as a model of a noble Roman matron and matriarch. Seated alone and to one side is Saladin, the Sultan of Egypt and Syria, the Muslim hero of the Third Crusade, praised by Christian writers for his magnanimity. Dante had referred to him with admiration in *Il Convivio*.[18]

Dante then lists examples from the world of learning. Supreme above all is Aristotle, *il maestro di color che sanno* ('the master of all those who know'), for whom he had repeatedly expressed reverence in *Il Convivio*. To see him seated among his philosophic kin, all of whom gaze at him in marvel and pay him homage, would indeed have been a matter of exultation. Nearest to him stand Socrates and Plato, the initiators of moral philosophy which Aristotle, Dante believed, had perfected.

Dante's joy in his study of philosophy is radiantly conveyed in *Il Convivio*. Here now are the masters who engaged his mind in the origins of the universe and the purpose of human life: Democritus, who believed the world was created by chance; Diogenes, the Cynic, about whom Dante had read in St Augustine; Anaxagoras, who rejected the materialistic explanation of the universe and held that mind was the cause of all things; Thales, the astronomer and mathematician; Empedocles, who first identified the four elements, earth, water, air and fire, of which all material bodies were held to be compounded; Heraclitus, who believed that fire was the primary form of matter and that all things were in a continual flux of becoming and perishing; Zeno, the founder of the Stoic school of philosophers, for whom the purpose of life was strict rectitude; Euclid, the geometer, Ptolemy the astronomer, Cicero, and Seneca, whom Dante calls 'the moralist', who wrote on ethics, philosophy and natural science. These last are mingled with two poets, Orpheus and Linus. Orpheus is of special importance, since he too had been down into Hell, in search of his wife Eurydice. Dante had read of him in Ovid's *Metamorphoses*, and in *Il Convivio* he had interpreted the power of his music over the natural world as an allegory of the influence of wisdom upon rational beings. He had read of Linus in Virgil's fourth eclogue, in the very context in which, it was believed, the birth of Christ is foretold. 'If only,' Virgil wrote, 'the last days of my life could be prolonged and breath enough remain, then neither Orpheus nor Linus could out-sing me, although Orpheus' mother was the muse Calliope and Linus had Apollo for his sire.'

A group of particular interest are the naturalists and physicians: Dioscorides, the herbalist, 'the good collector of simples', as Dante calls him; Hippocrates, the physician; Avicenna, who wrote on natural science; and Galen, the authority on medicine, whose works were in constant use in the Middle Ages. Mention of them reminds us that Dante was a member of the Guild of Physicians and Apothecaries. Like them, he was a healer and set himself to cure the sickness of the world. The list ends with a mention of Averroës, also a physician, but above all renowned for his commentary upon Aristotle. Thus we return full circle to the greatest sage of all.

All these philosophers, poets, moralists and scientists are Dante's intellectual credentials, his 'bibliography', his authorities for writing about Hell, Purgatory and the Heavens. His sponsors are five great poets of antiquity. In the story, Dante the character is portrayed as frightened, bewildered and in continual need of instruction and encouragement. Dante the writer is quite the reverse: no author can have set out upon a major work with greater confidence. His creative self-assurance is now immense.

One *spirito magno* is missing from Limbo, one whom above all great Romans Dante, it is to be imagined, would long to see: Cato of Utica, the Stoic, 'that glorious Cato', than whom no one could be a more worthy allegorical representation of God.[19] The omission is explained at the beginning of *Purgatorio*. Astonishingly, Dante has taken it upon himself to perform his own individual act of Hell-harrowing. As Christ released the figures of the Old Testament, so he, Dante Alighieri, has removed Cato the Roman from Limbo and made him the guardian of the lower slopes of the mountain. Whether at the Last Judgement he is also to be among the Blessed is left undetermined. The final word on the matter is implied in *Paradiso*.[20]

CHAPTER 14

Francesca da Rimini

In the primitive accounts of St Paul's visit to Hell a devil is described showing the souls a list of their sins, in which they read the place to which they are assigned. In some Doom paintings a devil is even seen ticking off a list with a pen as the souls pass onwards to their fate.[1] Dante takes over this detail and makes it still more grotesque. As the two travellers descend into the Second Circle of the vast funnel of Hell, they find Minos, in classical mythology a king of Crete and a lawgiver, in Virgil's Hades the judge who allots places to the souls according to their misdeeds. Dante transforms him into a snarling monster. The souls stand before him and confess their sins. Whipping his tail a number of times round his body, he indicates the circle to which the souls must fall:

> Cignesi con la coda tante volte
> quantunque gradi vuol che giù sia messa.
> Sempre dinanzi a lui ne stanno molte:
> vanno a vicenda ciascuna al giudizio;
> dicono e odono, e poi son giù volte.

> *He girds him with his tail as many times*
> *as are the circles he condemns them to.*
> *An endless crowd before him tell their crimes,*
> *each in his turn his judgment stands to learn:*
> *they speak, they hear and down are whirled betimes.*[2]

The narrative, crude in itself, is given extraordinary plasticity by Dante's handling of words. No translation can render adequately the slow, downward tumble of the line: *quantunque gradi vuol che giù sia messa*.

The souls speak, they hear the slapping of the tail, they are whirled down into the Abyss. Never before had the Italian vernacular conveyed such visual, aural and tactile effects as Dante achieves in his three-dimensional creation of Hell. It is evident that in writing his verse, he was listening to the effect it would have when read aloud. That is why he varies it in level and tone, making it now colloquial and conversational, now horrific, now delicate and lyrical, all styles inviting the acting talents of the reader, probably himself in the first instance.

Catching sight of a living man, Minos halts in his function to warn him of the dangers he will meet:

> 'Guarda com' entri e di cui ti fide:
>   non t'inganni l'ampiezza dell' entrare!'
>
> *'Mind how thou enterest, be on thy guard:*
>   *be not deceived by the wide open door!'*[3]

As to Charon, so now again to Minos, Virgil chants his formula of power:

> 'vuolsi così colà dove si puote
> ciò che si vuole, e più non dimandare.'
>
> *'thus it is willed where power and will are one,*
> *and so, as it behoves thee, ask no more.'*[4]

The judgement scene is followed by a hurricane and a sound of bellowing as of the sea buffeted by opposing winds. It whirls and drives the spirits, smiting and tormenting them. These are carnal sinners who allowed their desires to overcome their reason. As then, so now, they are without control. Dante the artist, however, is in control. Once again, he changes his style. The souls, like flocks of starlings flying south in winter, are borne onwards by the blast:

> Di qua, di là, di giù, di su li mena;
>   nulla speranza li conforta mai,
>   non che di posa, ma di minor pena.
>
> *Now here, now there, now down, now up again*
>   *it tosses them, uncomforted by hope*
>   *of any rest, nor even of less pain.*[5]

Some are like wailing cranes, strung in long lines across the sky. As St Paul questions the Archangel, so Dante asks: 'Master, who are these souls so scourged by the black air?'

Virgil begins his list of lustful souls with the names of women: Semiramis, the Queen of Assyria, so corrupted by licentious vice that she made lust lawful in her law;[6] Dido, who broke her vow of constancy to the ashes of her husband Sychaeus and killed herself for love; wanton Cleopatra; and Helen, the cause of so many evil years. With the introduction of the names of men, it is not lust that is mentioned: Achilles,[7] Paris and Tristan died as the result of love. Virgil continues, naming countless knights and ladies of old times who were likewise the victims of love. Dante the character is overcome with pity; he is also bewildered. Is love, then, a sin, as punishable as lust? Dante the writer's way of answering the question led him to create what has become perhaps the most famous episode in the *Commedia*.

Some time between 1283 and 1284, Gianciotto Malatesta, the lord of Rimini, murdered his wife Francesca and his younger brother Paolo, who had become lovers. Dante may have set eyes on Paolo when he was Capitano del Popolo in Florence in 1282. At the time of his affair with Francesca he was a married man of about 40, with two sons. Francesca, a daughter of the Polenta family of Ravenna, had married Gianciotto in about the year 1275 and was the mother of a child of nine. The actual facts suggest incestuous adultery and the outrage of a betrayed husband.

Dante chose to make of the scandal a romantic and tender relationship that has for centuries captured the imagination of painters, musicians, poets and dramatists. Seeing a pair of souls floating lightly on the wind, Dante asks to speak with them. Virgil consents and Dante lifts up his voice in compassionate appeal, the wind drops and the souls, like doves returning to their nest, are gently wafted towards him. The remainder of the canto, almost one half, consists of Francesca's account of her tragedy.

With her opening words we are transported out of Hell. Gracious and courtly, she readily agrees to tell Dante what he would know. She and her companion, 'who stained the world with blood', would pray to the king of the universe for him if they were not outcasts. And now her recitation begins. She does not give her name but indicates her place of birth as the city that lies on the outlet of the river Po. The panorama sets the scene for the enchantment that is to follow:

> 'Siede la terra dove nata fui
> sulla marina dove 'l Po discende
> per aver pace co' seguaci sui.'

> *My birthplace was a city on the sea,*
> *close to the strand where Po comes flowing down*
> *with all his streams to seek tranquillity.*'[8]

Each of the next three stanzas begins with the word *Amor*. It was love, quickly kindled in the gentle heart, that overcame her companion with the beauty of her body, which was taken from her in a way that still outrages her. It was love, which absolves no one beloved from loving, that overcame her with her lover's charms, and still holds her fast. It was love that brought them to a single death.

Dante the writer has given Francesca words from the poetry of the *Fedeli d'Amore*, even the concept of the poet Guido Guinizelli of the *cor gentile* ('gentle heart').[9] This is the kind of poetry Dante himself had written and was still writing in 1300. Looking back, in his 40s, he has come to see that such concepts can be distorted and misleading. To Francesca they are shown to be a source of self-deception and excuse.

The character Dante, overwhelmed by compassion, bows his head and remains mute. Asked by Virgil what he is thinking, he replies: 'Alas! What sweet thoughts, what longing led them to their grievous step!' And, knowing who she is, he calls her by her name: 'Francesca, thy torments make me weep in grief and pity:'

> 'Ma dimmi: al tempo de' dolci sospiri,
>   a che e come concedette amore
>   che conosceste i dubbiosi desiri?'

> *'But tell me: at the time of your sweet sighs,*
>   *how and by what did love concede to you*
>   *that hidden longings became certainties?'*[10]

Francesca takes up her story again, in words that must surely be among the most celebrated in literature. She introduces her tragedy as a loss of happiness:

> ... 'Nessun maggior dolore
> che ricordarsi del tempo felice
> nella miseria; e ciò sa il tuo dottore.'

> ... *'The greatest of all woes*
> *is to remember times of happiness*
> *in wretchedness; and this thy teacher knows.'*[11]

Dante now creates a scene as vivid as a miniature, a window opening into a room in the court of Rimini. The enamoured pair sit innocently together, reading an Arthurian romance out loud to each other: the story of Lancelot and Guinevere and of the kiss that led to their adultery.

> 'Noi leggevamo un giorno per diletto
>   di Lancialotto come amor lo strinse:
>   soli eravamo e senz'alcun sospetto.
> Per più fiate li occhi ci sospinse
>   quella lettura, e scolorocci il viso:
>   ma solo un punto fu quel che ci vinse.
> Quando leggemmo il disiato riso
>   esser baciato da cotanto amante,
>   questi, che mai da me non fia diviso,
> la bocca mi baciò tutto tremante.
>   Galeotto fu il libro e chi lo scrisse:
>   quel giorno più non vi leggemmo avante.'

> *'One day we read together for delight*
>   *of Lancelot and how love held him fast.*
>   *We were alone, without misgiving quite.*

Many a time our eyes were locked aghast
*   as we read on, our faces ashy pale,*
*   but one point only conquered us at last:*
when we had reached the moment in the tale
*   where smiling lips are kissed by such a woer,*
*   he then, who from my side will never fail,*
my mouth too kissed, trembling the while all o'er.
*   The book to us a Galleot was and he*
*   who authored it; that day we read no more.'*[12]

Francesca's lover, who is not named, speaks no word, but weeps throughout. Dante is so overcome that he faints and drops as a dead body falls:

e caddi come corpo morto cade.[13]

This is his second swoon within the space of two cantos.

One thing Francesca says is mysterious. Immediately after the line 'love brought us to a single death', she bursts out into a vindictive statement:

'Caina attende chi vita ci spense.'

'Caina waits for him who quenched our lives.'[14]

The words are not intelligible at this point, nor are they intended to be. It is not until we reach the Ninth Circle of Hell that we learn that Caina, named after Cain, is an area of damnation for traitors who murdered their kindred. It is the most prolonged cliff-hanger in the work. It is also troubling. First, how does Francesca know of such a place? Secondly, her husband was not a traitor, but a vengeful spouse, himself betrayed. Dante the writer cannot intend this fate for his soul.[15] At worst he belongs to the category of murderers among the violent in the Seventh Circle. Dante gives these words to Francesca for a reason: they are a key to her character, as is her use of poetry to justify her adultery and of Arthurian romance to blame for its influence.

The difference between Hell and Purgatory is repentance. The damned are those whose will was irretrievably fixed or who died before they could repent. They are in logic cut off for ever from God's mercy because they did not ask for it. But it is not God who decides who the damned souls are, nor Minos who allots the place. It is the author Dante. Such moral certainty in respect of individuals is difficult to accept. Creative art, however, is judgemental. Dante the artist chose to present Paolo and Francesca as unrepentant victims of murder. Dante Alighieri the man from Florence had no way of knowing whether or not they had time to repent before they died.

The appealing story, as created by Dante, has been further overlaid by romantic accretions. These began with Boccaccio. He was not only Dante's first biographer; he was also the first public lecturer on the *Commedia*.[16] His lectures, known as *Esposizioni*, were delivered in Florence between 1373 and 1374. They were intended to be a detailed commentary, literal and allegorical, on the entire work, canto by canto, but in January 1374, after the 59th lecture, Boccaccio fell ill and a year later he died.

In his commentary on the fifth canto we catch an unmistakable glimpse of the author of the *Decameron*, the consummate teller of tales. When he comes to Francesca's words, *Siede la terra dove nata fui*, he pushes Dante's text aside and launches into *his* version of the story, a version that has been accepted ever since, finding its way into commentaries and notes to the *Commedia*, as though it were authentic.

'Before I go any further,' Boccaccio begins, 'in order that you may understand what Francesca says, I will tell you who she was and how she came to die':

> E' adunque da sapere che costei fu figliuola di messer Guido vecchio da Polenta, signor di Ravenna ...

> *It must be known then that she was the daughter of Guido da Polenta the elder, lord of Ravenna ...*

In an attempt to make peace between Ravenna and Rimini, it was decided that she should be married to Gianciotto Malatesta, the son and heir of the lord of Rimini. But, Boccaccio goes on, a friend said to her father, 'Mind what you are doing. Your daughter has a will of her own. If she sees Gianciotto before the marriage she will not take him as her husband.' For though Gianciotto would one day become the lord of Rimini,[17] he was lame and ugly. So it was arranged that his brother Paolo should come to Ravenna to marry Francesca by proxy. Now Paolo was a handsome, attractive and charming man:

> Era Paolo bello e piacevole uomo e costumato molto.

As he approached the court of Ravenna, a lady-in-waiting pointed him out to Francesca through a loophole and said:

> 'Madonna, quegli è colui che dee esser vostro marito.'

> *'My lady, there is the man who is to be your husband.'*

The lady-in-waiting thought that it was so and Francesca at once fell in love with him and joyfully became his wife (as she believed) and went with him to Rimini. Not till the morning after the wedding night did she realize that she had been deceived. She was outraged and remained as much in love with Paolo as before.

In order to add verisimilitude to his own account, Boccaccio says Dante's story must be a fiction, for how could he know that the lovers had sat reading an Arthurian romance? According to Boccaccio, Paolo and Francesca became lovers and continued in adultery for some time, taking advantage of Gianciotto's absences from court. But one day a servant told him what was happening and advised him to pretend to go away and return unexpectedly. Gianciotto, deeply incensed, did so and saw Paolo enter his wife's room. He shouted her name and hurled himself against the locked portal. Paolo decided to escape through a trap-door in the floor which led to a room beneath. He leapt down, telling Francesca to open the door, but a fold of his jerkin caught on the bolt attached to the trap and he hung there, his head protruding above the floor. Francesca, not noticing this, opened the door to her husband, who strode in, sword in hand. Francesca flung herself between her lover and her husband and received the thrust with Gianciotto's full weight behind it. Gianciotto drew his sword from her breast and plunged it into Paolo, killing him. The lovers were buried the next morning, amid many tears, in a single tomb.

Such was the tale Boccaccio told one day in November 1374, in the church of Santo Stefano di Badia in Florence. This is the Boccaccio who, though elderly, has lost none of his skills. He still knows how to seize the dramatic moments and the vivid details and how to choose the words, style and pace best suited to the effect he wants to make. Here is an instance of a public reading of the *Commedia*, whether each canto as a whole, preceding the commentary, or a few verses at a time, we do not know, but it is by such means that the work became widely known before the age of printing.

Boccaccio's story made an impression five and a half centuries later, on Gabriele D'Annunzio. When he wrote his beautiful but somewhat over-blown poetic drama, *Francesca da Rimini*, he followed Boccaccio's (not Dante's) version, even to the extent of using Boccaccio's very words. Thus it was that the story came once more to life with Eleonora Duse acting out the climax, just as Boccaccio had told it, on a stage in Rome more than half a millennium later. The same story inspired the composer Riccardo Zandonai, whose opera *Francesca da Rimini*, based on D'Annunzio's play, was performed at Covent Garden in 1914.

When Francesca's nephew, Guido Novello da Polenta, became lord of Ravenna, he offered the homeless Dante a house of his own, which he accepted. It was to be his final refuge. Guido, a man of letters, had poetic leanings and took lessons from Dante in the writing of verse. In one of his exercises he quotes words which Dante had given to his wayward aunt:

... che mai da me non fia diviso

... who from me never will be parted,

an indication that he took no umbrage at Dante's presentation of her.[18]

CHAPTER 15

Dante in Danger

The contrast between the tender and delicate style of Francesca's narration and the repulsive description of the gluttons in the following canto shows Dante the craftsman at his most deliberate and self-aware. It is said repeatedly, and justly, that Italian is a beautiful language. Dante loved and cultivated its musical qualities; he also exploited its capacity to express the ugly and the crude.

The sinners in the Third Circle are depicted as wallowing in stinking mire beneath a pitiless deluge of rain, hail and snow. Over them stands the monster Cerberus, barking hound-like from his three gullets, his beard black and greasy, his belly swollen, his hands clawed, with which he tears, skins and dismembers the souls:

> Con tre gole caninamente latra ...
> graffia li spiriti, scuoia ed isquatra.[1]

These words are anything but beautiful, nor are they musical: they are harsh and coarse, but they are powerfully expressive. Nothing in English can quite render the effect of the repetition of broad a's and the phrase *caninamente latra*, the adverb ('hound-sounding') invented to increase the onomatopoeia of the verb *latra* ('barks').

The souls have no bodies; the description of their sufferings is a figurative image of the sin itself and of their spiritual and mental anguish. Dante the character, however, *is* in the body and he experiences with his living senses the claustrophobic enclosure of Hell; he sees despite the darkness, he hears, he touches and he smells. In a precisely structured setting Dante the writer places and moves his characters, rounded when it suits his purpose as though, like himself, they were substantial. This combination of bodiless souls and a tangible man is so convincing that we accept it and seldom stop to ask, as we read further on, how, for instance, Virgil can carry Dante in his arms, or how Dante can kick the head of a traitor protruding from the ice and tear the hair from his scalp. There are conventions for stories of this kind and on certain points, as Dante puts it, *è bello tacere* ('it is good manners to be silent'). Later in the work, an explanation of the corporeal semblance of souls is provided.[2]

Virgil quells Cerberus in the traditional manner, spreading out his hands and flinging something into his three jaws, in this instance fistfuls of miry ground, and the two travellers walk over the souls, which seem corporeal but are *vanità* ('nothingness'). One, seeing them pass, sits up and calls to Dante, asking if he knows him, but he is so altered that he has to identify himself. He is a Florentine, nicknamed Ciacco ('Hog'). He refers spitefully to the city, so full of envy, he declares, that it is like a sack running over. Dante now uses another convention: the dead, it was believed, had knowledge of the future.[3] It is therefore within the tradition that Dante should ask him what will become of Florence and why the city is so divided.

The *Commedia* is an allegory of damnation, repentance and beatitude and as such it has general application to Christian belief and human behaviour, as well as to Dante's own salvation; or one might call it a vast sermon with visual aids and sound effects. But it is also a diatribe against Florence and other cities, against the Papacy, against the monarchy of France and against the neglectful Emperors who have allowed Italy to degenerate into discord. In these interpolations, particularly those set within the awesome structure of Hell, it is Dante the publicist who writes. The more convincing he can make the literal story, the more compelling will be the message he has determined to use it to convey. The views he had already set forth and intended to develop further in *Il Convivio* in discursive, philosophic terms he now gives to his various created characters, reporting them with all the authority of someone fulfilling a divinely ordained mission. Here and there, briefly, and on one occasion at great length,[4] he steps outside his poem and speaks directly as himself.

In the conversation with Ciacco, the theme of Florence is introduced for the first time. Ciacco foretells that the two conflicting parties (the White and Black Guelfs) will come to bloodshed (as they did on May Day of the year 1300) and that the Whites will at first prevail and drive the others out. But within three years, the other party will return, aided by 'one who now prevaricates'. This oblique reference is one of many to Pope Boniface VIII, who within the timeframe of the story had not yet shown his hand in Florentine politics.

Ciacco alludes mysteriously to 'two righteous men whom no one heeds'. They have not been identified. Dante may simply have meant 'scarce one or two', or he may have meant himself and one other. It is possible that Giano della Bella, who reformed the laws of Florence, is intended. Dante asks where he will find other Florentines, whom he names. Are they in Hell or Heaven? Ciacco warns him that he will find them among the blackest souls in Hell. Thus the Florentine theme begins, on a small scale, with local politics and enquiries concerning a few individuals. As the work progresses it takes on proportions that link it with world history and ultimately with the universe.[5]

One of the features of the legendary material that Dante used was the resistance of the powers of the Underworld to an intruder from the world of the living. Charon and Minos have resisted Dante and now so does Plutus, in classical mythology the god of wealth, and here, like Minos, transformed into a monster, in charge of the souls of the avaricious in the Fourth Circle. His utterance is frightening gibberish:

'Papè Satàn, papè Satàn, aleppe!'

'Father Satan, Father Satan, help!'[6]

The word *aleppe* has never been convincingly decoded but the utterance appears to be a call to Father Satan for help against the intrusion of a living man. Virgil, *che tutto seppe* ('who knew all things'), reassures Dante, calling Plutus *maladetto lupo* ('accursed wolf'), the symbol of avarice, and taunting the monster with the memory of the defeat of the rebellious angels by the Archangel Michael, as though to say, 'It's no use expecting Satan to help you: remember how Michael dealt with him.' This so deflates Plutus that he collapses like the sails on a broken mast. As in the description of the gluttons, so here the language is harsh, with rhymes ending in *-occia* to suggest Plutus' spluttering speech, and rhymes in *-acca* to suggest the clatter of his collapse. The two opposite groups of the avaricious (the spendthrifts and the hoarders), pushing heavy boulders before them and clashing in conflicting bands, are given hurtling rhymes in double consonants: *viddi, Cariddi, riddi, intoppa, troppa, poppa.* Dante the technician, having riveted his audience's attention by the skilful use of sound, then moves to the visual aid of a picture of degraded souls, all so alike that they cannot be identified, except that by their tonsures the majority are seen to have been clerics. This is Dante's first attack in the *Commedia* upon the avarice of the Church.

Earlier tales of Underworld journeys included immersion of souls at different levels in foul rivers or marshes or streams of blood, incarceration in burning tombs, imprisonment in ice, the crossing of dangerous bridges, the tormenting of souls by devils with pitchforks, mutilation with swords and horrors involving snakes and serpents. All such elements, some of which are found also in the *Aeneid*, are used by Dante with increasing realism as *Inferno* progresses. The tension of danger also increases.

The Circle of the Wrathful is a marsh, across which Dante and Virgil are ferried by the boatman Phlegyas,[7] Dante's substantial body weighing down the boat. For the first time he is in physical danger. One of the wrathful rises up and confronts him. Dante knows him and curses him as rightly punished, whereupon the spirit reaches out to the boat with both his hands. Virgil pushes him off, saying: 'Away there, with the other dogs!' He then embraces Dante and kisses his cheek, rejoicing in his indignation, uttering the startling words: 'Blessed is the womb that conceived thee!'[8] Dante answers: 'Master, I'd dearly love to see him dipped in this broth before we go.' Virgil says that his wish will be gratified, and rightly. The soul is set upon by the muddied mob, who shout: 'Get Filippo Argenti!'

Filippo Argenti of Florence, as was said, was a man of violent temper, arrogant and so ostentatious that he shod his horse with silver. His dates are not known but he had evidently died by Easter Week of the year 1300. The Cavicciuli branch of the Adimari family, to which he was related, were Black Guelfs and are said to have been bitterly opposed to Dante's recall from exile. Commentators have done their best to elevate the outburst of vengeful wrath on the part of the character Dante, identifying it as righteous anger, repudiating sin, contrasted with the self-centred fury of the sinners in the mire. The fact cannot be evaded, however, that Dante the writer has shown his fictional self as exhibiting monstrous inhumanity. Up to now he has shown compassion: he has wept and swooned on hearing the tale of Francesca; he has wept at the condition of his Florentine friend Ciacco; unable to recognize any of the avaricious, he has conveyed scorn and abhorrence for all of them, that is to say, for the sin of avarice in general. But here he exhibits vindictive rage against an individual sinner, rejoicing in his sufferings, and is embraced and congratulated by Virgil for doing so, in words, moreover, that were used of Christ. Commenting on the episode in his own *persona*, Dante the writer says, *in the present tense*, that he still offers praise and thanks to God for what he saw:

> Dopo ciò poco vid'io quello strazio
> far di costui alle fangose genti,
> *che Dio ancor ne lodo e ne ringrazio.*

> *Soon after that I saw the muddy crew*
> *so fiercely set on him that even now*
> my praise and thanks to God I still renew.[9]

The quarrel between Dante and Argenti must have taken place before May Day 1300, when the White and Black Guelfs came to bloodshed, as Ciacco foretold that they would. It is therefore more likely to have been a personal than a political matter. There is more here than righteous indignation at the sin of wrath. This is Dante Alighieri, man alive, who in *Il Convivio* cursed those who denied belief in immortality and said that the only thing to do with someone who could not argue rationally was to take a knife to him.

The canto began with a twinkling of lights from a watchtower at the rim of the marsh. In answer, in the distance, a beacon flickered, and at this signal Phlegyas had come skimming across in his boat. When they reach the other side he sets the travellers down at the entrance to a walled city. Its turrets are red as fire and its walls are like iron. Virgil tells Dante that this is lower Hell, the City of Dis.[10] At the gates Dante sees countless devils, 'those who rained down from Heaven', that is, the rebellious angels. Their opposition to his approach exceeds all resistance so far. Virgil signals that he wishes to speak with them apart and they say, 'Come alone and let him who has dared to enter this kingdom go back, if he can find the way.' Dante's courage fails him and he begs Virgil to return with him quickly:

'ritroviam l'orme nostre insieme ratto'.

'let us retrace our steps together, quick'.[11]

Virgil tells him not to be afraid; no one can prevent their journey for it has been sanctioned by One above. He leaves Dante alone, promising not to desert him. Dante waits in fear and doubt. He cannot hear what Virgil says but sees the devils rush inside, shutting the gates in his face. Virgil returns to Dante with slow steps, gazing at the ground and saying to himself between sighs: 'Who are these that forbid my entrance into the abode of pain?' Then to Dante he says: 'Do not be dismayed. I will prevail. They have shown insolence before. And already one is descending without escort through the circles who will open the city to us.'

Dante has turned pale and Virgil alarms him further by his broken, mystifying phrases, conveying doubt, which he tries to conceal. Dante asks, indirectly, with subtle tact, whether anyone has ever descended from Limbo before. Virgil replies that it seldom happens but that he himself was conjured once by Erichtho, who sent him to the lowest depths of Hell to draw forth a spirit for her purposes. He knows the way: Dante need not fear.

Erichtho was a witch about whom Dante had read in Lucan's *Pharsalia*, where it is related that Pompey's son employed her to conjure up the soul of one of his dead soldiers to foretell the outcome of the war.[12] Similarly, in the *Aeneid*, the Sibyl reassures Aeneas that she has been guided by Hecate through all the penalties of Hades.[13] This was probably in Dante's mind, for it occurs at a point in the story that resembles the arrival at the City of Dis. Aeneas, too, has come to a large castle, with pillars of solid adamant, with an iron tower, from which groans are heard and the sound of a lash. Aeneas, rooted to the spot in terror, asks, 'What crimes are punished here? Why do they cry so loud?'

Three Furies now rise up on the battlements, blood-stained, girt with green hydras, with asps and adders writhing round their brows. Virgil points them out: on the right is Alecto, on the left Megaera and in the middle is Tisiphone. They beat their breasts and tear themselves with their nails, shrieking so loudly that Dante clings to Virgil in terror. 'Fetch Medusa!' they cry. 'We'll turn him to stone! Why did we not finish off Theseus when he attacked?'[14] At this threat Virgil turns Dante round and places his hands over his eyes and his own over them. If Dante looks on Medusa it will be all up with him. If the Furies represent remorse, Medusa is despair. Virgil protects him with all that he represents of wisdom, art and civilization.

At this point Dante speaks directly to his audience:

O voi ch'avete li 'ntelletti sani,
    mirate la dottrina che s'asconde
    sotto 'l velame de li versi strani.

O ye whose intellects are sane and sound
    note well the doctrine that beneath the veil
    of the mysterious verses can be found.[15]

There is only one other occasion in the *Commedia* where Dante draws his listeners' attention to an allegorical meaning hidden beneath the literal.[16] Both precede the arrival of angelic aid. Immediately following these lines a startling event occurs, the most striking in an already eventful canto.

Over the waves of the turbid marsh comes a crashing sound that sets both shores shaking, like the noise of a violent wind that assails a forest, breaking branches, flinging them down or carrying them away, scattering wild beasts and shepherds. Virgil releases Dante's eyes and tells him to peer over the ancient scum to where the fumes are most dense. As frogs before a snake scuttle to the bottom of a pond, so Dante sees countless souls hide from a figure who passes the marsh dry-footed, clearing the mist before his face with his left hand. Dante at once perceives that he is one sent from Heaven. He turns to Virgil who signs to him to keep silence and to bow down in reverence. With an air of superb scorn the messenger comes to the gates and with a little wand opens them. His voice is heard:

'O cacciati del ciel, gente dispetta',
    cominciò elli in su l'orribil soglia,
    'ond' esta oltracotanza in voi s'alletta?
Perchè recalcitrate a quella voglia
    a cui non può il fin mai esser mozzo,
    e che più volte v'ha cresciuta doglia?
Che giova nelle fata dar di cozzo?
    Cerbero vostro, se ben vi ricorda,
    ne porta ancor pelato il mento e 'l gozzo.'

> *'O outcasts from on high, despisèd crew',*
>   *thus he began upon that horrid sill,*
>   *'whence comes the insolence which dwells in you?*
> *Why do you kick against the sacred will*
>   *whose purpose never can be overborne,*
>   *and which has many times increased your ill?*
> *What does it profit you the fates to spurn?*
>   *Your Cerberus, if you recall aright,*
>   *still has his chin and gullet scraped and torn.'*[17]

The messenger then returns across the foul path, saying no word to Dante and Virgil, with the bearing of one who has other cares beyond the present.

No explanation of his identity is given, though attempts to name him have been made. Since in some versions of the tale of St Paul's visit to the Underworld he is accompanied by the Archangel Michael, the earliest audience and readers of *Inferno* would expect him to put in an appearance, or at least would feel no surprise if he did. He has moreover been mentioned at the beginning of Canto VII, where Virgil taunts Plutus by reminding him of the defeat of the rebellious angels by the Archangel. It is significant that the first lecturer on the *Commedia*, namely Boccaccio, did so identify him.

Whatever his identity, the allegorical meaning of the event, to which Dante has drawn attention, must be that Virgil, for all his wisdom and endowment of magical powers, is unable to overcome the worst of evil. For that, help from on high is needed and is provided.

CHAPTER 16

Dante the Taxonomist

In one version of the story of St Paul's journey into Hell, the Archangel Michael tells him to pause at one moment in order to accustom himself to the stench that rises from the abyss. St Paul does so, stuffing a fold of his mantle against his nostrils. Dante adopts this detail to provide an opportunity for Virgil to describe to Dante the layout of Hell. The moment is opportune. So many things have happened, monsters have been confronted, circles of Hell have been traversed, souls have been encountered. Dante senses that the audience now needs recapitulation and orientation.

After the dialogue with Farinata and Cavalcanti in the Circle of the Heretics,[1] Dante and Virgil take refuge behind the vault of a tomb containing the soul of Anastasius, a fifth-century Pope, said to have denied the divine nature of Christ. The tomb is perched on the edge of the abyss, from which the stench of sin rises, its position a symbol of the outrage on truth that Dante considered the heresy of a Pope to be. While the two poets rest, Virgil sets out with schematic precision the hierarchy and categories of sin.

It is not known whether Dante had intended to discuss the categories of sin in *Il Convivio*, but it is not unlikely. If so, this is a clear example of transference of material he had already prepared, either in his mind or more probably in notes, from the one work to the other. The prosaic nature of the verse strengthens this possibility.

His two authorities on the subject are Aristotle and Cicero. In Aristotle he had found wrongdoing divided into three categories: weakness of will, brutishness and malice. Cicero recognized only two: violence and fraud. Dante combines the two systems, adding to that of Cicero the category of 'Incontinence' (weakness of will), distinguished by Aristotle from sins that involve the deliberate use of the will.

Virgil begins his discourse with the three circles they will find below them, one of violence and two of fraud. The last two are distinguished according to the relationship between perpetrator and victim, the breaking of a bond of particular trust being defined as treachery. This involves a misuse of the intellect, a faculty with which only man is endowed, and is consequently the most offensive to God. Traitors therefore are in the lowest circle of all, the ninth.

The seventh, which they are about to enter, is divided into three zones, according to the victim against whom violence is used: one's neighbour, one's self, and God. Acts of violence against one's neighbour are listed as though by a teacher holding up a diagram to a class of pupils: murder, bodily harm, extortion, robbery, plunder, arson. In enumerating these categories, Dante could scarcely have avoided thinking of the wrongs he himself had suffered at the hands of the pillaging Black Guelfs in Florence who had destroyed and set fire to his home. Next comes the zone of those who do violence to themselves and to their own belongings: suicides, gamblers and wasters who destroy their own property, considered in Dante's age as an extension of the self. Violence against God is divided into blasphemy, outrage upon nature and upon man's industry. In this zone Dante groups together in one category, though distinguishing them, God-deniers, sodomites and usurers. The only blasphemer named is Capaneus, one of the seven kings who took part in the siege of Thebes and who while scaling the city wall boasted that not even Jove could stop him and who in his damnation still defies God. The inclusion of usury and sodomy together with blasphemy as violence against God requires some explanation for modern readers, as it evidently did for Dante's contemporaries, since he contrives for Virgil to justify it.

He does so by referring Dante to Aristotle's *Ethics*, where Nature is defined as the art of God, and man's industry as the offspring of Nature. Any abuse of man's material resources and of industry is consequently an offence against God. Aristotle had defined the use of money to generate more money as a barren activity, an image that is reflected in Dante's placing of usurers on barren sand. The Church condemned the lending of money for interest and so did Dante, although the wealth of Florence was enhanced by the development of banking, which made possible the organization of manufacture and industry. Dante's attitude to usury would seem to be an aspect of his condemnation of avarice as the greatest obstacle to man's social well being. It may be that his objection, as well as that of the Church, was levelled at exorbitant exactions by money lenders who held a monopoly and that he might have accepted what in modern terms is called a free market in financial services, subject to legal regulation. There were in Roman law rules on rates of interest, which Dante is likely to have held in respect. He can perhaps be compared to modern objectors to capitalism and in recent times to globalization. In any event he must have been aware of hardship suffered by victims of usury. During his exile he was himself obliged to borrow money. A striking example of atonement for the sin of usury, with which Dante was familiar, was the donation by Enrico Scrovegni of the chapel of the Madonna dell'Arena in Padua, which Dante's friend Giotto was engaged to decorate with his frescoes. Enrico is said to have been the son of Rinaldo degli Scrovegni who is placed among the usurers in Hell.[2] If this is so, the offering by Enrico, who is portrayed by Giotto holding up a model of the chapel, might be seen as a mediaeval example of the benefactions of millionaires of modern times.

The list of sins punished in the Eighth Circle, involving fraud practised against those with whom no special bond of trust exists, is rattled off in prosaic verse: hypocrisy, flattery, sorcery, impersonation, theft, simony, sexual exploitation, corruption, ending with the phrase *e simile lordura* ('and such-like filth'), as though the subject scarcely warranted the trouble of versifying further. The sins of the Ninth Circle, defined in general as treachery, are later found to be divided into four groups: treachery against kindred, treachery against political party or cause, treachery against guests and treachery against benefactors.

Dante asks Virgil about the circles they have already traversed. Why are those sins punished outside the City of Dis, which they have now entered? Virgil replies, somewhat testily:

> ... 'Perchè tanto delira',
> disse, 'lo 'ngegno tuo da quel che sole?
> O ver la mente dove altrove mira?'

> ... *'Why is thy mind,' he said,*
> *'so far away, unlike its usual self,*
> *what are thy wits about, where have they fled?'*[3]

He reminds Dante of the teaching of Aristotle, according to which the sins of weakness of will are less offensive than those incurring brutishness and malice. For this reason they are less severely punished.

During the time he spent at Bologna in the company of his jurist friend Cino da Pistoia, Dante is likely to have picked up some notions of civil law and of local tariffs of penalties, but canon law probably had more influence upon his classification of sins. Book V of the Gregorian Decretals is devoted to criminal law, with sections on forgery, heresy, homicide, arson, usury, adultery, theft, blasphemy and sorcery, among other offences. The writings of mediaeval canon lawyers are more philosophically and theologically nuanced than those of their civil law contemporaries.

Above all, his arrangement of sins, like much else in the *Commedia*, is influenced by numerology. The master concept of the entire structure is unity, represented by the figure one, a symbol of the union of the soul with its Maker, of time with eternity. To the seven ethical categories of wrong-doing in Inferno, he adds two: Limbo and Heresy (non-belief and wrong belief), making nine circles in all, to which is added the Vestibule of the Futile, bringing the main divisions to ten, which by mystic addition[4] is reducible to the figure one. This scheme is followed also in the structure of Mount Purgatory, with its two terraces and seven cornices, surmounted by the Garden of Eden. Likewise in Paradise there are nine heavens, to which is added the Empyrean. As has been shown, the figure three, the symbol of the Trinity or Three-in-One, is prevalent throughout. The rhyme scheme, *terza rima*, means that every canto is composed of a number of lines divisible by three, plus a concluding one, yet another return to unity. The 100 cantos that make up the entire work also represent the square of ten, regarded as the number of perfection.

Dante's numerical control of his material is particularly significant where Beatrice is involved. She is mentioned by name 63 times in the *Commedia*, a figure which, again by mystic addition, is reducible to nine. Her name is used as a rhyme word on nine occasions. She appears to Dante in the 30th canto of *Purgatorio*, which is the 64th canto of the whole *Commedia*, another figure reducible to ten, itself reducible to the figure of unity. It is preceded by 63 cantos (reducible to nine) and followed by 36 (also reducible to nine). The line in which she announces her identity, *Guardaci ben, ben sem, ben sem Beatrice* ('Look well, we are, we are Beatrice') is line 73 of the canto, while her first appearance occurs in lines 31–33. Such recurrent play of significantly Beatrician numbers could hardly be coincidence and must have been laid out structurally in advance.[5]

The number ten had particular significance. It can also be represented by a triangle which the Pythagoreans called the *tetrakis*. They regarded it as so holy that they swore oaths by it. Made up of 1 + 2 + 3 + 4, or 9 + 1, its components represented unity (1), duality (2), the harmonizing force that resolved duality (3) and completeness (4), as in the four elements of creation: earth, air, fire and water, and the four chief fluids (cardinal humours) of the body: blood, phlegm, choler and melancholy or black choler. Likewise the figure seven, of which the significant components are 3 + 4, was seen as a key to an understanding of the cosmos, as in the number of planets believed to circle the earth. From all such associations of numbers, Dante drew power for his creation and relied on it for the magical effect it would have on his contemporaries, whether consciously or unconsciously, as they read the *Commedia* or heard it read aloud. He himself also drew from it confidence in his structure as an image of truth.

From Pythagoras onwards, the Greeks had been fascinated by the beauty of number patterns and proportion. In their architecture they made use of what was known as the Divine Proportion, a discovery of the ratio between the length and breadth of a rectangle. The formula was forgotten for hundreds of years but works of art which were constructed according to it continued to prove the most pleasing to the eye. Music, too, was constructed in comparable patterns and continued to be so, whether the composer was aware of the formula or not. As Leibniz later said, 'Music is a secret arithmetical exercise and the person who indulges in it does not realize that he is manipulating numbers.'

The number seven, which is also a key feature in created works, is mathematically related to the spiral, a symbol of the journey of the soul. Spirals also occur in nature, in the arrangement of seeds, florets, types of fir cones and the shapes of certain shells, such as the nautilus and the ammonite, as well as other molluscs which are formed by the accretion of cells along the tangent to the curve of their growth.[6] Consequently the spiralling journeys of Dante through Hell, Purgatory and Paradise, whether consciously understood by him in this light or not, provide an imaginative experience that satisfies the very nature of our physical and spiritual being. It must have been an equally satisfying experience for Dante the maker to achieve by such methods of control the symmetry and harmony to which he aspired.

The *Commedia* was planned with minute precision but it is also a work that grew, like a living organism. Cantos of the same number echo and balance each other in content and significance between one *cantica* and another, but the symmetry is not rigid. There is no mid-point in 100, and so the perspective shifts, like an optical illusion. It was written over many years, probably between 1306 and 1321, and the events of the world succeeding in that period became part of it as it progressed. Dante, too, altered as he grew older. The author of *Inferno* is not the same person as the one who sailed over *migliori acque* ('better waters') to create *Purgatorio* or, shedding error after error in *Paradiso*, was at last enabled to construct a vision of God. As a craftsman he had planned his journey. As a poet he made discoveries as he went. This rescued the poem from static regularity and gave it the dynamism of experience.

CHAPTER 17

Creation of Character

Francesca da Rimini is the first and for some readers the most memorable of all Dante's characters in the *Commedia*. The second, Farinata degli Uberti, has already been mentioned in relation to the death of Guido Cavalcanti.[1] His magnificent unconcern for his torment in Hell, set against his continuing preoccupation with the fate of his fellow exiles in the first life, is contrasted with the lesser stature of his companion in heresy, Cavalcanti, the querulous father of Dante's friend Guido. Dante's talent in creating such portraits has held the fascinated attention of readers for centuries. It is not difficult to trace his description of Hell itself to earlier tales of the kind, but the selection of individual detail, the variations in speech and tone of voice, the ability to fix a mannerism and bring a character to life are tokens of a talent, largely histrionic, that goes beyond derivation. One after another of these master portraits, Francesca, Farinata, Pier delle Vigne, Brunetto Latini, Ulysses and Ugolino, are so vividly realized that an actor would require no further directions in order to represent them on the stage. Such is their animation that Dante must have heard them speaking as he wrote. When he read his cantos aloud he no doubt acted their voices. That he was a mimic is shown in the chapter on *De Vulgari Eloquentia*.

The setting of each of these figures reinforces the character drawing. Farinata, for instance, is seen against an austere background of a vast burial ground, like those at Arles and Pola,[2] with the difference that the tombs inside the wall of the City of Dis are heated by flames, all the lids stand open and lamentations issue from within. This is the Hell that Farinata, rising to his full height, appears to hold in scorn. Questioning Dante about his ancestors with aristocratic disdain, he raises his eyebrows a little and says, 'They were fierce enemies of mine, and of my forebears and of my party, and so twice I scattered them.' This is a portrait of a heroic Florentine, devoted to the city he saved from destruction when his victorious side proposed to raze it to the ground. It also tells us that Dante the person observed facial expression. That raising of the eyebrows 'a little' is a skilful touch. It has nothing to do with allegory, or with any of the major concerns of the work: it is pictorial art for its own sake. Farinata's response to the sound of a Tuscan voice, which brought him up from his tomb, provides another trait of character which is likewise memorable and shows Dante's imagination at its most vividly creative; so too is Farinata's regret that he may have caused too much anguish to the city he so loved. It is moments like this that make the *Commedia* much more than a mediaeval text of historical interest and Dante much more than a man of the Middle Ages. Here the creator's finger reaches out to make contact with us across the centuries.

Another such occasion occurs in the Seventh Circle. The setting is a lifeless wood, where souls who have committed suicide are transformed into trees and shrubs:

> Non fronda verde, ma di color fosco;
> non rami schietti, ma nodosi e 'nvolti;
> non pomi v' eran, ma stecchi con tosco.

> *No verdant foliage, but of dusky hue;*
> *no branches smooth and round, but warped and gnarled;*
> *no fruit was there, but thorns with poison grew.*[3]

Perched among the unnatural vegetation are Harpies, uttering laments. The sound of voices in distress makes Dante stand in wonder. Virgil does not explain but allows him to discover for himself what he is hearing. There follows one of the most visible and tangible similes of the work. Like the slight lift of Farinata's eyebrows, it brings us close to Dante as a person who communicates a vivid experience. Virgil instructs him to break off a twig from one of the plants:

> Allor porsi la mano un poco avante.
> e colsi un ramicel da un gran pruno;
> e 'l tronco suo gridò: 'Perchè mi schiante?'

> *My hand I then put forward, cautiously,*
> *and picked a little twig from a large thorn;*
> *and its trunk roared: 'Why this brutality?'*[4]

These lines are beautifully crafted for reading aloud: the timid hand reaching out to pick a little twig from a large thorn, the sonorous response of the trunk, with its contrasting vowel sounds. Seeping with dark blood, the plant continues: 'Hast thou no pity? We were once men and now are turned to trees. More merciful thy hand should be, had we been souls of serpents.'

The image of liquid oozing from the branch, together with the hiss of words, is compared by Dante the writer to a simple, everyday phenomenon. If a green branch is set alight, sap will issue from one end while from the other a squeal of air comes forth. Anyone who has burned green wood in a bonfire knows exactly what he means: the effect is startling. No wonder Dante the character drops the twig and stands in fear.

Virgil placates the injured soul, saying that if Dante had been able to believe what he had read in Virgil's own poem,[5] no such offence would have been necessary. In recompense he invites the soul to say who he was, so that the person who has injured him may make amends by reviving his fame in the world above.

The soul is that of Pier delle Vigne. Born in Capua about the year 1190, he was for many years Chancellor in the service of Emperor Frederick II of Sicily and became his most trusted adviser. He was in England between 1234 and 1235, negotiating the marriage between the Emperor and Isabella, a sister of Henry III. Two years later he fell from favour, being accused of conspiracy against Frederick. He was arrested, imprisoned and his eyes were put out. In 1249, in a prison at Pisa, he killed himself by dashing his brains out against a wall. Dante believed that he was the victim of slander. He chose him as an example of the sin of suicide in order to allow him to speak in his defence.

Pier was also a poet, of the so-called 'Sicilian School', from which the poetry of the *Fedeli d'Amore* developed, and was an early author of sonnets. Dante appropriately gives him words which might have come from one of his own elaborate poems:

'Sì con dolce dir m'adeschi,
    ch'i' non posso tacere; e voi non gravi
    perch'io un poco a ragionar m'inveschi.
Io son colui che tenni ambo le chiavi
    del cor di Federigo, e che le volsi,
    serrando e diserrando, sì soavi,
che dal secreto suo quasi ogn'uom tolsi:
    fede portai al glorioso offizio,
    tanto ch' i' i' ne perde' li sonni e' polsi.
La meretrice che mai dall'ospizio
    di Cesare non torse li occhi putti,
    morte comune, delle corti vizio,
infiammò contra me li animi tutti;
    e li 'nfiammati infiammar sì Augusto,
    che lieti onor tornaro in tristi lutti.
L'animo mio, per disdegnoso gusto,
    credendo col morir fuggir disdegno,
    ingiusto fece me contra me giusto.'

'Thy sweet words so beguile,
   I cannot silent stay; may it not displease
   if I am lured to speak a little while.

I am the one who once held both the keys
to Frederick's heart, which frequently I turned,
locking, unlocking with such gentle ease,
that almost none his confidence so earned:
faithful to such a glorious charge I stayed,
so that all loss of sleep and strength I spurned.
The harlot, who from Caesar's house ne'er strayed,
nor ever turned away her wanton eyes,
our common bane, of courts a vice inbred,
inflamed all hearts against me, and likewise
the inflamed so inflamed the Emperor with distrust
that joyful honours changed to baleful lies.
My spirit, in a temper of disgust,
thinking by my decease disdain to flee,
against my just self made myself unjust.' [6]

By this masterly pastiche Dante transports us from the wood of the suicides to the court of Frederick II and we hear the elaborate style of speech that characterized its cultivated members. Then with an immediate change of diction we are brought back to the unnatural wood, as the voice from the tree proclaims:

'Per le nuove radici d'esto legno
    vi giuro che già mai non ruppi fede
    al mio signor, che fu d'onor sì degno.'

'By the strange root-stock of this very tree
*   I swear I ne'er broke faith towards my lord*
*   who so deserving was of loyalty.'* [7]

Unjust accusation of a broken trust was something for which Dante felt deep sympathy: he himself had been similarly charged. Pier's declaration of innocence is thus made the more passionate and moving. Self-murder, however, is a sin, for which, in the system of Dante's Christian Hell, there is no mitigation. [8] It is identical with the wanton destruction of one's material belongings, property and wealth, another form of violence against the self which is the subject of the remainder of the canto.

The portrait of Brunetto Latini, Dante's guide and mentor in his early years, is drawn with love, pathos and a dignity that is the more compelling given the squalor of the punishment. In the third ring of the Seventh Circle of Hell we come to an area of sterile sand on which flames of fire unceasingly rain down, this being in itself an image of a reversal of nature, since fire burns upwards. This is the arena of the souls of sodomites and other sinners against the self. Dante and Virgil, having emerged from the wood of the suicides, are walking along an embankment which skirts a river of blood.

From this arises a pall of steam that protects Dante from the flakes of fire. Close to the bank a troop of souls come hurrying towards them, peering at them in the murky atmosphere, knitting up their brows as an old tailor squinnies at the eye of a needle. One of them recognizes Dante and reaches up from the sand to pull at the hem of his gown, crying: 'This is indeed a marvel!' Dante, bending down to peer into his face, is able, despite the scorched aspect and distorted features, to make out who it is. His response is dramatic:

> 'Siete voi qui, Ser Brunetto?'

> *Are* you *here, Ser Brunetto?'*[9]

In the rhythm of the verse there is a strong emphasis on the word *voi*, which conveys a moving effect of shocked surprise on the part of Dante the character. There has been some reluctance among modern commentators to acknowledge that Dante intended Brunetto's sin to be interpreted as sodomy.[10] Given the setting and context, however, it is difficult to see that there can be any doubt about it.

Brunetto Latini, who was born about the year 1220 and died in 1294, was a Florentine Guelf who represented for Dante the virtues of an earlier period of Florence. He was a notary and a man of learning, much respected by his fellow citizens and famed for his skill as an orator. He expounded the writings of Cicero as guidance in public affairs. There is a portrait of him in the Bargello in Florence, once reputed to be the work of Giotto, beside the one of Dante. The diminutive of his name, Bruno, may indicate that he was of small stature. He was much involved in the political life of Florence and was of sufficient standing to be sent to Seville on an embassy to Alfonso X, King of Spain, who had recently been elected Emperor but was never crowned. The Florentine Senate hoped that Brunetto would be able to gain his support against the threat of the Ghibellines of Siena. The mission was unsuccessful. On his return from Spain, travelling along the Pass of Roncesvalles, as he relates, he met a student from Bologna astride a bay mule, who told him of the disastrous defeat of the Guelfs at the Battle of Montaperti in 1260. As a result, Brunetto, like Dante, was exiled from his native city. He spent the next six years in France, where he wrote his great work, in French prose, *Le Livres dou Tresor*, an encyclopaedia or thesaurus of history, philosophy, moral instruction and science. He later produced an abridged version in Italian verse, known as *Il Tesoretto*.

From the dialogue in Canto XV it is evident that he was an important influence in Dante's early years. The relationship between them is interwoven with tender regard. Brunetto asks first, humbly, if he may keep him company, letting his group run on. Dante offers to sit down with him but that would

only increase Brunetto's penalty: he and the other souls are doomed to keep
moving aimlessly round the arena. Dante does not dare descend on to the
sand to walk beside him; all he can do is to bow his head towards him, like
someone showing reverence. Though Dante addresses him with the respectful pronoun *voi*, Brunetto uses the informal *tu*, as was no doubt their custom
when they spoke together in Florence:

> ... 'Se tu segui tua stella,
>   non puoi fallire a glorioso porto,
>   se ben m'accorsi nella vita bella;
> e s'io non fossi sì per tempo morto,
>   veggendo il cielo a te così benigno,
>   dato t'avrei all'opera conforto.'

> ... *'Follow but thy star,*
> *thy glorious port thou canst not fail to gain,*
> *if I saw truly in my life, once fair;*
> *had I not died so soon, since it was plain*
> *the heavens so propitious were to thee,*
> *thy champion and guide I would have been.'*[11]

These words have suggested to commentators that Brunetto once cast
Dante's horoscope. However that may be, he now proceeds, in obscure
imagery, to foretell his future. The malicious ingrates who of old descended
from Fiesole,[12] he says, will be his enemies, and with reason, for it is not
natural that among bitter sorbs the sweet fig should bear fruit. They are
reputed blind, avaricious, envious and proud. Let him beware, he warns, not
to be stained by them. His fortune holds for him such honour that both
parties will try to snatch and devour him, but the grass will be far from
the goat. Let Fiesole's wild beasts make fodder of themselves and leave the
plant, if on their dunghill any such spring up wherein is found the seed of
Romans who remained when it became the nest of so much ill.

Dante believed that the strife and disorder of Florence were due to the
intermarriage of intruders from Fiesole with the stock of Roman families
who founded the city.[13] The earthy, agricultural imagery in which he makes
Brunetto express this view may be characteristic of the man himself and of
his generation. It suggests someone of robust diction and opinion. Dante's
feeling towards him is devoutly filial:

> 'Se fosse tutto pieno il mio dimando',
>   rispuosi lui, 'voi non sareste ancora
>   dell'umana natura posto in bando;
> chè 'n la mente m'è fitta, e or m'accora,
>   la cara e buona imagine paterna
>   di voi quando nel mondo ad ora ad ora

m'insegnavate come l'uom s'etterna:
  e quant'io l'abbia in grado, mentr'io vivo,
  convien che nella mia lingua si scerna.'

'If all my prayers granted were', I said,
  'you, whom I so revere, would not yet be
  beyond our human nature banishèd;
for my heart aches when in my mind I see
  your dear, kind image, when from hour to hour,
  just like a father, you instructed me
how a man's gifts eternally may flower:
  my thanks for this, as long as I shall live,
  in plain and fitting language I will pour.'[14]

This picture of Brunetto instructing Dante has led commentators to assume that he was in some sense his tutor. This is unlikely but that there was an intellectual and affectionate bond between the elderly man and the young poet is clear. It was perhaps Brunetto who induced Dante to read Cicero and Boethius, as he says he did, after the death of Beatrice. It is also possible that Brunetto was Dante's guardian after the death of his father.

The squalor of Brunetto's sin and penalty is painful for Dante to visualize. He asks for information concerning the other souls and again Brunetto speaks in bluff, coarse words: they are clerics and scholars, he says, all fouled with the same sin, and if Dante is interested in 'such scurf', he names one or two: Priscian the grammarian, a lawyer from Bologna University and a bishop of Florence. Then seeing another group approach, with which he must not mingle, he runs off to join his own, calling out:

'Sieti raccomandato il mio Tesoro
  nel qual io vivo ancora, e più non cheggio.'

'Let my Thesaurus be thy care, I pray,
  in which I still live on: I ask no more.'[15]

As the scarred form runs off he seems to Dante like an athlete competing naked in the foot race in Verona for the prize of the green cloth, not like a loser but the winning runner.[16]

This portrait of Brunetto Latini is one of the most personally significant, providing a glimpse of Dante as a loyal friend who, though not evading the difference in God's sight between right and wrong, yet lovingly acknowledged the memory of benefits received.

CHAPTER 18

Down into the Depths

Of all the monsters and deformed mythological figures in *Inferno* the most terrifying is Geryon. The centaurs who guard the river of blood in the Seventh Circle, shooting arrows at the murderers, are picturesque in comparison. Nessus, who at Chiron's command, carries Dante on his back to the shore of the Wood of Suicides, is no formidable mount. Chiron himself, with whom Virgil converses, is a figure of classical dignity, parting his flowing beard with the notch of his arrow and remembered for his sublime role as the tutor of Achilles. But Geryon, who carries the poets down the chasm that divides the Seventh from the Eighth Circle, is repulsive as only an image of nightmare can be.

In Greek mythology Geryon was a monster in human form, with three heads, or with three conjoined bodies, who was killed by Hercules. Dante gives him three forms in one body, human, bestial and reptilian. He is the representation of fraud, having the face of a just man, a body dazzling with bright colours, the paws and forearms of an animal and a serpent's tail with a poisonous sting. As Dante and Virgil pause on the edge of the Seventh Circle they are stunned by the roar of water and blood falling into the abyss, draining from the circles above and representing the cruelty and suffering of humankind throughout the ages. At Virgil's command, Dante unties a cord he is wearing round his waist, with which, he says, he once hoped to capture the creature with the dappled pelt. This has been interpreted as a monk's girdle, symbolic of an attempt in youth to resist the temptations of the flesh, or even of a period when, it is said, Dante became a novice of the Franciscan Order, from which he later withdrew. It is possible that in its literal sense the cord is a rope, part of a climber's equipment, worn by Dante (so much as a matter of course that it was not worth mentioning at that point) when he began to ascend *il dilettoso monte* ('the mountain of joy').[1] The words in which he describes his unwinding of it suggest a cord of several coils:

Poscia che l'ebbi *tutta* da me sciolta,
   sì come 'l duca m'avea comandato,
   porsila a lui aggroppata e ravvolta.

> *When from myself I had loosed all the rope,*
>   *just as my leader had commanded me,*
>   *I gave it to him knotted and coiled up.*[2]

Earlier, if Dante had intended to use it, it had proved futile but now it is put to use: thrown by Virgil into the ravine with a vigorous right-hand swing, it serves as a signal to Geryon. The allegorical meaning may be that all self-sufficient and self-deceptive means of progress may as well now be abandoned, being useless against fraud, which has to be seen for what it is. Whatever its meaning, in the literal story it is never retrieved but lies forever somewhere in the Eighth Circle. Dante proceeds ungirt on his journey from now on until he arrives at the shore of the Mountain of Purgatory, where the guardian Cato will command Virgil to re-gird him with a rush, a symbol of humility.[3]

The effect of the signal is to bring Geryon up to the edge of the Seventh Circle. He comes up as though swimming through the thick, dark air, like a diver who has gone down into the sea to release an anchor from obstruction, stretching out his arms and drawing up his legs, an action Dante could have seen when on his travels near the coast. As a landsman he would have observed it with interest and remembered it, particularly if he had not learnt to swim himself, as seems likely.

The arrival of Geryon is preceded by an encounter with three other Florentine sinners against nature. Virgil and Dante were still walking along the embankment from which Dante had conversed with Brunetto Latini when three souls detached themselves from a group and came running towards him. They had recognized him from his dress as *alcun di nostra terra prava* ('someone of our depraved city').[4] This is an intriguing variation of the recognition of Dante as a Florentine by his speech.

Boccaccio, commenting on this line, says that in Dante's time 'almost every city or state had its own distinctive style of dress, for we had not then taken to dressing in German or English fashions'.[5] Giovanni Villani relates that the dress worn by Florentines was the most noble and dignified of all regional styles.[6] That of men was distinguished by the *lucco*, a long straight gown without folds, gathered at the waist, and by a cap, from which descended two bands at the side of the face, familiar from portraits of Dante. This is the first and only time his attire is mentioned in the *Commedia*.[7] The reference by the souls to his style of dress is the more striking in that they themselves, like Brunetto Latini, are naked and pitifully scarred by the flames:

Ancor men duol pur ch' i' me ne rimembri.

It grieves me yet when I remember them.[8]

For all the indignity of their condition, Virgil commands Dante to be courteous to them, saying that were it not for the flakes of fire it would be more fitting for him to hurry towards them than for them to show haste in approaching him.

They must not cease in their running and so, in order to converse with Dante, they form a circle, resembling wrestlers, naked and oiled, looking for a vantage from which to grip their opponents, each one with his head and feet turning perpetually in contrary directions. One of them asks Dante to reveal who he is. Their present aspect, he says, belies the fame they had on earth: the one in front of him is Guido Guerra, a Guelf nobleman who fought to expel the Ghibellines from Arezzo and after the Battle of Montaperti was himself banished from Florence. He was the grandson of a Florentine noblewoman, Gualdrada, famed for her beauty and virtue. The soul behind him is Tegghiaio Aldobrandini, another nobleman, of the Adimari family, who with Guido Guerra advised against the attack on Siena that ended in the defeat of the Florentines at Montaperti. The speaker names himself as Jacopo Rusticucci, whose bestial wife, more than all else, he says, has brought him to this pass.[9]

To the Dante of Florence these names, famous in the annals of his city, are of special significance. Familiar with them from childhood as heroic figures, he would gladly, he says, had it not been for the fire, have flung himself down on to the sand to embrace them:

'Di vostra terra sono, e sempre mai
   l' ovra di voi e li onorati nomi
   con affezion ritrassi e ascoltai.'

'I from your city am and long have known
   your deeds and honoured names and with full heart
   I heard and told the tales of your renown.'[10]

Jacopo begs Dante to tell them if courtesy and valour are still found in their city, for Guglielmo Borsiere, who has recently joined them, has brought troubling news.[11] Dante uses the enquiry to broaden the theme of the corruption of Florence. Lifting his face as though addressing the city itself, he denounces it for the influx of self-made men and for the quick-got gains that have generated luxury and arrogance, already a cause to others of deprivation and distress. The three souls look at each other like men who know the truth when they hear it. In their reply they congratulate Dante on being able to speak so freely and beg him, if he escapes from these dark regions and ever looks up at the star-lit sky again, to speak of them to living men. Then, on legs that seem like wings, they speed across the sand and disappear.

Noble and heroic they may have been in the first life, but (Dante evidently has reason to believe) they were guilty of sodomy and, in the case of Jacopo Rusticucci, probably of bestiality. His reference to his wife is deliberately equivocal:

'La fiera moglie più ch'altro mi nuoce.'

'My beast wife more than any does me harm.'[12]

The word *fiera* may be the feminine form of the adjective *fiero*, meaning savage, or feral, or it may be a noun, meaning a wild animal.

It is after this deeply emotional episode, with its mingling of heroism and depravity, its memories of Florence as a city of once valorous and courteous citizens, now degraded by avarice, that Dante and Virgil are confronted with the image of fraud, called up by the signal of the cord from Dante's waist. If this was simply a feature of the Florentine *lucco*, it may be that in discarding it Dante is dissociating himself from the Florence he has just denounced: an umbilical cord has been severed.

The monster clings to the edge of the Seventh Circle, like a boat lying part on land and part in water, or like a beaver which in German regions can be seen to settle to catch fish with its tail.[13] To reach it Dante and Virgil go towards the right and walk ten paces along the edge. While Virgil exerts his magical power over Geryon to compel him to carry them down, Dante is sent further along the edge to look at a third group of sinners of the Seventh Circle.

These are the usurers who sinned against natural resources and man's labour by the barren interchange of money, an example of the rapid gains that Dante has just deplored in his condemnation of present-day Florence. Distorted and deformed, they squat on the sand staring down at purses that hang round their necks. These are embroidered with the heraldic arms of their families, by which Dante is able to identify them. Flapping their hands, they try to shield themselves from the flakes of fire, as dogs do with their snout and paws in summer, when bitten by fleas or gnats or flies. The comparison is deliberately dehumanizing. A Paduan, identified as Rinaldo Scrovegni,[14] boasts that his neighbour Vitaliano will join him soon. Meanwhile, he says, Florentine usurers keep bawling in his ear, calling for *il cavalier sovrano* ('the peerless knight'), who will wear a pouch bearing the heraldic device of three goats: he has been identified as Giovanni Buiamonte dei Becchi, a notorious usurer, well known to Dante's contemporaries, as were two other Florentines, one of the Gianfigliazzi family and one of the Ubbriachi. The reference to Buiamonte as a *cavalier sovrano* is sarcastic, for this was a sobriquet used in chivalrous romance to denote a knight of supreme honour and valour. Having thus taunted Dante, Rinaldo distorts his mouth and sticks out his tongue like an ox licking its snout. By the use of such coarse vocabulary Dante, the master of language, exerts his control of the vernacular to express his contempt for the sin of usury.

The character Dante then returns to Virgil and finds him already seated on Geryon's back. Commanded to mount in front, he proves himself no *cavalier sovrano*, failing utterly in courage and shaking like someone with a quartan fever. Shame at last proving stronger than fear, he climbs up on the loathsome shoulders, trying the while to say 'Hold on to me', but no voice comes. Virgil has already clasped him in his arms and holds him steady. This is indeed necessary since, as previously at the gates of Dis, when threatened with the Gorgon, Dante is in extreme peril.

The description of the descent on the back of Geryon is Dante the writer's greatest feat so far in imaginative visualization. It begins with Virgil's words of command: 'Now move, Geryon, but slowly, in wide circles, remember the unusual burden on thy back.' As a little craft backs from its berth, so Geryon moves out from the cliff. (The modern equivalent might perhaps be the movement of a helicopter, having achieved lift, rolling slowly off the roof of a tall building and hanging in space.) Sensing itself in the clear, where its breast was it turns its tail, stretching and moving it like an eel, and draws air towards itself with its paws. Dante makes use of two mythical examples of disastrous flight to convey his fear: that of Phaethon who, driving his father's chariot of the sun, dropped the reins and set the sky ablaze, and that of Icarus who flew so near the sun that the wax on his feathers melted and he fell into the sea: neither felt greater terror than Dante. In the darkness he has at first no means of knowing that they are descending except for the sensation of wind blowing in his face from below (a remarkable feat of intuition on the part of Dante the writer and one which has recently been compared to Galileo's discovery of invariance). He hears the sound of the cataract falling from the circle above and cranes his head to look. Then the terror of alighting is worse even than being in mid-air, for he sees fires and hears sounds of wailing. He cowers back, trembling at the sight of torments now visible on all sides. At last, like a disappointed, sullen falcon that swoops slowly down, landing at a distance from its master, Geryon sets its passengers at the foot of the jagged cliff and immediately vanishes, like an arrow shot from a bowstring.

We have reached the Eighth Circle. Dante's three-dimensional imaginative power is now at its peak. His artistic task is to create an illusion of a vast structure, coiled into ten descending compartments or ditches, crossed by arched bridges, corresponding to ten sins that involve the use of fraud. These abstract notions have to be enlivened by varied pictures of suffering and by adventure-action, contrived to hold the audience in acute suspense from one ditch to the next.

In the first ditch are panders and seducers, that is, those who exploited women for gain or for sexual pleasure. For them Dante has devised a savage punishment. Divided into two groups, they circle the ditch, facing in two different directions, reminding him of the crowds in Rome at the time of the Jubilee, who formed two opposing lines as they crossed the bridge spanning the river Tiber between Castel Sant'Angelo and Mount Giordano, an ironic comment, perhaps, on the behaviour of the pilgrim-tourists. Many of the first audience would have seen this example of traffic control for themselves. The souls are cruelly lashed by horned demons as they pass. Dante takes satisfaction in recalling how they skipped and leapt to avoid a second blow. One face in particular he recognizes and he asks Virgil's consent to go back and scrutinize it. He knows the soul as Venedico Caccianemico, a powerful Guelf of Bologna, and asks him sarcastically how he has got himself into such *pungenti salse* ('stinging pickle'), a mocking reference to a place near Bologna where criminals were flogged and executed. The sinner admits that he pandered his sister to the Marquis of Este and boasts that there are many more pimps from that city in the same ditch with him, more even than all who say *sipa*, a contemptuous imitation of the Bolognese word for *sia* ('so be it').

This vindictive thrust at Bologna raises once more the question of Dante's attitude to those whom he selects as examples in Hell. He had said in *Il Convivio* that it was right to hate sin but not the sinner. It must be recognized, however, that in *Inferno* he does not always achieve this detachment. As in the case of Filippo Argenti,[15] so here in his choice of the first sinner in the Eighth Circle, Dante the writer shows personal resentment. The reason may be that the government of Bologna yielded to pressure from Florence to exile the White Guelfs who had taken refuge there; it may also be that he felt contempt for the lukewarm response of the Bolognese public to the banquet of learning he set before them. Whatever the explanation, resentment and contempt he certainly felt. 'If you don't believe me about the number of pimps here from Bologna,' says Venedico,

'rècati a mente il nostro avaro seno'.

just call to mind our avaricious hearts'.[16]

In our last glimpse of Venedico he is being lashed again by a demon, who gibes, 'Get along, you pander, there are no women here to exchange for coin!'

Dante returns to where Virgil is waiting for him and they climb up the rock and turn right until they reach the crest of a bridge. From there they look down on sinners passing below and are able to see the faces of those whose backs were turned to them before. From these indications we learn that the rule of the road in this ditch is to the right.

These are the seducers and they too are lashed by demons. The first, identified by Virgil, is Jason. Virgil points him out and comments on his kingly bearing and his courageous endurance of suffering. Here the separation between sin and sinner is clear. Jason is presented as a flawed heroic figure, whose indulgence in sexual pleasure involved him in the betrayal of both Medea and Hypsipyle, the *giovinetta* ('young woman') whom he left pregnant and alone (*soletta*) on the island of Lemnos. Dante, who had read of her in the *Thebaid* by Statius and in Ovid's *Heroides*,[17] visualized her with compassion, as may be seen from the affectionate diminutives he uses concerning her. Guilty as Jason was, he remains in Dante's eyes a tragic figure who loses nothing of his mythical stature as the leader of the Argonauts. Virgil explains how it is that so great a personage comes to be here: *tal colpa a tal martiro lui condanna*.[18] The use of the disjunctive pronoun *lui*, with the strong beat on the word, and the repetition of *tal* give particular emphasis, as though to say '*such* a man has been brought to *such* a torment by *such* guilt'.

In the same canto[19] another sin is introduced. The second ditch contains the souls of flatterers, who suffer the most repugnant punishment in the whole of *Inferno*. The sinners are immersed in excrement, snuffling and scratching at themselves with filthy hands. The sides of the ditch are encrusted with faeces, an offensive sight and stench. By flattery (*lusinghe*) Dante understands all forms of toadying and insincere adulation made use of for self-advancement. Ordure was an image of foul or deceitful speech (as the word 'crap' is used in English) and he has chosen this worst possible degradation to express his scorn. He must have observed much flattery in political life and seen with contempt how well it served those who demeaned themselves to employ it. Peering into the depths, he perceives one whose head is so heaped with filth he cannot tell whether it is tonsured or not. The soul shrieks: 'Why look at me, more than at the others?' Dante replies: 'I've seen you before, without shit on your head: you're Alessio Interminelli of Lucca, that's why I'm looking especially at you.'

Nothing is known about Alessio, except that he was a member of a prominent family who supported the White Guelfs in Lucca. Dante must have had a reason for choosing him to exemplify this sin. He knew him personally and despite his present degradation he still recognizes him. His close scrutiny of him now may imply that he had closely watched him in the world, advancing his career and gaining favours by falsely professing loyalty – very different from Dante's own uncompromising character. There is bitterness here, for by such means Dante might have been able to return to Florence, or might never have been exiled in the first place.

The example chosen from antiquity is that of a harlot, Thais, not the Athenian courtesan but a character in *Eunuchus*, a play by Terence, whose fulsome words to her lover Dante read in a quotation by Cicero. With a brief allusion to her, alternately standing and crouching in the dung and scratching herself with her filthy nails, Dante closes the canto with Virgil's dismissive words:

'E quinci sian le nostre viste sazie.'

'With what we've seen let us be satisfied.'[20]

CHAPTER 19

'Him of Alagna'

In 1300, the fictional date of the *Commedia*, Pope Boniface VIII was still alive; indeed that was the year of the great Jubilee. By the time Dante wrote Canto XIX of *Inferno* Boniface had been dead for several years, his demise having been caused in 1303 by the assault made on him by agents of the King of France.[1] Dante never relented in his animosity against Boniface. On the contrary, his hatred grew as the *Commedia* progressed, until the climactic moment when no less a figure than St Peter hurls at Boniface from the eighth sphere of Paradise a denial and a denunciation at which the heavens for very shame blush with the hues of sunrise and of sunset.[2] The venom with which Dante targets Boniface has never been fully accounted for.

Chronology made it impossible to construct a face-to-face encounter with Boniface in Hell, but Dante was determined to place him there in advance. The solution he contrived is ingenious and dramatic. Looking down from the crest of the bridge that spans the third ditch where the sin of simony is punished, he sees the gulley pitted with round holes. They remind him of the cylindrical containers in the font of his beautiful baptistery in Florence (*mio bel San Giovanni*).[3] From each of them protrude the feet and legs of sinners, visible up to the calf, the soles of their feet on fire, the rest of their body thrust down into the rock. Virgil carries Dante down the slope and places him by one of the holes so that he is able to speak with the sinner trapped inside. With scant courtesy Dante calls down to the soul:

> 'O qual che se' che 'l di su tien di sotto,
> anima trista, come pal commessa,'
> ... 'se puoi, fa motto.'

> *'O thou who down below dost hide thy top,*
> *stuck like a post, vile soul, whoe'er thou art,*
> *... if talk thou canst, speak up.'*[4]

With heartless indifference Dante compares himself to a priest standing over an assassin about to be put to death by being planted head down, who calls to the priest to hear his confession in order to put off the last terrible moment. The soul replies: 'What, fixed already, fixed already, Boniface? The future as I read it erred by several years. Already sated, art thou, with exploiting the Fair Bride seized by thee with guile?'[5] Dante stands bewildered and agape. Virgil interjects: 'Tell him quickly, "I'm not the one, I'm not the one thou takest me for."'

The soul writhes and twists his feet, then sighing and lamenting he replies: 'What dost thou want of me? If thou must know, I too once wore the great mantle. A son of the she-bear, I was so avid to enrich the cubs that up above I pouched coin and here below I pouched myself.'The soul is that of Nicholas Orsini.[6] Pope from 1277 to 1280, he too was held guilty of simony and nepotism. He explains that when a new soul arrives it thrusts the previous sinner further down the rock and waits, its legs protruding then, to be thrust down further in its turn. This mocking reversal of the normal dignity of a Pope is Dante's own personal assault upon Boniface, as well as upon others who likewise betrayed their sacred trust. Following Boniface, Nicholas foretells, will come *di ver ponente un pastor senza legge* ('from towards the west a lawless shepherd'). This will be Pope Clement V, a Gascon, elected in 1305 with the support of the King of France, to whom he had promised pecuniary concessions. He was responsible for transferring the Papal see from Rome to Avignon.

The picture of Boniface in Hell, the soles of his feet bright red with flame as they had been shod in life with rose-red slippers, is followed eight cantos later, in a dialogue with the soul of Guido da Montefeltro.[7] Here Boniface is shown as a wily intriguer, seeking advice from Guido as to how he might trick his personal enemies. Guido, a celebrated strategist, had withdrawn from worldly intrigues into the Franciscan Order, hoping to make his peace with God. But Boniface, as Dante constructs the story, sought him out, promising him absolution in advance for the sin he now tempted him to commit. Guido expresses for Dante all the venom against Boniface that he himself felt: *il gran prete, a cui mal prenda!* ('the great priest, whom ill befall!'), *lo principe de' novi Farisei* ('the prince of the new Pharisees'), being at war, not with Saracens or Jews, for every one of his enemies was Christian, heeded neither his supreme office nor Guido's vows as a Franciscan, reminding him that he held the keys of Heaven. Guido, trusting him, lapsed into sin again, with the result that he was now in Hell among the counsellors of fraud.[8]

The 19th canto opens with an oratorical outcry against simony, a sin named after Simon Magus, who tried to buy the gift of healing from the Apostles.[9] After the words of Nicholas Orsini, Dante resumes his tone of wrathful rebuke. Trafficking in sacred things is pilloried in images of sexual exploitation: simoniacs are those who prostitute for gold and silver the things of God which should be the brides of righteousness. How great is God's wisdom, how great His skill, in Heaven, on earth and in the evil world below, in His distinctions between sin and sin! The divisions between the sins punished in the ten ditches of the Eighth Circle are in fact subtle and Dante is drawing attention to his own discrimination. Avarice, in one form or another, links them all, as may be seen clearly already in the first three, but they have each particular characteristics that deserve separate retribution.

Dante, at first with some show of diffidence, takes centre stage. Was he too bold, he wonders now? He presents himself as being inspired beyond his immediate control, as though by a song or chant, as he suggests in the following lines:

> I' non so s' i' mi fui qui troppe folle,
> ch' i' pur rispuosi *lui* a questo metro.

> *I know not whether I was here too bold,*
> *that I replied to* him *in such a strain.*[10]

What follows is rebuke such as might have come from the lips of an early apostle:

'Tell me: how much treasure did our Lord ask of Saint Peter before He gave the keys into his charge? Truly he asked for nothing, saying only 'Follow me'. Neither did Peter or the others take gold or silver from Matthias when he was chosen for the place vacated by the evil soul.[11] Stay there, for thou art rightly punished. But for the reverence I feel for the sublime keys that thou didst hold in happier life, I'd use graver words still,

> chè la vostra avarizia il mondo attrista,
>   calcando i buoni e sollevando i pravi.
> Di voi pastor s'accorse il Vangelista,
>   quando colei che siede sopra l'acque
>   puttaneggiar coi regi a lui fu vista,
> quella che con le sette teste nacque,
>   e dalle diece corna ebbe argomento,
>   fin che virtute al suo marito piacque.
> Fatto v'avete Dio d'oro e d'argento:
>   e che altro è da voi all'idolatre
>   se non ch' elli uno, e voi ne orate cento?'

> *'for avarice like yours the world bereaves,*
> *trampling the good, exalting evil men.*
> *Shepherds like you the Evangelist perceives*
> *in her who over many waters spreads,*
> *the whore who kings seduces and depraves,*

> *the same who at her birth had seven heads,*
> *and from ten horns drew her authority,*
> *while virtue pleased her spouse in all his deeds.*
> *Silver and gold you make a deity:*
> *how do you differ from idolaters,*
> *who but to one, while you to hundreds pray?"*[12]

At this point, Dante reaches not only the climax of his inspired oration but the very core of the purpose of the *Commedia*: to proclaim the principles of justice by which the world should be governed. The Emperor Constantine, the first Christian Emperor, was believed to have endowed the Church with dominion over the western part of his empire. This act was set out in a text known as the Donation of Constantine, later proved to be a forgery but believed by Dante to be genuine. He regarded it as a grave error on the part of Constantine, well meant but disastrous for the future of the Church, which thereafter laid claims to temporal power:

> Ahi! Costantin, di quanto mal fu matre,
> non la tua conversion, ma quella dote
> che da te prese il primo ricco patre!

> *Ah, Constantine, that was indeed a curse,*
> *not thy conversion, but thy dower which*
> *first filled with wealth the Holy Father's purse!*[13]

All through this episode and his inspired remonstrance Dante has been under the spell of Virgil. It was he who carried Dante down the slope to reach the aperture from which the sinner's legs emerged, who stood beside him as he spoke, encouraging him to deny quickly that he was Boniface, and seemed by his smile to approve all that Dante said. He then carried him resting upon his breast, up the slope he had descended, nor did he tire before he reached the summit of the next bridge, where he set his burden down.

It was from reading Virgil that Dante had come to see the Roman Empire as divinely ordained for the righteous ordering of earthly life. The Christian Empire's independence of the Church in temporal matters, the clear distinction of its sphere of influence, formed a crucial part of Dante's political thinking and was to have been a major theme of *Il Convivio*, as it is of the *Commedia* and was later of his treatise on world government, *Monarchia*.[14] His surrender to Virgil's control is an image of his indebtedness to him as a convert to imperial authority. In the context of these great concerns, in the contrast between prophetic oratory and ridicule, such figures as Boniface dwindle to dwarf stature.

CHAPTER 20

Virgil and Sorcery

After simony comes sorcery, the distortion of the gift of prophecy for gain. Once more, avarice is the underlying motive. After his flight of oratory on the subject of simony, Dante reverts to his role of the bewildered onlooker and dissolves into tears at the hideous spectacle of souls whose heads are twisted backwards, their feet pointing forwards, their tears streaming down their backs to the cleft of their buttocks:

> Forse per forza già di parlasia
>   si travolse così alcun del tutto;
>   ma io nol vidi, nè credo che sia.
>
> *Perhaps the force of a paralysis*
>   *once twisted someone so completely round;*
>   *I never saw, nor can I credit this.*[1]

They tried to peer into the future; now they walk as slowly as a religious procession, looking behind them. Dante is sternly rebuked by Virgil for his sympathy:

> ... 'Ancor se' tu delli altri sciocchi?
> Qui vive la pietà quand'è ben morta.'
>
> *... 'Art thou another of those fools?*
> *Here piety survives when pity dies.'*[2]

This is Virgil's canto. He has been credited with magical power but a clear distinction is now drawn between him and those who pervert for their own benefit the sacred forces to which he has access. His prophecy of the birth of Christ, for instance, was believed to be divinely inspired. Similarly, the control he now has over the guardians and monsters of Hell has been granted him to enable Dante to convince believers and unbelievers of the truths of the Christian faith and to proclaim God's plan for the peace of the world. The reactions of listeners may have prompted this canto.

Belief in sorcery, necromancy, astrology, chiromancy, geomancy, augury was widespread in Dante's time, not only among the unlettered but also among the learned. It is significant that Dante makes Virgil dissociate himself from the examples drawn from antiquity. The first of these is Amphiaraüs, one of the seven kings who besieged Thebes, about whom Dante had read in the epic by Statius, the *Thebaid*.[3] Having knowledge of the future, he foresaw his own death in battle and when war came he concealed himself to avoid it. His hiding place was disclosed by his wife and on the battlefield the earth opened up and swallowed him, chariot and all, so that he fell, Virgil here adds, headlong as far as Minos, the judge of all who are damned:

'Mira, che ha fatto petto delle spalle;
    perchè volle veder troppo davante,
    dietro guarda, e fa retroso calle.'

'Look how his shoulders as his breast appear;
    because he tried to see too far ahead,
    he looks behind and walks not knowing where.'[4]

This is a very summary dismissal. Contemptuous too is Virgil's identification of Tiresias, the prophet of Thebes, of whose metamorphosis from male to female and back again Dante had read in Ovid.[5] Aruns is the next to be recognized, a renowned Etruscan augur, mentioned by Lucan,[6] who says that he foretold the civil war which was to end in the death of Pompey and the triumph of Caesar. He who once dwelt in a cave among the white marble of Carrara, looking out from it at the stars and the sea, is here described as having his back to the belly of Tiresias, a grotesque claustrophobic detail which robs the souls of all dignity. So much for them, Virgil seems to be saying, dismissing them as they shamble along in the dark, twisted and distorted.

The next to be identified is Manto, the daughter of Tiresias. Her loose tresses cover her breasts which, like her pubic hair, Dante cannot see. This degrading picture of a female sorceress is followed by a digression on the founding of Mantua, the city near which Virgil was born and which was held to have been named after Manto. Dante evidently considered it important to make clear that Manto's connection with the city, as stated by Virgil in a brief reference in the *Aeneid*,[7] did not imply a legacy of sorcery. He gives this refutation to the character Virgil in lines of serene beauty, evoking the natural elements from which the city was formed:

'Suso in Italia bella giace un laco,
    a piè de l'Alpe che serra Lamagna
    sovra Tiralli, c'ha nome Benaco.
Per mille fonti, credo, e più si bagna,
    tra Garda e Val Camonica, Apennino
    dell' acqua che nel detto laco stagna.'

'Up in fair Italy there lies a lake,
known as Benaco, at the foot of hills
which near Tyrol the German confines make.
Mount Apennine is by a thousand rills
between Camonica and Garda bathed,
the water which the lake I speak of fills.[8]

The memory of the landscape evokes in Virgil nostalgia for the region he once knew and he dwells lovingly on details, some of which he conjures up by preternatural foresight. In the lake is an island, in the centre of which is a place where pastors from Trent, Brescia and Verona might, if they passed that way, all make the sign of blessing.[9] Where the surrounding shore lies lowest stands the fortress of Peschiera, showing a bold front to the inhabitants of Brescia and Bergamo. At this point the lake, no longer called Benaco, becomes the river Mincio, flowing through green pastures as far as Governolo, where it falls into the Po. After a short course it comes to a level where it spreads out into a marsh, sometimes unwholesome in the summer. There Manto, Virgil relates, having wandered through many lands, found territory uninhabited and untilled, where she dwelt with her familiars to ply her arts, and where she died. Later came scattered inhabitants who built a city on that spot, defended on each side by bog land, and called it Mantua after her who had first lived there, but for no other reason. This is the truth about the founding of his city, which Virgil charges Dante to make known:

'Però t'assenno che se tu mai odi
    originar la mia terra altrimenti,
    la verità nulla menzogna frodi.'

'Therefore, be sure, since I have put thee wise,
if any of my city's birth say else,
to let no lie the truth of this disguise.'[10]

The purpose of this digression seems to be to establish that Virgil is no trumpery magician and that his city should not be tarnished by any reputation for sorcery, as it may have been in Dante's hearing.

After this refreshing scenic panorama of lake, mountains and river, we return to the squalors of the fourth ditch and more sorcerers are named. Eurypylus, his beard spreading from his cheeks over his swarthy shoulders, is the augur, Virgil here says, who together with Calchas advised on a propitious date for the Greeks to set sail from Aulis. 'I mention him somewhere in my high tragedy,' he adds casually, 'thou wilt know, who hast it all by heart.' Strangely Dante appears to have confused two episodes: the augury taken for the appropriate date for sailing from Aulis, which Virgil does not mention in the *Aeneid*, and the second augury taken by Eurypylus at Troy for the date of the Greeks' return, an incident Virgil does mention and in which he says Calchas was involved.[11]

The following examples of sorcerers are all of the Christian era, but Virgil nevertheless has no difficulty in naming them. The first is Michael Scot, described as being lean in the flanks (*ne' fianchi ... così poco*).[12] He is dismissed airily as being well up in the game of deception by magic. Michael Scot, a thirteenth-century seer from Balwearie in Scotland, was widely renowned in Europe for his magic arts. He was also praised as a philosopher, but Albertus Magnus wrote disparagingly of him and Dante may have come upon this reference. How he learnt that he was lean in the flanks we do not know.

After Michael Scot, two Italian soothsayers are pointed out: Guido Bonatti, an astrologer of Forlì, of whom Dante may have heard when he visited the court of Ordelaffi in that city. The other is Benvenuto, nicknamed Asdente ('Toothless'), a master cobbler of Parma, of the first quarter of the thirteenth century. Although illiterate, he is said to have possessed a good knowledge of astrology and of prophetic writings. Dante appears to have despised him, for he mentions him contemptuously in *Il Convivio* as an example of one who would be called noble, if notoriety conferred nobility.[13] 'He wishes he had stuck to his leather and thread,' says Virgil, 'but it's too late now.'

The last practitioners of magic arts to be mentioned are not named: they are women who neglected their needle and shuttle and distaff and took up with fortune-telling and making herbal potions and images. Thus the whole question of sorcery is brought down to a level of evil-doing and trivial super-stition, venerable Greek augurs being classed with unnamed witches.

St Thomas Aquinas had condemned superstitious practices, among which he included the use of astrology to foretell events. Rulers commonly kept astrologers in their service[14] to advise them when and when not to take action. A knowledge of astrology was expected of doctors, as it was of philosophers and other men of science. Dante is guided here by the opinion of Aquinas. It may be that he had previously venerated the augurs of antiquity, which is perhaps the reason why he represents Virgil as rebuking him for showing compassion for them in their present condition. The slight discrepancy between what Virgil says in the *Aeneid* about the founding of Mantua and what Dante gives to Virgil to say about it in this canto requires some clarification.

In Book X of the *Aeneid*, among the leaders who followed Aeneas from Etruria, there is mention of Ocnus, 'son of prophesying Manto and the Etruscan river, who gave to Mantua her walls and his mother's name'.[15] The adjective *fatidicus*, which Virgil applies to Manto, means simply 'prophetic, predicting the future'. There is no mention of sorcery, though the birth of a son by the Etruscan river confers on her a mythological status. Virgil's command that Dante should let no false tale about the origin of Mantua pervert the truth must mean that the city had gained a reputation for sorcery, which was traced to its association with the prophetess Manto.

Virgil in the *Commedia* has supernatural powers. Having been previously sought by the witch Erichtho to perform an errand for her in the depths of Hell,[16] he has now received the divinely authorized plea of Beatrice to go to Dante's rescue, for which unusual task help from on high has been promised. In order to pacify guardians and monsters he twice uses what is in its form a magic spell. He also commands the response of Ulysses by the use of a formal conjuration. He has the power of prophecy. This is first manifested in the introductory canto of *Inferno*, where he makes his oracular pronouncement about the coming of the *veltro*.[17] He has knowledge of people, events and places of Dante's time. In this he resembles other souls, in Purgatory and Paradise as well as Inferno, the last being able to see into the distant future, though they have only a confused knowledge of events near at hand. After the Day of Judgement all such knowledge will be denied to those in Hell. This belief was an accepted convention. It was also convenient for the story of the *Commedia* which, fixed in the timeframe of a single week in 1300, required a range comprehending Dante's life beyond that date. It was important that such extension should be seen to derive not from sorcery but from reputable and believable foreknowledge.

Virgil in the *Commedia* is also profoundly wise, a sage as well as a seer. The sense of awe that Dante experiences from being in his company is one of the most appealing features in the story. He has implicit faith in his advice and instruction, as when he agrees to obey his command about the truth of the origin of Mantua:

> … 'Maestro, i tuoi ragionamenti
> mi son sì certi e prendon sì mia fede,
> che li altri mi sarien carboni spenti.'

> … *'Master, thy every argument*
> *so certain is and so convinces me,*
> *others would be to me like embers spent.'*[18]

The writer Dante, imagining the marvel which such a companionship would be, is inspired to devise dialogue that holds the listener like a fascinated eavesdropper or a spectator of a compelling drama. But the audience is kept at arm's length. This is achieved by excluding them from the conversation from time to time, as they find themselves at the beginning of the next canto:

Così di ponte in ponte, altro parlando
    che la mia comedia cantar non cura,
    venimmo, e tenevamo il colmo ...

And so from bridge to bridge, of matters talking
    of which my comedy declines to sing,
    we went, towards another summit walking ...[19]

This is tantalizing, like our exclusion from the conversation between Dante and the five great poets in Limbo,[20] but it also has the effect of making the listener feel privileged to have been admitted so far into the poet's confidence and to have heard, if not everything, at least so much.

Such moments demonstrate that the showman Dante has his public continually in mind and that he knows how to manipulate his material in such a way as to arouse their curiosity and to hold their attention. For this purpose, in the following three cantos he adopts a startling change of style, proving that he has not lost touch with what pleases the 'groundlings'. His descent into rollicking and at one moment vulgar comic relief will be considered in the next chapter.

CHAPTER 21

Devil-Play

In the fifth ditch of the Eighth Circle are the souls of those who made money by trafficking in public offices, that is to say, those who were guilty of 'sleaze', as common then as now. They are plunged in boiling pitch. At first Dante can see nothing but a black, bubbling, glue-like substance. Contemplating it with detachment from the crest of the bridge, he is reminded of a scene he has witnessed in Venice, in winter, when sailors caulk and refit their ships.[1] There too he had seen bubbles of pitch rising and bursting and sinking again. As he gazes, Virgil catches hold of him and pulls him close, crying 'Look out! Look out!' As they hurry away, Dante, despite his fear, looks back and sees a black devil skimming up the cliff, his wings spread wide, his aspect fierce. Astride his high, narrow shoulders he carries a sinner, clutching him by the ankles. Reaching the bridge, he calls down to his fellow fiends: 'Hi, Evil-Claws, here's an alderman from St Zita [i.e. Lucca],[2] poke him under while I go back for more. They're all swindlers there, except Bonturo, of course':[3]

'del no per li denari vi si fa ita.'

'you can change no to yes for money there.'[4]

He flings the sinner down and wheels back along the stony cliff, faster than a mastiff after a thief. The soul plunges down and rises again to the surface, doubled up. Demons hidden under the bridge shout, 'There's no Holy Face[5] to pray to here! This is no Serchio to swim in.[6] Stay under or you'll feel our hooks.' They poke him down with their pitchforks, like scullions prodding meat in a cauldron:

> Non altrimenti i cuochi a' lor vassalli
> fanno attuffare in mezzo la caldaia
> la carne con li uncin, perchè non galli.

> *Just so do cooks make scullions prod the meat*
> *with forks, thrusting it down into the pot,*
> *so that it doesn't float above the heat.*[7]

Dante is thought to have been in Lucca between 1307 and 1308. He has already mentioned it as the city of Alessio Interminelli, the flatterer whom he recognizes although his head is covered with shit.[8] His attitude to Lucca was bitterly contemptuous when he wrote these cantos, perhaps because of the city's resistance to Henry VII.[9] When he returned later, probably in 1314, he received kindness from a lady named Gentucca, to whom he pays a grateful tribute in *Purgatorio*, as though to make amends.[10] We know nothing about her, but her name rhymed conveniently with the city.

Virgil now takes command of the situation. He needs to parley with the demons to obtain safe conduct along to the next bridge. He tells Dante to keep out of sight behind a rock and not to be afraid if he sees them threaten him,

> ... 'ch' i' ho le cose conte,
> e altra volta fui a tal baratta.'

> ... *'for I know how to handle this,*
> *and once before I met their trickery.'*[11]

This is an allusion to Virgil's earlier journey down into the depths of Hell, about which he told Dante when he met with resistance at the gates of Dis.[12] On that occasion too he left him alone as he went forward to talk with the devils.

Dante peers from behind the rock as Virgil goes down a slope towards the sixth bank, where evil sprites rush out from under the bridge, like dogs at a beggar. Virgil orders them to hold off until he has spoken with one of them. 'Let Malacoda go,' they say, and snarling as he comes, the demon mutters, 'What good does he think this will do him?'

Virgil addresses him in reasonable terms. 'Do you think, Malacoda, I'd have got as far as this without the help of Divine Will? Let us pass, for it is decreed in Heaven that I should conduct someone along this dangerous way.'

Malacoda is so crestfallen that he drops his pitchfork, saying to the others, 'Keep off him.' Virgil calls out to Dante in words that are deliberately comic, both in sound and meaning:

> ... 'tu che siedi
> tra li scheggion del ponte quatto quatto,
> sicuramente omai a me tu riedi.'

> ... *'thou hunched down on thy hunkers there*
> *between the broken boulders of the bridge,*
> *come out now, there is nothing more to fear.'*[13]

Dante stands up and goes quickly to Virgil. The devils surge towards him and he is terrified that they will disobey orders. He recalls seeing soldiers marched out after the siege of Caprona under truce, alarmed at finding themselves among so many enemies.[14] He cringes close to Virgil, not taking his eyes off the demons, whose looks are far from friendly. They lower their forks and one says to another, 'How if I poke him in the rump?' 'Yes,' say the others, 'give it him!' But Malacoda turns and says: 'Down, Scarmiglione, down!' He then tells Virgil that the nearest bridge over the sixth ditch is broken. They must go on to another by which they will be able to cross. Yesterday, he says, it was exactly 1,266 years since this bridge was broken. This is a reference to the earthquake that followed the Crucifixion on Good Friday in the year 34.[15] It sounds convincing but is only part of the truth, as will be seen. He summons a troop of his fellow demons to accompany the poets to the further bridge, where the path, he says, is unbroken. The names of the demons do not inspire confidence: Alichino, Calcabrina, Cagnazzo, Barbariccia, Libicocco, Draghignazzo, Ciriatto ('him with the tusks'), Graffiacane, Farfarello and mad Rubicante.

Attempts have been made to make sense of these ten names, together with those of Scarmiglione and Malacoda, even to the extent of identifying them as corruptions of the names of the 12 Black Priors who were in power in Florence in 1303, when Cardinal Niccolò da Prato failed to make peace.[16] Another suggestion has been that the names represent families in Lucca, among whom Corso Donati found support for his intrigue against Florence. Whatever Dante's first listeners made of them, it is evident that he is here avenging himself with relish on those who charged him unjustly of corruption while he was in office. The names, appearance and behaviour of the demons recall the grotesque images in mediaeval frescoes, carvings and sculptures. They were also familiar figures in the farcical scenes of miracle plays. Dante's audience would have welcomed them with hilarious gusto as old friends.

Malacoda commands the escort to keep an eye out for sinners rising above the pitch, and to take the travellers

> ... 'infino all'altro scheggio
> che tutto intero va sopra le tane.'

> ... *as far as the next ridge*
> *which goes unbroken across all the dens.'*[17]

At this the demons gnash their teeth and make threatening grimaces. Dante is alarmed and begs Virgil to go on with him alone, but Virgil is unperturbed. 'Let them gnash as much they like,' he says, 'they're only doing it to frighten the sinners.'

And so they move off. But first the demons put their tongues between their teeth, as though in a knowing sign to Barbariccia, who is to lead them. He, in his turn, sounds the advance, not with a bugle but with a fart. With this defiant raspberry, no doubt sounded by the reader, the canto comes to an end, to the rowdy response of the audience.

The following opens with Dante's ironic reflection that never in all his military experience had he heard so strange a signal, not from horsemen moving camp or starting an attack, or mustering, or beating a retreat, not in the forays of scouts, or in the clash of tournaments or the running of jousts; he had heard bells and drums and signals from the tops of castles and many a device, both Italian and foreign, but never had he seen cavalry or infantry move off or ships set sail to the sound of so strange a trumpet. 'Oh, well,' he says with a shrug:

> Noi andavamo con li diece demoni.
>   Ahi fiera compagnia! Ma nella chiesa
>   coi santi, ed in taverna co' i ghiottoni.

> *We went escorted by that troop of ten.*
>   *Fierce company! Ah well, with saints at church,*
>   *and in company with gluttons at an inn.*[18]

As they move along, Dante watches the sinners come up above the pitch for some relief, like dolphins when their humped backs warn sailors of approaching storm. They lie like frogs in a ditch with their muzzles poking out but as soon as Barbariccia draws near they dive down again. One wretched soul – Dante shudders to remember it – leaves it too late and Graffiacane hooks him by his tarry hair and holds him up. 'He looked to me,' Dante recalls, 'like an otter.' The demons shout to Rubicante to take the skin off him. Meanwhile Dante asks Virgil to find out who he is.

The wretched soul reveals himself as a native of Navarre, whose father had been a spendthrift and whose mother had placed him in the service of a nobleman; he later became a retainer of King Thibaut,[19] in whose service he was guilty of corruption, for which he is now paying the price. He does not give his name but early commentators identified him as Ciampolo, or Gian Polo, about whom nothing else is known. He refers to Thibaut as the *buon re* ('good king') and a reputation for virtue and valour is found also in accounts of him in mediaeval French poems. Dante must have read of an untrustworthy retainer in his service. He attributes to him a talent for trickery, for when Virgil asks him if he can name any Latin sinners in the pitch, he first refers to two of a neighbouring race, namely Sardinians,[20] Fra Gomita and Michele Zanche, who never stop talking about their native island.[21] This information is conveyed with difficulty, for as he speaks he is being mauled and maltreated by several demons. To escape them, he offers to bring up seven sinners from Tuscany and Lombardy. If his tormentors will back off a moment he will whistle to the sinners as a signal that all is clear, which is their custom if any of them gets to the surface. Cagnazzo doesn't trust him but Alichino says, 'Let's hide behind the bridge and he'll soon see we are more than a match for him.'

Dante announces the next scene with gusto:

O tu che leggi, udirai nuovo ludo.

Reader, a novel scene thou now wilt hear.[22]

The word *ludo* is a theatrical term, meaning a play or a scene, and the action he is about to describe is indeed a novel one.

Choosing his time well, Ciampolo plants his feet on the ground and with a sudden leap escapes into the pitch. Alichino flies after him but is too late, like a falcon which misses its prey and flies up again, vexed and discouraged. Calcabrina, enraged, sets upon Alichino and both fall into the boiling pitch, where they flounder, helpless. Barbariccia sends four other demons to the opposite bank to scoop them out with their grappling hooks. This is a rollicking piece of devil-play, worthy of clowns at a circus, showing the range of Dante's talents as a popular entertainer.

It is followed in the next canto by a contrasting moment of calm. As the two poets walk on alone, in silence, without an escort, one behind the other like Franciscan friars, Dante thinks of Aesop's fable of the frog and the mouse.[23] That story and what has just happened seem so alike that two words meaning the same thing could not be more so. This thought leads to another and Dante reflects, 'The fiends have been made ridiculous through us and I think this will greatly annoy them. They'll be after us faster than a dog after a hare.' He keeps looking behind him, his hair on end with terror. 'Master,' he says, 'best quickly hide us both. I'm afraid of the Evil-Claws and feel them behind us already.' Virgil in a stately and long-winded reply, which adds to the tension, agrees. The devils, wings outstretched, are already racing after them. Virgil snatches Dante in his arms, as a mother would a child from a burning house, and slides down the ravine with him:

Lo duca mio di subito mi prese,
    come la madre ch'al rumore è desta
    e vede presso a sè le fiamme accese,
che prende il figlio e fugge e non s'arresta,
    avendo più di lui che di sè cura,
    tanto che solo una camicia vesta;
e giù dal collo della ripa dura
    supin si diede alla pendente roccia,
    che l'un de' lati all'altra bolgia tura.

Non corse mai sì tosto acqua per doccia
a volger ruota di molin terragno,
quand' ella più verso le pale approccia,
come 'l maestro mio per quel vivagno,
portandosene me sovra 'l suo petto,
come suo figlio, non come compagno.

My leader then at once caught hold of me,
and as a mother, wakened by a noise,
who close at hand sees flames and instantly
her infant snatches to her breast and flees,
of herself heedless, caring more for him,
casting upon her only a chemise,
so down that rock-face from its topmost rim
he slithered on his back and came at last
where other ramparts the next gulley stem.
Never, I vow, through any sluice so fast,
to turn a land-mill's wheel, did water run,
even when closest to the blades it passed,
as did my Master down that slope rush on,
holding me to his bosom as he went,
not like his comrade then, but like his son.[24]

This moment of tenderness comes as a moving contrast to the coarse raillery that has preceded it, the more so as it is Virgil who was wrong about the devils and Dante who was right. They are safe now, however, for Providence, which set the fiends as guardians of the Fifth Circle, deprived them of all power to go beyond it. The last we see of them is as they stand thwarted on the top of the cliff looking down on their intended victims who have escaped. Another peril has passed.

A further masterly contrast now occurs. After the breakneck pace of the devil-play and the rapid escape of Dante and Virgil comes the slow, slow pacing of souls weighed down by heavy leaden cloaks. These are hypocrites, who used pretence of virtue to gain hidden ends. Their cloaks are gilded and their hoods, drawn over their eyes, are of the same style as the cowls worn by the monks of Cluny.[25] So burdensome are they that those which Frederick imposed were in comparison as light as straw:[26]

Oh in eterno faticoso manto!

Oh mantle, wearisome eternally![27]

The souls move so slowly that with every stride Dante and Virgil draw level with a new one. Dante asks Virgil to look behind as they go to see if any is known by name or deed. Someone behind them, recognizing Dante's Tuscan speech, calls out:

> ... 'Tenete i piedi,
> voi che correte sì per l'aura fosca!
> Forse ch'avrai da me quel che tu chiedi.'

> ... *'Slow down your speed,*
> *you two who go so quickly through the gloom!*
> *It may be I can satisfy thy need.'*[28]

Dante looks back and sees two who strive to catch up but are slowed down by their heavy cloaks and the narrow path. When they draw level, being unable to lift their heads, they look sideways at him for a while and one says to the other: 'This man seems to be alive, from the movement of his throat. If they are dead, by what privilege are they not wearing the heavy stole?' Then addressing Dante they say:

> ... 'O Tosco, ch'al collegio
> dell'ipocriti tristi se' venuto,
> dir chi tu se' non avere in dispregio.'

> ... *'Tuscan, who to the clan*
> *of melancholy hypocrites art come,*
> *to tell us who thou art do not disdain.'*[29]

Dante does not give his name but replies merely:

> ... 'I' fui nato e cresciuto
> sovra 'l bel fiume d'Arno alla gran villa,
> e son col corpo ch' i' ho sempre avuto.'

> ... *'I grew up and was born*
> *in the great town on Arno's lovely stream,*
> *and wear the body I have always worn.'*[30]

The reason for the insistence on Dante's Tuscan speech and Florentine origin is made plain when the two souls reveal who they are. In 1266, after the Battle of Benevento between Charles of Anjou and King Manfred of Sicily, there was turbulence in Florence between Guelfs and Ghibellines. In an attempt to settle matters, Catalano de' Malavolti, a Guelf, and Loderingo di Landolo, a Ghibelline, both of Bologna, were appointed jointly to the office of *podestà* in Florence. They were members of the Order of the Knights of Our Lady, known as the *Frati Gaudenti* (Jovial Friars). Owing to their maladministration, their term of office ended in an anti-Ghibelline rising in which the houses of the Uberti were sacked and burned.[31] Dante, who would have heard of these events in his boyhood, was evidently brought up in the belief that Catalano and Loderingo were hypocrites acting in their own interests. He is about to reply to them when he catches sight of a figure on the ground, crucified with three stakes. On seeing Dante he writhes and blows into his beard, sighing. Fra Catalano explains that this is he who advised that it was expedient that one man should die for the sake of the people.[32] This is Caiaphas, suffering the weight of all the leaden-mantled hypocrites who pass over him. In the same ditch is his father-in-law and all the members of the council who sowed so ill a seed for Jews. Virgil gazes in amazement at the crucified figure, 'racked so shamefully in everlasting exile'.

Caiaphas is here seen as the arch-hypocrite who gave what seemed like disinterested advice for concealed motives of political interest. He, together with Annas and the members of the Sanhedrin, bear the weight of all evil perpetrated in hypocrisy against the innocent, in this case against the Man without sin. Here is the supreme crime committed in the name of religion and the public good. The spectacle is left uncommented, being in itself sufficiently significant.

The canto ends with Virgil's realization of the true depth of the devils' trickery. He asks Fra Catalano if there is any route by which they can arrive at the next unbroken bridge. From his reply it is apparent that all the bridges across the sixth ditch are broken. Virgil is much put out. 'That was bad advice they gave us,' he says and Catalano, in his Bolognese accent, replies mockingly, 'I heard in Bologna that the devil was a master of lies.' Virgil moves off, piqued, with great strides. Dante follows dutifully,

dietro alle poste delle care piante.

the imprints following of those dear feet.[33]

CHAPTER 22

A Den of Thieves

C anto XXIV of *Inferno* opens with one of the loveliest similes of the work. The effect on Dante of the sudden clouding of Virgil's face and his return to serenity is compared to the feelings of a shepherd who seeing the ground covered in hoarfrost goes back in despair into his house, believing it is snow. Going out again, he sees the world transformed:

In quella parte del giovanetto anno
    che 'l sole i crin sotto l'Aquario tempra
    e già le notti al mezzo dì sen vanno,
quando la brina in su la terra assempra
    l'imagine di sua sorella bianca,
    ma poco dura alla sua penna tempra;
lo villanello a cui la roba manca,
    si leva, e guarda, e vede la campagna
    biancheggiar tutta; ond'ei si batte l'anca,
ritorna in casa, e qua e là si lagna,
    come 'l tapin che non sa che si faccia;
    poi riede, e la speranza ringavagna,
veggendo il mondo aver cangiata faccia
    in poco d'ora, e prende suo vincastro,
    e fuor le pecorelle a pascer caccia.
Così mi fece sbigottir lo mastro
    quand'io li vidi sì turbar la fronte,
    e così tosto al mal giunse lo 'mpiastro.

In the first quarter of the youthful year
    when in Aquarius the sun his locks
    refreshes and the nights departing are
towards the south, and when the hoarfrost mocks
    her snowy sister's image on the ground,
    though not for long her pen maintains its strokes,
the shepherd, rising early, gazes round
    in search of fodder, sees the land all white,
    and slaps his thigh, dismayed at what he's found.

> *He goes back in, lamenting at his plight,*
> *   restless, dismayed, knowing not what to do,*
> *   comes out, and gathers hope at a fresh sight:*
> *the world's face all at once has been made new.*
> *   Taking his crook in hand, he drives to pasture*
> *   his flock of sheep, as he intended to.*
> *So I lost courage when I saw my master,*
> *   his countenance all clouded with dismay,*
> *   and just as soon there came the healing plaster.*[1]

The 'plaster' that heals is the sweet look (*piglio dolce*) which Virgil turns on him, the same look, Dante says, that he first beheld at the foot of the mountain. This is an intimate detail of their relationship, reminding the reader of the *lieto volto* ('sweet look') with which Virgil encouraged Dante to enter the gateway of Hell. In a further touch of loving comradeship, Virgil, having carefully inspected the rocks up which they must climb, gathers Dante in his arms and lifts him up towards the top of a great boulder. 'Take hold of the next,' he says, 'but try first if it will hold you.' The strenuous climb is graphically described, the pauses in the second line skilfully conveying breathlessness:

> Non era via da vestito di cappa,
>   chè noi a pena, ei lieve, e io sospinto,
>   potevam su montar di chiappa in chiappa.

> *This was no way for heavy-mantled folk,*
> *   for we, he light, and I pushed from below,*
> *   could scarcely clamber up from rock to rock.*[2]

The rise, fortunately, is less steep than the one behind them, since the ditches of the Eighth Circle all slope downwards, their slant making each succeeding side lower than the one before. Even so, by the time they reach the top Dante is out of breath. Unable to go further, he sits down to rest.

But Virgil will have none of that. 'Lying on feathers under blankets is no way to fame,' he says. 'There is a steeper stair than this for us to climb.' This is an element of narrative structure that anticipates what is to come: the climb from the centre of the earth up through the southern hemisphere. At this point, however, the listener's curiosity is merely aroused. Dante puts on a brave face and, pretending to be less breathless than he is, talks as he goes along. The climb is still rugged and narrow and steep. At last they stand on the crest of a bridge but Dante can see nothing in the darkness. He asks, therefore, to cross the bridge and climb down some way into the ditch so that he can see as well as hear. Virgil consents. The sight that awaits them is repulsive in the extreme.

Snakes were a feature of the primitive tales about St Paul's vision of Hell. Dante now handles the subject with supreme mastery. Here are snakes to end all snakes. Here are serpents of all kinds: not Libya, Ethiopia or Arabia can compare, for all the reptilian monsters they may boast: chelydri, jaculi, pharae, cenchres and amphisbaena. He is quoting from the list of snakes in Lucan's *Pharsalia*,[3] a signal that he has taken up the challenge and intends to surpass all predecessors in bravura. Amid this *cruda e tristissima copia* ('cruel and repulsive plenitude') run the souls of thieves, naked and in terror, with no hope of hiding place or heliotrope.[4] Their hands are tied behind them with snakes, of which the heads and tails coil round their loins, forming a knot in front. As the poets watch, they see a soul run near them. A serpent stings him where his neck and shoulder join. Quick as a flash, or, as Dante says, his hand moving rapidly across his manuscript, 'quicker than O or I was ever written', the soul takes fire and burns away to ash. Immediately the ash reforms into the shape it had before.

As a relief to the description of this loathsome scene, Dante now decorates his page, as in a miniature, with a picture of a phoenix:

Così per li gran savi si confessa
   che la fenice more e poi rinasce,
   quando il cinquecentesimo anno appressa:
erba nè biada in sua vita non pasce,
   ma sol d'incenso lacrime e d'amomo,
   e nardo e mirra son l'ultime fasce.

Just so the phoenix dies and, as we hear,
   is born again, from what great sages tell,
   when it approaches its five-hundredth year:
no herbs nor any grain it eats at all
   but only drops of incense and amomum;
   while spikenard and myrrh provide its pall.[5]

Dante had read this description in Ovid's *Metamorphoses*.[6] It evidently pleased him for he quotes it almost word for word.

The mythical, exotic rebirth of the phoenix intensifies with its contrast the horror of the lurid re-forming of the soul from its pile of ash. Like someone felled to the ground by diabolic power or paralysing stroke, who on rising looks round in bewilderment, so the wretched soul appears when he stands up, an example of the power of God who rains such blows in vengeance. On being asked who he is, the soul, in a continuation of the metaphor, replies, 'I rained from Tuscany not long ago into this savage gullet.'

'Vita bestial mi piacque e non umana,
   sì che a mul ch' i' fui. Son Vanni Fucci
   bestia, e Pistoia mi fu degna tana.'

'A beast-like life I chose, not of a man,
*   just like the mule I was. I am that beast*
*   Vanni Fucci, of Pistoia, my just den.'*[7]

This is a name to strike horror into Dante's first listeners, especially Tuscans. Dante knew him as a murderer, 'a man of blood and rage', and asks Virgil what he is doing in this ditch, instead of among the violent in the Seventh Circle. Vanni Fucci overhears and is infuriated that Dante has found him here. Nevertheless he is not permitted to dissemble. Colouring with shame he admits that he stole from the sacristy of Pistoia Cathedral, famed for its treasure, and that an innocent man was blamed for the theft.

Pistoia is associated in Dante's mind with the disastrous beginnings of the feud in Florence between Black and White Guelfs, for it was from there that the division originally spread, leading ultimately to the domination of the Blacks and so to Dante's exile. To revenge himself for having to confess to Dante his sacrilegious crime, Vanni Fucci maliciously foretells that the Whites, having helped to drive the Blacks from Pistoia, will themselves be driven out of Florence:

'E detto l'ho perchè dolor ti debbia!'

'And I have told thee this to give thee pain!'[8]

With this spiteful gibe the canto ends, but not the episode of Vanni Fucci, who, sacrilegious thief that he is, opens the next canto by making an obscene gesture in the face of God:

Al fine delle sue parole il ladro
    le mani alzò con amendue le fiche,
    gridando: 'Togli, Dio, ch'a te le squadro!'

The thief, his words concluded, hands on high,
*   made with them both the sign of figs and shrieked:*
*   'God, take thou that, for thus I thee defy!'*[9]

No more obscene blasphemy could be devised for Vanni Fucci to commit. Dante's hatred of him is savage. He rejoices to see what happens next. Two snakes, friends to *him*, Dante says, coil themselves, one about Vanni's neck, stifling him, another about his arms, binding him so that he cannot move. Apostrophizing Pistoia, Dante calls on it to burn itself to ashes since it surpasses in wickedness those who founded it (an allusion to the tradition that the city was founded by the survivors of Catiline's army). His execration of Vanni Fucci is extraordinary: some personal resentment must underly it, the reasons for which are now unknown. Of all the sinners seen by him in Hell, he recalls, none did he see so arrogant in his defiance of God, not even Capaneus, the blasphemer.[10] Nor is his fate in Hell limited to being burned to ashes and reshaped. The centaur Cacus, relegated to this ditch for theft, instead of being in the company of his fellows in the Seventh Circle, comes raging past, shouting, 'Where is he, where is he, the evil-mouthing wretch?'[11] Cacus has more serpents coiled on his croup than there are in Maremma[12] and on his shoulders is a dragon, its wings stretched wide, and breathing fire. This is a dazzling mythological picture, like the phoenix and the winter panorama with which the canto begins, a decoration to the page, in this case heraldic.

The choreography of these transformations is masterly. Five thieves are identified, all Florentines: Agnello, Cianfa, Buoso, Francesco and Puccio. Hearing the name of one of them, Dante signals to Virgil to listen, laying a finger to his lips, *dal mento al naso* ('from chin to nose'), a glimpse of a gesture as vivid as if made before our eyes, probably made by the reader, perhaps Dante himself. What he is about to describe takes some believing, Dante warns: he hesitates to set it down, although he saw it. A serpent with six feet darts at one soul and fastens upon him. With its middle feet it grasps his belly, with its front paws it seizes his arms and sets its fangs in either cheek; the hind feet are spread over the thighs and its tail is thrust between them and stretched up over the loins behind:

Ellera abbarbicata mai non fue
   ad alber sì, come l'orribil fera
   per l'altrui membra avviticchiò le sue.
Poi s'appiccar come di calda cera
   fossero stati e mischiar lor colore,
   nè l'un nè l'altro già parea quel ch'era,
come procede innanzi dall'ardore
   per lo papiro suso un color bruno
   che non è nero ancora e 'l bianco more.

Never did ivy bind and cling so tight
   about a tree, as did that loathsome beast
   its members with the other's twine and plight.
Then, stuck together like hot wax, they dressed
   their several tints before my very eyes,
   till which was which I could not then have guessed,
just as when paper burns, as the flames rise
   we see a brown hue grow, not black as yet,
   although the white diminishes and dies.[13]

The six-footed monster turns out to be another thief, Cianfa, previously transformed. Two others, identified later as Buoso and Francesco, look on aghast and exclaim:

> ... 'Ohmè, Agnel, come ti muti!
> Vedi che già non se' nè due nè uno.'

> *... 'Alas, Agnel, how thou dost change!*
> *Already, look, thou'rt neither two nor one.'*[14]

Two heads now become one, two faces fuse, two arms and two fore-paws
swell to make two reptilian forequarters, thighs blend with legs, the belly
and the chest become such members as were never seen,

> e tal sen giò con lento passo.

> *and such, at a slow pace, it reeled away.*[15]

So far Dante has done little more than imitate Ovid when he describes the
sexual merging of Hermaphroditus with a Naiad:

> she entwines herself about him like a serpent ... as the ivy is wont to wind
> itself along the tall trunks of trees ... clinging to him with every limb as she
> holds fast ... the mingled bodies of the two are united, and one human shape
> is put upon them ... so when their bodies meet together in a firm embrace,
> they are no more two, and ... they can neither be styled woman nor boy; they
> seem to be neither and both.[16]

But now, as with a roll of drums, Dante calls the attention of his audience
to the way he is about to surpass both Lucan and Ovid. Lucan described
how of two soldiers, stung by serpents, Sabellus sank in putrefaction and
Nasidius swelled and burst inside his armour; Ovid described how Cadmus
killed a dragon sacred to Mars and was transformed to a serpent and how
the nymph Arethusa, pursued by a river-god, was changed into a fountain.
Dante envies neither poet:

> Taccia Lucano omai là dove tocca
>   del misero Sabello e di Nassidio,
>   e attenda a udir quel ch' or si scocca.
> Taccia di Cadmo e d'Aretusa Ovidio;
>   chè se quello in serpente e quella in fonte
>   converte poetando, io non lo 'nvidio.

> *Let Lucan silent be and talk not now*
>   *of poor Sabellus and Nasidius,*
>   *and listen to what shoots next from my bow.*
> *Let Ovid now no longer speak to us*
>   *of Cadmus, Arethusa, one a snake,*
>   *the other a fount: I am not envious.*[17]

Ovid never changed two forms face to face as Dante will now do.

The heavy line describing the blended monster is followed by a change of
pace and rhythm:

Come 'l ramarro sotto la gran fersa
   dei dì canicular, cangiando sepe,
   folgore par se la via attraversa
sì pareva, venendo verso l'epe
   delli altri due, un serpentello acceso,
   livido e nero come gran di pepe;
e quella parte onde prima è preso
   nostro alimento, all'un di lor trafisse;
   poi cadde giuso innanzi lui disteso.

Just as a lizard, with a quick, slick slither,
   flicks across the highway from hedge to hedge.
   fleeter than a flash, in the battering dog-day weather,
a fiery little monster, livid, in a rage,
   black as any peppercorn, came and made a dart
   at the guts of the others, and leaping to engage
one of the pair, it pierced him at the part
   through which we first draw food; then loosed its grip
   and fell before him, outstretched and apart.[18]

Now comes Dante's showpiece. Step by step he shows precisely how the serpent and the soul change forms. First the serpent splits its tail into a fork; the soul draws his feet together and the two legs merge into one without a seam; the forked tail takes on the shape of the other's vanished legs and its skin turns soft; arms draw into armpits and the serpent's paws are lengthened in proportion; the hind paws, twisted together, become the member which a man conceals; that of the wretched soul becomes two feet; smoke veils them both as they exchange colour; hair appears on one and on the other is stripped off; one stands, the other falls, both fixing the other with their *lucerne empie* ('baleful lamps'); the snout of the one that stands erect bulges into temples and of the superfluous matter two ears, a nose and lips are formed; the form that lies prostrate has its features elongated into a muzzle and inside its head it draws its ears,

come face le corna la lumaccia;

just like a snail when it pulls in its horns;[19]

the tongue which was whole and fit for speech divides and the forked one joins up; the smoke subsides.

Thus, Dante says, I saw that ballast change and interchange. Although bewildered by all the transformations, he recognizes Puccio by his limp and Francesco, who caused the Tuscan village Gaville much grief.

The whole canto is a demonstration of bravura, not only in the graphic descriptions but in the two contrasting pictorial interludes. Here is Dante displaying his skill, as in a master class. With assumed modesty, as though deprecating applause, he says, 'If my pen has been at fault, let the novelty of the events be my excuse.' From the episode of Vanni Fucci onwards, he is so much absorbed in rising to a challenge as a writer that he neglects to emphasize the message of the punishment of theft. A note of moral outrage is resumed in the following canto.

CHAPTER 23

Tongues of Fire

The 26th canto of *Inferno* opens with an imprecation against Florence. In addition to Vanni Fucci of Pistoia, Dante had chosen five Florentines as examples of the sin of theft. We now know nothing about them, except that they were all of noble families: Agnello dei Brunelleschi, Buoso degli Abati, Cianfa dei Donati, Francesco Guercio dei Cavalcanti and Puccio dei Galigai. Of 'squint-eyed' Francesco dei Cavalcanti it is said that he was murdered by the inhabitants of Gaville, a village in the Arno valley, and that his kinsmen avenged his death on the villagers. To Dante's contemporaries they would all five have been notorious. He now takes the occasion to reproach Florence for her ill fame, so widespread that her name is known throughout Hell:

> Godi, Fiorenza, poi che se' sì grande
> che per mare e per terra batti l'ali,
> e per lo 'nferno tuo nome si spande!
> Tra li ladron trovai cinque cotali
> tuoi cittadini onde mi ven vergogna,
> e tu in grande orranza non ne sali.
> Ma se presso al mattin del ver si sogna,
> tu sentirai di qua da picciol tempo
> di quel che Prato, non ch'altri, t'agogna.
> E se già fosse, non saría per tempo:
> così foss' ei, da che pur esser dee!
> chè più mi graverà, com' più m'attempo.

> *Florence, rejoice, so greatly art thou famed,*
> *o'er sea and land thy beating wings resound*
> *and even throughout Hell thou art proclaimed!*
> *Among the thieves five Florentines I found,*
> *whence, as I think of it, I feel disgrace,*
> *nor does great honour unto thee redound.*
> *But if near morning what we dream takes place,*
> *there will befall thee ere much time has gone*
> *what Prato and others crave will come apace.*

Were it so now, it would not be too soon:
  since it must be, so let it come to pass!
  The burden heavier weighs as time goes on.[1]

Dante is prophesying within the timeframe of the story and his phrase *picciol tempo* ('short space of time') is an allusion to the rioting that broke out on May Day 1300. Prato, a town in Tuscany about ten miles north-west of Florence, on the road to Pistoia, is cited as an example of the many enemies of Florence who enviously desire her downfall. His reference to his advancing age, however (*com' più m'attempo*), takes us to the period in which he is writing. In the years that had followed, many disasters befell Florence: not only the betrayal of the city by Charles of Valois and Corso Donati, followed by the exile of the White Guelfs, but later the collapse of a bridge that killed a great number of people, a fire in which over 2,000 houses were destroyed and many families ruined, as well as the deaths of the exiles who tried to return by force. All such doom he interprets as punishment for her corruption, a reflection that will the more grieve him the older he grows.[2]

After so many repulsive scenes, although he took pride in his skill in describing them, Dante the artist judged that the time had come to vary his effects. The ditches of the Eighth Circle have all been claustrophobic. In contrast he now opens up the scene by introducing a simile that lifts the imagination out of Hell to a peaceful hillside on a summer evening:

Quante il villan ch'al poggio si riposa,
  nel tempo che colui che 'l mondo schiara
  la faccia sua a noi tien meno ascosa,
come la mosca cede a la zanzara,
  vede lucciole giù per la vallea,
  forse colà dov' e' vendemmia ed ara;
di tante fiamme tutta risplendea
  l'ottava bolgia ...

As on a hillside where a serf at rest,
  when he whose beams of light upon us shine
  conceals his countenance from us the least,
when gnats replace the flies at day's decline,
  sees fireflies in the valley down below,
  where, it may be, he ploughs, and reaps the vine,
with flames of fire as many and just so
  the eighth ditch sparkled ...[3]

The flames conceal the souls of those who used their intellects to counsel deceit, leading others astray by means of their eloquence and cunning. Just as Elisha saw Elijah in his chariot vanish in a cloud of fire,[4] so every soul is hidden by a 'thievish' fire. One flame, divided at its tip, reminds Dante

of the pyre in which the two sons of Oedipus – Eteocles and Polynices
– died: such was their hatred of each other that the flames burning them
sprang apart. Virgil's reply introduces one of the most memorable episodes
in *Inferno*. Within the forked flame are the souls of Ulysses (Odysseus) and
Diomedes.

Dante did not read Greek. What he knew about the *Iliad* and the *Odyssey*
was derived from Latin sources, from Virgil's *Aeneid*, from Cicero and
from Horace, and from one other Roman author whose importance in this
connection will be discussed below. Dante had not read any of the twelfth-
or thirteenth-century accounts of the Trojan War. Nevertheless, he knew
that Ulysses and Diomedes were associated in various stratagems against
the Trojans and that Ulysses was held to be cunning. Virgil, the character
in *Inferno*, lists the misdeeds held against them: they beguiled Achilles to
desert Deidamia and join them in the war, concealing the prophecy of his
death; they stole the sacred image of Athene, believed to protect Troy; they
were associated in the trickery of the wooden horse. In the *Aeneid* Virgil
mentions only one of these three deeds as involving both Diomedes and
Ulysses, namely the theft of the image of Athene.[5] The deceiving of Achilles
is not mentioned in the *Aeneid* and in connection with the stratagem of the
horse Diomedes is not mentioned by name.

These joint actions do not alone explain the excitement Dante expresses
on hearing the identity of the souls:

> 'S'ei posson dentro da quelle faville
> parlar', diss'io, 'maestro, assai ten priego
> e ripriego, che il priego vaglia mille,
> che non mi facci dell'attender niego
> fin che la fiamma cornuta qua vegna:
> vedi che del disio ver lei piego!'

> *'If in those flames the souls have power of speech'*
> *said I, 'Master I beg thee and again*
> *I beg, a thousand times would I beseech*
> *that my entreaty thou wilt not disdain,*
> *to wait until the double flame draws near:*
> *see in my eagerness towards it I lean.'*[6]

Virgil consents. He has read the question in Dante's mind. But he tells
him to leave the talking to him. The reason for this was for a long time an
unsolved problem.

> 'Lascia parlare a me, ch'io ho concetto
> ciò che tu vuoi; ch'ei sarebbero schivi,
> perchè fuor greci, forse del tuo detto.'

'Leave me to speak to them, for I have guessed
  what thou dost want to know; and they, being Greeks,
  might be disdainful if by thee addressed.'[7]

Dante, an Italian, is a descendant of the Trojans, whom the Greeks defeated. But so is Virgil, a Roman. What, then, is the difference? The answer is twofold: Virgil has not only written of them in his *alti versi* ('noble lines'), he also has magical authority. The words he uses are in the form of a conjuration,[8] similar to those he has used to Charon and Minos:

'O voi che siete due dentro ad un foco,
  s'io meritai di voi mentre ch'io vissi,
  s'io meritai di voi assai o poco
quando nel mondo li alti versi scrissi,
  non vi movete; ma l'un di voi dica
  dove per lui perduto a morir gissi.'

'O you that in a single flame are two,
  if I deserved of you, ere life was spent,
  if much or little I deserved of you
when in the world I wrote with high intent,
  halt, I command: let one of you relate
  where, lost untimely, to his death he went.'[9]

What is this about a final, fatal voyage? In Homer's *Odyssey* Ulysses returns to Ithaca, slays the suitors of Penelope, quells a rebellion and settles down to resume his royal and domestic duties. This ending of the *Odyssey* was well known in the Middle Ages. The fourteenth-century commentator Benvenuto da Imola says that even schoolboys and dunces know that Ulysses got back to Ithaca and that Dante's account is not supported by any poetic tradition. In saying this Benvenuto, in common with modern commentators, strangely overlooked the origin of the story Dante tells.

In response to Virgil's command, the larger of the two horns of flame begins to toss and murmur as if blown by wind and the tip, waving to and fro like a tongue, flings forth a voice:

Indi la cima qua e là menando,
  come fosse la lingua che parlasse,
  gittò voce di fuori, e disse: 'Quando
mi diparti' da Circe, che sottrasse
  me più d'un anno là presso a Gaeta,
  prima che sì Enea la nomasse ...'

The tip, vibrating back and forth again,
  as if it were the tongue itself impelled
  to speak, threw out a voice, declaiming: 'When

from Circe I escaped, the same who held
me for a year and more, nearby Gaeta,
before thus by Aeneas it was called ...'[10]

Several questions arise. Why does Ulysses begin his tale at that point? Why
is he so precise about the length of time he was held by Circe? Why does he
mention Gaeta? Why does he refer to the fact that Aeneas named it thus?
The answers to these questions and to much else is to be found, not in Virgil,
not in Cicero, not in Horace, but in Ovid.

In the fifth story of Book XIII of the *Metamorphoses* Ovid begins a para-
phrase of the adventures of Aeneas, which, after interruptions, is resumed
in the second story of Book XIV. The two combine to form what might be
called a 'Reader's Digest' of the *Aeneid*. There is a summarized version of
Aeneas's departure from Troy, his arrival at Carthage and reception by Dido,
his departure from Africa and journey up the coast of Campania and arrival
at Cumae. A brief account is then given of Aeneas's visit to the Underworld
and his return to Cumae. When he reaches Gaeta, however, something
unexpected occurs which is not in the *Aeneid*.

In order to provide a link between the *Odyssey* and the *Aeneid*, Virgil had
introduced a survivor from among the Greeks. Coasting off Sicily, Aeneas
and his men put into harbour for the night, not far from Etna. The next
morning they come upon an unkempt stranger, his ragged clothes hooked
together with thorns, who approaches with arms outstretched in entreaty.
This is Achaemenides, from Ithaca, a comrade of Ulysses, who was left
behind in the cave of the Cyclops when the others made their escape. The
Trojans take him on board and receive from him an eyewitness account of
events that occurred in the *Odyssey*.

Ovid evidently admired this device, for he made use of it himself. When,
in his account of the Trojans' adventures, Aeneas and his men reach Gaeta,
they come upon yet another survivor from the crew of Ulysses. This is
Macareus of Neritos (mentioned neither in the *Odyssey* nor in the *Aeneid*).
He greets the Trojans and then in astonishment recognizes Achaemenides,
who gives him an account of the episode of Polyphemus, including a vivid
description of the escape of Ulysses and the surviving members of his crew,
with Polyphemus hurling rocks after the departing boats.

It is then the turn of Macareus. He takes up the story after the event of
the Cyclops, relating the episode of Aeolus and the winds, the arrival at the
ancient city ruled over by Antiphates, King of the giant cannibals (a city
later named Formia). One of their crew is devoured, the rest scurry to their
crafts, pursued by a shower of boulders which sink all but one boat. With
this depleted crew Ulysses proceeds to Circe's island. 'There,' says Macareus,
'we were detained for a year. During that long year I saw and heard many

things. Finally, when we were sluggish and inactive through idleness (*resides et desuetudine tardi*), we were ordered to embark once more. Circe had foretold that dangerous paths, a vast voyage and the perils of the raging sea awaited us. I was alarmed, I tell you frankly, and having reached Gaeta, here I stayed.' Here Macareus ended (*finierat Macareus*). Naturally, he had no more to tell.

This is the story Dante read in Ovid's *Metamorphoses*. It fired his imagination. What *happened* when Ulysses and his crew left Circe? How did they fare on that *iter vastum* ('vast journey'), the thought of which, Ovid said, so alarmed Macareus that he preferred to stay behind on the island? The storyteller in Dante responded to the storyteller in Ovid. *He* would continue the tale. He would make Ulysses number three in a series of eyewitnesses, beginning with Achaemenides and Macareus. That is why he makes Ulysses begin his story with the departure from Circe, why he refers to the length of time he was held prisoner by her, why he mentions Aeneas's naming of Gaeta. He is quoting Ovid almost word for word, and *he* will now complete the story that Ovid left unfinished. Once more he will surpass his distinguished predecessor.

Where does Dante send Ulysses on his *iter vastum*? Not home to Ithaca but on a vaster journey than any account related in stories taken from the *Odyssey*: he sends him to the southern hemisphere. Not only does he extend his exploration beyond all imagining, he extends the character of Ulysses too, from the conniving Greek hero to an image of unredeemed Man, who in his restless daring and thirst for discovery cannot be deterred from pushing beyond forbidden boundaries, who eats, that is, the fruit of the tree of knowledge. A contrast with Aeneas, divinely guided on *his* journey, is here implied.

The ancient world had declared the Ocean innavigable beyond the Pillars of Hercules, a region of *nulla aut ignota sidera* ('nothing but unknown stars'), which no human eye beholds (*humanus oculus non videt*), stated a twelfth-century map. The mediaeval imagination added monsters, excessive heat, excessive cold, magnetic rocks, violent winds and mountainous waves. Perhaps there was inhabited land, but *nullus nostrum ad illos, neque illorum ad nos pervenire potest* ('none of us can go to them, and none of them can come to us').[11] Not everyone, however, thought that the journey was impossible. Albertus Magnus said tantalizingly, *difficilis est transitus, non impossibilis* ('the crossing is difficult but not impossible').

Dante took from these hints and half-beliefs what he required for his own cosmology. At the antipodes of Jerusalem he visualizes rising from the ocean the highest mountain in the world. This is later revealed as the Mountain of Purgatory, on the summit of which is the Garden of Eden. To try to reach it across the southern ocean is an act of arrogance. The shaping spirit of Dante's imagination brings to Ovid's unfinished story not a Ulysses longing to return to his son, his father and his wife, but Ulysses the voyager in whom nothing can conquer the restless ardour to explore:

'Nè dolcezza di figlio, nè la pièta
   del vecchio padre, nè il debito amore
   lo qual dovea Penelopè far lieta
vincer poter dentro da me l'ardore
   ch'i' ebbi a divenir del mondo esperto,
   e delli vizi umani e del valore.'

'Not fondness for my son, not piety
   towards my agèd sire, not lawful love
   which should have gladdened my Penelope
could conquer in me the desire to rove
   about the world and to explore its ways,
   and human wickedness and worth to prove.'[12]

Ulysses recites the story of his foolhardy voyage. With but one ship and the few survivors of his crew, he set forth on the open sea. Sailing westwards on the Mediterranean they came to the outlet where Hercules set up his landmarks beyond which men were forbidden to pass. He and his companions were then old and weary: *Io e' compagni eravam vecchi e tardi* ... .[13] Dante here uses Ovid's very word *tardi*, an indication of how vivid the Latin account is in his mind. At this point Ulysses combines the daring voyager with the counsellor who gives evil advice. Urging on his men, he begged them, after so many perils passed, not to refuse this last experience of an unpeopled world:

'Considerate la vostra semenza:
   fatti non foste a viver come bruti,
   ma per seguir virtute e conoscenza.'

'Think of your lineage: men such as you
   have not been made to live the life of brutes,
   but fortitude and knowledge to pursue.'[14]

His 'little speech', Ulysses continued, so inspired his crew that he could then have scarcely held them back. With their stern pointing east, their oars like wings, they continued their *folle volo* ('mad flight'), losing sight of all northern stars except the Wain, seeing now only unknown stars. Five times they had seen the moon change from full to crescent, when, suddenly, dark in the distance, there loomed up a mountain higher than he had ever seen. They all rejoiced but soon their gladness turned to lamentation. A storm rose up from the new land and struck the forepart of the ship:

'Tre volte il fe' girar con tutte l'acque:
     alla quarta levar la poppa in suso
     e la prora ire in giù, com' altrui piacque,
infin che 'l mar fu sopra noi richiuso.'

'Three times the whirling waters round us sped,
     and at the fourth they lifted high the poop,
     the prow went under, as had been decreed,
till over us the engulfing sea closed up.'[15]

Here the canto ends.

This speech by Ulysses is one of the most celebrated in *Inferno*. The episode is quite unlike any other. It has nothing to do with party strife, the corruption of Florence or Dante's exile. The conception of a daring diso-bedience, undertaken for noble, inspiring reasons, presents Dante with a dilemma he feels the necessity to confront. He himself, like Ulysses, is filled with an ardour to pursue knowledge. He admits his own danger of being tempted beyond a boundary. He grieved then at what he saw, he grieves again at the memory:

e più lo 'ngegno affreno ch' i' non soglio
     perchè non corra che virtù nol guidi;
     sì che, se stella bona o miglior cosa
m'ha dato 'l ben, ch'io stesso nol m'invidi.

and more than I am wont my mind I curb,
     lest it may run where good does not permit;
     if by the stars or better things I'm blessed
with intellect, may I not forfeit it.[16]

The universality and timelessness of the theme make it a challenge still.[17]

CHAPTER 24

The Severed Head

We return from the wide ocean in which Ulysses perished to the deep valley of the Counsellors of Fraud. The waving, speaking tip, now upright, is silent and already the double flame, set free by Virgil's magic formula of dismissal, is moving on. Another flame approaches, drawn by the Lombard dialect it has recognized in the words in which Virgil releases Ulysses from his conjuration:

'Istra ten va; più non t'adizzo.'

'Now go; no longer do I conjure thee.'[1]

The word *istra* is a Lombardism for *now*. From this we learn that Dante imagined Virgil speaking in the patois and accent of his native Lombardy. This touch of realism stretches the conventional agreement between author and reader. We do not ask in which language Virgil speaks to Ulysses, a Greek. We accept that the souls of the dead can communicate with one another without being told what tongue they use and that, for purposes of narrative, all the dialogue is rendered in the language in which the author has chosen to write his work.[2] We are now led to assume that Virgil's Lombard speech was converted into Greek for the benefit of Ulysses and that Ulysses' speech, which must have been in Greek, was converted in its turn into Tuscan for Dante to report. From this it appears that arrangements in Hell have long anticipated those of the United Nations.

The flame approaching conceals the soul of Guido da Montefeltro, the leader of the Ghibellines of Romagna who lived from 1223 to 1298. He was famous for devious stratagems and acquired the nickname of 'The Fox'. He conspired repeatedly against the Papacy and was excommunicated. Later in life he repented and was reconciled to the Church, eventually entering the Franciscan Order.

Unable to see in his *cieco mondo* ('blind world'), he asks if the speaker has come recently from the sweet land of Italy and whether he can say if there is war or peace in Romagna. Dante is gazing down intently and Virgil nudges him, saying: 'Speak thou: he is Italian.' There is no risk of disdain here, nor any language problem. Dante reports that though the tyrants of Romagna always have war in their hearts, there was no warfare there when he left. After bringing the soul up to date concerning the present balance of power, he asks who he is. Believing that what he says can never be repeated on earth, the soul reveals his identity and relates the story of his damnation.

His account makes plain Dante's chief purpose in selecting him as a further example of the sin of counselling fraud: the deceitful involvement in his fate of Pope Boniface. Not content with ingeniously placing him among the Simonists before his death,[3] Dante again contrives his presence in *Inferno*. Guido da Montefeltro, now a Franciscan, had made his peace with God, having repented of his many wily deceptions, when he was approached by Boniface who asked him for advice in his war against his enemies, the Colonna family. 'The Prince of the new Pharisees', as Guido calls him, making war not on infidels in the Holy Land but on his fellow Christians, seduced him, a penitent, to commit further sin, tricking him into believing that he could grant him absolution there and then: 'Thou knowest I have the power to lock and unlock Heaven.' Guido yielded and advised a deceitful strategy, trusting in the Pope's assurance that all would be well. A sad awakening awaited him at death. St Francis came for him but was challenged by a black cherub, who said: 'No-one can be absolved who does not repent and no-one can repent and will to commit sin at the same time: the contradiction does not allow it.' He carried off the wretched Guido, saying 'Perhaps thou didst not think I was logical.' Brought before Minos, Guido watched him coil his tail eight times round his body. Then, biting it in rage, that connoisseur of evil proclaimed, 'Here's one for the thievish fire.'

The struggle between a good and evil spirit for the possession of a soul at death was often represented in mediaeval stories and paintings. Dante has returned to the devil-play in which he indulged in describing the fate of the swindlers, but there is no rollicking mockery here. The logic of the black cherub, a fallen member of the angelic order who have perfect knowledge of God, is weightier than the dishonest persuasion of a corrupt Pope in whom Guido had foolishly trusted. Is this a reflection of an attempt by Boniface to compromise Dante during his converse with him in 1301? Something lies at the back of this presentation of the Pope at his blackest: to connive at the damnation of another soul is worse than simony. It is Dante's triumph to have placed him, by implication, in two places in Hell at once. He is gradually settling a score but has not finished yet.

The battle between St Francis and the black cherub is balanced structurally by a similar battle for the soul of Guido's son, Buonconte da Montefeltro, which has a happier outcome.[4] This, the second anticipation of *Purgatorio*, immediately follows the glimpse of the Mountain in the speech of Ulysses in the preceding canto and is one of the many structural links that bind the work together.

The ninth ditch of the Eighth Circle, containing the souls of those who caused schism, is a gruesome image of war. This is one of the darkest moments in Dante's imagining of Hell. The unity of mankind is continually broken by the creators of discord, whether in religious schism, civil war, party strife or family feuds. The endless repetition of human conflict is evoked by an attempt to suggest the accumulated horror of battlefields from the beginning of history to Dante's own time:

> Chi porria mai pur con parole sciolte
>   dicer del sangue e delle piaghe a pieno
>   ch' i' ora vidi, per narrar più volte?
> Ogne lingua per certo verrìa meno
>   per lo nostro sermone e per la mente
>   c' hanno a tanto comprender poco seno.

> *Who, though with words from rhyme set free, could tell*
>   *of all the blood and wounds which I saw then,*
>   *though trying many times to no avail?*
> *All language, certainly, would be in vain;*
>   *our speech and memories have little room*
>   *so much to comprehend or to contain.*[5]

Here is Dante looking back, and indeed as we not only looking back but looking on around us also do, at the soul-defying inhumanity of man to man, helpless before the age-long and continuing spectacle of cruelty and carnage. All he can do is to represent it in images of butchery in his description of the punishment of those who spread discord and thus divide the unity of mankind. The chief of these, in his view, is Mahomet, the greatest renegade from Christianity. He and all the others proceed round the ditch, passing before a devil with an upraised sword, to be cleft and cleft again, their shadowy flesh uniting as they complete their circling. Dante's first sight of him reminds him of a broken wine vat:

> Già veggia, per mezzul perdere o lulla,
>   com' io vidi un, così non si pertugia,
>   rotto dal mento infin dove si trulla:
> tra le gambe pendevan le minugia;
>   la corata pareva e 'l tristo sacco
>   che merda fa di quel che si trangugia.

> *Never did wine-tub, losing stave or cant,*
>   *so split itself asunder as the one*
>   *I saw, from chin to fart-hole cleft and rent.*

Dangling between his legs his guts were shown,
  his vitals all exposed and the foul sack
  which turns to shit whatever we gulp down.[6]

Of all the lowly language Dante permits himself to use, these lines are among the most vulgar and the most coarse. We are among the maimed and mutilated; no illustrious vernacular will serve here. To produce a reaction of disgust Dante has recourse to images of butchery. He knew what he was describing: he had been in battle and had looked on carnage.

The soul, seeing Dante staring at him, rips his chest apart with his hands and says: 'See how I split myself! See how Mahomet is mangled! Ahead of me goes Ali, his face cloven from chin to forelock.'[7] He then asks Dante who he is, lingering on the ridge, perhaps to delay going to his own penalty. Virgil replies for him: 'Death does not bring him here, nor guilt, but I who am dead am charged to lead him down through Hell, from ring to ring, that he may learn it all.' At this more than a hundred souls, forgetting their torment in their amazement, stand still to stare at Dante. Mahomet, one foot raised, ready to move on, sends a cruelly ironic message to a certain Fra Dolcino, still alive, advising him to get in a good supply of food to ward against the snow, otherwise the victory of the Novarese will be gained too easily.[8] For us this is now meaningless, but contemporaries will have interpreted it easily, knowing that Fra Dolcino and his heretical sect known as the Apostolic Brothers, against whom Pope Clement V had ordered a crusade in 1305, held out against Papal forces in the hills near Novara and were forced to surrender in the snow for want of food. Having shot this spiteful bolt, Mahomet sets his foot to the ground and goes his way.

His place is taken by another soul, his throat slashed, his nose lopped off, one ear sliced away, his windpipe showing scarlet. He is Piero da Medicina, famed for creating discord between the Polenta and Malatesta families in Romagna. As a mischief maker, spreading lies, poking his nose into the affairs of others, listening to slander, he is punished symbolically in his mutilations. Dante may have known him personally, for Piero recognizes him and tells him to warn two noblemen of Fano of the terrible fate that awaits them:

'E fa sapere a' due miglior di Fano,
    a messer Guido e anco ad Angiolello,
    che se l'antiveder qui non è vano,
gittati saran fuor di loro vasello
    e mazzerati presso alla Cattolica
    per tradimento d'un tiranno fello.
Tra l'isola di Cipri e la Maiolica
    non vide mai sì gran fallo Nettuno,
    non da pirate, non da gente argolica.

Quel traditor che vede pur con l'uno
    e tien la terra che tal è qui meco
    vorrebbe di vedere esser digiuno,
farà venirli a parlamento seco;
    poi farà sì ch'al vento di Focara
    non sarà lor mestier voto nè preco.'

'And I advise, to Fano's two best men,
    Guido and Angiolello, let it be known
    that, if our future knowledge is not vain,
they will be seized and over shipboard thrown
    near La Cattolica, in a stone-filled sack,
    by a false tyrant tricked and left to drown.
From Cyprus to Majorca crime so black
    Neptune ne'er saw, neither by pirates done,
    nor Argonauts who ill fame do not lack.
That traitor, seeing with one eye alone,
    who rules the land that he beside me here
    wishes he ne'er had seen nor come upon,
will lure them unsuspecting to confer
    and will so deal that they Focara's wind
    need not propitiate with vow or prayer.'[9]

This passage contains the prophecy of a murder by the ruler of Rimini, 'one-eyed' Malatestino, of two noblemen of Fano who stood in the way of his ambition to gain possession of their city. He is said to have tricked them into sailing up the Adriatic to meet him for a parley and to have arranged for them to be seized and drowned before they reached the dangerous, windy promontory of Focara. Dante's use of the word *mazzerati* is graphic: it means 'tied into a sack weighted with stones' and gives a particularly horrifying touch to the crime. The outrage is said to have occurred in about 1312 and was therefore fresh in Dante's mind and in the minds of his first listeners. It is odd that he introduces it here, for the murder, sensational as it was, was not specifically a dividing of the body politic or a schism.

He gives it, however, august importance by linking it to an event in ancient Roman history, Curio's encouragement of Julius Caesar to take his army across the Rubicon: an example of the sin of spreading discord and so dividing the body politic.[10] His soul is beside that of Piero, who, on being asked by Dante to make his meaning plain, pulls down Curio's jaw and reveals his truncated tongue: once so bold of speech, he can no longer talk.

Another soul, lifting the mutilated stumps of both arms, from which the blood streams down over his face, identifies himself as Mosca dei Lamberti, whose fatal words, *capo ha cosa fatta* ('a thing done has an end'), led to the murder of Buondelmonte, who, betrothed to a daughter of the Amidei family, jilted her for one of the Donati. To this event Florentines traced the origin of the strife between Guelfs and Ghibellines in their city.

The last example chosen is the troubadour Bertran de Born,[11] who fomented a quarrel between Henry II of England and his son Prince Henry, an intervention that Dante compares to the action of Achitophel who made trouble between Absalom and David.[12] Bertran is shown as a truncated torso, carrying his head by the hair and swinging it like a lantern. As he draws near the bridge from which Dante is looking down, he holds the head up high so that its words may be heard:

> Io vidi certo, ed ancor par ch'io 'l veggia,
>   un busto sanza capo andar sì come
>   andavan li altri della trista greggia;
> e 'l capo tronco tenea per le chiome
>   pèsol con mano a guisa di lanterna;
>   e quel mirava noi, e dicea, 'Oh me!'

> *I plainly saw, and still I seem to see,*
>   *a headless bust which followed in the tread*
>   *of those who formed that wretched company;*
> *and by the hair it held the severed head,*
>   *swinging it like a lantern in its hand;*
>   *it looked at us and 'Woe is me!', it said.*[13]

Despite the sinister context, Dante cannot resist amusing himself with the rhymes *come, chiome*, culminating mockingly in Bertran's ejaculation: '*Oh me*'.

It is not known when Bertran's alleged machinations made such a dire impression on Dante. He mentions him favourably in *Il Convivio*, together with others, as an example of generosity who lives on in our hearts,[14] and in *De Vulgari Eloquentia* as an illustrious author of poetry on the subject of war.[15] Over 40 of Bertran's poems have been preserved, of which the most famous is a lament on the death of Prince Henry, son of Henry II. Nothing is known historically of the part played by Bertran in the rebellion of the young prince against his father. Dante's source of information appears to have been a biography of him in Provençal, in which it is related that King Henry II hated Bertran as the evil counsellor of his son and the cause of the conflict between them. This account evidently changed Dante's good opinion of him, making him appear a fitting example of the sin of fomenting schism.

What is remarkable about Dante's selection of examples is that he mingles a figure such as Mahomet with recent mischief makers of much less account, perhaps to imply that *all* sowers of discord are responsible for the disunity of mankind.

The last image, the head of Bertran de Born, held on high like a lighted pumpkin and speaking in mid-air, is the most memorable of all. No more striking image of disunity could be contrived and with it the canto ends.

CHAPTER 25

The Valley of Disease

Gazing at the vast number of souls with their horrifying wounds, Dante feels so overwhelmed that he is about to weep. Virgil asks him ironically if he is trying to count the souls. If so, he must realize that the ditch is 22 miles round. This is the first indication of measurement, and various attempts have been made to calculate from it the proportions of the Eighth Circle. More important is the sense of defeat that Dante's grief implies. To mourn and linger over the world's history of conflict is to despair.

But Dante has also a personal reason for distress. He had been searching among the souls for one who is related to him by blood. Virgil tells him to think no more about him. He has seen the soul in question beneath the bridge, pointing threateningly at Dante, and has heard him called Geri del Bello. Dante realizes that the soul (a cousin of his father) resents that no vendetta has been carried out for his murder and he is moved to compassion for him.

In his commentary on the *Commedia*, Dante's son Pietro says that Geri was murdered by Brodario Sacchetti of Florence; he adds that the murder was later avenged by Geri's nephews. The affair of honour, as it was termed, was finally settled in 1342, when an act of reconciliation between the two families was signed, one of the signatories being Dante's half-brother Francesco, representing himself, his two nephews Pietro and Jacopo, and other members of the Alighieri family. It is not known whether the vendetta had already been carried out by the time Dante was writing Canto XXIX of *Inferno*, but his emotional involvement in the sufferings of Geri, tempered by the rational withdrawal counselled by Virgil, represents his awareness of the dangers of family feuds.

The horrors of fraud, represented under ten aspects in the Eighth Circle, become darker and Dante's reactions more despondent the deeper down he goes. The last group, that of falsifiers and impersonators, are shown afflicted with disease, ranging from physical illness to raving madness. Their lamentations pierce him so painfully that he blocks his ears with his hands to prevent the sound reaching him:

Quando noi fummo sor l'ultima chiostra
   di Malebolge, sì che i suoi conversi
   potean parere alla veduta nostra,
lamenti saettaron me diversi,
   che di pietà ferrati avean li strali;
   ond'io li orecchi con le mani copersi.

There, from the crossing-span's high altitude,
   Malbowges' final cloister all appears
   thrown open, with its sad lay-brotherhood;
and there, such arrowy shrieks, such lancing spears
   of anguish, barbed with pity, pierced me through,
   I had to clamp my hands against my ears.[1]

If all the sick from the malarial districts of Valdichiana, Maremma and Sardinia[2] were piled together, it would resemble the scene that now meets his eyes, while the stench that arises is that which comes from festering limbs. They descend from the long ridge on to the last bank so that they can see more clearly what unerring Justice, the handmaid of the Lord, has prepared as punishment for the souls of falsifiers.

Not all that he has read of the pestilence sent by Juno to depopulate the island of Aegina[3] can compare with the spectacle before him. The diseased lie helpless, one on his belly, one across the shoulders of another, one crawling on all fours; two sit leaning against each other,

   com' a scaldar si poggia tegghia a tegghia

   like pan to pan, together propped to warm[4]

Covered with scabs from head to foot, they peel them off with their nails, like a stable-boy currying a horse or a fishmonger scraping the scales off a fish. The squalor of their condition is matched by the pettiness of their misdeeds. Griffolino of Arezzo pretended he could fly and was burned to death as a magician. Capocchio of Siena met the same fate for alchemy. Two impersonators are shown in the throes of madness: Myrrha who indulged an incestuous passion for her father, the King of Cyprus, and gained access to his bed in disguise,[5] and Gianni Schicchi, a Florentine, who was persuaded by Simone Donati to impersonate his father who had just died and to dictate a new will in favour of Simone. This Gianni obligingly did, taking care to bequeath to himself also a handsome legacy and the best mare in the stables. He is described as a raving maniac who seizes Capocchio by the scruff of the neck and drags him along so that his belly scrapes the bottom of the ditch.

Perhaps the most repulsive description is that of the counterfeiter of coins, Master Adamo of Brescia. Afflicted with dropsy, his body has swollen to the shape of a lute and his parched lips curl one towards his chin, the other upwards. In his longing for moisture, he dreams of the rivulets that flow from the green hills of the Casentino down into the Arno. It was in that region that Adamo issued gold florins with one-eighth of alloy, for which crime he was put to death by burning. He speaks bitterly of his patrons, the Conti Guidi, who induced him to commit this crime. He would gladly give up all hope of quenching his thirst or even the sight of Fonte Branda[6] if he could but see one of them, Guido or Alessandro or their brother,[7] in the same ditch. He has heard that one of them is there,[8] but how in his immobile state can he find him? If he could only move one inch every 100 years, though the ditch is 11 miles round and is not less than half a mile across, he would already have set off in search of him.

Dante sees two other souls lying near by, from whom a steam of fever rises, as mist is seen to rise from wet hands in winter weather. He asks Adamo who they are. He says that they have lain there motionless ever since he arrived and identifies them as falsifiers of words: Potiphar's wife who falsely accused Joseph,[9] and Sinon the Greek who tricked the Trojans into bringing the wooden horse within the walls of Troy.

A sordid squabble now occurs. Sinon, angered at being named, strikes Adamo on his leathery belly, which resounds like a drum. Adamo hits him in the face with his arm and they exchange squalid insults, mocking each other's sufferings with degraded cruelty. Dante listens fascinated until Virgil harshly reproves him:

> … 'Or pur mira!
> ch'è per poco che teco non mi risso.'

> … 'Keep on gloating then!
> A little more and I will row with thee.'[10]

Dante is stricken with remorse at this reproach and the shame of it is still vivid in his memory. Like someone dreaming that he is in danger and in his dream wishes that he were in truth only dreaming, he turns to Virgil, longing to ask forgiveness, unable to speak but doing so by his look alone. Virgil responds:

> 'Maggior difetto men vergogna lava,'
>   disse 'l maestro, 'che 'l tuo non è stato;
>   però d'ogne trestizia ti disgrava:
> e fa ragion ch'io ti sia sempre a lato,
>   se più avvien che fortuna t'accoglia
>   dove sien genti in simigliante piato,
> chè voler ciò udire è bassa voglia.'

'Less shame a greater fault would wash away,
   than thine has been', responded then my guide,
      'therefore cast off the weight of all dismay;
and bear in mind I'm always at thy side
   if chance again should bring thee to a place
      where disputants thus wrangle and deride;
the wish to hear such bickering is base.'[11]

In his description of the valley of disease Dante the writer seems both near and distant. On the one hand, he gossips about petty scandals connected with local personalities: Griffolino of Arezzo who made Alberto, the son of the Bishop of Siena, believe that he could fly. 'Were there ever such foolish people as the Sienese? Not even the French, by far!' exclaims Dante to Virgil. 'All except for Stricca,' chips in Capocchio ironically, 'and Niccolò, who started the expensive fashion of cooking with cloves, and Caccia of Asicano, who wasted his patrimony in vineyards and woodlands, and another nick-named *l'Abbagliato* (the Blunderer).' These individuals, who have nothing to do with the sin of falsification, were members of a group of Sienese known as the Spendthrift Brigade. The misdoing of Gianni Schicchi of Florence, who cunningly impersonated a dead man and arranged for a legacy for himself, is an episode which had its comic aspect for the composer Giacomo Puccini, who based his shrewd and entertaining one-act opera on it. All these minor anecdotes seem to admit us to the intimacy of everyday gossip, yet they are strangely out of proportion to the destabilizing crime of counterfeiting currency committed by Master Adamo. They are even more ill sorted with the ancient stories of Myrrha's incestuous deception of her royal father, of the false witness borne against Joseph by the wife of Potiphar and of the trickery of Sinon the Greek that brought about the fall of Troy. The homely similes of a stable-boy currying a horse in a hurry for an impatient master, of a scullion scraping the scales from a fish, of two cooking pots propped together to keep the contents warm, and of steam rising from wet hands in winter bring us close to Dante the living man: here are details he has glimpsed and remembered. Yet his grandiose comparisons of the grotesque madness of Myrrha and Gianni Schicchi (another strangely matched pair) with the tragic frenzy of Hecuba finding her son Polydore dead and with the homicidal madness of Athamas who, mistaking his wife and her two sons for a lioness and her cubs, seized one of them and dashed him against a rock, cause Dante to recede from us into a mythological world. Distant events from a heroic, Biblical and legendary past are here mingled with happenings scarcely worthy of headlines in the tabloid press. To Dante there was evidently no impropriety in such mingling of epic events with trivial and local incidents.

Though he represents himself in his character role as reprimanded by Virgil for listening to the wrangling between Master Adamo and Sinon the Greek, as a writer he shows a robust talent for coarse invective, sustained here for over one-fifth of the canto. It is evident that in a quarrel Dante the man could give as good as he got, or at least that he had listened attentively to such brawling as he walked about among the populace.

His reaction to illness is not one of compassion but of revulsion. Festering limbs give rise to stench, the helpless piles of the incurable and dying are objects of disgust. He may have witnessed such scenes in hospitals or along the streets at times of plague. All such horrors he takes as the image of a society in necrosis, suffering deservedly in its self-destruction.

The contrasts of this canto display not only Dante the man but also the public for whom he wrote. It is plain that he judged it necessary to entertain grossly as well as to edify. He did both with equal skill.

CHAPTER 26

Towering Giants

Dante now descends lower into Hell, to a pit of narrowing circumference, but the prelude to the descent engages the imagination in vast dimensions. As he walks with Virgil across the rampart that divides the Eighth from the Ninth Circle, in a twilight such as divides night from day, he hears the blast of a horn so loud that it would have made any thunderclap seem faint, more terrible even than the sound of Roland's horn after the tragic rout when Charlemagne's rearguard were slain.[1] Peering through the murky air in the direction of the sound, Dante sees in the distance what seem to be towers. He asks Virgil what city it is they are approaching. Taking him gently by the hand, Virgil replies: 'They are not towers, but giants, standing round the bank of the pit from the navel down':

> Poi caramente mi prese per mano,
>   e disse: 'Pria che noi siam più avanti,
>   acciò che 'l fatto ti paia men strano,
> sappi che non son torri, ma giganti,
>   e son nel pozzo intorno dalla ripa
>   dall'umbilico in giuso tutti quanti.'

> *Then by the hand he took me lovingly*
>   *and said: 'Before we further onwards go,*
>   *that what is fact may seem less strange to thee,*
> *they are not towers, but giants, thou must know,*
>   *around the rampart ranged, and in the pit,*
>   *all from the navel down, they stand below.'*[2]

Even with the reassurance of Virgil's handclasp, Dante the character experiences greater fear the closer he approaches and the more clearly he sees. Dante the writer, however, is again in perfect control. Once more he has judged that the time has come to vary his effects. His audience have had enough of sensational reporting of mutilations and of diseased bodies piled one upon another. He now sets himself the quite different task of evoking wonder and amazement at enormous size. To do so, he conjures for comparison things that he himself has seen and that his earliest listeners too may well have seen or could easily imagine. First he compares the giants to the towers that crown the circle of the walls of Monteriggioni, a castle near Siena.[3] Drawing near, he begins to distinguish the face of one of them, then gradually the shoulders, chest and belly and both arms hanging inert at his sides. The face, Dante says, is about as long and wide as the pine-cone at St Peter's in Rome, a bronze monument, about seven and a half feet in height at which the many thousands of pilgrims to Rome in the Jubilee year of 1300, Dante among them, would have gazed in the courtyard of the old Basilica.[4] The upper part of the body, which alone is visible, is so high that three Frieslanders, famed for their great stature, standing upright one upon another, would have difficulty in reaching to its hair. Altogether, Dante estimates, from where a man buckles his cloak, that is from the throat, down to the navel, the height of the giant was 30 *gran palmi* ('full palms'). Among various estimations it has been calculated that he intended to convey that the entire giant was 90 palms in height, or roughly 54 feet.

The lower part of the monster's body is screened, as by an apron, by the rampart. In describing the wall as an 'apron', Dante uses the word *perizoma*, from the Greek περίζωμα, which is found in the plural (*perizomata*) in the Vulgate,[5] in reference to the covering that Adam and Eve made for themselves on realizing they were naked. Thus Dante, with deliberate discretion, avoided the necessity of giving the measurements of the giant's genitals. Like his contemporaries, he did not doubt that 'there were giants in the earth in those days'.[6] Such creatures, he observes, no longer exist. Nature has prudently deprived Mars of such executives, producing now only such outsize creatures as elephants and whales, which, not possessing ill-intentioned intellect, pose less threat to mankind.

The first giant, identified by Virgil, is Nimrod. In believing him to have been a giant, Dante is following St Augustine.[7] He had already mentioned him in *De Vulgari Eloquentia*, where he also refers to him as a giant. The tradition that he was the builder of the Tower of Babel was well established in the Middle Ages, but Dante associates all mankind with this sin of pride:

> Incorrigible man, persuaded by the giant, presumed in his heart to surpass by his own skill not only nature, but even the very power that works in nature, who is God; and he began to build a tower in Sennear, which was afterwards called Babel, that is confusion, by which he hoped to ascend to heaven; intending in his ignorance, not to equal, but to surpass his Maker.[8]

Nimrod now gives voice; his words, as is suitable, are babel:

> 'Raphèl maÿ amèch zabì almì'[9]

They have never been decoded and Dante no doubt intended that we should believe Virgil when he says that nobody understands Nimrod's language, nor does he understand that of others, for this is he who in his pride in encouraging men to build a tower which should reach to Heaven deprived mankind of the possession of a single language.[10] To dispel Dante's fear, Virgil mocks him in words, which to Nimrod are, of course, meaningless:

> ... 'Anima sciocca,
> tienti col corno, e con quel ti disfoga
> quand'ira o altra passion ti tocca!
> Cercati al collo, e troverai la soga
> che 'l tien legato, o anima confusa,
> e vedi lui che 'l gran petto ti doga.'
> Poi disse a me: 'Ellii stesso s'accusa;
> questi è Nembròt per lui cui mal coto
> pur un linguaggio nel mondo non s'usa.
> Lascianlo stare e non parliamo a voto;
> chè così è a lui ciascun linguaggio
> come 'l suo ad altrui, ch'a nullo è noto.'

> ... *'Stupid soul,*
> *keep to thy horn and vent thyself with that*
> *when rage or other passions thee enthral!*
> *Feel round thy neck and thou wilt find the plait*
> *which holds it tied to thee, o soul confused,*
> *binding thy mighty torso like a slat.'*
> *Then he to me: 'He has himself accused;*
> *for this is Nimrod by whose evil plan*
> *throughout the world one language is not used.*
> *So we will leave him and not talk in vain,*
> *for gibberish to him is every tongue,*
> *as is his jargon, which to none is plain.'*[11]

They move along the rampart to the left and at the distance of a bowshot they come before a second giant, even more ferocious. From now on Dante uses his knowledge of giants in pagan mythology, drawing on the imaginary world of his fellow poets, Homer, Virgil, Ovid, Horace and Lucan, those among whose wisdom he was made sixth. The first, of whom he has read in Virgil and in Horace, is Ephialtes who with his brother giant fought against the gods, threatening to pile Mount Ossa on Olympus and Mount Pelion upon Ossa. In the *Aeneid* the Sibyl tells Aeneas that the giants are deep in Tartarus:

'Here the ancient sons of Earth, the Titan's brood, hurled down by the thunderbolt, writhe in the lowest abyss. Here, too, I saw the twin sons of Aloeus

[Ephialtes and Otus], giant in stature, whose hands essayed to tear down high Heaven and thrust down Jove from his realm above.'[12]

Horace also mentions them briefly as the brothers who tried to place Mount Pelion upon Olympus.[13] Neither Virgil nor Horace mention their names, but Servius, in his commentary on the *Aeneid*, which Dante knew, calls them Ephialtes and Otus and says that they were slain by Apollo and Diana.

Here are the shadowy elements from which Dante forms his impressively substantial and statuesque figures. Omitting Otus altogether, he concentrates upon Ephialtes, who is even larger and more ferocious than Nimrod. Dante summons the composure to marvel at the intricacy of his bonds:

A cinger lui qual fosse 'l maestro,
  non so io dir, ma el tenea soccinto
  dinanzi l'altro e dietro il braccio destro
d'una catena che 'l tenea avvinto
  dal collo in giù, sì che 'n su lo scoperto
  si ravvolgea infino al giro quinto.

Who was the craftsman who had girt him tight
  I cannot say, but his left arm was bound
  in front of him and at his back the right,
by one sole chain which was so closely wound
  from the neck down that on the part we saw
  above the brink the coils went five times round.[14]

Virgil identifies him with brief disdain, referring to him as the proud being who tried his strength against Jove: 'the arms he then plied he can no longer move'. Dante, his curiosity having now overcome his terror, asks if he may have the experience of setting eyes on *lo smisurato Briareo* ('the measureless Briareus'). Virgil the poet had compared the prowess of Aeneas in battle to this mighty giant, 'said to have a hundred arms and a hundred hands'.

Dante's brave desire is denied him. Briareus, Virgil tells him, is much further on; he is bound and formed like Ephialtes except that he looks more ferocious in the face. From this it is evident that Dante regarded Virgil's description of Briareus in the *Aeneid* as hyperbolic, not literal, but he took from Lucan the adjective *ferox*[15] and from Statius the adjective *immensus* (*smisurato*).[16] To have introduced a giant with a hundred arms and hands would have marred the symmetry of the apparent towers. Deprived of a glimpse at Briareus, Dante's spectators, so to call them, are compensated with a description of Ephialtes suddenly shaking himself, more violently than ever earthquake rocked a tower. At this, the terror of Dante the character is close to the fear of death, abated only by the sight of the fetters by which the giant is controlled. In a sobered state of mind, he is led before a third giant.

This is Antaeus, who stands five yards high, not counting his head. He is unfettered and is capable of speech. Associated in pagan legend with astounding feats, he was probably as familiar to Dante's contemporaries as the giants of fairy stories are to us. The son of Neptune and Gea (the Earth), he was a mighty wrestler, whose strength was derived from contact with his mother. Dante had read about him in Ovid's *Metamorphoses* and in Lucan's *Pharsalia* and had dwelt on his combat with Hercules in vivid detail in *Il Convivio*:

> We read in the stories of Hercules both in the Greater Ovid[17] and in Lucan and in other poets, that when the hero was fighting with the giant Antaeus, every time that the giant was weary and laid his body prostrate on the ground, whether of his own accord or because Hercules threw him, force and strength renewed, he rose again from the ground in which and from which he had been generated. Hercules perceiving this at last took hold of him, and clasping him tight and uplifting him from the ground held him without letting him come in contact with the earth, until by superior strength he conquered and slew him. And this combat took place in Africa as these writings testify.[18]

This earlier vivid visualization was to develop in the *Commedia* into a masterly feat of three-dimensional description.

Virgil requires the help of Antaeus. His words to him do not take the form of a command or a conjuration, but of a respectful request, referring to his heroic capture of a thousand lions in the valley in Libya where Scipio won his glorious victory over Hannibal at the Battle of Zama, details which Dante had also read in Lucan's *Pharsalia*:

'O tu che nella fortunata valle
    che fece Scipion di gloria reda,
    quand' Annibal co' i suoi diede le spalle,
recasti già mille leon per preda,
    e che se fossi stato all'alta guerra
    de' tuoi fratelli, ancora par che si creda
ch'avrebbero vinto i figli della terra;
    mettine giù e non ten vegna a schifo,
    dove Cocito la freddura serra. ...
però ti china, e non torcer lo grifo.'

'O thou who in the fateful vale which made
    Scipio an heir of glory in the fray
    when Hannibal with all his army fled,
didst once a thousand lions take as prey,
    and if thou too hadst been rebellious
    in the great war thy brethren waged, men say

the sons of earth had been victorious,
  do not disdain to set us down below
  where the cold ice has frozen Còcitus. ...
Bend down, and on thy face no grimace show.'[19]

Immediately the huge hands of Antaeus come down, hands which once grasped Hercules, and take hold of Virgil. Feeling himself thus seized, he calls to Dante, like a father to a child:

... 'Fatti qua, sì ch'io ti prenda.'

... *'Come here, let me catch hold of thee.'*[20]

The two tiny figures, huddled together in one bundle, are gathered up like toys. As Antaeus stoops, Dante recalls the sensation of standing beneath the leaning tower, Carisenda, in Bologna, when a cloud passes over it against the direction in which it inclines, resulting in the illusion that it is falling. 'Gladly,' says Dante, 'at that moment would I have gone by another road':

Ma lievemente al fondo che divora
  Lucifero con Giuda ci sposò;
    nè sì chinato lì fece dimora,
e come albero in nave si levò.

But gently on the floor which swallows up
  Judas and Lucifer ourselves he placed;
    and not for long he lingered in his stoop,
but rose erect as on a ship a mast.[21]

The first audience of this compelling scenic effect must have been spell-bound with amazement. Nothing so graphic and direct had ever been heard before. Dante the craftsman, acknowledging as his source the ancient poets he so much revered, has once again set out to surpass them, and has once again succeeded.

CHAPTER 27

The Frozen Lake

Dante now braces himself and his audience for a subject to which he fears his powers of expression cannot do justice. The dismal pit on which all other rocks of Hell bear down requires rhymes that are harsh and rugged, beyond any he can command, and he approaches his subject with misgiving. To describe the bottom of the universe is not an enterprise to be lightly taken in hand, nor is children's language fit for it. He entreats the Muses who helped Amphion to build a wall round Thebes to assist him, so that his words may encompass the truth.

His mention of Amphion and Thebes is significant. Amphion, the son of Zeus, was a musician who played so beautifully on the lyre that the stones of Mount Cithaeron came down of their own accord to hear him and placed themselves in the shape of a wall enclosing the city. Thebes was renowned for appalling atrocities and in particular for the bitter rivalry between two brothers, Eteocles and Polynices, which led to the war known as Seven Against Thebes, about which Dante read in Statius's *Thebaid*.[1] Dante's prayer is that he may now enclose Hell's city of treachery, the Ninth Circle, in words which will likewise of their own accord move into place.

It is not only the physical description of this last region of Hell that challenges his powers. The 'juice of his concept' which he would press out more fully, as he phrases it (*io premerei di mio concetto il suco/più pienamente*),[2] is the horror and outrage that treachery inspires in him. It is a freezing of all human bonds, of kinship, loyalty to country or party, hospitality, and gratitude for benefaction. Those who commit it are stuck fast in unsplinterable ice, the memory of which causes Dante still to shudder, not only in his body but in his soul.

Having descended to a level far below the feet of Antaeus, Dante is still looking up at the towering cliff when he hears a voice:

> ... 'Guarda come passi;
> va sì che tu non calchi con le piante
> le teste de' frati miseri lassi.'

> ... 'Take care
> *how thou dost walk, be mindful not to kick*
> *the heads of the two wretched brothers there.'[3]*

We do not learn whose voice this is. It is probably not Virgil's, as he would not have known that the souls in question are brothers. If it is the voice of another soul the note of compassion for the *frati miseri lassi* ('unhappy wretched brothers') is uncharacteristic of the other traitors.

Dante turns and sees at his feet a frozen lake, more like glass than water, formed from Cocytus, the fourth of the great rivers of Hell. The ice that covers it is thicker than any that ever sealed the river Danube or the Don, and if Mount Tambernic or Pietrapana were to fall on it not even the edge of it would crack. Mount Pietrapana has been identified with Petra Apuana, a mountain in the north-west of Tuscany. Mount Tambernic has eluded conclusive identification and has obviously been chosen for the sharp syllable with which the name ends. To give the impression of the crackling sound of walking on ice, Dante, always skilful in onomatopoeia, has used three masculine rhymes in *-ic*:[4]

> Non fece al corso suo sì grosso velo
>   di verno la Danoia in Osterlic,
>   nè Tanaì là sotto il freddo cielo,
> com'era quivi; chè se Tambernic
>   vi fosse caduto, o Pietrapana,
>   non avrìa pur dall'orlo fatto cric.

> *Never the Danube's course in Austria*
>   *in winter had a covering so thick,*
>   *nor yet the Don beneath cold skies afar;*
> *if Pietrapana or if Tambernic*
>   *had crashed on it, not even at the edge*
>   *would it have given forth the slightest creak.*[5]

The sinners with their muzzles sticking out of the ice are like frogs croaking in water at harvest time when a peasant woman dreams of abundant gleaning, but here in eternal winter their faces are livid and their teeth rattle like the chattering of the bill of a stork. At his feet are two so close together that their hair is intermingled. Dante asks them who they are and as they raise their heads their eyes gush with tears, flooding to their mouths, freezing immediately more firmly than ever wood was clamped to wood by iron bands. Such fury overcomes them that they butt against each other like two goats. Since they cannot speak, another soul, whose ears have been frozen off, reveals that they are the sons of the Count of Mangona, Napoleone and Alessandro, who quarrelled over their inheritance and killed each other:

'D'un corpo usciro; e tutta la Caina
   potrai cercare, e non troverai ombra
   degna più d'esser fitta in gelatina;
non quelli a cui fu rotto il petto e l'ombra
   con esso un colpo per la man d'Artù;
   non Foccaccia; non questi che m'ingombra
col capo sì ch' i' non veggio oltre più,
   e fu nomato Sassol Mascheroni;
   se tosco se', ben sai omai chi fu.'

'From one womb they came forth; and to be seen
   in all Caina not one soul is there
   more worthy to be fixed in gelatine:
not he whose breast and shadow fractured were
   by Arthur, not Foccaccia,[6] *and not he,*
   whose head so interrupts my view from here
that I beyond it further cannot see,
   called Sassol Mascheroni; who he was
   thou knowest well if thou a Tuscan be.'[7]

Sassol Mascheroni of Florence murdered his nephew for the sake of inheritance. On the discovery of his crime he was rolled through the streets of
Florence in a cask full of nails and afterwards beheaded. Many of the examples are likewise criminals of recent notoriety, now long forgotten but of
sensational interest at the time, as Jack the Ripper or any modern-day serial
killer is to us. The speaker is another such 'headline' murderer, Camicion dei
Pazzi, who says he awaits the coming of his kinsman Carlino, whose evil
deeds will surpass his own. He reveals that the first zone of the Ninth Circle
is called Caina, after Cain, the first fratricide. Virgil listed Abel among the
souls liberated by Christ from Limbo,[8] but, surprisingly, Cain himself is not
mentioned as being among murderers of kindred.

Another surprising omission is Gianciotto Malatesta, the husband of
Francesca. Now at last Dante's first listeners knew what she meant when
she said that he who murdered her and her lover Paolo was awaited in
Caina.[9] Whether Dante the writer intended such a destiny for the soul of
a cuckolded husband we do not know.[10] He makes no further reference to
Gianciotto's expected arrival (he did not die until 1304).

All round him he sees such a vast number of traitors' faces, grinning like
dogs with the cold, that the memory of them still makes him shudder whenever he now sees a frozen pool:

Poscia vid' io mille visi cagnazzi
   fatti per freddo; onde mi vien riprezzo,
   e verrà sempre, de' gelati guazzi.

> *A thousand faces there surrounded me,*
> *made dog-like by the cold: I shudder yet*
> *and always will, when frozen pools I see.*[11]

They move on down to the second zone, called Antenora, after Antenor, the Trojan who was said in mediaeval Latin versions of the *Iliad* to have betrayed Troy to the Greeks. As Dante walks between the innumerable heads, by chance or fate he cannot say, he strikes his foot hard against the face of one of them. The soul cries out: 'Why dost thou stamp on me? Is this some new revenge for Montaperti?' This brings Dante to a dead stop and he begs Virgil to wait. The word 'Montaperti' has led him to suspect who it is.

The soul refuses to give his name. He rejects Dante's offer to keep his fame alive on earth. That is the reverse of what traitors desire. Dante, suspecting still more strongly who he is, seizes him by the scruff of the neck and threatens to pull out all his hair if he does not reveal his identity. He has already torn out more than one tuft, the soul barking in protest, when another cries out:

> ... 'Che hai tu, Bocca?
> Non ti basta sonar con le mascelle,
> se tu non latri? Qual diavol ti tocca?'

> ' ... *'Bocca, what's got into thee?*
> *Art not content with clattering thy jaws,*
> *that thou must bark? What is this devilry?'*[12]

This is a name to make all Florentines shudder. Bocca degli Abati, originally a Ghibelline, fought on the side of the Guelfs at the Battle of Montaperti in 1260 and at a critical moment came up behind the standard-bearer of the cavalry and cut off his hand, thus bringing down the standard. The result was the rout of the Guelfs, with whose blood the river Arbia 'ran red with blood'.[13] Dante, in triumph, now knows all he needs to know and vows to relate on earth the fate of the *malvagio traditor* ('vile traitor'). Bocca vindictively tells him to add the names of several others, including Ganelon, the archetypal figure of a traitor in the Middle Ages.[14]

Dante's behaviour towards Bocca, as towards Filippo Argenti,[15] reveals a ferocious side of his character. No amount of allegorical interpretation can explain away his savage cruelty, displayed not only by the character Dante but left unmitigated by any expression of compunction by Dante the writer. Here are no tears, no fainting spells at the sight of the suffering of the damned. He rejoices in it and relishes the prospect of keeping their black fame alive on earth.

A further scene of savagery now follows. Another two souls, like the Mangona brothers, are fixed in a single hole. One of them, protruding like a hood, gnaws the skull of the other where the brain joins the nape, like some-one hungrily munching bread. This terrible spectacle is derived by Dante from the account he has read in the *Thebaid*[16] of Tydeus, King of Calydon, one of the Seven Against Thebes who, mortally wounded by the Theban warrior Menalippus, nevertheless killed him and ordered his head to be cut off and brought to him, when he gnawed the scalp and tore out the brains. Dante the character realizes that there must be some reason why the one soul is committing such an act of barbarity upon another: he asks him to explain, promising that if he is justified he will make his story known in the world above.

The theme of treachery has now developed into one of a devouring, munching cannibalism. Framed within it, in unexpected contrast, is a scene of piteous suffering, calling for horrified compassion. The ravenous soul who gnaws the skull of another is Ugolino della Gherardesca and his victim is Archbishop Ruggieri Ubaldini, both of Pisa and both guilty of political betrayal. Ugolino and his grandson Nino Visconti were the leaders of two Guelf parties who in 1288 held power in Pisa. Ugolino allied himself with the Archbishop, a Ghibelline, to drive Nino out. The Guelf party being thus weakened, the Archbishop turned against Ugolino and conspired to have him seized together with his two sons and two grandsons and imprisoned in a tower, where they remained until March 1289, when the Archbishop ordered the door to be nailed up. After eight days the tower was opened and the five bodies were found dead of starvation. This horrifying act of cruelty, involving Ugolino's innocent progeny as well as himself, was committed when Dante was 23 years old. The episode was well known in Florence, where Pisa was reviled as an example of barbarity.

In reply to Dante's question, the soul of Ugolino raises his mouth from his bestial meal, wiping it on the hair of the head he has ravaged with such ferocity:

La bocca sollevò dal fiero pasto
    quel peccator, forbendola a' capelli
    del capo ch'elli avea di retro guasto.
Poi cominciò: 'Tu vuo' ch'io rinovelli
    disperato dolor che 'l cor mi preme
    già pur pensando, pria ch'io ne favelli.
Ma se le mie parole esser dien seme
    che frutti infamia al traditor ch'i' rodo,
    parlare e lacrimar vedrai insieme.'

That sinner raised his mouth from the fierce feast,
    wiping it on the hair which grew atop the head
    which at the rear he'd ravaged like a beast.

'Thou dost desire me to renew', he said,
    the desperate grief which swells the heart in me,
    even to think of it, ere I proceed.
But if my words the seed of fruit may be
    which will defame the traitor I thus gnaw,
    one who sheds tears while speaking thou wilt see.'[17]

The style has changed from direct, brutal language to the diction of tragedy. What is more, the words echo those of Francesca da Rimini, who on being asked by Dante to say how her love for Paolo began replies:

> ... 'Nessun maggio dolore
> che ricordarsi del tempo felice
> nella miseria; e ciò sa il tuo dottore.
> Ma se a conoscer la prima radice
> del nostro amor tu hai cotanto affetto,
> dirò come colui che piange e dice.'

> ... *'The greatest of all woes*
> *is to remember times of happiness*
> *in wretchedness; and this thy teacher knows.*
> *But if a great desire on thee doth press*
> *to know the first root of our love, like one*
> *who weeps while he is speaking, I'll confess.'*[18]

Francesca's metaphor of the 'first root' of her love is echoed by Ugolino's 'seed of the fruit of infamy'. The words of both echo those of Aeneas to Dido, who bids him relate the treachery of the Greeks, the misfortunes of his comrades and his own wanderings. Aeneas consents:

> 'Terrible, o Queen, is the grief thou bidst me revive, but if thou hast such longing to learn of our disasters and in few words to hear of Troy's last agony, though my mind shudders to remember and recoils in grief, I will begin.'[19]

The lines in which Ugolino tells the story of his death are among the most famous in the *Commedia*. The atmosphere of terror, the moonlight filtering through a narrow slit in the tower, Ugolino's dream of the Archbishop as master of a hunt pursuing a wolf and its cubs with lean, eager, well-trained hounds, the tearing of the wolf and its young by the sharp fangs of the hounds, all presage what is to occur. On awakening, Ugolino heard his sons and grandsons crying out for food in their sleep and was filled with misgivings:

> 'Ben se' crudel, se tu già non ti duoli,
> pensando ciò ch' il mio cor s'annunziava:
> e se non piangi, di che pianger suoli?'

> *'Cruel thou art if thou dost not grieve now*
> *to think what my heart told me in advance:*
> *if not, by what impelled to weep art thou?'*[20]

The young men and boys were now awake and the hour was approaching when food was usually brought, but all of them, because of their dreams, were apprehensive. Then the sound was heard of nails being hammered into the door below. Ugolino turned to stone. He did not weep, although the others did and the youngest, *Anselmuccio mio* ('my little Anselm'), said:

> ... 'Tu guardi sì, padre: che hai?'

> ... *'Father, thou lookest so strange: what's wrong?'*[21]

Still Ugolino did not speak, nor did he weep, through all that day and night. The next morning, when the sun's ray filtered into the tower, he could see reflected in four faces an image of his own. At this he gnawed his hands in grief. The boys, thinking he did so in hunger, offered themselves as food:

> 'Padre, assai ci fia men doglia
> se tu mangi di noi: tu ne vestisti
> queste misere carni, e tu le spoglia.'

> ... *'Father, much less will we grieve*
> *if thou of us wilt eat; thou didst us clothe,*
> *now in return this wretched flesh receive.'*[22]

Not to grieve them further Ugolino calmed himself. That day and the next they all remained silent:

> 'Queta' mi allor per non farli più tristi;
> lo dì e l'altro stemmo tutti muti;
> ahi dura terra, perchè non t'apristi?'

> *'I calmed myself to let their grief subside;*
> *on that day and the next we all were mute;*
> *ah, cruel earth, why didst thou not gape wide?'*[23]

On the fourth day, Gaddo, one of the sons, threw himself at Ugolino's feet, and crying 'Father, why dost thou not help me?' he died. Between the fifth day and the sixth, he saw the other three die, one by one. For two days, Ugolino, himself now blind, groped over their bodies, calling their names,

> 'poscia, più che 'l dolor, potè il digiuno.'

> *'and hunger then did more than grief could do.'*[24]

This line is deliberately ambiguous. As Dante anticipated, it has been understood in two ways: either 'hunger, not grief, brought about my death', or, 'hunger, more powerful than grief, led me to eat their flesh'. There may have been a rumour that signs of this were noticed when the corpses were discovered. In the imaginary account he gives to Ugolino, Dante lifts the possibility to the level of epic by making the sons offer their bodies as food, relegating the realistic possibility to Ugolino's gnawing of Ruggieri's skull. No sooner has he finished his tale than he returns to his bestial repast:

> Quand'ebbe detto ciò, con li occhi torti
> riprese 'l teschio misero co' denti,
> che furo all'osso, come d'un can, forti.

> *When he had spoken thus, with eyes asquint,*
> *once more he took the skull between his teeth,*
> *which, like a dog's, were strong and violent.*[25]

At this point Dante the wrathful poet stands aside from his story and calls obliteration down upon all the inhabitants of Pisa, reviled in Florence as an example of barbarity:

> Ahi Pisa, vituperio delle genti
> del bel paese là dove 'l sì sona,
> poi che i vicini a te punir son lenti,
> muovasi la Capraia e la Gorgona,
> e faccian siepe ad Arno in su la foce,
> sì ch' elli annieghi in te ogni persona!

> *Ah, Pisa, shame of the community*
> *of the fair land where* sì *is heard to sound,*[26]
> *since slow thy neighbours are to punish thee,*
> *let Capraia and Gorgona*[27] *shift their ground*
> *and dam the river Arno's mouth until*
> *every last resident in thee is drowned!*[28]

This is the wrath of Jehovah who sent the Flood, but without the mercy shown to Noah. Pisa, a new Thebes, deserves in Dante's opinion to be utterly destroyed. He accepts the rumour that Ugolino was guilty of treachery in yielding certain Pisan strongholds to Florence and Lucca. It is for this and for other deeds of treachery that he places him among the traitors, but mercy should have been shown to Ugolino's sons and grandsons.

In the midst of the deepest savagery to which humans can sink, there comes a shaft of light. As the moon and sun filter their rays through the *pertugio* ('loophole') in the tower, so Ugolino's love and compassion for his sons and grandsons, their readiness to sacrifice themselves for him, their bond of kindred, offer hope of an escape, not for the unrepentant damned but for mankind. It is through another *pertugio* that Dante will emerge from Hell, to look once more upon the stars.[29]

But there is yet worse to come. Leaving Antenora, Dante and Virgil move on into the third zone of the Ninth Circle, where murderers of guests, betrayers of the ancient trust of hospitality, are frozen face upwards in the ice. The zone is named Tolomea, after Ptolemy, the captain of Jericho, who invited Simon the High Priest and his sons to a banquet and murdered them there.[30]

The eyes of these sinners are so caked with ice that, like a crystal visor, it fills up the cavity beneath the brows and tears well up behind it, increasing their anguish. One of the souls calls out, asking whoever is passing to remove the frozen crust from his eyes to grant him temporary relief. To this request Dante replies:

> ... 'Se vuo' ch' i' ti sovvegna,
> dimmi chi se', e s'io non ti disbrigo,
> al fondo della ghiaccia ir mi convegna.'

> *'First tell me who thou art: that is my price,*
> *and if I do not free thee from thy mask,*
> *may I be destined for the deepest ice.'*[31]

Since Dante is destined to travel, unharmed, down into the lowest pit of all, this is a pledge made in ill faith. The soul is deceived by it and reveals his identity:

> Rispuose adunque: 'I' son frate Alberigo;
> io son quel dalle frutte del mal orto,
> che qui riprendo dattero per figo.'

> *'I am Friar Alberigo', the soul said,*
> *'remembered for the evil garden's fruit,*
> *and here I am in dates for figs repaid.'*[32]

The mysterious reference to fruit is explained by early commentators who relate that Friar Alberigo[33] invited his brother and a nephew to a banquet and in revenge for an earlier insult, which he pretended to have forgiven, had them murdered, giving as a signal to his armed servants the command: 'Bring on the fruit!' Dante knew that he was still alive and expresses astonishment at finding his soul already in Hell. Alberigo explains that often when the bond of hospitality is betrayed the murderer's soul at once falls into Tolomea and for the rest of his life on earth his body is possessed by a demon. Alberigo also names the soul of Branca d'Oria of Genoa, whose soul has been there for many years. Dante does not believe him:

> 'Io credo', diss' io lui, 'che tu m'inganni;
> chè Branca d'Oria non morì unquanche,
> e mangia e bee e dorme e veste panni.'

'I think', I said, 'that thou art making fun,
*   'for Branca d'Oria is not dead at all,*
*   and eats and drinks and sleeps and puts clothes on.'*[34]

These three lines bring us very close to Dante the man. This is his voice, his everyday way of speaking, his refusal to be made a fool of. Alberigo assures him that Branca's soul dropped down into Tolomea even before that of his victim, his father-in-law Michele Zanche, reached the boiling pitch of the swindlers.[35] It is reported that the murder was committed about the year 1290 and that Branca, with the help of a nephew, conspired to invite his father-in-law to a banquet, where he had him killed in order to obtain the judicature of Logodoro in Sardinia which Zanche held. The nephew's soul is also in Tolomea, Alberigo adds, and his body too is possessed of a demon.

To allege that three living persons were possessed of demons was to place them in grave danger in a superstitious world. Why Dante elects to do so we do not know. Of all his contrivances for anticipating the damnation of individuals still alive, this is the most malicious. Vindictive too is his refusal, after his false pledge, to remove the ice from Alberigo's eyes:

e cortesia fu lui eser villano.

and villainy to him was courtesy.[36]

Nor do we know why Dante, finding in Tolomea, in company with 'the worst spirit of Romagna', two souls from Genoa, calls for the destruction of all the inhabitants:

Ahi Genovesi, uomini diversi
   d'ogne costume e pien d'ogni magagna,
   perchè non siete voi del mondo spersi?

Ah, Genoese, men utterly devoid
*   of all good custom and with every vice*
*   corrupt, how is it you are not destroyed?*[37]

Here Dante takes a stance not only of moral outrage but of moral vengeance.

CHAPTER 28

Lucifer

From his childhood Dante had been familiar with the image of Lucifer in the mosaic decoration of the cupola of the Baptistery in Florence. Work on these mosaics began in the first half of the thirteenth century and continued during Dante's early years. The design on the cupola consists of an apocalyptic vision of Christ in majesty presiding over the Last Judgement, the angelic hierarchy, events from the Old and New Testaments and scenes of damnation, arranged symmetrically in rectangular segments and culminating in a central triple-octagonal ornamentation. The image of Lucifer dominates a tumultuous scene in which souls of the damned are tormented by demons. Lucifer himself is a grotesque monster, horned and bearded, munching a soul whose legs and buttocks dangle from his mouth. From his ears protrude two snakes, also munching two souls, who dangle face forwards. Lucifer clenches other souls in his hands, held ready for the continuation of his meal. His feet are clamped on yet another two, and demons force others towards him and towards other snakes. A crude representation of his insides shows a soul being digested and about to be excreted. The devouring is thus represented as endlessly continuous.

Such a representation of Lucifer was conventional in Dante's time. It must have held a gruesome fascination for him as a boy. He may have seen it actually being put into place. The triple-mouthed head would have been recognized as a parody of the Trinity and the horrifying ugliness of the whole figure was a visual aid to sermons about the fate of the fairest and noblest angelic being who rebelled against the Creator.

This is the figure that Dante adopts for the climax of *Inferno*. It has been in his mind from the beginning. With characteristic control and orderliness, he improves on the crude mosaic picture while retaining essentials. His Lucifer has three faces, which, like the figure in the Baptistery, munch three souls, one with the legs dangling, the other two face forwards. To this extent he is faithful to his boyhood recollection. He adds, however, many details, which have significance for his imagined world.

In the mocking words of Virgil, with which the final canto opens, Lucifer is presented as the King of Hell:

Fig 5. The Cupola of the Baptistery in Florence

'*Vexilla regis prodeunt inferni*
   verso di noi; però dinanzi mira,'
   disse il maestro mio, 'se tu 'l discerni.'

'The banners of the king of Hell advance
   towards us, therefore to gain a glimpse of him,
   my master said, 'cast forward now thy glance.'[1]

Virgil (the pre-Christian) is here quoting, with the addition of the word
inferni, the first line of a Passion hymn sung in praise of the Cross. The
banners are Lucifer's six wings and it is not they which are advancing but
the poets who are moving towards them. Lucifer, the first and greatest of all
traitors, is stuck fast in the ice, both punished and punisher.

   Virgil and Dante are now in the fourth zone of the Ninth Circle, named
Judecca, after the arch-traitor Judas. Here the souls of betrayers of benefactors are completely immersed in the ice, like straws in glass, some supine,
others vertical, with head or feet uppermost, others arched like a bow. No
converse with them is possible and we do not learn who any of them are.
Dante becomes aware of what seems a vast edifice, like a windmill, glimpsed
in a thick fog. A chilling wind makes him draw back behind Virgil as his only
shelter. At a certain point Virgil steps aside to let him see *la creatura ch' ebbe
il bel sembiante* ('the creature who was once so fair'),[2] and says: 'Behold Dis;[3]
here is the place where thou must arm thyself with courage.'

   Dante has no literary predecessor for what he is about to describe. Up
to now he has drawn on Lucan and Ovid, claiming to surpass them, and
he has borrowed from Virgil, but here he is on his own. The fear which the
character Dante feels has its parallel in the soul of Dante the writer:

Com'io divenni allor gelato e fioco,
   nol dimandar, lettor, ch'i' non lo scrivo,
   però ch' ogni parlar sarebbe poco.
Io non mori' e non rimasi vivo:
   pensa oggimai per te, s' hai fior d'ingegno,
   qual io divenni, d'uno e d'altro privo.

How chilled I then became, how faint I grew,
   ask me not, Reader, for I cannot say,
   no words of any kind for this would do.
I did not die, alive I did not stay:
   think for thyself, if thou hast any wit,
   what I became, bereft in either way.[4]

'The Emperor of the woeful kingdom' rises mid-torso from the ice. Such is
his size that Dante compares better with a giant than giants compare with
his arms.

S' el fu sì bello com' elli è or brutto,
  e contra 'l suo fattore alzò le ciglia,
  ben dee da lui proceder ogni lutto.

If he as fair was as he now is foul
  and dared defy his Maker in revolt,
  well may he be the source of all our dole.[5]

Dante marvels to see three faces on his head, one in front and two over the middle of each shoulder, all joined at the crown. The one in front is red, the one on the right is white and yellow, the one on the left is the colour of people who inhabit the valley of the Nile. Beneath each are two wings, larger than any sails ever seen by Dante at sea; they have no feathers but are like a bat's. As they flap, they produce three winds, by which Cocytus is kept frozen. From six eyes he weeps and over three chins drip tears and bloody foam. In each mouth his teeth crush a sinner, like a hackle dressing flax, keeping all three of them in constant pain. For the sinner in the front mouth, the biting is exceeded by the clawing of nails which leave the spine stripped of all flesh.

This sinner, says Virgil, is Judas Iscariot. The other two are Brutus, who hangs from the black muzzle and says nothing, and Cassius, who seems strong-limbed.

'Ma la notte risurge, e oramai
  è da partir, chè tutto avem veduto.'

'But night is rising[6] *once again, and now*
the time has come to leave; we have seen all.'[7]

The economy with which Virgil announces the end of the tremendous journey through Hell is striking but we cannot take our leave of Lucifer without further comment. First, given his enormous height, which from Dante's indications has been calculated to be over 1,400 feet, and given that about one-half of him is visible above the ice, his three heads are about 700 feet above Dante's own. There is a conflict here between realistic description and poetic imagination, since from so far below and in such darkness it would be impossible for Dante to see, for instance, that Judas is being more scratched than bitten or that Cassius is sturdy of limb. It is possible that Dante here reproduces his childhood experience of looking up at the cupola of the Baptistery and knowing, from having been told, what is there although he cannot precisely see it from the ground. It is likely that in his childhood the image of Lucifer frightened him and haunted his dreams.

The presence of Judas as the worst of all human traitors requires no explanation, but that of Brutus and Cassius must have puzzled Dante's earliest listeners and has in fact given rise to controversy down the centuries. Readers

Fig 6. Lucifer in the Cupola of the Baptistery in Florence

of *Il Convivio* knew that Dante believed the Roman Empire to have been ordained by God for the peace of the world. Those who betrayed Caesar therefore (Cassius being the chief conspirator and Brutus once Caesar's closest ally) were in his view the secular equivalents of Judas who betrayed Christ. He takes no time at this point to expound this belief: the significance of the image will become clear as the work progresses. More important for his narrative is the immediate need to describe how the exit from Hell was managed. This explanation involves Dante's vision of the fall of Lucifer and the effect he imagined it had upon the globe of earth.

Obeying Virgil's instructions, Dante clasps him round the neck. Virgil watches Lucifer's flapping wings and when they are wide apart seizes the hair on his body and with Dante clinging to him descends from tuft to tuft between the monster and the icy crust. Reaching the point where the thigh-bone turns and the haunch swells, Virgil, with a great effort, turns upside down and pulls himself up, still clutching Lucifer's hair, so that to Dante it seems as if they are returning to Hell:

> 'Attienti bene, chè per cotali scale',
>> disse 'l maestro, ansando com' uom lasso,
>> 'conviensi dipartir da tanto male.'

'Hold tight, for it is by such stairs as these',
  my master said, weary and out of breath,
  'that we must leave such evil as this is.'[8]

Squeezing through a cleft, Virgil seats Dante on an edge of rock and then carefully steps across himself. Dante, looking up, expects to see Lucifer as he had left him and is dumbfounded to see instead that his legs are pointing upwards:

E s'io divenni allora travagliato,
  la gente grossa il pensi, che non vede
  qual è quel punto ch'io avea passato.

If I was then astonished and aghast,
  let stupid folk imagine, who don't see
  what point it is that I had then just passed.[9]

The point he has just passed is the middle of the earth.
Virgil commands Dante to get to his feet:

'Lèvati su', disse 'l maestro, 'in piede:
  la via è lunga e 'l cammino è malvagio,
  e già il sole a mezza terza riede.'

'Stand up', my master said, 'we must move on:
  the way is long, the path is rough and hard,
  already to mid-terce returns the sun.'[10]

Dante is now more perplexed than ever. Virgil had told him, before they began to climb down the body of Lucifer, that night was rising: how can it now be morning? Where is the ice, and why is Lucifer upside down?

Virgil explains that they are no longer in the northern hemisphere but have passed into the southern and are standing on a sphere of rock that forms the opposite surface of Judecca. When it is morning where they are, it is already evening in the north.

Dante now creates a legend to explain Lucifer's position in the ice and to describe the effect of his fall from Heaven upon the globe of the earth. No geological account of volcanic eruptions, of seismic convulsions or of tectonic changes resulting from continental shift, no science fiction, no space odyssey can match the magnificence of this titanic visualization.

When Lucifer fell from Heaven, Virgil explains, he collided with the southern hemisphere of our globe. At that time, all the land was in the southern sphere and the northern was covered with water. The land, in horror at the approach of Lucifer, shifted violently away from contact with him and reappeared in the north, while water rushed in to fill the void in the south. As the hideously transfigured archangel spiralled through the globe,

the earth inside rushed past him southwards in like horror, leaving a twisting hollow and forming a mountain which rose above the new covering of
waters. This violent re-arrangement of the face of the earth, the creative feat
of a single poet's imagination, surpasses all Ovid's fables of metamorphosis,
constituting a mythology on its own. It also raises the curtain on the cosmic
scene that forms the setting of *Purgatorio* and ultimately of *Paradiso*.

The earth's convulsive horror at the approach of Lucifer is likewise a
symbolic statement that mankind's habitat was created not for evil but for
good. He has contaminated it and now all sin, depicted in graphic realism in
the cantos of *Inferno*, flows from him. Nevertheless, there is a gleam of hope.
Light, which filtered through the *pertugio* of Ugolino's tower,[11] is seen again
by Dante as, climbing up the grotto in the darkness behind Virgil, guided by
the sound of a little stream, he emerges through another *pertugio* upon the
surface of the southern hemisphere, once more to behold the stars:

> Lo duca e io per quel cammino ascoso
> intrammo a ritornar nel chiaro mondo;
> e sanza cura aver d'alcun riposo
> salimmo su, el primo e io secondo,
> tanto ch'i' vidi delle cose belle
> che porta 'l ciel, per un pertugio tondo
> e quindi uscimmo a riveder le stelle.

> *My guide and I along that hidden route*
> *set forth, to see the world of light once more;*
> *and for repose or respite caring not,*
> *we climbed, he first, I second, as of yore,*
> *until the lovely things the heaven bears*
> *I could perceive through a round aperture,*
> *whence we came forth to see once more the stars.*[12]

CHAPTER 29

The Tragedy of Henry VII

On 27 November 1308 an event occurred that had an enormous impact upon Dante and his world. A new king of the Germans was elected. This was Henry, Count of Luxembourg, a member of a French-speaking aristocracy, renowned for their chivalry during the Crusades. The first of the family to rise to eminence, he was a courageous, idealistic prince on whom passionate hopes came to be fixed. One of his rivals for election had been Charles of Valois, supported by his brother King Philip IV of France. The fact that Henry's brother Baldwin in his office as Archbishop of Trier was one of the Electors no doubt influenced the result.[1]

Henry's first coronation, as the seventh of that name, took place at Aix-la-Chapelle on 6 January 1309. Three coronations were required to consecrate his election as, first, King of the Germans, next, King of the Romans and, finally, Emperor. The crown at the first ceremony was silver. On 2 June of that year he sent an embassy to Pope Clement V in Avignon, asking for his support. On 16 July Clement issued the first of two encyclicals confirming his election. One of Henry's first moves was to consolidate his relations with the Habsburgs, the family of his predecessor Albert I (who was murdered),[2] by marrying his son John to Elizabeth of Bohemia. King John of Bohemia, as he was then known, was later killed on the battlefield of Crécy in 1346.

In May 1310 Henry sent ambassadors to the rulers of Italian cities to announce his intention of coming to Rome to receive the imperial crown, a procedure that had been neglected by his predecessors for 60 years. It was made known that his intention was to reconcile the conflicting parties and to decree the return of political exiles to their cities of origin. There is a tradition that he said he would not permit the words Guelf and Ghibelline to be uttered in his presence.

The Florentines opposed him from the outset. On 3 July his ambassador arrived in Florence and met with a defiant rejection. By August the Florentine government had made alliances with King Robert of Naples[3] and with Guelf cities of Tuscany and Lombardy to resist Henry's advance through Italy. On 1 September Pope Clement issued a second encyclical

Fig 7. The Emperor Henry VII

calling on all good Christians, and Italians in particular, to receive and honour Henry as the Emperor. On 30 September King Robert arrived in strength from Naples to support the Florentine opposition. The battle lines were drawn.

On 10 October 1310 Henry arrived at Lausanne, where he was welcomed by ambassadors from a number of Italian cities, but not from Florence. That same month Henry with his German army crossed the Alps by Mount Cenis, reaching Susa on the 24th, and arrived in Turin on the 30th. Between 10 November and 12 December he was in Asti, where he received Guelf and Ghibelline exiles and appointed Imperial representatives (*vicari*) in various cities. By the end of November the Florentines were fortifying their walls, which had been allowed to fall into disrepair. On 23 December Henry entered Milan. He was received with acclamation and the Milanese made a donation of 100,000 florins in his support.

The effect on Dante of the news of these events can hardly be overstated. Here at last, it seemed, was the fulfilment of his hopes and dreams of peace and of his return to Florence. Such were the hopes and dreams too of many of his fellow exiles. He had broken away from those with whom he was involved in his first years of banishment and had played no part since then in political negotiation. Now he could no longer stand aside.

One of the first things he did was to travel with fellow supporters to Milan, where on 6 January 1311, in the church of Sant'Ambrogio, Henry received the 'iron crown'[4] of Charlemagne. Representatives from many Italian cities were present, but again none from Florence, nor from the Tuscan league of Guelfs.

Spare, small of stature and with a slight squint, his brow encircled with the crown which on Christmas Day in the year 800 had been set by Pope Leo III on the head of the first Holy Roman Emperor, here was the *veltro*, prophesied in *Inferno* and now materialized, the embodiment of the Monarch whom Dante had foreseen, who, as he wrote in *Il Convivio*,

> possessing everything, and having nothing left to desire, would keep kings confined within the borders of their kingdoms, so that peace would be maintained between them,[5]

who would establish justice, who would drive avarice from the earth. It must have been a hallowed moment for Dante when, kneeling in homage before this august personage, he touched his feet and paid tribute with his lips.[6]

Henry continued to instate representatives of imperial authority and attempted to reconcile Guelfs and Ghibellines. Already in January 1311 he had abrogated all sentences of banishment passed for political reasons, but the problem of the re-entry of exiles was proving intractable. By 20 February Cremona, incited by Florence, was rebelling against him, followed in March

by Brescia. His supporters resolved to try to influence rulers of Italian kingdoms and communes by despatching proclamations from eminent personages. Among them was Dante.

In all he wrote three letters. His first is addressed to 'Princes of Italy,[7]
Senators of Rome, Dukes, Marquises, Counts and Peoples'. Like the other
two, it is written in elegant Latin, in accordance with the rhetorical rules of
the *cursus*.[8] A question that comes to mind is: could these 'princes, senators,
dukes, marquises and counts' read Latin? Surely they are the very categories
of readers for whom *Il Convivio* was written in Italian:

> princes, barons, knights, and many other noble folk, not only men but women,
> numbers of both sexes who use the vulgar tongue and are not scholars.[9]

Even if such potentates were not 'scholars' (*literati*), protocol required
that such an epistle should be written in Latin. Literate members of secre-
tariats and chancelleries were in any event available to serve as translators.
Dante's letter was not the only one despatched, and teams of copyists must
have been engaged. This activity, as well as the cost of galloping messengers, had to be financed by some means. Dante was staying at the time in
the castle of Poppi in the Casentino region in Tuscany, the guest of Count
Guido Novello, with whom he took refuge after leaving Sarzana.[10] His
protectors were on terms of personal amity with the Emperor, as is shown
by correspondence between the Countess and the Empress,[11] and it is likely
that this powerful and wealthy family were among those who met the costs
of the campaign.

Dante's letter is expressed in high-flown metaphors: the sun of peace
is rising, justice, which has grown faint, will revive, another Moses has
been raised up to free his people. Let Italy now rejoice. Pitied even by the
Saracens, let her now welcome as her bridegroom Henry, the elect of God.
He will appoint officials to administer justice; he will grant amnesty to all
who submit but will punish those who resist. This is a reference to the rebellious opposition, especially in the north of Italy.

He rhetorically addresses the inhabitants of Lombardy, reviling them
as barbarians, descendants of the Scandinavians,[12] and calling on them to
summon what remains of their Trojan and Roman ancestry and offer allegiance to the Emperor. Let them not be misled by the wiles of avarice which
like the sirens of old can overcome their reason. This reference to avarice is
in line with Dante's thoughts on the subject in *Il Convivio* and in *Inferno*. It
also suggests that he is aware that opponents of Henry are being bribed to
stand against him.

To those who, like himself, have suffered injustice he counsels patience
and forbearance. He whose power, like that of St Peter and of Caesar, derives
from God, will show mercy and compassion. Let all the inhabitants of Italy

rise up to meet their king, not only as subjects to his sovereignty but as free peoples under his guidance. Again, as in *Il Convivio*, Dante asserts his conviction that the authority of the Roman Emperor was ordained by God from earliest times to the triumphs of Augustus, some achieved by the highest pitch of human endeavour, from which it is apparent that

> God at times has wrought through man as though through new heavens. For it is not always we who act, but sometimes we are the instruments of God; and the human will, in which liberty is by nature inherent, at times receives direction untrammelled by earthly affections, and subject to the Eternal Will unconsciously becomes the minister thereof.[13]

If this reasoning does not suffice, let those to whom he writes consider that during the period of 12 years of peace under the rule of Augustus, God the Son was made Man for the revelation of the Spirit and, preaching the gospel, apportioned the world to Himself and to Caesar, bidding that to each should be rendered that which was his.[14]

In an echo of his arrogant manner of arguing in *Il Convivio*, Dante concludes his letter with a challenge to any obstinate mind (*pertinax animus*) that does not yet assent to the truth: let it recall the words of Christ to Pilate who claimed vicarious authority over Him.[15] Let all, therefore, open the eyes of their minds and see how the Lord of heaven and of earth has appointed a king:

> This is he whom Peter, the Vicar of God, exhorts us to honour,[16] and whom Clement, the present successor of Peter, illumines with the light of the Apostolic benediction.[17]

The reference to the second encyclical of Pope Clement, which Dante echoes more than once, shows that this letter, which is undated, was written after 1 September 1310.

To Dante his arguments seemed unanswerable. Only obdurate minds, closed to reason, could reject them. They cut no ice, however, with Henry's opponents, who were more interested in *realpolitik* than in theological truth, ancient history and quotations from the Bible. By early 1311 the resistance of the Florentines had become so formidable that Dante next undertook to challenge them directly. The date of his second letter is 31 March of that year.

It opens with a form of address so insulting that it made it unlikely that those in power in Florence would ever re-admit him:

> From Dante Alighieri, a Florentine undeservedly in exile, to the most iniquitous Florentines within the city (*scelestissimis*[18] *Florentinis intrinsecis*).

The text of the letter begins with a renewed assertion of his conviction that the Roman Empire was a sacred institution, ordained by God for the peaceful governance of human affairs. Proof of this is to be found in Scripture, and the ancients, relying on reason alone, also bore witness to this truth. It is further confirmed by the fact that when the throne of the Emperor is vacant, the whole world goes awry, the helmsman and the rowers of the ship of Peter fall asleep, and unhappy Italy is tossed by such buffeting of winds and waves as no words can describe. He warns all who in mad presumption have risen up against the will of God that they will suffer divine retribution.

He accuses the Florentines of avarice, which leads them to resist the glory of the Roman Emperor, the King of the earth, the minister of God. He reviles them for their disobedience 'to most sacred laws' (*sacratissimis legibus*), made in the likeness of natural justice,

> the observance of which, if it be joyous, if it be free, is not only no servitude, but to him who observes with understanding is manifestly in itself the most perfect liberty.[19]

Dante holds the concept of law in religious reverence. He had come to do so already in Bologna, when in *Il Convivio* he set forth civil and canon law as the remedy for avarice.[20] That society will one day be justly ordered is certain to him not only as divine law but as a law of nature.

The Florentines presume to set up a separate kingdom in opposition to that of Rome. Such folly is comparable to that of setting up a second Holy See, or of creating a second moon and a second sun, the symbols of Papal and imperial power.[21] Let them reflect that the penalty for their crime is the loss not only of wisdom but of the beginning of wisdom, namely the fear of God. Florence, he prophesies, is heading for destruction. He mocks their confidence in their 'contemptible rampart'. What use will it be to them when, terrible in gold, the eagle shall swoop down upon them, as once it soared over the whole civilized world, from the Pyrenees, the Caucasus, the Atlas mountains, and gazed down upon the vast expanse of ocean?

He draws a terrifying picture of the walls of Florence crumbling beneath the battering rams of the imperial army, the city set on fire, the populace starving and in rebellion, the churches, where women take refuge, despoiled, children suffering in wonder and ignorance for the sins of their fathers:

> And if my prophetic soul be not deceived, which announces what it has been taught by infallible signs and incontrovertible arguments, your city, worn out by ceaseless mourning, shall be delivered at the last into the hands of the stranger, after the greater part of you have been destroyed in death or captivity; and the few that shall be left to endure exile shall witness her downfall with tears and lamentation.[22]

The letter concludes with further prediction of the destruction of Florence and of the triumph of Henry, the elect of God.

Dante was no diplomat. The only reaction to such a letter would be further defiance. This proved to be the case. Between April and May the Florentines recalled many of their Guelf exiles in order to weaken the opposition beyond their walls. Unsurprisingly Dante was not included in this amnesty; in fact, in a second proclamation, he was expressly excluded.

His third letter, dated 17 April 1310, addressed this time to the Emperor himself, advises him to delay no longer in the north but to attack Florence at once. From the form of address it is apparent that Dante wrote as a spokesman for 'all the Tuscans everywhere who desire peace', that is, the exiles who long for justice. New hope arose in their hearts when Henry crossed the Alps and they sang, like Virgil, of the return of a golden age. They are now perturbed by his delay but have not lost trust in him,

> and I too, who write as well for myself as for others, beheld thee most gracious and heard thee most clement, as beseems Imperial Majesty, when my hands touched thy feet and my lips paid their tribute.[23]

But they are puzzled that he has not yet moved against Tuscany. He seems to regard his kingdom as limited by the boundaries of Liguria, forgetting that the glorious dominion of the Romans was confined neither by the frontiers of Italy nor by the coastline of Europe.

At this point Dante introduces a further proof of his beliefs. This did not appear in *Il Convivio*, nor in his previous letters, but it is one which he will later make the cornerstone of his treatise *Monarchia*.[24] In the earlier form in which it appears in this letter, the reasoning is as follows: when Augustus issued a decree that all the world should be taxed, as Luke records, the fact that the Son of God willed to be made Man at that time proves that the decree came from the court of a most just prince. We catch here a glimpse of the cogitation of Dante's mind as he sets down the outline of an idea that will ultimately assume immense importance in his view of history and Divine Providence.

Urging Henry to move at once against Florence, Dante has recourse to classical parallels. Henry is a new Aeneas, whom Mercury once chided for his delay in Carthage; his son, the royal first-born and heir, is another Ascanius who will follow in his father's steps and fall like a raging lion upon the followers of Turnus, treating with gentleness the followers of Latinus. He cites the example of Hercules who in his attempt to kill the Hydra at first cut off one head after another, which, ever multiplying, sprouted again, stronger than before, until he finally attacked the root of its life, applying fire to the neck whence all the heads sprouted. Of what use is it to subdue Cremona? New rebellion will break out at Brescia or Pavia and, when that is quelled, at Vercelli or at Bergamo or somewhere else. Can his exalted Highness not perceive from his watch-tower that the source of resistance is Florence? She is the viper who rends her mother's vitals, the sick sheep that infects the flock, the abandoned and unnatural Myrrha, inflamed with passion for her father, and Amata, who killed herself rather than accept her daughter Lavinia's marriage to Aeneas. Mingled with these mythological examples are glimpses of actual events. Dante is aware that the Florentines are doing their best to win over bordering regions by bribes and lying propaganda; they are also trying to bring about a breach between Henry and the Pope, as well as negotiating with King Robert of Naples, unlawfully bartering rights which are not theirs.

The letter concludes with renewed exhortation to Henry to put an end to delay, bidding him overthrow this Goliath with the sling of his wisdom and the stone of his strength, thereby restoring to the lamenting exiles their rights as citizens.

Henry paid no attention to Dante's advice. Throughout September 1311 he besieged Brescia and razed its fortifications. Lucca, allied with Florence, strengthened its defences. Henry again sent ambassadors to the Florentines, who refused to receive them. In October he moved to Genoa and in November commanded that representatives from Florence should appear before him. They again refused. That same month, King Robert sent troops to help Florence and Lucca in their resistance. The Guelfs of Brescia again rose against the Emperor and were expelled by his heroic supporter Can Grande della Scala. Parma and Reggio, aided by Florentine and other Tuscan Guelfs, also rebelled. Just as Dante had predicted, the Hydra's heads were sprouting on all sides.

At the beginning of 1312 Cremona again rebelled and drove out the Imperial representative. In February Henry strengthened the position of Can Grande della Scala by making him Imperial Vicar of Vicenza but that same month Padua, aided by Florence and Bologna, rebelled and likewise ejected the Emperor's representative. Pope Clement, who had at first declared his support in two encyclicals, now under menaces from Philip IV of France felt obliged to leave Henry to carry on his task alone, unaided, if not actually opposed, by Papal authority.

It was at this unpropitious moment that Henry resolved to go to Rome to be crowned Emperor. In February he set sail from Genoa for Pisa. In readiness, King Robert sent his brother, Prince John, to Rome to join forces with the Orsini in opposition to Henry's arrival. On 28 April Henry left Pisa and travelled by way of the Maremma to Viterbo, thence on to Rome, where on 7 May, with the help of the Colonna family, enemies of the Orsini, he forced an entry. Prince John's troops and the Guelfs of Tuscany assembled in strength to oppose the coronation. Henry was forced to compromise. St Peter's being in the hands of hostile forces, he accepted coronation in the church of St John Lateran. The ceremony was performed on 29 June by Cardinal Niccolò da Prato[25] and two other cardinals. On this occasion the crown was gold.

In August Henry returned to Tuscany and set up camp in Arezzo, where it is thought Dante was among those who flocked to support him in his preparations for besieging Florence. He opened the siege on 19 September and his forces were ranged outside the walls until the end of October. The Florentines received large reinforcements from the Guelfs of Tuscany and Romagna but prudently did not venture out into battle, preferring a policy of masterly inactivity. On 31 October Henry, having achieved nothing, withdrew to San Casciano, where he remained until 6 January 1313. Later that month he moved to Poggibonsi and in March he set up camp in Pisa, where he issued a proclamation against Florence depriving the city of all dignities and privileges. In August he resolved to march south against King Robert of Naples. Leaving Pisa, he encamped on the banks of the river Arbia at Montaperti, the scene of the disastrous defeat of the Florentine Guelfs in 1260.

And here Henry fell ill, some say of malaria, others allege that he was poisoned. He was moved to Buonconvento, near Siena, where on 24 August he died. His body was taken to Pisa, where he was buried in the Cathedral. His monument, attributed to the sculptor Giovanni Pisano, is in the Campo Santo.

The Florentines were jubilant. They addressed an exultant letter to their allies, inviting them to rejoice at the death of their enemy, 'the savage tyrant, Henry Count of Luxembourg'. So much for his three coronations.

For his supporters there was mourning and lamentation and bitter regret for what might have been. Cino da Pistoia, Dante's friend, composed a *canzone* in lament. To Dante the catastrophe must have been overwhelming, but from the tragedy he managed to draw forth renewed resolve, stronger now than ever, to set forth in the *Commedia* his unshaken conviction that *one day* a supreme monarch would arise and bring peace and justice to the world.[26]

CHAPTER 30

Better Waters

How far had Dante advanced in his writing of *Inferno* when Henry VII crossed the Alps in 1310? We do not know, but the following is significant. In Canto XIX Pope Nicholas III foretells that Clement V will push Boniface VIII and himself like pot-holers along the rock:

'chè dopo lui verrà di più laida opra,
    di ver ponente un pastor senza legge,
    tal che convien che lui e me ricopra.
Nuovo Jason sarà, di cui si legge
    ne' Maccabei; e come a quel fu molle
    suo re, così fia lui chi Francia regge.'

'for after him will come, in deeds more foul,
    a lawless shepherd from the west, to trim
    the two of us and move us down this hole.
Another Jason he will be, like him
    we read of in the book of Maccabees,
    who'll bend the king of France to suit his whim.'[1]

These words must have been written after Pope Clement V, having at first supported Henry, treacherously withdrew his allegiance in compliance with pressure from Philip IV in 1312.

Dante is likely to have suspended work on the *Commedia* from about 1310 until Henry's death in 1313. As has been shown, he was deeply involved in lending his impassioned eloquence to bring about what he believed would establish justice in a disordered world. This was no time for withdrawal into imaginative composition; nor is it likely that he would then have gathered an attentive audience. After Henry's failure and death, and in the civil unrest in Italy that followed, the political elements in *Inferno* increase. Ironic gibes at public figures, rebukes to cities and regions, predictions of retribution multiply and become ever more reckless. Florence in particular, from the beginning a target for reproach, grows ever more so. The doom Dante foretold for her in his Epistle is echoed in Canto XXVI of *Inferno* in words that are almost a quotation.[2] The anti-Florence theme is given even more forceful expression in *Purgatorio* and reaches the last word in condemnation in *Paradiso*.[3]

Dante knew now that the Monarch he foresaw would not come immediately. There was nothing to be hoped for from Henry's successor, Louis IV of Bavaria,[4] whose battles with a rival candidate, Frederick of Austria, and subsequently with Frederick's brother Leopold, kept him occupied north of the Alps. Pope John XXII, who succeeded Clement V in 1316, refused to recognize either Louis or his rival Frederick and would later assert his right to administer the Empire himself.[5]

Despite these discouraging events, Dante never lost faith that one day an ideal Monarch would arise, and he saw it as his task to prepare public opinion for his coming. He came to believe more strongly than ever that, like the divine citizens of ancient Rome of whom he writes in *Il Convivio* and in his epistle to the rulers of Italy, he himself was an instrument of the will of God. His poem must also have been sponsored.

Henry had been a forerunner: the time for him had not been ripe. There is an oblique reference to this in *Purgatorio*. Sordello, pointing out the rulers in the Valley of the Late Repentant, indicates the Emperor Rudolph, who, he says, might have healed the wounds of Italy but neglected to do so and her recovery will now be deferred:

> sì che tardi per altro si ricrea.

> *not soon her health another will restore.*[6]

The enthronement-to-be of Henry VII in Paradise, confirming and surpassing his three coronations upon earth, is Dante's supreme obeisance to the man who might have been the Monarch he still foresees. He has no actual person in mind but he believes that it is God's law and a law of nature that a ruler must one day come who will establish justice in the world. In the meantime he has his prophetic vision to complete.

The dark, at times despairing images of Hell are now left behind:

> Per correr migliori acque alza le vele
> omai la navicella del mio ingegno,
> che lascia dietro a sè mar sì crudele;
> e canterò di quel secondo regno
> dove l'umano spirito si purga
> e di salire al ciel diventa degno.

> *On better waters now to navigate*
> *my little skiff of talent lifts her sail,*
> *leaving behind a sea so full of hate;*

and of that second realm my song will tell
   where human souls are purged and fit become
   to rise up into spheres celestial.[7]

Poetry, which has died in *Inferno*, will come to life again. To help him he invokes the Muses, whose devotee he is, and in particular Calliope, the epic Muse, for he is entering now upon a more heroic mode, though mindful of the presumption of the daughters of King Pierus who, challenging the Nine, were turned into idly chattering magpies. Dante had read the story in Ovid's *Metamorphoses*,[8] in which Calliope is described as *rising* to sing and *striking* the chords of her lyre with her thumb. Ovid's words are echoed:

E qui Calliopè alquanto *surga*,
   seguitando il mio canto con quel sono
   di cui le Piche misere sentiro
lo *colpo* tal, che disperar perdono.

And here let Calliopè awhile arise,
   accompanying my song with that same sound
   which struck *in punishment the wretched Pies,*
from which no pardon ever could be found.[9]

Dante still keeps Ovid at his elbow as he writes; likewise Lucan, as will be seen below.

The tale of a journey across the sea to an unknown island was almost as widespread in folklore as the tale of the underground journey into Hell. A well-known example was the *Navigatio Brendani* ('The Voyage of St Brendan'), a Celtic tale of sea adventure similar to the Imrama of Irish literature. Transmitted in Latin in the ninth century, it was adapted in prose and verse in Old French, Italian, Provençal and other languages. Dante may have read the Tuscan version, which dated from the early years of the fourteenth century. St Brendan's goal is the 'Promised Land of the Saints' and after prolonged search he finds it, but is sent back to Ireland where he tells his tale. In some versions, he makes several journeys. On the first he meets the Devil who takes him to the gate of Hell, where he sees 'a rough, hot prison, full of stench and filth and flame' and horrifying punishments. On the second he comes to an island where he meets an old man covered with white hair, like the feathers of a dove or a sea-mew, who has the speech of an angel. He admits Brendan to a land of Paradise, with radiant fields and fragrant flowers, where he hears melodies and shouts of joy. In other versions he comes to a Paradise of Birds. These are the neutral angels who upon the rebellion of Lucifer were neither for him nor for God. Being without active guilt they had been transformed into birds and relegated here to await the Resurrection.[10] It has been shown that Dante allots a more degrading fate to them in *Inferno*,[11] discreetly omitting all mention of them afterwards in *Paradiso*.

It is early dawn when Dante and Virgil emerge from the *pertugio tondo* ('round aperture') on to the shore of the Mountain of Purgatory. The sky is sapphire from the zenith to the horizon and Venus, the morning star, who incites all things to love, makes the east joyful as she veils the constellation of Pisces following in her train. Turning towards the south, Dante sees four stars, so brilliant that the whole sky seems to rejoice in their sparkling:

> Oh settentrional vedovo sito,
>> poi che privato se' di mirar quelle!

> *Oh widowed region of the northern sphere,*
>> *deprived of gazing on such stars as those!*[12]

These stars are strangely suggestive of the Southern Cross but since Dante says that they were never seen except by the *prima gente* ('first people'), that is, Adam and Eve,[13] it is unlikely that he had heard of them from Marco Polo and other travellers. It has slipped his mind that he has made Ulysses say that at one point all the stars of the southern sky were visible:

> 'Tutte le stelle già dell'altro polo
> vedea la notte …'

> *'Already all the stars of the south pole*
> *the night beheld …'*[14]

Turning his gaze towards the north, whence the Wain has already vanished, Dante sees the figure of an old man,

> degno di tanta reverenza in vista,
> che più non dee a padre alcun figliuolo.

> *so worthy in his bearing of respect,*
> *no son to father greater reverence owes.*[15]

His beard is long and streaked with white, and a double tress of silvered hair falls to his breast. Here is the old man of St Brendan's tale, as the audience would expect, but he is a great deal more than that. His face is so adorned with the light of the four holy stars that it seems as though the sun is shining on him. He does not welcome the travellers but sternly challenges them in deep, authoritative tones, shaking his venerable tresses as he speaks. It is interesting that here Dante calls his tresses *piume* ('feathers'), a word retained like a fossil from the earlier story of St Brendan:

> 'Chi siete voi che contro al cieco fiume
>> fuggita avete la pregione etterna?'
>> diss'el, movendo quelle oneste piume.

'Chi v'ha guidati, o chi vi fu lucerna,
    uscendo fuor della profonda notte
    che sempre nera fa la valle inferna?
Son le leggi d'abisso così rotte?
    O è mutato in ciel novo consiglio,
    che dannati venite alle mie grotte?'

'Who are you who upstream the hidden brook
    the eternal prison have escaped?' he said,
    shaking those reverend feathers as he spoke.
'Who was your guide, your lantern, when you fled
    the night profound which everlasting is,
    shrouding in black the valley of the dead?
Thus broken are the laws of the Abyss?
    Or does new law in Heaven now permit
    the damned to seek my grottoes as they please?'[16]

Virgil knows at once who this is: he has seen him before in Limbo. He takes hold of Dante and commands him to kneel and bow his head. The magic words with which he quelled Charon and Minos will not serve him now. He launches into an eloquent oration, in which, though his name is not mentioned, it is revealed that this is Cato of Utica, the 'god-like' Roman so revered by Dante. Virgil answers all Cato's questions, explaining that neither he nor Dante is among the damned, that his commission comes from on high, and asks for consent to lead his charge through the seven kingdoms under Cato's command. Dante meanwhile, kneeling in devout reverence, has his ears pricked.

'Libertà va cercando, ch' è sì cara,
    come sa chi per lei vita rifiuta.
    Tu 'l sai, che non ti fu per lei amara
in Utica la morte, ove lasciasti
    la vesta ch'al gran dì sarà sì chiara.'

'Freedom he seeks, which is so dear, as he
    who his own life renounces for it knows.
    Thou knowest, for in Utica for thee
death was not harsh when thou thy garb didst shed
    which glorified on the great day will be.'[17]

This forecast by Virgil of Cato's ultimate salvation is startling. Dante has allowed himself to imagine that Christ, when He released souls from Limbo, drew forth Cato, a pre-Christian Roman. Unlike the patriarchs and those who believed in Christ to come, he was not transported immediately to Heaven but must await the Last Judgement, serving in the meantime as guardian of the slopes of Mount Purgatory. This unorthodox addition to

Christian belief is the more challenging in that Cato had committed suicide rather than yield to Caesar after his defeat of Pompey, an act to which Virgil here refers in admiration, linking it with a dedication to liberty. Since the passport to Purgatory is repentance, the implication can only be that Cato has repented of his sin of suicide and purges it by the service he performs as guardian of those who arrive on the shore of the mountain on their way to Heaven.

Dante's idealized portrait of Cato was derived from Lucan: the great-hearted Cato of Stoic courage, who raised the morale of his troops before leading them on their march across the Libyan desert, the true father of his country who would one day be deified and Rome would have a god by whose name it need not be ashamed to swear.[18] Lucan left his epic poem unfinished, before reaching Cato's suicide, but Dante had read Cicero's comment, which he would later quote in *Monarchia*:

> Nature had bestowed on Cato an austerity beyond belief and he had strengthened it with unfailing constancy, and had always persisted in any resolve or plan he had undertaken. It was fitting therefore that he should die rather than submit to a tyrant.[19]

Such are the origins of Dante's historical and ethical view of Cato of Utica, but the episode in which this august figure appears in *Purgatorio* belongs not to history or to ethics but to poetry. 'Dead poetry' (*la morta poesia*), poetry that has been entombed with death and damnation, does indeed now come to life again.

The scene has a visual, almost theatrical quality. The three figures, Cato, with the starlight upon him, speaking in his deep, sonorous voice, Virgil, awe-struck and deferential, Dante, kneeling, his head bowed, in the presence of the two Romans he most greatly revered, are like characters in a play. Virgil, in a long, ornate speech, requests Cato's consent to proceed on their journey in the name of Cato's wife, Marcia, a fellow soul with Virgil in Limbo. Cato's response to Virgil's eloquence is one of the most memorable snubs in literature:

> 'Marzia piacque tanto alli occhi miei
>   mentre ch'io fui di là', diss'elli allora,
>   'che quante grazie volse da me, fei.
> Or che di là dal mal fiume dimora,
>   più muover non mi può, per quella legge
>   che fatta fu quando me n'uscì fora.'
>
> *'Marcia', said he, 'when I lived yonder there,*
>   *so pleased my eyes that any boon whatever*
>   *desired by her of me I granted her.*

Now that she dwells beyond the evil river
  she may not move me, by the edict made
  when from that place I took my leave forever.'[20]

'... but since a lady from on high is guiding thee, there is no need for flattery (*non c'è mestier lusinghe*), let it suffice to ask me in her name.'

This stern rebuff is in keeping with the Stoic personality of the historical Cato. So too is his lack of interest in Dante except as someone who is in no condition to appear before the heavenly beings he will meet. To Cato he is simply *costui* ('this man here') and he commands Virgil to take him to the water's edge and cleanse his face and gird him with a rush, which he will find growing at the margin of the island,

'là giù colà dove la batte l'onda'

'down there below where the wave laps the shore'[21]

a line which reveals Cato as a master of onomatopoeia. They are not to return the same way. The sun, which is rising, will show them where they can ascend the mountain more easily. Having given these terse instructions, he vanishes: *Così sparì.*[22]

This sudden disappearance of Cato belongs to fairytale. Indeed, this and the following canto of *Purgatorio* are written with a delicate enchantment that reveals a new aspect of Dante's poetic imagination.

As the light of dawn grows, the morning breeze departs and in the distance Dante can make out *il tremolar della marina* ('the trembling of the sea'). In a shady spot, where the dew still lingers, Virgil gently lays both hands outspread on the young grass:

Ambo le mani in su l'erbetta sparte
  soavemente 'l mio maestro pose:
  ond'io, che fui accorto di sua arte,
porsi ver lui le guance lacrimose ...

My master then extended both his hands,
  laying them gently on the tender grass:
  and I, like one who swiftly understands,
  towards him lifted up my tear-stained face ...[23]

This unforgettable scene is one of the most intimate moments in the *Commedia*.

Descending to the empty shore, Dante reflects that no man has ever sailed towards it who was subsequently able to return. He is thinking of Ulysses. He does not name him but the three rhyme-words in the context are the same with which he concludes the story of that doomed voyage: *acque, piacque, rinacque.*[24] Then, as Cato has commanded, Virgil girds Dante with a rush. The canto ends with another touch of fairytale; by a marvel the plant that is plucked grows up again immediately:

> Oh maraviglia! chè qual elli scelse
> l'umile pianta, cotal si rinacque
> subitamente là onde l'avelse.

> *O marvellous! the very stalk he chose*
> *amid the humble plant was born again,*
> *for where he plucked, the same at once arose.*[25]

CHAPTER 31

The Morning Sun

Dante the poet has now induced in his audience the responses of eagerness and hope, as also in the character whose role he plays. The early sun has reached the horizon. Standing beside Virgil at the water's edge, he sees a light which skims across the sea. As it grows brighter and larger, a whiteness appears to surround it. Virgil, who remains silent, discerns the figure of a winged pilot and exclaims to Dante:

> ... 'Fa, fa che le ginocchia cali:
> ecco l'angel di Dio: piega le mani;
> omai vedrai di sì fatti officiali.'

> ... 'Down, down upon thy knees,
> behold, this is God's angel, fold thy hands,
> henceforth thou'lt see such ministers as these.'[1]

This pilot needs neither oars nor sails. His wings, raised high, fanning the air, suffice *tra liti sì lontani* ('between such far-off shores').[2] As he draws near his brightness so increases that Dante's eyes are dazzled. The vessel comes to land, so light it draws no water. On the stern stands the heavenly steersman and in the boat sit more than a hundred souls, singing in unison the psalm *In exitu Israel de Aegypto* ('When Israel went out of Egypt').[3] Dante had chosen this text in *Il Convivio* as an example of spiritual allegory: while conveying a historical truth, it also signifies the release of the soul from sin.[4] The angel blesses the souls with the sign of the Cross, they disembark and he departs as swiftly as he came.

The new arrivals look about them not knowing which way to turn. Seeing Dante and Virgil they ask for directions. Virgil says they are strangers like themselves, having come by another route so rough and hard that to climb the mountain will seem easy in comparison. The souls notice from Dante's breathing that he is in the first life and grow pale with wonder. Like people crowding round a messenger who carries an olive branch, they press forward, eager to learn how this can be, as though forgetful of the purpose of their journey. One soul draws near to Dante, his arms outstretched. Dante responds but his arms three times fail to clasp the soul and fold back empty on his breast.

The metaphysics of the southern world are different from those in Hell; they are also variable. Virgil can seize hold of Dante and make him kneel before Cato, but Dante cannot touch this soul, who, smiling at his astonishment and repeated attempts, bids him desist. Dante then knows who he is and begs him to wait:

> Rispuosemi: 'Così come io t'amai
> nel mortal corpo, così t'amo sciolta:
> però m'arresto; ma tu perchè vai?'

> *'As in my mortal bonds', was his reply,*
> *'I loved thee, so, released, I love thee still:*
> *therefore I wait; but where goest thou and why?'*[5]

This is Casella, a singer, who is said to have set Dante's poems to music. When Dante wrote this canto, Casella had been dead for about 15 years. Since he died early in the year 1300,[6] Dante is obliged to explain how it is that he arrives only now, on Easter Sunday of that year.[7] Casella tells him that souls who die repentant gather at the mouth of the Tiber to await their passage to the southern hemisphere. For the last three months (since the proclamation of the Papal Jubilee) the angel-pilot has readily taken all who were eager to come. Casella's time of waiting, therefore, has not been lengthened but reduced.[8]

Asked if in his new state he can recall the songs of love with which he used to solace Dante's longings, Casella at once responds and his sweet voice sounds forth:

> *Amor che nella mente mi ragiona*
> cominciò elli allor sì dolcemente,
> che la dolcezza ancora dentro mi sona.

> Love which discourses to me in my mind
> *so sweetly he began to sing at my request,*
> *that in me still the sweetness is entwined.*[9]

Virgil and the hundred and more souls are likewise entranced, listening as if they had no other purpose for being there. They are interrupted by the stern tones of Cato, who reappears. Astonished to find the new arrivals dallying, he calls, in words resonant of a deep voice:

> ... 'Che è ciò, spiriti lenti?
> Qual negligenza, qual stare è questo?
> Correte al monte a spogliarvi lo scoglio
> ch' esser non lascia a voi Dio manifesto.'

> ... *'What now, you laggard souls,*
> *what dallying's this, what loitering behind?*
> *Off to the mount to strip away the scale*
> *which to the sight of God still makes you blind.'*[10]

Like doves startled at their feeding, the souls scatter, making for the slopes, going they know not where. Nor is the obedient departure of Virgil and Dante any less swift.

We know nothing of the poetry recitals that took place in Florence when Dante was a young man, but here, after many years in exile, he longingly evokes just such an occasion, recapturing his own trance-like pleasure in the sound of singing. There was evident affection between the two friends (*Casella mio*, Dante calls him), but those days are gone and he must not dwell nostalgically on the past. That is the meaning of Cato's harsh rebuke: there are urgent spiritual tasks ahead. Abashed, the souls disperse, Casella with them. Despite Cato, however, he has lingered for centuries in the imagination of readers, one of whom was Milton.

The *canzone* that Dante chooses for Casella to sing has a special significance at this point in the *Commedia*. Dante had provided it as the second dish of his banquet, *Il Convivio*.[11] A dedication of the intellect to divine Wisdom, it is also a love poem, inspired not by Beatrice, but by the *donna gentile*, identified by Dante in his commentary as Philosophy. In the first stanza, which we may hope Casella had time to sing, Dante conveys the difficulties he has met in his study of philosophy: his mind cannot inwardly express certain things and even what he can grasp he cannot adequately put into words. This is appropriate to the character Dante's unreadiness at the present stage in his journey: he still has many things to learn and many errors to shed, not only on Mount Purgatory but also in the spheres of Paradise. The second stanza draws the listeners' thoughts up into the heavens and to the movement of the sun in its apparent circling of the earth. In *Il Convivio* this had led to a long astronomical discourse, which he is about to transform into an engaging dialogue between himself and Virgil.

The doctrine of Purgatory released in Dante a sense of joyful elation. Despite all the evil that human beings commit, the arms of God's mercy are so wide that all who repent and seek forgiveness, even at the last moment before death, are saved from damnation, though the process of purgation they undergo may last for centuries. It is not sinful actions that are punished here, for those have been absolved, but sinful innate tendencies. These are known in theology as the Seven Capital (or Deadly) Sins: pride, envy, wrath, sloth, avarice, gluttony, lust. They are like illnesses of which the soul must be healed before it is fit to ascend to Heaven. The time of healing can be shortened by prayers offered by the living. It is for this reason that the souls on the Mountain, on realizing that Dante is still in the body and will return to the world they have left, are so eager to give him messages to take back about themselves.

To this orthodox doctrine, Dante adds an arrangement of his own. Below the seven cornices on which the Capital Sins are purged are two terraces where souls who died excommunicate, who delayed repentance owing to indolence or overriding concerns or who suffered sudden death are obliged to spend a preliminary period of waiting before entering on their purgation. This extension allows Dante to vary the personalities he meets and the circumstances in which he converses with them.

In Hell Dante was an observer. In Purgatory he is a participant, sharing, as a figure of mankind, a token purgation of all seven sins, which results in a bond between him and the souls. Love is an all-embracing element throughout this *cantica*, like the sunlight, in which his imagination flowers. He takes pleasure in constructing and adorning his three-dimensional world and visualizing himself moving about in it. We are now in the presence of Dante the scenographer.

He is particularly skilful with his lighting effects. As he and Virgil slow down their pace and walk towards the mountain, the sun is behind them. In front of him he sees his shadow, but only his. Alarmed, he turns, thinking that Virgil has left him. But Virgil is there, reassuring him and reproaching him for his lack of faith. He takes the opportunity to remind Dante of the time difference between the two hemispheres:

'Vespero è là colà dov' è sepolto
    lo corpo dentro al quale io facea ombra:
    Napoli l'ha, a da Brandizio è tolto.'

*'It is now twilight where my body lies,
    wherein I cast a shade, from Brindisi
    to Naples taken after my demise.'* [12]

He then begins a discourse on the insubstantial nature of souls, something which is beyond the grasp of philosophers, who yearn in vain for solutions to the mysteries of faith. 'I speak of Aristotle and Plato and many others', he says, and bows his head, seeming disquieted. This is a passing but structurally important allusion to Virgil's eventual return to the noble castle in Limbo, where the souls dwell in longing without hope.

Dante meanwhile has been looking up at the cliff and sees on the left a group of souls advancing slowly. He and Virgil have moved on a thousand paces, or 'about as far as a stone would fly from a good thrower's hand', when the souls stand still, pressing close together against the side of the cliff. Virgil addresses them with courtesy and respect:

'O ben finiti, o già spiriti eletti',
    Virgilio incominciò, 'per quella pace
    ch'i' credo che per voi tutti s'aspetti,
ditene dove la montagna giace
    sì che possibil sia l'andare in suso;
    chè perder tempo a chi più sa più spiace.'

Virgil began, 'O souls whose death was blessed,
    spirits already chosen for that peace
    which I believe awaits you, I request,
say where the mountain is less steep, to ease
    our upward path, for loss of time, the more
    one knows its value, must the more displease.'[13]

As sheep huddle behind their leader, stopping they know not why, so do the souls when those in front catch sight of Dante's shadow. Virgil at once confirms that his companion is a living man, privileged by power on high to make the journey. The souls, gesturing with the backs of their hands (a particularly Italian gesture), instruct them to turn and walk ahead of them.

They do so and a voice calls out: 'Whoever thou art, turn round and say if thou hast ever seen me yonder in the world.' Dante turns and looks at him fixedly:

Biondo era e bello e di gentile aspetto,
ma l'un de' cigli un colpo avea diviso.

Blond, beautiful and nobly born he seemed,
but one brow had been severed by a blow.[14]

Dante humbly disowns ever having seen him. The soul shows him a wound on his breast and, smiling, says, 'I am Manfred, grandson of the Empress Constance.'

This is a royal personage of high standing. The natural son of the Emperor Frederick II, he was a scion of the Hohenstaufen, a Germanic dynasty, from whom he inherited his blond good looks. On his father's death in 1250 he became ruler of Apulia and Sicily and was a powerful supporter of the Imperial cause. Pope Clement IV excommunicated him and established Charles, Count of Anjou, the son of King Louis of France, in his place. Charles defeated Manfred at the Battle of Benevento, at which he was slain, in 1266.

Manfred relates that on receiving two mortal blows he turned in tears to God:

'Orribil furon li peccati miei;
    ma la bontà infinita ha sì gran braccia
    che prende ciò che si rivolge a lei.'

'Horrible were the sins I did commit;
  but infinite good has such wide-open arms
  that it receives whoever turns to it.'[15]

Manfred was alleged to have committed several murders in his attempt to hold on to power[16] but the chief barrier to his redemption was his excommunication. Dante has undertaken to save him from damnation by decreeing in *his* Purgatory that those who die repentant, though excommunicate, are redeemed, though obliged to spend there 30 times the number of years they remained in contumacy with the Church. Manfred asks Dante to give his daughter Constance, mother of the kings of Sicily and Aragon, the joyful news that he is not in Hell. When Dante wrote these words, Constance had been dead for many years.[17] They are, in effect, addressed to the Papacy, defying the orthodox belief that excommunication ineluctably damned a soul to Hell.

Chroniclers had recorded that Manfred's body was not found for some days after the battle, when a camp follower recognized it, flung it across an ass and went about calling, 'Who will buy King Manfred?' It was brought before King Charles, who, at the request of Manfred's barons who had been taken prisoner, gave him an honourable burial. Having been excommunicated he could not be interred in consecrated ground, but a pit was dug at the foot of a bridge near Benevento and every soldier cast one stone over it, building up a cairn. When the Pope heard what had been done, he ordered the Archbishop of Cosenza to dig up the body and scatter the remains along the bank of the river Verde, beyond land belonging to the Church. 'If the Archbishop had read God's page more carefully,' Manfred says, 'my bones would still lie at the bridgehead near Benevento under the shelter of the heavy cairn.'[18]

His choice of King Manfred as an example of a redeemed excommunicate is significant. He had formed from chroniclers a romantic concept of him as a courtier, a poet, a musician, a valiant soldier and a royal personage of outstanding beauty. In *De Vulgari Eloquentia*[19] he had referred to him and his father as the founders of the Sicilian school of poetry:

> Those illustrious heroes, the Emperor Frederick[20] and his well-born[21] son Manfred, displayed the nobility and righteousness of their character, as long as fortune remained favourable, ... and those who were of noble heart and endowed with grace strove to attach themselves to the majesty of such great princes. Consequently, in their time whatever the best Italians attempted first appeared at the court of these mighty sovereigns.

He had then begun a diatribe against their successors, strangely irrelevant to the subject of the text, as he himself admits, saying, 'But it is better to return to our subject than to speak in vain.' The degeneracy of their followers is a matter he will resume with renewed emphasis in *Purgatorio*, not this time, he hoped, in vain.[22]

Whatever Dante's ultimate opinion of Frederick II and of his descendants, it is evident that he was susceptible to the glamour of royal personages and to male beauty. Manfred was defeated in battle but Dante invests him nevertheless with an aura of victory. His wounds were honourably received facing the enemy and his soul has defeated the anathema of a Pope. When other details fade from our attention, in the single line

biondo era e bello e di gentile aspetto

King Manfred still shines from the page like a golden heraldic figure in the light of the morning sun.

CHAPTER 32

From Humour to Invective

At a certain point, the excommunicate souls point out a gap where Virgil and Dante can ascend to the next level. The ascent is strenuous and Dante is left exhausted and breathless. To recover, he sits on a ledge and looks east, first down at the shore and then up at the sun. To his astonishment it is on his left. Virgil notices his surprise and there follows a dialogue which is a delightful game of mockery, of the audience and of Dante himself.[1]

The explanation is simple: they are south of the equator, where, if one turns to the east, the sun at mid-morning is on one's left, whereas north of the equator it is on one's right. Dante makes Virgil provide a long and involved account, a parody of learned writings on the subject. 'If Castor and Pollux,' he begins, 'were in company with the mirror that carries its light upwards and downwards, the glowing Zodiac wheel would be still closer to the Bears, unless it departed from its ancient track. To understand clearly how this may be, imagine Zion and this mountain so placed that they have one horizon in common and different hemispheres. It will then be plain that the highway[2] on which Phaethon failed to drive must necessarily pass this mountain on the one side and that on the other side, if thou wilt give thy mind to it carefully.'

In simple terms, if it were summer, the sun would be still further north; and since Mount Zion and the Mountain of Purgatory are exactly opposite to each other, the sun is always to the south of Zion and to the north of Purgatory. Dante's reply, also needlessly involved, is devised to produce still more confusion and to demonstrate his own nimble wits. With smug complacency he answers, 'Truly, Master, I never saw anything so clearly as I now discern what I failed to grasp before, that the mid-circle of the celestial motion, which is called the equator in astronomy, always lies between the sun and winter, and is as far northward from us here now as the Hebrews saw it towards the torrid regions.'

Eager now to proceed, he asks how much further they have to go, for the mountain soars beyond his sight. Virgil encourages him by saying the climb will seem easier the higher he goes, until when he reaches the top it will be like going downstream in a boat. At this moment a voice is heard close by:

> ... 'Forse
> che di sedere in pria avrai distretta!'

> ... *'Maybe*
> *before then thou'lt have need to sit awhile.'*[3]

They turn and notice a large boulder, in the shade of which souls are resting. One of them sits clasping his knees and holding his face down between them. Dante calls Virgil to look at this picture of indolence. The soul, scarcely moving his head along his thigh, says, 'Go on up, thou who art so strong!' Dante then knows who he is and, although still weary, moves towards him. The soul raises his head a little and says mockingly, 'Hast thou taken in how the sun drives his chariot on thy left?'

The soul is that of Belacqua, another friend from Dante's Florentine days, a maker of musical instruments, so lazy that he was said never to walk when he could sit. The genial banter between them evokes a happy relationship, so much so that Dante, the censorious moralist, relaxes for a moment and smiles. This sudden, intimate self-portrait has caught at the heart of many readers: Dante, stooping over the hunched figure of his lazy friend, smiling indulgently at his foible, as perhaps he did when he visited him in his workshop, pleased now to find him not in Hell but among those who will ultimately be blessed. But why, he asks, does he delay? Belacqua answers: 'What would be the use of going up?' He has to wait until the length of his earthly life has passed before the 'angel of God who sits in the doorway'[4] will let him in, unless prayers from a soul in grace shorten the time. 'What other prayers are of use?' Belacqua asks, with characteristic resignation.

But Virgil is calling. They must move on:

> ... 'Vienne omai: vedi ch' è tocco
> meridian dal sole ed alla riva
> cuopre la notte già col piè Morocco.'

> ... *'Make haste, see how*
> *the sun has touched meridian, and night*
> *at the far shore bestrides Morocco now.'*[5]

In this brilliant stanza we see the whole globe of earth, the southern hemisphere ablaze with noon-day light, the northern swathed in midnight black.

Following in Virgil's steps, Dante hears a soul call out, 'Look, the rays of the sun are blocked on the left of the one below', a nice example of stage-management, indicating that he has now turned direction. He looks back, his attention self-centredly held by the amazement of the souls. Virgil sternly rebukes him:

> 'Perchè l'animo tuo tanto s'impiglia',
>   disse 'l maestro, 'che l'andare allenti?
>   Che ti fa ciò che quivi si pispiglia?
> Vien dietro a me, e lascia dir le genti:
>   sta come torre ferma, che non crolla
>   già mai la cima per soffiar de' venti.'

> *'Why do thy wits so wander in a snare',*
>   *my master said, 'that thou dost lag behind?*
>   *If they are whispering, why shouldst thou care?*
> *Follow, and let them talk as they've a mind.*
>   *Stand like a solid tower that never bows*
>   *its head for all the buffeting of wind.'*[6]

Dante, blushing with shame, can only reply, 'I come'.

They now meet souls who died in battle or in murder. Having put off repentance until the last moment they, like the indolent, must spend time equal to their years on earth before they are admitted to the cornices of purgation. Among them is Buonconte da Montefeltro, a Ghibelline warrior killed on the battlefield of Campaldino, where Dante himself had fought.[7] Buonconte's body was never recovered and Dante invents an explanation, drawing a deliberate contrast between Buonconte and his father Guido da Montefeltro, the fate of whose soul, like that of his son, was in a critical balance at the point of death.[8] It is possible that Dante may himself have slain Buonconte or have seen him slain: they were both fighting in the cavalry, on opposing sides. The reference to the fatal wound in the throat suggests one or the other possibility. If so, the story he gives Buonconte to relate concerning his final moments takes on a personal poignancy.

As a guest in the castle of Poppi, Dante had many opportunities to revisit the plain of Campaldino and to recall the battle in which he had fought as a young man. In stormy weather he could have watched the river Archiano gushing in full spate into the Arno, causing it to overflow its banks.[9] Was this, he may have pondered, how Buonconte's body disappeared? 'Where the stream joins the river,' Buonconte relates, 'I arrived, unhorsed, my throat cut, my blood staining the ground.' There he lost the power of sight and managing only to utter the single word 'Mary':

> 'caddi e rimase la mia carne sola'.

> *'I fell and my dead flesh alone was left.'*[10]

This vivid picture of a body emptied of its soul further suggests Dante's memories of seeing death in combat, possibly even the death of Buonconte.

As in the case of his father, Buonconte's soul was the object of dispute between an angel and a devil. The angel claimed him and the devil bitterly complained:

'Tu te ne porti di costui l'etterno
   per una lacrimetta che 'l mi toglie;
   ma io farò dell'altro governo!'

'Thou carriest off the eternal part of him
   for one small tear by which thou robbest me;
   but with the other I will have my whim!' [11]

The devil conjured up a mist that hung between the mountains of Pratomagno and the Apennines, such as Dante must have often seen when he was in the region. This so charged the sky that the air was turned to water. Down came the rain, swirling in torrents that poured full spate into the Arno. The Archiano reached Buonconte's stiffened body and swept it along, loosening its arms from the cross it had formed at the moment of death and rolling it over and over between the banks until it was covered with weed.

The vividly imagined fate of Buonconte's body is followed by the brief, plaintive words of another soul. This is Pia dei Tolomei, said to have been murdered by her husband. She is forever memorable for the courteous words in which she asks Dante to pray for her:

'Deh, quando tu sarai tornato al mondo
   e riposato della lunga via',
     seguitò il terzo spirito al secondo,
'ricorditi di me che son la Pia:
   Siena mi fè; disfecemi Maremma:
   salsi colui che 'nnanellata pria
disposando m'avea con la sua gemma.'

'I beg, when thou the world once more hast gained
   and rested art from thy long journeying,'
   another spirit added at the end,
'the name of Pia to thy memory bring.
   Siena gave me life, Maremma death,
   as he well knows who wed me with his ring,
having, betrothed to me, first pledged his faith.' [12]

Pia's womanly thought for Dante's need of rest after his journey offers a glimpse of the pleasure he took in feminine sympathy. Coming as it does immediately after the memory of the brutal masculinity of battle it is peculiarly touching.

The other souls who clamour round him, eager that he should take back messages to their relatives on earth, are less self-effacing. Dante, comparing himself to a winner at a game of dice, around whom a crowd gathers hoping for a share, names only six of them, briefly and dismissively. 'When I had rid myself of one and all,' he says with somewhat callous detachment, 'I questioned Virgil as to the efficacy of prayer.' Virgil draws a distinction between prayers from souls who are in grace and those who are not (as indeed Belacqua has already done) and says this must suffice until Beatrice is able to expound the matter further: Dante will see her upon the summit of the mountain, smiling and blessed.

At the mention of her name all Dante's detachment vanishes. He is at once eager to hurry on. Virgil tells him that things are otherwise than he thinks. They can advance as long as there is light but before they reach the mountain's crest they will again see the sun, which is now hidden by the slope, so that Dante no longer casts a shadow. This adroit change in the lighting arrangement serves conveniently to remove Dante from the centre of attention.

Seated to one side is a majestic figure. Gazing disdainfully at the travellers, he is about to let them pass, watching them like a lion couched. Virgil, however, approaches him and asks the way to the easiest ascent. The soul does not reply but asks only where they come from and who they are. Virgil begins: 'Mantua ...' and the soul at once leaps up, crying 'O Mantuan, I am Sordello of thy city!' and they embrace each other.

At this point Dante steps outside the narrative, like a modern broadcaster who leaves the autocue, and speaks in his own person: Dante the exile, Dante the public figure, Dante the champion of imperial authority. For the rest of the canto he rails, as through a megaphone, against Emperors who have neglected Italy and against Florence, his city still ('my Florence'), which has lapsed into turmoil. The time from which he speaks is 1300, but he is writing more than a decade later, not long after the tragic failure of Henry VII and the resistance Florence had mounted against him.[13]

The power of the invective is all the stronger for being unexpected. It is the brotherly love of the two Mantuans, evoked by the mere mention of their city's name, which releases the outburst. Dante the character in the story stands unobserved, in shadow, a silent onlooker. Dante the writer stands forward in dramatic prominence and gives vent to his personal wrath, bringing into evidence the political aim of his work. This is the Dante who at the time of Henry's coming addressed letters to the rulers of Italy, to the Florentines and to Henry himself: all to no avail. With apocalyptic fury he denounces the irresponsible Emperors and foretells the assassination of Albert, calling it a just judgement; with grief he enumerates the feuds by which Italy is torn;[14] with frenzied sarcasm he mocks the Florentines for their lawlessness and for their continual changes of legislation.

The diatribe is given immense force by cumulative alliteration. Read aloud for the first time it must have held his listeners spell-bound, a striking example of Dante's demagogic power. The similes are overpowering: Italy is an abode of grief, a ship without a pilot in a raging storm, no longer ruler of domains but a common hireling,[15] a riderless horse. Of what use is the bridle of laws refitted by Justinian if the saddle is empty? Or worse, if it is mounted by the clergy who usurp the authority of Caesar? The remedy is long in coming and at the time of writing Dante seems almost to have given up hope: has God turned His eyes away, or is He preparing some good in the secret abyss of His counsel? The bitterness of the outburst, inspired by the recent tragedy of Henry's failure and by the thought of what might have been, is deeply moving. After seven centuries the force of his resentment and of his desire for vengeance has not diminished.

Some explanation of Sordello's function as the trigger of this invective is required. Sordello, the poet, was born in Goito, near Mantua, in about the year 1200 but spent most of his life in Provence. About 40 of his poems are extant, all in Provençal. Dante speaks of him admiringly in *De Vulgari Eloquentia*,[16] as being distinguished by his eloquence both in poetry and in other writings, from which it is apparent that Dante had read certain prose works by Sordello which have not been preserved. One poem in particular, known as the *Lament for Blacatz*, is a denunciation of the foremost princes of Europe. It is perhaps from this that Dante derived the concept of him as a figure appropriate to associate with his own invective.

Dante returns to the poem as narrator in the following canto. The gestures of greeting between the two Mantuans are repeated three and four times before Sordello draws back and asks, 'But you, who are you?'[17] Virgil replies, 'Before souls worthy to ascend to God had approached this mountain my bones were buried by the Emperor Octavian. I am Virgil, and for no other fault I was deprived of Heaven but for lack of faith.'

Overcome by the marvel of Virgil's presence, Sordello bows, embracing him *là 've 'l minor s'appiglia* ('where the humble clasp the great'):[18]

'O gloria de' Latin' disse, 'per cui
    mostrò ciò che potea la lingua nostra,
    o pregio etterno del loco ond'io fui,
qual merito o qual grazia mi ti mostra?
    S'io son d'udir le tue parole degno,
    dimmi se vien d'inferno, e di qual chiostra.'

'O glory of the Latins', he exclaimed,
    'through whom our tongue showed all that it could do,
    for whom my birthplace is forever famed,

what grace or merit thee to me doth show?
    If I deserving am to hear thy words,
    art thou from Hell, and from which quire below?'[19]

In Virgil's reply, in which he tells Sordello of his place in Limbo and of his journey, sanctioned by divine power, he omits all mention of the fact that Dante is a living man. Here is another example of well-contrived stage-management: the revelation is reserved for a later moment when it will not draw attention away from Virgil and will make its own more dramatic impact.

Night is now approaching and Sordello, stooping to the ground, draws a line with his finger, saying, 'Once the sun goes down there can be no going up, not even past this mark, but only down and round the hillside.' He conducts the two travellers to a valley where they can rest and await the new day. There follows a beautiful scene, filled with colour, fragrance and the sound of singing.

CHAPTER 33

Close of Day and a New Dawn

The first day on Mount Purgatory begins and ends with song. Seated on the slopes of the valley to which Sordello leads Virgil and Dante are the souls of kings, princes and other rulers whose responsibilities and worldly cares led them to delay repentance. They too must wait the length of their earthly lives before entering the gate to the cornices of purgation. Sordello identifies the souls from a bank, from which vantage point the poets can see them well, a scene which balances a similar moment in Limbo.[1] There Dante and the five poets had looked down upon a meadow of bright green grass, peopled with illustrious souls; here Dante and the two poets look down on green turf, also peopled with illustrious souls and starred with flowers, the colours of which surpass all that a painter could contrive, giving forth a blended sweetness unknown in this world. The souls are singing the Compline hymn to the Virgin, *Salve Regina*.

Among them is the Emperor Rudolph, bitterly reproached by Dante in his recent invective, seated beside his former enemy, King Ottocar of Bohemia. Also reconciled are Peter of Aragon and his former enemy, Charles of Anjou. Seated a little apart from the others is Henry III of England, reputed to be of modest life, whose son, Edward I, excelled him. The moral is drawn that the worth of these rulers, once so powerful, resided not in their ancestry but in themselves, a view asserted in *Il Convivio*.[2]

The next canto begins with a very beautiful and famous evocation of the melancholy of evening, which sets the mood of the audience

> Era già l'ora che volge il disio
> > ai navicanti e 'ntenerisce il core
> > lo dì c'han detto ai dolci amici addio,
> e che lo novo peregrin d'amore
> > punge, se ode squilla di lontano
> > che paia il giorno pianger che si more.

> *It was the hour which touches longingly*
> > *and melts the hearts of those who said farewell*
> > *to friends that day as they set out to sea,*

> *and the new traveller who hears a bell*
> *   from far away is pierced with love, as though*
> *   of the departing day it tolled the knell.*[3]

One soul rises and with palms held high begins to sing the evening hymn *Te lucis ante terminum* ('Before the ending of the light'), in which prayers are offered for protection during sleep from phantoms and from the Evil One. The sound is so beautiful that Dante, as when he listened to Casella, feels carried out of himself. He draws attention here, as he did once before in *Inferno*,[4] to the meaning beneath the veil: souls in Ante-Purgatory, being only recently repentant, are, like new converts in the first life, still vulnerable to temptation, against which they must pray for God's protection during the night.

There follows a colourful scene, managed as though upon a stage equipped with flying apparatus. From on high descend two angels, bearing truncated swords[5] and clad in raiment green as newly unfurled leaves. Their garments, trailing behind them, are fanned by their green wings. They alight on opposite banks, guarding the company between. Looking up at them, Dante perceives their golden hair but their faces are so dazzling he cannot see them. 'They come from Mary's bosom to guard the valley from the serpent which will soon arrive,' Sordello explains. At this Dante is terrified and presses close to Virgil's shoulders. Sordello, unheeding, suggests that they should descend a little into the valley to speak with the rulers. They have gone about three paces when Dante sees a soul peering at him in the darkling air, as though in recognition.

It proves to be Nino Visconti, Judge of Gallura in Sardinia, whom Dante had known in Florence.[6] They greet each other joyfully and Dante, in retrospect, recalls his delight at finding Nino on his way ultimately to beatitude. Nino, not realizing that Dante is still in the body, asks how long it is since he came across the distant waters to the shore of the Mountain. Dante replies:

> ... 'per entro i luoghi tristi
> venni stamane, e sono in prima vita,
> ancor che l'altra, sì andando, acquisti.'

> ... *'from the sad, evil reign*
> *I came this morn and am in the first life,*
> *hoping the other I may thus attain.'*[7]

At these astonishing words, Sordello and Nino both turn, one back to Virgil and the other in the opposite direction to a soul who is seated near by, calling, 'Currado, rise, and come to see what God has granted by His grace.' This elegant duple movement is another example of Dante's choreographic management of his figures, which he moves about in his imagination as though upon a model stage. Nino, renouncing all hope of understanding the strange miracle, begs Dante to ask his daughter Giovanna to pray for him. He speaks resentfully of his wife Beatrice, who has married again[8] and will live to regret it:

> 'Per lei assai di lieve si comprende
>   quanto in femmina foco d'amor dura,
>   se l'occhio o 'l tatto spesso non l'accende.'

> *'One learns by her example easily*
>   *how long love's fire in females lasts, unless*
>   *by sight or touch they often kindled be.'*[9]

Dante speaks so seldom of marriage that the slightest reference to it is intriguing. In Nino's disillusioned words, love in women is limited to sensuality. Did Dante share this view and did he doubt his wife's constancy in his absence? We are here a long way from the idealization of women in *La Vita Nuova*.

Dante's gaze moves skyward and he contemplates with wonder three stars that now illumine the South Pole. Virgil tells him they have replaced the four they beheld that morning. He can say no more about them, for they represent the three theological graces, faith, hope and love, the Christian meaning of which is unknown to him, while the previous group of four stars that illumined the face of Cato symbolize justice, prudence, temperance and fortitude, the cardinal virtues which were within the scope of the ancient world.

At this moment Sordello draws Virgil's attention to the arrival of the serpent, 'perhaps the very same that tempted Eve':

> Tra l'erba e i fior venia la mala striscia,
>   volgendo ad ora ad or la testa, e 'l dosso
>   leccando come bestia che si liscia.

> *Through grass and flowers slid the evil streak,*
>   *turning its head from time to time, its back*
>   *to lick, just as a beast itself will sleek.*[10]

The angels are so swift that Dante does not see them move but he does hear their green wings cleave the air. The serpent withdraws and the angels fly back to resume their guard during the night.

Throughout this spectacle Currado's attention has been fixed on Dante. He is a cousin of Franceschino Malaspina, who was Dante's host and protector in Sarzana in Lunigiana, and of Moroello the warrior and Dante's friend.[11] Currado asks for news of the region of Valdimagra.[12] Dante disclaims ever having been there but speaks admiringly of the Malaspina family, renowned for their military valour and generosity. Currado replies in cryptic words: 'Not seven years will pass before thy courteous opinion will be hammered into thy brain with stronger nails than words.'[13] With this new prophecy of Dante's exile and oblique expression of gratitude to his future protectors the canto concludes.

He opens the next with a mythological adornment of his own creation. Since Aurora, the solar-dawn, is the wife of Tithonus,[14] Dante calls the lunar-dawn his concubine:

> La concubina di Titone antico
> > già s'imbiancava al balco d'oriente
> > fuor delle braccia del suo dolce amico;
> di gemme la sua fronte era lucente
> > poste in figura del freddo animale
> > che con la coda percuote la gente.

> *The concubine of old Tithonus now*
> > *gleamed white upon the eastern balcony,*
> > *emerging from her lover's arms, her brow*
> *adorned with gems of sparkling finery,*
> > *set in the form of the cold animal*
> > *which with its tail does men an injury.*[15]

In this silvery light the company of five recline upon the grass. Dante, who shares, as he says, the burden of Adam's mortality, falls asleep.

Just before morning he has a dream. He seemed to be on Mount Ida, where Ganymede was carried up to Olympus to be cupbearer to the gods. A golden eagle, hovering for a while, swooped down upon him, terrible as lightning, and carried him up into the sphere of fire where he and it together burned, and he awoke.

Only Virgil is beside him now, the sun is more than two hours high and before him is the sea. Virgil reassures him. He is at the entrance to Purgatory. As he slept St Lucy came and carried him up the remainder of the approach and set him down close to the gate.

The usual identification of St Lucy with the martyr of Syracuse, who died in 303 and was revered as the patron of those who suffered from poor sight, leaves out of account her representation as an eagle in Dante's dream. The eagle is an important figure in the *Commedia*. It will recur in two key passages in *Paradiso*, once as the symbol of imperial authority and again as the symbol of divine justice.[16] Dante's conversion to the belief that the Roman Empire was divinely ordained, to which he came during his study of philosophy, was an important step in his search for truth. It is possible that St Lucy is the figure of the *donna gentile*, symbolic, as she was, of Dante's philosophical studies and of philosophy itself. In this role, St Lucy, patron saint of vision, can be said to have opened his eyes.[17] In art St Lucy is represented as a type of divine wisdom with a lighted lamp in her hands, an appropriate figure for philosophy and for one to whom Dante avows himself a *fedele* ('devotee').[18]

Approaching a gap in the mountain wall, he perceives a gate with three steps of different colours leading up to it. On the top step an angelic guardian, holding a naked sword, is seated on a throne of adamant. Both his face and the sword are so radiant that Dante cannot keep his gaze on them. The guardian challenges the two visitors: 'Where is your escort?' he demands, from which it is evident that souls approaching the entrance are usually sponsored, perhaps by an angelic being. Virgil, who has learnt from Cato to be brief and to the point, says only: 'A lady from Heaven, *di queste cose accorta* ('with knowledge of these things'), instructed us to approach.'[19] The guardian is satisfied and bids them move forward to the steps.

In the year 1300, as has been said, Dante went on a pilgrimage to Rome to participate in the general remission of sins offered in celebration of the Jubilee to those who in true repentance made full confession at the shrines of St Peter and St Paul.[20] At least 12 years have passed but that solemn occasion is still fresh in his memory. His prostration now at the feet of the guardian, striking himself three times on the breast in token of confession, contrition and reparation, is a re-enactment in his memory of that earlier spiritual abasement. So far in the story Dante the writer has shown himself in possession of moral certainty. The focus from now on will be on him as an individual sinner, in need of guidance and instruction. The guardian with his sword outlines the letter P (for *peccatum*, sin) seven times on Dante's forehead, commanding him to see that one is erased on each of the seven cornices he is about to traverse. Dante thus links himself with the sinful nature of all mankind.

From beneath his vesture of ashen hue, the guardian draws two keys, one gold, one silver. There is something homely about his words as he explains their function, almost as though he were an earthly porter at some castle gate:

'Quandunque l'una d'este chiavi falla,
   che non si volga dritta per la toppa',
   diss'elli a noi, 'non s'apre questa calla.
Più cara è l'una; ma l'altra vuol troppa
   d'arte e d'ingegno avanti che diserri,
   perch' ella è quella che nodo digroppa.
Da Pier le tegno; e dissemi ch' i' erri
   anzi ad aprire ch'a tenerla serrata,
   pur che la gente a' piedi mi s'atterri.'

> *'If one or other of these keys', said he,*
>   *'should turn awry and make the tumblers block,*
>   *this passage will not open; though one be*
> *more costly, yet the other needs a stock*
>   *of skill and wisdom in the handling ere*
>   *the knot of sinfulness it will unlock.*
> *Peter I had them from; he bade me err*
>   *more in the opening than in keeping shut,*
>   *if souls kneel in repentance to me here.'*[21]

It is an engaging character sketch, based perhaps on priest confessors Dante had known.

The keys represent the two steps to absolution: repentance and reconciliation. The golden key is the divine authority given to the Church to remit sin. It is the more costly because it was bought at the price of Christ's death. The silver key loosens the entanglement of sin in the heart and requires special skill on the part of the confessor. Having imparted this information, the guardian pushes open the door, warning the travellers not to look back, else they will find themselves outside again. No distinction is made between Dante the living man and Virgil the disembodied soul. The guardian addresses them both impartially and shows no interest in their identities.

The door grides on its hinges. Inside there is a sound of voices singing *Te Deum laudamus*, but indistinctly, as when singers are accompanied by an organ, so that the words are sometimes distinguished and sometimes not. Dante is now inside Purgatory itself.

This turning point of *Purgatorio* occurs in the ninth canto, as does the turning point of *Inferno*, with the entrance into lower Hell. Dante the writer has firm control over the architecture of his poem. This will become still more apparent as he proceeds.

CHAPTER 34

Pride and Humility

After a strenuous climb, Dante and Virgil reach the First Cornice. They find it empty. This provides an opportunity for them to examine the face of the cliff. Of pure white marble, it is sculpted in high relief with figures representing humility. No human artistry has ever come near it. The first image is of the Annunciation. The Archangel Gabriel and the Virgin Mary are so life-like that the words *Ave* and *Ecce ancilla Dei* seem to be breathed forth from the stone. Next is the image of David dancing in humility before the Ark of the Covenant, with his wife Michal looking on in contempt from a window.[1] Ranged round the cart on which the Ark is carried and the oxen which pull it are a company of people divided into seven choirs. Dante both hears and does not hear their singing, just as he is uncertain whether he can smell the incense he sees rising. The third image represents a legendary episode in the life of the Emperor Trajan, who humbled himself to grant a widow's request for vengeance for her son.[2] The scene is described as though it were a *tableau vivant*. The beseeching widow stands at the bridle of the Emperor's horse in an attitude of grief. The area about them is trampled and thronged by knights on horseback and the Roman eagles on golden banners flutter in the wind.[3] The converse between Trajan and the widow is reported as though the marble is speaking.

Realistic sculpture had replaced the static formalism of Byzantine art in the second half of the thirteenth century. Nicola Pisani and his son Giovanni[4] were famous in Pisa, Siena, Pistoia and elsewhere for their richly carved scenes of episodes from the Bible and from legends, which decorated tympana, architraves, doors and walls. The most celebrated of their works were pulpits, alive, as though rustling, with figures that served as visual aids to sermons and readings from Scripture. Dante, attending Mass, must often have meditated on the multiple impression made on the senses by words and sculpture combined. The Pisani, both father and son, were skilful in producing an effect of swirling drapery, fluttering flags, above all an impression of movement rippling through the sensuous forms, vigorous gestures and expressive postures of the crowded figures. In his description of the divinely created sculptures on the wall of Mount Purgatory, Dante adds to the impression of movement the illusion of sound: *visibile parlare* ('visible speech'), he calls it, an uncanny forecast of what our modern era would eventually produce, first by the combination of photography and soundtrack, and then by three-dimensional computer graphics.

In the distance a curious procession is seen advancing. Neither Virgil nor Dante can at first make out what the figures are. Dante is reminded of carvings of distorted forms, knees joined to breasts, bearing the weight of ceiling or roof, so convincing that the unreal causes real pain to the spectator. They are the souls of the proud, bowed down by boulders, weeping and beating their breasts. Among the carvings by Giovanni Pisani on a pulpit in Pistoia there is a figure of Atlas, a type of pride, bowed beneath a column.

Approaching slowly, they recite the Lord's Prayer, expanded into a homily on the dependence of mankind upon the grace of God. Virgil requests one of the souls to tell them where an ascent can be found which a living man can scale. The soul who replies is Omberto Aldobrandesco, a member of a powerful Ghibelline family of Santafiora, near Siena. They were attacked by the Sienese in 1259, when Omberto was murdered in his castle. He is an example of pride in ancestry, a sin of which Dante acknowledged that he too was guilty. Significantly, to speak with Omberto he is obliged to bend down, as though he also were burdened by a block of stone. When, in *Paradiso*, he comes into the presence of his illustrious Crusader ancestor, Cacciaguida, we learn for the first time that Cacciaguida's son, Dante's great-grandfather, Alighiero, from whom his surname came, has been circling the First Cornice of Mount Purgatory for a hundred years. Cacciaguida bids Dante pray for him, that his time of purgation may be shortened.[5] It is not known on what evidence Dante attributed the sin of pride to this ancestor, nor why he does not mention him in *Purgatorio*. The reference back to him in *Paradiso* is an oblique statement that not only Dante but his ancestors too plumed themselves on their birth. To a man unjustly impoverished and humiliated this thought must have helped to restore self-esteem, however reprehensible the sin of pride.

A conversation is next held with Oderisi of Gubbio, an example of pride in artistic achievement. Oderisi was an illuminator of manuscripts. Dante would have seen examples of his work in Bologna, as well as of Oderisi's successor, Franco Bolognese.[6] Oderisi, twisting his face beneath his burden, recognizes Dante and calls his name. Dante in turn recognizes him:

'Oh!' diss' io lui, 'non se' tu Oderisi,
    l'onor d'Agobbio e l'onor di quell'arte
    ch'alluminar chiamata è a Parisi?'

'Art thou not Oderisi', I exclaimed,
    'honour of Gubbio and of that art
    which in Paris is illumination named?'[7]

In these lines the hand of Dante the versifier is seen to hover for a moment over the page. A rhyme for Oderisi? Yes: Parisi; and this gives him an opportunity to exhibit his knowledge of the term *alluminare*, derived from French. In the fourteenth century Paris had become the centre of the art of illustrating manuscripts.

Here is a meeting between two craftsmen, knowledgeable about each other's work. Dante also painted, as we know from *La Vita Nuova*.[8] Passed now to the life of the spirit and progressing in his release from pride, Oderisi generously admits the superiority of his rival, Franco of Bologna, something, he says, he could not have done in his earthly life. This leads him to a discourse on the impermanence of fame:

'Oh vana gloria dell'umane posse!
    Come poco verde in su la cima dura,
    se non è giunta dall' etati grosse!
Credette Cimabue nella pintura
    tener lo campo, e ora ha Giotto il grido,
    sì che la fama di colui è scura:
così ha tolto l'uno all'altro Guido
    la gloria della lingua; e forse è nato
    chi l'uno e l'altro caccerà del nido.'

'Oh, empty glory of our human deeds!
    How brief its green upon the topmost bough,
    unless perhaps some grosser age succeeds!
In painting Cimabue thought as how
    he held the field; but Giotto rules today,
    so that obscure the other's fame is now.
One Guido from the other took the bay,
    the poet's crown of glory, and perhaps
    one's born who'll from their nest chase both away.'[9]

Oderisi here comes very close to home. Giotto was a friend of them both. Of the two Guidos, Guinizelli and Cavalcanti, the latter was Dante's beloved friend in his days in Florence and still alive in Easter 1300. The one, perhaps already born, who may supplant them both, is obviously Dante himself. There has been a strange reluctance among commentators to admit this, but it presumes false modesty on Dante's part to think otherwise. He knew his literary powers. In 1300, when the words are fictionally spoken, he was already acclaimed as the leading poet of Florence. At the time of writing, probably about 1315, although only half way through his major work, he was well aware that he had surpassed all who had ever written in the vernacular. What he must guard against is self-glorification. His genius is a gift from God, mediated to him through the Muses, whose help he is careful to entreat. Oderisi's next comment is a direct personal challenge. Fame is but a breath of wind, constantly changing direction: what more renown will he, Dante, have in a thousand years, if he dies in old age rather than while he still prattled in his infancy? And what are a thousand years compared to eternity?

Almost 700 years have passed since Dante's death. Whether the ages that succeed are gross or enlightened, it is likely that in another three centuries, if there is not an overthrow of all cultural values, Dante will still be held as one of the greatest poets of European literature. T.S. Eliot said, 'Dante and Shakespeare divide the modern world between them; there is no third.'[10] This is more than Dante himself, in his most prideful moments, could have anticipated.

The next example, a soul inching along in front of them, is identified by Oderisi as Provenzano Salvani, once a powerful Sienese Ghibelline, who after the Battle of Montaperti was among those who urged the destruction of Florence:

> ... 'quando fu distrutta
> la rabbia fiorentina, che superba
> fu a quel tempo sì com' ora è putta.'

> ... 'when was brought low
> the rage of Florence, as overweening then
> as she corrupt and prostitute is now.'[11]

In his first life his name resounded throughout all Tuscany; now it is scarcely whispered in Siena. Dante, knowing that Provenzano had remained arrogant until the day of his death, asks how it is that he is not in Ante-Purgatorio. Oderisi relates that one heroic act, of begging in public in Siena for money to ransom a friend who had been taken prisoner, gained him release. This deed of self-abasement caused him such humiliation that he trembled in every pulse. Oderisi adds that in a short time Dante too will know the ignominy of having to beg for money.

Resentment at being dependent on charity rankled deep in Dante's soul. In the early years of his exile he had written bitterly in his odes and in *Il Convivio* of the injustice and humiliation of poverty. Now, a decade later, though having received generous hospitality and support from the Malaspina family and others, he still feels the need to express his chagrin. He, a descendant of distinguished ancestors, an outstanding poet, and one who once held high office in Florence, had been obliged to humble himself, trembling, like Provenzano, in every pulse, as he asked for help. It is something he never forgave.

At Virgil's command, Dante leaves the procession of burdened souls and walks erect. The joyful bounce of three final *ms* in the following line conveys physical relief and exhilaration:

già mostravam com' eravam leggieri …

nimbly we moved and light we seemed of limb …[12]

Dante's pleasure in pattern and design is shown vividly in the illustrations he next creates of fallen pride. Like funeral slabs on the floors of churches recalling the illustrious dead, here on the pavement of the First Cornice are 13 inlaid scenes excelling any upon earth. Arranged in four groups of 12 stanzas and ending with a climax in three lines, the examples are chosen from the Old Testament and from classical legend. The initial letters of the first lines of the stanzas, V, O, M, form an acrostic reading UOM (the Italian for 'man', V and U being interchangeable in ancient and mediaeval script). In the 13th stanza, all three initials are brought together, providing a key. Such manipulation of words to form a significant pattern was then a usual part of a writer's repertoire.

The first group displays Lucifer, the noblest of created beings, falling like lightning from Heaven, Briareus who tried to overthrow the gods, the giants who attempted to scale Olympus, and Nimrod who tried to reach Heaven by building the Tower of Babel. The second group represents the arrogant conviction of superiority, punished by disaster: Niobe, Saul, Arachne and Rehoboam.[13] The third group represents over-confidence, or hubris, punished by overthrow: Eriphyle, Sennacherib, Cyrus and Holofernes.[14] The final image represents the fall of Troy, the initial letters spelling the Italian for 'man':

Vedea Troia in cenere e in caverne:
  O Ilion, come te basso e vile
  Mostrava il segno che lì si discerne!

My eyes saw Troy, in ash and craters strewn.
  Alas, proud Ilium, how vile and base
  Now in that inlaid image thou wert shewn![15]

Dante is stirred to amazement by the verisimilitude of the figures: *morti li morti e i vivi parean vivi* ('the dead seemed dead, the living seemed alive').[16] No human artist could have achieved such truth, not even Giotto, his admired friend, whom it is said Dante saw working on his frescoes in the Scrovegni Chapel in Padua, some time between 1304 and 1305. Dante had not then even begun on the *Commedia*,[17] but the memory of Giotto's work may have contributed to it later. The naturalism of the narrative scenes, the interaction of sharply individualized figures, arranged as in *tableaux*, so new and striking in the frescoes, are features which Dante also adopts, not only in his descriptions of divine art but in his own arrangement of characters and events.

Dante's meditation on the scenes of pride overthrown ends with a sarcastic challenge, addressed in his own *persona*, to mankind in general, *figliuoli d'Eva* ('the sons of Eve'),[18] bidding them hold their heads high and avoid looking down at the evil path they tread. In his role as Dante the character he is about to undergo an exalting experience. An angel comes towards him, beautiful and clothed in white, his face as radiant as a star at dawn. His arms and wings spread wide, he leads the travellers to a cleft in the rock where the climbing will be easy. He then brushes Dante's forehead with his wing and promises him a safe journey. This is the Angel of Humility.

Dante the character, listening to Oderisi, acknowledged that his words had abated in him a great swelling of pride:

> … 'Tuo vero dir m'incora
> bona umiltà, e gran tumor m'appiani.'
>
> … '*Thy truly spoken words*
> *humble my heart and prick my swollen pride.*'[19]

He had known humility in the presence of Beatrice and she herself was always benignly clothed in that virtue on hearing herself praised.[20] Dante's return to this state, after years of spiritual turmoil, is moving and convincing. As he ascends to the Second Cornice he is aware of a lightness he cannot understand and asks Virgil for an explanation. Virgil tells him that one of the Ps with which his forehead had been wounded has been healed. Dante, like people unaware of something on their head, prompted by the gestures of others, spreads out his fingers and explores his brow: only six letters remain. At this his fond companion smiles.

This is a pleasing episode, showing the character Dante in an endearing light. The writer Dante is another person. All through the *Commedia* there is a personal agenda of vendetta. Among his principal targets are the Florentines, against whom he looses shaft after shaft. Having already given Oderisi bitter words to speak concerning their pride and corruption, he now, describing the ascent to the Second Cornice, compares it to the steps leading up to the church of San Miniato which looks down on Florence – *la ben guidata* ('the well-governed city'), he calls her, in bitter sarcasm – steps that were hewn at a time when measures and records were not tampered with.[21] This is a contemptuous allusion to two petty frauds, one committed by an official in charge of the Salt Import Department who reduced the size of the bushel-measure, and another by two public officials who tore a page from a ledger to conceal their pilfering.

Humility is a blessed state; to attain it Dante is eager to undergo purgation. But humiliation is another matter. The rancour he feels at what he has suffered in this respect runs like molten lava in his veins, erupting at fault-lines in his work, even, as will be shown, at moments of sublime exaltation in *Paradiso*.

CHAPTER 35

Evil and the Freedom
of the Will

A violent and sustained eruption of Dante's unforgiving rancour occurs on the Second Cornice of Mount Purgatory. Here the souls are purged of *invidia*, the sin that first sent avarice out into the world.[1] It is usually translated into English as *envy*. It means not only covetousness, however, but hatred of the sight of good fortune and happiness of others. Those guilty of the sin are purged by having their eyes sealed, while words recalling instances of generosity and of malevolence go echoing past them as they sit huddled against each other, like blind beggars outside a church. Sapia, who lived in Siena at the time of the Florentine defeat of the Sienese in 1249,[2] tells the story of her malicious delight in the misfortunes even of her fellow citizens, for whose defeat she prayed. Her late repentance would have led her to be detained in Ante-Purgatory had it not been for the prayers of a saintly character known as Peter the Comb-Seller. His honesty was so scrupulous that he was said to throw any defective combs among his merchandise into the river Arno rather than sell them even at a reduced price. This is a picturesque glimpse of local street-selling but much more important is the conversation that next arises.

Two souls leaning against each other are curious to know who the passer-by can be. They have heard him tell Sapia that he is still in the body and will return to earth and that when he dies he too will have his eyes sealed, but only for a short while, for he has but seldom looked spitefully on the good fortune of others; far greater is his fear of the time he will have to spend on the Cornice of Pride. On being asked who he is Dante says:

'Per mezza Toscana si spazia
   un fiumicel che nasce in Falterona,
   e cento miglia di corso nol sazia.
Di sovr'esso rech'io questa persona;
   dirvi ch'i' sia, sarìa parlare indarno,
   chè 'l nome mio ancor molto non sona.'

'*Through Tuscany there spreads a rivulet:*
from Falterona first its waters came,
and scarce a hundred miles suffice for it.
From off its shore I bring this mortal frame.
To tell you who I am would useless be,
for I have won as yet but small acclaim.'[3]

The soul who has addressed him replies, 'I think, if I have understood correctly, that river is the Arno.' His neighbour asks: 'Why does he conceal its name as if it were something too horrible to be mentioned?' The other answers: 'I do not know, but it is fitting indeed that the name of such a valley should perish.'

There follows a deadly denunciation of the whole of Tuscany, uttered not by Dante the character but by the soul who questioned him. Along the whole length of the Arno, from its source in the mountains to its outlet at the sea, virtue is shunned as if it were a snake, either by some misfortune of the region or because of evil deeds. The inhabitants of the vile valley have so changed their nature that it is as though Circe held them in pasture. In the Casentino live foul pigs, more worthy of acorns than of any human food; Arezzo is populated by snarling curs, at which the river *da lor disdegnosa torce il muso* ('in scorn turns its snout away');[4] the further it descends, the deeper it fills *la maladetta e sventurata fossa* ('the accursed and ill-starred ditch'); coming to Florence it finds the dogs turned to wolves; plunging still further through many a steep-cut gorge it reaches Pisa, the home of foxes so cunning that they fear no trap.

This abhorrent picture of the whole of Tuscany is followed by a prophecy of a doom that is about to overtake Florence. The speaker, who later reveals himself, is Guido del Duca, a member of the Onesti family of Ravenna. The soul huddled beside him is Rinieri da Calboli of the distinguished Guelf family of Forlì, grandfather of the notorious Fulcieri da Calboli, who was *podestà* of Florence in 1302 and again in 1312. Guido foretells the atrocities Fulcieri will commit against the White Guelfs and the Ghibellines, selling their flesh while they are still alive and slaughtering them like cattle, emerging stained with blood from the *trista selva* ('evil and wretched wood') and leaving it so deforested that not for a thousand years will it recover.

The phrase *trista selva* is a deliberate echo of the *selva oscura* in which, in the opening lines of *Inferno*, Dante says that he was lost. The entire invective marks a renunciation of his Tuscan identity, a matter of deep sadness. Several times in the story he has been recognized by his accent as a Tuscan. His descriptions of Tuscan landscape show that he loved the region, and though he deplored what had happened in Florence he longed to return there. He is likely to have left Tuscany for good when he wrote this invective.

The panoramic view suggests a final judgement from a distance, and the sorrowful tone is that of a bitterly regretful farewell. Perhaps he was then the guest of Can Grande della Scala of Verona.

Leaving his native region offers no escape from evil, however. Romagna too has deteriorated, as Guido del Duca regrets in his continuing lament. Gone are the virtuous men of yesteryear, replaced now by those who are corrupt, the soil so filled with poisonous shoots that it would take long tillage to destroy them:

'Oh Romagnoli tornati in bastardi!'

'Oh Romagnoles, turned to a bastard breed!'[5]

Both Guido's nostalgic speech about Romagna and his denunciation of the evil valley of the Arno (the two passages have the same number of lines), contain, however, seeds of hope. The Tuscans have *changed*; once the inhabitants of Romagna were noble and chivalrous. Guido weeps as he remembers them,

'le donne e ' cavalier, li affanni e li agi
    che 'nvogliava amore e cortesia
    là dove i cuor son fatti sì malvagi.'

*'the ladies, cavaliers, the toils, the games
    inspired in us by love and courtesy,
    where now malevolence our hearts inflames.'*[6]

Confessing his own sin of envy, which would formerly have turned him livid at the sight of a joyful man, Guido asks an important rhetorical question:

'O gente umana, perchè poni 'l core
    là 'v' è mestier di consorte divieto?'

*'O human race, why do ye covet things
    which by their nature partnership exclude?'*[7]

The words are enigmatic, deliberately so, and climbing up to the next cornice Dante asks Virgil to explain them. Virgil answers in the next canto:

... 'di sua maggior magagna
    conosce il danno; e però non s'ammiri
    se ne riprende perchè men si piagna.
Perchè s'appuntano i vostri desiri
    dove per compagnia parte si scema,
    invidia move il mantaco a' sospiri.'

*... 'he knows the cost of his worst fault;
    that he deplores it should be no surprise,
    hoping less cause for sorrow will result.*

> *Because your longing for possessions flies*
> *where sharing means that fewer can be owned,*
> *envy becomes the bellows to your sighs.'*[8]

If men directed their desires towards the highest sphere they would discover that the more there are who say 'ours', the more of good there is to share. To Dante the character, his mind still set on earthly possessions, this seems a contradiction. Virgil's explanation provides a fore-glimpse of Heaven. The sharing of spiritual goods and the reciprocity of love increase eternal goodness, just as mirrors reflect light one from the other. Dante the writer here extends Virgil's spiritual understanding beyond that to which his fellow inmates of Limbo could attain. As though recalling this in time, he restores Virgil's pre-Christian status by causing him to say, 'If my words do not content thee, thou shalt see Beatrice who will deliver thee from this and every need to understand.'

Virgil's discourse is the first section of an intricately devised centrepiece that crowns the structure not only of *Purgatorio* but of the whole of the *Commedia*. Here are the ingredients of the intellectual feast Dante had prepared for his banquet, *Il Convivio*: spiritual, in place of earthly possessions; the wrong choices made by humanity; the means of returning to the right path; the freedom of the will; and the force which underlies all, which is love. The inter-related subjects proceed step by step from Canto XIV to XX, Canto XVII being the central, culminating peak. They reach back to *Inferno* and forward to *Paradiso*: the result is an architectural design of three edifices, of which the central one, *Purgatorio*, is spanned by an elegantly constructed arch.

Engulfed in the smoke that is the purgation of the wrathful, Dante and Virgil hear the voices of souls. One of them assures them that they are going in the right direction, and on learning that Dante is in the first life asks for his prayers. The words in which he reveals his identity lead on to a discourse that is fundamental to the entire work.

> 'Lombardo fui, e fu' chiamato Marco:
>   del mondo seppi, e quel valore amai
>   al quale ha or ciascun disteso l'arco.'

> *'I was a Lombard, Marco was my name.*
>   *I knew the world, and virtue loved, at which*
>   *all bowmen of today have ceased to aim.'*[9]

Guido del Duca, in denouncing Tuscany, had already said that virtue there was shunned as though it were a snake, 'either from misfortune or from evil deeds'. Marco Lombardo's words bring to a head a question to which Dante the character longs to know the answer: what is the cause of evil in the world?

'Lo mondo è ben così tutto diserto
   d'ogne virtute, come tu mi sone,
   e di malizia gravido e coverto;
ma priego che m'addite la cagione,
   sì ch'i' la veggia e ch'i' la mostri altrui;
   chè nel cielo uno, e un qua giù la pone.'

'The world of every good is void indeed,
   as thou to me just now didst indicate,
   pregnant with vice, with evil overspread;
but what the cause is, tell me, I entreat,
   that I may see it and to others show,
   which some in heaven, some on earth locate.'[10]

Marco sighs deeply and laments the blindness of those who attribute
all things to the influence of the stars. If this were so, there would be no
justice in reward for virtue or punishment for vice. This subject had been a
matter of debate for centuries and still is: Nature or Nurture? Heredity or
Environment? What part does individual decision play in our actions? By
the 'stars' Dante and his contemporaries understood the fixed conditions
of our birth and upbringing. Such conditions 'initiate your impulses' says
Marco: 'I do not say all, but even if it were so, there exists a power of discernment between good and evil, which, if rightly exercised, gains control.' (As
astrologists still say, 'The stars impel, they do not compel.')

'A maggior forza ed a miglior natura
   liberi soggiacete; e quella cria
   la mente in voi, che 'l ciel non ha in sua cura.
Però, se 'l mondo presente disvia,
   in voi è la cagione, in voi si cheggia;
   e io te ne sarò or vera spia.'

'A greater force, a better law there is
   which forms your minds and freely you obey;
   no power the stars have over you in this.
So if the present world has gone astray,
   in you the cause is, seek for it in you;
   thy true guide now I'll be in what I say.'[11]

In this rejection of determinism Dante makes one of the most positive statements of his belief in moral autonomy. Whatever the conditions into which
we are born, our souls are the direct creations of God and we are responsible
for our deeds.

   In *Il Convivio* Dante had written of the soul entering upon its path in
life, directing its gaze towards the goal of supreme good, being drawn first
by trifling things:

So we see little children fixing their chief desire on an apple; then as they go farther they desire a small bird; then going farther still, fine clothes; after that a horse, then a mistress; after that riches, then greater and still greater wealth.[12]

Years before, Dante had seen his children develop from infancy. In the tenderness of these words and of those he now gives to Marco Lombardo we perhaps catch a glimpse of Dante remembering his time as a father. If this is so, the glimpse is a rare one:

'Esce di mano a lui che la vagheggia
    prima che sia, a guisa di fanciulla
    che piangendo e ridendo pargoleggia,
l'anima semplicetta che sa nulla,
    salvo che, mossa da lieto fattore,
    volentier torna a ciò che la trastulla.
Di picciol bene in pria sente sapore;
    quivi s'inganna, e dietro ad esso corre,
    se guida or fren non torce suo amore.'

'Forth from His hand who fondly looks on her
    from her first origin, like a small child,
    crying, laughing, as if a babe she were,
the little, simple soul is born; beguiled
    by her Creator's joy, she follows all
    that pleases her or is delightful styled.
At first of trifling good she heeds the call,
    and, thus deceived, sets out in quest of it,
    unless a guide or rein her longing stall.'[13]

For this reason, law was needed to set a curb, a king was needed who could at least discern the tower of the true city. Laws there are, but who enforces them? Nobody, because the shepherd who leads cannot discriminate between the spiritual and the temporal. Thus Marco, in reply to Dante's question, puts the blame squarely on Papal secular ambition:

'Ben puoi veder che la mala condotta
    è la cagion che 'l mondo ha fatto reo,
    e non natura che 'n voi sia corrotta.'

'Thou canst see plainly that ill-guidance is
    the cause of evil in the world, not that
    your nature is corrupt beyond redress.'[14]

The central position of this denunciation of the temporal greed of the Papacy gives powerful emphasis to Dante's diagnosis of the ills of the world. They are not predestined, nor are they unavoidable: they can be cured. It was to prescribe the cure that Dante first felt called to write *Il Convivio*. This work having failed to gain a public, it is with the same purpose that he now transfers the message to the *Commedia*, having chosen a form that rivets the attention. The hammer is in his hand and he wields it with vigour. Marco Lombardo rams home the command:

> 'Dì oggimai che la chiesa di Roma,
>   per confondere in sè due reggimenti,
>   cade nel fango e sè brutta e la soma.'

> *'Say here and now, the Church of Rome, encoiling*
>   *two governments in one, falls in the mire,*
>   *herself befouling and her burden soiling.'*[15]

Here is the central message of the *Commedia*, set in the very centre of the work.

CHAPTER 36

Love, Natural and Rational

During his exile, when he entered on his great undertaking, *Il Convivio*, Dante had pondered deeply the nature of love and had come to identify it as the natural propensity of all created things. He developed this concept in his commentary on his *canzone* beginning *Amor che nella mente mi ragiona* ('Love which discourses to me in my mind.'):

> Love, truly understood and subtly considered, is nothing else than a spiritual union of the soul with the loved object; and to this union the soul, by virtue of its nature, runs swift or slow according as it is free or impeded ... for instance, simple bodies have in themselves a love inspired by nature for their own proper place, and therefore earth always tends downwards to the centre; fire has a natural love for the circumference above, adjoining the heaven of the moon, and therefore always leaps up towards that.

> The primary composite bodies, such as minerals, have a love for the place which is adapted for their generation, and grow in that and derive strength and potency from that. ...

> Plants ... still more evidently have a love for a certain place in accordance with the requirements of their constitution; and therefore we see that certain plants almost always do well by water, certain others on the ridges of mountains, certain others on the shore or at the foot of mountains, which if they are transplanted either die altogether or live as it were sadly, like things detached from the place they love. Dumb animals not only more plainly have a love for their place, but we see that they have a love for one another.

> Mankind have their own love for all perfect and noble things. [Sharing with all created things the properties which make them susceptible to gravity and to love of their place and time of generation] everyone is naturally of more vigorous body in the place where he was born and at the time when he was conceived. Likewise, man has affection for certain food, not because it acts on the senses but because it is nutritious. ... And therefore we see that certain food makes men shapely and large-limbed and of a good healthy colour, and that certain other food produces an effect contrary to this. ... Man feels love also according to appearance, like the animals, and this love in man most of all

has need of control on account of its excessive activity, chiefly in the pleasures of taste and touch. Lastly, rational man has affection for truth and virtue; and from this affection springs true and perfect friendship, derived from what is honourable.[1]

This section in *Il Convivio* brings us close to Dante the person. The style is informal and engaging, as though he were speaking to an audience. To read this passage, especially in the original, is to feel, after seven centuries, that we are members of that audience and are seeing the shabbily dressed, unjustly impoverished exile and hearing his Florentine voice as he recalls feeling more vigorous in the place where he was born and at the time of year when he was conceived and benefiting from certain foods more than from others. Like plants removed from their natural habitat, he lives sadly, detached from the place he loved.

As in *Inferno*, so now in *Purgatorio*, a stage has been reached when it is necessary to explain the arrangement of the sins. Ascending from the Cornice of Wrath, Dante and Virgil reach the top step of the stairway leading to the Cornice of Sloth. Night has now fallen and by the law of the mountain they are prevented from going up further. Virgil uses the time of waiting by discoursing on sloth and its relationship to the sins below it and above. He first defines sloth as insufficient zeal for the love of good. Then, in order that Dante may fully understand, he expounds the relationship between love and all the Seven Deadly Sins:

'Nè creator nè creatura mai',
    cominciò el, 'figliuol, fu sanza amore,
    o naturale o d'animo; e tu 'l sai.
Lo naturale è sempre sanza error,
    ma l'altro puote errar per mal obietto
    o per troppo o per poco di vigore.'

'No creature, no creator', he outlined,
    'was ever without love, my son, and this
    thou knowest, natural or of the mind.
The natural love unerring always is,
    the other by a faulty aim may err,
    or by defect of zeal, or by excess.'[2]

From this it follows, Virgil continues, love is the seed of every virtue and of every vice, according to that to which it is attached and to its degree of attachment. Those who love glory desire to be supreme and are thus guilty of the sin of pride; those who love their own good fortune and are afraid it may be diminished in comparison with that of others are guilty of the sin of envy; those who suffer wrong and desire vengeance are guilty of the sin of wrath. This triform love is purged on the three cornices below. Those who love the good, but insufficiently, are guilty of the sin of sloth. Those who love what is good, though not the supreme good, may love it to excess: they are guilty of the sins of avarice, gluttony and lust, which are purged on the three cornices above, as will be shown.

Dante has clearly understood Virgil's discourse so far but now he needs to understand the nature of love itself and how it operates in the human soul. He entreats Virgil to explain further:

> 'Però ti prego, dolce padre caro,
>   che mi dimostri amore, a cui reduci
>   ogni buono operare e 'l suo contraro.'

> *'I beg thee, father, gentle and most dear,*
>   *to demonstrate the love thou sayest is*
>   *the source of every action whatsoe'er.'*[3]

Virgil bids him fix on him the penetrating eyes of his intellect, when he will see clearly that those who have said that all love is blameless have been in error. Virgil's discourse from here on resembles scholastic disputations between masters and pupils in which Dante may have taken part. The minute definitions and distinctions reveal the nature of thought processes characteristic of his time. The mind, Virgil explains, being created to love readily, is susceptible to everything that it finds pleasing. This pleasure is not in itself love but it awakens the mind to activity that may become love. But if, asks Dante, love is a compulsion that moves us from without, how can we be responsible for what we do? Virgil replies that he can explain only in terms of reason; beyond that, it is a matter of faith and only Beatrice can take it further. Every independent being (in mediaeval terms a 'substance') is possessed of a fundamental character (a 'form'), which gives a being its separate existence. The 'substantial form' of mankind is the intellective soul, which is different from matter but united with it. Of this, the specific faculty is the instinct that comprises innate knowledge and a disposition to love. Such faculty is not perceived except in operation, nor is it ever revealed except by its results, as life in a plant is known by its green leaves. We do not know whence comes understanding of the first axiomatic truths, nor love for the first objects of desire, which are innate, like the instinct in bees to make honey. Such first desire (*prima voglia*) is another term for 'natural love'. In order that every other desire shall be rightly related to the first blameless longing for what is good,

> 'innata v'è la virtù che consiglia,
>   e dell'assenso de' tener la soglia.'

> *'innate in you a counselling power resides*
>   *and should the threshold of consent command.'*[4]

This is the inborn liberty, perceived by philosophers who allowed the existence of ethics:

'Onde, poniam che di necessitate
    surga ogni amor che dentro a voi s'accende,
    di ritenerlo è in voi la podestate.'

'Let us suppose that, of necessity,
    arises every love that kindled in you is,
    to curb it you possess the faculty.'[5]

This noble faculty Beatrice calls free will, which Virgil bids Dante bear in
mind if she should speak to him of it.

Virgil's role has here reached its most profound and comprehensive.
What he has expounded to Dante is the distinction between natural and
rational love. He has also reached the most moving stage in his relationship with Dante. Virgil is here the loving father, earnestly scanning Dante's
face, intent to see if he has understood; Dante is the loving son, the reverent
pupil, eager to absorb all that he can from his master. In creating this scene,
Dante is drawing upon his sense of the loss of his father. He had found such
a figure as a boy in his mentor, Brunetto Latini, and as a young poet in his
friend and adviser, Guido Cavalcanti. His friendship with Cino da Pistoia
and the discussions on law and justice he probably held with him in Bologna
is another example of the importance in his intellectual growth of converse
with those from whom he could learn.

As Dante learnt not only from his contemporaries but also from the
masters of the past, so he desired to pass on his understanding to others.
Such intellectual transmission became for him a form of love. It was the
love that prompted him to offer a banquet of learning to those who had had
no opportunity to acquire 'the bread of angels' for themselves. When this
offering ceased to attract, he re-arranged the courses he had prepared in the
form of story and dialogue, violent and dramatic in *Inferno*, appealing and
engaging in *Purgatorio*, ethereal and ecstatic in *Paradiso*.

This transformation led him to create a new form of literary art, of universal and timeless significance, but presented in immediate, human terms. It
also led him to see that truth and the freedom to choose between good and
evil were apprehended by and mediated through the 'substantial form' of
mankind, created by God as body, rational mind and soul. Exchange of mind
between such beings was therefore a sacred trust. In writing the *Commedia*,
Dante's desire was to serve that trust and to enable others to do likewise. To
this task he brought, to the utmost of his talent, both natural and rational
love.

CHAPTER 37

The Mountain Trembles

Two-thirds of the way up the Mountain of Purgatory that superb showman, Dante Alighieri, realizing that his audience have had a surfeit of abstract thought, springs a surprise. At the end of Canto XX the mountain shakes as though it is falling. Dante the character feels chilled as with the fear of death. On all sides a great shout goes up: *Gloria in excelsis Deo*[1] and Virgil draws his terrified companion close to his side. They both stand motionless and in suspense. The first listeners who heard this canto read aloud were also left in suspense: they had to wait until the next canto was read before they learnt the solution to this (literal) cliff-hanger.

Dante and Virgil stand gazing at the souls on the Cornice of Avarice who lie face down on the ground, able to see only earth, as their minds had been fixed only upon the earthly things that wealth can buy. A soul walks up behind them and greets them with the words, 'God give you peace, my brothers.' Virgil replies with the gracious courtesy of a soul who is in Limbo to one who is on his way to beatitude. After explaining that Dante is still in the body and what his own task has been, 'drawn forth from the wide throat of Hell for his guidance', he asks the soul to say why the mountain trembled and why shouts from all the souls seemed to rise as far as from its ocean shore.

The soul explains that when a penitent is released from purgation the mountain shakes and all the other souls cry out for joy. We still do not know who the released soul is: Dante, a skilful narrator, does not spoil his effects by telling us too soon. In reply to Virgil's further enquiry, he says he has lain for 500 years and more on the Cornice of Avarice and only now has he felt his will free to move on towards a happier threshold.

Virgil next asks him directly who he was. The soul replies that he lived in the time of Titus, who avenged the wounds whence flowed the blood that was betrayed by Judas.[2] He bore the title that longest endures and bestows most honour (that of poet) and received the myrtle crown in Rome. And now at last he tells his name:

'Stazio la gente ancor di là mi noma:
    cantai di Tebe, e poi del grande Achille;
    ma caddi in via con la seconda toma.'

'Statius by people yonder I'm named still:
    I sang of Thebes, of great Achilles next,
    but carrying the second load I fell.'[3]

Statius, the author of the *Thebaid*, an epic poem in 12 books on the history of the war against Thebes, lived from *c.* AD 45 to 96. He also began an epic on Achilles and the Trojan War, but this remained unfinished. As in the case of Cato, so once again Dante takes it upon himself to place an ancient Roman not in Limbo, but on the Mountain of Purgatory. He knew from the *Thebaid* that Statius had great admiration for the *Aeneid*, for at the conclusion he says, addressing his epic, 'Do not attempt to rival the divine *Aeneid*, but follow from afar, ever revering its footsteps.'[4] It is appropriate therefore that he now makes Statius say that the *Aeneid* was mother and nurse to him in poetry:

'Al mio ardor fuor seme le faville,
    che mi scaldar, della divina fiamma
    onde sono allumati più di mille;
dell' Eneida dico, la quale mamma
    fummi e fummi nutrice poetando:
    sanz'essa non fermai peso di dramma.'

'The sparks which my poetic ardour lit
    from the divine flame rose inspiringly,
    and more than a thousand kindled were by it:
the Aeneid *I mean, which nurtured me*
    as poet like a mother and a nurse;
    without it scarce a drachm my weight would be.'[5]

And he adds: 'Gladly would I have spent another year in Purgatory if only I could have lived when Virgil did.'

This is a supreme moment of dramatic irony. Our attention is fixed on the three actors as on a lighted stage. Virgil turns immediately to Dante with an expression that commands silence. But laughter and tears, Dante says, are the least subject to the will in those who are the most sincere. He smiles like someone conveying a hint. Statius looks him fixedly in the eyes and asks why he is laughing. Every reader who comes on this scene for the first time experiences a shock of delight at being admitted into Dante's living presence. We see him as he stands hesitating between the other two, the one commanding silence, the other conjuring him to answer. He sighs. Virgil hears him and relents. Given permission to speak, Dante addresses Statius:

... 'Forse che tu ti maravigli,
antico spirto, del rider ch'io fei;
ma più d'ammirazion vo' che ti pigli.
Questi, che guida in alto gli occhi miei,
è quel Virgilio dal qual tu togliesti
forza a cantar delli uomini e de' dei.'

... 'It may be that amazed thou art,
o ancient soul, by my display of mirth,
but greater wonder yet would I impart:
this man who bids me seek the highest worth
is Virgil, he from whom thou strength didst draw
to sing of gods and mortals upon earth.'[6]

At this revelation, Statius kneels to embrace Virgil's feet, but is dissuaded from the attempt. 'Brother, desist, thou art a shade and a shade thou seest.' Statius replies, 'Now thou canst understand the measure of my love for thee, since I forget our emptiness, treating shades as though they were substantial.'

The metaphysics of Mount Purgatory vary, as has been seen, from place to place. On the shore, Dante and Casella are unable to embrace; on the terrace of the late-repentant, Sordello and Virgil succeed in doing so; on the Fifth Cornice Statius cannot embrace Virgil's feet. Dante sees no necessity to reconcile these inconsistencies, which add to the mysteriousness of the mountain. The curiosity his readers may feel concerning the nature of spirit-bodies is, in fact, about to be satisfied.[7]

The three characters ascend to the Sixth Cornice, where the souls of gluttons undergo purgation. The fifth scar is erased by an angel's wing from Dante's forehead and he feels lighter than before. Meanwhile, a delightfully realistic conversation is taking place between Virgil and Statius. 'Ever since Juvenal[8] joined us in Limbo,' says Virgil, 'I have known of thy love for me and I have loved thee in return. But tell me, as friend to friend, how could avarice take root in thy soul?' Statius smiles a little and then remarks that appearances can be deceptive. It was not for miserliness that he was confined to the Cornice of Avarice, but for its opposite, prodigality. In *Inferno* also these two extremes in the mismanagement of wealth are shown to be aspects of the same sin.[9] Certain lines in Virgil's *Aeneid*[10] led him to see the error of his ways, else he too would have found himself among the hoarders and spendthrifts in Hell.

Virgil, who seems to have learnt something of the *Thebaid* from Juvenal in Limbo, then remarks that it does not appear in that work that Statius had been brought to the faith without which virtuous deeds are not in themselves sufficient:

'Se così è, qual sole o quai candele
　　ti stenebraron, sì che tu drizzasti
　　poscia di retro al pescator le vele?'

'If that is so, what candles or what sun
　　dispersed the dark, that thou thy sails didst raise
　　behind the fisherman then and thereon?'[11]

Dante evidently imagines that details concerning the spread of Christian belief could have reached Virgil from souls who joined him in Limbo during the first century: from them he has learnt of St Peter, the fisher of men.

The reply of Statius to this enquiry is the supreme climax of the episode. Virgil was not only his guide in poetry; he had shown him also the way to faith:

　　　　　　　　... 'Tu prima m'inviasti
　　verso Parnaso a ber nelle sue grotte,
　　e prima appresso Dio m'alluminasti.
Facesti come quei che va di notte,
　　che porta il lume dietro e sè non giova,
　　ma dopo sè fa le persone dotte,
quando dicesti: "Secol si rinova;
　　torna giustizia e primo tempo umano,
　　e progenie scende da ciel nova."
Per te poeta fui, per te cristiano.'

　　　　　　　　　　... *'Thou first it was*
　　who bade me drink upon Parnassus' height,
　　Thou wert like one who goes abroad by night,
　　his lamp behind him, and thus cannot see,
　　only to those who follow giving light,
　　when thou didst say: "The world renewed will be,
　　justice returns and the first age of man,
　　from heaven descends a wondrous progeny."
　　Poet through thee I was, and Christian.'[12]

Statius confesses that he kept his conversion a secret, fearing the persecutions of the Emperor Domitian, though he wept for the victims and did his best to succour them. For his insufficiency of zeal he has spent more than 400 years on the Cornice of Sloth. This length of time, added to the 500 years spent on the Cornice of Avarice, accounts for about 950 of the 1,200 years since his death. Where he spent the other 250 years we are not told: perhaps on one of the terraces in Ante-Purgatory.

But now, while they still have time, Statius asks Virgil for news of fellow poets: Terence, Caecilius, Plautus and Varius. Are they damned and, if so, in which circle? 'They are all,' replies Virgil, 'and Persius too, with many more, in the First Circle,[13] where Homer is, and often we talk of that mountain where those who nurtured us[14] still dwell. Euripides is with us and many Greeks who once wore the laurel crown.' And Virgil goes on to name several characters from Statius's epic who are also in Limbo, a conversation Dante must have taken pleasure in devising.

They reach the Cornice of the Gluttons and turn with confidence with the edge of the mountain on their right, as they have always done, but now with the reassurance of Statius. The two ancient poets walk ahead and Dante follows behind, listening to their conversation on the art of poetry. This picture is of great significance, equal to the moment in Limbo when Dante is made 'sixth among such wisdom' on being admitted to the company of Homer, Ovid, Lucan, Horace and Virgil.[15] Here are two great authors of epic, one the master of the other, now conversing as equals, with Dante following and learning from them: his place in the great line of poets, as he sees it, could hardly be more explicit.

CHAPTER 38

Dante and Forese Donati

The pleasant converse (*le dolci ragioni*) of the two ancient poets (to which we are not admitted) is interrupted when they are obstructed by a tree bearing sweet-smelling fruit. Nearby, a clear stream flows from a high rock, watering the leaves. They are now on the Cornice of the Gluttons.

Virgil and Statius approach and a voice is heard among the boughs, intoning 'You may not eat of this food.' It then recites examples of virtuous temperance, of the Virgin Mary at the wedding at Cana, of women of ancient Rome who abstained from drinking wine, and of Daniel who despised food and gained wisdom. Next it utters praises of the age of gold, when hunger made acorns appetizing and thirst made nectar of every brook, and finally St John the Baptist who fed on locusts and wild honey.

Dante meanwhile has drawn near the tree and is peering into its foliage, like one who wastes his time on hawking. For this he is gently rebuked by Virgil:

> Lo più che padre mi dicea: 'Figliuole,
> vienne oramai, chè 'l tempo che n' è imposto
> più utilmente compartir si vuole.'
>
> *'My son', my more-than-father said to me,*
> *come now away, for our allotted time*
> *more usefully than this deployed must be.'*[1]

Dante readily follows the two sages, the more so since they continue their conversation, which it gives him pleasure to overhear. As they proceed they hear the words *Labia mea Domine*[2] chanted in lamentation. A crowd of souls come up behind them and, passing on, look back in wonder. They are pale and so emaciated that their skin reveals the shape of their bones. So skeletal are their faces that the word 'OMO' seems to be written upon them.[3]

We are here back among the gruesome distortions of Hell. One soul, peering at Dante from his sunken eyes, calls out in amazement, *qual grazia m' è questa?* ('what grace do I receive?'). The encounter is startlingly remi-

Fig 8. Face of a Glutton in *Purgatorio*

niscent of Dante's meeting with Brunetto Latini, who exclaims, on seeing
Dante, *qual maraviglia!* ('what a marvel!'), as he snatches at the hem of his
garment.[4] Dante first recognizes the voice and then, just as he made out
his beloved master Brunetto beneath his scorched features, so beneath the
emaciated face before him now he makes out the soul of his Florentine
friend Forese Donati.[5]

Relations between them in their young days had not been edifying, and
in this canto Dante candidly admits and regrets it. Their playful exchange of
abusive sonnets[6] had included on Dante's part gibes against Forese's wife, his
incapacity as a husband and his indulgence in gluttony. Dante grieves to see
the face that once he mourned so wasted and disfigured and begs to know
the reason. Forese explains that the fragrance of the fruit and the spray from
the water induce in the penitent gluttons a craving to eat and drink, which
thus reduces them.

Dante then asks another question: 'Forese, not five years have gone by
since thou didst exchange the world for a better life.[7] How can it be that
thou art here already? I thought to find thee down below, where time is
made good by time.' This enables Forese to pay tribute to his wife, by whose
prayers he has been furthered in his progress towards Heaven. This is Dante's
way of making amends for having denigrated her:

> … 'Sì tosto m'ha condotto
> a ber lo dolce assenzo de' martiri
> la Nella mia con suo pianger dirotto.
> Con suoi prieghi devoti e con sospiri
> tratto m'ha della costa ove s'aspetta,
> e liberato m'ha delli altri giri.
> Tanto è a Dio più cara e più diletta
> la vedovella mia, che molto amai,
> quanto in bene operare è più soletta.'

> *… 'It was my Nella by her floods of tears*
> *who brought me here so soon to drink the sweet*
> *tormenting wormwood; with her sighs and prayers*
> *she drew me from the slopes where souls must wait*
> *and with her constant pleading for my sake*
> *from other cornices did liberate.*
> *So much the greater pleasure does God take*
> *in my dear little widow, whom I loved,*
> *as virtues an exception of her make.'*[8]

Forese now bursts out in a bitter condemnation of the women of Florence, accusing them of being more flagrant in their immodesty than those who dwell in the wild hills of Barbagia,[9] flaunting their bosoms down to their very paps. A time is not far off, he prophesies, when they will be denounced from the pulpit and retribution will descend on them. If they but knew what awaited them,

> 'già per urlare avrien le bocche aperte.'

> *'ready to howl, their mouths they'd open now.'*[10]

This denunciation of Florence is even more disturbing than those already uttered, in that it is directed solely at women. The crude words are given to Forese but they are Dante's own. It would appear that in his late 40s, the age he was when he wrote this canto, Dante had reached a time of life in which he felt a revulsion against the allurements of the flesh. Questioned by Forese, he expresses remorse for their early years together in words that, as has already been remarked,[11] suggest a homosexual relationship:

> … 'Se tu riduci a mente
> qual fosti meco, e qual io teco fui,
> ancor fia grave il memorar presente.'

> *… 'If thou wilt call to mind*
> *what thou with me and I with thee once was,*
> *the memory thou wilt yet a burden find.'*[12]

The similarity between his meeting with Brunetto and his present encounter with Forese would seem to make the sexual meaning of these lines more than probable. Another explanation could be that of coincidence, but, given Dante's meticulous control of his material, this is unlikely, especially since there is a second similarity between Brunetto's departure and that of Forese.[13]

Moving on to an explanation of his present condition, Dante informs Forese that he has been guided through the profound night of the truly dead and up the mountain that straightens those whom the world has made crooked. His guide will remain until he arrives where Beatrice is and must then depart. Virgil he names, but not Statius, saying only that it was on his release that the mountain trembled. Once again Dante the writer keeps skilful control of his material.

The dialogue between Dante and Forese has the casual informality of the exchange of news between friends. He even mentions the name of Beatrice with no more ado than if he were alluding to someone they both knew in Florence, as was the case. He next enquires as to the whereabouts of Forese's sister, Piccarda. 'Oh, she is in Heaven,' he replies, and, after paying brotherly tribute to her beauty and her virtue, proceeds to name some of his fellow gluttons, of whom the most significant is the poet Bonagiunta of Lucca. There then takes place the dialogue about Dante's love poetry and the defining of his style as the *dolce stil nuovo* ('new sweet style'), which has already been discussed.[14]

There is a rushing movement as the emaciated souls pass them like a flock of birds streaming at speed along the river Nile. Forese, however, continues to keep pace slowly with Dante in order to go on talking with him. 'How long will it be until I see thee again?' he asks. Dante's reply is an expression of deep sadness, reflecting what he felt at the time of writing rather than in the year 1300:

'Non so', rispuos'io, 'quant' io mi viva;
   ma già non fia 'l tornar mio tanto tosto
   ch'io non sia col voler prima alla riva;
però che 'l loco u' fui a viver posto
   di giorno in giorno più di ben si spolpa,
   e a trista ruina par disposto.'

'How long I have to live, I am not sure,
   but not so soon', I said, 'shall I return
   as in desire I long to reach the shore;
the place where I was destined to be born
   from day to day denudes itself of good,
   intent upon its ruin and forlorn.'[15]

Forese agrees that this is true and foretells the death, not long off, of his own brother Corso, who, within the timeframe of the story, is about to plot the downfall of the White Guelfs.

Forese then takes leave of Dante, saying that he must no longer walk slowly beside him, for time is precious and he must catch up with his fellow penitents. Just as Brunetto, who had turned back along the burning sand to talk with Dante, was obliged to run off to rejoin his companions in sin, seeming, Dante said, like a winner in the race for the green cloth in Verona, so now Forese, moving off with longer strides, is ennobled by a comparison to a horseman who leaves a troop of cavalry to gain the honour of a first encounter. Dante follows him with his eyes, thinking of his words, until he sees him no more.

These parallels, between the recognition and departure of Forese and the same two moments in the episode of Brunetto, cannot be other than deliberate. Their significance with regard to Dante's sexual relationship with Forese has been overlooked, but once pointed out can hardly be dismissed. The question remains: why did Dante choose thus to inculpate himself? The answer may be that his involvement with Forese was already known, in Florence and in other cities.

Another tree stands in the way, also green and laden with fruit. A group of souls lift up their hands towards the foliage, like children reaching for something they desire, while someone dangles it out of their grasp. This charming simile seems to evoke Dante's memories of playing with his children. But this is no game. A voice from the tree sternly commands them to pass on. This plant, it says, was raised from a tree above from which Eve plucked the apple. At this the three poets draw closer together and walk along by the mountain's side. The voice continues, reciting reminders of examples of gluttony: the centaurs who became drunk at the wedding of Pirithous and Hippodamia and were defeated, a story which Dante had read in Ovid,[16] and the rejection by Gideon of those of his troops who swilled, face down, from a stream instead of remaining alert in soldierly fashion and lapping from the palms of their hands.[17]

During the personal and intimate exchange between Dante and Forese, the two great poets of antiquity, Virgil and Statius, are removed from focus. It is time now to bring them back. Dante does so by describing how they all three walk thoughtfully in single file, listening to the ancient tales of gluttony. A voice calls out:

'Che andate pensando sì voi sol tre?'

'What are you pondering, you three alone?'[18]

The scene has been set with timely clarity. The section of the path on which they walk is now deserted. Dante jumps at the voice, like a startled animal, and looks up. What he beholds is a dazzling being, brighter red than any glass or metal seen in a furnace. Dante the poet is perhaps remembering the description of the angel who appeared to Daniel after his three weeks' fast: 'His body also was like the chrysolite and his face as the appearance of lightning, and his eyes as lamps of fire, and his arms and his feet like in colour to polished brass.'[19] He may also be thinking of glass-blowers he could have seen in Venice, or blacksmiths he may have watched, as they removed their products red-hot from the fire.

This wondrous personage is the Angel of Temperance, arrived to guide them to the steps that lead up to the next cornice. Like a breeze in May at dawn, which spreads the fragrance of the grass and flowers, his wing brushes Dante's brow as with the odour of ambrosia, removing yet another of the seven scars. At the same time, the Angel pronounces the Benediction, 'Blessed are they that hunger after righteousness.'[20]

The sun has declined from noon and it is no moment for delay. The three figures walk quickly up the stairway, which is so narrow that they must continue in single file. Despite their need for haste, Dante cannot hold back from asking a question as they climb. It is indeed a question that can be deferred no longer. It takes the combined wisdom of Virgil and Statius to answer it.

CHAPTER 39

Body and Soul

T he question Dante now asks has been at the back of the reader's mind from the beginning: how can bodiless forms suffer bodily anguish?[1] The emaciated condition of the souls of gluttons acts as a trigger: how, Dante longs to know, is it possible to become lean if there is no need for nourishment?

Virgil in reply suggests two parallel phenomena. Meleager, the son of the King of Calydon, was doomed by the Fates to die when a certain log of wood was consumed by fire: as it fell to ashes, his soul fled into the air.[2] But this is an example of a relationship between two corporeal objects, a burning log and a living body; it does not explain how unsubstantial forms can waste away in consequence of the growth of fruit and foliage. Virgil's second parallel is that of a body and its image in a mirror, which he offers as comparable to the relation between a soul and the body it represents. This is as far as Virgil, the pre-Christian, can go. That Dante may be fully satisfied he refers the matter to Statius, who, in graceful homage to his great master, obeys his request:

> 'Se la veduta etterna li dislego',
>   rispuose Stazio, 'là dove tu sie,
>   discolpi me non potert' io far nego.'

> *'If in thy presence I to him expound*
>   *eternal verities', Statius replied,*
>   *'my pardon be: to obey thee I am bound.'*[3]

This brings Statius centre stage as Dante's mentor not only on the corporeal semblance acquired by spirits after death but also on human procreation and the divine origin of the soul. In assigning to him this important role, Dante the author makes plain the difference between the pagan and the Christian mind. The conversion of Statius in the first century of the Christian era gave him access to truths that were beyond Virgil, for all his wisdom. Strangely, it even enabled him to be aware of issues that were debated for centuries since his time on earth. By Dante's day, certain doctrines had been shown to be essential to the Christian faith: the direct creation by God of the individual soul, the unity of rational man who shared the faculties of vegetative and animal forms but possessed in addition intellectual faculties, and the autonomy of the human soul endowed both before and after death with memory, intelligence and will. It is to expound these verities that Dante detains Statius, a soul who would otherwise have departed immediately to enter into blessedness in the Empyrean.

The long discourse by Statius is of interest chiefly for the evidence it provides of Dante's understanding of embryology, derived from Aristotle, and of the nature of spirit forms. Here is another example of the father–son relationship. Statius, like Virgil, addresses Dante as 'son' and his tone is loving.

The link between procreation and the formation of the soul after death is what Statius calls the *virtute informativa* ('formative power') of 'perfect blood', that is, the semen, which unites with the blood of the female, forming first an embryo, which it quickens into life. This then undergoes four stages of development: that of a vegetative soul, *qual d'una pianta* ('as of a plant'), with the difference that the soul of a plant is completely developed. The embryo next moves to the intermediary stage between a plant and an animal, *come fungo marino* ('like a sea fungus'). After that comes the animal soul, followed finally by the rational:

'Or si spiega, figliuolo, or si distende
	la virtù ch' è dal cor del generante,
	dove natura a tutte membra intende.
Ma come d'animal divenga fante,
	non vedi tu ancor: quest' è tal punto,
	che più savio di te fè già errante.'

And now the force from the begetter's heart,
	my son, spreads and develops wheresoe'er
	nature intends for every limb and part.
So far, however, thou art not aware
	how reason it acquires, and here it was
	one wiser than thou art was led to err[4]

Statius is now given the role of proclaiming one of the most important tenets of the Christian faith. Nothing that Dante learns from Beatrice in *Paradiso* is of greater significance:

'Apri alla verità che viene il petto;
	e sappi che, sì tosto come al feto
	l'articular del cerebro è perfetto,

lo motor primo a lui si volge lieto
  sovra tant'arte di natura, e spira
  spirito novo di vertù repleto,
che ciò che trova attivo quivi, tira
  in sua sustanzia, e fassi un'alma sola,
  che vive e sente e sè in sè rigira.'

'Open thy mind to what is true and know:
  when the articulation of the brain
  has been perfected in the embryo
by Nature's doing, the First Mover then,
  joyful, breathes into it a spirit, rare
  and new, filled with a power to entrain
into itself what it finds active there,
  which with its substance forms a single soul,
  living and feeling, of its self aware.'[5]

To help Dante to understand how this can be, Statius asks him to consider the heat of the sun which turns the juice of the grape into wine.

When the soul is set free from the body, it carries with it the same *virtute informativa* ('formative power') which the pure blood (semen) had possessed. That is, the soul possesses in potential both the human and the divine faculties; the physical senses being now inactive, memory, intelligence and will are keener than before. The 'formative power' enables the soul to imprint upon the atmosphere that surrounds it the image of the body it formerly occupied, just as the air, when it is moist with rain, becomes adorned with the colours of a rainbow. Then, like a flame that follows fire wherever it moves, this image follows the spirit and by the 'formative power' acquires a semblance of organs for every sense and for every feeling:

'Quindi parliamo e quindi ridiamo noi;
  quindi facciam le lacrime e' sospiri
  che per lo monte aver sentiti puoi.
Secondo che ci affiggono i disiri
  e li altri affetti, l'ombra si figura;
  e quest'è la cagion di che tu miri.'

'Thence do we speak, thence laugh, and thence we make
  our tears and sighs which thou didst hear and see
  as thou thy way along the mount didst take.
Whate'er our feelings and desires may be,
  the shade takes form and this the reason is
  of all that has seemed marvellous to thee.'[6]

On the Seventh Cornice the souls of the lustful are purged in a wall of fire. Divided into two bands, of natural and unnatural lust, they meet and chastely kiss each other, like ants nuzzling to exchange messages. Dante's shadow cast on the fire makes the souls marvel and one entreats him to explain. He identifies himself as Guido Guinizelli.[7]

Dante expresses joy at this encounter in terms which yet again convey the father–son relationship which marks his gratitude to all those from whom he has learnt the art of poetry. In particular, Guinizelli is not only *his* father but the father of all who have written sweet and pleasing rhymes of love:

> ... il padre
> mio e delli altri miei miglior che mai
> rime d'amore usar dolci e leggiadre ...

> *... to me a father and to those*
> *as well, my betters, who before and since*
> *sweet, pleasing rhymes of love did e'er compose ...*[8]

Guinizelli, who has heard of his veneration, asks why it is he holds him dear. Dante replies, using the honorific *voi*:

> ... 'Li dolci detti vostri,
> che, quanto durerà l'uso moderno,
> faranno cari ancora i loro inchiostri.'

> *... 'Master, I think*
> *your sweetly crafted verses will endear,*
> *as long as our style lasts, their very ink.'*[9]

Guinizelli points to an ancestor of them all, the Provençal troubadour Arnaut Daniel, who surpassed in craftsmanship all those who wrote in any of the languages of Romance.[10] In a self-conscious display of his sense of heritage, Dante, in homage to this forebear, casts Arnaut's greeting into Provençal.

We do not know on what evidence (if any) he relegates Guinizelli and Arnaut Daniel to the Cornice of the Lustful, but he has shown from the canto of Francesca da Rimini onwards[11] that love, even of the 'gentle heart', can go astray and may need to be purged in the refining fire. Dante's admiration for the poetry of Arnaut Daniel had led him to compose four of his most intricate, including one of his most erotic, poems, inspired by an unrequited sexual passion for a woman referred to as Pietra.[12] Who she was we do not know: the name 'Pietra' probably refers to her stony-hearted indifference to Dante. It is possible that he intended to comment on these poems in *Il Convivio*, in the context of the need for reason to restrain the excesses of lust. He does not, however, refer to them directly anywhere in the *Commedia*. What next occurs may be his way of purging this episode from his soul.

The fire serves a double purpose. It not only purges those who exceeded in their loves but, since love is the seed of all action, good or evil, as Virgil has shown, *all* the souls who are released from the Mountain of Purgatory have to go through this fiery barrier to reach the summit, on their way to beatitude.

Dante, in his mortal body, is terrified. He clasps his hands and gazes at the fire, vividly imagining bodies he has seen burned. Virgil tries to reassure him, reminding him how he protected him upon the back of Geryon. Here may be torment but not death, the fire cannot burn him; let him test it himself with the edge of his garment:

'Pon giù omai, pon giù ogni temenza:
    volgiti in qua; vieni ed entra sicuro!'
    E io pur fermo e contra coscienza.

'Put fear aside, put every fear aside:
    turn and draw near; come, enter here with trust!'
    But I, against my will, stood petrified.[13]

Virgil, a little troubled, says, 'Look, my son, between thee and Beatrice is this wall.' At this, Dante's stubbornness gives way and he turns to his wise leader, who shakes his head and says, as though tempting a child with an apple, 'So, are we to remain here, on this side?' He then enters the fire himself and bids Statius, who for long had walked between them, to bring up the rear.

The sensation of burning is so fierce that Dante relates that he would gladly have thrown himself into boiling glass to get cool. Virgil speaks continually of Beatrice to hearten him:

Lo dolce padre mio, per confortarmi,
    pur di Beatrice ragionanado andava,
    dicendo, 'Li occhi suoi già veder parmi.'

My loving father, to encourage me,
    of Beatrice kept talking as he went:
    'Her eyes already now I seem to see.'[14]

Dante's participation in the purgation of the lustful appears to be a confession on his part of remorse for lapses from his highest ideals. This is Dante, close on his 50th year, looking back at himself as a young man, judging himself and suffering an agony of repentance. Only the thought of Beatrice gives him the strength to endure what he now suffers. He is guided too by a voice singing beyond the flame. On emerging he knows that the song is the beatitude 'Come, ye blessed of my Father, inherit the kingdom prepared for you.'[15]

The sun sets and the three poets spend the night asleep on the steps, Dante protected like a goat between two shepherds. During his sleep he has a prophetic dream in which he sees a beautiful young woman gathering flowers and singing. She names herself as Leah, whose sister Rachel remains gazing at herself in a mirror, she with contemplation, Leah with action, being satisfied.[16] With the coming of dawn, the three poets rise and mount to the top of the last stairway. Before them lies the Garden of Eden.

This is a moment of fulfilment and transition. Dante has travelled through Inferno and up Mount Purgatory. All seven scars of sin have been erased from his brow. Virgil can help him no further and, though Dante does not realize it at the time, he now bids him farewell:

> ... 'Il temporal foco e l'etterno
> veduto hai, figlio; e se' venuto in parte
> dov'io per me più oltre non discerno.
> Tratto t'ho qui con ingegno e con arte;
> lo tuo piacere omai prendi per duce:
> fuor se' delle erte vie, fuor se' dell'arte.
> Vedi il sol che in fronte ti riluce;
> vedi l'erbetta, i fiori e li arbuscelli,
> che qui la terra sol da sè produce.
> Mentre che vegnan lieti li occhi belli
> che, lacrimando, a te venir mi fenno,
> sederti puoi e puoi andar tra elli.
> Non aspetta mio dir più nè mio cenno:
> libero, dritto e sano è tuo arbitrio,
> e fallo fora non fare a suo senno:
> per ch'io te sovra te corono e mitrio.'

> ... 'the temporal fire and the eterne
> thou hast beheld, my son, and come thou art
> where of myself no further I discern.
> I've brought thee here with knowledge and with art;
> let pleasure be thy only guide from now:
> from steep and narrow ways thou mayst depart.
> See now the sun which shines upon thy brow,
> the grass, the flowers and the trees, which here
> spontaneously from the terrain grow.
> Till those fair, joyful eyes to thee appear,
> which, weeping, bade me come to rescue thee,
> amid the garden rest and wander there.
> No longer wait for word or sign from me.
> Upright and whole and free thy will has grown,
> not to obey it would an error be:
> hence over thee I mitre thee and crown.'[17]

CHAPTER 40

The Christian Sibyl

Outdoor theatrical spectacles, allegorical pageants, masques and processions were frequent in Florence and other Italian cities in Dante's time. Saints' days and other communal events were celebrated with colour, costume, dance and song, not only in the streets but on the river. It is not surprising that Dante should decide to organize his own pageant in the *Commedia*. The place he chose was the Garden of Eden.

His arrival there is the final climax of *Purgatorio*. Followed by Virgil and Statius, he steps eagerly forward into a green and shady wood, where birds are singing in the topmost branches. They come to the brink of a clear stream. On the opposite side, over grass which is bright with red and yellow flowers, there moves a beautiful woman singing and gathering a nosegay. Audience anticipation is aroused. Can this be Beatrice? It is not, and who she is we are never told, except that her name is Matilda.[1] To Dante the sight of her recalls Proserpina in the meadow when she was seized by Pluto; she is as beautiful as Venus when she was pierced by Cupid's arrow, or as Hero for whom Leander braved the Hellespont. He asks her to draw near that he may hear what she is singing. Moving delicately like a dancer, she comes to the water's edge and stands upright, her hands full of flowers. As she raises her eyes she smiles.

Thinking this may surprise them, since they are newly arrived, she tells them why she smiles: this is the place that God created for man's eternal peace but through his fault his stay was short. She explains the miraculous way in which the plants are generated and how the water flows from a supernatural and unfailing spring. This is perhaps, she adds, what the ancient poets imagined when they sang of the age of gold. Dante looks back to see how 'his' poets have taken this and sees that they too are smiling.

This pastoral prelude gives no clue of what is to follow. Walking along on opposite banks of the stream, they follow its curve and come to face the east. Matilda says: 'My brother, look and listen.' A sudden brightness, like lightning, sweeps through the forest and a sweet melody sounds through the shining air, which, as the light increases to a blaze of fire, is heard to be songs. In the distance Dante sees what he at first takes to be seven golden trees.

Nearer they prove to be candlesticks and voices are heard singing 'Hosanna'. Dante in astonishment turns back to Virgil but he, for the first time, has no explanation and can only return a look filled likewise with amazement. There approaches slowly a procession of figures clothed in white. Above them the flames from the candlesticks stream like pennons, in the seven colours of the rainbow, ten paces apart and vanishing into the distance.

Beneath the radiant sky 24 elders walk two by two, crowned with lilies. They sing: 'Blessed art thou among the daughters of Adam and blessed forever be thy beauty!'[2] After them come four living creatures, crowned with green leaves; each one has six wings and in their plumage are six eyes.[3] In a space between these four, a two-wheeled chariot is drawn by a Gryphon, part lion, part eagle, whose wings stretch up between the coloured pennons. Its bird-like part is gold, its lion-part is white and red. Not Scipio Africanus, not Augustus had so magnificent a triumph car, and even the chariot of the sun would seem pale beside it. At the right wheel three women dance and sing a roundelay; one is as red as fire, one seems made all of emerald, and one is as white as newly fallen snow. As they dance they sing, taking their measure, fast or slow, from the one who leads the song in turn. At the left wheel four other women dance, clothed in purple, taking their time from one who has three eyes.[4] Bringing up the rear are two old men, one with the aspect of a physician, the other with a sword, 'so bright and sharp' that Dante feels afraid of it even from across the stream. Four others follow, of humble aspect, and an old man alone, walking as though asleep but with an alert countenance. All seven are crowned like the preceding 24, but instead of lilies their wreaths are of roses and other vermilion flowers, so that from a distance they seem on fire above their brows. When the chariot draws opposite to Dante it stops. There is a clap of thunder and the pageant comes to a halt.

The voice of one of the elders is heard calling three times: *Veni, sponsa, de Libano* ('Come with me from Lebanon, my spouse')[5] and all the others then join in. At this, more than a hundred angels rise from the chariot and cry: *Benedictus qui venis* ('Blessed art thou that comest').[6] Casting flowers into the air, they also chant: *Manibus o date lilia plenis* ('O give lilies with full hands').[7] At this moment, amid the cloud of flowers, Dante sees a figure crowned with an olive wreath over a white veil and clad in a garment-like flame, covered with a green mantle. Never before, or since, has such a magnificent entry been prepared for a *prima donna*.

Dante the dramatist here takes over from the pageant-master. The scene that follows is the most masterly piece of drama in a work that is largely dramatic. Dante the character at once senses, before he actually knows, that this is Beatrice:

E lo spirito mio, che già cotanto
    tempo era stato che alla sua presenza
    non era di stupor tremando affranto,
sanza delli occhi aver più conoscenza,
    per occulta virtù che da lei mosse,
    d'antico amor sentì la gran potenza.

My spirit, which through such a span of years,
    of trembling, that o'ercame it quite
    when in her presence, had put by its fears,
needing no more assurance from my sight,
    by secret power that from her came forth
    my old love felt again in all its might.[8]

As he has done so many times before, he turns to Virgil, like a child to its
mother, for support. He says: 'Not a drop of blood in my veins but does not
tremble. I know the embers of an ancient flame.' In these last words, *conosco i
segni dell'antica fiamma*, he is quoting from Dido's confession of her love for
Aeneas to her sister Anna, a moving tribute to his beloved poet.[9]

But Virgil has gone. Without a word he has just vanished. Dante's shock
and grief are so great that he has forgotten even Beatrice. Not all the beauty
of Eden, forfeited by Eve, can recompense him for his loss and he breaks
down in bitter tears.

Beatrice, instead of consoling him, addresses him sternly, calling him by
his name (the only occasion on which it is used in the *Commedia*):

'Dante, perchè Virgilio se ne vada,
    non pianger anco, non piangere ancora;
    chè pianger ti conven per altra spada.'

'Dante, weep not for Virgil's going, keep
    as yet from weeping, weep not yet, for soon
    another sword shall give thee cause to weep.'[10]

In the role that Beatrice here plays she is the lady in the traditional quest
narrative who rebukes her lover for his infidelity. But the scene is more than
a literary trope. The use of Dante's name indicates that it is personal: Beatrice
here represents his guilty conscience. He portrays her as a severe, authoritative figure, like an admiral who inspects his fleet, moving from stern to
prow, surveying and urging on the work of the crews. Royal and stern in her
demeanour, she says, 'Look on us well, we are, we are Beatrice.'

The use of the plural is startling and significant.[11] 'I am Beatrice,' she
seems to be saying, 'and I am also as you behold me now.' It is as though
the son of a queen, on beholding his mother crowned, sees her now as his
mother, now as his monarch, yet she is always one person. And indeed Dante

speaks of the mother–son relationship at this point:

> Così la madre al figlio par superba,
>   com' ella parve a me; perchè d'amaro
>   sent' il sapor della pietade acerba.

> *And even as a little boy may think*
>   *his mother harsh, she seemed so then to me;*
>   *stern pity is a bitter-tasting drink.*[12]

The speech of accusation that Beatrice now makes is addressed not to him but to the angels. But they, who partake of God's eternal vision, do not need to be informed: her words are for Dante's benefit. This indirect mode has the effect of a drama with a chorus, or, to compare it to a modern setting, of a scene in a court of law. She recalls Dante's natural endowments, which in his 'new life'[13] promised such marvellous results. But the more favourable the ground, the more the weeds flourish if bad seeds fall upon it. For a while he was uplifted and led aright by her face and the beacons which were her eyes. But when, on the threshold of her second age,[14] she changed one life for another (*mutai vita*), he turned from her to someone else. Though her beauty and virtue were then enhanced, he loved her less and wandered from the path of truth, following false phantoms of the good. All her attempts to call him back by dreams and other signs were of no avail. He fell so low that every means to save his soul had failed, except to show him the damned in Hell.

> 'Per questo visitai l'uscio de' morti
>   e a colui che l'ha qui su condotto
>   i preghi miei, piangendo, furon porti.
> Alto fato di Dio sarebbe rotto
>   se Lete si passasse e tal vivanda
>   fosse gustata sanza alcun scotto
> di pentimento che lagrime spanda.'

> *'For this the gateway of the dead I sought,*
>   *and weeping, made request of him by whom*
>   *he has been raised thus far and hither brought.*
> *It would do violence to God's high doom*
>   *if Lethe could be passed, and evil-doers*
>   *to taste this blessed fare could straightway come*
> *without some forfeit of repentant tears.'*[15]

With a superb sense of timing, Dante here ends both Beatrice's speech to the angels and the canto.

With no preamble, the next canto opens with the sword of her rebuke pointed straight at Dante himself, *che pur per taglio m' era paruto acro* ('which even from its edge towards me had seemed sharp'). She calls on him to say whether her accusations are true. He is so broken in spirit that he cannot speak. All he can do is to form the word 'Yes' with his lips but no voice comes, only sobs. But she continues, mercilessly. In answer to her question as to what allurements had led him astray, he manages to stammer amid tears:

> Piangendo dissi: 'Le presenti cose
>   col falso lor piacer volser miei passi
>   tosto che 'l vostro viso si nascose.'

> *'Things transitory, with their false delight',*
>   *weeping I said, 'enticed my steps aside,*
>   *soon as your face was hidden from my sight.'*[16]

His confession of guilt is to his credit but still she continues her reproaches. Nothing surpassed the beauty of her body, which now lies buried in the earth. How could he then have been enticed by something less? At the first shaft of temptation he should have taken flight to pursue her memory, not waited for the next, some *pargoletta*, or other passing fancy.

Standing ashamed and silent, like a child, his eyes fixed on the ground, Dante is still unable to reply. She humiliates him further:

>   ... 'Quando
> per udir se' dolente, alza la barba,
> e prenderai più doglia riguardando.'

>   ... *'If*
> *hearing only grieves thee, raise thy beard,*
> *and thou by looking shalt feel greater grief.'*[17]

Dante feels the sting of her allusion to his beard: he is not a child but a grown man. With an enormous effort he lifts up his chin and looks at her across the stream; still veiled, she is now gazing at the Gryphon. As her beauty outshone that of all other women when she was on earth, she now outshines her former self so far that all other past objects of his love he now hates. Remorse and self-reproach so gnaw his heart that, overwhelmed, he falls in a dead faint. When he comes to himself he is being plunged by Matilda in the stream, which we later learn is the river Lethe, the water of which washes away the memory of all sin.

This prolonged scene of rebuke and confession is placed in a central position in the *Commedia*. From its nature it would seem to have actual, as well as allegorical, meaning; that is to say, Dante is here the living man, writing in his late 40s, looking back on himself. He suffers remorse when he recalls that after the death of Beatrice he failed to live up to the ideal of the *cor gentile*, the love that ennobles. There seems to be an admission that he erred in this regard in connection with the *donna gentile*. When Beatrice says that at her death he turned away and gave himself to someone else, this surely refers to the conflict he described in *La Vita Nuova*. He had tried to reconcile this in *Il Convivio* but had not totally succeeded. His love for the *donna gentile* seems to have merged eventually with his enamoured study of philosophy but there had been an earlier period when the passion of the body had predominated over the passion of the mind. This is what he now confesses to Beatrice, as well as acknowledging trivial entanglements which are reflected in minor poems. In the drama that he here constructs, Beatrice is a severe prosecutor; in reality it is Dante Alighieri who is severe upon himself.

In one aspect of this scene Beatrice is also herself. That is, Dante portrays her as the woman he had come to imagine her to be. But in the pageant and in the following episodes, continuing until the end of *Purgatorio*, he casts her for roles that go far beyond her actual self, as though she were masqued like someone performing in an allegorical production, such as he must often have seen in Florence and elsewhere.

The theme of the pageant so far has been divine revelation. Dante does not interpret the figures who compose it, for his contemporary readers (or, in this case, 'spectators') would have been familiar with them. The candlesticks with seven lights represent the seven gifts of the Spirit: wisdom, understanding, counsel, might, knowledge, piety and fear of the Lord. The 24 elders are the books of the Old Testament (as reckoned by St Jerome). They sing in praise of the Virgin, of whom the books were believed to be full of prophecy. The four winged creatures are a man, a lion, an ox and an eagle, the symbols of the Evangelists. The triumph car is the Church. The Gryphon, twyform, represents the theological concept of Christ, the mystery of the divine and human nature in one. The three dancers at the right wheel of the chariot are the theological virtues, Faith, Hope and Charity, in their symbolical colours. The four at the left wheel are the cardinal virtues, Prudence, Courage, Justice and Temperance, clothed in purple, the colour of empire. The two old men represent the Acts of the Apostles by Luke, 'the beloved physician', and the writings of St Paul, armed with 'the sword of the spirit, which is the word of God'. The four who follow represent the General Epistles and the man walking as though asleep represents Revelations.

The cry of the angels: *Benedictus qui venis* ('Blessed art thou who dost come'), adapted from the words of St Mark, is a line from the hymn sung before the sacring of the Mass. At this moment, 'the one who comes' is Beatrice. Dante has left unchanged the masculine ending (*-us*) to show that at this supreme climax she represents not a woman but something beyond her gender.

One of the most important religious processions of Dante's time celebrated the (then) recently renewed observance of the office of Corpus
Christi. This festival, like Dante's pageant, had chants and lights; flowers too
were scattered. A Papal Bull had ordered: 'Let faith sing psalms, let hope
dance, let charity exult.'[18] Such correspondences have a meaning that indeed
surpasses 'what has been written in verse of any woman': the glorification of
Beatrice as the image of the Host.[19] As in the Corpus Christi procession the
Host was the centre, carried under a baldachin, so in Dante's pageant the
centre is Beatrice carried in the chariot that represents the Church.

Emerging from the river Lethe on to the opposite bank, Dante is led
by the four cardinal virtues into the presence of Beatrice. Gazing into her
now unveiled eyes, the *smeraldi* ('emeralds'), he sees reflected in them the
Gryphon, now wholly eagle, now wholly lion, though being itself unchanged.
Dante's soul, 'full of amazement and gladness', tastes of the food that satisfies
yet creates for itself still further appetite (the Eucharist). At the entreaty of
the theological virtues, Beatrice unveils her smiling mouth. The canto ends
with an admission that no poet could ever summon the ability to render her
as she then appeared.

In the next canto, Dante, resuming his skill as pageant-master, rises to
heights worthy of an earl marshal. As a military man he understood how
a body of soldiery was manoeuvred. The 'glorious army' turns on its right
flank, so that the seven flames are in their faces, together with the sun, now
mounting to its noonday height. As a squadron beneath its shields wheels
with the colours before the whole vanguard can change direction, so the
heavenly militia moves before the pole can turn the chariot round. The seven
virtues again take their places beside the wheels. The Gryphon moves the
blessed burden on and not a feather of its plumage is disturbed. Matilda,
Statius and Dante follow at the right wheel, which describes the smaller arc.
This is troop management indeed.

In time to angelic music, the procession paces through the lofty glade.
When they have advanced about as far as the distance of three arrow flights,
Beatrice descends from the car, thus ending her representation of the Host.
A murmur of the name 'Adam' rustles through the ranks, as though in
reproachful memory of his sin of disobedience. The procession halts, encircling a tree which is bare of all flowers and leaves. Of immense height, its
topmost branches spread the widest. The company address the Gryphon:
'Blessed art thou that with thy beak dost never pluck from this tree, which,
sweet to taste, makes the belly writhe in pain.'

And now an unimaginable thing occurs. The Gryphon, the heraldic
emblem of the two natures of Christ, is heard to speak – a single sentence
only, of cryptic and enigmatic portent:

'Sì si conserva il seme d'ogni giusto.'

'Thus is preserved the seed of all that is just.'[20]

The utterance of so sublime a being, it is evident, is likely to have the utmost significance, and so it proves to be. First, it is an echo of the words of Jesus to St John the Baptist at the moment of His baptism:

'Thus it becometh us to fulfil all righteousness.'

or, as Dante read them in the Vulgate:

'Sic enim decet nos implere omnem iustitiam.'[21]

In both the Italian and the Latin, the reference is to Justice. The words also echo those of St Paul:

As by one man's disobedience many were made sinners, so by the obedience of one shall many be made righteous.[22]

Adam had betrayed the sense of right, implanted originally by God in human nature. This Christ restored by His incarnation and death under the jurisdiction of Empire and by His 'refusal of the kingdoms of the world and the glory of them'.

Having made its arcane pronouncement, the Gryphon pulls the shaft of the car to the foot of the despoiled tree and attaches it there with a withy of the tree itself. At once it blossoms into flowers, less crimson than the rose, more purple than the violet. This bonding of the chariot to the tree (the Tree of Knowledge) is a picture of perfected human order under an ideal union of Church and Empire. The company burst into song but Dante does not comprehend the words nor hear the music to the end.

The reason was, he fell asleep: how, he cannot describe but passes to his awakening. A shining splendour breaks his slumber and a voice calls: 'Arise! What art thou doing?' as when Peter, James and John after the Transfiguration were awakened by the touch and voice of Jesus. Over him stands Matilda and in sudden fear Dante asks: 'Where is Beatrice?' Matilda replies: 'See where she sits beneath the new foliage at the foot of the tree; see the company surrounding her [the seven virtues, who now hold the candle-sticks]; the Gryphon and the others are ascending to the sound of a sweeter and profounder song.'

Beatrice has now moved to her next role. As guardian of the union between the chariot and the tree, she becomes a mistress of ceremony, in command of the masque which will display to Dante the history of the Church and Empire, from the age of persecution to the present time. It is also her function to predict Dante's ultimate salvation:

'Qui sarai tu poco tempo silvano;
   e sarai meco sanza fine cive
   di quella Roma ove Cristo è romano.'

'Briefly the woodland world will be thy home;
   with me eternal citizen thou'lt be
   where Christ is Roman in that other Rome.'[23]

But while still in 'the woodland world', Dante has a mission to fulfil. It is a world that has gone much awry and for its sake he will be shown things now which he must note and write on his return. Beatrice commands him to fix his eyes on the chariot and he obeys. This is the first time that the purpose of his journey, other than his own redemption, is made plain, and it comes in the context of the restoration of justice.

A rapid sequence of violent *coups de théâtre* now takes place. First, the bird of Jove swoops down like lightning on the tree, stripping it of its new foliage and flowers: this represents the persecutions of the early Christians. Next, a lean and starving fox pollutes the car and is driven off by Beatrice (the heresies of the early centuries). Next, the eagle returns, leaving the car feathered with its plumage (the well-meant but in Dante's view disastrous Donation of Constantine, as well as enrichments of the Church by Pepin and Charlemagne).[24] The voice of St Peter is heard lamenting from Heaven: 'O my little vessel, with how much evil art thou burdened!' Next, the earth opens between the chariot wheels and a dragon appears. Driving its tail up through the car, it drags away part of the floor (the schism brought about by Mohammed). There follows a distortion of the chariot. Seven heads appear, three on the pole and one on each corner, the three horned like oxen and the four with a single horn on each forehead (an image taken from the Beast of the Apocalypse 'having seven heads and ten horns').[25] This represents the corruption of the Church. Seated on the car is a harlot, her clothes awry. Beside her is a giant, with whom she fornicates. She leers at Dante, which angers the giant, who belabours her and drags her off into the forest.[26]

The final canto of *Purgatorio* opens with the lamentations of the seven virtues. Beatrice, listening to them, is filled with grief, like Mary at the Cross. She rises to her feet and speaks in Latin:

'Modicum, et non videbitis me;
   et iterum …
   modicum, et vos videbitis me.'

'A little while and ye shall not see me;
   again …
   a little while, and ye shall see me.'[27]

In quoting these words of Jesus to His disciples concerning His death and Resurrection, Beatrice is foretelling the transference of the Papacy to Avignon and its longed-for return to Rome, an event that did not occur in Dante's lifetime.[28]

With the seven virtues walking ahead of her and followed by Matilda, Dante and Statius, Beatrice now moves away from the Tree of Knowledge. When she has advanced ten paces, she commands Dante to draw level with her, so that he may hear what she will tell him. He does so with reverence and breathless awe. She speaks to him now in solemn and mysterious words. The broken chariot 'was and is not'[29] but he who is to blame shall not escape vengeance. The eagle that left its plumes upon the car will not remain without an heir.

She then utters an enigmatic prophecy, which she commands Dante to report: the time is coming, she foretells, when one sent by God, *un cinquecento diece e cinque* ('a five hundred ten and five') will slay the harlot and the giant. If her obscure sayings now cloud his mind, events will clarify their meaning. She bids him note and relate her exact words to the world. Above all he is to describe what he saw happen to the tree, for whoever robs it commits blasphemy. She knows that his intellect has turned to stone and is so darkened that her speech bewilders him. Nevertheless he is to remember it, if not in words, at least in pictures.

Dante replies that his brain is stamped like wax with the impression of all which he has seen and heard, and asks why her words so far out-soar his understanding. She replies that he may now see how remote from God's truth are the studies he has made.[30] Dante, interpreting this to mean that he has been estranged from Beatrice, says he cannot recall that this was ever so. Smiling, she says: 'Thou hast today drunk the waters of Lethe. If fire may be inferred from smoke, this thy forgetfulness implies that thou wast indeed at fault.' Henceforth, she says, her words will be as plain as is required for the meaning to penetrate his obtuse mind.

No longer a figure in a pageant or a masque, she has now entered on her function as Dante's guide, a role she will continue throughout *Paradiso*. Her oracular words, above all her arcane prophecy, make plain the nature of her Sibylline role.

Her mysterious words, *un cinquecento diece e cinque* ('a five hundred ten and five'), have never been convincingly explained, though many ingenious and fantastic attempts have been made. One valid but incomplete interpretation, long accepted, is that the numbers written as the Roman numerals DXV can be arranged to read DVX, that is, the Latin word *dux*, meaning leader. This, however, does not get us far. Another acceptable interpretation reads DXV as the initials of Dominus Christus Victor, but this also leaves the immediate significance unsolved.

There is a further interpretation, never previously perceived, which I here present. The number *cinquecento*, usually printed as a single word, is interpreted as 500. But it can also be read as three words: *cinqu' e cento* ('five and one hundred'), that is, 105. The following numbers *diece e cinque*, 10 and 5, can also, by mystic addition, form 105. The two sets of figures, therefore: *un cinqu'e cento* (one, five and a hundred) and *diece e cinque* (ten and five) can both be read as a reference to the line in *Inferno*, in which Virgil ends his prophecy of the *veltro*, that is, Canto I, line 105:

e sua nazion sarà tra feltro e feltro.

'twixt felt and felt his naissance will be found.[31]

The repetition of the number 105 in the second half of the line makes it possible also to read the figures as the Roman numerals DXV; in this case the figure *un* (one) becomes the indefinite article.

This simple solution is in keeping with Dante's fascination with the meanings that can be read into numbers. The figures 1, 5, 100 also form by mystic addition the number 7, the total of 3 plus 4, representing the theological and the cardinal virtues, the symbol of the ideal organization of the world. The solution also links Virgil and Beatrice as prophets, both of whom foretell the coming of one who will remedy the ills of the world, visualized by Dante in *Il Convivio* as a supreme emperor. It is significant that he introduces this prophecy both at the beginning of the first and at the end of the middle section of the *Commedia*, that is, where Virgil, the pagan sage, is about to lead Dante down into Hell and where Beatrice, the Christian sibyl, is about to lead him up into Heaven. Finally, the arcane words may be seen as a farewell to the character Virgil. Beatrice has replaced him but she takes on his message, like a baton. Failure to recognize its simplicity and once again, as in the case of the *veltro*, the assumption that Dante is referring to a specific person, have obscured its meaning for seven centuries in a wilderness of tangled comment.

CHAPTER 41

Who is Matilda?

D
ante the dramatist, Dante the pageant-master and Dante the creator of masques are all to be found in the spectacular events that take
place in the Garden of Eden. There is also Dante the poet. At the
beginning of *Purgatorio*, after the horrific descriptions of the punishments
in Hell, Dante had invoked the Muses, that poetry might arise again from
the dead:

Ma qui la morta poesì resurga,
o sante muse ...

But here let poetry from death arise,
o sacred muses ...[1]

Throughout this second *cantica* there have been many tender, lyrical
moments, full of colour and imagery, in which the expressive powers of the
volgare illustre have been developed to the utmost. Here in the Garden of
Eden, where the first words of Adam were spoken,[2] Dante manifests some
of his finest poetic skills.

The beauty of the garden is evoked with a delicacy that recalls his most
melodious *canzoni*. The dense, green forest, tempering the rays of the early
sun, the fragrance of the plants, the gentle breeze, the singing of the birds
in the tree-tops, accompanied by the fluttering of leaves, draw the reader in,
with Dante, as he moves slowly forward to explore. The sudden appearance
of a *bella donna*, singing and gathering flowers, with which all her path was
painted (*ond'era pinta tutta la sua via*)[3] is a picture such as might have come
from Dante's own brush in the days when he painted figures of angels upon
boards.[4]

The identity of this figure has been and is still the subject of controversy.
In order to analyse the problem and possibly to arrive at a conclusion, it is
necessary to examine every reference to her more minutely than has been
done in the preceding chapter.

In response to Dante's entreaty, she draws near the bank of a stream
which divides them, still singing, moving delicately like a dancer:

Come si volge con le piante strette
  a terra ed intra sè donna che balli,
  e piede innanzi a piede a pena mette,
volsesi in su i vermigli ed in sui gialli
  fioretti verso me non altrimenti
  che vergine che li occhi onesti avvalli.

Just as a dancer, when she pirouettes,
  her feet down pointed and together close,
  and one before the other tightly sets,
so she, amid the flowers, gold and rose,
  towards me turned, her modest eyes cast down,
  moving demurely as a maiden does.[5]

It is possible that Dante is here evoking the performance by dancers of one of his *ballate*, such as the one he sent to Beatrice, to be sung and danced to her in hope of a reconciliation.[6]

The beautiful and mysterious *donna* then raises her eyes and smiles. Thinking some explanation of her joy is needed, she tells the three newcomers that this is the garden created as the dwelling for humanity; the psalm *Delectasti* ('Thou, Lord, hast made me glad through thy work') will perhaps dispel all surprise from their minds.[7] She then addresses Dante directly, saying that she will tell him whatever he wishes to know, for she has come prepared to do so.[8] From this it is reasonable to draw a working hypothesis: she is one of the several guides sent to assist or instruct Dante on his journey; unlike Cato at the foot of the mountain, and unlike the porter at the gate to the cornices, she is not permanently present; like St Bernard who appears at Dante's side when Beatrice resumes her throne in the Celestial Rose, she has been sent for a special purpose and will return to Paradise.[9]

Dante wishes first to know the source of the water and of the breeze in the garden, for he has been informed (by Statius)[10] that above the gateway to the cornices there are no atmospheric disturbances. The lady's explanation, delivered in didactic style, links the mountain with the movement of the heavenly spheres, which, as they circle, produce a soft breeze, which carries the seeds of plants, spontaneously generated here, to the northern hemisphere, where they are self-sown. The water issues by God's will from a constant unvarying fount, dividing into two streams: the nearer one, named Lethe, takes from the soul all memory of sin; the other, named Eunoë,[11] restores the memory of every good deed, its taste by far surpassing all else in its sweetness.

The lady then adds what she calls a 'corollary': the poets who wrote of the age of gold and its happy state were perhaps dreaming of this place when they wrote of the Golden Age:

'Qui fu innocente l'umana radice;
    qui primavera sempre ed ogni frutto;
    nettare è questo di che ciascun dice.'

'Here mankind's origin was innocent;
    here was eternal spring and every fruit,
    and what by nectar every poet meant.'[12]

Like a woman in love, she continues singing[13] and moves along the bank upstream, Dante matching his steps to hers on the opposite side. So they proceed until the arrival of the pageant. After the disappearance of Virgil it is she who instructs Dante where to fix his gaze. She is a witness of his humiliation and confession and when he drops in a swoon it is she who plunges him into the river Lethe. She accompanies the procession to the Tree and is present throughout the sequence of masques. When Dante falls asleep it is she who awakens him and reassures him when he looks about him in search of Beatrice. When Dante is summoned to Beatrice's side, she walks behind with Statius. As they come to the second branch of the stream, Dante asks what this water is. And now at last the mysterious lady's name is revealed. Beatrice replies, *Prega/Matelda che 'l ti dica* ('Ask Matilda to tell thee').[14] The lady replies that she has already told him this and many other things and is sure that the water of Lethe cannot have washed the memory from him. 'Perhaps a greater care has clouded his mind,' Beatrice answers. 'But there is Eunoë. Lead him to it *e come tu se' usa* ("and as thou art accustomed") revive his weakened powers.' The lady takes Dante by the hand and bidding Statius to come with him leads him to Eunoë. From its sacred water he emerges 'remade, like plants renewed with new leaves',

    puro e disposto a salire alle stelle.

pure and disposed to rise up to the stars.[15]

With this repetition of the last rhyme of *Inferno*, the second *cantica* ends.

Who is Matilda? Why is her name revealed only at the end of her role and then with no explanation? What do the words *come tu se' usa* convey? Do they imply that it is her permanent function to immerse penitent souls in the two streams and, if so, was Statius also immersed? (Nothing is said concerning him in this regard.) Or does it simply mean that she is now to plunge Dante in Eunoë as she has already plunged him in Lethe? Is she a person or merely a symbol? If a symbol, what does she signify?

The earliest commentators, including Dante's son Pietro, identified her as Matilda, Countess of Tuscany, and for many centuries this identification was uncontested. In recent times objections have been raised to it, so many that it is surprising that it remained unchallenged for so long.

The historical Matilda of Tuscany (1046–1115) was an ally and supporter of Pope Gregory VII and a generous benefactress to the Church, bequeathing to it her vast territories. In 1077 she played an important role in the confrontation between the Pope and the Emperor Henry IV, a celebrated event that was played out at Matilda's castle of Canossa.[16] The conflict arose as a result of a decree passed by the Pope forbidding the appointment of ecclesiastics by secular authorities. This challenged a lucrative traffic and was bitterly contested by Henry IV.

Matters came to a head over the archbishopric of Milan, to which Henry had nominated his own candidate, ignoring the Pope's choice. Gregory could not overlook such defiance and demanded the withdrawal of Henry's nominee. Henry refused. In 1076, at a meeting at Worms, attended by 24 bishops and the archbishops of Mainz and Trier, Gregory was declared deposed. This was followed by a meeting at Piacenza, at which Lombard bishops issued a similar declaration. The news was conveyed to Gregory at a Lenten synod at which there was an outburst of wrath among the assembly. The unfortunate messenger was set upon and would have been killed but for the intervention of Gregory. His next step was to excommunicate Henry and to declare him deposed as Emperor.

A decision was taken to hold a meeting at Augsburg, attended by Gregory, at which Henry should face his accusers. To forestall this danger, Henry secretly crossed the Alps with a few attendants in the midst of winter and arrived outside the gates of the castle of Canossa, where the Pope was staying as a guest of the Countess Matilda, on his way to Augsburg. Henry knelt in penitence, barefoot in the snow, for three days. Matilda is said to have interceded for him and the Pope finally absolved him from his excommunication.

This striking event remained for centuries a dramatic icon of Papal and Imperial conflict, resolved in reconciliation at the mediation of 'the Great Countess'. In view of Dante's concern with the balance of power between Pope and Emperor, it is surprising that no mention is made of this episode in the *Commedia*, nor in his treatise *Monarchia*.[17] The question is: has he made indirect allusion to it in the figure of Matilda in the scene of reconciliation between himself and Beatrice in the Garden of Eden?

If so, one question can be provisionally answered: why Dante does not reveal the identity of Matilda until the end of the episode. To have done so would have distracted attention from Beatrice and from the central scene. With his strong sense of dramatic structure, Dante always knows better than to anticipate his effects.

Other problems remain, however. One objection was powerfully expressed by the Dante scholar Francesco D'Ovidio[18] who could not accept that Dante's Matilda represented 'a fiery and imperious old woman of seventy who had been twice married'. He was convinced that if anything was certain about Matilda it was that she was *not* the Countess of Tuscany. Another objection, which has seemed insurmountable to some commentators, is the bequest by the Countess of wealth and territories to the Church. As against this, however, although Dante deplored the Donation believed to have been made by the Emperor Constantine to Pope Sylvester, it did not prevent him from exalting the soul of Constantine to Paradise among rulers who loved and exercised justice.[19]

Numerous other candidates have been proposed: two nuns, Matilda of Hackeborn and Matilda of Magdeburg, both authors of mystical writings; the Empress Matilda, wife of Henry I; Matilda, daughter of Henry I. Another category of suggestions offers a range of women mentioned in the *Vita Nuova*: one of the screen-ladies; one of the companions of Beatrice; the lady loved by Cavalcanti, known as Giovanna or Primavera; the *donna gentile*. Another desperate solution propounds the theory that she is a purely fictitious symbol; if this were so, she would be unique among all the characters in the *Commedia*.

The case for the Countess may be approached from another angle. Leaving on one side what is known of the historical personage, it is worth considering what impression Dante himself might have formed of her. What was his source of information?

Between the years IIII and III2 the chaplain of Matilda, named Domnizo, completed a chronicle in Latin verse relating her virtuous deeds. Referring to her as 'the worthy daughter of Peter', he describes her as follows: 'she is tall, with the beautiful features of her mother and her father's southern complexion'; 'she shines as brightly as the star Diana'; 'she is upheld, irradiated and wonderfully sustained by hope'; 'she loves greatly the Divine Word by whom all things are created'; 'she has always a cheerful, smiling countenance and a calm and peaceful mind;' 'she delights in and praises those of her servants whom she finds full of humility and they honour and obey her with reverence'; 'prudence accompanies her every action'; 'prosperity does not alter her, nor do misfortunes disturb her'.

The tradition that she was beautiful lived on after her. Riccobaldo, a historian of Ferrara of the thirteenth century, describes her as possessing great beauty which she retained even to the last years of her life. She was known to be an influential patron of art and was involved in the rebuilding of Modena Cathedral. She promoted the reform of the Cluniac Order, of which several monasteries were rebuilt under her patronage. Her tomb[20] was first placed in the monastery of San Benedetto Polirone, near Mantua, in the Oratory of the Blessed Virgin, which formed part of the ancient church founded by Tedaldo, Matilda's grandfather. The walls were adorned with frescoes and in the pavement round the sarcophagus was a series of mosaics depicting figures symbolic of Matilda and her qualities. Four stately female figures represent the cardinal virtues: Prudence, Justice, Fortitude and Temperance. On the left of them is a man with a spear in his hand which he aims at a dragon; on the right are a unicorn and a bird with webbed feet and an animal's head.

From these elements of biography and iconography Dante may well have fashioned his idyllic picture of Matilda. A further source, that of epigraphy, could be the origin of the mysterious phrase *come tu se' usa* ('as thou art accustomed'), uttered by Beatrice when she commands Matilda to revive Dante in the water of Eunoë. Near Pisa, at Acqua, were certain baths, beside which, on a wall, an inscription commemorated their renewal by the Countess Matilda:

> MATHELDIS
> Comitissa insignis
> Ob Humanam Valetudinem
> Instaurandam, Praeservandamque
> Amena Haec ab Aquis salubria
> Balnea
> In omnigentium Hominum Usum
> Omni cum ornatu cultuque
> Dicavit A
> A.D. MCXII. K. Maias

> (The renowned Countess Matilda, for the establishment
> and preservation of human health, dedicated with every
> decoration and care these pleasant and salubrious baths
> for the use of men of all races, in the year A.D. 1112 in
> the Kalends of May.)

The words *in omnigentium hominum usum* ('for the use of men of all races') appear to be echoed by those of Beatrice, *come tu se' usa*, as though health-giving waters for the refreshment of mankind were associated with the bounty of Matilda.

From these fragments it is perhaps possible to strengthen the case for the identification of Dante's Matilda as the Countess of Tuscany, presented in delicate, idyllic allegory as a figure of the active life, as anticipated by the figure of Leah in Dante's dream.[21] If so, Beatrice, anticipated by Rachel in the same dream, represents the contemplative life. The allegory is, however, many-layered. The central scene between Dante and Beatrice is above all one of self-abasement and reconciliation, mediated by her handmaid Matilda: it is, perhaps, by subtle implication, Dante's own Canossa.[22]

Fig 9. Mosaics Adorning the Tomb of the Countess Matilda

CHAPTER 42

Dante and His Patrons

O f all Dante's patrons, the most powerful and influential was Can Grande della Scala.[1] The third son of Alberto della Scala, the Ghibelline ruler of Verona, he became joint lord with his brother Alboino on the death of their elder brother Bartolommeo in 1308. When Alboino died in 1311 Can Grande became sole ruler of Verona, at the age of 20.

A champion of Henry VII, he was present at Milan on 6 January 1311 when Henry received the second of his three crowns, and Dante could have seen him there.[2] He was about to embark at Genoa for Rome to support Henry's third coronation when news reached him of the death of Alboino and he returned at once to Verona. From there he continued to campaign in support of Henry and was appointed Imperial Vicar of Verona and of Vicenza. He was a brilliant and successful general. Within a short period he added Vicenza, Padua, Cremona, Mantua and Treviso to his territories.

Can Grande's court in Verona had a reputation for magnificence and it was his policy to offer shelter to prominent exiles. A chronicler named Sagacio Mucio Gazata, who was one of his guests, provided the following description of his hospitality:

> Different apartments, according to their condition, were assigned to the exiles in the Scala palace. Each had his own servants and a well-appointed table served in private. The various apartments were marked with various devices and figures, such as Victory for soldiers, Hope for exiles, Muses for poets, Mercury for artists and Paradise for preachers. During meals in common, musicians, jesters and jugglers performed. ... The halls were decorated with pictures representing the vicissitudes of fortune. On occasion Can Grande invited certain of his guests to his own table, notably Guido da Castello ... and the poet Dante Alighieri.[3]

It is not known precisely when Dante entered the household of Can Grande, perhaps between 1315 and 1316, but he contrives for Marco Lombardo to mention Guido da Castello in *Purgatorio*[4] as one of three *vecchi* ('elders') in whom virtue still survives. Born between 1233 and 1238, Guido was in his early 60s in 1300. He is said to have been still living in 1315 so it is possible that he and Dante met at the court of Verona and dined together at Can Grande's table. Dante had referred to him as a model of nobility of character in *Il Convivio*,[5] but whether he had met him by then or merely knew of his reputation it is not possible to say.

There are several stories of coarse buffoonery of which Dante was sometimes the victim, but Gazata's description of individual apartments gives an impression of dignity and comfort, conditions which make it probable that Dante wrote and read aloud part of *Purgatorio* there. Can Grande may have been lavish in his hospitality but he was also pragmatic. Dante was by then celebrated as the author of an ongoing and compelling work that championed the Imperial cause and reviled its opponents, particularly the Papacy. Can Grande was successfully establishing his power but he had enemies, particularly among the Paduans, who, having recently suffered from the atrocities of the tyrant Ezzelino da Romano,[6] feared the rise of Can Grande as another such despot. Dante's support of Empire as divinely ordained was an aid to Can Grande in his ambition to be established as the principal Ghibelline ruler of an extensive area of Italy.

Exactly how Dante's cantos were made public we do not know, but it is likely that Can Grande provided copyists, organized public readings and arranged for the work to be distributed, at least in its later stages. It would have been to his advantage to do so. He was aware of Dante's persuasive skills as a publicist and on one occasion he made use of them, as will be shown later in this chapter. It has been said that after some time relations between them became strained (possibly the buffoonery of the Verona court became more than Dante could endure) but he never lost his admiration and gratitude towards the valiant young ruler of Verona. His outspoken condemnation in his poem of so many public figures earned him enemies also[7] and the protection and sponsorship of someone as powerful as Can Grande were worth cultivating. They were each of use to the other.

The dependence of potentates upon poets for their fame, both during their lives and in posterity, is an ancient tradition. Such patronage worked both ways. It was an advantage to a poet to hitch his wagon to a star, and the more illustrious a poet became the greater the patron's renown and hope of immortality. Such a system brought writers into relation with an influential social and political élite and obliged them to confront political and social concerns. In this relationship poets functioned as spokesmen (what are now called 'spin doctors') for public relations, receiving in return financial benefit, protection and hospitality, as well as the circulation of their works with a prestigious *imprimatur*. In later centuries the system deteriorated into a form of courtly literature in which the flattery of rulers became servile.

Can Grande was a patron of artists as well as poets. He is said to have invited Giotto to Verona and to have sponsored architects. He organized festivities and pageants to celebrate his victories, splendid in décor, apparel and allegorical panache. Dante placed great hopes in him as the champion of Henry VII and, when that enterprise failed, of the next Emperor ordained to take his place, whoever and whenever that should be. Many commentators have identified Can Grande himself as the *veltro* ('hound'),[8] chiefly because of the punning coincidence of his name, but from *Il Convivio* onwards Dante had seen the necessity for an Emperor whose power would be supreme over the Holy Roman Empire, in command of all other secular rulers, on whom he could depend to implement and maintain the laws, both canon and civil, against avarice. For this fulfilment Dante looked to the eventual but not the immediate future. Not much was to be hoped from the unresolved rivalry between Louis of Bavaria and Frederick of Austria, as a result of which the office of Emperor remained vacant for the rest of Dante's life.[9] Nevertheless, he never gave up hope and regarded it as his mission as a poet-prophet to provide in his writings a structure of conviction and readiness among his readers, both popular and learned, for what would come to pass.[10]

The timeframe of the story of the *Commedia* permitted only a future glimpse of Can Grande, for he was a boy of nine in 1300, but Dante introduces him in a context of heroic significance. In the central canto of *Paradiso*, in the Heaven of Mars, Dante's crusader ancestor Cacciaguida foretells that Dante in his 'first refuge' (Verona)[11] will set eyes on one whose noble deeds are destined to become renowned:

> 'Non se ne son le genti ancora accorte
>   per la novella età, chè pur nove anni
>   son queste rote intorno di lui torte;
> ma pria che 'l Guasco l'alto Arrigo inganni,
>   parran faville della sua virtute
>   in non curar d'argento nè d'affanni.
> Le sue magnificenze conosciute
>   saranno ancora, sì che i suoi nemici
>   non ne potran tener le lingue mute.
> A lui t'aspetta ed a' suoi benefici;
>   per lui fia trasmutata molta gente,
>   cambiando condizion ricchi e mendici.'

> *'Of him the world as yet is unaware*
> *   for he is young, these circles having turned*
> *   for nine years only round his life so far;*
> *but of his prowess sparks will be discerned*
> *   before the Gascon the great Harry cheats.*
> *Toil will be scoffed, desire for fortune spurned;*

the marvels of his many benefits
  so famous will become, his very foes
  will scarce be mute about his valiant feats.
Await him and his bounties as time goes;
  by him will many fortunes altered be,
  the poor he will exalt, the rich depose.'[12]

In 1317 or thereabouts Dante received an offer of hospitality from the ruler of Ravenna. At that time Ravenna was nominally a republic but in reality the government was under the control of the head of the Polentani family who with the title of *podestà* was absolute ruler. In June 1316 Guido da Polenta the Younger (Guido Novello) succeeded to this position. A nephew of the notorious Francesca da Rimini, he evidently appreciated Dante's compassionate account of his aunt's adultery and death in Canto V of *Inferno*.[13] Himself a versifier, he admired Dante as a poet and regarded his presence an asset to his court.

He provided Dante with a house of his own, the first since his banishment from Florence in 1302. Dante's sons Pietro and Jacopo, on whom sentence of exile had become effective when they reached the age of 14, joined him. The dates of their births are not known. They may have taken refuge in Verona while their father was the guest of Can Grande. In the fresh sentence of banishment passed against Dante on 6 November 1315 both his sons were included in the threat of public beheading if they re-entered Florence. His daughter Antonia also joined him in Ravenna and after her father's death became a nun in the convent of Santo Stefano degli Ulivi under the name of Sister Beatrice,[14] an indication of the reverence in which the name of Dante's great love was held in his family circle. It is possible also that Dante's wife Gemma joined the household but there is no certainty of this, nor, on the other hand, is there evidence to the contrary, and some commentators believe that she did.

Whatever his domestic arrangements in Ravenna, Dante found it possible to write the last cantos of *Purgatorio* there and the whole of *Paradiso*. It has been suggested that the beauty of the pine forest nearby, known as the Pineta, contributed to Dante's imaginative creation of the Garden of Eden. Certainly the Byzantine and early Christian art in the city of Theodoric and Justinian and the sparkling mosaics in the churches representing in hieratic splendour the rulers of the past can be seen reflected in the iconic qualities of *Paradiso*.

The Studio, or University, of Ravenna, provided Dante with an opportunity to add to his income by teaching and lecturing. Among his colleagues were two fellow Florentines, Dino Perini and a physician, Fiduccio de' Milotti. Florentine voices and Florentine accents resounded therefore within the walls of Dante's house and Florentine affairs were no doubt a subject of discussion. It is said that private pupils sought his guidance in the art of writing verse in the vernacular, among them being Guido Novello himself. There is a tradition that Giotto visited Dante in Ravenna between 1317 and 1320 and certain frescoes in the church of San Giovanni Evangelista have, rightly or wrongly, been attributed to him.

Dante's last years in Ravenna appear to have been congenial. They were certainly productive. Not only did he complete the *Commedia* during that period, he also wrote a number of minor works in Latin. The most important was his treatise in support of imperial authority, entitled *Monarchia*.

On 20 April 1314 Pope Clement V died. A conclave of 24 cardinals assembled at Carpentras to elect a successor. Of these, only six were Italian, the rest being French, mainly Gascons, eager to maintain the policies of the late Pope. The Italian cardinals hoped to secure the election of the Bishop of Palestrina, who had pledged to restore the Papacy to Rome and rescue it from Gascon domination. In May or June 1314 Dante, either on his own initiative or, more probably, commissioned by sponsors, had written a fiery and bitterly reproachful epistle to the Italian cardinals,[15] urging them to withstand the Gascons and to restore the Papacy to Rome. The Gascon party, fearing the election of the Bishop of Palestrina, organized an armed irruption into the conclave and, shouting 'Death to the Italian cardinals!', forced them to take refuge. The See remained vacant for two years, until 7 August 1316, when Jacques d'Euse of Cahors, Bishop of Avignon, was elected as Pope John XXII.

The new Pope at once set about challenging the legitimacy of the title of Imperial Vicar, conferred by Henry VII on Can Grande and on several other Italian rulers: Visconti in Milan, Bonaccolsi in Mantua and Estensi in Ferrara. The Pope, determined to dissolve this powerful alliance of Ghibelline supporters, issued a decree from Avignon on 31 March 1317, warning that while the office of Emperor was vacant all jurisdiction was transferred to the Papal see and the title of Imperial Vicar was no longer valid. Those who persisted in acknowledging it would be excommunicated and placed under an interdict. On 6 April 1318 Can Grande, Matteo Visconti and Passarino Bonaccolsi were individually targeted: they were given two months to appear before a Papal judge and submit to the Pope's decree. They refused to do so and the dispute continued for the following 20 years.[16]

This was a serious challenge to the position of Can Grande. It was essential to convince the clergy of Verona that the decree had no validity and that they could rightly disregard the threat of excommunication and interdict. It was a moment of crisis. An authoritative statement was needed proving that the Pope had no political authority over the Emperor. The obvious person to turn to was Dante.

His views on the subject were well known, not only from the letters he had written in support of Henry VII in 1310,[17] but from his earlier work, *Il Convivio*.[18] More recently, in *Purgatorio*, he had plainly attributed the ill organization of the world to the intrusion of the Pope into secular affairs.[19] It is possible that Can Grande called on Dante's assistance as early as 1317. Dante did not fail him.

For centuries it has been maintained that the treatise known as *Monarchia* was contemporary with the letters Dante wrote in support of Henry VII in 1310, but recent scholarship has shown that this, always unconvincing, theory is invalid.[20] In the first of the three books of which the work is composed,[21] Dante refers to a canto of *Paradiso*, in which, he says, he has already written of free will, as he does now in *Monarchia*, as 'the greatest gift conferred by God on human nature: *sicut in Paradiso Comedie iam dixi* ("as I have already said in *Paradiso* in the *Commedia*")'. This is a reference to the words of Beatrice in the fifth canto:

'Lo maggior don che Dio per sua larghezza
  fesse creando ed alla sua bontate
  più conformato e quel ch' e' più apprezza,
fu della volontà la libertate;
  di che le creature intelligenti
  e tutte e sole, fuoro e son dotate.'

'The greatest gift which God creating made,
  and to His bounty most akin, which He
  most precious holds of all that He conveyed,
was freedom of the will, that liberty
  with which all creatures made intelligent
  were and are each endowed, and only they.'[22]

Scholars who hold to the earlier dating have refused to acknowledge the authenticity of the reference to *Paradiso*, explaining it away as an interpolation by another hand or by Dante at a later date. Recent study of the manuscripts has shown the reference to be authentic.[23]

The treatise *Monarchia* was written, then, to serve an immediate purpose: to defend the position of Can Grande della Scala by proving that the decree issued by Pope John XXII was without authority. At the same time, and more importantly, the challenge provided Dante with an opportunity to set out in a form appropriate for the attention of prelates and other learned readers the views he had already presented for general readers in *Il Convivio* and was continuing to convey in narrative and allegorical form in the *Commedia*. The disguise of the expedient purpose in the midst of philosophical, historical and theological arguments was a skilful strategy. If the authority of the

Emperor could be shown convincingly in abstract argument to be directly received from God, no concrete specific refutation of the Pope's decree was required: its invalidity would be subsumed in a universal truth. The treatise also provided a firm underpinning of the *Commedia*, particularly of the political agenda of *Paradiso*, several cantos of which were already written.

The *Monarchia*, more than any other work, brings Dante before us as an intellectual and a publicist. We see how he was trained, how his mind worked, how he disputed with opponents. He had learnt from his studies of Aristotle to argue from first principles. His debating skills were finely honed and his eye for a fallacy in a syllogism was sharp. It is possible that he had acquired these skills during his student years, perhaps even from Brunetto Latini, and that he later took part in disputes with fellow intellectuals in Bologna and elsewhere, possibly at Can Grande's court and in Ravenna. Such competence does not come and is not maintained without training and practice.

There are, however, many differences between his way of thinking and ours. His use of examples is selective; he accepts evidence from history, Scripture, ancient literature and legends on an equal footing; his interpretation of events of the past does not constitute proof, though he presents it as such. The triumphs of the ancient Romans become the triumphs of Dante's contemporary world, the centuries melt away, the past is adjusted to fit the present. To defend the position of Can Grande it was necessary to demonstrate that the authority of the Emperor, which the Ghibelline ruler represented, was derived directly from God. The task was twofold: he had to prove that arguments supporting the secular supremacy of Papal authority were fallacious and he had himself to put forward convincing arguments for the independence of Imperial power. In an elegant construction, he approaches the subject from three points of view, set out in three books.

In the first book, mankind is considered as a whole. For the fulfilment of human potential a single leader is required, the principle of oneness mirroring the oneness of God. Such a leader, set over all others, is essential for the resolution of conflict and the abolition of avarice; his power alone, being absolute, can ensure that justice is enforced; he is the peacekeeper and lawgiver, indeed, the embodiment of the concept of law, the only means by which the freedom of the will, God's greatest gift to mankind, can be exercised. The first book concludes with a reminder of the time in history when mankind enjoyed universal peace, under a universal monarchy, the moment of Christ's birth under the *imperium* of Augustus, an argument that is given special prominence in the second book.

This is concerned with Roman history. If it can be shown that the Roman Empire was founded on right it follows that it was founded in accordance with God's will. Dante here uses again material he had already set out in *Il Convivio*. In the earlier work he had written with passion and wonder of the divine pattern. In *Monarchia*, a more disciplined and formal presentation, the fervour still shines through. He believes, not only by philosophic and historical argument but with ardent faith, that Roman history presented clear signs of God's will in operation. He corroborates his belief by (selective) quotations from historians, reinforced by others from the ancient poets, particularly Virgil, who had perceived the truth.

The most powerful and to his opponents[24] the most objectionable argument, already mentioned at the end of Book I, is aimed at Christian believers and, for the express purpose of the work, at the clergy: if the domination of the world by Romans was not legitimate, it follows that Christ's Redemption of all mankind was invalid. This view, propounded first by Orosius, had been mentioned briefly by Dante in his letter to Henry VII.[25] Here he brings it forth in full force, a challenge he held to be unanswerable:

> If Christ had not suffered under a qualified judge, that suffering would not have been a punishment. And the judge could not have been qualified had he not had jurisdiction over the whole human race; since it was the whole human race that was to be punished in that flesh of Christ, who was bearing and sustaining our griefs. And Tiberius Caesar, whose vicar Pilate was, would not have had such jurisdiction unless the Roman empire had been of right.[26]

In the third book, Dante proceeds to demolish the arguments of his opponents. His purpose is to show that if the Emperor were subject to the Pope's authority this would be contrary to nature's intention and hence to the will of God. He identifies three classes of people who oppose the truth: first, the Pope and other prelates, who, perhaps out of zeal rather than insolence, oppose the truth he is about to demonstrate; secondly those whose

> stubborn greed has put out the light of reason, who declare themselves devout, but, being the sons of Satan, stir up contention and, hating the sacred title of princedom, impudently deny the first principles ...

and thirdly, the Decretalists, who regard the Decretals[27] as the only source of truth concerning the authority of the Church.

With the third group he deals as follows:

> the Decretalists, strangers to and ignorant of every kind of theology and philosophy, who carp at the empire, putting all their reliance on the decretals (which, as it happens, I revere) and regarding them as supreme. I have heard one of them declare ... that the traditions of the church are the foundation of the faith, may which impious thought be extirpated from the minds of men ... for the traditions of the church were in Christ the Son of God, either He that was to come or He that was present and had already suffered.[28]

This is the angry, combative Dante, whose fury against opponents is aroused even in a formal treatise, the same Dante who ten years previously in *De Vulgari Eloquentia* had said that if anyone disagreed with him he did not consider him worthy of any reply[29] and in *Il Convivio* of another opponent that the only way to deal with him was to take a dagger to him,[30] the same Dante who had cursed the presumption of those 'most foolish and degraded beasts' who did not acknowledge the wisdom of God in bringing together in time the birth of Rome and the birth of David,[31] and who had described those who denied belief in immortal life as 'most brutish, vile, foolish and pestilent'.[32]

At the beginning of the second book of *Monarchia* Dante refers to a time when he believed that the Roman Empire had been established by force. When he perceived the truth he was filled with derisive contempt not only for his own previous folly but towards all those who persist in the same error and 'oppose their Lord and his anointed Prince'.[33] It is now his intention to lay aside derision and instead 'to pour forth the light of instruction and to break the chains of the ignorance of kings and princes ... who usurp to themselves public government, as they falsely suppose the Romans did'.[34] His intention is laudable but his characteristic impatience with those who oppose his views causes him to break into outbursts of wrath. It is not known who the Decretalist was whom he heard proclaim the 'impious thought' that the Decretals were the foundation of the faith, but the occasion may have been a public dispute in which Dante took part. If so, the dispute is likely to have been intemperate.

In the third book, Dante controls his wrath and demolishes, one by one, without derision or contempt, the arguments on which his opponents relied for their belief in the supremacy of the Papacy over the authority of Empire. His last paragraph is conciliatory: the Emperor, he allows, is in some respect subject to the Pope, as earthly happiness is subordinate to immortal happiness. For the fulfilment of the two goals of mankind, the exercise of moral intellectual virtues and the exercise of theological virtues, two guides are needed. If perfect co-operation between Emperor and Pope can be achieved, there will be temporal peace on earth and eternal peace in the afterlife. This is Dante's undying hope and it is for this that he writes the *Commedia*.

The *Monarchia* did not win Can Grande's conflict for him. It was, however, considered a dangerous book by the Church. In about 1327, only six years after Dante's death in 1321, a Dominican priest, Guido Vernani, wrote a denunciation of it, entitled *De Reprobatione Monarchiae*. In 1329 the book was ritually burned. As late as 1554 it was officially placed on the Vatican's Index of prohibited books, from which, presumably owing to inertia, it was not removed until 1881.

Dante wrote this remarkable work in Ravenna, in the grace and favour house granted to him by Guido da Polenta, where he lived with his sons Jacopo and Pietro and his daughter Antonia. It is striking that the balance between Church and Empire for which Dante hoped is mirrored in microcosm in the choice of professions made by his offspring: Jacopo became a priest, Pietro became a judge, Antonia became a nun.

CHAPTER 43

Prelude to *Paradiso*

Of the three sections of the *Commedia*, the least read is *Paradiso*. Many, heeding Dante's warning, have turned back to seek the safety of the shore.[1] Although the most demanding, it is in some ways the most rewarding. Here Dante the mature man is to be found, his conflicting aspects integrated and brought at last into harmony with the will of God, or, as he says in his final line, with *l'amor che move il sole e l'altre stelle* ('the love which moves the sun and the other stars').[2] He knows that he is attempting what has never been tried in poetry before and that he needs a different audience: only those who have reached out to seize the bread of angels (philosophy and theology) will now be able to follow him. Yet he is still showman enough to hold the attention of those who have so far been captured by the story; at one point he even teases them, saying, 'If I stopped now, how disappointed you would be!'

> Pensa, lettor, se quel che qui s'inizia
> non procedesse, come tu avresti
> di più savere angosciosa carizia.
>
> *Think, reader, if what here I have begun*
> *did not proceed, with what anxiety*
> *thou wouldst desire to know how it goes on.*[3]

Although what he experienced in Heaven is beyond the comprehension of many, even, as he says, beyond his own capacity to put into words, Dante the craftsman still knows how to hold his audience with descriptions, portraits and dialogue, beguiling them with his poetry, as well as rousing them with his denunciation of evil-doers, as wrathful in its expression as anything in *Inferno* or *Purgatorio*. The construction of the story, too, is beautifully designed: as Dante ascends, souls descend from the Empyrean, where in timelessness they all dwell, to greet him as he ascends in the time-space of the narrative in a succession of planetary spheres, a duple movement that achieves dynamic variety and at the same time disproves the Platonic belief that souls returned for ever to the stars whence they first came.

Not long after writing *Monarchia*, Dante addressed to Can Grande[4] what has been called an epistle, in Latin, in which he dedicated and commended to him this final section of his poem. In gratitude for the bounty he has many times received, it is now his desire to reciprocate by presenting as a gift this most exalted of his writings. In a formal and public gesture, Dante is in effect requesting official promotion of the work by his patron, whose friendship he values as a precious possession. He refers to his first visit to Can Grande's court, to which he was drawn by the fame of its splendour, as the Queen of Sheba had been drawn to visit the temple of Solomon, and found, as she did, that report fell short of the truth. In his opening words he salutes Can Grande not only as 'magnificent' and 'most victorious' but also as Imperial Vicar of Verona and Vicenza, thereby disregarding the decree issued by Pope John XXII, which he had recently shown in *Monarchia* to be invalid.[5] In this act of public defiance he risked calling down excommunication upon himself.

After the opening salutation, the text develops into the first instalment of a commentary on *Paradiso* and on the allegory of the *Commedia* as a whole. The commentary was never continued but what exists provides evidence that Dante hoped to proceed. In its formal style it has the appearance of a public lecture; in fact, looked at with a fresh mind, it can be seen to be not an epistle at all but an oration, written to be read at the court of Verona. There are even indications in the text that Dante delivered it himself.[6] This would not have been a unique event. On 20 January 1320 he visited Verona to deliver a lecture on the relative levels of water and earth on the globe, having previously attended a lecture at Mantua on the same subject, with which he disagreed.[7]

Reading the text as an oration one can imagine oneself a member of the audience in Verona, hearing the Florentine voice of Dante Alighieri, a lean figure in his 50s, five feet five inches tall, now slightly bowed, white-bearded and white-haired. Just as in *La Vita Nuova* and in *Il Convivio* he had analysed his poems in both their literal and allegorical meaning, so, once again, in his characteristic manner, he defines, divides and expounds his text. He begins by explaining the meaning of the whole work, which he terms 'polysemous', that is, having several meanings: the literal and, as he here terms them, the 'mystical'. He illustrates this distinction by expounding the psalm: 'When Israel went out of Egypt, the house of Jacob from a people of strange language; Judah was his sanctuary, and Israel his dominion.'[8] In the literal sense, these words refer to the escape of the Israelites from Egypt in the time of Moses; in the allegorical sense, they signify our redemption through Christ; in the moral sense, the conversion of the soul from the sorrow and misery of sin to a state of grace; in the anagogical[9] sense, the passing of the sanctified soul from the bondage of corruption of this world to the liberty of everlasting glory. All three non-literal meanings, he says, may be termed 'allegorical' in a general sense, in that they differ from the literal; at the same time (and confusingly), he also applies the word in a specific sense to the first of the interpretations, as distinct from the moral and the spiritual.

Dante had used the same psalm as an example in *Il Convivio*, but in the earlier work he did not appear to consider, as he does in the present, that a single text can be expounded in four senses. In *Purgatorio* he had used it again: it is the psalm sung by the hundred and more souls who approach the mountain, piloted by the angel. Of his *Commedia*, he now identifies only two meanings, literal and allegorical:

> The subject, then, of the whole work, taken in the literal sense only, is the state of souls after death. … On and about that argument the whole work turns. If, however, the work is regarded from the allegorical point of view, the subject is man according as by his merits or demerits in the exercise of his free will he is deserving of reward or punishment by justice.[10]

The aim of the whole work as well as of the third part is 'to remove those living in this life from a state of misery and to bring them to a state of happiness': from this it follows that the branch of philosophy to which it belongs is that of morals and ethics, but the speculation to which it gives rise has a practical rather than a theoretical purpose.

His exposition is orderly and systematic. He begins by explaining the title of the whole work. Relying on a dictionary of etymology in use at the time,[11] he derives the word *comoedia* from *comus*, a village, and *oda*, a song: 'whence comedy is, as it were, a rustic song'. The word *tragoedia* is derived, he says, from *tragos*, a goat, and *oda*, a song, and is therefore fetid, like a goat, 'as may be seen in the tragedies of Seneca'. A tragedy begins tranquilly but its end is foul and terrible; a comedy begins with adverse conditions but ends happily. In illustration of this, he quotes a proverbial greeting: 'I wish you a tragic beginning and a comic end.'[12]

He moves next to differences in style: the language of tragedy is high-flown and sublime, that of comedy unstudied and lowly. His *Comedy* is written not in Latin but in the vernacular, in which even humble women talk to one another: *locutio vulgaris, in quae et mulierculae comunicant*. In this deprecating reference to women, Dante uses the word *mulier*, a woman, as distinct from *domina*, a lady or mistress of a household. He uses it, moreover, in the diminutive, conveying the disparaging sense of uneducated women of low estate. For all his idealization of women in his love poems, there was an element in Dante of what is now called chauvinism.

Having defined the subject matter of *Paradiso*, he moves to the division of the text into prologue and narrative. The prologue he further divides into two parts: a forecast of what is to follow and an invocation to Apollo. He had learnt from Cicero that a good exordium should meet three requirements: the hearer should be rendered favourably disposed, attentive and willing to learn; this is especially so if the subject is unusual. To show how well he has followed the advice of Cicero, he refers to the first 12 lines of *Paradiso*, of which he quotes the first, in Latin:[13]

La gloria di colui che tutto move
    per l'universo penetra e risplende
    in una parte più e meno altrove.
Nel ciel che più della sua luce prende
    fu'io, e vidi cose che ridire
    nè sa nè può chi di là su discende;
perchè appressando sè al suo disire,
    nostro intelletto si profonda tanto,
    che dietro la memoria non può ire.
Veramente quant'io del regno santo
    nella mia mente potei far tesoro,
    sarà ora matera del mio canto.

The glory of Him who moves all things whate'er
    shines through the universe and light bestows
    in one part more, less bounteously elsewhere.
In that heaven where His radiance most glows
    was I, and saw things he who thence returns
    no knowledge has, nor power to disclose.
For, drawing near to that for which it yearns,
    our mind is plunged so deep, our memory
    cannot recall nor tell what it discerns.
Yet, all that which has granted been to me
    of the blessed realm to treasure in my thoughts
    the matter of my song from now will be.[14]

He moves next to the second part of the prologue, namely the invocation. Orators, he says, give a summary of what they are about to say, in order to gain the attention of their hearers. Poets do this also, but in addition they feel the need to petition superior beings for what is beyond the range of human powers. In *Inferno* he had invoked the Muses in general, in *Purgatorio* he had invoked them again, and in particular Calliope, the Muse of epic poetry; for the crowning section of his work he entreats the aid of Apollo.

Referring in the third person to the author-character of the poem and speaking as commentator, he expounds the metaphysical truth behind the statement that God's light shines in every part of the universe, but more in some parts than in others. In this demonstration we obtain further insight, as in *Monarchia*, into Dante's intellectual procedures. *Ratio sic*, he begins, 'the reasoning is as follows': everything that exists has its being either from itself or from some other being; the only self-existent being is God, the primal cause; all other beings have their origin in Him; the causal power derived in sequence from all other beings is like rays of light derived ultimately from God, as though reflected from mirrors; since beings exist in differing degrees of excellence, it is evident that the light of God is variously received.

The heaven that receives the most of God's light is the highest, itself everlastingly at rest but from which all movement is ultimately derived. This is called the Empyrean, which Dante describes as glowing with fire or heat, not material but spiritual, which is to say, with holy love. This is the abode of God. He names as his authorities for these concepts Aristotle and the so-called Dionysius, believed to be the author of *On Celestial Hierarchy*, as well as Scripture, from which he quotes Jeremiah, the Psalms, Ecclesiasticus and St Paul's Letter to the Ephesians. He is here repeating in condensed form what he had already set out in greater detail in *Il Convivio*.[15]

Dante the commentator confirms that Dante the character was in that part of Heaven where he saw things which he was later powerless to relate. The reason for this he explains as follows: when the mind reaches a certain degree of exaltation, memory fails, for it has transcended the range of human faculty. In support, he quotes St Paul's Letter to the Corinthians:

> I know a man (whether in the body or out of the body, I cannot tell; God knoweth) how that he was caught up to the third heaven, and heard unspeakable words, which it is not lawful for a man to utter.[16]

He quotes also from St Matthew's account of the Transfiguration, in which it is related that the three disciples fell on their faces and afterwards could record nothing as though their memory had failed them.[17] For further corroboration he refers also to Richard of St Victor in his work *On Contemplation*, to St Bernard in his work *On Consideration* and to St Augustine in his work *On the Capacity of the Soul*. Dante the commentator seems here to be on the defensive. Twice he refers resentfully to those who may doubt what he says. Once he calls them 'envious', *Et ubi ista invidis non sufficient* ... ('And if this should not satisfy the envious ...'); on a second occasion he refers to those who may rant and bluster because of the sinfulness of the speaker: *Si vero ... propter peccatum loquentis oblatrarent*. Such forceful expressions (the Latin verb *oblatrare* means literally 'to howl against') suggest that he may have been challenged by sceptics and that he is here taking the opportunity to vent his wrath against them by means of this public rebuff.

As to his own unworthiness (and here he identifies himself with the character Dante), he cites the example of Nebuchadnezzar, who was granted knowledge of divine truths by means of dreams, which he later could not recall – a somewhat puzzling example, since Nebuchadnezzar had periods of insanity, eating grass and believing himself to be an animal. Beside this may be set another strange example in the first canto of *Paradiso*, in which he compares himself to Glaucus,[18] who through eating a herb was transformed into a sea-god, as he, Dante, was 'transhumanized' on ascending into Heaven. Gazing at Beatrice, he was changed within, he says:

> ... qual si fè Glauco nel gustar dell'erba
> che 'l fè consorte in mar delli altri dei.
> Transumanar significar per verba
> non si porìa; però l'essemplo basti
> a cui esperienza grazia serba.

> ... *like Glaucus who a herb was said to taste*
> *and so an ocean-deity became.*
> *Transhumanizing could not be expressed*
> *in words, so let the example serve, the same*
> *who with the said experience was graced.*[19]

These two references, to Nebuchadnezzar and to Glaucus, who both consumed herbs, may be oblique allusions to stimulants which produced effects comparable to what Dante claims to have experienced. He was familiar with the Latin version of the work of Dioscorides, the first-century Greek physician, *il buon accoglitor del quale* ('the good collector of simples'), as he calls him when he sees him in Limbo.[20] Knowledge of herbs and medicinal potions was passed from country people and herb-gatherers to apothecaries, and herb gardens were a common feature of monasteries. From the early fourteenth-century manuscript *Tractatus de Herbis*[21] it is evident that the plant Canapa (*Cannabis sativa*) was known and available. So too was *Aloe vera*, from which a substance called aloes was obtained and used medically. Another plant was called 'grains of Paradise'. If Dante partook of some such psychedelic substance, perhaps in the company of the *Fedeli d'Amore*, when they gathered to perform and discuss their poems, this might partly account for his (and their) experiences of heightened awareness, as described in *La Vita Nuova*. Aldous Huxley, to take a twentieth-century example, experimented with altered states of consciousness by taking mescalin (obtained from the aloe). He seemed to see 'what Adam had seen on the morning of his creation, the miracle moment by moment of naked existence':

> [Plato] could never have seen [as I was seeing] a bunch of flowers shining with their own inner light and all but quivering under the pressure of the significance with which they were charged; could never have perceived that what rose and iris and carnation so intensely signified was nothing more,

and nothing less, than they were – a transience that was yet eternal life, a perpetual perishing that was at the same time pure Being, a bundle of minute, unique particulars in which, by some unspeakable and yet self-evident paradox, was to be seen the divine source of all existence. ... Words like Grace and Transfiguration come to my mind, and this of course was what, among other things, they stood for.[22]

Towards the end of his oration, referring again to the Invocation, Dante says that he will not at present expound its meaning further, nor will he say more about the narrative that follows, except that it will be by ascent from heaven to heaven and that an account will be given of the blessed spirits who are met with in each sphere and of whom things of great profit and delight will be asked. His reason for not continuing at present is given at the end of his oration:

Urget enim me rei familiaris angustia, ut haec et alia utilia rei publicae derelinquere oporteat.

Anxiety as to my domestic circumstances presses upon me so heavily that I am obliged to defer this and other tasks of public utility.

He expresses the hope, however, that his Magnificence may grant him the opportunity at some future date to continue this useful exposition.

This is an overt appeal for financial support and can be viewed as the mediaeval equivalent of an application to a university for a grant. It was said that it was Dante's custom to send batches of cantos to Can Grande as his work progressed. If this is true, it was not just a question of courtesy but an arrangement whereby he relied on Can Grande to publicize his work and to provide subsidy. This may have generated some addition to his income but it was evidently not enough to liberate him from other paid activities, such as lecturing and teaching at Ravenna, or commissions carried out for Guido Novello. We do not know what his domestic anxieties were at this time, but evidently they were such that he did not see his way to complete *Paradiso* and at the same time to continue his exposition of it.

Indeed, his time was more limited than he knew.

CHAPTER 44

Beatrice in Heaven

By the time Dante was at work on *Paradiso*, Beatrice Portinari had been dead for more than 25 years. He believed that her soul was in the Empyrean, the abode of God, where she enjoyed, with the other souls of the blessed, the experience of timelessness and the contemplation of the Beatific Vision. He also believed that she had knowledge of him in the finite world and continued to watch over the welfare of his soul. In his spiritual life he identified her with all that guided him towards repentance and the acceptance of salvation. In the role allotted to her in *Purgatorio* she brings him to a final stage of contrition and purification from sin. In the role of a Christian Sibyl she presides over the masque representing the vicissitudes of the Papacy and she prophesies, as Virgil had done in the first canto of *Inferno*, the coming of one who would re-instate peace and order in the world.[1]

In *Paradiso* her role grows more and more exalted. In her exposition of doctrine, she represents Dante's intellect, clarified and illuminated by his meditation, perhaps also by mystical experience, whether or not heightened by stimulants. Since it was in order to understand a vision of Beatrice that Dante says he undertook his intensive programme of study, in this sense it was she who had led him to the understanding of truths that are the subject of *Paradiso*. Appropriately, therefore, in the story, she now communicates those truths to the character Dante as he ascends from heaven to heaven.

The weight of Dante's body is a realistic feature of the narrative of *Inferno* and *Purgatorio*. At the beginning of *Paradiso*, still in the body, he finds himself rising above the earth. Beatrice, knowing that he is puzzled as to how this can be, explains the law of spiritual gravitation: all created things are governed by order, wherein resides the likeness of the universe to God; the natural law by which fire burns upwards, heavy bodies are drawn earthwards, and brute creatures are impelled by instinct, is the same by which creatures endowed with love and understanding (angels and men) are drawn upwards to their appointed site, the abode of God: since Dante has now been purged of sin and his will is rightly fixed, the fact that he is ascending towards Heaven should no more surprise him than the sight of a stream rushing down hill.[2]

This explanation which Dante gives to Beatrice to expound is a restate-ment in verse of words by St Augustine:

> In Thy gift shall we rest; there shall we enjoy Thee, our rest, our place. Love lifts us up thither, and Thy good Spirit exalts our humbleness from the gates of death. In good will is our peace.[3] The body by its own weight strives towards its own place. Weight is not downward only, but to its own place. ... My weight is my love; by that I am borne, wherever I am borne. By Thy gift we are inflamed, and are borne upward; we are kindled, and we go. We ascend by the ascents of the heart, and sing a song of degrees.[4]

The achievement of *Paradiso* is not simply a matter of the versification of doctrine: it is also a supreme feat of poetic imagination. Dante's entrance into the moon beguiles the reader into an entranced acceptance of ethereal experience:

> Quali per vetri trasparenti e tersi,
>   o ver per acque nitide e tranquille,
>   non sì profonde che i fondi sien persi,
> tornan di nostri visi le postille
>   debil sì, che perla in bianca fronte
>   non vien men tosto alle nostre pupille;
> tali vid'io più facce a parlar pronte.

> *As from a mirror, polished, terse and clear,*
>   *or water, limpid in tranquillity,*
>   *but not so deep that shallows disappear,*
> *an image of our face so faint we see,*
>   *just as a pearl on a white brow our sight*
>   *deceives, so in a throng appeared to me*
> *faces in converse eager to unite.*[5]

Confused, like Narcissus in reverse, Dante thinks they must be reflections of people behind him. Turning round, he discovers his mistake, whereupon Beatrice smiles.

The smile of Beatrice, the radiance of her eyes and her increasing beauty are part of the spiritual gravitation by which Dante is continually impelled upwards. The effect of her smile and of her miraculous beauty had been conveyed in several sonnets in *La Vita Nuova*[6] and to these the mind of Dante the poet returns in his further exaltation of her in *Paradiso*. In *Paradiso*, as she clarifies his doubts, 'bringing the fair face of truth to light,'[7] his joy is progressively intensified.

One of his first doubts concerns the location of souls in Heaven: do they feel discontent in relation to other souls who, it seems, dwell higher up? He puts this question to the soul which seems most eager to converse with him. This is Piccarda de' Donati, the sister of Forese and Corso Donati, about whom Forese has spoken on the Cornice of the Gluttons on Mount Purgatory.[8] As a young woman she entered the convent of St Clare, but Corso forced her to break her vows and marry Rossellino della Tosa in order to achieve a political alliance. Soon after her marriage she fell ill and died.

Dante has chosen her as an example of souls who were guilty of inconstancy to vows. Their status is indicated by their manifestation to him in the sphere of the moon, the planet nearest the earth and a symbol of inconstancy. Piccarda's gentleness and sweetness of disposition, touchingly conveyed in her words, make her a fitting image of the nature that yielded in the first life to the pressure of others and lacked the steadfastness to remain constant to the will's resolve. Now in Heaven, she, like all the souls, repentant and purified, rejoices in the will of God. All possibility of their wills being in conflict with His has been removed. This is the essential nature of love:

'Frate, la nostra volontà quieta
virtù di carità, che a volerne
sol quel ch'avemo, e d'altro non ci asseta.'

'Brother, our love has laid our will to rest,
making us long only for what is ours,
and by no other thirst to be possessed.'[9]

'Remember,' Piccarda seems to be saying to Dante, 'all that you have experienced and learned of love, and know now that in Paradise to love is to dwell within the love of God, with which our own wills are made one.' And she continues with an utterance that is famous and frequently quoted for its simplicity and completeness:

'E la sua volontade è nostra pace:
ell' è quel mare al qual tutto si move
ciò ch' ella cria e che natura face.'

... 'And His will is our peace:
this is the sea whereunto all things move
that it creates and nature furnished has.'[10]

At the conclusion of her exposition of the nature of Heaven, Piccarda, singing *Ave Maria*, vanishes like a heavy weight into deep water. Dante strains his sight to follow her as long as possible, then turns to look at Beatrice. She is so radiant that he cannot keep his gaze upon her and is obliged to wait before questioning her further.

He is held in hesitation between two perplexing concerns: do the souls, as Plato is believed to have taught, return to the planets which had most influence over them in their first life? And if Piccarda and the other souls manifested to him in the moon were forcibly prevented from fulfilling their vows, is it just that they, as it appears, should enjoy less beatitude? Beatrice reads these two doubts in his mind and answers them both, taking first the location of souls as being the more important.

All souls, she tells him are in the Empyrean, the abode of God, all share beatitude to the extent of which each is capable. Since Dante can apprehend only with his senses what his intellect then receives, the souls will be shown to him in the spheres to which he ascends:

'Qui si mostraron, non perchè sortita
    sia questa spera lor, ma per far segno
    della cestial c'ha men salita.
Così parlar conviensi al vostro ingegno,
    però che solo da sensato apprende
    ciò che fa poscia d'intelletto degno.
Per questo la Scrittura condescende
    a vostra facultate, e piedi e mano
    attribuisce a Dio, ed altro intende;
e Santa Chiesa con aspetto umano
    Gabriel e Michel vi rappresenta,
    e l'altro che Tobia rifece sano.'

'They're shown thee here, not that they here reside,
    allotted to this sphere; their mansion
    being less exalted, is thus signified.
This way of speech best suits your apprehension,
    which knows but to receive reports from sense
    and fit them for the intellect's attention.
So Scripture stoops to your intelligence:
    it talks about God's "hand" and "feet", intending
    that you should draw a different inference;
and so does Holy Church, in pictures lending
    a human face to Michael, Gabriel,
    and him by whom old Tobit found amending.'[11]

These lines reveal something very important concerning Dante: he did not believe that Hell, Purgatory and Paradise could be apprehended directly by humankind as they truly are. Thus it is that Scripture presents us with images of God and, for example, of the Archangels Gabriel, Michael and Raphael, which we can recognize. These signs, not to be taken literally, imprint perceptions on the imagination which in its operation leads to intellectual understanding and so to love. Using means similar to those of Scripture,

Dante renders the three worlds of the afterlife intelligible in terms of sense, imagination and intellect. For complete apprehension another category of vision will be required.

Beatrice next solves the second doubt, explaining the distinction between absolute and conditioned will. Her words are a celebration of the freedom of the soul, which bring joy to Dante's mind and inspire him with still further eagerness to learn and understand:

> 'O amanza del primo amante, o diva',
>   diss'io appresso, 'il cui parla m'inonda
>   e scalda sì, che più e più m'avviva,
> non è l'affezion mia sì profonda,
>   che basti a render voi grazia per grazia;
>   ma quei che vede e puote a ciò risponda.'

> *'O loved', said I, 'of the First Lover! O*
>   *most heavenly Lady, by whose words I live*
>   *more and yet more, bathed in their quickening glow,*
> *my love's whole store is too diminutive*
>   *too poor in thanks to give back grace for grace;*
>   *may He that sees and has the power, so give!'*[12]

Dante now sees that the intellect can never be satisfied until it reaches the all-inclusive truth of God, for in its pursuit new doubts spring up like shoots from a tree. And as he asks yet another question, the eyes of Beatrice, sparkling with love, grow so divine that he is almost lost and must cast down his gaze before continuing.

More than once his mental leap of enlightenment is expressed in terms that are erotic. His enamoured mind, he says, plays endless court to his lady:

> La mente innamorata, che donnea
>   con la mia donna sempre ...

> *My mind, in love, which to my lady paid*
>   *perpetual court ...*[13]

On another occasion their mutual joy is conveyed in overtly sexual imagery, as when Beatrice says:

> 'L'alto disio che mo t'infiamma e urge,
>   d'aver notizia di ciò che tu vei,
>   tanto mi piace più quanto più turge.'

> *'The deep desire, which in thee flames and leaps,*
>   *to understand still more what thou dost see,*
>   *the more delights me as it tumescent keeps.'*[14]

From this it appears that in his pursuit of truth and release from error Dante's creative intellect was seized from time to time by a spiritual equivalent of orgasm, something not unknown to mystics or to scholars in their discovery of truth. A further clue to his mental exhilaration can be seen in the rapturous words he had previously used to describe the desire for knowledge. In *Il Convivio* he discoursed at length on the way in which such longing increases: 'properly speaking, this is not growth but a transition from something small to something large ...', the final object of desire being God.[15] In *Purgatorio*, he referred to 'the natural thirst which nothing quenches' (that is, the desire for knowledge),[16] an image further developed in *Paradiso* at the moment of ascent:

> La concreata e perpetua sete
> del deiforme regno cen portava
> veloci quasi come 'l ciel vedete.

> *The inborn thirst which is perpetual*
> *for God's own kingdom carried us aloft*
> *as swiftly almost as the heavens roll.*[17]

There is, however, a problem connected with Beatrice, the conveyor of theological truths, in whose eyes Dante sees the light which is God, the paradisiacal being whose beauty impels him higher and higher through the heavenly realms towards the Beatific Vision. In no fewer than three instances in *Paradiso*[18] Dante the author presents her in yet another role, one which it is difficult to reconcile with her idealized, transhuman self. In a mode that is startlingly out of character, she becomes a harsh critic of human wrongdoing; in a criticism of the sermons of incompetent preachers she uses language suitable for the market-place, and her very last words are a vicious gibe at the ultimate fates of Popes Clement V and Boniface VIII. Such utterances have nothing to do with the Beatrice of *La Vita Nuova*, of *Purgatorio*, or of the rest of *Paradiso*, and nothing whatever to do with Beatrice Portinari, the gently nurtured young woman of Florence. Why did Dante give these invectives to her to pronounce, rather than to some other character, as he does, for instance, in his denunciation of the moral degeneracy of monasticism? These occasions, far from being part of a sustained ascent, are sudden lurches into the world below. How did Dante the maker come to admit them to the sublime fabric of his Beatrician vision? Was it a failure in artistic judgement? If so, how was it that Dante committed such a lapse, he who elsewhere so skilfully portrays the identity of his characters and so appropriately adjusts his dialogue to their personalities?

The words that Beatrice speaks at these moments are not hers or those of any of the mystics, but the words of Dante Alighieri, the Florentine, uttered in an explosion of wrath, which bursts through the frame of fiction, regardless of artistic integrity. They belong, in fact, to another category: the personal and public agenda of *Paradiso*.

This subject will be discussed in the following chapter.

CHAPTER 45

Propaganda in *Paradiso*

ante had a powerful political motive in writing the *Commedia*. This is especially obvious in *Inferno*, still apparent in *Purgatorio*, and startling when it breaks cover in *Paradiso*. Bearing in mind that *Paradiso* was dedicated to Can Grande and was sent to him in batches of a few cantos at a time, it is interesting to consider which, if he had time to read them, are likely to have caught his attention as being in support of his interests. An immediate answer which comes to mind is the canto of Justinian.[1]

Living in Ravenna and visiting the church of San Vitale, where the mosaic figures of Justinian and his retinue gleam from the walls, Dante could not have been other than responsive to all that he signified. Emperor in Constantinople from 527 to 565, Justinian made a valiant effort to bind together the east and west sections of the Empire. With the support of his generals, Belisarius and Narses, he overthrew the Vandals in Africa and the Ostrogoths in Italy. His aim was to rebuild the Empire of Augustus, on the foundation of ancient sovereignty but in accordance with the new faith. He is celebrated above all for appointing a commission of jurists to draw up a codification of Roman law, as a result of which, to quote Gibbon, 'the public reason of the Romans has been silently or studiously transfused into the domestic institutions of Europe, and the laws of Justinian still command the respect or obedience of independent nations'.[2] In the establishment of Justinian's government at Ravenna, Dante saw the divinely willed restoration of Imperial rule in western Europe and the promise of his own hopes: what had happened once could happen again.

Entering the Heaven of Mercury, Dante finds himself in the presence of a brilliant radiance, within which he is able to discern the eyes and smile of a soul.[3] In response to Dante's enquiry as to who he is, the soul reveals himself:

'Cesare fui e son Giustinano.'

'Caesar I was and am Justinian.'[4]

In a speech that occupies almost an entire canto he traces the history of

Fig 10. The Emperor Justinian and His Retinue

Rome from its beginnings to the time of Charlemagne. Mingled in contrast with the epic splendour of his heroic roll-call are disparaging references to the petty contemporary feuds between Guelfs and Ghibellines, of which, like all the souls in Heaven, he has present knowledge.

Dante's method in *Paradiso* of securing assent to his political convictions is to set them within the framework of the universe. What is true of the heavens is true of what he learns there; what is contrary to them is contrary to nature and to the will of God. Justinian begins by defining the departure of Constantine to the Eastern Empire as 'turning back the eagle' (the symbol of Roman authority) 'against the course of heaven':

'Poscia che Costantin l'aquila volse
    contr' al corso del ciel, ch' ella seguìo
    dietro all'antico che Lavinia tolse,
cento e cent'anni e più anni l'uccel di Dio
    ne lo stremo d'Europa si ritenne,
    vicino a' monti de' quai prima uscìo;
e sotto l'ombra delle sacre penne
    governò 'l mondo lì di mano in mano,
    e, sì cangiando, in sua la mia pervenne.'

'When Constantine turned back the eagle's flight
   against the heavens whose course it kept of yore,
   following Lavinia's bridegroom and the light,
a hundred and a hundred years and more
   the bird of God on Europe's last confine
   dwelt near the hills that taught it first to soar;
thence ruled the world, as line succeeded line
   under the sacred wings' o'ershadowing span,
   and passed from hand to hand to light on mine.'[5]

Since the heavenly spheres revolve diurnally from east to west, and
Constantine had transferred the seat of Empire from west to east, his action
was contrary to the rule of the cosmos. It was contrary also to the course
from east to west taken by Aeneas, the predestined founder of the Roman
Empire. Against such celestial *exempla*, ranged unassailably by Dante in
support of his thesis, there can be no opposition. It was God's will that the
heavens should revolve from east to west, it was His will that Aeneas should
move from east to west, it was against His will that Constantine should
remove the power of Empire from west to east; when 200 years had passed,
it was His will that Justinian should restore it to the west. It was His will also
that Justinian should re-establish the valid provisions of Roman law, adapt-
ing them to the conditions of the Christian Empire. Having previously held
the heretical view that only the divine nature, not also the human, existed
in Christ, Justinian was converted to the truth that he now sees as clearly as
it can be seen that of two contradictory propositions one must be true, one
false. There could be no more authoritative witness to the axiom that the
Roman Empire was ordained by right.

All the fervour and passion with which Dante had conjured the names
of Roman heroes and the succession of heroic events, first in *Il Convivio*,
later in his letter to Henry VII and in *Monarchia*, vibrate also in the words
of Justinian, this time with epic force. The diction is vigorous and resonant,
sweeping all doubt aside. The heraldic image of the eagle, the symbol of
Roman might and justice, soars over the historic sequence which culminates
in the establishment of world peace under Augustus. But of all the eagle's
achievements, the greatest of all was that which came to pass when it lighted
upon the hand of Tiberius, in whose reign Christ was crucified. This identifying of the right of the Roman Empire with the Redemption of mankind
was also used by Dante in *Monarchia*.[6] He here takes the argument forward
a final step, beyond which nothing more can be said:

'Ma ciò che 'l segno che parlar mi face
   fatto avea prima e poi era fatturo
   per lo regno mortal ch'a lui soggiace,

diventa in apparenza poco e scuro,
  se in mano al terzo Cesare si mira
  con occhio chiaro e con affetto puro;
chè la viva giustizia che mi spira,
  li concedette, in mano a quel ch'i' dico,
  gloria di far vendetta alla sua ira.
Or qui t'ammira in ciò ch'io ti replico:
  poscia con Tito a far vendetta corse
  della vendetta del peccato antico.'

'Yet what this banner that I speak about
  had done and was to do in every land
  that called it lord, the mortal world throughout,
seems but a dim and paltry thing, if scanned
  with a clear eye and with a heart entire,
  to what it did in the third Caesar's hand;
for in that hand, the life which I respire,
  the Living Justice, granted it to win
  the glory of wreaking vengeance for His ire.
Marvel how plea meets counter-plea herein:
  for afterward, in Titus' time it sprang
  to avenge the vengeance for the ancient sin.'[7]

In the last three lines Justinian refers to the destruction of Jerusalem by the Emperor Titus in the year 70. Dante accepts the view of the historian Orosius that by this act Titus avenged the death of Christ. Justinian, appropriately, speaks in legal terms: *or qui t'ammira in ciò ch'io ti replico* ('marvel how plea meets counter-plea herein'). In Roman law a defendant pleading special circumstances was said to put forward an *exceptio*. If the plaintiff countered this, his reply was termed a *replicatio*. What is in question here is the guilt attributed to the Jews for the Crucifixion of Christ. The *exceptio* that could be put forward was that the Crucifixion was the Atonement for the Fall. The counter-plea (*replicatio*) would be that this in no way justified the execution of an innocent man. Thus, Justinian maintains, the eagle in the hand of Titus, that is, *la viva giustizia* ('the living justice'), justly avenged 'the vengeance for original sin'.

This cryptic utterance is clarified in the following canto. Beatrice reads in Dante's mind that he is mystified as to how 'just vengeance' (atonement for the sins of mankind) can in its turn be justly avenged. To explain this she enters first on a discourse concerning the Redemption. Concerning the apparent paradox in the words of Justinian, she explains that if the nature assumed by God in the Incarnation is considered, no penalty was ever so just as the Cross; but if the Person who suffered it is considered, no penalty was ever so unjust:

'Non ti dee oramai parer più forte,
    quando si dice che giusta vendetta
    poscia vengiata fu da giusta corte.'

*'No longer now should it seem hard to thee
    that the just vengeance was by a just court
    avenged, as afterwards it came to be.'*[8]

Dante has inextricably united belief in the Redemption and belief in the divine ordainment of the Roman Empire. To unravel them, in his conviction, would be heresy. Both are manifestations of God's justice.

This is the most powerful and conclusive of all Dante's pronouncements on world affairs. Within the logic of his intellectual structure, disregarding inexorable changes in world history, it is unanswerable. There is no doubt that he believed it but the use he made of it is not contemplative. It is directed to a purpose: that of leading the world to achieve order and peace. It is, in other words, propaganda, of a noble kind, but still propaganda. The cartoon-like gibes at the Ghibellines and Guelfs which also find a place in Justinian's speech seem scarcely worthy of that splendid Imperial icon, making his proclamation from the wall of San Vitale rather than from the sphere of Mercury, surely the most impressive public-relations speech of all time.

CHAPTER 46

The City Walls

To live in a walled city is to be embraced. This is a physical sensation lost to most of us in modern times and to visit a city such as Carcassonne is to realize that exile was a deprivation of a deeply physical kind, like being excluded from the arms of a parent. Many who suffered exile in Dante's time came to terms with it eventually. One example was the father of the poet Petrarch, who was exiled from Florence at the same period as Dante. He made the best of his situation and took employment as a notary in Provence. His son Francesco recalled in adult life that he had set eyes on Dante. This was probably in Pisa, between 1311 and 1312. We can visualize the group, the boy of eight, looking up at the two exiles, his father and another man, who must have seemed much older, though this was not the case.[1] Dante had aged quickly as a result of his misfortune. In fact, he never recovered from it.

Dante suffered not only emotional deprivation; he was deeply scarred by the humiliation of poverty and loss of public esteem.[2] People in such a position often hug to themselves the comfort of dwelling upon an illustrious ancestry, real or imaginary. His dearest pride and consolation was the thought of his crusader ancestor, Cacciaguida.[3] The three cantos in which the soul of Cacciaguida is present occupy a central position in *Paradiso*.[4] Canto XVII, which is precisely central, contains some of the most intimate and personal lines in the entire work.

In the Heaven of Mars Dante has been gazing at a group of lights which form the pattern of a cross. From its white bars, pricked out with fiery splendours, each one a soul, dancing like particles caught in a beam of sunshine, there flashes into Dante's mind a vision of Christ. Dante himself had been a soldier, in combat in defence of Florence against the Ghibellines, but here are the warriors of God, saints who died in defence of the Faith. One of them, like a shooting star, detaches itself from the right arm of the cross, spinning to the foot, where it glows like flame behind an alabaster screen. With equal eagerness, Dante recalls, did the soul of Anchises move to greet his son Aeneas in Elysium.

This comparison is significant. As Aeneas was called to found what would become the Empire of Rome, so Dante believed himself called to re-establish Rome in the minds of his contemporaries as the centre of the Christian world. He is the new Aeneas, as he is the new St Paul: the disclaimer made with such diffidence to Virgil at the beginning of *Inferno*[5] is here finally and totally withdrawn. In astonishment he hears words in Latin issuing from the light that has come to greet him:

'O sanguis meus, o superinfusa
  gratia Dei, sicut tibi, cui
  bis unquam coeli janua reclusa!'

'O my own blood! O grace of God beyond
  all measure poured! To whom else, as to thee,
  were Heaven's gates twice opened ever found?'[6]

The answer to Cacciaguida's rhetorical question is, of course, St Paul.

Dante looks back at Beatrice and sees in her eyes such joy that he feels he has plumbed the depth of bliss. The soul continues to speak, in words which at first soar beyond mortal comprehension. At last his meaning becomes clear.

The encounter between Dante and his illustrious ancestor is one of the most poignant moments in the poem. Of all the souls he has met throughout his journey, this is the one from whom his life-blood flows, through whom he is intimately linked with the history of Florence. Cacciaguida addresses him as his 'blood', his 'seed', his 'son', 'his branch'. Never can derivation have been more insistently emphasized:

'O fronda mia in che io compiacemmi
  pur aspettando, io fui la tua radice.'

'O branch of mine, whose coming in delight
  I long awaited have, I was thy root.'[7]

Unexpectedly, he asks Dante to pray for his great-grandfather, Cacciaguida's own son, who for a hundred years and more has circled the Cornice of Pride on the Mountain of Purgatory, unexpectedly because there has been no mention of him before. This request gathers Dante up into the network of his kin, connecting him closely with the memories of his ancestors.

Cacciaguida begins by telling him of Florence as she once was, enclosed within her ancient circle of walls, *in pace, sobria e pudica* ('at peace, sober and chaste'), like a stately matron, unadorned with bracelet, tiara, embroidered gown, or costly girdle.[8] Dowries did not then impoverish fathers, no homes were large beyond the needs of a family, no bedrooms were scenes of wantonness. Men dressed in plain buff coats, girt with leather, fastened with bone buckles. Women wore no makeup as they sat contented at their spindle, tending the cradle, soothing their children, telling them in words fond parents love to use the tales of Troy, Fiesole and Rome, not deserted in their beds by husbands travelling for trade to France, and knowing where at death they would be laid to rest.

In this idyllic picture Dante expresses his longings for a peaceful community life, as he imagines it may once have been, now long gone. Into such a city his ancestor was born:

'A così riposato, a così bello
    viver di cittadini, a così fida
    cittadinanza, a così dolce ostello,
Maria mi diè, chiamata in alte grida;
    e nell'antico vostro Battisteo
    insieme fui cristiano e Cacciaguida.'

'Into this life, so peaceful and so fair,
    where every man was a true citizen,
    into a dwelling-place so sweet and dear,
Mary, called by my mother in her pain,
    delivered me; in your ancient Baptistery
    Cacciaguida I became and Christian.'[9]

The Baptistery in Florence, Dante's *bel San Giovanni*, as he called it, was the hallowed place where his ancestors were christened, where he too was received into the Faith and where he longed one day to receive the poet's laurel crown.[10]

Addressing his illustrious forebear as 'father' and using the honorific pronoun *voi* in respect for his rank (a vanity at which Beatrice smiles), he asks him to tell him yet more about the early years of Florence. Cacciaguida does so, speaking sweetly and gently, and in a vernacular now out of date.[11] He recalls the names of virtuous Florentines long gone, and of Florentines more recent and depraved. They mean little to us but the list must have been followed with eager interest when this canto was first read. He attributes the degeneracy of the city to its growth beyond the early walls and to the pollution of the original inhabitants by the influx of outsiders from neighbouring regions:

'La confusion delle persone
    principio fu del mal della cittade,
    come del corpo il cibo che s'appone.'

'Strains intermingled the beginning were
    and cause of evil in the city's life,
    as excess food in bodies will incur.'[12]

From these words it is evident that Dante believed in protecting the purity of the blood-line, a view which seven centuries later would be termed politically incorrect, if not racist. All the misfortunes that have befallen Florence are attributed to the greed and corruption of incomers of base stock.

At last Dante the character summons the courage to question his ancestor about his future. What is the meaning of the many grave warnings he has heard on his journey, while in the company of Virgil? With no oracular evasion, in plain, precise words, spoken with fatherly love, Cacciaguida reveals the truth: as Hippolytus was driven from Athens by his cruel and lying step-mother, so will Dante be driven from Florence. This is already planned and contrived and will soon be accomplished by one who meditates upon it where Christ is daily bought and sold, a clear reference to Boniface VIII:

> 'Tu lascerai ogni cosa diletta
>   più caramente; e questo è quello strale
>   che l'arco dello essilio pria saetta.
> Tu proverai sì come sa di sale
>   lo pane altrui, e come è duro calle
>   lo scendere e 'l salir per l'altrui scale.'

> *'Thou shalt abandon each and every thing*
> *   most dear to thee; that shaft's the first that e'er*
> *   the bow of exile looses from the string.*
> *Thou shalt by sharp experience be aware*
> *   how salt the bread of strangers is, how hard*
> *   the up and down of someone else's stair.'*[13]

Dante had been in exile for over 15 years when he wrote those words. He expresses not only his own pain but the sorrow of refugees throughout history and the world over. Peculiar to him is the hatred which Cacciaguida tells him he will nourish towards his fellow exiles, who will turn against him and defame him. Dante has never forgiven *la compagnia malvagia e scempia ... tutta ingrata, matta ed empia* ('the evil and senseless company ... all ungrateful, mad and impious'). Soon they, not Dante, will be put to shame and of their bestial folly their doings will give proof: bitter words after so long an interval. His loving forefather congratulates him upon the decision he will make to form a party by himself. He goes on to predict, as has been shown,[14] the hospitality and protection his beloved descendant will receive at the court of Verona and the fore-glimpse he will have there of the noble youth who will grow up to become Can Grande della Scala. It is strange that Dante makes no mention, neither here nor anywhere in the *Commedia*, of Guido Novello da Polenta, lord of Ravenna, the one patron who provided him with a home of his own, making it possible for his sons and a daughter to join him and possibly also his wife, where the bread was surely more palatable and the stairs at last familiar beneath his feet. It may be that Dante resented the calls Guido made upon his time, the last of which was destined to be fatal.

Dante the character is presented as receiving this forecast of his exile with fortitude, but now he asks advice. If he must leave the place most dear to him, what must he do not to be driven out also from other places by what he writes? If he relates what he has seen and heard in Hell, Purgatory and Paradise, his words will taste to many like bitter herbs; and yet if he is not faithful to the truth, he will lose the respect of future readers.

Cacciaguida's advice is forthright; in fact it is a command. Those who are guilty will indeed find his words offensive, but he has been commanded to disregard all probable reaction:

'ma nondimen, rimossa ogni menzogna,
    tutta tua vision fa manifesta;
    e lascia pur grattar dov' è la rogna.'

'nevertheless, give lies the quick despatch;
    make thy whole vision freely manifested
    and where men feel the itch there let them scratch.'[15]

This last line has given offence to fastidious readers. How could Dante include such a coarse expression among his illustrious ancestor's words, evoking as they do a time when people carried fleas and lice? There is a similar problem, as has been said, with words he gives to Beatrice. It appears that occasionally Dante loses sight of the characters he creates, putting into their mouths words of his own which jar, the more so that they are so memorable in their force and passion. It could, on the other hand, be argued that in this instance it is perhaps characteristic of a bluff army veteran to speak so crudely.

Dante knew that the *Commedia* would arouse hostility towards him (how could it be otherwise?) and that he might even be in some danger. Nevertheless, he is determined to speak out. As he makes his ancestor foretell:

'Questo tuo grido farà come vento,
    che le più alte cime più percuote;
    e ciò non fa d'onor poco argomento.
Però ti son mostrate in queste rote,
    nel monte e nella valle dolorosa
    pur l'anime che son di fama note.'

'Thy cry will beat as beats the wind, most rough
    against the loftiest tops; this will redound
    much to thine honour, and is cause enough

> *why, in these wheels, and on the mount, and round*
> *about the dolorous vale, thou hast been shown*
> *only those souls whose fame has made some sound.'*[16]

From the fulfilment of this (self-appointed) commission Dante did not shrink. On the contrary, he fulfilled it with relish.

CHAPTER 47

Justice Unfathomed

Dante suffered grave injustice at the hands of his political enemies and it rankled with him bitterly. He never forgave them but as time went on he arrived at a concept of ideal justice which brought him some measure of philosophic and religious peace.

A magnificent heraldic presentation of this ideal occurs in the Heaven of Jupiter, where a series of lights form one letter after another which spell out a command in Latin:

DILIGITE JUSTITIAM QUI IUDICATIS TERRAM

Love Justice Ye Who Judge the Earth

This brilliant spectacle in the sky may have been suggested to Dante's imagination by fireworks, since classical times in use in warfare and continued in Dante's time in celebrations of victory and on other festive occasions.

When the final M appears, the initial of Monarchy, which for Dante is synonymous with Empire, the gothic shape of the letter undergoes a series of transformations. The lower section, in the shape of the fleur-de-lis of France, which the Guelf party also displayed on their arms, merges stage by stage with the upper until the whole finally takes the shape of an eagle, the emblem of Roman authority, already glorified in the words of Justinian.[1] The changes clearly figure the submission of the kingdom of France and the Guelf powers to become an integral part of a supreme Monarchy.[2] In its final, composite form it represents a concord of just rulers, who maintain the liberty of the people they judge while accepting one authority, a sovereign prince embodying the general principles of justice. This notion, expressed by Dante in his treatise *Monarchia*, was perceived by him as manifested in the legal systems of Italian republics and communes. All such systems, however imperfect, were derived from Roman law, which is to say *scritta ragione* ('written reason'), as he defined it in *Il Convivio*, God's gift to mankind of justice on earth. He displays the notion here in dazzling heraldry.

As he gazes on the blaze of gold against the silvery background of the planet, to his astonishment the bird's beak gives voice. This is something never before described or even imagined:

Fig 11. Transformations of the Letter 'M'

Fig 12. Transformations of the Letter 'M'

E quel che mi convien ritrar testeso,
  non portò voce mai, nè scrisse inchiostro,
  nè fu per fantasia già mai compreso;
ch'io vidi e anche udi' parlar lo rostro,
  e sonar nella voce e 'io' e 'mio',
  quand'era nel concetto 'noi' e 'nostro'.

And what my duty now is to relate
  was never penned in ink, nor voice could speak,
  nor ever fancy frame or contemplate;
for I beheld and heard the eagle's beak
  both 'I' and 'mine' proclaim, although in truth
  in 'we' and 'ours' its meaning was to seek.[3]

This is one of Dante's most exalted concepts. The constellated souls, each like a ruby reflecting the sun's rays, all speak as one. Signifying singly the gradual attempts throughout history to establish justice in the world, they form together its divine and perfect image. Dante experiences amazement at this moral miracle.

He eagerly asks the emblem to satisfy *il gran digiuno/che lungamente m'ha tenuto in fame* ('the great fast that has long kept me hungry'), that is, the desire to comprehend justice.[4] The word *lungamente* ('for a long time') is significant. The story is set in Easter Week, 1300. Five years previously, having attained full citizenship at the age of 30, Dante had entered public life. From then on, he had concerned himself with the question of just government in Florence, the 'Ordinances of Justice', introduced by Giano della Bella in 1293, having recently made the matter one of urgent concern.[5] But the great fast that had long kept him hungry takes the reader beyond the year 1300, to embrace the period of his exile and the composition of the *Commedia*.

During the time Dante spent in Bologna in the company of Cino da Pistoia and other legal scholars,[6] Dante would have become familiar with the meanings of *iustitia* in Roman law: 'a constant and permanent will to render to each his own',[7] 'the precepts of the law are these: to live honestly, not to harm others and to render each his own',[8] and 'Law/Right is the art of the good and equal'.[9] It was for him chiefly a cardinal virtue and *vir iustus* ('a just man') corresponded to the *pius Aeneas* of the *Aeneid*.[10]

In two early allegorical *canzoni* Dante had lamented the exile of justice and the inequitable distribution of wealth.[11] In *Inferno*, the word *giustizia* is used almost always in the wider sense of the just consequences of sin. No matter how terrible the punishments, they are *justified*. The word is sometimes broadened to signify the righteous visitation of divine power upon sinners and strengthened by the adjectives 'divine' and 'infallible'. This is the meaning of the first use of the word, found in the inscription on the gateway to Hell:

Giustizia mosse il mio alto fattore.

Justice my supernal Maker moved.[12]

In *Purgatorio*, as in *Inferno*, the meaning is usually that of penance, sometimes extended to convey the rightness of the penance, or what is just and right in general. On one occasion it is used in the sense of the Last Judgement. In *Paradiso*, the word is used once in the sense of rightful possessions, once in the sense of desire for what is just and once in the sense of the Last Judgement. In all other nine instances, it signifies God's justice, described as 'divine', 'sempiternal' and 'living'.

This extended range of meaning indicates a deepening over the years of Dante's concept of justice. He came to see that in its divine sense it was unfathomable. This is what the Eagle now tells him: God's wisdom, being the archetypal idea of all things possible, remains in infinite excess of all things created. Thus it is that the mind of humans can penetrate divine justice only as little as the eye can penetrate the depths of the sea. Even the vision of the souls in Heaven comes short.

Dante's eagerness to comprehend is prompted also by a long-held doubt concerning justice in Heaven. The Eagle reads this in his mind and defines it. The problem is the case of a man born on the bank of the Indus, who has never heard of Christ, and who, despite a virtuous life, dies unbaptized and excluded from beatitude: what can be the justice of this? In reply the Eagle curtly rebukes Dante for his presumption:

'Or tu chi se' che vuo' sedere a scranna,
    per giudicar di lungi mille miglia,
    con la veduta corta d'una spanna?'

'Now who art thou who from thy bench wouldst scan,
    thinking to judge a thousand miles away,
    with sight that is restricted to a span?'[13]

The minds of earthly creatures are gross, unable to understand that Divine Goodness is the only source and only measure of justice and that it can itself be judged only by itself: only God's will is just and what is just is God's will.

The problem of the virtuous unbaptized had troubled many theologians, including St Thomas Aquinas, and was a matter of recurrent debate. Dante reflects this concern. He related that great grief filled his heart when he entered the castle in Limbo, for he knew that noble souls from antiquity were present there.[14] The theme of Virgil's eventual return to Limbo runs poignantly through the story, reaching its climax in his sudden departure at the summit of Mount Purgatory and Dante's overwhelming grief.[15]

There is unfinished business here. It is significant that in the preceding canto Dante again brought Virgil's name to the fore when he asked advice as to how much he should relate of all he had seen when in his company.[16] Answering Dante's unspoken question, the Eagle says that no soul ever entered Heaven who did not believe in Christ, either before or after His Crucifixion. Yet many who assert belief will be further from Him at the Last Judgement than some who never knew Him. There follows a list of unjust rulers who will find their infamies inscribed in the Book of Judgement and themselves excluded from Heaven.

In naming them, Dante is following the command of Cacciaguida to strike out at the highest.[17] The Eagle's long roll-call, from the Emperor Albert of Austria, Philip IV of France, the quarrelling kings of England and Scotland, the King of Spain, the King of Bohemia, the King of Naples, the King of Sicily, the King of the Balearic Islands, the King of Aragon, the King of Portugal, the King of Norway, the King of Dalmatia, down to an insignificant French ruler of Cyprus, all condemned by their evil deeds, is a scorching indictment. As in the canto describing the Cornice of Pride the acrostic VOM (that is, UOM, meaning 'man') joins together 13 stanzas,[18] so here the acrostic LUE (meaning 'plague') links another nine, giving once again sculptural prominence to the lines as though they were embossed on a monument.

In contrast to the iniquitous rulers (the 'pestilence' of Europe), the Eagle next draws Dante's attention to six lights which shine, one in the pupil of its eye, and the other five in the shape of an arch above it.[19] All except one are rulers who delighted in justice. In the pupil is David, the first true king of the chosen people. First in the arch, nearest to the Eagle's beak, is the Emperor Trajan, believed to have been restored to life and converted by the prayers of Pope Gregory the Great. Next to him is Hezekiah, King of Judah, who was granted an extended lease of life in response to prayer and penitence.[20] Beside him is the Emperor Constantine, who, despite his (believed) Donation of the western part of his Empire to the Papacy, dwells in beatitude undiminished by the evil consequences of his well-intentioned act. Next is William II, the last of the Norman kings of Sicily, known as 'William the Good'.

The climax of the six is Rhipeus the Trojan. Here is the complete answer to Dante's doubt. An obscure Trojan warrior, slain during the sack of Troy, described by Virgil in the *Aeneid* as 'the most just (*iustissimus*) of all the Trojans and the strictest observer of right',[21] is in Heaven. How can this be?

The legend concerning Trajan was widely believed but the instance of Rhipeus is Dante's own invention. The words of St Peter, 'In every nation he that feareth Him, and worketh righteousness [*iustitiam* in the Vulgate]

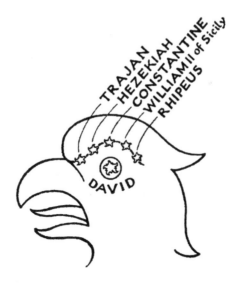

Fig 13. The Eye of the Eagle

is acceptable to God',[22] were deemed to give Scriptural authority for such a possibility. Dante also has in mind the teaching of St Thomas Aquinas concerning the salvation of virtuous pagans: God will reveal what is necessary either by instruction or by interior inspiration.

Though not understanding, yet believing, Dante cannot prevent his joy at the presence in Heaven of both Trajan and Rhipeus from bursting from his lips: *Che cose son queste?* ('What are these things I hear?')[23] At this all the souls forming the Eagle flash in bright revelry and in collective voice explain that both souls left their bodies not as Gentiles but as Christians, both believers, one in the Crucifixion to come, the other in the Crucifixion that had come to pass:

'De' corpi suoi non uscir, come credi,
   gentili, ma cristiani, in ferma fede
   quel de' passuri e quel de' passi piedi.'

       ... *'these put the body off,*
not gentiles, as thou deemest, but complete
in Christian faith, clinging as each had scope
to the passion-pierced, to the yet-to-be-possible Feet.'[24]

God, the Eagle continues, opened the eyes of Rhipeus to our coming Redemption, rescuing him from the stench of paganism, so that he rebuked those who perversely clung to it (an inventive extension of Virgil's words on Dante's part). Already possessed of the cardinal virtues, he received by grace the virtues of Faith, Hope and Love, the three theological virtues that Dante had seen as figures dancing at the right wheel of the chariot in the Garden of Eden.[25] Why this had come about is one of the mysteries of predestination, which like divine justice is far removed from mortal gaze and even from the vision of the souls in bliss:

> 'E voi, mortali, tenetevi stretti
>   a giudicar; chè noi, che Dio vedemo,
>   non conosciamo ancor tutti li eletti.'

> *And mortals, keep your judgment straitly checked,*
>   *for here we see God face to face, and still*
>   *we know not all the roll of His elect.'*[26]

As the Eagle speaks, the two lights which are the souls of Trajan and Rhipeus, like two eyes in the same head blinking together, accompany the words with flicks of flame, another display of divine pyrotechnics.

The question of Virgil is left open. At the Last Judgement he may be included in the roll of God's elect. It is not for Dante, or for us, to know. The blessed souls themselves do not know and such ignorance is sweet to them, for what God wills they also will, an echo of the words of Piccarda,

> 'e la sua voluntade è nostra pace.'

> *'and His will is our peace'.*[27]

It is also an anticipation of Dante's own integration with divine love with which the *Commedia* will end.

CHAPTER 48

Dante and Monasticism

In *Il Convivio* Dante, writing of old age, said those men were wise who then withdrew from active to religious life: 'Even those who are married may so do, since God requires only the profession of the heart.' This is perhaps an indication that Dante was considering the possibility of doing so himself in his final years. There is a tradition that in his youth he became a novice of the Franciscan Order and later withdrew. However that may be, the question of monasticism is frequently raised in *Paradiso*. The first soul who converses with Dante is Piccarda, a nun who broke her vows, and the first moral question on which Beatrice instructs him concerns atonement for broken vows.

According to Catholic faith, as Dante believed it, all the souls in Heaven are already in the enjoyment of timelessness. Until the Last Judgement, however, they will also be aware of the joys and sorrows, the sins and virtues of mortals, both of the past and of the future. In the Heaven of Saturn, into which Dante and Beatrice ascend from Jupiter, Dante sees a golden ladder stretching far beyond his sight. Thronging upon it are the souls of Contemplatives. Jacob's ladder was quoted by preachers as a figure of monastic life and the souls 'ascending and descending on it' were interpreted as signifying the monks who climbed by contemplation up to God and those who descended by compassion among men. Owing to their continuing knowledge of life on earth, they are not withdrawn but deeply incensed by the corruption of the religious orders of which they were members.

This theme was first introduced in the Heaven of the Sun,[1] where a circle of 12 lights, followed by a second and a third circle, encloses him and Beatrice, revolving round them three times, singing so sweetly that the beauty is beyond description. These are the souls of theologians, preachers, scholars and writers, many of whom disagreed with one another on earth, perceiving only part of the truth, but who now see it whole and rejoice in knowing it in harmony together. St Thomas Aquinas, the greatest of Dante's teachers of Christian doctrine, identifies himself and goes on to relate the tale of St Francis of Assisi and his heroic espousal of poverty. This leads him to utter a stern rebuke of both the Franciscan and the Dominican Orders for their decline from the ideals of their founders. There follows a similar rebuke from St Bonaventure who deplores the corruption and dissension among Franciscans.

In the world of monastic discipline which Dante now enters there is first of all silence. He hesitates to break it. One soul draws near and in answer to a question Dante asks as to why he, from among so many, has been chosen to approach him, speaks of the unfathomable depths of predestination and warns Dante, bidding him also to warn others, against seeking to probe exalted mysteries. He reveals himself as Peter Damian. Born in Ravenna at the beginning of the eleventh century, he entered the Benedictine monastery of Fonte Avellana on the slopes of Mount Catria in Umbria, of which in 1041 he became Abbot and was later created Cardinal and Bishop of Ostia. He became a celebrated preacher and a zealous reformer of Church discipline. He is said to have addressed a letter to certain cardinals reproaching them for their indulgence in costly clothing, fine horses and armed escorts. There is a tradition that Dante stayed for a time at the monastery on Mount Catria. If so, he may have heard of the letter, and the words he gives to Peter Damian are perhaps an echo of it. However this may be, he would have found the memory of Peter cherished in Ravenna, where Dante wrote this canto, and if he gave a public reading of it there it would have been received with particular interest.

Recalling the poverty of the first followers of Christ, Peter Damian contrasts it with the greed of modern prelates:

'Venne Cefas e venne il gran vasello
    dello Spirito Santo, magri e scalzi,
    prendendo il cibo da qualunque ostello.
Or voglio quinci e quindi chi li rincalzi
    li moderni pastori e chi li meni,
    tanto son gravi, e chi di retro li alzi.
Cuopron de' manti loro i palafreni,
    sì che due bestie van sott'una pelle:
    o pazienza che tanto sostieni!'

'Barefoot and lean came Cephas, came the great
    Vessel of the Holy Ghost; and they would sup
    at whatsoever house they halted at.
Pastors today require to be propped up
    on either side, one man their horse to lead
    (so great their weight!) and one their train to loop.
Over their mounts their mantles fall, full-spread;
    two beasts beneath a single hide they go.
    O patience, is thy meekness not yet fled?'[2]

At the conclusion of these words, there is a blaze of light as more and more souls cluster and circle round. They give vent to such a roar of anger that Dante almost swoons and has to turn to Beatrice as a little boy runs for comfort to his mother, something he perhaps remembered from his own childhood, or seeing his children do. She tenderly restores his confidence and foretells that before his death he will see the sword of punishment fall.

When Dante wrote these words Boniface VIII had suffered the outrage at the hands of Philip IV of France that had led to his death and the Curia had undergone the humiliation of the transference to Avignon. No doubt he had these events in his mind but he leaves the prophecy undefined. What is remarkable is the shout of wrath that goes up among the Contemplatives at the words of Peter Damian, showing that righteous zeal, as well as silence, is a mark of true spiritual contemplation.

Dante next brings forward St Benedict, 'the largest and most lustrous of these pearls', the founder of monasticism in the Western Church. Together too approach his brother monks, Romualdus, also of Ravenna, who founded the Order of Reformed Benedictines in Camaldoli in the eleventh century, and Maccarius, said to be a founder of monasticism in the East. Identifying himself, St Benedict tells of his founding of his monastery in Cassino and in words which echo those of Peter Damian he passes to still more severe denunciation of the corruption into which his Order has passed:

> ... 'mo nessun diparte
> da terra i piedi, e la regola mia
> rimasa è per danno delle carte.
> Le mura che solìeno esser badia
> fatte son spelonche, e le cocolle
> sacca son piena di farina ria.
> Ma grave usura tanto non si tolle
> contra 'l piacer di Dio, quanto quel frutto
> che fa il cor de' monaci sì folle;
> chè quantunque la Chiesa guarda, tutto
> è della gente che Dio dimanda;
> non di parenti nè d'altro più brutto.
> La carne de' mortali è tanto blanda,
> che giù non basta buon cominciamento
> dal nascer della quercia al far la ghianda.
> Pier cominciò sanz' oro e sanz'argento,
> e io con orazione e con digiuno,
> e Francesco umilmente il suo convento.
> E se guardi là il principio di ciascuno,
> poscia riguardi là dov'è trascorso,
> tu vederai del bianco fatto bruno.'

... 'to crown
iniquity, there in my house men sit,
    smirching with wasted ink my Rule's renown.
Dens are the buildings once for abbots fit;
    rancid the meal, and the cowls in which they dress
    are like so many sacks stuffed full with it.
Gross usury bears lighter the impress
    of God's displeasure than the well-filled purse
    which monkish hearts now covet to excess.
Whatever wealth the Church is called to nurse
    belongs to those who ask it in God's name,
    not to the families of monks, or worse.
The yielding flesh of man is much to blame:
    more than a good beginning was required
    ere ever acorn from an oak-tree came.
Peter, to found his house, no wealth desired,
    nor I, by fasting and by prayer made rich,
    nor Francis, by humility inspired.
If thou wouldst contemplate the point from which
    each one set out, and where their followers are,
    thou wilt perceive how white has changed to pitch.'[3]

St Benedict, like Beatrice, foresees that God will punish the wrongdoers: the turning back of Jordan and the drying up of the Red Sea were even greater miracles than retribution for such avarice would be.

Dante, addressing St Benedict as 'Father', had asked if he might behold him in his true form. This is the only occasion on which he makes such a request in *Paradiso*. In reply, St Benedict, addressing him as 'Brother', tells him that his yearning will be granted in the last sphere, as will be the case of all the blessed:

'Ivi è perfetta, matura ed intera
    ciascuna disianza; in quella sola
    è ogni parte là ove sempr' era,
perchè non è in loco e non s'impola;
    e nostra scala infino ad essa varca,
    onde così dal viso ti s'invola.'

'There and there only every longing has
    final attainment, perfect, ripe and whole,
    and there each part is where it always was,
for it is not in space and has no pole;
    wherefore our ladder, at its full extent,
    steals from thy view, since yonder is its goal.'[4]

Thus St Benedict gives Dante the character a foretaste of the final blessedness in the Empyrean, where there is no finite space and all time is present.
By calling him 'Brother', he admits him into their company in anticipation
of the stage when, in the story, Dante himself becomes a Contemplative.
With regard to Dante the man, it may be a hint that in an ideal world
his hope would be one day to be admitted to the contemplative life of the
Benedictine Order. This was possibly in his mind for the years to which he
looked forward, years which he was not to know in this life.

CHAPTER 49

The Theme's Great Weight

The concluding cantos of *Paradiso* represent Dante's literary skills brought to their highest pitch: variety of narrative, compelling dialogue, surprise, ethereal pictorial similes, rich and colourful imagery, visions of the universe, together with startling contrasts in style, changing suddenly from the sublime to invective. His mind and soul are represented as growing more exalted the higher he ascends, but Dante the writer is still a craftsman who is alert to the attention span of his new, select audience, who, though more responsive, still require variety of narrative and characterization.

Rising swiftly to the Heaven of the Fixed Stars, Dante enters his own natal constellation of Gemini:

> O gloriose stelle, o lume pregno
>   di gran virtù, dal quale io riconosco
>   tutto, qual che sia, il mio ingegno,
> con voi nasceva e s'ascondeva vosco
>   quelli ch' è padre d'ogni mortal vita,
>   quand' io sent' di prima l'aere tosco;
> e poi, quando mi fu grazia largita
>   d'entrar nell'alta rota che vi gira,
>   la vostra region mi fu sortita.
> A voi divotamente ora sospira
>   l'anima mia, per acquistar virtute
>   al passo forte che a sè la tira.

> *O stars of glory, from whose light on high*
>   *a mighty virtue is poured forth, to you*
>   *I owe such talents as within me lie;*
> *with you there rose and with you sank from view*
>   *he who is father of all life below*
>   *when my first breath of Tuscan air I drew,*
> *and when by grace I rose at last into*
>   *the lofty sphere in which you circle, then*
>   *your region it was granted me to know.*

To you my soul devoutly sighs, to gain
the power and courage for the hardest step,
which pulls her onwards to itself amain.[1]

Dante the poet now summons all his innate gifts, derived not only from his stars but also from the region, Tuscany, where he first drew breath. In so doing, he reminds his readers that he is no abstract symbol but an individual self, formed by destiny and environment. He also prepares them for the *passo forte*, the most difficult part of his task. To complete it, he needs not only poetic skill but light to comprehend both spiritual and material truths.

Accordingly, Beatrice first commands him to cast his eyes down towards the earth. Obediently he retraces with his gaze (for this endowed with supernatural power) the course he has taken through the seven planetary spheres, until it rests at last upon our puny globe, *l'aiuola che ci fa tanto feroci* ('the threshing-floor which renders us so fierce'), *tal ch'io sorisi del suo vil sembiante* ('such that I smiled it seemed so base a thing').[2]

Like a mother-bird alert on an open spray, awaiting the dawn that it may feed its young, Beatrice, erect and in suspense, gazes towards the east as the sky grows more and more resplendent. Suddenly, her face aflame with love and her eyes filled with joy, she exclaims:

> … 'Ecco le schiere
> del triunfo di Cristo e tutto il frutto
> ricolto del girar di queste spere!'
>
> … *'Behold Christ's hosts in triumph! Lo,*
> *the fruit all garnered here which ripened has*
> *beneath these circling spheres on earth below!'*[3]

In the Earthly Paradise Dante had seen the Pageant of the Church Militant, imaged in symbols in the very scene of man's Fall.[4] So now, in the Heaven of the Fixed Stars, the highest region visible from earth, he beholds the Church Triumphant, manifested to him as a myriad of lights which he defines in a rich and lovely image as the fruits of the circling spheres. They are all kindled by one sun, as on a clear night the moon smiles on the eternal nymphs who deck the sky. This is the Redeemer, in whose brilliance Dante glimpses a shining substance, so bright that his eyes cannot endure it.

This is Dante's third vision of Christ. The first was in the Garden of Eden, as the Gryphon; the second was in the Heaven of Mars, where he beheld the warriors of Christ, including his own ancestor, Cacciaguida.[5] Beatrice tells him that what dazzles him is *la sapienza e la possanza* ('the wisdom and the might'), which opened between Heaven and earth the paths that were so long desired. At these words, Dante describes what may have been an actual experience in one of those moments of higher consciousness at which he has hinted earlier, and to which a number of references have been made in the course of the present work:

> Come foco di nube si diserra
>   per dilatarsi sì che non vi cape,
>   e fuor di sua natura in giù s'atterra
> la mente mia così tra quelle dape
>   fatta più grande, di sè stessa usciò,
>   e che si fesse rimembrar non sape.

> *As fire from a cloud must soon explode,*
>   *if it dilate and prove untenable,*
>   *and downward flies, against its natural mode,*
> *my soul, grown heady with high festival,*
>   *gushed and o'erbrimmed itself, and what strange style*
>   *it then assumed, remembers not at all.*[6]

Beatrice tells Dante to look back at her and see her as she truly is. Now that he has looked on Christ he is able to withstand her smile but what she truly is defeats his powers of description. He is like someone waking from a dream who tries in vain to recall it. Likewise, in picturing Paradise, he must leap over much, like one who finds obstructions in a path:

> Ma chi pensasse il ponderosa tema
>   e l'omero mortal che se ne carca
>   nol biasmerebbe se sott'esso trema.
> Non è pileggio da picciola barca
>   quel che fendendo va l'ardita prora,
>   nè da nocchier ch'a sè medesmo parca.

> *But one who called to mind the theme's great weight,*
>   *and mortal shoulder which supports the strain,*
>   *if it should shake, would lay no blame on it.*
> *No sea for cockle-boats is this great main*
>   *in which my prow now boldly carves its ways,*
>   *nor for a pilot sparing toil or pain.*[7]

At the command of Beatrice, Dante turns to behold a garden flowering in the rays of Christ, like a meadow seen beneath shafts of sunlight striking through the clouds, the rose in which the divine Word was made flesh, the lilies for whose fragrance the true path was followed. By these images Dante signifies that he is granted a vision not only of the light that is Christ but also of the splendours that are the Virgin Mary, to whom he prays every morning and evening, the Apostles and the redeemed of the Old and New Testaments. As he gazes on the Virgin's light, a brilliant torch descends from on high, circling about her like a crown. A burst of melody, compared with which the sweetest ever heard on earth would seem like thunder, accompanies the torch as it swirls round the sapphire light and the sky itself turns blue. The torch (which is later revealed as the Archangel Gabriel) sings a joyful greeting:

'Io sono amore angelico, che giro
   l'alta letizia che spira del ventre
   che fu albergo del nostro desiro;
e girerommi, donna del ciel, mentre
   che seguirai tuo figlio, e farai dia
   più la spera suprema perchè li entre.'
Così la circulata melodia
   si sigillava, e tutti li altri lumi
   facean sonare lo nome di Maria.

'I am angelic love who circle round
   the joy sublime, breathed from the womb wherein
   for our desire a shelter once was found.
Thus, heavenly Lady, I will thee entwine
   till with thy Son to enter thou hast willed
   the highest sphere thy presence makes divine.'
Thus the encircling melody was sealed.
   All other lights together sang aloud
   and through the sphere the name of Mary pealed.[8]

The Virgin moves aloft, the other lights reaching up towards her as an infant stretches out its arms to its mother when it has fed at her breast. Lingering still in Dante's sight, they continue singing *Regina coeli* so sweetly that the delight has never left him.

What is remarkable is the tender imagery by which Dante conveys these celestial apparitions. This is no static heraldry or pageantry, but love and the beauty of the natural world, within the range of human experience: the mother-bird, fruit harvested, a garden, a rose, lilies, the moon on a clear night among the stars, shafts of sunlight striking through the clouds on a flowery meadow, a baby stretching its arms towards its mother. Yet this vision surpasses anything Dante has been privileged to experience so far. Souls have descended from the Empyrean to converse with him in the planetary spheres, but here, amid his own constellation, Christ, the Virgin Mary, the Apostles, the Archangel Gabriel and thousands of redeemed souls have come to welcome him, a mortal man.

Beatrice too has undergone a change beyond the power not only of Dante's words but of all sacred poetry ever written. This must signify that Beatrice here represents his apprehension of divine truth.[9] It may be that his study of theology carried him beyond doctrine to an intensified awareness of the divine which exceeded the intellect. It may also be that in his prayers he sometimes entered an altered state of consciousness. As has been suggested, it is also possible that such extensions of the mind, associated with physical ecstasy, were heightened still further by means employed by mystics.

However arrived at, the vision is presented as an actual experience, a state of being, the theme under whose great weight his mortal shoulder trembles. This is not surprising. Like divine justice, the Logos is unfathomable.

CHAPTER 50

Faith, Hope and Love

T he spotlight is now on Dante the Christian believer. Here the poet and the character are one, but within the fiction he contrives exalted communion between himself and three of Christ's disciples: St Peter, St James and St John. No more sublime confessors could be imagined. Beatrice presents her protégé, humbly requesting the saints to test him in his understanding of Faith, Hope and Love. According to St Thomas Aquinas, before the soul can attain to participation in the Beatific Vision, these three theological virtues, mediated by divine light, must first prepare it for this final goal.

There are perhaps personal implications in the threefold interrogation that follows. According to an early tradition, Dante was once brought under enquiry by the Inquisition for heresy. If this is so, or if the tradition merely represents rumours as to the unorthodoxy of his beliefs, Dante here devises an opportunity to set the matter right beyond all possible doubt. It has also been said that he underwent some such formal examination during his theological studies, possibly during an early period in Bologna, or, as some commentators have maintained, in Paris. However that may be, the heavenly Tripos he here creates, not to mention the examiners, surpass those of any earthly university.

In *Il Convivio* Dante had used the image of a banquet for the acquisition of knowledge, expressing his desire to share with others less fortunate than himself what little he had acquired:

> I who am not seated at the table of the blessed, but am fed from the pasture of the common herd, and at the feet of those who sit at that table am gathering up of that which falls from them, perceive how wretched is the life of those whom I have left behind by the sweetness which I taste in that which little by little I obtain.[1]

Many years had passed since he wrote those words. Now he gives them in more exalted form to Beatrice, who thus addresses the saints still assembled in the Eighth Heaven:

'O sodalizio eletto alla gran cena
   del benedetto Agnello, il qual vi ciba
   sì che la vostra voglia è sempre piena,
se per grazia di Dio questi preliba
   di quel che cade della vostra mensa,
   prima che morte tempo li prescriba,
ponete mente all'affezione immensa,
   e roratelo alquanto: voi bevete
   sempre del fonte onde vien quel ch'ei pensa'.

'O fellowship of the elect who sup
   with Christ the Lamb, Who doth so nourish you
   that full to overflowing is your cup,
if God by grace admits this man unto
   the broken meats that from your table fall,
   before the hour prescribed by death is due,
the boundless measure of his love recall.
   Bedew him with some drops! Your fountainhead,
   whence comes what he thinks, is perpetual.'[2]

The feast of *Il Convivio* is here transformed to a celestial banquet, of which Dante is both creator and participant. He is no longer asking questions, as previously throughout *Paradiso*: he is answering them, with clarity and precision. There is a halt, for the moment, to professions of inability to find words for what he saw and heard.

The souls respond with joy to the request of Beatrice, flaming like comets, revolving some slowly and some fast. To enable the reader to visualize the scene, Dante uses a practical simile drawn from the latest advancement in mechanical science: the train of wheels of a striking clock, revolving at different speeds, a recent invention that had evidently caught his imagination. The simile is not only vivid: it carries the mind from the Eighth Heaven to earth, where time is measured and theological belief, an intellectual conviction, is in conformity with reason and accessible to the senses of mortals.

The soul of St Peter approaches and a brisk question-and-answer dialogue follows. When Dante argues convincingly for the truth of Christ's miracles, all the saints in their whirling circles break into the *Te Deum*, the song of salvation written by St Ambrose on the occasion of St Augustine's conversion. Dante had heard it indistinctly sung on entering the gateway to the seven cornices of Purgatory. Now the souls in Heaven sing it in accepting him as truly grasping the foundations of belief, and the light of St Peter, singing blessings on his soul, circles round him three times.

St James then joins St Peter and the two lights mingle in mutual bliss. Dante is now to be examined in his understanding of Christian hope. Beatrice presents him as one abundantly possessed of this second virtue, by virtue of which he has been granted his journey:

'La Chiesa Militante alcun figluolo
   non ha con più speranza, com' è scritto
   nel Sol che raggia tutto nostro stuolo:
però li è conceduto che d'Egitto
   vegna in Jerusalemme, per vedere,
   anzi che 'l militar li sia prescritto.'

'No child of the Church Militant can vie
   with him in hope; this blazoned in the Sun,
   the light of all our host, we may descry.
Hence, leave to come from Egypt he has won,
   to see Jerusalem, though many a year
   his soldiering on earth has yet to run.'[3]

It is hope that has earned for Dante the privilege of ascending to Heaven
in the body, Christian hope arising from faith, hope for mankind, for the
Empire, for Italy, for the regeneration of the Church, and, despite bitter
disappointments, hope still for his honourable recall to Florence. At the
end of his examination by St Peter he has expressed this personal hope in
moving words that show that at the date of writing them he still looked
forward to a day when the Florentines will invite him home to receive the
laurel crown at his font of baptism:

Se mai continga che 'l poema sacro
   al quale ha posto mano e cielo e terra,
   sì che m'ha fatto per più anni macro,
vinca la crudeltà che fuor mi serra
   del bel ovile ov'io dormi' agnello,
   nimico ai lupi che li danno guerra,
con altra voce omai, con altro vello
   ritornerò poeta, ed in sul fonte
   del mio battesmo prenderò 'l cappello.

If it should chance that e'er the sacred song
   to which both Heaven and earth have set their hand,
   whence I am lean with labouring so long,
should touch the cruel hearts by which I'm banned
   from my fair fold where as a lamb I lay,
   foe to the wolves which leagued against it stand,
with altered voice, with altered fleece today
   I shall return, a poet, at my font
   of baptism to take the crown of bay.[4]

He expressed the same hope when a poet of Bologna, known as Giovanni
del Virgilio, addressed to him a poem in Latin urging him to cease wasting

his talents by writing in the vernacular on subjects that the unlearned could not appreciate, and to compose in Latin an epic on a subject that could earn him a poet's crown from the University of Bologna. Dante replied, also in Latin, in the mock pastoral form of an eclogue, promising to send Giovanni samples of his work and expressing the hope that he would receive the laurel crown in Florence:

> Nonne triumphales melius pexare capillos
> et patrio redeam si quando abscondere canos
> fronde sub inserta solitum flavescere Sarno?

> *More glorious, were it not, to groom my hair,*
> *now become white which formerly was fair,*
> *concealed in leaves entwined on Arno's shore,*
> *when to my homeland I return once more?*[5]

The intriguing reference to the light shade of Dante's hair in his youth, now turned white, echoes the reference in *Paradiso* to the *altro vello* ('altered fleece') with which he imagines himself returning to Florence after an absence of many years, an old man now, white-haired and lean with labouring on his great work. The lines are also evidence that he continued to cherish hope of a recall, until, as will be seen later, something caused him to relinquish it for ever.

In May 1315 an amnesty had been issued by the government of Florence, offering pardon and freedom of return to exiles under certain conditions. One, known as the *oblatio*, was a ceremony in which a malefactor, clothed in sackcloth, wearing a mitre on his head and carrying a candle, was conducted to the Baptistery and presented by a sponsor at the altar for official pardon. Those who had been exiled for political offences were subjected to a modified but still degrading form of the ceremony and were required to pay a sum of money. News of this amnesty is said to have been communicated to Dante by a nephew and by friends. The brother of his wife, Teruccio di Manetto Donati, a member of a religious order, also wrote urging him to comply, discreetly concealing from him the conditions of the pardon. Dante's answer was gracious but indignant:

> Is this, then, the recall of Dante Alighieri to his native city, after the miseries of almost fifteen years of exile? Is this the reward of innocence manifest to all the world, and of the sweat and toil of unremitting study? Far be it from one who has followed philosophy to submit to such humiliation. ... Far be it from one who has preached justice and who has suffered wrong to pay money to those who wronged him, as though they had been his benefactors.

> No, father, not by this path will I return to my native city. If some other can be found, by you in the first instance and then by others, which does not dero-

gate from the fame and honour of Dante, that I will tread with no lagging footsteps. But if by no such path Florence may be entered, then I will enter Florence never again. Can I not anywhere gaze upon the face of the sun and the stars? Can I not anywhere contemplate the sweetest truths without first returning to Florence disgraced, even dishonoured, in the eyes of my fellow-citizens? Indeed, I shall not lack for bread!⁶

It was not in sackcloth with a mitre on his head that Dante later visualized himself, presented by his sponsor Beatrice, to the disciples of Christ before the assembly of souls in his natal constellation. Yet, even there, he acknowledged a blindness to the truth.

When the soul of St John draws near, a light which seems equal in radiance to the sun itself, Dante commits the error of peering into its depths. St John rebukes him:

>   … 'Perchè t'abbagli
> per veder cosa che qui non ha loco?
> In terra è 'l mio corpo, e saragli
> tanto con li altri, che 'l numero nostro
> con l'etterno proposito s'agguagli.
> Con le due stole nel beato chiostro
> son le due luci sole che saliro;
> e questo apporterai nel mondo vostro.'

>   … *'Why treatest thou so ill*
> *thy sight, seeking in me what thy world keeps?*
> *Earth in the earth my body lies, and will*
> *so lie with others till our total count*
> *be equal God's great purpose to fulfil.*
> *Two only who straightway to heaven did mount*
> *in our blessed cloister in both robes are clad.*
> *This truth unto the world shalt thou recount.'*⁷

Turning to look once more on Beatrice, Dante finds that he has gone blind.

The belief in St John's assumption in the body originated in the Eastern Church and gained limited credence in the West. St Thomas Aquinas called it 'a pious belief'. It is possible that the painting by Giotto in Santa Croce of the assumption of St John may have been commissioned by the Florentines to defy Dante's refutation of the legend. It would seem that Dante himself once believed it and here represents himself as blind for having done so.

St John reassures him that his sight will be restored to him by Beatrice, as St Paul's sight was restored to him by the hand of Ananias. In the meantime St John commands him to expound the nature of his love and its origin. In the question-and-answer dialogue that follows Dante states that God is the beginning and end of all his loves and defines the sources of his knowledge that God is the ultimate good. St John acknowledges that Dante's love is based both on revelation and on reason, but goes on to ask what other loves bind him to the divine. Dante enumerates the blessings by which God has manifested His goodness:

> ... 'l'essere del mondo e l'esser mio,
>   la morte ch' el sostenne perch' io viva,
>   e quel che spera ogni fedel com' io,
> con la predetta conoscenza viva,
>   tratto m'hanno del mar dell'amor torto,
>   e del diritto m'han posto alla riva.
> Le fronde onde s'infronda tutto l'orto
>   dell'ortolano etterno, am' io contanto
>   quanto da lui a lor di bene è porto.'

> *'The being of the world and my own state,*
>   *the death he died that I might live the more,*
>   *the hope in which I, by faith, participate,*
> *the living truth which I conveyed before,*
>   *have dredged me from the sea of wrongful love*
>   *and of the right have set me on the shore.*
> *Thus through the garden of the world I rove,*
>   *enamoured of its leaves in measure solely*
>   *as God the Gardener nurtures them above.'*[8]

At the conclusion of these words, Beatrice and the heavenly choir fill the heaven with sweet song, chanting 'Holy, holy, holy', and Dante's sight is restored to him, clearer than ever. A fourth light now blazes brilliantly where three had been. This is the soul of Adam.

Dante is awed, even more than by the presence of Christ's disciples. He knows that the First Ancestor of the human race reads his heart and mind and begs him to tell him what he would know. The soul quivers in glad eagerness and speaks. Dante's unspoken desire is to know how long ago God set Adam in the earthly Paradise, how long he remained there, what occasioned God's great displeasure (in other words, what was the cause of the Fall) and the language which he spoke. Adam states first the nature of the Fall. It was not the tasting of the forbidden fruit that incurred exile but the transgression from the path, the haste to know good and evil. Dante follows the teaching of Genesis as regards the length of his life: 'And all the days that Adam lived were nine hundred and thirty years.' He also follows the chronology devised by Eusebius, who puts the birth of Christ 5,198 years and His Crucifixion 5,232 years after the Creation. In the year 34 Adam was removed from Limbo by Christ, 'whence thy lady to thee Virgil sent'.

The language Adam spoke was something that Dante had already pondered in his treatise *De Vulgari Eloquentia*. He said there that it was Hebrew and that this language was spoken by all Adam's descendants until the building of the Tower of Babel. From then on only the sons of Heber spoke it, from whose name it was called Hebrew, and this, Dante believed, was the language of Christ. Dante's opinion then changed and he concluded that Adam's language was not a divine creation but the result of human reason and consequently susceptible of change and decay.

Adam finally answers Dante's desire to know how long he dwelt in Eden. Many theologians had meditated upon this and Dante chooses the view of Petrus Comestor that the duration was six hours, from the first hour to the seventh, when the sun, having run through a quarter, or 90 degrees of its circle, moved into its second quadrant. With this disclosure, Adam's words come to an end.

The four lights continue to blaze in Dante's sight and the heavenly choir rejoice in his enlightenment, singing a hymn of praise to the Three-in-One. Dante participates in the joy and, as though beholding a smile of all creation, by ear and eye he draws the inebriate rapture in.

It is at this sublime moment that the writer Dante chooses to place the most terrible of all his indictments of Pope Boniface VIII.

CHAPTER 51

Hatred in Heaven

Dante's hatred for Boniface VIII reaches an intensity which in modern terms would be diagnosed as a monomania. It reaches its highest pitch at a moment of the highest joy. At the conclusion of the words of Adam, the souls sing so sweet a song of triumph that Dante's senses are as though drunk:

> O gioia! Oh ineffabile allegrezza!
>> Oh vita integra d'amore sicura di ricchezza!
>> Oh santa brama sicura di ricchezza!

> *Oh joy no tongue can tell! Oh ecstasy!*
>> *Oh perfect life fulfilled of love and peace!*
>> *Oh wealth past want, that ne'er shall fade nor fly!*[1]

At this moment Dante the writer sees fit to open the vials of his wrath. The joyful choirs fall silent, the light of St Peter changes colour and he speaks in another tone:

> ... 'Se io mi trascoloro
> non ti maravigliar; chè, dicendo io,
> vedrai trascolorar tutti costoro.'

> ... *'If I change colour as I do,*
> *marvel not thou, for thou shalt see apace,*
> *while I shall speak, all these change colour too.'*[2]

With startling abruptness he launches into a diatribe against his present successor:

> 'Quelli ch'usurpa in terra il loco mio,
>> il loco mio, il loco mio, che vaca
>> nella presenza del Figliuol di Dio,
> fatt' ha del cimitero mio cloaca
>> del sangue e della puzza; onde 'l perverso
>> che cadde di qua su, là giù si placa.'

> '*He that on earth has dared usurp that place*
>   *of mine, that place of mine, that place of mine,*
>   *which now stands vacant before God's Son's face,*
> *has made my burial-ground a running rhine*
>   *of filth and blood, which to the Renegade*
>   *down there, who fell from here, is anodyne.*'[3]

St Peter here gives vent to all Dante's contempt for Boniface, who gained by craft the Papal throne, which in God's sight stands vacant, who by his avarice and worldly ambition has made the burial-place of St Peter a sewer of blood and filth, a source of gratification to Lucifer who fell from Heaven to Hell. The ugly rhymes, with their broad open vowels, *vaca, cloaca, placa*, the frenzied triple shriek, *il loco mio, il loco mio, il loco mio,* the crude imagery of the sewer, the filth, the stench, belong not to the disciple of Christ but to the diction of *Inferno.* Even more startling is the deep red, like clouds at sunset and sunrise, with which the sky, and Beatrice's modest visage too, are suffused in shame, as dark, Dante says, as the eclipse that occurred when Christ died on the Cross. This verges on profanity, if not on blasphemy.

But St Peter has not finished yet. Looking back to the martyrs among his early virtuous successors and prophesying the disgrace of the transference of the Papacy to Avignon, he rails against the avarice of later holders of the sacred Office and foretells divine retribution:

> 'Non fu la sposa di Cristo allevata
>   del sangue mio, di Lino e quel di Cleto,
>   per essere ad acquisto d'oro usata:
> ma, per acquisto d'esto vivo lieto,
>   e Sisto e Pio e Calisto e Urbano
>   sparser lo sangue dopo molto fleto.
> Non fu nostra intenzion ch'a destra mano
>   de' nostri successor parte sedesse,
>   parte dall'altra popol cristiano;
> nè che le chiavi che mi fuor concesse
>   divinisser signaculo in vessillo
>   che contra battezzati combattesse;
> nè ch'io fossi figura di sigillo
>   a privilegi venduti e mendaci,
>   onde' io sovente arrosso e disfavillo.
> In vesta di pastor lupi e rapaci
>   si veggion di qua su per tutti i paschi:
>   o difesa di Dio, perchè pur giaci?
> Del sangue nostro Caorsini e Guaschi
>   s'apparecchian di bere: o buon principio,
>   a che vil fin convien che tu caschi!

Ma l'alta provedenza che con Scipio
   difese a Roma la gloria del mondo
   soccorrà tosto, sì com'io concipio.'

'The blood of Linus, Cletus and myself
   was shed to foster her who is Christ's bride,
   not that she should be used for gain of pelf;
rather, to gain this life beatified,
   Sixtus, Pius, Calixtus, Urban spilled
   their blood and in long torment, weeping, died.
Never by our intention was it willed
   that Christendom should sit on either hand
   of those who after us our office held;
nor that the keys bequeathed to me should stand
   as emblem on a banner waging war
   against the baptized in a Christian land;
nor that a signet which my features bore
   should seal the lying privileges sold,
   whence, coruscating, I blush red the more.
Rapacious wolves in shepherds' garb behold
   in every pasture! Lord, why dost Thou blink
   such slaughter of the lambs within Thy fold?
Gascons and Cahorsines prepare to drink
   our blood. Beginning that so far didst show,
   to what vile ending wast thou doomed to sink!
But Providence, which once through Scipio
   the glory of the world and Rome's renown
   secured, will swift lend aid, as I foreknow.'[4]

Denunciation of the clergy was no uncommon theme in Dante's time or in later centuries, even long after the Reformation. Just as he set himself to surpass his classical predecessors in his description of snakes, and in other *tours de force*, so now Dante gathers all his mastery of the vernacular he is creating to surpass all diatribes. It is not only that he gives his words to St Peter: within the fiction, it is St Peter who commands Dante to report 'his' words when, at the end of his privileged journey into Heaven, he shall have returned to earth:

'E tu, figliuol, che per lo mortal pondo
   ancor giù tornerai, apri la bocca,
   e non asconder quel ch'io non ascondo.'

'And thou, my son, whose weight must draw thee down
   to earth once more, open thy mouth and speak:
   the things which I hide not, see thou make known.'[5]

He had received a similar command from Beatrice in the Earthly Paradise and from his ancestor Cacciaguida in the Heaven of Mars. He is now commanded by St Peter himself. Such is the measure of the aggrandized role that Dante allots to himself in the sight of Heaven.

He wrote these lines in Ravenna as he approached the end of his great work. He had many more joyful concepts to communicate, some beyond his capacity to express. This intrusion of violence into the ethereal reveals an instability of mood, arising perhaps from the contrast between what could be and what is and from the disappointment of frustrated hopes. At the same time, Dante still has faith that the causes of Church and Empire are in God's hand. This faith he contrives for Beatrice to express when he ascends with her into the Primum Mobile, or Crystalline Heaven, the boundary of space and time and the outermost limit of the created universe that is subject to change. The first moved of all the spheres, it spins at infinite speed in the desire of all its parts to be in contact with the Empyrean. Thus its motion is distributed to the other spheres, by whose motions time is measured. The whole structure is as ordered and as unquestionable, Beatrice says, as the truth that two and five are the dividends of ten.

In this context of the perfection of the divinely structured universe, Beatrice departs temporarily from her ethereal role and, in terms which are nearer Dante's than her own, rebukes human avarice and degeneracy:

'Oh cupidigia che i mortali affonde
    sì sotto te, che nessuno ha podere
    di trarre gli occhi fuor delle tue onde!
Ben fiorisce nelli uomini il volere;
    ma la pioggia continua converte
    in bozzacchioni le susine vere.
Fede ed innocenzia son reperte
    solo ne' parvoletti; poi ciascuna
    pria fugge che le guance sian coperte.
Tale, balbuziendo ancor, digiuna,
    che poi divora, con la lingua sciolta,
    qualunque cibo, per qualunque luna.
Tale balbuziendo, ama e ascolta
    la madre sua, che, con loquela intera,
    disia poi di vederla sepolta.
Così si fa la pelle bianca nera
    nel primo aspetto della bella figlia
    di quel ch'apporta mane e lascia sera.
Tu, perchè non ti facci maraviglia,
    pensa ch'n terra non è chi governi;
    onde si svia l'umana famiglia.'

'Cupidity! Thou dost engulf the race
    of mortal men so deep, not one may then
    above the o'erwhelming waters raise his face.
Fair is the blossom of the will of men,
    but the true fruit is swollen and made weak
    by drenchings of interminable rain.
In little children only mayst thou seek
    true innocence and faith, and both are flown
    before the down has grown upon the cheek.
He who the fast-days as a child has known
    will every dish in every season have
    ere out of baby-talk he scarce has grown;
or who affection to his mother gave
    in lisping childhood, learning at her knee,
    in manhood longs to see her in her grave.
Thus the white skin of the fair progeny
    of him who brings the morn and leaves the night
    darkens upon exposure instantly.
And thou, lest thou shouldst marvel at such plight,
    reflect: since there be none to govern you,
    how can the human household run aright?'[6]

But there is hope. As Beatrice foretold in the Earthly Paradise, a leader will come who will restore order to Church and Empire, so now she ends her speech with renewed assurance:

'Ma prima che gennaio tutto si sverni
    per la centesma ch'è là giù negletta,
    raggeran sì questi cerchi superni
che la fortuna che tanto s'aspetta,
    le poppe volgerà u' son le prore,
    sì che la classe correrà diretta;
e vero frutto verrà dopo 'l fiore.'

'Ere January be unwintered, through
    the hundredth of a day which men neglect,
    these lofty circles shall give vent unto
such roaring, that the storm we long expect
    shall whirl the vessels round upon their route,
    setting the fleet to sail a course direct;
and from the blossom shall come forth true fruit.'[7]

It is possible that by now Dante the man, though still hopeful, had resigned himself to a distant fulfilment of his dream of justice and peace.

CHAPTER 52

The Creation

D ante's two visions of God, first as an indivisible point and finally as three circles, may, like his visions in the Heaven of the Fixed Stars, represent actual experiences. Many commentators have believed that this is so. Whether or not this is true (and there is no certainty either way), Dante the writer remains throughout in conscious poetic control. The metaphysics of Heaven, the account of the creation of the universe, the river of time transformed to the Circle of Eternity, the scenic arrangement of the Blessed in the Celestial Rose, the final vision of the Trinity, all of which, as he ascends, take the character Dante and, with him, the reader from marvel to marvel, are deliberately planned and stage-managed by Dante the writer, the same showman who first led his listeners *dentro alle le segrete cose* ('in among the secret things').[1]

The final cantos are also in large part a versification, sometimes word for word, of texts from which Dante derived his concepts of Heaven and his belief in the reality of ecstatic contemplation. It may be that he experienced intellectual *ebbrezza* (inebriation) as a result of reading Aristotle and St Thomas Aquinas, as well as the mystics, such as Richard of St Victor, St Bernard and St Augustine. By making Beatrice the exponent of his rational understanding of their concepts, he gives his mental illumination an intensely personal visionary dimension.

When he moves up into the Ninth Heaven, which, as it whirls to unite with the Empyrean, the abode of God, imparts movement to all the other spheres, he sees reflected in the eyes of Beatrice an indivisible and immeasurable point of light. On turning to look at it directly he sees revolving round it nine circles of flame. These, she informs him, are the orders of angelic beings.

This vision was shaped by his reading of several authors. Aristotle, for example, in his *Metaphysica* speaks of the indivisibility of the Godhead and writes as follows of the Prime Mover, or God:

> The Prime Mover, which causes motion without itself being moved, must be eternal, must be Essence, and must be Actuality. It must be the first object of

desire and the first object of will. ... Without it, good or perfection cannot be had; it is what it is absolutely, without possibility of being otherwise. ... From a principle of this kind depend the Heaven and all Nature.[2]

Dante puts that last sentence, word for word, into the mouth of Beatrice:

'*Da quel punto depende il cielo e tutta la natura.*'[3]

It is evident that what he read in the abstract Dante converted to visible terms, by which he created a diagram of the cosmos for his better understanding. He says that he first sees the Point (which is God) reflected in the eyes of Beatrice, who represents Theology. This is appropriate since he had found God thus represented in the writings of theologians. By the nine angelic orders, manifested as fiery circles wheeling round the Point, he conveys visually the notion of a vast encompassing spiritual order, one Divine Providence which is operative continuously and variously in the lives of men. What (in the story) he says puzzles him is the comparative speed at which the circles rotate about the Point, the inmost being the fastest moving of the nine. This is the reverse of the speed at which the heavenly spheres were conceived to circle the earth, the Primum Mobile being the fastest, the Heaven of the Moon the slowest.

Beatrice tells him that if he will consider the power of each angelic order, instead of the apparent circumference of each celestial sphere, he will see that each heaven is controlled by the angelic order most suited to it: the Seraphim move the Primum Mobile, the Cherubim move the Eighth Circle and so on down to the angels who move the Heaven of the Moon. Hence, swiftness and brightness being the measure of the excellence of the angelic circles, and size the measure of the excellence of the heavenly spheres, the correspondence between the two spatial presentations can be seen to be perfect. It would appear that Dante in real life had been bemused by the theological notion of God as the centre of the universe as well as the all-embracer. Beatrice's answer to the apparent contradiction may be Dante's own solution. The joyful and triumphant simile by which he conveys his intellectual illumination seems to suggest this:

> Come rimane splendido e sereno
>   l'emisperio dell'aere, quando soffia
>   Borea da quella guancia ond' è più leno,
> per che si purga e risolve la roffia
>   che pria turbava, sì che 'l ciel ne ride
>   con le bellezze d'ogni sua paroffia;
> così fec'io, poi che mi provide
>   la donna mia del suo responder chiaro,
>   e come stella in cielo il ver si vide.

As when the dome of air more lovely grows,
    by Boreas serene and shining made,
        when from his milder cheek he softly blows,
purging and scattering the murky shade
        wherewith the sky was stained until, made clean,
            it smiles, with all its pageantry displayed,
so did my understanding there grow keen
        soon as I heard her luminous reply,
            and, like a star in heaven, the truth was seen.[4]

When Beatrice has paused, Dante beholds a sparkling of scintillas in each circle, representing such an increase of angels that their total exceeds by thousands the figure arrived at by the progressive doubling of the chessboard squares. In order to convey the idea of innumerableness Dante the writer has recourse to an ancient Eastern legend, according to which a Brahmin brought to a king the game of chess, with which he was so delighted that he offered the Brahmin in return anything he might ask. The Brahmin said he would take only a grain of wheat, doubled as many times as there are squares on a chessboard. By geometric progression (i.e. 1 + 2 + 4 + 8, etc.) the total goes into millions. At the same time there is a burst of singing as *Hosanna* resounds from choir to choir, in glory of the Point which holds them, and ever shall, in the place where they have ever been. The diagram here comes to life; the truth is experienced as light and song; Dante the character rejoices, as does Dante the poet.

Many years before, in *Il Convivio*, in his role as educator, Dante had discussed the number of angels in connection with Plato's theory of 'ideas':

> There were others, like Plato … who assumed not only that there are as many Intelligences [angelic beings] as there are movements of the heavens, but also that as the Intelligences of the heavens are producers of these movements, each one of its own, so these other Intelligences are producers of everything else, and exemplars each one of its own species; and Plato called them 'ideas'.[5]

He then proceeded to demonstrate by argument that the Intelligences 'who live only by contemplation' are much greater in number than those who produce the effects that man can apprehend. It is possible therefore that when Dante came to describe the angelic circles in *Paradiso* he intended to convey that those he first beholds are the movers of the heavens, while the myriad countless sparks which secondly appear are the contemplative angels of each order. However this may be, it is probable that Dante had long visualized these abstract notions in scenic terms.

When both kinds of each angelic order have manifested themselves, Beatrice proceeds to name them. Dante had altered his mind since writing *Il Convivio*, and had accepted the order attributed to Dionysius the

Areopagite, who, Dante makes Beatrice say, learnt the truth from St Paul who had been caught up into the Third Heaven. The matter of the angelic orders is also discussed at length by St Thomas Aquinas in *Contra Gentiles* and in the *Summa*.[6]

Dante also follows St Thomas in a matter of still greater importance: does love of God spring from knowledge of Him, or knowledge of Him from love? The question was much debated. Dante's approach to God was through his intellect, as the result of reasoned and objective consideration of life and reality. He found in St Thomas confirmation that this was fundamental to the life of the spirit. Thus he speaks of Beatrice as 'she who *my mind* imparadises'.[7] It is his thinking that she raises to Heaven; he is both learner and lover of divine things. The Empyrean is intellectual light:

> 'luce intellettual, piena d'amore;
>   amor di vero ben, pien di letizia,
>   letizia che trascende ogni dolzore.'

> *'pure intellectual light, fulfilled with love,*
>   *love of the true good, filled with all delight,*
>   *transcending sweet delight, all sweets above.'*[8]

Beatrice has yet to teach him concerning the Creation. The question in his mind is 'Why did God create?' Her answer is that God created not to increase His good, which cannot be, but in order that His reflected light might shine back to Him self-existing and in self-awareness. There were no successive stages in the act of Creation. Time did not exist before 'the spirit of God moved upon the face of the waters': the angels, primal matter and the material heavens all issued simultaneously into being:

> Nè prima quasi torpente si giacque;
>   chè nè prima nè poscia procedette
>   lo discorrer di Dio sovra queste acque.
> Forma e matera, congiunte e purette,
>   usciro ad esser che non avia fallo,
>   come d'arco tricordo tre saette.
> E come in vetro, in ambra od in cristallo
>   raggio resplende sì, che dal venire
>   all'esser tutto non è intervallo,
> così 'l triforme effetto del suo sire
>   nell'esser suo raggiò insieme tutto
>   sanza distinzione in essordire.

> *Nor did He lie before this as at ease,*
>   *for neither first nor after did proceed*
>   *the movement of God's Spirit on the seas.*

Pure form, pure matter, form and matter wed,
  came forth to being without blemish as
  three arrows from a three-stringed bow are sped.
And as through crystal, amber, or plain glass
  a sunbeam floods its all-pervading fire,
  not gradual, but instantaneous,
so the three-fold creation of the Sire
  from its beginning without sequences,
  rayed into being, instant and entire.[9]

'Pure form' is pure mind, that is, the angels; 'pure matter' is the primal stuff of the elements; 'form and matter wed' are the material heavens. In this Dante is following Aristotle who in *De Anima* ('On the Soul')[10] distinguishes between three orders of existence: form or act, matter or potency, form and matter combined. He is also repeating, through the words of Beatrice, what he has caused Aquinas to say in the Heaven of the Sun concerning the divine creative light which operates on primal matter through the angelic orders and the spheres that they control, and produces earthly creatures.[11]

Dante, speaking still through Beatrice, proceeds to correct a number of errors, which he may himself formerly have held. One is the opinion of St Jerome who said that angels existed long before the rest of the universe. Dante here follows St Thomas and considers that he is supported by Scripture; he also argues independently in terms of reason: how could the movers exist without function, there being no spheres for them to move? Beatrice tells him that the rebellious angels fell immediately upon being created. Dante had already said this in *Il Convivio*[12] but added there that some were lost from each order, a statement which he now omits, as he drops all mention of the neutral angels he had seen in the Vestibule of Hell.[13] He may by then have come to accept that belief in them was heretical. He also makes Beatrice deny that angels were possessed of memory, as attributed to them by St Thomas and others. In so doing, Dante follows an earlier concept, that angels, dwelling with God in eternity, hold the knowledge of past and future in an enduring present. The souls of the Blessed also see all things at once, though in *Purgatorio* they are said to possess memory, intelligence and will.[14] The merit of angels and of men is the willing acceptance of grace, and the reward of that merit is yet more grace; the root and essence of sin is pride which refuses the bonds of grace and rebels against the order of the universe.[15]

After this imaginative presentation of inherited beliefs, conveyed in radiant words by Beatrice, Dante the writer, still speaking through her, launches into a sarcastic condemnation of preachers who in their trivial sermons betray such glorious truths. Although it is appropriate for the figure of theology to condemn unworthy preaching, the style of this diatribe, as has been said, is out of keeping with Beatrice in any of her roles and in irreconcilable conflict with the idealized portrait of her that follows soon afterwards. The final words in particular stand out like a sore thumb. The trivial jokes on which ignorant preachers rely and the sale of pardons without authority delight the devil hiding in their cowls and make fools of their congregations:

'Di questo ingrassa il porco sant'Antonio
e altri assai che sono ancor più porci,
pagando di moneta senza conio.'

'That's how St Anthony fattens his pig,
as many others do, more pig-like still,
paying with currency not worth a fig.'[16]

This expression of exasperation and contempt would come suitably from Dante himself. From Beatrice it is as grotesque as a gargoyle.

CHAPTER 53

The Departure of Beatrice

After her contemptuous speech about facetious clergy, Beatrice, seeming almost to apologize for her digression, reverts to her sublime function of expounding the infinitude of angels and the unity of God. For this concept she has recourse to the Book of Daniel:

'Ma perchè siam digressi assai, ritorci
    li occhi oramai verso la dritta strada,
    sì che la via col tempo si raccorci.
Questa natura sì oltre s'ingrada
    in numero, che mai non fu loquela
    nè concetto mortal che tanto vada;
e se tu guardi quel che si rivela
    per Daniel, vedrai che 'n sue migliaia
    determinato numero si cela.
La prima luce, che tutta la raia,
    per tanti modi in essa si recepe.
    quanti son li splendori a ch' i' s'appaia.
Onde, però che all'atto che concepe
    segue l'affetto, d'amar la dolcezza
    diversamente in essa ferve e tepe.
Vedi l'eccelso omai e la larghezza
    dell'etterno valor, posica che tanti
    speculi fatti s'ha in che si spezza,
uno manendo in sè come davanti.'

'Since of digression we have had our fill,
    our eyes upon the straight path let us bend;
    as time grows short, our way we must curtail.
The numbers of angelic beings extend
    so far beyond the range of mortal mind,
    no words or thought have ever reached the end.
And in the book of Daniel thou wilt find,
    for all the thousand thousands he there states,
    no fixed and final figure is assigned.

The Primal Light the whole irradiates,
    and is received therein as many ways
    as there are splendours wherewithal it mates.
Since, then, affection waits upon the gaze
    and its intensity, diversely bright
    therein the sweets of love now glow, now blaze.
Consider well the breadth, behold the height
    of the eternal Goodness, seeing that o'er
    so many mirrors It doth shed Its light,
yet one abideth as It was before.'[1]

The wonder of the concept of God's unity in diversity elates both the mind of Dante the character and Dante the poet, who here merge without distinction into one and the same, a tendency that increases as *Paradiso* draws to its close.

The angelic circles fade one by one from sight. Dante turns once more to look at Beatrice and finds her so transfigured that, once again, he has insufficient power to describe her. Many years before, in his *canzone* inspired by the *donna gentile* beginning *Amor che nella mente mi ragiona*, Dante had professed his inability to grasp and adequately put into words what Love conveyed to his mind. The blame for this he attributed to weakness of intellect and faculty of speech which are unable to record all that Love says. Later, in his commentary on this poem in *Il Convivio*, he again affirmed this inability:

... la lingua mia non è di tanta facondia che dir potesse ciò che nel pensiero mio se ne ragiona.

... *my tongue has not such eloquence as to be able to express that which in my thought is said* [*about my Lady*].[2]

But in this context, the Lady (the *donna gentile*) signifies Philosophy, while in *Paradiso* Beatrice signifies Theology. It is evident that in Dante's experience philosophic truths, no less than theological, had soared beyond the grasp of his intellect and powers of expression.

They have now left the Primum Mobile and ascended to the Empyrean, the abode of God, where Dante will behold both hosts of Heaven: the angels in traditional figuration and the souls of the departed in the semblance of their earthly bodies. At first unable to bear the radiance that pours in on him from every side, he cannot discern anything. Beatrice tells him that Divine Love always thus prepares the soul for the vision of Himself, like a candle made ready for its flame:

'per far disposto a sua fiamma il candelo.'

'so is the candle for its flame made apt.'[3]

A new force now enters him. He describes it as a sense of rising above his usual power:

> ... io compresi
> me sormontar di sopra a mia virtute.

> ... *I became aware*
> *that I surmounted what my power was.*[4]

This is as close as Dante comes to sharing with us his experience of heightened consciousness, an extension of his perceptions beyond the rational. It may also signify a leap beyond the normal of his imaginative and creative powers.

He first sees light in the form of a river, flowing between flowery banks, from which arise vivid sparks. This is yet another recollection of the Book of Daniel: 'A fiery stream issued and came forth before him.'[5] Beatrice tells him to look his fill at the scene of stupendous beauty, in which the flowers, like rubies set in gold, with the brilliant sparks diving amongst them and into the stream, are but shadow-prefaces of what he will next behold. Like a baby, awakened beyond its usual hour, mouthing hungrily for its mother's breast, Dante bends over the stream, filling his eyes to his very eyelids. The river turns into a circle (a symbol of eternity), so wide that its circumference would exceed that of the sun, while the sparks and flowers, like people in a masquerade who tear off their disguise, are changed into the two courts of Heaven, the angelic and the human.

Dante now utters a prayer for power to say what he then saw, giving emphasis to the word *vidi* ('I saw') by making it an identical rhyme in three lines. No longer does he invoke the Muses or Apollo, but God Himself. The threefold emphasis has been interpreted as an assertion that he did in reality see what he is about to describe; it may also be an echo of the words of St John, 'That which we have seen ... we have seen ... we have seen ... declare we unto you.'[6]

Brilliant light shines on the convex surface of the Primum Mobile, which receives from it all its power of movement as it whirls the circles below it. Dante beholds thousands and thousands of tiers containing thrones on which are seated the souls of the Blessed. The whole structure is in the form of a rose with white petals, spread out before him in the form of an amphitheatre, the rings nearest him so wide that he is unable to imagine the extent of the most distant. Beatrice leads him to the golden centre of the rose and says:

> ... 'Mira
> Quanto è 'l convento delle bianche stole!
> Vedi nostra città quant' ella gira,

> vedi li nostri scanni sì ripieni,
> che poca gente più ci si disira.'

> *'Behold how great the white-robed company!*
> *Look on our city, see its gyres full-spread!*
> *Behold our thrones, that are so nigh complete*
> *few souls they lack for whom they're covenanted.'*[7]

It is now, in a speech already quoted, that Beatrice indicates the empty throne, marked with a crown, destined for the soul of the Emperor Henry VII, rejected by Italy, a hungry, petulant infant,[8] (in contrast with the other hungry infant who was Dante as he drank eagerly at the stream). This reference to the rejection of Henry, a memorial to Dante's disappointed hopes, written eight years after the Emperor's death, is also an expression of his faith that beatitude would reward the heroic monarch, a coronation more sublime than his three earthly ones, while retribution awaits two miscreant Popes: Clement V who betrayed him and Boniface VIII who betrayed Florence. As Beatrice continues:

> 'E fia prefetto nel foro divino
>   allora tal, che palese e coverto
>   non anderà con lui per un cammino.
> Ma poco poi sarà da Dio sofferto
>   nel santo officio; ch' el sarà detruso
>   là dove Simon mago è per suo merto,
> farà quel d'Alagna intrar più giuso.'

> *'Then o'er the sacred forum will preside*
> *   one whose allegiance will be proved infirm,*
> *   feigning support, but stepping then aside.*
> *Him in the Holy Office no long term*
> *   will God endure, but thrust him down below*
> *   where Simon Magus pays his score, to squirm*
> *behind the Anagni man, who'll deeper go.'*[9]

These, though Dante the character does not know it, nor does the reader, are the last words of Beatrice, in strident and inexplicable conflict with the idealization to which her *persona* has so recently been exalted.

Eager, as he was in the Terrestrial Paradise, to enter this new scene of wonder, Dante lets his gaze range over the spectacle before him. The angels fly down to the saints as bees to flowers and fly back to God as bees to their hive, conveying peace and burning love. Their countenances are aflame, their wings are gold, their raiment as white as snow. For all their thousands, they present no impediment to Dante's vision of every detail. The poet Dante invokes the Trinity, entreating it to shine on those who are tossed on the tempest of earthly life. Filled with awe, he compares his amazement to the stupefaction of barbarians from the north seeing Rome and all its wonders. It is at this stupendous moment, as his creation draws to its sublime close, that Dante the embittered exile strikes his final and most savage blow at Florence, ending thereby all possible hope of ever returning:

> Io, che al divino dall'umano,
>   all'etterno dal tempo era venuto,
>   e di Fiorenza in popol giusto e sano,
> di che stupor dovea esser compiuto!

> *I, coming to holiness from the profane,*
>   *to the eternal from the temporal,*
>   *from Florence to a people just and sane,*
> *into what stupor, then, must I needs fall!*[10]

His eyes wander in amazement, 'now upwards and now down, and now circlewise'. He turns then to look back at Beatrice, exactly as in the Terrestrial Paradise he had turned to look back at Virgil, and, exactly in the same way, he finds her gone. This master stroke of balance is once again evidence of the perfect control Dante the writer had over the structure of his narrative. Despite his many misgivings as to the inadequacy of his powers of expression, this he never loses.

CHAPTER 54

Approach to the Final Vision

Without a word of farewell, Beatrice has returned to her throne among the Blessed. Under her guidance as the figure of Theology, Dante has been granted anticipatory visions of the glory of God. Now, having been first blinded and then kindled to new sight by the light of that glory, he has been made apt, like a candle for a flame, to participate in a vision of the Trinity. In her allegorical function, Beatrice has fulfilled her task. Dante has passed beyond intellectual comprehension of theology and is about to enter a mode of contemplation. For this he needs the help of one who can implore intercession by the Virgin Mary for this ultimate grace. Dante the poet too needs all his finest skills to take his audience with him to this final climax.

Beatrice has been replaced by the figure of a venerable elder whose countenance displays the tenderness of holy love. This is the soul of St Bernard of Clairvaux, the impassioned promoter of the Second Crusade, in which Dante's ancestor Cacciaguida fought and died. A type of the mystical contemplative, he was known from his sermons and other writings to have been ardent in his veneration of the Virgin Mary. He was also believed by some theologians to have had a vision of God while still in his earthly life. It is for these reasons that Dante has chosen him as his last guide. The story is now coming full circle: as St Lucy, first commanded by the Virgin Mary, sent Beatrice to the rescue of Dante, Beatrice now sends St Bernard to enlighten Dante still further on the ultimate stage of his journey.

Thus to the many paternal figures in the *Commedia* is now added St Bernard:

> Diffuso era per gli occhi e per le gene
> di benigna letizia, in atto pio
> quale a tenero padre si convene.

> *His eyes and face diffused with gladness were,*
> *such kindly piety his air conveyed*
> *such as we see a loving father bear.*[1]

Like his predecessors in this role, he too addresses Dante as *figliuol* ('son'), the affectionate diminutive of *figlio*.[2] The filial relationship that Dante the character bears to several figures in the *Commedia* (Virgil, Brunetto Latini, Cacciaguida, Statius and Guinizelli) suggests that Dante himself had nostalgic memories of his father, and that he looked throughout his life for substitutes for him in older men. If this is so, his father would appear to have been a just and loving parent, whose loss, together with that of his mother at an earlier age, left Dante with a permanent sense of orphaned bereavement. His exile from Florence, which he compared to the betrayal of Hippolytus by his step-mother Phaedra, was consequently the more wounding.[3] Some such psychological syndrome contributed to the yearning for privileged sonship, which is so marked a feature of the *Commedia*. It may even underlie, at a subconscious level, his longing for the return of an authoritative world ruler who will one day restore peace and happiness to mankind.

When Virgil suddenly departs in *Purgatorio* Dante breaks down in a passion of weeping. The disappearance of Beatrice, on the contrary, occasions no tears, only bewilderment, as when, having fallen asleep in the Terrestrial Paradise, he anxiously asks Matilda where Beatrice is, a moment anticipatory of his present startled exclamation:

E 'Ov' è ella?' subito diss' io.

And 'She, where is she?' instantly I said.[4]

The elder, who has not yet revealed his identity, replies that he has been sent by Beatrice to bring Dante's quest to final fulfilment. He instructs him to look up towards a distant circle, the third from the highest tier, where he will see her seated on the throne to which merit has assigned her. Dante does so and, despite the vast space that now separates them, greater than the distance between the region of thunder and the bottom of the sea, he is able to see her, crowned and reflecting from herself the light of glory. In the last words he speaks to her, he expresses his loving gratitude for her guidance and prays that she will continue in her bounty towards him during his remaining years in the body.[5] It is immensely moving that in these last words he addresses her, for the first time, with the intimate pronoun *tu*, something he had not done even in the poems addressed to her in *La Vita Nuova*.

St Bernard now says who he is. Dante compares his awe and amazement to the feelings of a pilgrim from a primitive region of Christendom, as it might be Croatia, who gazes at the veil of St Veronica in Rome, believed to have been imprinted with the features of Christ when she wiped the sweat and blood from His face as He passed on His way to Calvary. This relic, an object of deep veneration, was displayed at St Peter's during January and Holy Week. Dante had referred to it in *La Vita Nuova*[6] in connection with his sonnet about pilgrims passing through Florence on their way to Rome. The two comparisons of his feelings, first to those of barbarians from the north visiting pagan Rome, and secondly to those of a pilgrim gazing at a sacred relic in Christian Rome, bring the theme of the divinely ordained political and spiritual centre of the world into a final focus:

> Qual è colui che forse di Croazia
> viene a veder la Veronica nostra,
> che per antica fama non sen sazia,
> ma dice nel pensier, fin che si mostra:
> 'Signor mio Gesù Cristo, Dio verace,
> or fu sì fatta la sembianza vostra?'
> tal era io mirando la vivace
> carità di colui che 'n questo mondo,
> contemplando, gustò di quella pace.

> *Like one perhaps who from Croatia came*
> *to see the veil of our Veronica*
> *and held, unsated, by its ancient fame*
> *looks all he may, musing the while with awe:*
> *'Lord Jesus Christ, true God, this semblance of*
> *Thy face those who beheld Thee truly saw?',*
> *so I there marvelled at the living love*
> *of him who tasted, while a mortal man,*
> *by contemplation, of that peace above.*[7]

As Beatrice had several times directed Dante's gaze from her face to the souls who had come to converse with him, so now St Bernard bids him look away from him to the highest row where he will see the Mother of God.

This is Dante's second vision of the Virgin Mary. He had first seen her as a sapphire light among the Pageant of the Church Triumphant in the Heaven of the Fixed Stars.[8] Now in bodily form, like the other saints, she is yet conveyed in imagery that shrouds and at the same time reveals her as all but divine. She is the Queen of Heaven, to whom all the saints are subject, yet with them she too is one of redeemed humanity:

> Io levai gli occhi; e come da mattina
> la parte oriental dell'orizzonte
> soverchia quella dove 'l sol declina,
> così, quasi di valle andando a monte
> con li occhi, vidi parte nello stremo
> vincer di lume tutta l'altra fronte.

> *I looked above and, as the orient scene*
> *at dawn exceeds the beauty of the west,*
> *where the declining sun has lately been,*

> *so, mounting as from vale to mountain-crest,*
> *these eyes beheld, at the remotest rim,*
> *a radiance surpassing all the rest.*[9]

The radiance is the glory of the Virgin. About her Dante sees more than a thousand angels with wings outspread, each distinct in brightness and function, making festival in glad revelry and joyful songs. Beaming out upon them is the beauty of the Virgin, diffusing joy into the eyes of all the saints. Once again, Dante the writer renounces all attempt to describe the least part of such gladness. St Bernard, seeing Dante's eyes fixed upon the Virgin's light, turns his own upon her with an ardour which increases Dante's still further.

There is still more to come. First, Dante's understanding of his vision has to be set in order. St Bernard, in the role of a *dottore* ('teacher'), like a guide in a sacred edifice, names the figures in the celestial scene.

It is a static scene, like a mosaic or a fresco, such as Dante must often have contemplated in Ravenna and elsewhere, representing the figures of the Old and New Covenants, those who believed in Christ to come and those who believed in Him in His incarnation. It provides an iconic balance to the Limbo and to the lesser assemblage of rulers in the valley of Ante-Purgatory. Here in the Empyrean are souls whom Virgil saw drawn by Christ from Limbo when He descended into Hell. Eve, who inflicted on mankind the wound that led to the Fall, and Mary who healed it, often coupled in sermons and homilies, are seen here as the fountain-heads of original sin and Divine Redemption. The whole assembly represents the fulfilment of God's plan for mankind. Those who in one way or another were involved in the Redemption are named. John the Baptist, the Forerunner, is seated above a line of three who continued his work of preparing the way: Francis, the most Christ-like among the saints, Benedict who founded Western monasticism, seen now by Dante in semblance of bodily form, as he had promised, and Augustine, eminent among Christian confessors. Adam, the first to be drawn from Limbo, and Peter the first head of the Church, Moses the leader of the chosen race, Anna the mother of the Virgin, and all the others named, as well as the ranks of children, saved by the merits of Christ alone, form a perfectly balanced arrangement, divided into four sections, each one of which is a complete semicircle. At the Day of Judgement the total numbers of believers of the Old and New Dispensation will be equal. St Bernard draws Dante's attention to the supreme skill manifested here by God the Designer:

> 'Or mira l'alto proveder divino,
> chè l'uno e l'altro della fede
> egualmente empierà questo giardino.'

> *'Now marvel at God's plan, for on each hand*
> *both aspects of the faith will, when complete,*
> *in equal number in the garden stand.'*[10]

Into this formal, precise geometrical pattern, Dante introduces a discourse by St Bernard on predestination and the elective gift of grace, a matter as inscrutable as divine justice, as if to convey that though the result of God's handiwork can be laid out in a diagram, His will eludes all attempts to define and measure it.

The most important stage in Dante's vision is now approaching. For the third time he beholds the Virgin. Poised before her he sees the Archangel Gabriel, gazing into her eyes, while all the court of Heaven sings 'Hail, Mary'. Not only is she supreme among mortals; it was she who set in motion the whole process of Dante's awakening to the realities of sin, repentance and salvation. More than that, she is here called by St Bernard *Augusta*, which is to say, the Empress of *questo impero giustissimo e pio* ('this most just and holy empire.')[11] Dante here raises his philosophical belief as to the right ordering of the world to the sublime height of the Empyrean, as though God Himself, Creator and Son of the Empress, were the predestined Emperor, the *veltro* and the DVX. To this near-blasphemous climax Dante's obsession has now brought him.

St Bernard tells Dante that his entrancement is now drawing to a close:

> 'Ma perchè 'l tempo fugge che t'assonna,
>   qui farem punto, come buon sartore
>   che com' elli ha del panno fa la gonna;
> e drizzerem li occhi al primo amore,
>   sì che, guardando verso lui, penetri
>   quant' è possibil per lo suo fulgore.'

> *'But since the time of thy entrancement doth*
> * grow short, like the good tailor we hear of,*
> * we'll cut our coat according to our cloth,*
> *and here will stop, to turn our eyes above*
> * that thou, as far as may be, with thy gaze*
> * mayst penetrate into the Primal Love.'*[12]

Thus, in simple, homely words, St Bernard bids Dante prepare himself for the vision of the Trinity.

CHAPTER 55

The Vision of the Trinity

V*ergine madre, figlia del tuo figlio* ('Virgin mother, daughter of thy son'): with these celebrated words St Bernard begins his prayer to the Mother of God. It is a prayer such as St Bernard in life might have offered, extolling her at once as lowly and yet the most exalted of all creatures, the mediatrix to whom all mankind should turn, in whom compassion, mercy and all human goodness are combined, who so ennobled human nature that its Creator did not disdain to become Himself His creature. He now entreats her to intercede for Dante that he may attain to a vision of God and that thereafter, under her protection, his affections and impulses may be directed aright:

'vedi Beatrice con quanti beati
per li miei preghi ti chiudon le mani.'

*'see Beatrice and all the many blessed
with folded hands my prayers supplicate.'*[1]

This is our final sight of Beatrice.

The Virgin, gazing first upon Bernard, shows how welcome his devout prayer is to her and then turns her eyes to the eternal Light. Dante, now nearing the fulfilment of his desire, his sight made clear, penetrates further and further into the supreme light which in itself is truth. From then onwards, what he sees surpasses all human speech and even memory fails, as when a dreamer awakes:

Qual è colui che somniando vede,
    che dopo il sogno la passione impressa
    rimane, e l'altro alla mente non riede,
cotal son io, chè quasi tutta cessa
    mia visione, ed ancor mi distilla
    nel core il dolce che nacque da essa.
Così la neve al sol si disigilla;
    così al vento nelle foglie levi
    si perdea la sentenza di Sibilla.

> *As from a dream one may awake to find*
> *that passion felt in sleep does not depart,*
> *although all else is cancelled from the mind,*
> *so of my vision now but little part*
> *remains, and yet within me still I know*
> *the sweetness it engendered in my heart.*
> *So the sun melts the imprint on the snow,*
> *even so the Sibyl's wisdom that was penned*
> *on light leaves vanished on the winds that blow.*[2]

Here, with his use of the present tense, *quasi tutta cessa/la mia visione … ed ancor mi distilla*, Dante the character is again merged with Dante the poet. And it is the poet now who prays that God may grant him power to convey some small spark of what he saw that those who come after him may have a clearer understanding of His victory:

> O somma luce che tanto ti levi
> da' concetti mortali, alla mia mente
> ripresta un poco di quel che parevi,
> e fa la lingua mia tanto possente,
> ch' una favilla sol della tua gloria
> possa lasciare alla futura gente;
> chè per tornare alquanto a mia memoria
> e per sonare un poco in questi versi,
> più si conceperà di tua vittoria.

> *O light supreme, by mortal thought unscanned,*
> *grant that Thy former aspect may return;*
> *once more a little of Thyself relend.*
> *Make strong my tongue that in its words may burn*
> *one single spark of all Thy glory's light*
> *for future generations to discern.*
> *For if my memory but glimpse the sight*
> *of which these lines would now a little say,*
> *more will be comprehended of Thy might.*[3]

Here at last is the unequivocal statement of the ultimate purpose of his work: to bring men to a better understanding of the glory of God, by which means, as he said in his 'epistle' to Can Grande della Scala, 'to remove those living in this life from a state of misery and to bring them to a state of happiness'.[4]

In the story, Dante the character undergoes long preparation for this ultimate vision. Dante the writer had undergone even longer preparation. For years he had meditated on the writings of the mystics and had perhaps shared something of their experiences. This is evident not only in *Il Convivio*.

Even as far back as the days in which he was writing *La Vita Nuova*, as has been shown, he had already experienced heightened states of consciousness in which his intellect could not follow him. He had many predecessors in this.

The so-called Dionysius in his work *Mystical Theology* wrote:

> My argument now rises from what is below up to the transcendent and the more it climbs, the more language falters, and when it has passed up and beyond the ascent, it will turn silent completely, since it will finally be at one with him who is indescribable.[5]

Dionysius did not ascribe to himself a personal experience of the divine presence but he appealed to the witness of those to whom it had been granted, such as Moses and St Paul. Since Dante, like his contemporaries, believed that Dionysius was the convert of St Paul, his words held indisputable truth for him.

There was also Hildegard of Bingen, the twelfth-century visionary and prophet, known as the Sibyl of the Rhine, who wrote letters to Popes and prelates denouncing their abuses and warning them of wrath to come. She described one of her visions as follows:

> Heaven was opened and a fiery light of the greatest brilliance came down and filled my whole head, my whole heart, and my whole breast, like a flame, not so much burning as warming.[6]

St Bernard said that her gifts were divinely inspired. Her visions were of a transforming contact with God, providing ineffable knowledge and deep sense of union. St Augustine believed that visions could be corporeal, spiritual or intellectual. In his *Confessions* he said:

> I saw with my soul's eye ... an unchanging Light above that same soul's eye, above my mind. With the fine point of the mind we are able to gaze upon something unchangeable, though hastily and in part.

He believed that such experiences could never be adequately expressed, but only hinted at through verbal strategies designed to suggest but not to circumscribe the mystery of God. There occurred special acts of grace, in which 'the soul is snatched away from the body's senses'. At such moments the soul sees nothing by way of the senses, being totally intent on imaginative or intellectual seeing, the intellectual being the higher:

> There the brightness of the Lord is seen, not through a symbolic or corporeal vision – but through a direct vision ... as far as the human mind elevated by God's grace can receive it.[7]

St Augustine's theories of ecstatic vision had a long-lasting influence on other mystics, especially on Richard of St Victor, who taught that contemplation begins with images formed in the mind, when reason rises from the material to an understanding of the spiritual. To progress further, the seeker must make intense efforts in prayer and meditation. By God's grace, the human reason may then succumb to what it beholds of the divine light, when it is lifted above itself and rapt in ecstasy.[8] He wrote also of 'the free penetration of the mind, hovering in wonder, into the manifestation of Wisdom'.[9] The ultimate purpose of such contemplation was to increase man's love of God and of one's neighbour.

There can be little doubt that from such writings Dante derived the belief that it was possible to have a vision of God in the first life, and formed some of idea of what such a vision could be like. The question still remains: did he himself experience one? If so, was it an hallucination caused by a pathological condition induced by prolonged prayer and fasting, or by some psychedelic stimulus?

There is a striking similarity between Dante's description of his visions throughout *Paradiso* and accounts of experiences resulting from drugs.[10] In a heightened state of consciousness, induced by chemical changes, time is perceived as an eternal present of infinite duration, reality takes on a sacramental significance, and everything in the universe seems to be grasped in one single act of comprehension as of an all-enclosing design of interlinked phenomena. An artist or a poet, endowed naturally with exceptional powers of vision, especially if stimulated further by artificial means, may become aware of the glory and wonder of existence to a degree beyond even the highest art to express. To sustain such an experience, the mind has to remain concentrated on what it perceives as a divine light which inspires an increasing urge to transcend the limitations of selfhood and achieve unity with the infinity of God.

Such visions are experienced also by mystics who, with or without the help of stimulants, are known to have brought about an alteration in consciousness by fasting,[11] sleep-deprivation, mortification of the body by flagellation and other disciplines, and by the prolonged repetition of prayers and chants. Images of precious jewels, colours brilliant beyond the normal and dazzling light are among the features of pictures that come into their minds. Vision-inducing arts such as fireworks, pageantry, civic and religious processions, theatrical spectacles, one scene turning into another, transfiguration, masquerades, music and dance serve to heighten a sense of the paranormal and induce a transition from one mode of perception to another.

Visions can, of course, occur, in normal circumstances, spontaneously, without stimulus of any kind. Those who experience them speak of a sense of the immanence of the supernatural in all that they behold. An example occurs in the autobiography of Pamela Hansford Johnson. She describes the experience as follows:

> It was … a radiant late afternoon in Spring. I was looking, lack-lustre, out
> of the train windows. Then the glory opened. I can only weakly describe it.
> The trees sprang to three times their normal height and burst out in blossom.
> … All was a golden enormity, beyond everything I had ever seen or ever can
> conceive. Size and gold. A sky golden all over. Familiar and yet unfamiliar,
> something of almost insufferable beauty.[12]

Dante's intellectual grasp of the meditations of mystics, the tradition of
geometrical images representing the divinity, the symbol of three entwined
circles representing the Trinity in a manuscript entitled *Liber Figurarum*,
attributed to Joachim of Flora,[13] as well as pictorial and sculpted works of
other-world significance provided material for his poetic imagination to
work on. An archetype of all such apprehensions is the vision of Ezekiel:

> Upon the likeness of the throne was the likeness of the appearance of man …
> and I saw as the colour of amber, as the appearance of fire round about within
> it … and it had brightness round about. As the appearance of the bow that is
> in the cloud in the day of rain, so was the appearance of the brightness round
> about. This was the appearance of the likeness of the glory of the Lord.[14]

It is also possible that the final canto may be the result of the interaction
of an actual mystical experience with the symbolism of Dante's allegorical method and his conscious poetic creativeness. As is often the case, the
simplest explanation is perhaps the one from which all the others derive: his
mystic awareness of the divine arose, as he said it did, from his early sight of
a beautiful Florentine girl.

Dante's vision of the Trinity, the crown and climax of the *Commedia*, is
presented as two revelations. First he perceives in the Divine Light the form
of all creation. All things that exist in themselves, all aspects of being, all
mutual relations are seen as though bound together in one single volume.
The Universe is in God. Dante is convinced that he saw it because as he
writes he feels such joy, although the memory of it seems as distant as the
25 centuries which divide the present from the voyage of the *Argo*. What he
next sees eludes his power of words, as if he were an infant, his tongue still
milky at the breast.

Having glimpsed the whole of creation, he beholds the Creator. He sees
three circles of three colours, yet of one dimension. One is reflected from
another, the third, like flame, derives equally from both: thus he perceives
the Three-in-One, Father, Son and Holy Ghost. As he gazes, the reflected
circle shows within itself the human form, coloured with the circle's own
hue. He strives in vain to understand how the human image is united with
the circle that is the Son:

Qual' è 'l geometra che tutto s'affige
     per misurar lo cerchio, e non ritrova,
     pensando, quel principio ond' elli indige,
tal era io a quella vista nova:
     veder volea come si convenne
     l'imago al cerchio e come s'indova.

As the geometer his mind applies
     to square the circle, nor for all his wit,
     finds the right formula, howe'er he tries,
so strove I with that wonder – how to fit
     the image to the sphere; so sought to see
     how it maintained the point of rest in it.[15]

At this instant a flash of light floods his mind and he understands how the human and the divine are joined in the Incarnation. Here the highest power of his imagination failed and he can say only that his will and desire were moved as in a circle by divine love:

All'alta fantasia qui mancò possa,
     ma già volgeva il mio disio e 'l velle,
     sì come rota ch'igualmente è mossa
l'amor che move il sole e l'altre stelle.

High fantasy lost power and here broke off;
     and as a wheel in a smooth motion whirs,
     my will and my desire were turned above
by love that moves the sun and the other stars.[16]

Dante is now at one with the universe. The future, his own and that of the world, is with God and he is content that it is so. His work, concluding, like *Inferno* and *Purgatorio*, with the rhyme-word *stelle*, significant of destiny, has come full circle.

Epilogue

Soon after Dante wrote the final words of his *Commedia* peace was shattered. Trouble sprang up between Venice and Ravenna. Some Venetian ships were seized by the Ravennese and Venetian sailors were killed. The Doge of Venice formed an alliance with Rimini and Forlì and prepared to make war on Ravenna. Dante's patron, Guido da Polenta, the lord of Ravenna, was in no position to meet the challenge. He accordingly sent an embassy to negotiate terms. Dante was included, commissioned because of his renown as an orator and his experience in negotiation. This is an indication of the extent to which Guido called upon his services, this time with fatal result.

Before leaving, Dante placed the manuscript of his last 13 cantos, of which he had not had time to make copies, inside a wall-cupboard in the room where he had been working. His long task was done and his mind must have felt fulfilled as he set out in aid of his patron.

The delegates travelled to Venice by sea along the Adriatic coast and were successful in averting war. They (or Dante alone, it is not certain) returned to Ravenna by land, through the lagoons of Comacchio and across the northern extremity of the Pineta, the pine forest said to have inspired the description of the Terrestrial Paradise in *Purgatorio*. On this journey Dante caught malaria and arrived home ill. He died during the early hours of 14 September 1321. He was 56 years old.

After the funeral ceremonies, his sons Pietro and Jacopo turned their minds to setting his papers in order. To their dismay, they were unable to lay hands on the last 13 cantos of *Paradiso*. They were certain that their father had finished the work, but the manuscript did not go beyond Canto XX. Where was the rest of it? They knew that it was his practice to send batches of cantos to Can Grande della Scala but enquiries made in that quarter were fruitless. In a state of desperation they were persuaded by friends to try to finish *Paradiso* themselves. They knew their father's work well and would later write commentaries on it. They had also tried their hand at verse. Nevertheless, the task was far beyond their abilities.

After about eight months, Jacopo had a dream one night in which his

Fig 14. Mask of Dante

father appeared to him. On being asked by Jacopo if he had finished his poem, Dante replied, 'Yes, I finished it.' He then took his son by the hand and showed him a room in a house and touched part of the wall, saying: 'Here is what you have been looking for.' On waking, Jacopo went with a friend to the house and there they found, in a recess in a wall, concealed by a flap of material, a pile of manuscript covered with mildew. They lifted it out and brushed it clean: it was the missing 13 cantos.

This story was related by Giovanni Boccaccio, the first biographer of Dante.[1] He was a child of eight when Dante died and never even set eyes on him, but when he began to read the *Commedia* he was an immediate enthusiast. The first version of his biography was brought out in 1351, when he was 38 years old. In preparation he had collected a great deal of what is now called 'oral history'. He interviewed Giovanni Villani, the chronicler and a neighbour of Dante, Cino da Pistoia, Dante's close friend and fellow poet, Andrea Poggio, Dante's nephew, and many others. He travelled to places mentioned by Dante. He went to Ravenna and talked there with Dante's sons and others who had known him in his last years.

It might appear at first sight that Boccaccio's admiration for Dante should be taken for granted. What is surprising about it? The answer to this involves several factors. One is the attitude of the Humanists. Two examples will suffice: Giovanni del Virgilio, Professor of Rhetoric at the University of Bologna, and the poet Petrarch. The first is an example of a conventional academic mind. He wrote to Dante while he was living in Ravenna, reproaching him with wasting his talents on a work of vulgarization. Will he not write an epic in Latin on a subject likely to win academic approval? If so, he might even be in the running for an honorary degree at the University of Bologna.

In Petrarch we have the fastidiousness of a learned poet confronted by an art very different from his own. Boccaccio, who also admired Petrarch's poetry and became a close friend, was dismayed by his reluctance to take a position concerning the merit of a fellow Tuscan. He sent him a copy of the entire *Commedia*, written in his own hand, accompanied by a letter asking him to read the poem and make his opinion of it known. Petrarch eventually wrote a letter in which he praised Dante but it was not the enthusiastic response for which Boccaccio had hoped.

Another factor that deterred public acknowledgement of Dante's greatness was the attitude of the Florentines. They had exiled him, unjustly, and when a community has committed an injustice towards one of its members it is not swift to make amends. There were also several affronted families among them; there were the extremist Guelfs who were opposed to Dante's championing of the Empire; and there were the ecclesiastics. In 1335 the

Florentine Chapter of the Dominicans forbade the friars to read his works. Guido Vernani, a learned theologian who taught at Bologna, denounced him as a *vas diaboli* and repudiated the *Monarchia*, which was ceremonially burned in public.

There were thus many reasons why a man of letters who cared for his reputation would be evasive on the subject of Dante. Boccaccio was not evasive. He is an example of the enthusiast who boldly commits himself, without waiting for a body of opinion to be established, to which he can with safety add his murmur of assent. He was moved to write his biography by a burning sense of indignation against his fellow Florentines,[2] who had made no amends: no statue had been raised, no monument.[3] He, with humility, undertook to make good the omission and to do honour to that *chiarissimo uomo* ('most illustrious man'), who deserved acclamation for his virtue, his learning and his good deeds, but had received only injustice, exile, alienation of his property and slander. He prevailed upon the Florentines to make some recompense to Dante's daughter, Sister Beatrice, who had entered a convent in Ravenna, and it was he who went there to present her with ten gold florins. She was then an elderly woman.

The divulgation of Boccaccio's biography had its effect. In 1373 a petition was made by the citizens of Florence to the Priors for the establishment of a year's daily public lectures on the *Commedia*. The petition was granted and Boccaccio was appointed the first official public lecturer on Dante. He was then 60 years of age. He died before completing the task.

Boccaccio did not take the *Commedia* seriously as a prophetic work, nor did he share Dante's obsessive vision of world order established under the supreme authority of an Emperor of Europe. The important thing about Boccaccio's biography and his *Esposizioni*, as his lectures have been entitled, was his immediate recognition of Dante's living power as a writer and of his creative mastery of the Tuscan language, particularly his range and diversity of styles: narrative, dramatic, lyrical, oratorical and vituperative. This is a view that has survived for 700 years: Dante, the artist and creator of modern literature. It is for his poetic genius that we still read him and for his vision of divine love. As the nineteenth-century poet Giosuè Carducci wrote:

Muor Giove, e l'inno del poeta resta.

Jove dies, the poet's hymn survives.[4]

To Boccaccio's generosity and courage, to his ardent dedication we owe a great deal: not only the copies he made of the *Commedia* and the information he gathered, but especially the example of an independent mind arriving at its own judgement and not afraid to proclaim it. To Boccaccio also we owe the adjective *divina*, which he first applied to the *Commedia*.

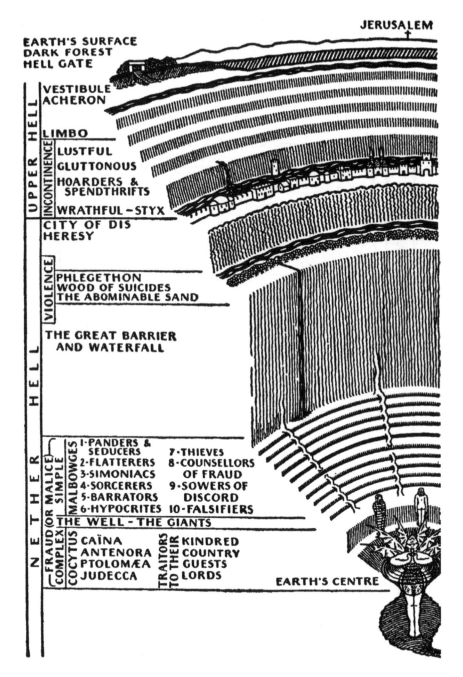

Fig 15. Diagram of Inferno

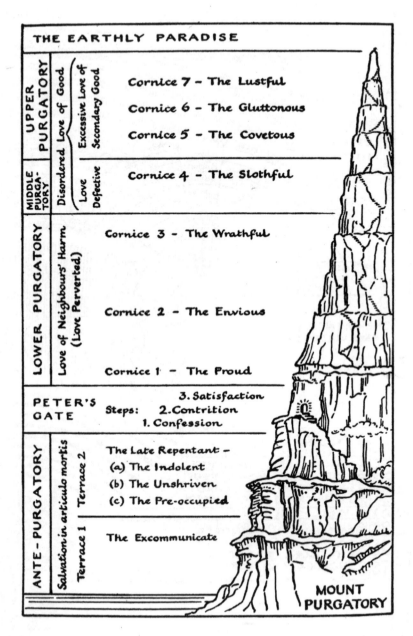

Fig 16. Diagram of Purgatory

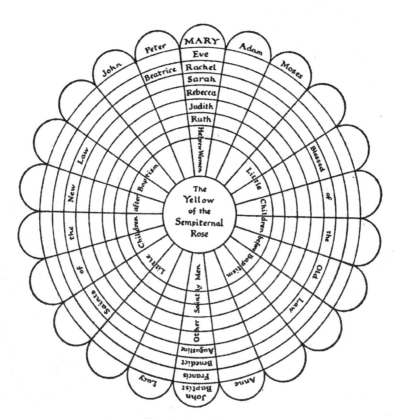

The Celestial Rose.

Fig 17. Diagram of Heaven

Appendices

1. Chronology of Dante's Life and Works

1265	between May and June	Birth of Dante in Florence.
1266	January	Birth of Beatrice Portinari.
1273?		Death of Dante's mother.
1274	traditionally 1 May	First meeting of Dante and Beatrice.
1277		Betrothal of Dante and Gemma Donati.
1278?		Death of Dante's father.
1280–82		Dante composes and circulates his earliest sonnets.
1282?		Beginning of friendship with Guido Cavalcanti and other members of the *Fedeli d'Amore*.
1285		Dante takes part in an expedition of Florentine militia in support of Tuscan Guelfs against the castle of Poggio di Santa Cecilia, roused to rebellion by Ghibellines.
1289	11 June	Battle of Campaldino against the Ghibellines of Arezzo. Dante fights among the first rank of the cavalry.
	31 December	Death of Beatrice's father.
1290	8 June	Death of Beatrice.
1292?		Dante first sees the *donna gentile* looking at him with compassion from a window. He becomes enamoured and writes poems about her.
1293?		Vision of Beatrice in Heaven. Dante resolves to write no more love poetry concerning Beatrice but to study philosophy.
1294	spring	Visit to Florence of Charles Martel, King of Hungary.
1294?		Dante composes *La Vita Nuova*.
1295		Dante enters political life. He continues to write poetry, but of philosophical and moral content.

1300	May	Guelf party in Florence, split into two opposing factions, known as the Whites and the Blacks, comes to bloodshed.
	15 June–15 August	Dante holds office as Prior.
	August	Death of Guido Cavalcanti.
1301	autumn	Dante and others sent to negotiate with Pope Boniface VIII concerning the threat to Florence of intervention of Charles of Valois.
		Florence taken over by Charles of Valois, with the connivance of the Pope, supported by Black Guelfs led by Corso Donati. White Guelfs, including Dante, are exiled. Violence and burning of property.
	November	Dante, returning from Rome, hears of betrayal and joins fellow exiles at Garganza, near Siena.
1302	February	Meeting between exiled White Guelfs and exiled Ghibellines.
	June–March 1303	Unsuccessful attempts by exiles to return to Florence by force.
1303?	May, June	Dante at court of Bartolommeo della Scala, Verona.
1303	September	Outrage of Anagni.
	12 October	Death of Pope Boniface VIII.
1304	January	Cardinal Niccolò da Prato appointed peacemaker in Florence; exiles have hopes of returning.
	March	Death of Bartolommeo della Scala.
		Dante in Arezzo, HQ of White Guelfs.
		Dante writes letter to Cardinal da Prato on behalf of fellow exiles.
		Cardinal's attempt at peacemaking fails.
1304	20 July	Last attempt by exiles to enter Florence by force. Disastrous defeat.
		Dante quarrels with fellow exiles.
1304–6		Dante in Bologna; renews contact with Cino da Pistoia.
		Dante writes *De Vulgari Eloquentia* and *Il Convivio*, both left unfinished.
1306	autumn?	Dante begins writing the *Commedia*.
1306–7?		Dante in Sarzana, guest of Malaspina family.
1307		Dante in Casentino region, guest of Guidi family.
1308	November	Henry of Luxembourg elected King of the Germans.
1311	6 January	Henry crowned in Milan with the crown of Charlemagne. Dante present at ceremony.
		Resistance of Florence and allies to Henry's claim to authority.

1311–13		Dante writes three letters in support of Henry; probably suspends work on *Inferno* during this period.
1312	29 June	Henry crowned Emperor in Rome.
1313	24 August	Death of Henry VII.
1314	May or June	Dante writes letter to Italian cardinals urging support of Italian successor.
1315–16?		Dante in Verona as guest of Can Grande della Scala. He writes part of *Purgatorio* there.
1317?		Dante writes *Monarchia* in challenge to Pope John XXII and in support of Can Grande as Imperial representative.
1319?		Dante offered home in Ravenna by Guido Novello da Polenta. He continues *Purgatorio* there and begins *Paradiso*.
		Dante writes address to Can Grande concerning *Paradiso*; possibly gives it personally as an oration.
1320	20 January	Dante in Verona to give lecture entitled *De Aqua et Terra*.
		Exchange of Latin poems with Giovanni del Virgilio. He has by then completed at least ten cantos of *Paradiso*.
1321	summer– autumn?	Dante finishes *Paradiso*.
		Threat of war between Venice and Ravenna. Dante is chosen as member of delegation to negotiate with the Doge on behalf of Guido da Polenta. He travels with fellow delegates to Venice.
	autumn	The delegates return to Ravenna. Dante falls ill with malaria on journey home.
	14 September	Death of Dante in Ravenna.

2. Guelfs and Ghibellines

The words 'Guelf' and 'Ghibelline' are derived from the German names 'Welf' and 'Weiblingen'. They were first adopted in Italy at the beginning of the thirteenth century by two leading factions that divided the cities of Lombardy. The overriding contest was between the Pope and the Emperor in their attempt to maintain control of areas of the Italian peninsula. Those who supported the policies of the Pope were known as Guelfs; those who supported the Emperor were known as Ghibellines.

For most of Dante's lifetime, Florence was under the control of the Guelf party. Five years before his birth, in 1260, a terrible battle had been fought between Guelfs and Ghibellines, known as the Battle of Montaperti. The Guelfs met with disastrous defeat, to the extent, Dante said, that the river Arbia ran red with their blood. The leader of the Ghibellines was Farinata degli Uberti, who alone defied the victors who had resolved to raze Florence to the ground. This heroic figure appears in *Inferno*.

In Florence the Guelf party split into two bitterly opposed factions, known as

Blacks and Whites. Dante was a member of the Whites, said to be the less militant of the two. On May Day 1300 the two parties came into violent conflict which led within two years to the overthrow of the Whites and to Dante's exile.

3. List of Popes in Dante's Lifetime

Clement IV (1265–1268)
Gregory X (1271–1276)
Innocent V (February–June 1276)
Hadrian V (July 1276)
John XXI (1276–1277)
Nicholas III (1277–1280)
Martin IV (1281–1285)
Honorius IV (1285–1287)
Nicholas IV (1288–1292)
Celestine V (July–December 1294)
Boniface VIII (1294–1303)
Benedict XI (1303–1304)
Clement V (1305–1314)
John XXII (1316–1334)

4. Holy Roman Emperors Referred to by Dante

Charlemagne (800–814)
Otto I (962–973)
Henry II (1002–1024)
Conrad III (1138–1152)
Frederick I (1152–1190)
Henry VI (1190–1197)
Frederick II (1211–1250)
Rudolf I (1273–1291)
Adolf (1292–1298)
Albert I (1298–1308)
Henry VII (1308–1313)

5. The *Canzone*

A *canzone* is a poem written to be set to music and sung to the accompaniment of a musical instrument. Its form is governed by the nature of the tune that is chosen. This can be of two kinds: (1) the tune is continuous, without division or repetition, throughout each stanza; (2) the tune is divided into two melodic sections, termed *odi*, in which one of the sections must be and both may be repeated. The transition from the first to the second *ode* is termed a *diesis* or *volta*. If the repetition occurs before the *diesis*, the stanza is said to have two *piedi*, followed by a *sirma* or *coda*. If the repetition occurs after the *diesis*, the stanza is said to have a *fronte*, followed by two *versi*.

The rhyme scheme must remain uniform throughout the poem. Lines of any number of syllables, not exceeding 11, may be used, but the 11-syllable line (*endecasil-labo*) should predominate.

A *canzone* may be concluded by a *tornata*, corresponding to an *envoi*, in which the poet personifies the poem and bids it address itself to certain persons.

The nature of the diction that Dante considered suitable for a *canzone* is defined by him in *De Vulgari Eloquentia* (see Chapter 5 of the present work). Dante considered the *canzone* the highest form of vernacular poetry and deeply respected its dignity and complexity, which he regarded as a check on facile versifying.

Notes

Chapter 1: The Early Years

1. *Paradiso* XXII, 112–115.
2. *Ibid.*, XV, 133–135.
3. See Figure 1.
4. See Chapter 49 of the present work.
5. See Figure 2.
6. *Inferno* XIX, 21.
7. Giovanni Boccaccio, *Trattatello in Laude di Dante*, trans. Philip H. Wicksteed (adapted). See also translation by J.G. Nichols, Hesperus Press, 2002.
8. *Ricognizione delle Ossa di Dante*, Reale Accademia Nazionale dei Lincei, Serie Quinta, Volume XVII, Fascicolo 1, Rome, 1923.
9. *Ibid.*, pp 24–25. Petrarch's cranial capacity has been calculated as 1,481 cubic centimetres and the probable weight of his brain as 1,288 grams.
10. Seymour Kirkup (1788–1880), an amateur artist, lived in Florence for a time and was a member of the English colony there. The sketch he made of the portrait by Giotto was reproduced by chromolithography and published by the Arundel Society. See Frontispiece.
11. See Chapter 2 of the present work.
12. *Il Convivio*, Book I, Chapter 13. All translations of this work are by W.W. Jackson, Oxford, Clarendon, 1909, with occasional adaptations.
13. The reference to his conception in *Inferno* VIII, 45, where Virgil exclaims 'Blessed is the womb that bare thee!', is an allusion to his mother but it is scarcely a memory of her.
14. See *Il Convivio*, Section IV, Chapter 24. It is not known who the guardian was. See also Chapter 8 of the present work, note 32.
15. '*Io sono stato con Amore insieme*', K. Foster and P. Boyde, *Dante's Lyric Poetry*, Oxford, Clarendon, 1967, pp 198–201.
16. '*E' m'incresce di me sì duramente*', stanza 5, K. Foster and P. Boyde, *Dante's Lyric Poetry*, pp 56–58.
17. *Inferno* V, 142.
18. The two elder sisters, Beatrice and Ravignana, were both married during their father's lifetime. The younger sisters were named Vanna, Pia, Margarita and Castoria. The sons were named Manetto, Ricovero, Pigello, Gherardo and Iacopo. Their mother was Cilia de' Caponsacchi.

19. *La Vita Nuova*, Chapters XXXII and XXXIII.

20. This hospital, one of the earliest in Europe, still exists but has been moved to the Piazza Santa Maria Nuova. The original building, in Via Folco Portinari, is now a library.

21. The house in Florence said to be Dante's is a modern reconstruction.

22. His wife may have joined him. There is no proof that she did not.

23. *Paradiso* XII, 137.

24. *Inferno* XV, 109. Priscian was a sixth-century grammarian.

25. Of the third century AD.

26. *Inferno* XV. See also Chapter 17 of the present work.

27. *Ibid.*, 81–85.

28. His name was Belacqua. See *Purgatorio* IV, 106–135 and Chapter 31 of the present work.

29. *Purgatorio* II, 76–133. See also Chapter 32 of the present work.

30. *La Vita Nuova*, Chapter XII.

31. See also Chapter 5 of the present work.

32. *La Vita Nuova*, Chapter XXXIV.

33. *Purgatorio* VIII, 28–36.

34. *Ibid.*, 73–75.

35. *Purgatorio* V, 85–129. See also Chapter 32 of the present work.

36. *Inferno* XXI, 94–96.

37. See Mauro Cursietti, *La Falsa Tenzone di Dante con Forese Donati*, Anzio, 1995. See also Chapter 38 of the present work.

38. Born *c.*1230, he died before 1300.

39. See Chapter 43 of the present work.

40. The examination of urine had long been employed in diagnosing disease. Urine could be tested for sugar, an indication of diabetes, and for sexual infections. Instructions to physicians emphasized the importance of observing the consistency of the urine, the colour and the deposits contained in it. Residue of herbal potions and narcotics is likely to have been noticeable, and Dante of Maiano's advice may be a sly hint to this effect.

41. Born between 1250 and 1255, he died in 1300.

42. *Guido Cavalcanti: Rime*, edited by Guido Favati, Ricciardi, Milan, 1957, p 277. It was translated by Dante Gabriel Rossetti, *Dante and His Circle*, London, Ellis and Elvey, 1892, p 116.

43. *Inferno* X. See also Chapter 2 of the present work.

44. This is not to say that Virgil is to be identified with Guido Cavalcanti, but Dante's grief at the sudden disappearance of Virgil in *Purgatorio* perhaps evokes his deep sense of loss at the death of Cavalcanti.

45. *Inferno* X. See Chapters 3 and 16 of the present work.

46. *Purgatorio* VI, 61–66.

47. *Paradiso* IX, 25–36.

48. *c.*1280–1348.

49. *Cronica* I, 19, 15–27.

50. See Chapter 15 of the present work.

51. *Inferno* XIX, 49–51.

52. In *Inferno* XVI, 45, Jacopo Rusticucci's words, *la fiera moglie più che altro mi nuoce*

('my fierce wife above all else causes me harm') are probably a reference to bestiality. See Chapter 18 of the present work.

53. See Figure 6.
54. *Inferno* XXXIV, 28–69.
55. See Chapter 10 of the present work.
56. *Cronica* VIII, 76.
57. Boccaccio's *Esposizioni sopra la 'Commedia' di Dante Alighieri*, a commentary on Canto V of *Inferno*.
58. *Purgatorio* XXIII. See also Chapter 38 of the present work.
59. *Paradiso* XV, 97–124. See also Chapter 46 of the present work.
60. Early fourteenth century, a contemporary of Dante.
61. Translation by Dante Gabriel Rossetti, *Dante and His Circle*, pp 333–341.
62. Translation by Dante Gabriel Rossetti.

Chapter 2: Dante and Guido Cavalcanti

1. *Il Convivio*, Section II, Chapter 2.
2. *Purgatorio* XXX, 115–117.
3. This particular sonnet may indicate that the *tenzone* was changing to the vituperative mode, as in the case of the *tenzone* between Dante and Forese Donati. (See Chapter 1 of the present work.)
4. i.e. in the vernacular.
5. *La Vita Nuova*, Chapter XXV.
6. *Ibid.*, XXX.
7. *Purgatorio* II, 106–117.
8. *La Vita Nuova*, Chapter XXIV, sonnet beginning *Io mi sentii svegliar dentro a lo core.*
9. *Ibid.*, XIV.
10. *Purgatorio* XXIV, 49–54.
11. *Inferno* XXXI, 136–138.
12. *La Vita Nuova*, Chapter XX.
13. The words *dire* and *dettare*, as Dante uses them in this context, signify 'to write in verse'.
14. The Bardi home was situated across the river Arno, near the Rubaconte Bridge.
15. *La Vita Nuova*, Chapter XXX.
16. The custom is found also in Wales.
17. *La Vita Nuova*, Chapter XXIII.
18. *Ibid.*, VIII. On this occasion he seems to have mingled with women mourners or possibly with women who ministered to the body.
19. Not that the *lady* is the enemy of reason, as is often wrongly interpreted.
20. See also Chapter 6 of the present work.
21. By 'mystic' addition 19 = 1 + 9 = 10.
22. See Chapter 16 of the present work.

Chapter 3: Disaster

1. Giovanni Villani, *Cronica* VIII, xiii.
2. The *canzone* beginning *Voi ch'ntendendo il terzo ciel movete* ('Ye who by intellect the third Heaven move'), written while Dante was still torn between his love for

Beatrice and his love for the *donna gentile*.

3. *Paradiso* VIII, 37.
4. The names were derived from a conflict in Pistoia, the leaders of two factions being descended from two wives of the same husband, one of whom was called Bianca.
5. See Chapter 1 of the present work.
6. A district in the north-west corner of Tuscany, between the Apennines and the Ligurian border.
7. *Inferno* X, 22–120.
8. *Ibid.*, 60.
9. *Ibid.*, 63. The meaning has been much disputed. Possibly Dante intended it to be enigmatic.
10. *Inferno* XV.
11. *Purgatorio* XXVI.
12. *Paradiso* XV–XVIII. See also Chapter 8 of the present work.
13. *Cronica* VIII, 36.
14. *Paradiso* XV, 109.
15. *Inferno* XVIII, 28–33, where the rule is 'keep to the right'. It is not known what the rule was in Rome 1300, but it is likely to have been 'keep to the left', as being convenient for travellers on horseback, armed with swords.
16. *Il Convivio*, Section IV, Chapter 5.
17. See Figure 3.

Chapter 4: The First Years of Exile

1. Spelled Alagna in Dante's time.
2. It is perhaps the building which has been incorporated into the seventeenth-century Palazzo Traietto.
3. As was necessary. See also note 22.
4. *Purgatorio* XX, 73–74.
5. See Chapter 31 of the present work.
6. One of the valleys of Tuscany, watered by the Sieve.
7. See *Paradiso* XVII, 70–73, where Bartolommeo is referred to as 'the great Lombard', whose courtesy is such that he will bestow gifts before being asked.
8. See *Dante e Verona*, Museo di Castelvecchio, 1965, Introduction by Antonio Scolari, p xiii.
9. See Chapter 3 of the present work.
10. *Ibid.*
11. Altichiero di Domenico da Zevio (*fl.*1369; *d.* before 10 April 1393), painter of Verona, a member of the Scala household.
12. See for instance the exchange of sonnets with Aldobrandino of Padua, discussed in Chapter 5 of the present work. See also the discussion of the erotic *canzone* in Chapter 10.
13. Translated from the Latin and quoted by T.S.R. Boase, *Boniface the Eighth*, Constable, 1933, pp 346–347. It was not the intention of the attackers to cause the Pope's death but to force certain concessions from him. Hundleby's despatch was dated 27 September, two weeks before the Pope died.
14. The exact date of his birth is not known.
15. Related by the chronicler Giovanni Villani, *Cronica* VIII, 63.

16. *Purgatorio* XX, 87–90 (Sayers' translation).
17. The earliest of Dante's extant letters, it is in Latin. See edition by Paget Toynbee, Oxford, Clarendon, 1920, pp 1–10. The translation is by Toynbee.
18. Alessandro da Romena, said by Leonardo Bruni to have been elected by the Florentine exiles as their captain. His name, like that of 'Brother L.', is indicated only by the initial A. This was a convention in official letters. See also note 20.
19. This phrase is a translation of the Latin *Preceptis salutaribus moniti*, words which precede the Lord's Prayer in the Mass.
20. Toynbee, pp 11–13. This letter is also in Latin.
21. Dante describes himself thus in the headings of four of his letters.
22. The Latin words are *equis armisque*. Anyone travelling was advised to ride accompanied and carrying arms.
23. Clement V (1305–1314), a native of Gascony. It was during his pontificate that the Papal see was transferred to Avignon.
24. *Paradiso* XVII, 69.
25. *Ibid.*, 55–69.
26. 1270?–1336. His full name was Guittoncino di Francesco dei Sigisbuldi.
27. 1314. *Readings in the Codex.*
28. See Chapter 2 of the present work. The sonnet in question is now attributed to Terino di Castelfiorentino.
29. *De Vulgari Eloquentia*, Book II, Chapter 6. See Chapter 5 of the present work.
30. It was founded in 1088.
31. *Purgatorio* XI, 73–84. See also Chapter 34 of the present work.

Chapter 5: Language and Poetry

1. Only three manuscripts of this work, which is unfinished, are known to exist. The work attracted little attention until 1529, when Gian Giorgio Trissino published an Italian translation of it, which was at first believed to be a fabrication. The Latin text was not published until 1577.
2. His poetry was already known in Bologna. Part of his *canzone* beginning *Donne ch'avete intelletto d'amore* had been copied into a Bolognese official document dating from 1292.
3. It is evident that Dante had no understanding of blindness. Blind people have 'facial vision', which prevents them from imagining that things in front of them are behind them.
4. *De Vulgari Eloquentia*, Book I, Chapter 1.
5. *Paradiso* XXVI, 124–138.
6. *De Vulgari Eloquentia*, Book I, Chapter 7. Compare this with Dante's description of Venetian sailors repairing their ships, *Inferno* XXI, 7–15.
7. *Ibid.*, Chapter 9.
8. Derived from the Latin *ille est*.
9. Derived from the Latin *hoc est*.
10. Derived from the Latin *sic*. It is said that Latin had no word for 'yes', but there were several ways of expressing the affirmative. Another form was *ita*, 'thus'.
11. *De Vulgari Eloquentia*, Book I, Chapter 11.
12. *Ibid.*
13. *Ibid.*

14. *Ibid.*, Chapter 13.

15. *Ibid.*, Chapter 15.

16. *Ibid.*, Chapter 14.

17. The Latin words of this phrase, *revolventes volumina*, evoke the image of an ancient scroll and also throw light on the words of Dante to Virgil in *Inferno* I, 84: *che m'ha fatto cercar il tuo volume*. This is usually translated as 'which has made me search thy volume', but the word *cercare* in mediaeval Italian (like *circare* in Vulgar Latin) was a term derived from hunting, referring to hounds closing in a circle upon their prey.

18. *De Vulgari Eloquentia*, Book I, Chapter 6.

19. *Ibid.*, Chapter 13.

20. Guittone of Arezzo (1230?–1294), a lyric and didactic poet, is the author of a lament on the defeat of the Florentine Guelfs at the Battle of Montaperti in 1260. Dante began by imitating his style but later disparaged him.

21. See Chapter 2 of the present work.

22. Gallo of Pisa was a contemporary of Bonagiunta of Lucca. Two of his *canzoni* are extant.

23. Mino Mocato of Siena has been identified with Bartolommeo Mocati, author of a *canzone* found in a manuscript in the Vatican.

24. *Inferno* XV. See also Chapter 17 of the present work.

25. The original Latin words are: *Transeuntes nunc humeros Apennini frondiferos*. It is interesting to find Dante speaking here of the shoulders of the mountains, as he was to do in *Inferno* I, 16–17.

26. Sonnet beginning *Per quella via che la bellezza corre*.

27. His dates are 1244–1278.

28. He is said to have been a nephew of the Fabbro mentioned in *Purgatorio* XIV, 100, a member of the Lambertazzi family, a noble and distinguished soldier, a wise man and prudent in counsel.

29. Onesto degli Onesti, known as Onesto Bolognese, was born in Bologna around 1240. He entered into a *tenzone* (an exchange of sonnets) with Cino da Pistoia.

30. *De Vulgari Eloquentia*, Book I, Chapter 16. It was believed that the panther by its fragrant breath attracted other animals to itself in order to devour them.

31. The Latin for hinge is *cardo*.

32. i.e. *De Vulgari Eloquentia*, Book II.

33. *Ibid.*, Book II, Chapter 1.

34. *Ibid.*

35. *Ibid.*

36. This is said to be the reason why no musical accompaniment is preserved in manuscripts of *ballate*.

37. *De Vulgari Eloquentia*, Book II, Chapter 2. See also Chapter 9 of the present work.

38. Dante's original is printed as *hoc opus et labor est*, probably a scribe's error, which has been perpetuated by modern editors.

39. *Aeneid* VI, 126–129.

40. *De Vulgari Eloquentia*, Book II, Chapter 6.

41. *Purgatorio* XIII, 73–74.

42. Frontinus, of the first century AD, was the author of a manual on the art of war, a

surprising work to find on Dante's reading list at this period.

43. In modern Italian the initial *h* is silent. In the Florentine accent a hard initial *c*, as in *casa*, is pronounced as an *h*. This cannot have been the case in Dante's time, otherwise he would have excluded it.

44. Shakespeare, *Love's Labour's Lost*, V, i.

45. *De Vulgari Eloquentia*, Book II, Chapter 9.

46. See Appendix 5 of the present work.

Chapter 6: Invitation to a Banquet

1. *Il Convivio*, Section I, Chapter 9.

2. *Ibid.*, Section IV, Chapter 6.

3. *Ibid.*, Chapter 25. The word *adorna* is the feminine form of the adjective *adorno*. It could also have been mistaken for a noun, a feminine object adorned.

4. *Ibid.*, Section I, Chapter 3.

5. Guittone of Arezzo had used his Aretine dialect in writing discourses and letters to public personages. Ristoro, also of Arezzo, wrote a treatise on astronomy in the same vernacular. Giamboni, a Florentine judge, translated works from Latin and French into Florentine.

6. *Il Convivio*, Section I, Chapter 11.

7. *Ibid.*, Chapter 5.

8. See Chapter 5 of the present work.

9. The possibility that such aliens might understand Italian does not occur to him.

10. *Il Convivio*, Section I, Chapter 7. It would seem that Dante believed that the poems of Homer were composed to be sung.

11. *Ibid.*, Chapter 9.

12. *Ibid.*, Chapter 12.

13. See Chapter 3 of the present work.

14. *Paradiso* VIII, 37.

15. Perhaps because she was still alive.

16. See Chapter 2 of the present work.

17. *La Vita Nuova*, Chapter XLII.

18. See also Chapter 2 of the present work.

19. Mystical or spiritual.

20. See Chapter 43 of the present work.

21. *Il Convivio*, Section III, Chapter 9. Dante was probably suffering the results of uncorrected presbyopia (a decreasing ability of the lens to focus). I am indebted for this diagnosis to Mr John Keast-Butler, FRCS, who wrote: 'Normal-sighted patients are universally presbyopic enough to have anything from moderate to serious difficulties with close work by the age of 45 or so. Dante seems to me to describe very accurately what uncorrected presbyopia is like.'

22. He was born at Fergana (in Samarkand), from which his name was derived.

23. There are 20 manuscript copies of this text in Oxford (in the Bodleian Library and in various college libraries), three in the Cambridge University Library and one in the British Library.

24. See cover illustration.

25. *Inferno* I, 72.

26. i.e. Beatrice, of whom he says it is not his purpose to speak further in *Il Convivio*.

27. *Inferno* II, 94–105. Lucia is the celebrated Santa Lucia, whose body has recently been transferred from Venice to Naples, where she lives on in the famous song.

28. *Purgatorio* XIX, 25–30.

29. *Paradiso* XXXII, 136–138. See also Chapter 53 of the present work.

Chapter 7: Main Dishes and Trenchers

1. See Chapter 6 of the present work.

2. *Purgatorio* II, 105–133.

3. See end of Chapter 6 of the present work.

4. *Purgatorio* IV, 58–84.

5. Lines 27–29, 55–56, 59–62 of the *canzone*.

6. See Chapter 6 of the present work.

7. Lines 71–72 of the *canzone*.

8. *Inferno* II, 97–100.

9. See Chapter 2 of the present work.

10. See Chapter 3 of the present work.

11. Grandson of Frederick Barbarossa and son of the Emperor Henry VI and Constance of Sicily, he was elected Emperor in 1212. He died in 1250. Known as the *stupor mundi* ('the wonder of the world'), he was admired for his dedication to the advancement of learning, sciences and arts. His opinion, therefore, was worthy of respect.

12. See Chapter 5 of the present work.

13. *Il Convivio*, Section IV, Chapter 17. It is strange that Dante does not know (or has forgotten) that the Emperor Frederick II derived his definition of nobility from the supreme authority, Aristotle: 'ancient wealth and virtue' (*Politics*).

14. *Inferno* IV, 131–133.

15. *Il Convivio*, Section IV, Chapter 4.

16. *Ars Poetica*: *Omne tulit punctum qui miscuit utile dulci,/Lectorem delectando pariterque monendo* ('He has gained every vote who has mingled profit with pleasure by equally delighting the reader and instructing him').

17. Proverbs VIII, 6.

18. *Il Convivio*, Section IV, Chapter 5.

19. *Ibid.*

20. *Ibid.*

21. See Chapter 42 of the present work.

22. *Paradiso* VI, 34–111. See also Chapter 45 of the present work.

23. Chapter I, 1.

24. *Paradiso* XVIII, 88–93. See also Chapter 47 of the present work.

25. *Inferno*, XXXIII, 136–147. See also Chapter 27 of the present work.

26. *Il Convivio*, Section IV, Chapter 9.

Chapter 8: The True Definition of Nobility

1. A central peak in the Tuscan Apennines, north-east of Florence. In Roman law, under rules formulated during the reign of the Emperor Hadrian, those who found buried treasure by chance were permitted to take half of it, sharing with the owner of the land upon which it was found, so long as they announced the find. In contrast those who deliberately sought buried treasure on another's land could

not obtain any right to it: all went to the owner of the land. Historically the rule was probably established in order to encourage chance finds to be reported (so that the owner of the land could get something). In Dante's terms it means that only chance and not deliberate labour produces such results.

2. *Il Convivio*, Section IV, Chapter 12. By the *cominciamenti* Dante is probably referring to the Ten Commandments (Exodus 20, 15 and 17: Thou shalt not steal. Thou shalt not covet) and the Twelve Tables of Roman Law (451BC), from which respectively the idea of canon and civil law arose.

3. *Inferno* I, 100–105. See Chapter 12 of the present work for an interpretation of their meaning.

4. *Il Convivio*, Section IV, Chapter 12.

5. *Inferno* I, 1–3.

6. *Il Convivio*, Section IV, Chapter 24.

7. *Inferno* I, 31–60.

8. *De Consolatione Philosophiae*, Book IV, Prose 3.

9. *Il Convivio*, Section IV, Chapter 12.

10. See Chapter 9 of the present work.

11. *Purgatorio* XVI, 121–126, 133–138.

12. Lines 74–75 of the *canzone*.

13. *Purgatorio* VIII, 61–63.

14. *Il Convivio*, Section IV, Chapter 15.

15. St Thomas's words are: *Totam Naturam divinam se reputant suo intellectu posse metiri* ('They consider that all Nature can be measured by their intellect').

16. There is a delightful glimpse of such a person in E.M. Forster's short story, 'Other Kingdom': '"Surely" – said Miss Beaumont. She had been learning Latin for not quite a fortnight, but she would have corrected the Regius Professor.'

17. Mediaeval lawyers divided the text of the *Digest* into three parts of which the second was called 'Infortiatum'.

18. The law quoted by Dante is D.28.1.2: *In eo qui testatur, ejus temporis quo testamentum facit, integratis mentis, non sanitas corporis exigenda est.*

19. Psalm 8, I, 4–6.

20. *Il Convivio*, Section IV, Chapter 19.

21. *Ibid.*, Chapter 21. The quotation is from St Paul's Epistle to the Romans, XI, 33.

22. *Purgatorio* XXV, 37–60. See also Chapter 39 of the present work.

23. *Paradiso* XXVII, 88.

24. Isaiah XI, 2.

25. *Il Convivio*, Section IV, Chapter 21.

26. i.e. impulse. Dante uses this word twice, as though pleased with his knowledge of it.

27. For the last two quotations, *Il Convivio*, Section IV, Chapter 22.

28. Dante himself must have had a guardian after the death of his father. Who it was we do not know. Brunetto Latini is a possibility. There is an apparent anomaly in the fact that adolescents who are under restriction until 25 are deemed old enough to be punished at 14. The explanation lies in the various legal limitations in play. From infancy (defined as 0–7 in Roman law) until the age of puberty (14 for boys and 12 for girls) a minor is presumed incapable. From 14 to 25 he is competent in criminal and civil law, but until he reaches 25 he can be relieved from the effects of

a bad bargain if the transaction is not overseen by a guardian.

29. *Il Convivio*, Section IV, Chapter 25.

30. For the last two quotations, *ibid.*, Chapter 26.

31. Lucan said of Cato: 'It was the unswerving rule of the rigid Cato ... not to believe himself born for himself but for all the world' (*Pharsalia* II, 383). See also below concerning Cato and the Mountain of Purgatory.

32. *Il Convivio*, Section IV, Chapter 27.

33. *Ibid.* He has already said that in the same penultimate section he will deal with the question why poets chose to conceal their true meaning in allegory (Section II, Chapter 1).

34. *De Senectute*, Chapter 19.

35. A Mediterranean craft of the sort Dante had in mind had a large lateen which was let down when not in use. Large Atlantic ships have square sails which are furled up when not in use.

36. *Il Convivio*, Section IV, Chapter 28.

37. For the last two quotations, *ibid.*

38. *Inferno* XXVII, 79–81. See also Chapter 24 of the present work.

39. See Chapter 48 of the present work.

40. *Pharsalia* II.

41. *Il Convivio*, Section IV, Chapter 28. In *Purgatorio* Dante introduces Cato as the stern guardian of the lower slopes of the mountain. See Chapter 30 of the present work.

Chapter 9: Injustice and Avarice

1. *Il Convivio*, Section I, Chapter 18.

2. *De Vulgari Eloquentia*, Book II, Chapter 2.

3. See Chapters 11 and 40 of the present work.

Chapter 10: Dante the Showman

1. A district in the north-west of Tuscany, between the Apennines and the border of Liguria, ruled over in Dante's time by the Malaspina family.

2. *Inferno* XV, 110. He lived from 1225 to 1294. A renowned professor of jurisprudence at Bologna University, he was also invited to teach at Oxford.

3. *Ibid.*, XVIII, 48–61.

4. *Ibid.*, XXIII, 103–104.

5. See Chapter 3 of the present work. Cavalcanti may have taken refuge with the Malaspina family, as Dante did.

6. Formerly an Etruscan town, on the left bank of the river Macra, in ruins in Dante's time, though the episcopal see was named after it.

7. *Purgatorio* VIII, 121–129.

8. *Inferno* XXIV, 145.

9. See Chapter 1 of the present work.

10. *Ibid.*

11. See Figure 4. For an English translation of a Latin version see Montague Rhodes James, *The Apocryphal New Testament, Apocalypse of Paul*, Oxford, Clarendon, 1924, pp 525–555. See also Alison Morgan, *Dante and the Medieval Other World*, Cambridge University Press, 1990.

12. Dante uses this image in *Purgatorio*, in the purgation of the gluttons (Canto XXII).
13. *Aeneid* VI.
14. i.e. St Paul.
15. *Inferno* II, 32
16. cf. the ghost in *Hamlet*.
17. *Inferno* II, 73–75.
18. *Ibid.*, I, 79–80.
19. *Ibid.*, 89.
20. *Ibid.*, III, 21.

Chapter 11: The Return of Beatrice

1. See Dorothy L. Sayers in *Introductory Papers on Dante*, 'The Fourfold Interpretation of the *Comedy*', Methuen, 1954, p 109.
2. *Inferno* X, 127–133.
3. See Chapter 46 of the present work.
4. *Inferno* II, 70.
5. *Ibid.*, 105.
6. *La Vita Nuova*, Chapter XLI.
7. *Ibid.*, Chapter XLII.
8. *Ibid.*, Chapter XLI.
9. See Chapter 44 of the present work.
10. *Ibid.*
11. *Ibid.*
12. *Paradiso* XXX, 16–33 (Sayers' translation).
13. *Ibid.*, XXXI 79–90.
14. See Chapter 40 of the present work.

Chapter 12: The Story Begins

1. *De Vulgari Eloquentia*. See Chapter 5 of the present work.
2. *Ibid.*
3. *Inferno* I, 97–99.
4. *Ibid.*, 100–105.
5. See Chapter 8 of the present work.
6. *Ibid.*
7. *Il Convivio*, Section IV, Chapter 4. See also Chapter 8 of the present work.
8. *Ibid.*, Chapter 12. See also Chapter 8 of the present work.
9. The technological information which follows was provided by George McCandless in a letter to *The Times Literary Supplement*, 12 July 2002, p 17, replying to an article by the present author, 'Dante De-Felted: A Solution to a 700-Year-Old Mystery', *ibid.*, 21 June 2002, p 16. For further information, see Dard Hunter, *Papermaking: The History and Technique of an Ancient Craft*. See also Arsenio Frugoni, 'Il canto XXXIII del *Purgatorio*' in *Nuove letture dantesche*, V (1969–1970), Florence, Le Monnier, 1972, pp 235–253: 'La carta, chi non lo sa, tra feltro e feltro viene fabbricata', p 241.
10. *Il Convivio*, Section III, Chapter 9 (italics added). See also Chapter 6 of the present work.

11. *Inferno* I, 136.
12. *Inferno* II, 121–126.
13. *Ibid.*, 127–130.
14. *Ibid.*, 140.

Chapter 13: Limbo

1. *Inferno* III, 1–9.
2. *Ibid.*, 18. In *Il Convivio* Dante quotes Aristotle as saying, 'Truth is the good of the intellect'.
3. Francesco Botticini (1446–1498). The painting is in the National Gallery, London.
4. A line which T.S. Eliot absorbed into *The Waste Land*: 'A crowd flowed over London Bridge, so many/I had not thought death had undone so many.'
5. See Chapter 3 of the present work.
6. *Inferno* III, 51.
7. *Ibid.*, III, 84–87.
8. *Ibid.*, 88–89.
9. *Ibid.*, 94–96.
10. *Ibid.*, 102–107.
11. *Inferno* IV, 22.
12. See Chapter 47 of the present work.
13. *Inferno* IV, 46–50.
14. *Ibid.*, 52–54.
15. *Ibid.*, 80–81.
16. *Ibid.*, 100–102.
17. *Aeneid* VI, 637–665.
18. *Il Convivio*, Section IV, Chapter 11.
19. See Chapter 8 of the present work.
20. See Chapter 47 of the present work.

Chapter 14: Francesca da Rimini

1. As in St Andrew's Church, East Chesterton, Cambridge, England.
2. *Inferno* V, 11–15.
3. *Ibid.*, 19–20.
4. *Ibid.*, 23–24.
5. *Ibid.*, 43–45.
6. Dante had read of her in *Histories Against the Pagans* by Orosius, from which he is here quoting.
7. In Homer's *Iliad*, Achilles was killed at the siege of Troy, but according to a later tradition, which Dante follows here, he became enamoured of Polyxena, daughter of King Priam, and was promised her hand on condition that he joined the Trojans. Tricked by this promise he entered a Trojan temple unarmed and was assassinated by Paris.
8. *Inferno* V, 97–99.
9. See Chapters 2 and 39 of the present work.
10. *Inferno* V, 118–120.
11. *Ibid.*, 121–123.
12. *Ibid.*, 127–138.

13. *Ibid.*, 142.

14. *Ibid.*, 107.

15. Gianciotto is not mentioned as being awaited in the Circle of Caina when Dante reaches it. See Chapter 27 of the present work.

16. But see Chapter 43 of the present work.

17. He died in 1304, predeceasing his father and his eldest brother.

18. See Chapter 42 of the present work.

Chapter 15: Dante in Danger

1. *Inferno* VI, 14, 18.

2. *Purgatorio* XXV. See also Chapter 39 of the present work.

3. See *Inferno* X for Farinata's foreknowledge. See also Chapter 3 of the present work.

4. *Purgatorio* VI, 76–151.

5. See Chapter 49 of the present work.

6. *Inferno* VII, 1. The archaic Tuscan verb *leppare* meant to remove or to escape.

7. In Greek mythology Phlegyas was a king of Boeotia, the son of Mars by a human mother. His daughter Coronis was loved by Apollo, and Phlegyas in a rage set fire to Apollo's temple (*Aeneid* VI, 618).

8. Luke XI, 27: 'Blessed is the womb that bare thee.'

9. *Inferno* VIII, 59–60 (italics added).

10. In Greek mythology Dis was another name for Hades and for the King of the Underworld, also known as Pluto. Here the name is limited to Nether Hell, distinguished from the upper circles by the fact that the sins punished are those in which the will is actively involved. See *Inferno* XI and Chapter 16 of the present work.

11. *Inferno* VIII, 102.

12. *Pharsalia* VI, 508–830.

13. *Aeneid* VI, 564–565.

14. Theseus, King of Athens, tried to rescue Persephone from Hades. He failed but if the Furies had killed him then other living men would have been deterred from entering the Underworld.

15. *Inferno* IX, 61–63. See also Chapter 8 of the present work.

16. *Purgatorio* VIII, 19–21.

17. *Inferno* IX, 91–99. Hercules, as the last of his labours, brought Cerberus out of Hell, damaging his throat as he did so.

Chapter 16: Dante the Taxonomist

1. See Chapter 3 of the present work.

2. *Inferno* XVII, 64–75.

3. *Ibid.*, XI, 76–78.

4. An example of 'mystic addition' is 19 = 1 + 9 = 10. See also Chapter 2 of the present work.

5. See William Anderson, *Dante the Maker*, Routledge and Kegan Paul, 1980, pp 284–286.

6. See K.R. Imeson, *The Magic of Number*, printed privately, distributed by the Mathematical Association, Chapters III and IV. See also David Well, *The Penguin Dictionary of Curious and Interesting Numbers*, Penguin, 1987.

Chapter 17: Creation of Character

1. See Chapter 3 of the present work.
2. Arles in Provence, where many ancient tombs were said to contain the bodies of Charlemagne's soldiers killed in battle against the Saracens at Aleschans; Pola, on the Adriatic coast, was said to contain about 700 tombs of Slavonians.
3. *Inferno* XIII, 4–6.
4. *Ibid.*, 31–33.
5. In the *Aeneid* (III, 22 et seq.) Aeneas relates to Dido that soon after setting out from Troy he came upon a mound on which cornel and myrtle bushes were growing. Wishing to place some boughs upon an altar he began to tear up the shrubs. From the roots black blood trickled and a piteous groan was heard from the mound and the words: 'Alas! Aeneas, why do you ravage me?' The voice is that of the soul of Polydorus.
6. *Inferno* XIII, 55–72. The *meretrice* ('harlot') is slander.
7. *Ibid.*, 73–75.
8. Cato of Utica, the Stoic who killed himself rather than accept the rule of Caesar, is seen by Dante as a man of great nobility, whose soul he entrusts with the guardianship of the lower reaches of the Mountain of Purgatory.
9. *Inferno* XV, 30. The title *Ser* is an abbreviation of *Messer*, which was a customary form of address to a notary.
10. It has been interpreted, for instance, as blasphemy towards the Italian language because Brunetto wrote his principal work in French. It is said that there is no evidence that he was a sodomite. It is also pointed out that in his Italian work, *Il Tesoretto*, he condemns sodomy as one of the worst sins. Neither objection rules out the possibility that he was guilty of it himself.
11. *Inferno* XV, 55–60.
12. Fiesole is on a hill about three miles north-east of Florence. It was one of the 12 Etruscan towns.
13. See Cacciaguida's words on the same subject in *Paradiso* XVII. See also Chapter 46 of the present work.
14. *Inferno* XV, 79–87.
15. *Ibid.*, 119–120.
16. The greeting and departure of Brunetto are echoed in the episode of Forese Donati in *Purgatorio* XXIII. See Chapter 38 of the present work.

Chapter 18: Down into the Depths

1. *Inferno* I, 77.
2. *Ibid.*, XVI, 109–111 (italics added).
3. *Purgatorio* I. See also Chapter 30 of the present work.
4. *Inferno* XV, 8.
5. *Esposizioni*, Canto XVI.
6. *Cronica* XII, 4.
7. Apart, that is, from the mention of the hem of his garment which Brunetto Latini seizes, and Cato's command concerning the rush. In *De Vulgari Eloquentia* Dante had commented on the variations in dress from region to region. (See Chapter 5 of the present work.)
8. *Inferno* XVI, 12.

9. See below in this chapter.

10. *Inferno* XVI, 38–40.

11. Boccaccio, in his *Esposizioni*, says that Guglielmo was a maker of purses (hence his name Borsiere, from *borsa*, a purse), who later became a broker of marriages and other alliances. He made him the subject of a story in his *Decamerone* (Day 1, Tale 8).

12. *Inferno* XVI, 45.

13. Dante's son Pietro, commenting on this simile, explains that the beaver agitates the water with its tail, exuding drops of fat and oil, thereby attracting fish. Dante believed the beaver to be a creature of northern Europe.

14. Said to be an ancestor of Enrico Scrovegni. See Chapter 16 of the present work.

15. See Chapter 15 of the present work.

16. *Inferno* XVIII, 63.

17. Epistle VI, from Hypsipyle to Jason.

18. *Inferno* XVIII, 95.

19. *Ibid.*, 100–136.

20. *Ibid.*, 136.

Chapter 19: 'Him of Alagna'

1. See Chapters 3 and 4 of the present work.

2. See Chapter 48 of the present work.

3. *Inferno* XIX, 17. See also Chapter 1 of the present work.

4. *Ibid.*, 46–48.

5. Dante believed that Boniface VIII had guilefully persuaded Pope Celestine V to abdicate.

6. The Italian word *orsa* means a she-bear.

7. *Inferno* XXVII, 67–111.

8. See also Chapter 24 of the present work.

9. Acts VIII, 9–24.

10. *Inferno* XIX, 88–89. Dante's use of the disjunctive pronoun *lui* is equivalent to putting it into italics: he is, after all, addressing a former Pope.

11. i.e. Judas (Acts I, 13–26).

12. *Inferno* XIX, 104–111.

13. *Ibid.*, 115–117. The *primo ricco patre* ('first rich father') was Pope Sylvester, believed to have cured Constantine of leprosy, in return for which Constantine endowed the Church with Imperial dominion in the west when he removed his government to Byzantium.

14. See Chapter 42 of the present work.

Chapter 20: Virgil and Sorcery

1. *Inferno* XX, 16–18.

2. *Ibid.*, 26–27.

3. *Thebaid* VIII, 147 et seq.

4. *Inferno* XX, 37–39.

5. *Metamorphoses* III, Fable 5, lines 324–331.

6. *Pharsalia* I, 584–638.

7. *Aeneid* X, 198–200.

8. *Inferno* XX, 61–66. Mount Apennine is not the Apennine range but a spur of the Rhoetian Alps, near Lake Garda (formerly Benaco).

9. The three dioceses of Trent, Brescia and Verona meet on an island in the lake.

10. *Inferno* XX, 97–99.

11. *Aeneid* II, 114–119.

12. *Inferno* XX, 115.

13. *Il Convivio*, Section IV, Chapter 16.

14. As did Hitler, it has been said. The same has also been alleged of Ronald Reagan.

15. *Aeneid* X, 198–200.

16. *Inferno* IX, 23.

17. See Chapter 10 of the present work.

18. *Inferno* XX, 100–102.

19. *Inferno* XXI, 1–3.

20. See Chapter 13 of the present work.

Chapter 21: Devil-Play

1. *Inferno* XXI, 7–15. This may be a sly allusion to corruption in Venice.

2. 'Evil-Claws' is a translation of *Malebranche*, which is the collective name of the devils in the fifth ditch. St Zita is the patron saint of Lucca. A maidservant, she died in about 1275 and her body is preserved in a tomb in a chapel of the church of San Frediano.

3. The reference to Bonturo (Dati) is sarcastic, for he was renowned for his corruption. He was still alive in 1300, so the implication is that the demon will be ready for him when the time comes.

4. *Inferno* XXI, 42. The word *ita*, meaning 'yes', is a Latinism for the more usual Italian word *sì*. It seems to have been current usage in Lucca.

5. The Holy Face (*Santo Volto*) is a crucifix carved in cedar wood. It was believed to have been begun by Nicodemus, who fell asleep and woke to find the work miraculously completed. It was said to have been transferred from the Holy Land to Lucca in 782. The people of Lucca offered prayers and oblations to it when in trouble. The words of the demon are thus particularly offensive.

6. The Serchio is a river near Lucca.

7. *Inferno* XXI, 55–57.

8. *Ibid.*, XVIII 115–126. See Chapter 18 of the present work.

9. See Chapter 29 of the present work.

10. *Purgatorio* XXIV, 37–48.

11. *Inferno* XXI, 62–63.

12. *Ibid.*, IX 22–27. See Chapter 15 of the present work.

13. *Ibid.*, XXI 87–89.

14. The Pisan fortress of Caprona was seized by Tuscan Guelfs in 1289. The implication is that Dante was among the besiegers.

15. This was mentioned by Virgil as having heralded Christ's entry into Hell and caused the landslide between the Sixth and Seventh Circles (Canto XII, 34–45).

16. See Chapter 4 of the present work.

17. *Inferno* XXI, 125–126.

18. *Ibid.*, XXII, 13–15. Lines 14–15 contain what sounds like a proverbial expression.

19. Count Thibaut V of Champagne, King Thibaut II of Navarre from 1253 to 1270.

20. Dante did not consider Sardinians to be Italians and said that when their own language died out they took to imitating Latin like apes. (See Chapter 5 of the present work.) Sardinia, occupied by Saracens for several centuries, was later under the control of Pisa.

21. Fra Gomita of Gallura, a province of Sardinia, was appointed deputy by Nino Visconti of Pisa and hanged for corruption. Michele Zanche, Governor of Logoduro, another Sardinian province, was murdered by his son-in-law, Branca d'Oria, a scandal to which Dante refers later (*Inferno* XXVIII). What Michele's peculations and pilfering amounted to is not known.

22. *Inferno* XXII, 118. It is interesting that Dante here uses an address to the 'reader', who is also a listener.

23. In a fable, which Dante here attributes to Aesop, a frog offers to carry a mouse across a pond, tied to its leg. Half-way across the frog dives and drowns the mouse. A hawk swoops down and devours them both. In one version, the mouse escapes.

24. *Inferno* XXIII, 37–51.

25. The monks of Cluny were said to wear lavish robes. Some editors read Cologne, of which a similar charge was made.

26. The Emperor Frederick II is said to have punished traitors by having them encased in lead and thrown into a cauldron.

27. *Inferno* XXIII, 67.

28. *Ibid.*, 77–79.

29. *Ibid.*, 91–93.

30. *Ibid.*, 94–96.

31. See Chapter 3 of the present work.

32. John XI, 49–50.

33. *Inferno* XXIII, 148.

Chapter 22: A Den of Thieves

1. *Inferno* XXIV, 1–18.

2. *Ibid.*, 31–33.

3. *Pharsalia* IX, 708–733.

4. A precious stone, a chalcedony, believed to render the bearer invisible.

5. *Inferno* XXIV, 106–111.

6. *Metamorphoses* XV, 392–402.

7. *Inferno* XXIV, 124–126. Vanni Fucci was the illegitimate son of Fucci de' Lazzari, of a noble family of Pistoia. Dante takes a sly dig at his illegitimacy by making him call himself a mule, the hybrid of a horse and an ass.

8. *Ibid.*, 151.

9. *Inferno* XXV, 1–3. The gesture called 'the figs' is made by placing the tip of the thumb between the first two fingers, in imitation of the male genitals.

10. Seen in Canto XIV, 43–72.

11. Cacus was a giant in mythology, not a centaur. Virgil calls him 'semi-human' and this may have misled Dante. He stole the oxen of Geryon which Hercules was bringing from Spain as one of his 12 labours, and dragged them backwards to his den, leaving a misleading set of hoof-prints. Hercules heard them bellowing, killed Cacus and recovered the herd.

12. Maremma was a swampy district along the coast of Tuscany.

13. *Inferno* XXV, 58–66.
14. *Ibid.*, 68–69.
15. *Ibid.*, 78.
16. *Metamorphoses* IV, 361–379.
17. *Inferno* XXV, 94–99.
18. *Ibid.*, 79–87 (Sayers' translation).
19. *Ibid.*, 132.

Chapter 23: Tongues of Fire

1. *Inferno* XXVI, 1–12.
2. See also Chapter 29 of the present work.
3. *Inferno* XXVI, 25–32.
4. 2 Kings II, 11–12, 23–24.
5. *Aeneid* II, 162–168.
6. *Inferno* XXVI, 64–69.
7. *Ibid.*, 73–75.
8. This was first noticed by Dorothy L. Sayers. See her article, 'The Eighth Bolgia', first delivered as a lecture in August 1946 (*Further Papers on Dante*, Methuen, 1957, pp 102–118).
9. *Inferno* XXVI, 79–84.
10. *Ibid.*, 88–93.
11. Guillaume de Conches, quoted by J.L. Lowes, *The Road to Xanadu*, Constable, 1951, p 118.
12. *Inferno* XXVI, 94–99.
13. *Ibid.*, 106.
14. *Ibid.*, 118–120.
15. *Ibid.*, 139–142.
16. *Ibid.*, 21–24.
17. My discovery of Dante's source of his tale of the last voyage of Ulysses was first published in 1960: 'Dante's Tale of Ulysses', *Annali dell'Istituto Universitario Orientale, Sezione Romanza*, Naples, pp 49–65.

Chapter 24: The Severed Head

1. *Inferno* XXVII, 21.
2. There are three exceptions to this: in *Purgatorio* XXVI, 140–147 Arnaut Daniel speaks in Provençal, in XXXIII, 20–22 Beatrice speaks in Latin and in *Paradiso* XV, 28–30 Dante's ancestor Cacciaguida greets him in Latin.
3. See Chapter 19 of the present work.
4. *Purgatorio* V, 85–129.
5. *Inferno* XXVIII, 1–6.
6. *Ibid.*, 22–27.
7. *Ibid.*, 30–33. Ali, the son-in-law of Mahomet, was the leader of a schism within the followers of the Prophet himself.
8. The Apostolic Brothers preached communal ownership of property and women. Fra Dolcino was burned alive in 1307.
9. *Inferno* XXVIII, 76–90.
10. Caius Scribonius Curio, said by Lucan to have urged Julius Caesar to cross the

Rubicon and so declare war on the Republic.

11. Bertran de Born (*c.*1140–1215), a Provençal troubadour and warrior.
12. 2 Samuel, XV–XVII.
13. *Inferno* XXVIII, 118–123.
14. *Il Convivio*, Section IV, Chapter 11.
15. *De Vulgari Eloquentia*, Book II, Chapter 2.

Chapter 25: The Valley of Disease

1. *Inferno* XXIX, 40–45 (Sayers' translation).
2. Valdichiana is the valley of the river Chiana in Tuscany, then a district infected with malaria, especially in the summer months. The same was true of the Maremma, a wild marshy region along the coast of Tuscany. Concerning the island of Sardinia, of which Dante had no personal experience, early commentators said that the air was pestilential and that few travellers to the island survived there for more than a year.
3. *Metamorphoses* VII, 523–657.
4. *Inferno* XXIX, 74.
5. *Metamorphoses* X, 298 et seq.
6. Probably the spring that once rose near the castle of Romena.
7. Identified as Aghinolfo.
8. i.e. Guido, who died in 1292. Counterfeiting or corrupting the currency was seen as a serious crime because it damaged confidence in the State.
9. Genesis XXIX, 6–23.
10. *Inferno* XXX, 131–132.
11. *Ibid.*, 142–148.

Chapter 26: Towering Giants

1. *La Chanson de Roland.* When Charlemagne was returning from fighting the Saracens in Spain, his rearguard, led by his nephew Roland, was slaughtered at the Pass of Roncevaux in the Pyrenees. With his last breath Roland blew his ivory horn so loud that Charlemagne heard it eight miles away.
2. *Inferno* XXI, 28–33.
3. Built in 1213 to defend the commune against the attacks of the Florentines and furnished with 14 towers between 1260 and 1270. The towers are now reduced almost to the level of the castle wall.
4. It is now in the Vatican.
5. Genesis III, 7.
6. Genesis VI, 4. Dante would have read these words in the Latin of the Vulgate: *Gigantes autem erant super terram in diebus illis.* St Augustine and St Thomas of Aquinas also refer to giants.
7. *De Civitate Dei* XVI, 3.
8. *De Vulgari Eloquentia*, Book I, Chapter 7. See also Chapter 5 of the present work.
9. *Inferno* XXXI, 67.
10. For the building of the Tower of Babel and the consequent confusion of tongues, see Genesis XI.
11. *Inferno* XXXI, 70–81.
12. *Aeneid* VI, 582–584.

13. *Carmina* III, 4, 51–52.
14. *Inferno* XXXI, 85–90.
15. *Pharsalia* IV, 596.
16. *Thebaid* II, 596.
17. i.e. in Ovid's greater work, *Metamorphoses*.
18. *Il Convivio*, Book IX, 183–184.
19. *Inferno* XXXI, 115–123, 126.
20. Ibid., 134
21. Ibid., 142–145.

Chapter 27: The Frozen Lake

1. See also *Inferno* XXVI and Chapter 23 of the present work for a reference to the hatred between Polynices and Eteocles.
2. *Inferno* XXXII, 4–5.
3. Ibid., 19–21.
4. Printed in some editions as feminine rhymes in *-icche*.
5. *Inferno* XXXII, 25–30.
6. King Arthur killed his treacherous nephew Mordred with a single blow of his lance which let light through his body and his shadow.
7. *Inferno* XXXII, 58–66. Focaccia, of Pistoia, a traitor.
8. *Inferno* IV, 56.
9. Ibid., V, 107.
10. See Chapter 14 of the present work.
11. *Inferno* XXXII, 70–72.
12. Ibid., 106–108.
13. Ibid., 85–87.
14. He who betrayed the cause of Charlemagne and brought about the defeat and death of Roland at Roncevaux.
15. *Inferno* VIII. See Chapter 15 of the present work.
16. *Thebaid* VIII, 740–763
17. *Inferno* XXXIII, 1–9.
18. Ibid., V, 121–126.
19. *Aeneid* II, 3–13.
20. *Inferno* XXXIII, 40–42. Dante here dissociates the image of the wolf from the she-wolf which represents avarice in *Inferno* I.
21. Ibid., 51.
22. Ibid., 61–63.
23. Ibid., 64–66.
24. Ibid., 75.
25. Ibid., 76–78. It has been reported recently that the body of Ugolino della Gherardesca has been exhumed. Examination indicates that his last meals were of coarse bread only.
26. In *De Vulgari Eloquentia* Dante had defined Provençal, French and Italian according to their affirmatives, as, respectively, the language of *oc*, the language of *oïl* and the language of *sì*. See Chapter 5 of the present work.
27. Two islands near the mouth of the Arno, then belonging to Pisa.
28. *Inferno* XXXIII, 79–84.

29. *Ibid.*, XXXIV, 138–139.
30. 1 Maccabees, XVI.
31. *Inferno* XXXIII, 115–117.
32. *Ibid.*, 118–120.
33. Of the Manfredi family of Faenza, he was a member of the *Frati Gaudenti* ('Jovial Friars'), who have been mentioned in *Inferno* XXV.
34. *Inferno* XXXIII, 139–141.
35. *Ibid.*, XXII, 88–89. See also Chapter 21 of the present work.
36. *Ibid.*, XXXIII, 150.
37. *Ibid.*, 151–153.

Chapter 28: Lucifer

1. *Inferno* XXXIV, 1–3.
2. *Ibid.*, 18.
3. This is the classical name for the King of the Underworld, called by Dante Beelzebub, Lucifer and Satan. It is also the name for Hades, as Dante uses it in *Inferno* VIII.
4. *Inferno* XXXIV, 22–27.
5. *Ibid.*, 34–36. See Figure 6.
6. i.e. it is about 7.30 pm.
7. *Inferno* XXXIV, 68–69.
8. *Ibid.*, 82–84.
9. *Ibid.*, 91–93. The protruding legs of Lucifer recall the legs of the Simonists in Canto XIX.
10. *Ibid.*, 94–96. Terce, the first of the four canonical divisions of the day, lasted from sunrise (6 am at the equinox) until 9 am. The time was therefore about 7.30 am.
11. See Chapter 27 of the present work.
12. *Inferno* XXXIV, 133–139.

Chapter 29: The Tragedy of Henry VII

1. There were seven Electors to the office of Emperor: the Prince-Bishops of Trier, Mainz and Cologne, the Duke of Saxony, the Count-Palatine of the Rhine, the Margrave of Brandenburg and the King of Bohemia.
2. By his nephew, from whom he had wrongfully withheld inheritance.
3. Robert, Duke of Calabria, the third son of Charles II of Anjou and Naples, was King of Naples from 1309 to 1343. As a leader of the Guelfs he opposed Henry VII, who proclaimed him a rebellious vassal.
4. So called because it was reinforced by a band of iron and constructed so that it could be folded.
5. *Il Convivio*, Section IV, Chapter 4. See also Chapter 7 of the present work.
6. Epistola VII, paragraph 2, addressed to the Emperor. The 'tribute of Dante's lips' signifies a kiss on the ground before the Emperor's feet.
7. The 'princes' were the King of Sicily (Frederick II of Aragon) and the King of Naples (Robert of Anjou).
8. The *cursus* is the rhetorical term for the metrical arrangement of the ending of clauses and sentences in classical Latin prose. The mediaeval *cursus*, descended from the classical, is accentual and rhythmical, instead of being metrical, as in the

prosa numerosa of Cicero. (See *The Letters of Dante*, ed. Paget Toynbee, Oxford, Clarendon, 1966, pp 224–247.)

9. *Il Convivio*, Section I, Chapter 9.

10. See Chapter 10 of the present work.

11. They are said to have been written by Dante on behalf of the Countess, for whom he acted as secretary. All three, in Latin, are ceremonious replies to epistles from the Empress. Margaret of Brabant, daughter of John I, Duke of Brabant, married Henry, Count of Luxembourg, in 1292. On his election she accompanied her husband on his campaign in Italy and died at Genoa on 14 December 1311, where she is buried.

12. The tradition that the Lombards were of Scandinavian origin was recorded by Paulus Diaconus in his *Historia Longobardorum*, a work which Dante knew.

13. Epistola V, paragraph 8.

14. Matthew XXII, 21.

15. 'Then saith Pilate unto him, "Speakest thou not unto me? Knowest thou not that I have power to crucify thee, and have power to release thee?" Jesus answered, "Thou couldest have no power at all against me, except it were given thee from above."' (John XIX, 10–11).

16. 'Honour all men. Love the brotherhood. Fear God. Honour the king' (Peter I, ii, 17).

17. Epistola V, paragraph 10.

18. The Latin adjective *scelestus*, used here in the superlative, has a very strong denunciatory meaning.

19. Epistola VI, paragraph 5.

20. See Chapter 8 of the present work.

21. Dante at first regarded the sun, the greater light, as the symbol of Papal power, and the moon, the lesser light, as the symbol of Empire. He later reversed this view in his political treatise *Monarchia*.

22. Epistola VI, paragraph 4.

23. Epistola VII, paragraph 2.

24. See Chapter 42 of the present work.

25. See Chapter 4 of the present work.

26. For further information, see W.M. Bowsky, *Henry VII in Italy*.

Chapter 30: Better Waters

1. *Inferno* XIX, 82–87. Pope Clement V, who came from Gascony ('the west'), had intrigued with Philip IV to gain election to the Papacy (then in Avignon), as Jason had bribed Antiochus Epiphanes to make him High Priest. In a nice touch of editing, Dante distinguishes between the two Jasons, as though to say, 'I don't mean the leader of the Argonauts, but the one we read about in Maccabees' (IV, 7 et seq.).

2. See Chapter 23 of the present work.

3. *Purgatorio* VI, 127–151; *Paradiso* XXXI, 37–40. See Chapter 49 of the present work.

4. Elected King of the Germans on 20 October 1314 and crowned at Aix-la-Chapelle on 25 November.

5. See Chapter 43 of the present work.

6. *Purgatorio* VII, 96.

7. *Ibid.*, I, 1–6.
8. *Metamorphoses* V, 294–678.
9. *Purgatorio* I, 9–12 (italics added).
10. C.S. Boswell, *An Irish Precursor of Dante*, London, David Nutt, 1908.
11. Canto III. See also Chapter 13 of the present work.
12. *Purgatorio* I, 26–27.
13. It is later revealed that the Garden of Eden is situated on the summit of the Mountain of Purgatory.
14. *Inferno* XXVI, 127–128.
15. *Purgatorio* I, 32–33.
16. *Ibid.*, 41–48.
17. *Ibid.*, 71–75.
18. *Pharsalia* IX.
19. *De Officiis* I, 31, quoted in *Monarchia*, Book II, Chapter 5.
20. *Purgatorio* I, 85–93.
21. *Ibid.*, 101.
22. *Ibid.*, 109.
23. *Ibid.*, 124–127. This is a remarkable mirror-image of the description of Virgil's hands spread out on the mire of the Circle of the Gluttons: *Lo duca mio distese le sue spanne* (*Inferno* VI, 25). See Chapter 15 of the present work.
24. See the conclusion of *Inferno* XXVI.
25. *Purgatorio* I, 134–136.

Chapter 31: The Morning Sun

1. *Purgatorio* II, 28–30.
2. That is, from the port of Rome (Ostia) to the Mountain of Purgatory, as we later learn. This is the vessel on which Charon prophesied it would be the destiny of Dante's soul to travel (*Inferno* III, 91–93).
3. Psalm 114.
4. *Il Convivio*, Section II, Chapter 1.
5. *Purgatorio* II, 88–90. See Chapters 15 and 39 of the present work.
6. The exact date of his death is not known.
7. According to Dante's chronology of his journey.
8. This is a reference to the Papal indulgences granted to pilgrims visiting Rome in 1300. (See Chapter 3 of the present work.) The Bull of Jubilee was promulgated on 22 February 1300 but extended retrospectively to Christmas Day 1299. By the time of Dante's vision, set in Easter Week 1300, the indulgences had been operative for three months. The period of waiting that souls have to spend at Ostia may be associated with the belief that some spirits are earthbound after death.
9. *Purgatorio* II, 112–114.
10. *Ibid.*, 120–123.
11. See Chapter 7 of the present work.
12. *Purgatorio* III, 25–27. Virgil died in Brindisi, in Apulia, returning from Greece, where he became ill. His body was taken by order of Augustus to Naples for burial. His supposed tomb is still to be seen on the road to Pozzuoli.
13. *Ibid.*, 73–78.
14. *Ibid.*, 107–108.

15. *Ibid.*, 121–123.
16. Dante had read in Brunetto Latini's *Tresor* that Manfred had murdered his father, his brother, his nephew and attempted to murder his great-nephew.
17. She died in Barcelona in 1302.
18. The reference is to John VI, 37: 'Him that cometh unto me I will in no wise cast out.' Manfred has quoted these words in lines 122–123.
19. See Chapter 5 of the present work.
20. He was to consign the Emperor Frederick II to the burning tomb of a heretic in Hell (*Inferno* X). It is significant that Manfred avoids mentioning his father.
21. The original word is *benegenitus*, an unexpected epithet in view of Manfred's illegitimacy.
22. See Chapter 32 of the present work.

Chapter 32: From Humour to Invective

1. For Dante's study of astronomy, see Chapter 6 of the present work.
2. i.e. the ecliptic, the sun's path along the Zodiac, which lies mid-way between any point on earth and its antipodes.
3. *Purgatorio* IV, 98–99.
4. i.e. the angel who guards the entrance to the seven cornices of Purgatory proper. See Chapter 33 of the present work.
5. *Purgatorio* IV, 137–139. The 'shore' is that of the river Ganges.
6. *Purgatorio* V, 10–15.
7. See Chapter 1 of the present work.
8. *Inferno* XXVII. See also Chapter 24 of the present work.
9. Dino Compagni, the chronicler, states that the sky was overcast on the day of the battle (*Cronica* I, 10).
10. *Purgatorio* V, 102.
11. *Ibid.*, 106–108.
12. *Ibid.*, 130–136.
13. See Chapter 29 of the present work.
14. Including the feud of the Montagues and Capulets.
15. The Italian word *bordello*, which means brothel, had another meaning, now archaic, namely 'hired hand' or 'stable-boy'. It is possible that Dante intended a contrast between *donna di provincie* (a person) and a lowly member of a household (another person).
16. *De Vulgari Eloquentia*, Book I, Chapter 15. See also Chapter 1 of the present work.
17. Sordello here uses the plural pronoun *voi*, referring to both of them.
18. i.e. round the feet.
19. *Purgatorio* VII, 16–21.

Chapter 33: Close of Day and a New Dawn

1. *Inferno* IV. See Chapter 13 of the present work.
2. See Chapters 8 and 46 of the present work.
3. *Purgatorio* VIII, 1–6.
4. *Inferno* IX. On both occasions he addresses his listeners in the plural, as an audience.
5. The blunted swords are usually interpreted as signifying mercy rather than

judgement.

6. He was the grandson of Ugolino della Gherardesca. See *Inferno* XXXIII and Chapter 27 of the present work.
7. *Purgatorio* VIII, 58–60.
8. Her second husband was Galeazzo Visconti of Milan. Misfortunes overtook the Visconti family from 1302 onwards.
9. *Purgatorio* VIII, 76–78.
10. *Ibid.*, 100–103.
11. See Chapter 10 of the present work.
12. The valley of the river Macra in Lunigiana.
13. Dante was a guest of the Malaspina family in 1306.
14. Tithonus, brother of King Priam of Troy, was the spouse of Aurora, the Dawn, who obtained for him from the gods the gift of immortality. She forgot, however, to ask also for perpetual youth, so Tithonus grew older and older.
15. *Purgatorio* IX, 1–6. The 'cold animal' is the constellation of Scorpio.
16. *Paradiso* VI and XVIII–XX. See Chapter 47 of the present work.
17. See also Chapter 8 of the present work.
18. *Inferno* II, 97–108.
19. Virgil's description of St Lucy as *accorta* reinforces her association with knowledge.
20. See Chapter 3 of the present work.
21. *Purgatorio* IX, 121–129.

Chapter 34: Pride and Humility

1. 2 Samuel VI.
2. See Chapter 47 of the present work.
3. Dante, misled by painted and sculptured representations, believed the Roman Imperial standards to be flags showing a black eagle on a gold field, whereas they were poles surmounted by bronze figures.
4. Nicola Pisani was born about 1220 and died before 1284. His son Giovanni was born about 1245 and died before 1319. See G.H. and E.R. Crichton, *Nicola Pisano and the Revival of Sculpture in Italy*, Cambridge University Press, 1938.
5. *Paradiso* XV, 91–96. See Chapter 46 of the present work.
6. Oderisi of Gubbio, whose date of birth is unknown, is said to have died by 1299. It is thought that Dante may have met him during an early visit to Bologna in 1287. The dates of Franco of Bologna are unknown but it is evident that he was younger than Oderisi; he is believed to have lived into the first decade of the fourteenth century.
7. *Purgatorio* XI, 79–81.
8. *La Vita Nuova*, Chapter XXXIV.
9. *Purgatorio* XI, 91–99.
10. *Dante*, Faber and Faber, paperback edition, 1965, p 46.
11. *Purgatorio* XI, 112–114.
12. *Ibid.*, XII, 12.
13. Niobe, who had 14 children, boasted of her superiority to Latona who had borne by Jove only Apollo and Diana, who killed her and all her children with their arrows. Saul, the first king of Israel, was defeated by the Philistines on Mount Gilboa and

fell upon his sword. Arachne challenged Minerva to a contest in weaving and was changed into a spider for her presumption. Rehoboam, King of Israel, boasted that he would prove a greater tyrant than his father Solomon and was obliged to flee from his people who rebelled against him.

14. Alcmaeon slew his mother Eriphyle, who had betrayed his father for the bribe of a necklace. Sennacherib of Assyria, oppressor of Jerusalem, defeated by Hezekiah, was killed by his own sons. Cyrus, the Persian tyrant, murdered the son of Tomyris, Queen of Scythia, who killed him and threw his head into a vessel of blood. Holofernes, captain of the army of Nebuchadnezzar, was seduced by Judith, who cut off his head.

15. *Purgatorio* XII, 61–63.

16. *Ibid.*, 67.

17. Giotto was born some time between 1267 and 1275 and died in 1337.

18. *Purgatorio* XII, 71.

19. *Ibid.*, XI, 118–119.

20. See *La Vita Nuova*, Chapters XI, XXIII, XXVI and XXVIII.

21. *Purgatorio* XII, 100–105.

Chapter 35: Evil and the Freedom of the Will

1. As Virgil told Dante in *Inferno* I, 111: *là onde invidia prima dipartilla* ('there whence envy first despatched it', i.e. avarice). Cf. 'Through envy of the devil came death into the world' (*Book of Wisdom* II, 24).

2. The Sienese were led by Provenzano Salvani. See Chapter 34.

3. *Purgatorio* XIV, 16–21. Mount Falterona, on the borders of Romagna, is the source of the river Arno. Dante has noted Oderisi's words about pride, but *ancor* ('as yet') shows that he knows he will win renown.

4. Above Arezzo the Arno makes a bend eastward, passing a few miles to the north of the city.

5. *Purgatorio* XIV, 99.

6. *Ibid.*, 109–111.

7. *Ibid.*, 86–87.

8. *Ibid.*, XV, 46–51.

9. *Ibid.*, XVI, 46–48. Not much is known of Marco Lombardo. Early commentators agree that he lived in Venice and was a noble-minded man, though evidently inclined to wrath.

10. *Ibid.*, 58–63.

11. *Ibid.*, 79–84.

12. *Il Convivio*, Section IV, Chapter 12.

13. *Purgatorio* XVI, 85–93.

14. *Ibid.*, 103–105.

15. *Ibid.*, 127–129.

Chapter 36: Love, Natural and Rational

1. *Il Convivio*, Section III, Chapters 2–3.

2. *Purgatorio* XVII, 91–96.

3. *Ibid.*, XVIII, 13–15.

4. *Ibid.*, 62–63.

5. *Ibid.*, 70–72.

Chapter 37: The Mountain Trembles

1. 'Glory to God in the Highest' (Luke II, 9).
2. Titus was Roman Emperor from AD 79–81. In AD 70, serving under his father Vespasian, he besieged and destroyed Jerusalem, thereby avenging, as was believed, the death of Jesus upon the Jews.
3. *Purgatorio* XXI, 91–93.
4. *Thebaid* XII, 816–817: ... *nec tu divinam Aeneidam tenta/sed longe sequere, et vestigia adora.*
5. *Purgatorio* XXI, 94–99.
6. *Ibid.*, 121–126.
7. See Chapter 38. See also Chapter 15.
8. A Roman satirical poet, who died aged 80 some time before AD 61. He mentions Statius in his seventh satire.
9. *Inferno* IV.
10. *Aeneid* III, 56–57: *quid non mortalia pectora cogis,/auri sacra fames!* ('to what dost thou not drive the hearts of men, O accursed hunger for gold!').
11. *Purgatorio* XXII, 61–63.
12. *Ibid.*, 64–73. Statius is here quoting words from Virgil's fourth eclogue.
13. i.e. Limbo.
14. i.e. the Muses.
15. *Inferno* IV.

Chapter 38: Dante and Forese Donati

1. *Purgatorio* XXIII, 4–6.
2. Psalm 51, 15: 'O Lord, open thou my lips and my mouth shall forth thy praise.' The words serve as a reminder that the mouth is intended for other things besides eating and drinking.
3. i.e. the eyes represent the two Os, the line of the cheeks, eyebrows and nose form the M. See Figure 8.
4. *Inferno* XV, 24. See Chapter 17 of the present work.
5. See Chapter 1 of the present work. Forese is said to have been a cousin of Dante's wife.
6. *Ibid.*
7. Forese Donati died in July 1296.
8. *Purgatorio* XXIII, 85–93.
9. The inhabitants of Barbagia, a hilly region in central Sardinia, had the reputation of living like brute beasts. Dante more than once speaks with contempt of Sardinia.
10. *Purgatorio* XXIII, 108.
11. See Chapter 1 of the present work.
12. *Purgatorio* XXIII, 115–117.
13. See below.
14. See Chapter 2 of the present work.
15. *Purgatorio* XXIV, 76–80. Dante seems to imply that he will return to the Cornice of the Gluttons. By 'the shore' he probably means the shore of the Mountain of

Purgatory, or possibly the port of Ostia where penitent souls wait to be ferried across to the southern hemisphere.

16. *Metamorphoses* XII, 210–535.
17. Judges VII, 1–7 et seq.
18. *Purgatorio* XXIV, 133.
19. Daniel X, 6.
20. Matthew V, 6.

Chapter 39: Body and Soul

1. See Chapter 15 of the present work.
2. Dante had read the story in Ovid's *Metamorphoses* VIII, 451 et seq.
3. *Purgatorio* XXV, 31–33.
4. *Ibid.*, 58–63. The 'one wiser than thou art' is Averroës, the Muslim commentator of Aristotle, who finding no organ for the intellect which distinguishes man from the animals stated that man's rational soul was not individual but universal. His view was disputed by Aristotle.
5. *Purgatorio* XXV, 67–75.
6. *Ibid.*, 103–108.
7. See Chapter 2 of the present work.
8. *Purgatorio* XXVI, 97–99.
9. *Ibid.*, 112–114.
10. i.e. derived from Latin.
11. *Inferno* V. See Chapter 14 of the present work.
12. See Foster and Boyde, *Dante's Lyric Poetry*, Volume I, pp 158–175.
13. *Purgatorio* XXVII, 31–33.
14. *Ibid.*, 52–54.
15. Matthew XXV, 34.
16. In mystical writings, the two wives of Jacob were interpreted as allegories of the active and contemplative life. Dante's dream anticipates his coming meeting with Matilda and Beatrice.
17. *Purgatorio* XXVII, 127–142.

Chapter 40: The Christian Sibyl

1. Spelled 'Matelda' in accepted manuscripts. For a discussion of her identity see Chapter 41, of which see also note 14 for an interpretation of her name.
2. Adapted from the angel's greeting to Mary: 'Hail, thou that art highly favoured, the Lord is with thee: blessed art thou among women' (Luke I, 28).
3. Adapted from the four beasts of the Apocalypse, Revelations IV, 6–8, and the four living creatures of Ezekiel I, 4–14; X, 8–14.
4. The third eye, denoting wisdom, is a Buddhist conception and is also found in the Western iconographical tradition.
5. The Song of Solomon, IV, 8. The Spouse of Lebanon is an image of the soul espoused to God.
6. Adapted from Matthew XXI, 9: 'Blessed is he that cometh in the name of the Lord.'
7. *Aeneid* VI, 883.
8. *Purgatorio* XXX, 34–39.

9. *Agnosco veteris vestigia flammae. Aeneid* IV, 23

10. *Purgatorio* XXX, 55–57 (Sayers' translation).

11. Not all manuscripts have the plural but it is now usually accepted.

12. *Purgatorio* XXX, 99–101 (Sayers' translation, adapted).

13. Perhaps an allusion to his work *La Vita Nuova*. See Chapter 2 of the present work.

14. Beatrice died when she was 24.

15. *Purgatorio* XXX, 139–145 (Sayers' translation, adapted).

16. *Ibid.,* XXXI, 34–36.

17. *Ibid.,* 67–69.

18. From the Bull issued on Corpus Christi by Pope Urban in 1264.

19. This identification was first pointed out by John D. Sinclair, *The Divine Comedy of Dante Alighieri*, II. *Purgatorio*, John Lane, 1948, pp 414–416.

20. *Purgatorio* XXXII, 48.

21. Matthew III, 15.

22. Epistle to the Romans V, 19.

23. *Purgatorio* XXXII, 100–102. See also St Bernard's identification of the Virgin Mary as 'Augusta' (Chapter 53 of the present work).

24. *Inferno* XIX, 115–117 and Chapter 19 of the present work.

25. Revelations XVII, 3.

26. This represents the removal of the Papacy to Avignon, which occurred in 1305.

27. cf. John XVI, 16.

28. The return did not take place until 1377, 56 years after Dante's death.

29. 'The beast that thou sawest was, and is not' (Revelations XVII, 8).

30. This would seem to be an admission by Dante that he had once separated the study of philosophy from that of theology.

31. See Chapter 12 of the present work.

Chapter 41: Who is Matilda?

1. *Purgatorio* I, 7–8.

2. *Paradiso* XXVI, 124–138.

3. *Purgatorio* XXVIII, 40–42.

4. *La Vita Nuova*, Chapter XXXIV.

5. *Purgatorio* XXVIII, 52–57.

6. *La Vita Nuova*, Chapter XII.

7. Psalm 92, 4.

8. *Purgatorio* XXVIII, 83–84.

9. *Paradiso* XXXI–XXXIII.

10. *Purgatorio* XXI.

11. The name appears to be Dante's invention, formed from two Greek words meaning 'good knowledge'.

12. *Purgatorio* XXVIII, 142–144.

13. She now sings Psalm 32, 1 (in the Vulgate 31, 1): 'Blessed are they [whose transgressions are forgiven and] whose sins are covered.'

14. *Purgatorio* XXXIII, 118–119. The Italian form of her name, Matelda, has been interpreted as an anagram of the Latin words *ad letam*, 'to Lethe', the river into which she plunges Dante when he is unconscious. This may be so, but her functions are

more multiple than that.

15. *Ibid.*, 145.
16. A castle situated on a hill, south-west of Reggio dell'Emilia, destroyed in 1255.
17. See Chapter 42 of the present work.
18. 1849–1925.
19. *Paradiso* XX, 55–57. See also Chapter 47 of the present work.
20. Now in the Vatican. See Figure 9.
21. See Chapter 39 of the present work.
22. Adapted from 'La Matilda de Dante', *Mélanges ... à Rita Lejeune*, Duculot, s.d.

Chapter 42: Dante and His Patrons

1. Can Francesco della Scala, known as Can Grande, 1291–1329.
2. See Chapter 29 of the present work.
3. *Dante Dictionary*, Paget Toynbee, art. Can Grande della Scala, Oxford, Clarendon, 1908.
4. *Purgatorio* XVI, 125–126.
5. *Il Convivio*, Section IV, Chapter 16.
6. A ruthless tyrant (1194–1259), guilty of mass atrocities, ruler of the March of Treviso for over 30 years. Dante places him among the violent in the first zone of the Seventh Circle of Hell (*Inferno* XII, 109–110).
7. It is said that relatives of Branca d'Oria threatened to molest Dante in Genoa. See Chapter 27 of the present work.
8. *Inferno* I. See Chapter 12 of the present work.
9. Louis was not crowned Emperor in Rome until 1328, seven years after Dante's death.
10. See Chapter 49 of the present work.
11. A reference to Dante's first visit to Verona in 1303, at the invitation of Bartolommeo. See Chapter 4 of the present work.
12. *Paradiso* XVII, 79–90. The 'Gascon' is Pope Clement V (Bertrand de Goth, a native of Gascony) who at first supported Henry VII but, yielding to the pressure of Philip IV of France, later secretly opposed him. This is the first of two mentions of Henry VII. On both occasions Dante uses the familiar form of his name, Arrigo, equivalent to our Harry. See also Chapters 29 and 46 of the present work.
13. See Chapter 14 of the present work. In one of his poems Guido quoted the line from *Inferno* V, in which Francesca refers to Paolo's undying love: *che mai da me non fia diviso* ('who never from me will be parted').
14. It was formerly said that Dante had two daughters, Antonia and Beatrice, but scholars are now satisfied that only one is known for certain: Antonia, who is believed to have taken the name of Suor Beatrice when she became a nun.
15. Epistola VIII, ed. Paget Toynbee, Oxford, Clarendon Press, second edition, 1966, pp 121–147.
16. A successor of Can Grande made peace finally in 1339, agreeing to accept the title of Papal instead of Imperial Vicar.
17. See Chapter 29 of the present work.
18. See Chapter 7 of the present work.
19. See Chapter 35 of the present work.
20. See Richard Kay, *Dante's Monarchia, Translated with a Commentary*, Introduction,

Toronto, 1998, Pontifical Institute of Mediaeval Studies. See also the edition and translation by Prue Shaw, Cambridge University Press, 1995, and Charles Till Davis, *Dante and the Idea of Rome*, Appendix II, Oxford, Clarendon Press, 1957, pp 263–269.

21. *Monarchia*, Book I, Chapter 12.
22. *Paradiso* V, 19–24.
23. See Richard Kay, *Dante's Monarchia*, pp xxiii–xxv
24. Guido Vernani, the earliest critic of the work, denounced this argument as *vile et derisibile* ('base and ludicrous').
25. See Chapter 29 of the present work.
26. *Monarchia*, Book II, Chapter 13.
27. i.e. the corpus of Papal decrees which are the basis of ecclesiastical law.
28. *Monarchia*, Book III, Chapter 3.
29. See Chapter 5 of the present work.
30. *Il Convivio*, Section IV, Chapter 12. See Chapter 8 of the present work.
31. *Ibid.*, Chapter 5. See Chapter 7 of the present work.
32. See Chapter 6 of the present work.
33. *Monarchia*, Book II, Chapter 1.
34. *Ibid.*

Chapter 43: Prelude to *Paradiso*

1. *Purgatorio* II, 1–6.
2. *Paradiso* XXXIII, 145.
3. *Ibid.*, V, 109–111.
4. Epistola X, ed. Paget Toynbee, Oxford, Clarendon Press, 1920, pp 160–211. The authenticity of this epistle has been a matter of controversy but the majority of Dante scholars are convinced that it is genuine. For my reasons for agreeing with them, see Introduction to *Paradise*, Penguin Classics, 'The Epistle to Can Grande', revised edition, 2004.
5. See Chapter 42 of the present work.
6. He refers to himself as the speaker, and to his address as 'the present occasion'.
7. The lecture, entitled ʃ ⌐ ɪ, was delivered at the church of Sant'Elena in Verona.
8. Psalm 114 (in the Vulgate 113). See also Chapters 6 and 31 of the present work.
9. i.e. spiritual.
10. Translation by Paget Toynbee.
11. *Derivationes* by Uguccione da Pisa.
12. Still in existence in the theatrical convention of wishing a fellow 'Break a leg!' and, in the German equivalent, 'Hals und Beinbrech!'
13. All the quotations from *Paradiso* in the oration are in Latin.
14. *Paradiso* I, 1–12.
15. See Chapter 6 of the present work.
16. 2 Corinthians XII, 2–4.
17. Matthew XVII, 1–8.
18. Glaucus, a fisherman of Boeotia, on seeing fish revive in contact with a certain herb, ate some himself and was moved to plunge into the sea and became a sea-god. Dante read of him in Ovid's *Metamorphoses* XIII, 920–968.

19. *Paradiso* I, 68–72.
20. *Inferno* IV, 139–140.
21. London, Folio Society, 2002.
22. *The Doors of Perception*, Chatto and Windus, 1954, p 12. See also Chapter 54 of the present work.

Chapter 44: Beatrice in Heaven

1. See Chapter 40 of the present work.
2. *Paradiso* I, 136–138.
3. Compare the words of Piccarda, *ibid.*, III, 85.
4. *Confessions* XIII, 9.
5. *Paradiso* III, 10–16.
6. *La Vita Nuova*, Chapter XXI.
7. *Paradiso* III, 2.
8. *Purgatorio* XXIV. See also Chapter 38 of the present work.
9. *Paradiso* III, 70–72 (Sayers' translation).
10. *Ibid.*, 85–87.
11. *Ibid.*, IV, 37–48 (Sayers' translation).
12. *Ibid.*, 118–123 (Sayers' translation).
13. *Paradiso* XXVII, 88–89. The archaic word *donneare* meant 'to flirt, to play the gallant, to woo'.
14. *Ibid.*, XXX, 70–72.
15. *Il Convivio*, Section IV, Chapter 13.
16. *Purgatorio* XXI, 1.
17. *Paradiso* II, 19–21.
18. *Paradiso* XXVII, XXIX, XXX.

Chapter 45: Propaganda in *Paradiso*

1. *Paradiso* VI.
2. *The History of the Decline and Fall of the Roman Empire*, 'Justinian and the Roman Law', Volume V, Chapter 44. When Gibbon wrote, there were many legal systems in Europe that drew directly upon Roman law. Codification has long since changed that (except for Andorra and San Marino).
3. Beyond the Heaven of the Moon the souls appear only as lights. The human form, apart from Dante and Beatrice, is not manifested again until they reach the souls in the Empyrean.
4. *Paradiso* VI, 10.
5. *Ibid.*, 1–9 (Sayers' translation).
6. See Chapter 42 of the present work.
7. *Paradiso* VI, 82–93 (Sayers' translation).
8. *Ibid.*, VII, 49–51.

Chapter 46: The City Walls

1. This was the only occasion on which Petrarch set eyes on Dante. There was a difference of about ten years in age between Dante and Petrarch's father.
2. See *Il Convivio*, Section I. See also Chapter 6 of the present work.
3. See Chapter 1 of the present work.

4. *Paradiso* XV–XVII.
5. *Inferno* II, 32.
6. *Paradiso* XV, 28–30.
7. *Ibid.*, 88–89.
8. *Ibid.*, 99–102.
9. *Ibid.*, 130–135.
10. *Ibid.*, XXV 1–9.
11. This would naturally occur to the author of *De Vulgari Eloquentia*. See Chapter 5 of the present work.
12. *Paradiso* XVI, 67–69.
13. *Paradiso* XVII, 55–60 (Sayers' translation).
14. See Chapter 42 of the present work.
15. *Paradiso* XVII, 127–129 (Sayers' translation).
16. *Ibid.*, 133–138 (Sayers' translation).

Chapter 47: Justice Unfathomed

1. *Paradiso* VI. See Chapter 45 of the present work. The command is to love justice, not merely to enforce it.
2. See Figures 11–12.
3. *Paradiso* XIX, 6–12.
4. *Ibid.*, 25–26.
5. See Chapter 3 of the present work.
6. See Chapters 5 and 6 of the present work.
7. Justinian's Codex, Dig. 1.1. 10pr.
8. *Ibid.*, Dig. 1.1.10.1.
9. *Ibid.*, Dig. 1.1. 1pr.
10. See also Patrick Boyde, *Human Vices and Human Worth in Dante's Comedy*, Cambridge University Press, 2000, 'Justice', pp 198–224.
11. See Chapter 9 of the present work.
12. *Inferno* III, 4.
13. *Paradiso* XIX, 79–81.
14. See Chapter 13 of the present work.
15. See Chapters 39 and 40 of the present work.
16. See Chapter 46 of the present work.
17. *Ibid.*
18. *Purgatorio* XII, 25–63. See also Chapter 33 of the present work.
19. See Figure 13.
20. 2 Kings XX, 1–6 and 2 Chron. XXXII, 26.
21. *Aeneid* II, 426–427.
22. Acts X, 35.
23. *Paradiso* XX, 82.
24. *Ibid.*, 103–105 (Sayers' translation).
25. See Chapter 40 of the present work.
26. *Paradiso* XX, 133–135 (Sayers' translation).
27. *Ibid.*, III, 85. See also Chapter 44 of the present work.

Chapter 48: Dante and Monasticism

1. *Paradiso* X.
2. *Ibid.*, XXI, 127–135.
3. *Ibid.*, XXII, 73–93.
4. *Ibid.*, 64–69 (Sayers' translation).

Chapter 49: The Theme's Great Weight

1. *Paradiso* XXII, 112–123.
2. *Ibid.*, 135, 151.
3. *Ibid.*, XXIII, 19–21.
4. *Ibid.*, XIV. See also Chapter 46 of the present work.
5. See Chapter 40 of the present work.
6. *Paradiso* XXIII, 40–45 (Sayers' translation).
7. *Ibid.*, 64–69.
8. *Ibid.*, 103–111.
9. In *La Vita Nuova*, Chapter XXIV, Dante interpreted Beatrice as signifying Christ.

Chapter 50: Faith, Hope and Love

1. *Il Convivio*, Section I, Chapter 1.
2. *Paradiso* XXIV, 1–9.
3. *Ibid.*, XXV, 52–57.
4. *Ibid.*, 1–9.
5. Wicksteed and Gardner, *Dante and Giovanni del Virgilio*, Constable, 1902, p 154.
6. Epistola IX, in Paget Toynbee (ed), *The Letters of Dante*, translation by Toynbee, adapted.
7. *Paradiso* XXV, 122–129. The 'two only' who ascended to Heaven in the body are Christ and the Virgin Mary.
8. *Ibid.*, XXVI, 58–66.

Chapter 51: Hatred in Heaven

1. *Paradiso* XXVII, 1–3 (Sayers' translation).
2. *Ibid.*, 19–21 (Sayers' translation).
3. *Ibid.*, 22–27 (Sayers' translation).
4. *Ibid.*, 40–63. 'Gascons and Cahorsines' refers to the election of Pope Clement V (a Gascon) and Pope John XXII (of Cahors).
5. *Ibid.*, 64–66.
6. *Ibid.*, 121–141.
7. *Ibid.*, 142–148. The 'hundredth of a day' is the error in the Julian calendar, according to which the length of the year was 365¼ days. This was too long by 11 minutes and 14 seconds, roughly 1/100 of a day. By Dante's time January had advanced more than eight days nearer the end of winter and would eventually have become 'unwintered', i.e. become a spring month. Beatrice here, by a rhetorical figure, substitutes a long period for a short one, as though to say, 'It will not take till doomsday.'

Chapter 52: The Creation

1. *Inferno* III, 21.
2. *Metaphysica* VII, 1075a, 5–7.
3. *Paradiso* XXVIII, 41–42.
4. *Ibid.*, 79–87. The 'milder cheek' of Boreas is the north-east wind, by which the skies of Italy are blown clear.
5. *Il Convivio*, Section II, Chapter 5.
6. *Summa Theologiae*, Part I, question 108.
7. *Paradiso* XXVIII, 3.
8. *Ibid.*, XXX, 40–42 (Sayers' translation).
9. *Ibid.*, XXIX 19–30.
10. *De Anima* II, ii.
11. *Paradiso* XIII, 52–87.
12. *Il Convivio*, Section II, Chapter 4.
13. *Inferno* III, 37–40.
14. *Purgatorio* XXV, 79–84.
15. See J.D. Sinclair, *Paradiso*, London, Bodley Head, p 426.
16. *Paradiso* XXIX, 124–126. St Anthony of Egypt, the hermit (251–356), is said to have kept herds of swine, fattened on proceeds from the sale of pardons.

Chapter 53: The Departure of Beatrice

1. *Paradiso* XXIX, 127–145. The passage in the Book of Daniel to which Beatrice refers is the following: 'The Ancient of days did sit ... thousand thousands ministered unto him, and ten thousand times ten thousand stood before' (VII, 9–10).
2. *Il Convivio*, Section III, Chapter 4.
3. *Paradiso* XXX, 54.
4. *Ibid.*, 55–56.
5. Daniel VII, 20.
6. John I, 1–3.
7. *Paradiso* XXX, 129–132.
8. See Chapter 30 of the present work.
9. *Paradiso* XXX, 133–141.
10. *Ibid.*, XXXI, 37–40.

Chapter 54: Approach to the Final Vision

1. *Paradiso* XXXI, 61–63.
2. *Ibid.*, 112.
3. See Chapter 46 of the present work.
4. *Paradiso* XXXI, 64. See also Chapter 40 of the present work.
5. See Chapter 11 of the present work.
6. *La Vita Nuova*, Chapter XL.
7. *Paradiso* XXXI, 103–111.
8. See Chapter 50 of the present work.
9. *Paradiso* XXXI, 118–123.
10. *Ibid.*, XXXII, 37–39.
11. *Ibid.*, 117–119. Beatrice has also spoken of Christ as Roman in Heaven. See Chapter 40 of the present work.

12. *Ibid.*, 139–144.

Chapter 55: The Vision of the Trinity

1. *Paradiso* XXXIII, 38–39.
2. *Ibid.*, 58–66.
3. *Ibid.*, 67–75.
4. See Chapter 43 of the present work.
5. See Bernard and Patricia McGinn, *Early Christian Mystics*, New York, The Crossroad Publishing Company, 2001, p 113.
6. From the Prologue of a work entitled *Scivias* ('Know the Ways of God'). It is interesting that Hildegard, like other mystics, was knowledgeable about herbs, of which she names about 140 in her work *Liber subtilitatum diversarum naturarum creaturarum.*
7. *Confessions* VII, 10.
8. Richard, born in Scotland in the twelfth century, entered the hermitage of St Victor outside Paris, where he became teacher, Sub-prior and finally Prior.
9. Richard of St Victor, *Twelve Patriarchs.*
10. See Aldous Huxley, *The Doors of Perception, Heaven and Hell*, in one volume, Chatto and Windus, 1960. See also Chapter 44 of the present work.
11. Dante wrote of being *macro* ('lean') from working on his poem (*Paradiso* XXV, 3). This is perhaps an allusion to fasting.
12. Pamela Hansford Johnson, *Important to Me: Personalia*, London, Macmillan, 1974, p 27. A still more remarkable experience is described by Jill Paton Walsh in her novel *Lapsing*, Weidenfeld and Nicolson, 1983, pp 83–85.
13. See Margery E. Reeves. 'The *Liber Figurarum* of Joachim of Fiore', *Mediaeval and Renaissance Studies*, Volume II, pp 57–81.
14. Ezekiel I, 26–28
15. *Paradiso* XXXIII, 133–138 (Sayers' translation).
16. *Ibid.*, 142–145.

Epilogue

1. See *Giovanni Boccaccio: Life of Dante*, translated by J.G. Nichols, Hesperus Press, 2002.
2. He is said to have been born in Certaldo, a village near Florence.
3. No monument to Dante was raised in Florence until 1830. The poet Giacomo Leopardi composed a reproachful *canzone* on the subject.
4. The last line of the sonnet 'Dante' by Giosuè Carducci (1835–1907).

Select Index

Note: Major references are in **bold** type.